D0772946

ARISTOTLE

XXIII

LCL 199

ARISTOTLE
POETICS

EDITED AND TRANSLATED BY
STEPHEN HALLIWELL

LONGINUS
ON THE SUBLIME

TRANSLATION BY W. H. FYFE
REVISED BY DONALD RUSSELL

DEMETRIUS
ON STYLE

EDITED AND TRANSLATED BY
DOREEN C. INNES
BASED ON W. RHYS ROBERTS

HARVARD UNIVERSITY PRESS
CAMBRIDGE, MASSACHUSETTS
LONDON, ENGLAND
1995

Library of Congress Cataloging-in-Publication Data

Aristotle.
[Poetics. English]
Poetics / Aristotle; edited and translated by Stephen Halliwell.
On the sublime / Longinus; edited and translated by
W. Hamilton Fyfe; revised by Donald Russell.
On style / Demetrius; edited and translated
by Doreen C. Innes; based on the translation by W. Rhys Roberts.
p.   cm. — (Loeb classical library; L199)
Includes bibliographical references and index.
ISBN 0–674–99563–5
1. Greek literature—Translations into English.
2. Greek literature—History and criticism—Theory, etc.
3. Style, Literary—Early works to 1800.
4. Literary form—Early works to 1800.
5. Aesthetics, Ancient.   6. Sublime, The.
PA3621.A75   1995   94–5113   808.2—dc20

Typeset by Chiron, Inc, Cambridge, Massachusetts.
Printed in Great Britain by St Edmundsbury Press Ltd,
Bury St Edmunds, Suffolk, on acid-free paper.
Bound by Hunter & Foulis Ltd, Edinburgh, Scotland.

CONTENTS

ARISTOTLE
POETICS

EDITED AND TRANSLATED BY
STEPHEN HALLIWELL

INTRODUCTION

Aristotle's *Poetics* occupies a highly special, indeed unique, position in the long history of Western attitudes to literature. It is, in the first place, the earliest surviving work to be exclusively concerned with the discussion and analysis of poetry as an art, and this fact has turned it into a document standing apparently near the very beginning of, and effectively inaugurating, an entire tradition of literary theory and criticism. In part, this is the result of considerable contingency, since there had been earlier Greek authors who had devoted writings (now lost) to the subject of poetry, as well as thinkers, above all Plato, who had examined literary works in relation to differently defined sets of concerns (philosophical, historical, biographical, etc.). Moreover, if the *Poetics* inaugurated a tradition of thought, it is far from obvious that it did so in virtue of any direct or persistent influence upon subsequent critics of antiquity. In the ancient world itself, the treatise seems never to have been widely known or read, though that is not to deny the existence of recurrent elements of Aristotelianism within the development of Greco-Roman literary criticism.[1] What may now look to

---

[1] This Aristotelianism may have stemmed partly from Ar.'s published dialogue *On Poets*, as well as from the writings of Peripatetics such as Theophrastus and Neoptolemus of Parium.

our retrospective gaze to be the "inaugural" significance of the *Poetics* owes much to the way in which the work was rediscovered, disseminated, and established as canonical by certain sixteenth-century Italian theorists and their successors elsewhere in Europe. In that sense, the book's uniqueness is far from being a pure reflection of its original creation or purpose, and is intimately bound up with its involvement in the construction of competing views of literary criticism since the Renaissance.

Yet it would, for all that, be superficial to suppose that the status of the *Poetics* is irredeemably a consequence of historical accident and arbitrariness. We need only consider that even since its decline from the preeminence and authority with which, as late as the eighteenth century, it had been endowed by neoclassicists, it has continued tenaciously to provide a valuable point of reference within the debates of literary criticism and theory—even, often enough, for those who have found its contents uncongenial. At the very least, therefore, we need to recognise that the work's own character, despite the many difficulties which it has always posed for interpreters, lends itself with peculiar force to use (and abuse) in urgent, continuing disputes about the nature, form, and value of literature. To try to understand this character, we need to approach it against the background of the work's historical setting.

The *Poetics*, like virtually all the extant works of Aristotle, represents something in the nature of teaching materials or "lecture notes," produced not as a text for private reading by anyone interested, but for instructional use in an educational context. In view of this circumstance, with its implication of a less than tidy occasion of

4

composition (still less, "publication"), it is not surprising that we cannot safely date the work to a single point in Aristotle's career. An indefinite amount of revision and redrafting is readily conceivable, especially given some of the work's many loose ends; and certain sections may originally have been compiled at appreciably different times from one another. Chs. XX–XXII, for example, which discuss "diction," *lexis*, in terms that are more linguistic than stylistic, are closely related to bk III of the *Rhetoric* and to *De Interpretatione*, both of which there is some reason to suppose were of relatively early date. But other elements in the *Poetics*, such as the views on the relation between action and character in ch. VI, might suggest a more mature stage of Aristotle's thinking—in this particular case, a stage reflected in some of the ideas of the ethical treatises. We can be fairly confident that the *Poetics* was mostly compiled later than both the dialogue *On Poets* (to which 54b18 is probably a reference) and the six book discussion of interpretative difficulties in Homer, *Homeric Problems* (of which *Poetics* ch. XXV appears to provide a summary). All in all, it is highly plausible that the *Poetics*, whatever its history of composition, was at any rate available for use during the final phase of Aristotle's career, after the founding of his own school, the Lyceum, at Athens in 335.[2]

Why should Aristotle, whose supreme intellectual interests lay elsewhere, have concerned himself philosophically with poetry? We can identify, to begin with, both a general and a more specific impetus behind his

[2] Halliwell (1986), appendix 1, collects views and evidence on the date of the *Poetics*.

decision to address (and, indeed, to help define) the subject: the first, a response to poetry's vital, long established importance within Greek culture and education, and its consequent interest for a philosopher widely concerned with the forces influencing the life and mind of his society; the second, a reaction to the passionate critique—by turns, moralistic, psychological, political, and religious—which Plato had directed, especially in bks. 2–3 and 10 of his *Republic*, against both Homeric epic and Athenian drama. Within the immediate context of Athenian culture, where he was first a member of Plato's Academy (367–47) and later the head of the Lyceum (335–23), Aristotle even came to develop a documentary interest in the history of Attic drama. Whatever the relationship of the *Poetics* to the works which he compiled on theatrical records,[3] it is clear that he discerned an importance in drama which prompted him to make it, together with the two great Homeric epics, the basis of a fresh and distinctive approach to "poetry in general" (47a8)—an approach which expresses not only his divergences from Plato's and other earlier thinkers' views on the subject, but also the concepts, methods, and tendencies of his own philosophical outlook.

In attempting to characterise what was distinctive about the *Poetics*, we cannot do better than concentrate on what might be called its "foundational" strategy. By this I mean its explicit attempt to scrutinise poetry in a systematic and analytic manner—beginning, in typical Aristotelian fashion, from what are taken to be the most fundamental propositions about the field of enquiry

[3] Details in *DFA*[2], pp. 70–71.

("first principles," 47a12–13); developing an argument
whose main stages are carefully signalled, often by the
introduction and definition of key terms, and whose progressive plan is highlighted by a large number of cross references; and striving, if less than perfectly (at any rate in
the surviving state of the text), to make the connections
between its basic tenets and its individual judgements as
tight as possible. This foundational quality, with its
implicit faith in a rational procedure of criticism, has
elicited admiration in some readers, and discomfort in
others. What is pertinent here is that it is this aspect
more than any other which, so far as we can tell, marked
off Aristotle's undertaking from those of his predecessors,
and which has made the *Poetics* an abiding paradigm of
the application of intellectual method and conceptual
precision to the interpretation of literature.

If we seek to clarify what is entailed by Aristotle's
attempt to construct a stable framework for the understanding of Greek poetry, at least three essential elements
in his perspective can be isolated. The first is the placing
of poetry, alongside the visual arts, music, and dancing,
within a general category of artistic mimesis or representation. This dimension of the work, which gives its
thought a breadth of reflectiveness that was not lost on
post-Renaissance developers of mimeticist aesthetics, is
initially prominent in the principles and distinctions set
out in chs. I–IV. But it recurs at a number of later points,
including the repeated analogies between poetry and
painting, and the pregnant remarks on the multiple relationship of mimetic art to "life" in ch. XXV. Ideas of
mimesis had been active in a great deal of earlier Greek
thinking about poetry and other arts. Aristotle has debts

to this tradition; his account of mimetic modes in ch. III, for example, is closely related to Plato *Republic* 3.392d ff. But unlike Plato, or indeed any other predecessor of whom we know, Aristotle perceives a function for mimesis which does not threaten to reduce it to a static or inflexible model of artistic activity. Without ever offering a definition of the term (a perhaps sagacious reticence), Aristotle employs mimesis as a supple concept of the human propensity to explore an understanding of the world—above all, of human experience itself—through fictive representation and imaginative "enactment" of experience. His views are sketched, not fully elaborated, but we can see that they hope to connect art to a vital part of human nature (48b5 ff) and that they discern in poetry a capacity to convey ideas whose depth Aristotle regards as reaching towards the significance of the "universal" (ch. IX).

The second distinctive element in the *Poetics*' perspective is the recognition that poetry has a history of its own, and that this history is indispensable for the interpretation of certain conventions and possibilities of poetic practice. Literary criticism and literary history are here simultaneously delineated and conceptually intertwined. This aspect of Aristotle's approach is particularly obvious in chs. IV–V, where he reconstructs the patterns of cultural evolution which saw tragedy and comedy emerge from the earlier branches of serious and humorous poetry. It must be added that, somewhat ironically (given his own comments, in chs. IX and XXIII, on the chronicle-type character of history), Aristotle's perspective on poetic history is hardly straightforward or neutrally factual. It is, on the contrary, permeated by an interpretative vision—a vision of poetic history as an area in which "nature," working of course through *human* nature (48b4–5) yet promoting practices which have a dynamic of their own (49a15, 24, 60a4), brings into being the distinct cultural forms, the poetic kinds or genres, which count as the primary material for Aristotle's analysis of poetry.

The mention of genres brings us to the third, and in some ways the most important, element of the *Poetics* which deserves to be highlighted in an introduction. The establishment and deployment of a concept of genre lies at the basis of Aristotle's enquiry; the main purpose of the scheme of mimetic media, objects, and modes in chs. I–III is precisely to suggest how genres can be delimited in terms of their particular combinations of these features. It is also the steadiness of focus upon genres which was to be subsequently responsible for a large part of the work's appeal to, and influence on, neoclassical trends of thought. By organising discussion around juxtaposed and interlinked consideration of his chosen "species" of poetry, Aristotle aims to ensure that the judgement of particular poems is controlled by standards which refer to the character and goals of a shared generic "nature" (cf. 49a15).

This quasi-naturalistic framework, which we have already seen to be associated with Aristotle's view of literary history, is reinforced by a central emphasis on form and structure as fundamental to the understanding of poems as "objects" in their own right. This point, which contrasts so strongly with the overtly moral and political approach to poetry typically urged by Plato, should be perceived on a theoretical not a practical level. Aristotle does not in fact undertake anything like a close analysis of any individual work; "explication de textes" is scarcely glimpsed in the *Poetics*. What he does do, in a way which itself epitomises what I have called his foundational strategy, is to assert the significance of formal design and unity for both the composition and the appreciation of literary works, and to offer a conception of artistic form which relates it to the organic forms crucial to his understanding of nature (50b34–51a6).

In one sense, therefore, it might seem tempting to call the *Poetics*' perspective "formalist." But this term inevitably brings with it implications of views which treat form as guaranteeing a self-sufficient and autonomous nature for literary works. This, indeed, is the kind of view which has often been overtly ascribed to Aristotle. Yet it remains vital to see that the formal emphases of the treatise are coupled with concepts which make it hard to sustain such a reading of its author's position: such concepts include the "necessity and/or probability" which provide criteria of what makes coherent sense in the dramatic depiction of human life (51a12–13, etc.); the "universals" which poetry has the potential, according to ch. IX, to convey or intimate; and the emotions, pity and fear in the case of tragedy (and epic too), which help to define the essential nature of particular genres. Given all this, it seems appropriate to suggest that Aristotle's concern with form is with nothing less than the shaping and structuring of poetic meaning.

In each of the three respects I have picked out—the general or "aesthetic" category of artistic mimesis; the sense of poetry's history/evolution; the centrality of concepts of genre and form—there were partial antecedents

10

in Plato and others for Aristotle's attitudes and emphases.[4] But the *Poetics* combines these and other salient
concerns with a new argumentative firmness and detail,
and the result is a work which demarcates poetry as an
independent subject for study, and does so in a manner
copious, if sometimes frustratingly unclear, in philosophical and conceptual implications. Aristotle's original plan
(49b21–2) was evidently to elaborate his argument by
concentrating on each of three genres: epic, whose sur-
passing Homeric achievements made it an inescapable
focus of attention; and both of the branches of Attic
drama, tragedy and comedy. But this intention has, from
the point of view of modern readers, been overshadowed
by two factors: one, the loss of the discussion of comedy,
which belonged to what some ancient critics called the
Poetics' "second book";[5] the other, Aristotle's decision to
make the treatment of epic (chs. XXIII–XXV) subordinate to that of tragedy, on the grounds that tragedy could
be judged to have carried to superior fulfilment certain
goals which had been powerfully adumbrated, but not
wholly crystallised, in the poetry of Homer.[6] The combined result of these two factors, one contingent and one
conceptual, is that the *Poetics* now stands as above all a
treatise on tragedy; and it is to the discussion of this genre

[4] Lucas pp. xiv–xxii and Halliwell (1986) pp. 6–27 summarise
the *Poetics'* relation to earlier Greek writings on poetry.

[5] The most recent attempt to reconstruct parts of the second
book is that of Janko (1987) pp. 43–55 (with notes, pp. 159–74),
building on the more specialised treatment in Janko (1984). The
subject remains inevitably speculative and controversial.

[6] See esp. 49b9–20, and the comparison of the two genres in
ch. XXVI.

(VI–XXII) that some further introductory remarks must therefore be devoted.

Modern attitudes to tragedy, especially in the wake of such German theorists as Hegel, Schopenhauer, and Nietzsche, have been predominantly influenced by metaphysical and existentialist inclinations to identify a dark essence, an irreducible conception of "the tragic," at the heart of the matter. Such attitudes were in a sense prefigured by Plato, who, as an opponent of the psychological power of tragedy (within which, like Aristotle after him, he sometimes included Homeric epic), saw in it an expression of corrosive despair over the possibility of true happiness.[7] Aristotle's distance from this Platonic view, as well as from many later theories of tragedy, can perhaps best be regarded as part of a more general disinclination to discover a single core of significance in Greek tragic drama. Aristotle's treatment of tragedy has many facets, and is not the formulation of one dominant insight into the genre. It combines, as does the whole work, descriptive and prescriptive elements. It brings to bear, above all in identifying the six "components" of tragedy (ch. VI), the analytic method which functions throughout Aristotle's approach to poetry. It contains many principles—such as the priority of action over character (ch. VI), the requirements of structural unity (chs. VII–VIII), and the criteria of necessity and probability (e.g. ch. IX)—whose applicability is much wider than tragedy as such. We should not, therefore, expect the *Poetics* to yield a neatly circumscribed account of the quintessentially tragic.

[7] See esp. *Republic* 10.605c–6b.

Rather than the identification of a hard kernel of tragic meaning, Aristotle's goal can best be seen as the progressive demarcation of an area of possibilities which simultaneously codifies existing achievements of the tragedians, and legislates for the ideal scope of tragedy. This demarcation is initially embodied in the definition of the genre (49b24–8), which accentuates two features peculiar to tragedy (and to its Homeric adumbration): the structure of an "elevated" action, and the arousal of "pity and fear." The first of these features, both of which are elucidated and refined in the subsequent chapters, represents partly a generic gravity of tone, but also (or at the same time) a matter of ethical intensity. "Elevated," *spoudaios*, is the term used to denote the typical level of characterisation found in tragedy and epic (chs. II–III); the subject matter of serious in contradistinction to comic poetry (48b34, 49b10); and the quasi-philosophical universality of poetry, as opposed to history's particularity (51b6). As the definition indicates, the elevation of tragedy is a quality principally of its *action*, and a quality which will arise, in Aristotle's terms, from events involving and determining the lives of characters who can be generally regarded as striving for both practical success and ethical virtue.[8]

But "elevation," with its implications for tone and ethical interest, delimits the range of tragic action in only the broadest fashion. Aristotle narrows this range further by employing a model—deeply embedded in Greek

[8] Ar.'s views leave no real room for tragedies that hinge around seriously corrupt characters: this is the cumulative implication of 48a16–18, 52b36 ff, 54a16–17. Only 56a21–23, a very obscure passage, appears to contemplate plays whose central figures have substantial vices.

13

tragedy's own language of human experience — of movement or "transformation" (*metabasis*)[9] between extreme
poles of fortune: "prosperity" (*eutuchia*) and "adversity"
(*atuchia*, *dustuchia*). This polarity, first mentioned at the
end of ch. VII (51a13–14), provides a formula which
attempts to capture the crucial life-affecting shifts in the
status of tragedy's central characters. One striking fact
about Aristotle's use of the formula is that he more than
once appears to leave open the direction in which a tragic
transformation may take place.[10] But although this
involves him in the perhaps problematic preference for
plays of averted catastrophe in ch. XIV (54a4–9), its general import is not as paradoxical as might at first appear.
Aristotle assumes that any tragic transformation from
adversity to prosperity must give prominence to the first
of these extremes, and will take place in the context of
events entailing, or threatening, great suffering: at
54a12–13 the "families which such sufferings have
befallen" include those whose life histories contain the
plots of averted catastrophe which have just been singled
out for praise. Whatever one may feel about the fore-
grounding of such plots, they are not an invention of the
Poetics but a fact about the established possibilities of

[9] Ar. applies *metabasis* (52a16–18), with its cognate verb, to
the movement of fortune which he regards as essential to all
tragedy; *metabolē* (52a23, 31), "change," also with its cognate
verb (51a14 being an exception), is reserved for the more abrupt
twists which characterise the elements of the "complex" plot.
But what Ar. means by *metabasis* is often expressed, in tragedy
itself and elsewhere, by *metabolē*.

[10] See 51a13–14, 52a31 (perhaps), 55b27–8, as well as ch.
XIV's preference for averted catastrophe.

Greek tragedy itself.

The centrality of "transformation" in Aristotle's conception of tragedy links up with his estimation of the "complex" plot (chs. X–XI etc.) as the ideal for the genre. The elements of the complex plot—recognition and reversal—are themselves defined in terms of dramatic, sharp twists in the action. They are, in other words, hinge-like junctures at which the general tragic pattern of transformation is encapsulated in a particularly intense and decisive manner. Accordingly, they exemplify in a special degree the way in which, within the *Poetics'* account of tragedy, the idea of a change of fortune is closely related to two further elements: on the one hand, pity and fear; [11] on the other, the exhibition of human fallibility, for which *hamartia* is Aristotle's chosen expression in ch. XIII.

Pity and fear were traditionally held to be the combination of emotions appropriately evoked by tragedy, in life as well as fiction. Aristotle gives his own definitions of them in *Poetics* XIII, and much more fully in *Rhetoric* II.5 and II.8. He takes them to be felt for the undeserved afflictions of those "like ourselves" (53a5–6), and this condition implies a response to sufferings of kinds to which we can, implicitly at any rate, imagine ourselves too as vulnerable. The combination of pity and fear therefore represents tragedy as tapping a deep and quasi-universal [12] sense of human vulnerability—a vulnerability which

---

[11] Both 52a3–4 and 52a36–b3 allude, in effect, to the special capacity of complex plots to arouse the tragic emotions.

[12] Part of the importance of tragic fear, which is focussed on the dramatic characters (53a4–5) but contains a tacitly self-regarding element, lies in its connection with the "universals"

15

is dramatically projected by events in which transformations of fortune, and thus great swings in the potential happiness[13] of the central agents, are dominant. Tragedy, on this view, contains patterns of suffering which explore the experience of limitations upon human control of life. But it enlarges and heightens this experience by focussing it upon events that are typically "awesome"[14] in scope and impact, and by connecting it with characters who, while "like us" in their basic nature, are nonetheless "better than our normal level" (48a4) in the heroic scale and sweep of their lives.

When, therefore, in *Poetics* XIII Aristotle prescribes that the tragic agent should fall into adversity not "because of evil and wickedness, but through some kind of error (*hamartia*)" (53a8–10), it is not easy to see how *hamartia*, repeated a few lines later, can serve as much more than a token for the various sources of fallibility which could activate a tragic calamity, while still falling short of serious ethical culpability on the character's own part. *Hamartia* can perhaps most readily be construed as involving a piece of profound ignorance, particularly given the requirements of a complex plot (for reversal

---

that poetry has the power to intimate (51b6–7): to regard tragic agents as "like ourselves" is to move towards perceiving the universal significance latent in their stories.

[13] Ar. does not take tragedy to be concerned with all the details of "happiness," *eudaimonia*, which he examines in his own ethical writings. But he does see it as concerning itself with the decisive impingement of material circumstances, "prosperity" and "adversity," upon the possibilities for realising happiness in action: see esp. 50a16–20.

[14] See on 52a4.

and recognition) which Aristotle has in mind in this context (cf. 52b30–32). But neither the larger shape of the argument, nor the list of examples at 53a20–21, allows one to restrict *hamartia* to matters of factual ignorance; elements of limited culpability on the agent's part, including certain deeds of passion, cannot be ruled out.[15] Rather, in any case, than a precise formula for a quintessential tragic causality, *hamartia* can best be understood as designating a whole area of possibilities, an area unified by a pattern of the causal yet unintended implication of tragedy's characters in the pitiable and terrible "transformation" of their own lives. *Hamartia*, in short, embraces all the ways in which human vulnerability, at its extremes, exposes itself not through sheer, arbitrary misfortune (something inconsistent with the intelligible plot structure which Aristotle requires of a good play), but through the erring involvement of tragic figures in their own sufferings.

The *Poetics* repeatedly emphasises that the exhibition of tragic vulnerability or mutability is the ground of pity and fear. Only once, yet that in the definition of the genre, does Aristotle add that the experience of these emotions conduces to catharsis ("through pity and fear accomplishing the catharsis of such emotions," 49b27–8). In these circumstances, it is not surprising that the Greek term *katharsis*, whose senses include "cleansing," "purification," and "purgation," has long been the most vexed in the entire work. Opinion has been divided over the extent to which interpretative help can be found in *Poli-*

[15] See Stinton's article, the most thorough and cogent modern contribution to the longstanding argument over *hamartia*; cf. also Nussbaum (1986), pp. 382–3.

tics VIII.7, where Aristotle mentions catharsis in connection with certain kinds of music, associates it with both religious and medical forms of experience, and promises further elucidation of it "in my treatment of poetry." It is not inconceivable that this cross reference is to part of the lost second book of the *Poetics*, but more likely that it is to the early dialogue *On Poets*, where Aristotle may have explicitly introduced catharsis to block the Platonic charge that the arousal of emotions by tragedy tended dangerously to increase susceptibility to the same emotions in life.[16] If catharsis was conceived in anything like this spirit, then we should expect its function to emphasise resistance *both* to the idea of emotions as dangerous *and* to the notion of increased susceptibility.

Such dissension from Plato's position would draw on Aristotle's general and positive view, as revealed especially in his ethical writings, that emotions are cognitively based responses to experience, and can correspondingly be justified if the judgements which occasion and underlie them are themselves appropriate to the objects of the emotions.[17] It is evident throughout the *Poetics* that pity and fear are regarded as apt and indeed necessary emotions to be felt towards the suffering characters of tragedy. This alone makes it difficult to sustain what was for long the dominant modern view that catharsis is purely a matter of emotional outlet and release (the

[16] The attribution of a statement on catharsis to *On Poets* is accepted by e.g. W. D. Ross, *Aristotelis Fragmenta Selecta* (Oxford: Clarendon Press, 1955), p. 69, fr. 5. The Platonic doctrine in question is developed especially at *Republic* 10.603c–6d.

[17] This aspect of Ar.'s moral psychology is discussed by Nussbaum (1992).

extreme "purgation" view).[18] Such a function would be a contingent by-product of tragedy, not the essential element which ought to explain its presence within ch. VI's definition. While, in the absence of an Aristotelian elucidation of the term for tragedy, the significance of catharsis cannot be conclusively established, we are more likely to approximate to the truth if we keep in view the ethical importance of emotions for Aristotle, the *Poetics'* treatment of tragic pity and fear as the basis of a special form of pleasure (53b10–13), and, finally, the wider principle that the pleasure derived from mimetic works of art rests on an underlying process of comprehension. This configuration of factors allows us, however tentatively, to make of catharsis a concept which is interconnected with various components in Aristotle's theory of tragedy, and which in some sense completes his account of the genre by framing the experience of it as psychologically rewarding and ethically beneficial. Tragedy, on this reading, may revolve around the exhibition of sufferings which stem from profound human fallibility, yet by engaging the understanding and the emotions in contemplation of those phenomena it succeeds in affording an experience which deeply fulfils and enhances the whole mind.

The selective and highly compressed survey of some major features of the *Poetics* has taken us from an initial concern with the systematic and "foundational" strategy of the work, to the discussion of ideas—most notably, *hamartia* and catharsis—which, not least by their intriguing elusiveness, provide material for ongoing controversy. It may now be worth drawing the explicit moral that this

[18] For this and other interpretations of catharsis, see Halliwell (1986) ch. 6 and appendix 5.

combination of the methodical and the suggestive, the analytic and the elliptical, is surely one of the main reasons why the treatise has recurrently stimulated such interest and such sharp reactions, both positive and negative, from literary critics and theorists between the sixteenth century and the present. Partly because of its frequent terseness, partly on account of the damaged state in which it has reached us, the *Poetics* is a document which somewhat offsets its intellectually orderly and progressive approach with elements which have the effect of encouraging an indefinite process of reflection and reinterpretation. For this and other reasons the treatise has, since its late Renaissance "rediscovery" in Italy, maintained a persistent status as a conspicuous point of reference—a repeatedly cited model (whether for good or bad, depending on the interpreter's own allegiances) of certain kinds of assumptions and judgements about the nature of literary works, yet a model which never quite permits the reading of its arguments to reach a point of equilibrium.

No other document has had a history parallel to that of the *Poetics*: a canonical text for neoclassical thinkers, and in fields beyond those of literature itself, over a period of two and a half centuries; a locus of keenly contested debate, as well as a certain amount of revisionist interpretation, during the rise of Romantic conceptions of art; and a sporadically cited work even in the heavily ideological era of modern hermeneutics and literary theory.[19] It is

[19] I have discussed aspects of the *Poetics'* reception in three publications: Halliwell (1986) ch. 10, (1987) pp. 17–28, and the Epilogue in Rorty (1992), pp. 409–424.

tempting to say that this long, sometimes fraught story has left its scars on the work's standing. But it has also marked it out as a somewhat indomitable "survivor," whose historically formative role and continued salience no one interested in the development of Western attitudes to literature can afford to ignore.

Text and translation

The text printed has been broadly based on the edition by Rudolf Kassel, *Aristotelis de Arte Poetica Liber* (Oxford: Clarendon Press, 1965; corr. repr., 1968). But as well as sometimes preferring different readings from Kassel's, I have occasionally repunctuated the text and introduced some additional paragraph divisions. I have also deliberately printed as "clean" a text as possible, minimising such things as editorial brackets.

In keeping with the aims of the Loeb series, the apparatus criticus is highly selective; its guiding purpose is not to give full information about the textual tradition, but to notify (or remind) interested readers of salient elements of textual uncertainty. The apparatus is accordingly limited largely to those contexts where a conjectural emendation is printed, or where the manuscript evidence contains variants with substantive implications for the sense. It should be noted, additionally, that I do not mention places where readings taken from *recentiores* involve a practically certain correction of the medieval manuscripts; I do not record differences between A and B which are inconsequential for the meaning, even where they may be important for understanding the textual tradition as such; and I cite the medieval Latin translation and the Arabic translation only for a few striking points, not as supplementary evidence to the manuscripts.

The following abbreviations are used in the apparatus; the introduction to Kassel's edition should be consulted for further details:

A: 10th cent. ms., Parisinus gr. 1741.

Arab.: readings implied by the 10th cent. Arabic translation from an earlier Syriac translation of the *Poetics*.

B: 14th cent. ms., Riccardianus gr. 46 (which has substantial lacunae at 1447a8–48a29, and 1461b3–62a18).

Lat.: readings implied by the Latin translation of William of Moerbeke, completed in 1278.

rec.: readings of one or more Renaissance ms. (15th/16th cent.)

The translation printed here was drafted without reference to the version which I published in 1987 (see Bibliography). While subsequent comparison of samples yielded some similarities of wording between the two, in most cases I have not taken any active steps to remove these. The present translation aims to give a somewhat closer rendering than the earlier, though I have continued to follow the principle of preferring, wherever reasonable, intelligibility in English to a literalness which requires knowledge of Greek to decode.

The following conventions in the translation should be noted:

< > = words deemed to be missing from the Greek text and conjecturally supplied by editors.

( ) = parts of the text conveniently rendered as parentheses; round brackets are used more often in the translation than in the Greek text.

INTRODUCTION

[ ] = transliterated Greek terms or translations of such terms, included to clarify verbal points.

BIBLIOGRAPHY

The following abbreviated references are used in the notes to the translation (abbreviations for ancient authors and works generally follow the *Oxford Classical Dictionary*, see below, though I use Ar. not Arist. for Aristotle).

*DFA*²: Pickard-Cambridge, Arthur. *The Dramatic Festivals of Athens*, rev. J. Gould and D. M. Lewis. Oxford: Clarendon Press, 1968.

DK: Diels, H., and W. Kranz edd. *Die Fragmente der Vorsokratiker*. 7th ed. Berlin: Wiedmann, 1954.

Gigon: Gigon, O. ed. *Aristotelis Opera III: Librorum Deperditorum Fragmenta*. Berlin: de Gruyter, 1987.

Nauck: Nauck, August *Tragicorum Graecorum Fragmenta*. 2nd ed. Leipzig: Teubner, 1889.

OCD: *The Oxford Classical Dictionary*, ed. N. G. L. Hammond & H. H. Scullard. 2nd ed. Oxford: Clarendon Press, 1970.

PCG: Kassel R. and C. Austin edd. *Poetae Comici Graeci*. Berlin: de Gruyter, 1983–.

PMG: *Poetae Melici Graeci*, ed. D. L. Page. Oxford: Clarendon Press, 1962.

P. Oxy.: *The Oxyrynchus Papyri*. London: Egypt Exploration Society, 1898–.

TrGF: *Tragicorum Graecorum Fragmenta*, ed. B. Snell et al. Göttingen: Vandenhoeck & Ruprecht, 1971–.

Rose: Rose, V. *Aristotelis qui ferebantur librorum fragmenta*. Leipzig: Teubner, 1886.

West: West, M. L. *Iambi et Elegi Graeci*. 2nd ed. Oxford: Clarendon Press, 1989–92.

23

The following selection of publications is restricted to writings in English; works in other languages can be traced through the bibliographies in many of the items listed here.

Commentaries

Bywater, Ingram. *Aristotle on the Art of Poetry*. Oxford: Clarendon Press, 1909.

Else, Gerald F. *Aristotle's Poetics: the Argument*. Cambridge, Mass.: Harvard University Press, 1957.

Lucas, D. W. *Aristotle Poetics*. Oxford: Clarendon Press, 1968.

Monographs

Belfiore, Elizabeth S. *Tragic Pleasures: Aristotle on Plot and Emotion*. Princeton: Princeton University Press, 1992.

Halliwell, Stephen. *Aristotle's Poetics*. London: Duckworth, 1986.

House, Humphrey. *Aristotle's Poetics*. London: Rupert Hart-Davis, 1956.

Translations

The following contain extensive annotation or commentary.

Golden, Leon, and O. B. Hardison. *Aristotle's Poetics: a Translation and Commentary for Students of Literature*. Englewood Cliffs: Prentice-Hall, 1968.

Halliwell, Stephen. *The Poetics of Aristotle: Translation and Commentary*. London: Duckworth, 1987.

Hubbard, Margaret. "Aristotle: *Poetics*." in D. A. Russell and M. Winterbottom. *Ancient Literary Criticism*. Oxford: Clarendon Press, 1972.

Hutton, James. *Aristotle's Poetics*. New York: Norton, 1982.

Janko, Richard. *Aristotle Poetics*. Indianapolis: Hackett, 1987.

Other works

Cave, Terence. *Recognitions: A Study in Poetics*. Oxford: Clarendon Press, 1988.

Gallop, David. "Animals in the *Poetics*." *Oxford Studies in Ancient Philosophy* (Oxford), 8 (1990), 145–171.

Halliwell, Stephen. "The Importance of Plato and Aristotle for Aesthetics." In J. J. Cleary (ed.) *Proceedings of the Boston Area Colloquium in Ancient Philosophy*, vol. 5. Lanham: University Press of America, 1991, pp 321–348.

——— "Aristotelian Mimesis Reevaluated." *Journal of the History of Philosophy* (Chicago), 28 (1990), 487–510.

Heath, Malcolm. "Aristotelian Comedy." *Classical Quarterly* (Oxford), 39 (1989), 344–354.

——— "The Universality of Poetry in Aristotle's *Poetics*." *Classical Quarterly* (Oxford), 41 (1991), 389–402.

Janko, Richard. *Aristotle on Comedy: Towards a Reconstruction of Poetics II*. London: Duckworth, 1984.

Kennedy, George A., ed. *The Cambridge History of Literary Criticism vol. 1: Classical Criticism*. Cambridge: Cambridge University Press, 1989.

Lear, Jonathan. *"Katharsis."* *Phronesis* (Oxford), 33 (1988), 297–326.

Nussbaum, Martha C. *The Fragility of Goodness: Luck and Ethics in Greek Tragedy and Philosophy*. Cambridge: Cambridge University Press, 1986.

——— "Tragedy and Self-Sufficiency: Plato and Aristotle on Fear and Pity." *Oxford Studies in Ancient Philosophy* (Oxford), 10 (1992), 107–159.

Richardson, Nicholas. "Aristotle's Reading of Homer and Its Background." in Lamberton, R. W., and J. Keaney edd. *Homer's Ancient Readers*. Princeton: Princeton University Press, 1992, 30–40.

Rorty, Amélie Oksenberg, ed. *Essays on Aristotle's Poetics*. Princeton: Princeton University Press, 1992.

Stinton, T. C. W. *"Hamartia* in Aristotle and Greek Tragedy." *Classical Quarterly* (Oxford), 25 (1975), 221–254.

ΠΕΡΙ ΠΟΙΗΤΙΚΗΣ

ΠΕΡΙ ΠΟΙΗΤΙΚΗΣ

1447a
I

10

Περὶ ποιητικῆς αὐτῆς τε καὶ τῶν εἰδῶν αὐτῆς, ἥν τινα δύναμιν ἕκαστον ἔχει, καὶ πῶς δεῖ συνίστασθαι τοὺς μύθους εἰ μέλλει καλῶς ἕξειν ἡ ποίησις, ἔτι δὲ ἐκ πόσων καὶ ποίων ἐστὶ μορίων, ὁμοίως δὲ καὶ περὶ τῶν ἄλλων ὅσα τῆς αὐτῆς ἐστι μεθόδου, λέγωμεν ἀρξάμενοι κατὰ φύσιν πρῶτον ἀπὸ τῶν πρώτων.

15

20

ἐποποιία δὴ καὶ ἡ τῆς τραγῳδίας ποίησις ἔτι δὲ κωμῳδία καὶ ἡ διθυραμβοποιητικὴ καὶ τῆς αὐλητικῆς ἡ πλείστη καὶ κιθαριστικῆς πᾶσαι τυγχάνουσιν οὖσαι μιμήσεις τὸ σύνολον· διαφέρουσι δὲ ἀλλήλων τρισίν, ἢ γὰρ τῷ ἐν[1] ἑτέροις μιμεῖσθαι ἢ τῷ ἕτερα ἢ τῷ ἑτέρως καὶ μὴ τὸν αὐτὸν τρόπον. ὥσπερ γὰρ καὶ χρώμασι καὶ σχήμασι πολλὰ μιμοῦνταί τινες ἀπεικάζοντες (οἱ μὲν διὰ τέχνης οἱ δὲ διὰ συνηθείας), ἕτεροι δὲ διὰ τῆς φωνῆς, οὕτω κἀν ταῖς εἰρημέναις τέχναις ἅπασαι μὲν ποιοῦνται τὴν μίμησιν ἐν ῥυθμῷ καὶ λόγῳ καὶ ἁρμονίᾳ, τούτοις δ' ἢ χωρὶς ἢ

[1] ἐν Forchhammer: γένει A

[a] A major genre of choral lyric, performed in honour of Dionysus; cf. 49a10–11 for its relation to tragedy.

28

POETICS

We are to discuss both poetry in general and the capacity of each of its genres; the canons of plot construction needed for poetic excellence; also the number and character of poetry's components, together with the other topics which belong to the same enquiry—beginning, as is natural, from first principles.

Now, epic and tragic poetry, as well as comedy, dithyramb,[a] and most music for aulos[b] and lyre, are all, taken as a whole, kinds of mimesis.[c] But they differ from one another in three respects: namely, by producing mimesis in different media, of different objects, or in different modes. Just as people (some by formal skill, others by a knack) use colours and shapes to render mimetic images of many things, while others again use the voice,[d] so too all the poetic arts mentioned produce mimesis in rhythm, language, and melody, whether separately or in

[b] A reed pipe (akin to an oboe) used to accompany parts of drama and some other forms of poetry, but also for purely instrumental music; cf. 48a9, 61a18, b31.

[c] The foundational aesthetic concept of the *Poetics*; my translation generally retains the Greek noun, but sometimes, to avoid awkwardness, I use the verb "represent." See the Introduction.

[d] For vocal mimicry, including that of actors; cf. *Rh.* 1404a21–3.

μεμιγμένοις· οἷον ἁρμονίᾳ μὲν καὶ ῥυθμῷ χρώμεναι
μόνον ἥ τε αὐλητικὴ καὶ ἡ κιθαριστικὴ κἂν εἴ τινες
ἕτεραι τυγχάνωσιν οὖσαι τοιαῦται[1] τὴν δύναμιν,
25 οἷον ἡ τῶν συρίγγων, αὐτῷ δὲ τῷ ῥυθμῷ[2] χωρὶς
ἁρμονίας ἡ[3] τῶν ὀρχηστῶν (καὶ γὰρ οὗτοι διὰ τῶν
σχηματιζομένων ῥυθμῶν μιμοῦνται καὶ ἤθη καὶ
πάθη καὶ πράξεις)· ἡ δὲ[4] μόνον τοῖς λόγοις ψιλοῖς ἢ
τοῖς μέτροις καὶ τούτοις εἴτε μιγνῦσα μετ' ἀλλήλων
1447b εἴθ' ἑνί τινι γένει χρωμένη τῶν μέτρων ἀνώνυμος[5]
τυγχάνει οὖσα[6] μέχρι τοῦ νῦν· οὐδὲν γὰρ ἂν ἔχοιμεν ὀνομάσαι κοινὸν τοὺς Σώφρονος καὶ Ξενάρχου
10 μίμους καὶ τοὺς Σωκρατικοὺς λόγους, οὐδὲ εἴ τις διὰ
τριμέτρων ἢ ἐλεγείων ἢ τῶν ἄλλων τινῶν τῶν τοιούτων ποιοῖτο τὴν μίμησιν. πλὴν οἱ ἄνθρωποί γε συν-
άπτοντες τῷ μέτρῳ τὸ ποιεῖν ἐλεγειοποιοὺς τοὺς δὲ
ἐποποιοὺς ὀνομάζουσιν, οὐχ ὡς κατὰ τὴν μίμησιν
15 ποιητὰς ἀλλὰ κοινῇ κατὰ τὸ μέτρον προσαγορεύον-
τες· καὶ γὰρ ἂν ἰατρικὸν ἢ φυσικόν[7] τι διὰ τῶν
μέτρων ἐκφέρωσιν, οὕτω καλεῖν εἰώθασιν· οὐδὲν δὲ
κοινόν ἐστιν Ὁμήρῳ καὶ Ἐμπεδοκλεῖ πλὴν τὸ

---

[1] τοιαῦται rec.: om. A
[2] ῥυθμῷ μιμοῦνται A: μιμ. del. Spengel (om. Arab.)
[3] ἡ rec.: οἱ A
[4] δὲ ἐποποιία A: ἐπ. del. Ueberweg (om. Arab.)
[5] ἀνώνυμος add. Bernays (Arab.)
[6] τυγχάνει οὖσα Suckow: τυγχάνουσα A
[7] φυσικόν Heinsius (Arab.): μουσικόν A

combinations. That is, melody and rhythm alone are used by music for aulos and lyre, and by any other types with this capacity, for example music for panpipes; rhythm on its own, without melody, is used by the art of dancers (since they too, through rhythms translated into movements, create mimesis of character, emotions,[a] and actions); while the art which uses either plain language or metrical forms (whether combinations of these, or some one class of metres) remains so far unnamed.[b] For we have no common name to give to the mimes of Sophron and Xenarchus[c] and to Socratic dialogues; nor even to any mimesis that might be produced in iambic trimeters[d] or elegiac couplets[e] or any other such metres. Of course, people attach the verbal idea of "poetry" [*poiein*] to the name of the metre, and call some "elegiac poets," others "epic poets." But this is not to classify them as poets because of mimesis, but because of the metre they share: hence, if writers express something medical or scientific in metre, people still usually apply these terms. But Homer and Empedocles[f] have nothing in common *except*

[a] Or perhaps "sufferings."

[b] Ar. notes the lack of a collective name for mimesis in prose or metre, and rejects the standing equation of "poetry" with verse.

[c] Sicilian authors, father (late 5th cent.) and son, of prose mimes, i.e. comic sketches; cf. Ar. *On Poets*, fr. 15 Gigon/72 Rose. Sophron allegedly influenced Plato's dialogues: e.g. D. L. 3.18, *P. Oxy.* XLV 3219 fr. 1.

[d] The metre both of some "iambic" poetry (e.g. Archilochus; cf. 48b31–2) and of dialogue in drama (49a21–28).

[e] Used mostly in "elegiac" poetry such as that of Theognis.

[f] E. (c. 495–35) composed two philosophical/scientific works, *On Nature* and *Purifications*, in hexameters.

μέτρον, διὸ τὸν μὲν ποιητὴν δίκαιον καλεῖν, τὸν δὲ
φυσιολόγον μᾶλλον ἢ ποιητήν. ὁμοίως δὲ κἂν εἴ τις
20 ἅπαντα τὰ μέτρα μιγνύων ποιοῖτο τὴν μίμησιν
καθάπερ Χαιρήμων ἐποίησε Κένταυρον μικτὴν
ῥαψῳδίαν ἐξ ἁπάντων τῶν μέτρων, καὶ ποιητὴν
προσαγορευτέον. περὶ μὲν οὖν τούτων διωρίσθω
τοῦτον τὸν τρόπον. εἰσὶ δέ τινες αἳ πᾶσι χρῶνται
τοῖς εἰρημένοις, λέγω δὲ οἷον ῥυθμῷ καὶ μέλει καὶ
25 μέτρῳ, ὥσπερ ἥ τε τῶν διθυραμβικῶν ποίησις καὶ ἡ
τῶν νόμων καὶ ἥ τε τραγῳδία καὶ ἡ κωμῳδία· διαφέρουσι δὲ ὅτι αἱ μὲν ἅμα πᾶσιν αἱ δὲ κατὰ μέρος.
ταύτας μὲν οὖν λέγω τὰς διαφορὰς τῶν τεχνῶν ἐν
οἷς[1] ποιοῦνται τὴν μίμησιν.

II Ἐπεὶ δὲ μιμοῦνται οἱ μιμούμενοι πράττοντας,
1448a ἀνάγκη δὲ τούτους ἢ σπουδαίους ἢ φαύλους εἶναι
(τὰ γὰρ ἤθη σχεδὸν ἀεὶ τούτοις ἀκολουθεῖ μόνοις,
κακίᾳ γὰρ καὶ ἀρετῇ τὰ ἤθη διαφέρουσι πάντες),
ἤτοι βελτίονας ἢ καθ᾿ ἡμᾶς ἢ χείρονας ἢ καὶ τοιού-
5 τους, ὥσπερ οἱ γραφεῖς· Πολύγνωτος μὲν γὰρ κρείτ-
τους, Παύσων δὲ χείρους, Διονύσιος δὲ ὁμοίους
εἴκαζεν. δῆλον δὲ ὅτι καὶ τῶν λεχθεισῶν ἑκάστη
μιμήσεων ἕξει ταύτας τὰς διαφορὰς καὶ ἔσται ἑτέρα
τῷ ἕτερα μιμεῖσθαι τοῦτον τὸν τρόπον. καὶ γὰρ ἐν

---

[1] οἷς Vettori: αἷς A

---

[a] 4th cent. tragedian (*Rh.* 1413b13, *TrGF* I no. 71); *Centaur*
was probably a polymetric drama, perhaps meant only for recital
(hence "rhapsody," elsewhere used of epic recitals). Cf. 60a1–2.

their metre; so one should call the former a poet, the other a natural scientist. Equally, even if someone should produce mimesis in a medley of all the metres (as Chaeremon[a] did in composing his *Centaur*, a hybrid rhapsody containing all the metres), he ought still to be called a poet. In these matters, then, we should make discriminations of this kind. There are also some arts which use all the stated media—rhythm, melody, metre—as do dithyramb and nomes,[b] tragedy and comedy. They differ in that some employ all together, others use them in certain parts. So these are the distinctions between the arts in the media in which they produce mimesis.

Since mimetic artists represent people in action, and the latter should be either elevated[c] or base (for characters almost always align with just these types, as it is through vice and virtue that the characters of all men vary), they can represent people better than our normal level, worse than it, or much the same. As too with painters: Polygnotus depicted superior people, Pauson inferior, and Dionysius those like ourselves.[d] Clearly, each of the kinds of mimesis already mentioned will manifest these distinctions, and will differ by representing

[b] Nomes were traditional styles of melody, for string or wind instrument, to which various texts could be set; by Ar.'s time the term covered elaborate compositions closely related to dithyramb: cf. 48a15.

[c] See on 49b24.

[d] Polygnotus: major mid-5th cent. wall painter; cf. 50a27, with *OCD* s.v. Pauson (cf. *Pol.* 1340a36): identity uncertain; a painter of caricatures? Dionysius: more than one painter of this name is known; perhaps D. of Colophon (Ael. *VH* 4.3).

ὀρχήσει καὶ αὐλήσει καὶ κιθαρίσει ἔστι γενέσθαι
10 ταύτας τὰς ἀνομοιότητας, καὶ περὶ τοὺς λόγους δὲ
καὶ τὴν ψιλομετρίαν, οἷον Ὅμηρος μὲν βελτίους,
Κλεοφῶν δὲ ὁμοίους, Ἡγήμων δὲ ὁ Θάσιος ὁ τὰς
παρῳδίας ποιήσας πρῶτος καὶ Νικοχάρης ὁ τὴν
Δειλιάδα χείρους· ὁμοίως δὲ καὶ περὶ τοὺς διθυράμ-
βους καὶ περὶ τοὺς νόμους, ὥσπερ γὰρ[1] Κύκλωπας
15 Τιμόθεος καὶ Φιλόξενος μιμήσαιτο ἄν τις. ἐν αὐτῇ
δὲ τῇ διαφορᾷ καὶ ἡ τραγῳδία πρὸς τὴν κωμῳδίαν
διέστηκεν· ἡ μὲν γὰρ χείρους ἡ δὲ βελτίους μιμεῖσθαι βούλεται τῶν νῦν.

III ″Ετι δὲ τούτων τρίτη διαφορὰ τὸ ὡς ἕκαστα τούτων μιμήσαιτο ἄν τις. καὶ γὰρ ἐν τοῖς αὐτοῖς καὶ τὰ
20 αὐτὰ μιμεῖσθαι ἔστιν ὁτὲ μὲν ἀπαγγέλλοντα ἢ ἕτερόν τι γιγνόμενον ὥσπερ Ὅμηρος ποιεῖ, ἢ ὡς τὸν
αὐτὸν καὶ μὴ μεταβάλλοντα, ἢ πάντας ὡς πράττοντας καὶ ἐνεργοῦντας τοὺς μιμουμένους. ἐν τρισὶ δὴ
ταύταις διαφοραῖς ἡ μίμησίς ἐστιν, ὡς εἴπομεν κατ'
25 ἀρχάς, ἐν οἷς τε καὶ ἃ καὶ ὥς. ὥστε τῇ μὲν ὁ αὐτὸς
ἂν εἴη μιμητὴς Ὁμήρῳ Σοφοκλῆς, μιμοῦνται γὰρ
ἄμφω σπουδαίους, τῇ δὲ Ἀριστοφάνει, πράττοντας
γὰρ μιμοῦνται καὶ δρῶντας ἄμφω. ὅθεν καὶ δράματα καλεῖσθαί τινες αὐτά φασιν, ὅτι μιμοῦνται
δρῶντας. διὸ καὶ ἀντιποιοῦνται τῆς τε τραγῳδίας

---

[1] γὰρ Vahlen: γᾶς A: Γαλατείας καὶ Eden

[a] Minor tragic poet; cf. 58a20 and *Rh*. 1408a15.
[b] Probably late 5th cent.; cf. *OCD* s.v.

different objects in the given sense. In dancing too, and in music for aulos and lyre, these variations can occur, as well as in prose writings and metrical works without melody: for example, Homer represented superior people, Cleophon[a] those like ourselves, Hegemon of Thasos[b] (the first composer of parodies) and Nicochares[c] (author of the *Deiliad*) inferior characters. Likewise with dithyrambs and nomes: for one could represent Cyclopses as did Timotheus and Philoxenus.[d] This very distinction separates tragedy from comedy: the latter tends to represent people inferior, the former superior, to existing humans.

There is, beside these, a third distinction—in the *mode* of mimesis for these various objects. For in the same media one can represent the same objects by combining narrative with direct personation, as Homer does; *or* in an invariable narrative voice; *or* by direct enactment of all roles. These, then, are the three distinctions underlying mimesis, as we said at the outset: media, objects, modes. Accordingly, in one respect Sophocles could be classed as the same kind of mimetic artist as Homer, since both represent elevated characters, but in another the same as Aristophanes, since both represent people in direct action. Hence the assertion some people make, that dramas are so called because they represent people in action.[e] Thus, the Dorians actually lay claim to

[c] Probably late 5th cent.: *Deiliad* is a mock-epic title (cf. e.g. *Iliad*), "tale of a coward."

[d] Timotheus, c. 450–360; his *Cyclops*: *PMG* nos. 780–83. Philoxenus, roughly contemporary; see *PMG* nos. 815–24. Both were musico-stylistic innovators.

[e] The noun *drama* derives from the verb *dran*, "do" or "act" (cf. 48b1).

35

30 καὶ τῆς κωμῳδίας οἱ Δωριεῖς (τῆς μὲν γὰρ κωμῳδίας
οἱ Μεγαρεῖς οἵ τε ἐνταῦθα ὡς ἐπὶ τῆς παρ' αὐτοῖς
δημοκρατίας γενομένης καὶ οἱ ἐκ Σικελίας, ἐκεῖθεν
γὰρ ἦν Ἐπίχαρμος ὁ ποιητὴς πολλῷ πρότερος ὢν
Χιωνίδου καὶ Μάγνητος· καὶ τῆς τραγῳδίας ἔνιοι
τῶν ἐν Πελοποννήσῳ) ποιούμενοι τὰ ὀνόματα
35 σημεῖον· αὐτοὶ[1] μὲν γὰρ κώμας τὰς περιοικίδας
καλεῖν φασιν, Ἀθηναίους[2] δὲ δήμους, ὡς κωμῳδοὺς
οὐκ ἀπὸ τοῦ κωμάζειν λεχθέντας ἀλλὰ τῇ κατὰ
1448b κώμας πλάνῃ ἀτιμαζομένους ἐκ τοῦ ἄστεως· καὶ τὸ
ποιεῖν αὐτοὶ μὲν δρᾶν, Ἀθηναίους δὲ πράττειν
προσαγορεύειν. περὶ μὲν οὖν τῶν διαφορῶν καὶ
πόσαι καὶ τίνες τῆς μιμήσεως εἰρήσθω ταῦτα.

IV Ἐοίκασι δὲ γεννῆσαι μὲν ὅλως τὴν ποιητικὴν
αἰτίαι δύο τινὲς καὶ αὗται φυσικαί. τό τε γὰρ μιμεῖ-
5 σθαι σύμφυτον τοῖς ἀνθρώποις ἐκ παίδων ἐστὶ καὶ
τούτῳ διαφέρουσι τῶν ἄλλων ζῴων ὅτι μιμητικώτα-
τόν ἐστι καὶ τὰς μαθήσεις ποιεῖται διὰ μιμήσεως
τὰς πρώτας, καὶ τὸ χαίρειν τοῖς μιμήμασι πάντας.
σημεῖον δὲ τούτου τὸ συμβαῖνον ἐπὶ τῶν ἔργων· ἃ
10 γὰρ αὐτὰ λυπηρῶς ὁρῶμεν, τούτων τὰς εἰκόνας τὰς
μάλιστα ἠκριβωμένας χαίρομεν θεωροῦντες, οἷον
θηρίων τε μορφὰς τῶν ἀτιμοτάτων καὶ νεκρῶν.

---

[1] αὐτοὶ Spengel: οὗτοι AB
[2] Ἀθηναίους anon. Oxon., Spengel: -αίοι AB

---

[a] Mid-6th cent., much earlier than the introduction of comedy into dramatic festivals at Athens (cf. 49b1–2).

tragedy and comedy (comedy being claimed by the
Megarians both here on the mainland, contending it
arose during their democracy,[a] and in Sicily, the home-
land of the poet Epicharmus, a much earlier figure than
Chionides and Magnes;[b] and tragedy being claimed by
some of those in the Peloponnese);[c] and they cite the
names as evidence. They say that they call villages *kōmai*,
while the Athenians call them *dēmoi*; their contention is
that comic performers [*komodoi*] got their name not from
revelling [*kōmazein*] but from wandering through villages
when banned from the city. And they say their own word
for acting is *dran*,[d] while the Athenians' is *prattein*. So
much, then, by way of discussion of the number and
nature of the distinctions within mimesis.

It can be seen that poetry was broadly engendered by
a pair of causes, both natural. For it is an instinct of
human beings, from childhood, to engage in mimesis[e]
(indeed, this distinguishes them from other animals: man
is the most mimetic of all, and it is through mimesis that
he develops his earliest understanding); and equally natural that everyone enjoys mimetic objects. A common
occurrence indicates this: we enjoy contemplating the
most precise images of things whose actual sight is painful
to us, such as the forms of the vilest animals and of

[b] C. and M. were, between them, active at Athens in the 480s
and 470s (see on 49b3); E.'s dates are disputed: his career probably spanned the late 6th and early 5th cent.

[c] Cf. the "tragic choruses" at Sicyon, Hdt. 5.67.

[d] See on 48a28.

[e] Here a genus of activities including imitative behaviour and
artistic "image-making" as two of its species.

37

αἴτιον δὲ καὶ τούτου,[1] ὅτι μανθάνειν οὐ μόνον τοῖς
φιλοσόφοις ἥδιστον ἀλλὰ καὶ τοῖς ἄλλοις ὁμοίως,
ἀλλ' ἐπὶ βραχὺ κοινωνοῦσιν αὐτοῦ. διὰ γὰρ τοῦτο
15 χαίρουσι τὰς εἰκόνας ὁρῶντες, ὅτι συμβαίνει θεω-
ροῦντας μανθάνειν καὶ συλλογίζεσθαι τί ἕκαστον,
οἷον ὅτι οὗτος ἐκεῖνος· ἐπεὶ ἐὰν μὴ τύχῃ προεωρα-
κώς, οὐχ[2] ᾗ μίμημα ποιήσει τὴν ἡδονὴν ἀλλὰ διὰ
τὴν ἀπεργασίαν ἢ τὴν χροιὰν ἢ διὰ τοιαύτην τινὰ
ἄλλην αἰτίαν.

κατὰ φύσιν δὲ ὄντος ἡμῖν τοῦ μιμεῖσθαι καὶ τῆς
20 ἁρμονίας καὶ τοῦ ῥυθμοῦ (τὰ γὰρ μέτρα ὅτι μόρια
τῶν ῥυθμῶν ἐστι φανερόν) ἐξ ἀρχῆς οἱ[3] πεφυκότες
πρὸς[4] αὐτὰ μάλιστα κατὰ μικρὸν προάγοντες ἐγέν-
νησαν τὴν ποίησιν ἐκ τῶν αὐτοσχεδιασμάτων. διε-
σπάσθη δὲ κατὰ τὰ οἰκεῖα ἤθη ἡ ποίησις· οἱ μὲν
25 γὰρ σεμνότεροι τὰς καλὰς ἐμιμοῦντο πράξεις καὶ
τὰς τῶν τοιούτων, οἱ δὲ εὐτελέστεροι τὰς τῶν φαύλων, πρῶτον ψόγους ποιοῦντες, ὥσπερ ἕτεροι ὕμνους
καὶ ἐγκώμια. τῶν μὲν οὖν πρὸ Ὁμήρου οὐδενὸς
ἔχομεν εἰπεῖν τοιοῦτον ποίημα, εἰκὸς δὲ εἶναι πολλούς, ἀπὸ δὲ Ὁμήρου ἀρξαμένοις ἔστιν, οἷον ἐκείνου
30 ὁ Μαργίτης καὶ τὰ τοιαῦτα. ἐν οἷς κατὰ τὸ ἁρμόττον καὶ τὸ ἰαμβεῖον ἦλθε μέτρον—διὸ καὶ ἰαμβεῖον

---

[1] τούτου Lat.: τοῦτο A   [2] οὐχ ᾗ Ellebodius: οὐχὶ AB
[3] οἱ B: om. A   [4] πρὸς B: καὶ A

[a] I.e. in a portrait—a deliberately rudimentary instance of an
interpretative process which could take more complex forms.

corpses. The explanation of this too is that understanding gives great pleasure not only to philosophers but likewise to others too, though the latter have a smaller share in it. This is why people enjoy looking at images, because through contemplating them it comes about that they understand and infer what each element means, for instance that "this person is so-and-so."[a] For, if one happens not to have seen the subject before, the image will not give pleasure *qua* mimesis but because of its execution or colour, or for some other such reason.

Because mimesis comes naturally to us, as do melody and rhythm (that metres are categories of rhythms is obvious), in the earliest times[b] those with special natural talents for these things gradually progressed and brought poetry into being from improvisations. Poetry branched into two, according to its creators' characters: the more serious produced mimesis of noble actions and the actions of noble people, while the more vulgar depicted the actions of the base, in the first place by composing invectives[c] (just as others produced hymns and encomia).[d] Now, we cannot name such an invective by any poet earlier than Homer, though probably many poets produced them; but we can do so from Homer onwards, namely the latter's *Margites*[e] and the like. In these poems, it was aptness which brought the iambic metre too

[b] Lit. "from the beginning": the point is *a priori* rather than strictly historical.

[c] Satirical lampoons on individuals.

[d] Poems in praise of gods and outstanding humans.

[e] A (lost) burlesque epic, named after its crass "hero," composed in a mixture of hexameters and iambic trimeters. It is not now, and was not always in antiquity, attributed to "Homer."

καλεῖται νῦν, ὅτι ἐν τῷ μέτρῳ τούτῳ ἰάμβιζον ἀλλήλους. καὶ ἐγένοντο τῶν παλαιῶν οἱ μὲν ἡρωικῶν οἱ
δὲ ἰάμβων ποιηταί. ὥσπερ δὲ καὶ τὰ σπουδαῖα
μάλιστα ποιητὴς Ὅμηρος ἦν (μόνος γὰρ οὐχ ὅτι εὖ
35 ἀλλὰ καὶ μιμήσεις δραματικὰς ἐποίησεν), οὕτως καὶ
τὰ[1] τῆς κωμῳδίας σχήματα πρῶτος ὑπέδειξεν, οὐ
ψόγον ἀλλὰ τὸ γελοῖον δραματοποιήσας· ὁ γὰρ
Μαργίτης ἀνάλογον ἔχει, ὥσπερ Ἰλιὰς καὶ ἡ
1449a Ὀδύσσεια πρὸς τὰς τραγῳδίας, οὕτω καὶ οὗτος πρὸς
τὰς κωμῳδίας. παραφανείσης δὲ τῆς τραγῳδίας καὶ
κωμῳδίας οἱ ἐφ᾽ ἑκατέραν τὴν ποίησιν ὁρμῶντες
κατὰ τὴν οἰκείαν φύσιν οἱ μὲν ἀντὶ τῶν ἰάμβων
κωμῳδοποιοὶ ἐγένοντο, οἱ δὲ ἀντὶ τῶν ἐπῶν τραγῳ-
5 δοδιδάσκαλοι, διὰ τὸ μείζω καὶ ἐντιμότερα τὰ σχήματα εἶναι ταῦτα ἐκείνων.

τὸ μὲν οὖν ἐπισκοπεῖν εἰ ἄρα ἔχει ἤδη ἡ τραγῳδία τοῖς εἴδεσιν ἱκανῶς ἢ οὔ, αὐτό τε καθ᾽ αὑτὸ
κρῖναι[2] καὶ πρὸς τὰ θέατρα, ἄλλος λόγος. γενομένη[3] δ᾽ οὖν ἀπ᾽ ἀρχῆς αὐτοσχεδιαστικῆς (καὶ αὐτὴ
10 καὶ ἡ κωμῳδία, καὶ ἡ μὲν ἀπὸ τῶν ἐξαρχόντων τὸν
διθύραμβον, ἡ δὲ ἀπὸ τῶν τὰ φαλλικὰ ἃ ἔτι καὶ νῦν

[1] τὰ . . . σχήματα A Lat.: τὸ . . . σχῆμα B
[2] κρῖναι Forchhammer: κρίνεται ἢ ναί A: κρίνεται εἶναι B
[3] γενομένη rec.: -ένης AB

[a] Cf. on 47b11.
[b] See on 49b24.
[c] I.e. containing much direct/personative speech; cf. 48a21–
2, 60a5–11.

into use—precisely why it is called "iambic" now, because it was in this metre that they lampooned [*iambizein*] one another.[a] Of the older poets some became composers of epic hexameters, others of iambic lampoons. Just as Homer was the supreme poet of elevated[b] subjects (for he was preeminent not only in quality but also in composing dramatic[c] mimesis), so too he was the first to delineate the forms of comedy, by dramatising not invective but the laughable: thus *Margites* stands in the same relation to comedies as do the *Iliad* and *Odyssey* to tragedies. And when tragedy and comedy had been glimpsed,[d] those whose own natures gave them an impetus towards either type of poetry abandoned iambic lampoons to become comic poets, or epic to become tragedians, because these newer forms were grander and more esteemed[e] than the earlier.

To consider whether or not tragedy is even now sufficiently developed in its types—judging it intrinsically and in relation to audiences—is a separate matter.[f] Anyhow, when it came into being from an improvisatory origin (that is, both tragedy and comedy: the former from the leaders of dithyramb,[g] the other from the leaders of the

[d] I.e. potentially, within the nature of Homer's poetry.

[e] This applies principally to Athens, and to creation of new works rather than abstract estimation of poems.

[f] A curious remark, in view of 14–15 below; but the emphasis here may fall on "types" (cf. 55b32) rather than tragedy's essential "nature."

[g] See on 47a14. Ar. probably assumes that the Athenian Thespis took the crucial step, c. 534 B.C., of adding an individual voice (the first actor) to the traditional chorus of dithyramb: cf. *TrGF* I 62, T6.

ἐν πολλαῖς τῶν πόλεων διαμένει νομιζόμενα), κατὰ
μικρὸν ηὐξήθη προαγόντων ὅσον ἐγίγνετο φανερὸν
αὐτῆς· καὶ πολλὰς μεταβολὰς μεταβαλοῦσα ἡ τρα-
15 γῳδία ἐπαύσατο, ἐπεὶ ἔσχε τὴν αὐτῆς φύσιν. καὶ τό
τε τῶν ὑποκριτῶν πλῆθος ἐξ ἑνὸς εἰς δύο πρῶτος
Αἰσχύλος ἤγαγε καὶ τὰ τοῦ χοροῦ ἠλάττωσε καὶ τὸν
λόγον πρωταγωνιστεῖν[1] παρεσκεύασεν· τρεῖς δὲ καὶ
σκηνογραφίαν Σοφοκλῆς. ἔτι δὲ τὸ μέγεθος· ἐκ
μικρῶν μύθων καὶ λέξεως γελοίας διὰ τὸ ἐκ σατυρι-
20 κοῦ μεταβαλεῖν ὀψὲ ἀπεσεμνύνθη, τό τε μέτρον ἐκ
τετραμέτρου ἰαμβεῖον ἐγένετο. τὸ μὲν γὰρ πρῶτον
τετραμέτρῳ ἐχρῶντο διὰ τὸ σατυρικὴν καὶ ὀρχηστι-
κωτέραν εἶναι τὴν ποίησιν, λέξεως δὲ γενομένης
αὐτὴ ἡ φύσις τὸ οἰκεῖον μέτρον εὗρε· μάλιστα γὰρ
λεκτικὸν τῶν μέτρων τὸ ἰαμβεῖόν ἐστιν· σημεῖον δὲ
25 τούτου, πλεῖστα γὰρ ἰαμβεῖα λέγομεν ἐν τῇ διαλέκτῳ τῇ πρὸς ἀλλήλους, ἑξάμετρα δὲ ὀλιγάκις καὶ
ἐκβαίνοντες τῆς λεκτικῆς ἁρμονίας. ἔτι δὲ ἐπεισ-

---

[1] πρωταγωνιστεῖν Sophianus: -ιστὴν AB

[a] Sung to accompany processional carrying of phallic icons in
ritual contexts; normally obscene and scurrilous: cf. Aristoph.
Ach. 241–79.

[b] Not consistently, as his surviving plays show, but in broad
relation to his predecessors.

[c] The third actor was probably introduced in the 460s, early
in Soph.'s career; it is required in Aesch. *Oresteia* of 458. Scene
painting: decoration of the stage building (*skēnē*), to give it an
active dramatic status.

phallic songs[a] which remain even now a custom in many
cities), it was gradually enhanced as poets developed the
potential they saw in it. And after going through many
changes tragedy ceased to evolve, since it had achieved its
own nature. Aeschylus innovated by raising the number
of actors from one to two, reduced the choral component,[b] and made speech play the leading role. Three
actors and scene painting came with Sophocles.[c] A further factor was grandeur: after a period of slight plots and
laughable diction, owing to development from a satyric[d] ethos, it was at a late stage that tragedy acquired
dignity, and its metre became the iambic trimeter instead
of the trochaic tetrameter.[e] To begin with they used the
tetrameter because the poetry was satyric and more associated with dancing; but when spoken dialogue was
introduced,[f] tragedy's own nature[g] discovered the appropriate metre. For the iambic trimeter, more than any
other metre, has the rhythm of speech: an indication of
this is that we speak[h] many trimeters in conversation with
one another, but hexameters only rarely and when diverg-
ing from the colloquial register. Further changes con-

[d] I.e. with the tone of a satyr play. Did Ar. connect this tone
with the early dithyrambs from which tragedy developed
(49a10–11)?

[e] Trimeter: see on 47b11; trochaic tetrameter: apparently the
main metre of early tragedy, used sporadically by later tragedians; cf. 59b37, *Rh.* 1404a30–31.

[f] Ar. seems to imply that in the earliest tragedy everything
was musically accompanied.

[g] Cf. 49a15 above; see 60a4 for "natural" appropriateness of
metre to genre.

[h] Sc. unintentionally.

43

οδίων πλήθη. καὶ τὰ ἄλλ' ὡς ἕκαστα κοσμηθῆναι
λέγεται ἔστω ἡμῖν εἰρημένα· πολὺ γὰρ ἂν ἴσως
30 ἔργον εἴη διεξιέναι καθ' ἕκαστον.

V Ἡ δὲ κωμῳδία ἐστὶν ὥσπερ εἴπομεν μίμησις
φαυλοτέρων μέν, οὐ μέντοι κατὰ πᾶσαν κακίαν,
ἀλλὰ τοῦ αἰσχροῦ ἐστι τὸ γελοῖον μόριον. τὸ γὰρ
γελοῖόν ἐστιν ἁμάρτημά τι καὶ αἶσχος ἀνώδυνον καὶ
35 οὐ φθαρτικόν, οἷον εὐθὺς τὸ γελοῖον πρόσωπον
αἰσχρόν τι καὶ διεστραμμένον ἄνευ ὀδύνης. αἱ μὲν
οὖν τῆς τραγῳδίας μεταβάσεις καὶ δι' ὧν ἐγένοντο
οὐ λελήθασιν, ἡ δὲ κωμῳδία διὰ τὸ μὴ σπουδάζε-
1449b σθαι ἐξ ἀρχῆς ἔλαθεν· καὶ γὰρ χορὸν κωμῳδῶν ὀψέ
ποτε ὁ ἄρχων ἔδωκεν, ἀλλ' ἐθελονταὶ ἦσαν. ἤδη δὲ
σχήματά τινα αὐτῆς ἐχούσης οἱ λεγόμενοι αὐτῆς
ποιηταὶ μνημονεύονται. τίς δὲ πρόσωπα ἀπέδωκεν ἢ
προλόγους ἢ πλήθη ὑποκριτῶν καὶ ὅσα τοιαῦτα,
5 ἠγνόηται. τὸ δὲ μύθους ποιεῖν[1] τὸ μὲν ἐξ ἀρχῆς ἐκ
Σικελίας ἦλθε, τῶν δὲ Ἀθήνησιν Κράτης πρῶτος
ἦρξεν ἀφέμενος τῆς ἰαμβικῆς ἰδέας καθόλου ποιεῖν
λόγους καὶ μύθους.

---

[1] ποιεῖν Ἐπίχαρμος καὶ Φόρμις AB: Ἐ. κ. Φ. secl.
Susemihl (om. Arab.)

---

[a] Early tragedy's plots were shorter, less complex (cf. "slight
plots," 49a19).

[b] 48a17–18; cf. 48b26.

[c] *Aischros*, "shameful," also covers "ugly," and is so translated
in the next sentence.

44

cerned the number of episodes.[a] And we shall take as read the ways in which other features of tragedy are said to have been embellished; it would no doubt be a large task to discuss them individually.

Comedy, as we said,[b] is mimesis of baser but not wholly vicious characters: rather, the laughable is one category of the shameful.[c] For the laughable comprises any fault or mark of shame which involves no pain or destruction: most obviously, the laughable mask is something ugly and twisted, but not painfully. Now, tragedy's stages of development, and those responsible for them, have been remembered, but comedy's early history was forgotten because no serious interest was taken in it: only at a rather late date did the archon grant a comic chorus;[d] previously performers were volunteers. It is from a time[e] when the genre already had some formal features that the first named poets of comedy are remembered. Who introduced masks, prologues, various numbers of actors, and everything of that kind, has been lost. The composition of plots originally came from Sicily; of Athenian poets Crates was the first to relinquish the iambic manner and to create stories and plots with an overall structure.[f]

[d] The archon (a major magistrate) chose plays, and arranged funding, for official production at the City Dionysia festival: this happened first for comedy only in 487/6; tragedies had been so performed since the late 6th century.

[e] The 480s/70s, the era of e.g. Chionides and Magnes; see on 48a34.

[f] Sicily was home of Epicharmus (see on 48a33). Crates was active in the 440s and 430s; "iambic manner" implies satire of individuals (cf. 48b31–2). "Overall structure," *katholou*, is the same term used for "universals" at 51b7.

45

ἡ μὲν οὖν ἐποποιία τῇ τραγῳδίᾳ μέχρι μὲν[1] τοῦ
μετὰ[2] μέτρου λόγῳ μίμησις εἶναι σπουδαίων ἠκο-
10 λούθησεν· τῷ δὲ τὸ μέτρον ἁπλοῦν ἔχειν καὶ ἀπαγγελίαν εἶναι, ταύτῃ διαφέρουσιν· ἔτι δὲ τῷ μήκει· ἡ
μὲν ὅτι μάλιστα πειρᾶται ὑπὸ μίαν περίοδον ἡλίου
εἶναι ἢ μικρὸν ἐξαλλάττειν, ἡ δὲ ἐποποιία ἀόριστος
τῷ χρόνῳ καὶ τούτῳ διαφέρει, καίτοι τὸ πρῶτον
15 ὁμοίως ἐν ταῖς τραγῳδίαις τοῦτο ἐποίουν καὶ ἐν τοῖς
ἔπεσιν. μέρη δ' ἐστὶ τὰ μὲν ταὐτά, τὰ δὲ ἴδια τῆς
τραγῳδίας· διόπερ ὅστις περὶ τραγῳδίας οἶδε σπουδαίας καὶ φαύλης, οἶδε καὶ περὶ ἐπῶν· ἃ μὲν γὰρ
ἐποποιία ἔχει, ὑπάρχει τῇ τραγῳδίᾳ, ἃ δὲ αὐτῇ, οὐ
20 πάντα ἐν τῇ ἐποποιίᾳ.

VI   Περὶ μὲν οὖν τῆς ἐν ἑξαμέτροις μιμητικῆς καὶ
περὶ κωμῳδίας ὕστερον ἐροῦμεν· περὶ δὲ τραγῳδίας
λέγωμεν ἀναλαβόντες[3] αὐτῆς ἐκ τῶν εἰρημένων τὸν
γινόμενον ὅρον τῆς οὐσίας. ἔστιν οὖν τραγῳδία
μίμησις πράξεως σπουδαίας καὶ τελείας μέγεθος
25 ἐχούσης, ἡδυσμένῳ λόγῳ χωρὶς ἑκάστῳ[4] τῶν εἰδῶν
ἐν τοῖς μορίοις, δρώντων καὶ οὐ δι' ἀπαγγελίας, δι'
ἐλέου καὶ φόβου περαίνουσα τὴν τῶν τοιούτων
παθημάτων[5] κάθαρσιν. λέγω δὲ ἡδυσμένον μὲν

[1] μὲν τοῦ Tyrwhitt: μόνου AB
[2] μετὰ μέτρου λόγῳ Kassel: μέτρου μετὰ λόγου B: μέτρου
μεγάλου A
[3] ἀναλαβόντες Bernays: ἀπο- AB
[4] ἑκάστῳ Reiz: -ου AB
[5] παθημάτων B: μαθημάτων A Lat.

Epic matches tragedy to the extent of being mimesis of elevated matters[a] in metrical language; but they differ in that epic has an unchanging metre and is in narrative mode.[b] They also differ in length; tragedy tends so far as possible to stay within a single revolution of the sun, or close to it, while epic is unlimited in time span and is distinctive in this respect (though to begin with the poets followed this same practice in tragedy as in epic). Epic and tragedy have some components in common, but others are peculiar to tragedy. So whoever knows about good and bad tragedy knows the same about epic, as epic's resources belong to tragedy,[c] but tragedy's are not all to be found in epic.

VI   We shall later discuss the art of mimesis in hexameters,[d] as well as comedy.[e] But let us now discuss tragedy, taking up the definition of its essence which emerges from what has already been said. Tragedy, then, is mimesis of an action which is elevated,[f] complete, and of magnitude; in language embellished by distinct forms in its sections; employing the mode of enactment, not narrative; and through pity and fear accomplishing the

---

[a] Or "characters"; for "elevated" see on 49b24.

[b] Cf. the distinctions in chs. I–III; Homer's combination of narrative with personation (48a21–2) is here left aside.

[c] Cf. 62a14–15.

[d] I.e. epic; cf. 59a17.

[e] The discussion of comedy is lost; cf. on 62b19, and see the Introduction at n. 5.

[f] *Spoudaios*, the same adj. used for characters at e.g. 48a2; it denotes ethical distinction and gravity of tone. Cf. the Introduction.

λόγον τὸν ἔχοντα ῥυθμὸν καὶ ἁρμονίαν,[1] τὸ δὲ
χωρὶς τοῖς εἴδεσι τὸ διὰ μέτρων ἔνια μόνον περαίνε-
30 σθαι καὶ πάλιν ἕτερα διὰ μέλους. ἐπεὶ δὲ πράττον-
τες ποιοῦνται τὴν μίμησιν, πρῶτον μὲν ἐξ ἀνάγκης
ἂν εἴη τι μόριον τραγῳδίας ὁ τῆς ὄψεως κόσμος·
εἶτα μελοποιία καὶ λέξις, ἐν τούτοις γὰρ ποιοῦνται
τὴν μίμησιν. λέγω δὲ λέξιν μὲν αὐτὴν τὴν τῶν
μέτρων σύνθεσιν, μελοποιίαν δὲ ὃ τὴν δύναμιν
35 φανερὰν ἔχει πᾶσαν. ἐπεὶ δὲ πράξεώς ἐστι μίμησις,
πράττεται δὲ ὑπό τινων πραττόντων οὓς ἀνάγκη ποιούς τινας εἶναι κατά τε τὸ ἦθος καὶ τὴν διάνοιαν
(διὰ γὰρ τούτων καὶ τὰς πράξεις εἶναί φαμεν ποιάς
1450a τινας,[2] καὶ κατὰ ταύτας καὶ τυγχάνουσι καὶ ἀπο-
τυγχάνουσι πάντες), ἔστιν δὲ τῆς μὲν πράξεως ὁ
μῦθος ἡ μίμησις, λέγω γὰρ μῦθον τοῦτον τὴν σύνθεσιν τῶν πραγμάτων, τὰ δὲ ἤθη, καθ᾽ ὃ ποιούς
5 τινας εἶναί φαμεν τοὺς πράττοντας, διάνοιαν δέ, ἐν
ὅσοις λέγοντες ἀποδεικνύασίν τι ἢ καὶ ἀποφαίνονται
γνώμην. ἀνάγκη οὖν πάσης τῆς[3] τραγῳδίας μέρη
εἶναι ἕξ, καθ᾽ ὃ ποιά τις ἐστιν ἡ τραγῳδία· ταῦτα δ᾽
ἐστὶ μῦθος καὶ ἤθη καὶ λέξις καὶ διάνοια καὶ ὄψις
10 καὶ μελοποιία. οἷς μὲν γὰρ μιμοῦνται, δύο μέρη
ἐστίν, ὡς δὲ μιμοῦνται, ἕν, ἃ δὲ μιμοῦνται, τρία, καὶ
παρὰ ταῦτα οὐδέν. τούτοις μὲν οὖν οὐκ ὀλίγοι

---

[1] ἁρμονίαν καὶ μέλος AB: καὶ μ. del. Tyrwhitt
[2] post τινας seq. πέφυκεν αἴτια δύο τῶν πράξεων εἶναι,
διάνοια [-αν, A] καὶ ἦθος in AB: πέφυκεν . . . ἦθος secl. Else
[3] τῆς B: om. A

catharsis[a] of such emotions. I use "embellished" for language with rhythm and melody, and "distinct forms" for the fact that some parts are conveyed through metrical speech alone, others again through song. Since actors render the mimesis, some part of tragedy will, in the first place, necessarily be the arrangement of spectacle;[b] to which can be added lyric poetry and diction, for these are the media in which they render the mimesis. By "diction"[c] I mean the actual composition of the metrical speech; the sense of "lyric poetry"[d] is entirely clear. Since tragedy is mimesis of an action, and the action is conducted by agents who should have certain qualities in both character and thought (as it is these factors which allow us to ascribe qualities to their actions too, and it is in their actions that all men find success or failure), the plot is the mimesis of the action—for I use "plot" to denote the construction of events, "character" to mean that in virtue of which we ascribe certain qualities to the agents, and "thought" to cover the parts in which, through speech, they demonstrate something or declare their views. Tragedy as a whole, therefore, must have six components, which give it its qualities—namely, plot, character, diction, thought, spectacle, and lyric poetry. The media of the mimesis are two components, its mode one, and its objects three;[e] there are no others. Now, these

---

[a] The term (the most controversial in the work) is never defined; cf. the Introduction. [b] I.e. the visual aspects of the action, esp. the appearance of the agents; cf. the end of ch. VI and the start of ch. XIV. [c] *Lexis*: see chs. XIX-XXII. [d] *Melopoiïa* covers the sung parts of tragedy. [e] This matches the components with chs. I-III's scheme: media = diction, lyric poetry; mode = spectacle (i.e. enactment); objects = plot, character, thought.

ARISTOTLE

αὐτῶν¹ κέχρηνται τοῖς εἴδεσιν· καὶ γὰρ ὄψεις² ἔχει
πᾶν ὡς εἰπεῖν¹ καὶ ἦθος καὶ μῦθον καὶ λέξιν καὶ
μέλος καὶ διάνοιαν ὡσαύτως. μέγιστον δὲ τούτων
15 ἐστὶν ἡ τῶν πραγμάτων σύστασις. ἡ γὰρ τραγῳδία
μίμησίς ἐστιν οὐκ ἀνθρώπων ἀλλὰ πράξεως³ καὶ
βίου, καὶ εὐδαιμονία καὶ κακοδαιμονία ἐν πράξει
ἐστίν, καὶ τὸ τέλος πρᾶξίς τις ἐστίν, οὐ ποιότης·
εἰσὶν δὲ κατὰ μὲν τὰ ἤθη ποιοί τινες, κατὰ δὲ τὰς
πράξεις εὐδαίμονες ἢ τοὐναντίον. οὔκουν ὅπως τὰ
20 ἤθη μιμήσωνται πράττουσιν, ἀλλὰ τὰ ἤθη συμπερι-
λαμβάνουσιν διὰ τὰς πράξεις· ὥστε τὰ πράγματα
καὶ ὁ μῦθος τέλος τῆς τραγῳδίας, τὸ δὲ τέλος μέγιστον ἁπάντων. ἔτι ἄνευ μὲν πράξεως οὐκ ἂν γένοιτο
τραγῳδία, ἄνευ δὲ ἠθῶν γένοιτ' ἄν· αἱ γὰρ τῶν νέων
25 τῶν πλείστων ἀήθεις τραγῳδίαι εἰσίν, καὶ ὅλως
ποιηταὶ πολλοὶ τοιοῦτοι, οἷον καὶ τῶν γραφέων Ζεῦξις πρὸς Πολύγνωτον πέπονθεν· ὁ μὲν γὰρ Πολύγνωτος ἀγαθὸς ἠθογράφος, ἡ δὲ Ζεύξιδος γραφὴ
οὐδὲν ἔχει ἦθος. ἔτι ἐάν τις ἐφεξῆς θῇ ῥήσεις ἠθι-
κὰς καὶ λέξει⁴ καὶ διανοίᾳ εὖ πεποιημένας, οὐ ποιή-
30 σει ὃ ἦν τῆς τραγῳδίας ἔργον, ἀλλὰ πολὺ μᾶλλον
ἡ καταδεεστέροις τούτοις κεχρημένη τραγῳδία,
ἔχουσα δὲ μῦθον καὶ σύστασιν πραγμάτων. πρὸς

¹ αὐτῶν ὡς εἰπεῖν AB: ὡς εἰπεῖν post πᾶν (a13) transpos.
Bywater
² ὄψεις rec.: ὄψις AB
³ πράξεως A: -εων B
⁴ λέξει καὶ διανοίᾳ Vahlen: λέξεις καὶ διανοίας AB

have been used by a majority of poets as their basic elements,[a] since practically every drama has items of spectacle, character, plot, diction, lyric poetry, and thought, alike. The most important of these things is the structure of events, because tragedy is mimesis not of persons[b] but of action and life; and happiness and unhappiness consist in action, and the goal[c] is a certain kind of action, not a qualitative state: it is in virtue of character that people have certain qualities, but through their actions that they are happy or the reverse. So it is not in order to provide mimesis of character that the agents act; rather, their characters are included for the sake of their actions. Thus, the events and the plot are the goal of tragedy, and the goal is the most important thing of all. Besides, without action there could be no tragedy, but without character there could be: in fact, the works of most of the recent poets are lacking in character, and in general there are many such poets (as with Zeuxis' relationship to Polygnotus among painters: Polygnotus is a fine depicter of character, while Zeuxis' painting contains no character).[d] Again, if someone lays out a string of speeches that express character and are well composed in diction and thought, he will not achieve the stated function of tragedy; much more successful will be a tragedy which, though deficient in these other elements, has a plot and structure of events. In addition, tragedy's most

[a] Text and sense are here greatly disputed; cf. 52b14.

[b] I.e. not of personal qualities *per se*.

[c] Of either drama or life: Ar. may mean both.

[d] Zeuxis (late 5th cent.) pioneered new techniques of realism; cf. 61b12 (idealisation of human form). Polygnotus: see on 48a5.

δὲ τούτοις τὰ μέγιστα οἷς ψυχαγωγεῖ ἡ τραγῳδία
τοῦ μύθου μέρη ἐστίν, αἵ τε περιπέτειαι καὶ ἀναγνω-
ρίσεις. ἔτι σημεῖον ὅτι καὶ οἱ ἐγχειροῦντες ποιεῖν
35 πρότερον δύνανται τῇ λέξει καὶ τοῖς ἤθεσιν ἀκρι-
βοῦν ἢ τὰ πράγματα συνίστασθαι, οἷον καὶ οἱ πρῶ-
τοι ποιηταὶ σχεδὸν ἅπαντες.

ἀρχὴ μὲν οὖν καὶ οἷον ψυχὴ ὁ μῦθος τῆς τραγῳδίας, δεύτερον δὲ τὰ ἤθη (παραπλήσιον γάρ ἐστιν
καὶ ἐπὶ τῆς γραφικῆς· εἰ γάρ τις ἐναλείψειε τοῖς
1450b κ αλλίστοις φαρμάκοις χύδην, οὐκ ἂν ὁμοίως εὐφρά-
νειεν καὶ λευκογραφήσας εἰκόνα)· ἔστιν τε μίμησις
πράξεως καὶ διὰ ταύτην μάλιστα τῶν πραττόντων.
τρίτον δὲ ἡ διάνοια· τοῦτο δέ ἐστιν τὸ λέγειν δύνα-
5 σθαι τὰ ἐνόντα καὶ τὰ ἁρμόττοντα, ὅπερ ἐπὶ τῶν
λόγων τῆς πολιτικῆς καὶ ῥητορικῆς ἔργον ἐστίν· οἱ
μὲν γὰρ ἀρχαῖοι πολιτικῶς ἐποίουν λέγοντας, οἱ δὲ
νῦν ῥητορικῶς. ἔστιν δὲ ἦθος μὲν τὸ τοιοῦτον ὃ
δηλοῖ τὴν προαίρεσιν, ὁποῖά[1] τις ἐν οἷς οὐκ ἔστι
δῆλον ἢ προαιρεῖται ἢ φεύγει (διόπερ οὐκ ἔχουσιν
ἦθος τῶν λόγων ἐν οἷς μηδ’ ὅλως ἔστιν ὅ τι προαι-
10 ρεῖται ἢ φεύγει ὁ λέγων), διάνοια δὲ ἐν οἷς ἀποδει-
κνύουσί τι ὡς ἔστιν ἢ ὡς οὐκ ἔστιν ἢ καθόλου τι
ἀποφαίνονται. τέταρτον δὲ τῶν μὲν λόγων ἡ λέξις·
λέγω δέ, ὥσπερ πρότερον εἴρηται, λέξιν εἶναι τὴν
διὰ τῆς ὀνομασίας ἑρμηνείαν, ὃ καὶ ἐπὶ τῶν ἐμμέ-
τρων καὶ ἐπὶ τῶν λόγων ἔχει τὴν αὐτὴν δύναμιν.
15 τῶν δὲ λοιπῶν ἡ μελοποιία μέγιστον τῶν ἡδυσμά-

[1] ὁποῖά τις AB: ὁποία τις Lat.

potent means of emotional effect are components of plot, namely reversals and recognitions.[a] A further pointer is that apprentice poets can achieve precision in diction and characterisation sooner than structure the events, as likewise with almost all the early poets.

Plot, then, is the first principle and, as it were, soul of tragedy, while character is secondary. (A similar principle also holds in painting: if one were to cover a surface randomly with the finest colours, one would provide less pleasure than by an outline of a picture.) Tragedy is mimesis of action, and it is chiefly for the sake of the action that it represents the agents.[b] Third in importance is thought: that is, the capacity to say what is pertinent and apt, which in formal speeches is the task of politics and rhetoric. The earliest poets made people speak politically, present day poets make them speak rhetorically. Character is that which reveals moral choice—that is, when otherwise[c] unclear, what kinds of thing an agent chooses or rejects (which is why speeches in which there is nothing at all the speaker chooses or rejects contain no character); while thought covers the parts in which they demonstrate that something is or is not so, or declare a general view. Fourth is the diction of the spoken sections: as stated earlier, I define diction as expression through choice of words—something which has the same capacity in both verse and prose. Of the remainder, lyric poetry is the greatest embellishment, while spectacle

[a] See ch. XI for definitions.
[b] The same principle as 50a16–17.
[c] Sc. from the action; cf. 54a17–19.

των, ἡ δὲ ὄψις ψυχαγωγικὸν μέν, ἀτεχνότατον δὲ καὶ
ἥκιστα οἰκεῖον τῆς ποιητικῆς· ἡ γὰρ τῆς τραγῳδίας
δύναμις καὶ ἄνευ ἀγῶνος καὶ ὑποκριτῶν ἔστιν, ἔτι δὲ
κυριωτέρα περὶ τὴν ἀπεργασίαν τῶν ὄψεων ἡ τοῦ
20 σκευοποιοῦ τέχνη τῆς τῶν ποιητῶν ἐστιν.

VII   Διωρισμένων δὲ τούτων, λέγωμεν μετὰ ταῦτα
ποίαν τινὰ δεῖ τὴν σύστασιν εἶναι τῶν πραγμάτων,
ἐπειδὴ τοῦτο καὶ πρῶτον καὶ μέγιστον τῆς τραγῳδίας ἐστίν. κεῖται δὴ¹ ἡμῖν τὴν τραγῳδίαν τελείας
καὶ ὅλης πράξεως εἶναι μίμησιν ἐχούσης τι μέγε-
25 θος· ἔστιν γὰρ ὅλον καὶ μηδὲν ἔχον μέγεθος. ὅλον
δέ ἐστιν τὸ ἔχον ἀρχὴν καὶ μέσον καὶ τελευτήν.
ἀρχὴ δέ ἐστιν ὃ αὐτὸ μὲν μὴ ἐξ ἀνάγκης μετ᾽ ἄλλο
ἐστίν, μετ᾽ ἐκεῖνο δ᾽ ἕτερον πέφυκεν εἶναι ἢ γίνε-
σθαι· τελευτὴ δὲ τοὐναντίον ὃ αὐτὸ μὲν μετ᾽ ἄλλο
πέφυκεν εἶναι ἢ ἐξ ἀνάγκης ἢ ὡς ἐπὶ τὸ πολύ, μετὰ
30 δὲ τοῦτο ἄλλο οὐδέν· μέσον δὲ ὃ καὶ αὐτὸ μετ᾽ ἄλλο
καὶ μετ᾽ ἐκεῖνο ἕτερον. δεῖ ἄρα τοὺς συνεστῶτας εὖ
μύθους μήθ᾽ ὁπόθεν ἔτυχεν ἄρχεσθαι μήθ᾽ ὅπου
ἔτυχε τελευτᾶν, ἀλλὰ κεχρῆσθαι ταῖς εἰρημέναις
ἰδέαις. ἔτι δ᾽ ἐπεὶ τὸ καλὸν καὶ ζῷον καὶ ἅπαν
πρᾶγμα ὃ συνέστηκεν ἐκ τινῶν οὐ μόνον ταῦτα
35 τεταγμένα δεῖ ἔχειν ἀλλὰ καὶ μέγεθος ὑπάρχειν μὴ
τὸ τυχόν· τὸ γὰρ καλὸν ἐν μεγέθει καὶ τάξει ἐστίν,
διὸ οὔτε πάμμικρον ἄν τι γένοιτο καλὸν ζῷον
(συγχεῖται γὰρ ἡ θεωρία ἐγγὺς τοῦ ἀναισθήτου
χρόνου γινομένη) οὔτε παμμέγεθες (οὐ γὰρ ἅμα ἡ
1451a θεωρία γίνεται ἀλλ᾽ οἴχεται τοῖς θεωροῦσι τὸ ἓν καὶ

is emotionally potent but falls quite outside the art and is not integral to poetry: tragedy's capacity is independent of performance and actors, and, besides, the costumier's[a] art has more scope than the poet's for rendering effects of spectacle.

Given these definitions, let us next discuss the required qualities of the structure of events, since this is the principal and most important factor in tragedy. We have stipulated that tragedy is mimesis of an action that is complete, whole, and of magnitude (for one can have a whole which lacks magnitude). A whole is that which has a beginning, middle, and end. A beginning is that which does not itself follow necessarily from something else, but after which a further event or process naturally occurs. An end, by contrast, is that which itself naturally occurs, whether necessarily or usually, after a preceding event, but need not be followed by anything else. A middle is that which both follows a preceding event and has further consequences. Well-constructed plots, therefore, should neither begin nor end at an arbitrary point, but should make use of the patterns stated. Besides, a beautiful object, whether an animal or anything else with a structure of parts, should have not only its parts ordered but also an appropriate magnitude: beauty consists in magnitude and order, which is why there could not be a beautiful animal which was either minuscule (as contemplation of it, occurring in an almost imperceptible moment, has no distinctness) or gigantic (as contemplation of it has no cohesion, but those who contemplate it lose a sense of

---

[a] Responsible, above all, for mask-making.

[1] δή Bywater: δέ AB

τὸ ὅλον ἐκ τῆς θεωρίας), οἷον εἰ μυρίων σταδίων εἴη
ζῷον· ὥστε δεῖ καθάπερ ἐπὶ τῶν σωμάτων καὶ ἐπὶ
τῶν ζῴων ἔχειν μὲν μέγεθος, τοῦτο δὲ εὐσύνοπτον
5 εἶναι, οὕτω καὶ ἐπὶ τῶν μύθων ἔχειν μὲν μῆκος,
τοῦτο δὲ εὐμνημόνευτον εἶναι. τοῦ δὲ μήκους ὅρος
ὁ¹ μὲν πρὸς τοὺς ἀγῶνας καὶ τὴν αἴσθησιν οὐ τῆς
τέχνης ἐστίν· εἰ γὰρ ἔδει ἑκατὸν τραγῳδίας ἀγωνί-
ζεσθαι, πρὸς κλεψύδρας ἂν ἠγωνίζοντο, ὥσπερ ποτὲ
καὶ ἄλλοτέ φασιν. ὁ δὲ κατ' αὐτὴν τὴν φύσιν τοῦ
10 πράγματος ὅρος, ἀεὶ μὲν ὁ μείζων μέχρι τοῦ σύνδη-
λος εἶναι καλλίων ἐστὶ κατὰ τὸ μέγεθος· ὡς δὲ
ἁπλῶς διορίσαντας εἰπεῖν, ἐν ὅσῳ μεγέθει κατὰ τὸ
εἰκὸς ἢ τὸ ἀναγκαῖον ἐφεξῆς γιγνομένων συμβαίνει
εἰς εὐτυχίαν ἐκ δυστυχίας ἢ ἐξ εὐτυχίας εἰς δυστυ-
15 χίαν μεταβάλλειν, ἱκανὸς ὅρος ἐστὶν τοῦ μεγέθους.

VIII   Μῦθος δ' ἐστὶν εἷς οὐχ ὥσπερ τινὲς οἴονται ἐὰν
περὶ ἕνα ᾖ· πολλὰ γὰρ καὶ ἄπειρα τῷ ἑνὶ συμβαίνει,
ἐξ ὧν ἐνίων οὐδέν ἐστιν ἕν· οὕτως δὲ καὶ πράξεις
ἑνὸς πολλαί εἰσιν, ἐξ ὧν μία οὐδεμία γίνεται πρᾶξις.
διὸ πάντες ἐοίκασιν ἁμαρτάνειν ὅσοι τῶν ποιητῶν
20 Ἡρακληίδα Θησηίδα καὶ τὰ τοιαῦτα ποιήματα
πεποιήκασιν· οἴονται γάρ, ἐπεὶ εἷς ἦν ὁ Ἡρακλῆς,
ἕνα καὶ τὸν μῦθον εἶναι προσήκειν. ὁ δ' Ὅμηρος
ὥσπερ καὶ τὰ ἄλλα διαφέρει καὶ τοῦτ' ἔοικεν καλῶς

---

¹ ὁ add. Ellebodius

ᵃ The ref. is obscure, but Ar.'s rejection of contingent conventions is clear.

unity and wholeness), say an animal a thousand miles long. So just as with our bodies and with animals beauty requires magnitude, but magnitude that allows coherent perception, likewise plots require length, but length that can be coherently remembered. A limit of length referring to competitions and powers of attention is extrinsic to the art: for if it were necessary for a hundred tragedies to compete, they would perform them by water clocks, as they say happened once before.[a] But the limit that conforms to the actual nature of the matter is that greater size, provided clear coherence remains, means finer beauty of magnitude. To state the definition plainly: the size which permits a transformation to occur, in a probable or necessary sequence of events,[b] from adversity to prosperity or prosperity to adversity,[c] is a sufficient limit of magnitude.

VIII   A plot is not unified, as some think, if built round an individual.[d] Any entity has innumerable features, not all of which cohere into a unity; likewise, an individual performs many actions which yield no unitary action. So all those poets are clearly at fault who have composed a Heracleid, a Theseid, and similar poems: they think that, since Heracles was an individual, the plot[e] too must be unitary. But Homer, in keeping with his general superiority, evidently grasped well, whether by art or nature, this

[b] Probability and necessity: Ar.'s recurrent criteria of what makes "natural" sense within human lives.

[c] On alternative directions of "transformation," see esp. chs. XIII–XIV.

[d] I.e. unity of "hero" is not a sufficient (or even necessary) condition for unity of plot.

[e] Sc. of H.'s life.

ἰδεῖν, ἤτοι διὰ τέχνην ἢ διὰ φύσιν· Ὀδύσσειαν γὰρ
25 ποιῶν οὐκ ἐποίησεν ἅπαντα ὅσα αὐτῷ συνέβη (οἷον
πληγῆναι μὲν ἐν τῷ Παρνασσῷ, μανῆναι δὲ προσ-
ποιήσασθαι ἐν τῷ ἀγερμῷ), ὧν οὐδὲν θατέρου γενο-
μένου ἀναγκαῖον ἦν ἢ εἰκὸς θάτερον γενέσθαι, ἀλλὰ
περὶ μίαν πρᾶξιν οἵαν λέγομεν τὴν Ὀδύσσειαν
συνέστησεν, ὁμοίως δὲ καὶ τὴν Ἰλιάδα. χρὴ οὖν,
30 καθάπερ καὶ ἐν ταῖς ἄλλαις μιμητικαῖς ἡ μία μίμησις ἑνός ἐστιν, οὕτω καὶ τὸν μῦθον, ἐπεὶ πράξεως
μίμησίς ἐστι, μιᾶς τε εἶναι καὶ ταύτης ὅλης, καὶ τὰ
μέρη συνεστάναι τῶν πραγμάτων οὕτως ὥστε μετα-
τιθεμένου τινὸς μέρους ἢ ἀφαιρουμένου διαφέρεσθαι
καὶ κινεῖσθαι τὸ ὅλον· ὃ γὰρ προσὸν ἢ μὴ προσὸν
35 μηδὲν ποιεῖ ἐπίδηλον, οὐδὲν μόριον τοῦ ὅλου ἐστίν.

IX   Φανερὸν δὲ ἐκ τῶν εἰρημένων καὶ ὅτι οὐ τὸ τὰ
γενόμενα λέγειν, τοῦτο ποιητοῦ ἔργον ἐστίν, ἀλλ᾽
οἷα ἂν γένοιτο καὶ τὰ δυνατὰ κατὰ τὸ εἰκὸς ἢ τὸ
ἀναγκαῖον. ὁ γὰρ ἱστορικὸς καὶ ὁ ποιητὴς οὐ τῷ ἢ
1451b ἔμμετρα λέγειν ἢ ἄμετρα διαφέρουσιν· εἴη γὰρ ἂν
τὰ Ἡροδότου εἰς μέτρα τεθῆναι καὶ οὐδὲν ἧττον ἂν
εἴη ἱστορία τις μετὰ μέτρου ἢ ἄνευ μέτρων· ἀλλὰ
τούτῳ διαφέρει, τῷ τὸν μὲν τὰ γενόμενα λέγειν, τὸν
5 δὲ οἷα ἂν γένοιτο. διὸ καὶ φιλοσοφώτερον καὶ
σπουδαιότερον ποίησις ἱστορίας ἐστίν· ἡ μὲν γὰρ
ποίησις μᾶλλον τὰ καθόλου, ἡ δ᾽ ἱστορία τὰ καθ᾽
ἕκαστον λέγει. ἔστιν δὲ καθόλου μέν, τῷ ποίῳ τὰ
ποῖα ἄττα συμβαίνει λέγειν ἢ πράττειν κατὰ τὸ

point too: for though composing an *Odyssey*, he did not
include every feature of the hero's life (e.g. his wounding
on Parnassus, or his feigned madness in the call to arms),[a]
where events lacked necessary or probable connections;
but he structured the *Odyssey* round a unitary action of
the kind I mean, and likewise with the *Iliad*. Just as,
therefore, in the other mimetic arts a unitary mimesis has
a unitary object, so too the plot, since it is mimesis of an
action, should be of a unitary and indeed whole action;
and the component events should be so structured that if
any is displaced or removed, the sense of the whole is dis-
turbed and dislocated: since that whose presence or
absence has no clear significance is not an integral part of
the whole.

It is also evident from what has been said that it is not
the poet's function to relate actual events, but the *kinds* of
things that might occur and are possible in terms of probability or necessity. The difference between the historian
and the poet is not that between using verse or prose;
Herodotus' work could be versified and would be just as
much a kind of history in verse as in prose. No, the difference is this: that the one relates actual events, the other
the kinds of things that might occur. Consequently,
poetry is more philosophical and more elevated[b] than history, since poetry relates more of the universal, while history relates particulars.[c] "Universal" means the kinds of
things which it suits a certain kind of person to say or do,

---

[a] Wounding: described, but only as recollection, at *Od.*
19.392–466. The *Od.* never mentions Odysseus' madness,
feigned to avoid joining the Trojan expedition.

[b] Of greater ethical import (by philosophical standards); see
on 49b24.   [c] On history and particulars cf. 59a21–9.

εἰκὸς ἢ τὸ ἀναγκαῖον, οὗ στοχάζεται ἡ ποίησις ὀνό-
10 ματα ἐπιτιθεμένη· τὸ δὲ καθ' ἕκαστον, τί Ἀλκιβιά-
δης ἔπραξεν ἢ τί ἔπαθεν. ἐπὶ μὲν οὖν τῆς κωμῳδίας
ἤδη τοῦτο δῆλον γέγονεν· συστήσαντες γὰρ τὸν
μῦθον διὰ τῶν εἰκότων οὕτω τὰ τυχόντα ὀνόματα
ὑποτιθέασιν, καὶ οὐχ ὥσπερ οἱ ἰαμβοποιοὶ περὶ τὸν
καθ' ἕκαστον ποιοῦσιν. ἐπὶ δὲ τῆς τραγῳδίας τῶν
15 γενομένων ὀνομάτων ἀντέχονται. αἴτιον δ' ὅτι πιθανόν ἐστι τὸ δυνατόν· τὰ μὲν οὖν μὴ γενόμενα οὔπω
πιστεύομεν εἶναι δυνατά, τὰ δὲ γενόμενα φανερὸν
ὅτι δυνατά· οὐ γὰρ ἂν ἐγένετο, εἰ ἦν ἀδύνατα. οὐ
μὴν ἀλλὰ καὶ ἐν ταῖς τραγῳδίαις ἐν ἐνίαις μὲν ἓν ἢ
20 δύο τῶν γνωρίμων ἐστὶν ὀνομάτων, τὰ δὲ ἄλλα
πεποιημένα, ἐν ἐνίαις δὲ οὐθέν, οἷον ἐν τῷ Ἀγάθωνος Ἀνθεῖ·[1] ὁμοίως γὰρ ἐν τούτῳ τά τε πράγματα
καὶ τὰ ὀνόματα πεποίηται, καὶ οὐδὲν ἧττον εὐφραί-
νει. ὥστ' οὐ πάντως εἶναι ζητητέον τῶν παραδεδο-
μένων μύθων, περὶ οὓς αἱ τραγῳδίαι εἰσίν, ἀντέχε-
25 σθαι. καὶ γὰρ γελοῖον τοῦτο ζητεῖν, ἐπεὶ καὶ τὰ
γνώριμα ὀλίγοις γνώριμά ἐστιν, ἀλλ' ὅμως εὐφραί-
νει πάντας. δῆλον οὖν ἐκ τούτων ὅτι τὸν ποιητὴν
μᾶλλον τῶν μύθων εἶναι δεῖ ποιητὴν ἢ τῶν μέτρων,
ὅσῳ ποιητής κατὰ τὴν μίμησίν ἐστιν, μιμεῖται δὲ
τὰς πράξεις. κἂν ἄρα συμβῇ γενόμενα ποιεῖν, οὐθὲν
30 ἧττον ποιητής ἐστι· τῶν γὰρ γενομένων ἔνια οὐδὲν

---

[1] Ἀνθεῖ Welcker: ἄνθει AB

[a] Names denote particulars.

in terms of probability or necessity: poetry aims for this,
even though attaching names[a] to the agents. A "particular" means, say, what Alcibiades did or experienced. In
comedy, this point has by now[b] become obvious: the
poets construct the plot on the basis of probability, and
only then supply arbitrary names; they do not, like iambic
poets, write about a particular person.[c] But in tragedy
they adhere to the actual[d] names. The reason is that the
possible seems plausible: about the possibility of things
which have not occurred we are not yet sure;[e] but it is evident that actual events are possible—they could not otherwise have occurred. Yet even in some tragedies there
are only one or two familiar names, while the rest are
invented; and in certain plays no name is familiar, for
example in Agathon's *Antheus*:[f] in this work, events and
names alike have been invented, yet it gives no less pleasure for that. So adherence to the traditional plots of
tragedy should not be sought at all costs. Indeed, to seek
this is absurd, since even the familiar subjects are familiar
only to a minority, yet nonetheless please everyone. It is
clear from these points, then, that the poet should be
more a maker of plots than of verses, in so far as he is a
poet by virtue of mimesis,[h] and his mimesis is of actions.
So even should his poetry concern actual events, he is no
less a poet for that, as there is nothing to prevent

[b] Some time in the mid-4th cent.: see the Introduction.

[c] See on 49b8.

[d] I.e. supplied by the traditional myths (cf. 51b24–5); Ar.
treats this, by simplification, as synonymous with historical fact.

[e] The sentence characterises an ordinary mentality.

[f] Nothing else is known about this work (*TrGF* I 161–2);
Agathon was active c. 420–400.   [g] *Poiētēs* means both
"maker" and "poet."   [h] Cf. 47b15.

κωλύει τοιαῦτα εἶναι οἷα ἂν εἰκὸς γενέσθαι καὶ
δυνατὰ γενέσθαι, καθ' ὃ ἐκεῖνος αὐτῶν ποιητής
ἐστιν.

τῶν δὲ ἁπλῶν[1] μύθων καὶ πράξεων αἱ ἐπεισοδιώ-
δεις εἰσὶν χείρισται· λέγω δ' ἐπεισοδιώδη μῦθον ἐν
ᾧ τὰ ἐπεισόδια μετ' ἄλληλα οὔτ' εἰκὸς οὔτ' ἀνάγκη
35　εἶναι. τοιαῦται δὲ ποιοῦνται ὑπὸ μὲν τῶν φαύλων
ποιητῶν δι' αὐτούς, ὑπὸ δὲ τῶν ἀγαθῶν διὰ τοὺς
ὑποκριτάς·[2] ἀγωνίσματα γὰρ ποιοῦντες καὶ παρὰ
1452a　τὴν δύναμιν παρατείνοντες τὸν μῦθον πολλάκις δια-
στρέφειν ἀναγκάζονται τὸ ἐφεξῆς. ἐπεὶ δὲ οὐ μόνον
τελείας ἐστὶ πράξεως ἡ μίμησις ἀλλὰ καὶ φοβερῶν
καὶ ἐλεεινῶν, ταῦτα δὲ[3] γίνεται καὶ μάλιστα[4] ὅταν
γένηται παρὰ τὴν δόξαν δι' ἄλληλα· τὸ γὰρ θαυμαστὸν οὕτως ἕξει μᾶλλον ἢ εἰ ἀπὸ τοῦ αὐτομάτου καὶ
5　τῆς τύχης, ἐπεὶ καὶ τῶν ἀπὸ τύχης ταῦτα θαυμασιώ-
τατα δοκεῖ ὅσα ὥσπερ ἐπίτηδες φαίνεται γεγονέναι,
οἷον ὡς ὁ ἀνδριὰς ὁ τοῦ Μίτυος ἐν Ἄργει ἀπέκτεινεν
τὸν αἴτιον τοῦ θανάτου τῷ Μίτυι, θεωροῦντι ἐμπε-
σών· ἔοικε γὰρ τὰ τοιαῦτα οὐκ εἰκῇ γίνεσθαι· ὥστε
10　ἀνάγκη τοὺς τοιούτους εἶναι καλλίους μύθους.

X　Εἰσὶ δὲ τῶν μύθων οἱ μὲν ἁπλοῖ οἱ δὲ πεπλεγμέ-
νοι· καὶ γὰρ αἱ πράξεις ὧν μιμήσεις οἱ μῦθοί εἰσιν
ὑπάρχουσιν εὐθὺς οὖσαι τοιαῦται. λέγω δὲ ἁπλῆν

---

[1] ἁπλῶν AB (om. Arab.): ἀτελῶν Essen
[2] ὑποκριτάς AB: κριτάς rec.
[3] δὲ A: om. B
[4] μάλιστα καὶ μᾶλλον AB: καὶ μ. del. Ellebodius

some actual events being probable as well as possible, and it is through probability that the poet makes his material from them.

Of simple[a] plots and actions, the episodic are worst. By "episodic" I mean a plot in which the episodes follow one another without probability or necessity. Such plays are composed by bad poets through their own fault, and by good poets for the sake of the actors: for in composing show pieces,[b] and stretching the plot beyond its capacity, they are often forced to distort the continuity. Given that the mimesis is not only of a complete action but also of fearful and pitiable matters, the latter arise above all when events occur contrary to expectation yet on account of one another. The awesome[c] will be maintained in this way more than through show of chance and fortune, because even among chance events we find most awesome those which seem to have happened by design (as when Mitys' statue at Argos killed the murderer of Mitys, by falling on him as he looked at it;[d] such things *seem* not to occur randomly). And so, such plots are bound to be finer.

Plots can be divided into the simple and complex, since the actions which plots represent are intrinsically of these kinds. I call "simple" an action which is continuous,

[a] The term is defined in ch. X; its occurrence here has been questioned.

[b] Works designed to lend themselves to histrionic brilliance.

[c] Awe (or "wonder") will be aroused by something astonishing and suggestive of deeper significance: cf. 60a11–18.

[d] Or "when he was visiting the festival"; the story is otherwise unknown, but M. (if the same) is mentioned at Dem. 59.33.

μὲν πρᾶξιν ἧς γινομένης ὥσπερ ὥρισται συνεχοῦς
15 καὶ μιᾶς ἄνευ περιπετείας ἢ ἀναγνωρισμοῦ ἡ μετάβασις γίνεται, πεπλεγμένην δὲ ἐξ ἧς μετὰ ἀναγνωρισμοῦ ἢ περιπετείας ἢ ἀμφοῖν ἡ μετάβασίς ἐστιν.
ταῦτα δὲ δεῖ γίνεσθαι ἐξ αὐτῆς τῆς συστάσεως τοῦ
μύθου, ὥστε ἐκ τῶν προγεγενημένων συμβαίνειν ἢ
20 ἐξ ἀνάγκης ἢ κατὰ τὸ εἰκὸς γίγνεσθαι ταῦτα· διαφέρει γὰρ πολὺ τὸ γίγνεσθαι τάδε διὰ τάδε ἢ μετὰ
τάδε.

XI Ἔστι δὲ περιπέτεια μὲν ἡ εἰς τὸ ἐναντίον τῶν
πραττομένων μεταβολὴ καθάπερ εἴρηται, καὶ τοῦτο
δὲ ὥσπερ λέγομεν κατὰ τὸ εἰκὸς ἢ ἀναγκαῖον, οἷον
ἐν τῷ Οἰδίποδι ἐλθὼν ὡς εὐφρανῶν τὸν Οἰδίπουν καὶ
25 ἀπαλλάξων τοῦ πρὸς τὴν μητέρα φόβου, δηλώσας
ὃς ἦν, τοὐναντίον ἐποίησεν· καὶ ἐν τῷ Λυγκεῖ ὁ μὲν
ἀγόμενος ὡς ἀποθανούμενος, ὁ δὲ Δαναὸς ἀκολου-
θῶν ὡς ἀποκτενῶν, τὸν μὲν συνέβη ἐκ τῶν πεπρα-
γμένων ἀποθανεῖν, τὸν δὲ σωθῆναι. ἀναγνώρισις
δέ, ὥσπερ καὶ τοὔνομα σημαίνει, ἐξ ἀγνοίας εἰς
30 γνῶσιν μεταβολή, ἢ εἰς φιλίαν ἢ ἔχθραν, τῶν πρὸς
εὐτυχίαν ἢ δυστυχίαν ὡρισμένων· καλλίστη δὲ ἀναγνώρισις, ὅταν ἅμα περιπετείᾳ[1] γένηται, οἷον ἔχει ἡ
ἐν τῷ Οἰδίποδι. εἰσὶν μὲν οὖν καὶ ἄλλαι ἀναγνωρί-
σεις· καὶ[2] γὰρ πρὸς ἄψυχα καὶ τὰ τυχόντα ἔστιν[3]

---

[1] περιπετείᾳ γένηται Gomperz: περιπέτεια γένηται B:
περιπέτειαι γίνονται A
[2] καὶ γὰρ . . . ἀναγνωρίσαι om. B
[3] ἔστιν ὡς ὅπερ Spengel: ἐστὶν ὥσπερ A

64

in the sense defined,[a] and unitary, but whose transformation[b] lacks reversal and recognition; "complex," one whose transformation contains recognition or reversal or both. And these elements should emerge from the very structure of the plot, so that they ensue from the preceding events by necessity or probability; as it makes a great difference whether things happen because of, or only after, their antecedents.

Reversal is a change to the opposite direction of events, as already stated[c] and one in accord, as we insist, with probability or necessity: as when in the *Oedipus* the person who comes to bring Oedipus happiness, and intends to rid him of his fear about his mother, effects the opposite by revealing Oedipus' true identity.[d] And in the *Lynceus*,[e] the one figure is led off to die, while Danaus follows with the intention of killing him, yet the upshot of events is Danaus' death and the other's survival. Recognition, as the very name indicates, is a change from ignorance to knowledge, leading to friendship or to enmity,[f] and involving matters which bear on prosperity or adversity. The finest recognition is that which occurs simultaneously with reversal, as with the one in the *Oedipus*.[g] There are, of course, other kinds of recognition too, since what has been stated[h] occurs, after a fashion, in

[a] In ch. VII's schema of beginning, middle, end.

[b] Between prosperity and adversity; see on 51a13–14.

[c] An unclear back ref.: 52a4, "contrary to expectation," is the likeliest point.   [d] Soph. *OT* 924–1085; Ar. refers to two stages in the scene (cf. 989 ff, esp. 1002–3).   [e] Probably Theodectes'; see on 55b29.   [f] See on 53b15.   [g] Unclear: the reversal begins at Soph. *OT* 924 (cf. 52a24–6); Jocasta sees the truth by 1056, Oedipus only in the lead-up to 1182.   [h] I.e. in the preceding definition.

35 ὡς ὅπερ εἴρηται συμβαίνει, καὶ εἰ πέπραγέ τις ἢ μὴ
πέπραγεν ἔστιν ἀναγνωρίσαι. ἀλλ' ἡ μάλιστα τοῦ
μύθου καὶ ἡ μάλιστα τῆς πράξεως ἡ εἰρημένη ἐστίν·
ἡ γὰρ τοιαύτη ἀναγνώρισις καὶ περιπέτεια ἢ ἔλεον
1452b ἕξει ἢ φόβον, οἵων πράξεων ἡ τραγῳδία μίμησις
ὑπόκειται· ἔτι[1] δὲ καὶ τὸ ἀτυχεῖν καὶ τὸ εὐτυχεῖν ἐπὶ
τῶν τοιούτων συμβήσεται. ἐπεὶ δὴ ἡ ἀναγνώρισις
τινῶν ἐστιν ἀναγνώρισις, αἱ μέν εἰσι θατέρου πρὸς
τὸν ἕτερον μόνον, ὅταν ἦ δῆλος ἅτερος τίς ἐστιν, ὁτὲ
5 δὲ ἀμφοτέρους δεῖ ἀναγνωρίσαι, οἷον ἡ μὲν Ἰφιγέ-
νεια τῷ Ὀρέστῃ ἀνεγνωρίσθη ἐκ τῆς πέμψεως τῆς
ἐπιστολῆς, ἐκείνου[2] δὲ πρὸς τὴν Ἰφιγένειαν ἄλλης
ἔδει ἀναγνωρίσεως.

δύο μὲν οὖν τοῦ μύθου μέρη ταῦτ' ἐστί, περιπέτεια καὶ ἀναγνώρισις· τρίτον δὲ πάθος. τούτων δὲ
10 περιπέτεια μὲν καὶ ἀναγνώρισις εἴρηται, πάθος δέ
ἐστι πρᾶξις φθαρτικὴ ἢ ὀδυνηρά, οἷον οἵ τε ἐν τῷ
φανερῷ θάνατοι καὶ αἱ περιωδυνίαι καὶ τρώσεις καὶ
ὅσα τοιαῦτα.

XII   Μέρη δὲ τραγῳδίας οἷς μὲν ὡς εἴδεσι δεῖ χρῆσθαι πρότερον εἴπομεν, κατὰ δὲ τὸ ποσὸν καὶ εἰς ἃ
15 διαιρεῖται κεχωρισμένα τάδε ἐστίν, πρόλογος ἐπεισόδιον ἔξοδος χορικόν, καὶ τούτου τὸ μὲν πάροδος τὸ
δὲ στάσιμον, κοινὰ μὲν ἁπάντων ταῦτα, ἴδια δὲ τὰ
ἀπὸ τῆς σκηνῆς καὶ κομμοί. ἔστιν δὲ πρόλογος μὲν
μέρος ὅλον τραγῳδίας τὸ πρὸ χοροῦ παρόδου, ἐπ-

---

[1] ἔτι δὲ AB: ἐπειδὴ Vahlen
[2] ἐκείνου Bywater: -ω AB

relation to inanimate and even chance things, and it is also possible to recognise that someone has or has not committed a deed. But the kind most integral to the plot and action is the one described: such a joint recognition and reversal will yield either pity or fear, just the type of actions of which tragedy is taken to be a mimesis; besides, both adversity and prosperity will hinge upon such circumstances. Now, because recognition is recognition between people,[a] some cases involve only the relation of one party to the other (when the other's identity is clear), while in others there is need for double recognition: thus, Iphigeneia was recognised by Orestes through the sending of the letter, but for Iphigeneia to recognise his relation to herself required a further recognition.[b]

These, then, are two components of the plot—reversal and recognition. A third is suffering. Of these, reversal and recognition have been explained, and suffering is a destructive or painful action, such as public deaths, physical agony, woundings, etc.

We spoke earlier[c] of the components of tragedy that must be used as basic elements; but its formal and discrete sections are as follows: prologue, episode, exodos, choral unit (further divisible into parodos and stasimon). These are common to all plays, but actors' songs and kommoi are special to some. The prologue is the whole portion of a tragedy prior to the chorus' parodos; an episode

[a] Ar. ignores recognition of inanimate objects, mentioned above.
[b] Eur. *IT* 727–841.
[c] Cf. esp. 50a9–14.

67

20 εἰσόδιον δὲ μέρος ὅλον τραγῳδίας τὸ μεταξὺ ὅλων
χορικῶν μελῶν, ἔξοδος δὲ μέρος ὅλον τραγῳδίας
μεθ' ὃ οὐκ ἔστι χοροῦ μέλος· χορικοῦ δὲ πάροδος
μὲν ἡ πρώτη λέξις ὅλη[1] χοροῦ, στάσιμον δὲ μέλος
χοροῦ τὸ ἄνευ ἀναπαίστου καὶ τροχαίου, κομμὸς δὲ
θρῆνος κοινὸς χοροῦ καὶ ἀπὸ σκηνῆς. μέρη δὲ τρα-
25 γῳδίας οἷς μὲν ὡς[2] εἴδεσι δεῖ χρῆσθαι πρότερον
εἴπαμεν, κατὰ δὲ τὸ ποσὸν καὶ εἰς ἃ διαιρεῖται κεχωρισμένα ταῦτ' ἐστίν.

XIII Ὧν δὲ δεῖ στοχάζεσθαι καὶ ἃ δεῖ εὐλαβεῖσθαι
συνιστάντας τοὺς μύθους καὶ πόθεν ἔσται τὸ τῆς
τραγῳδίας ἔργον, ἐφεξῆς ἂν εἴη λεκτέον τοῖς νῦν
30 εἰρημένοις. ἐπειδὴ οὖν δεῖ τὴν σύνθεσιν εἶναι τῆς
καλλίστης τραγῳδίας μὴ ἁπλῆν ἀλλὰ πεπλεγμένην
καὶ ταύτην φοβερῶν καὶ ἐλεεινῶν εἶναι μιμητικήν
(τοῦτο γὰρ ἴδιον τῆς τοιαύτης μιμήσεώς ἐστιν),
πρῶτον μὲν δῆλον ὅτι οὔτε τοὺς ἐπιεικεῖς ἄνδρας δεῖ
μεταβάλλοντας φαίνεσθαι ἐξ εὐτυχίας εἰς δυστυ-
35 χίαν, οὐ γὰρ φοβερὸν οὐδὲ ἐλεεινὸν τοῦτο ἀλλὰ μια-
ρόν ἐστιν· οὔτε τοὺς μοχθηροὺς ἐξ ἀτυχίας εἰς εὐτυχίαν, ἀτραγῳδότατον γὰρ τοῦτ' ἐστὶ πάντων, οὐδὲν
γὰρ ἔχει ὧν δεῖ, οὔτε γὰρ φιλάνθρωπον οὔτε ἐλεει-
1453a νὸν οὔτε φοβερόν ἐστιν· οὐδ' αὖ τὸν σφόδρα πονη-
ρὸν ἐξ εὐτυχίας εἰς δυστυχίαν μεταπίπτειν· τὸ μὲν
γὰρ φιλάνθρωπον ἔχοι ἂν ἡ τοιαύτη σύστασις

---

[1] ὅλη Susemihl: ὅλου AB   [2] ὡς εἴδεσι rec.: om. AB

[a] Usually accompanying their entrance onto the scene.

is the whole portion of a tragedy between complete
choral songs; the exodos is the whole portion of a tragedy
following the final choral song. Of choral units, the parodos is the first complete utterance[a] of the chorus; a stasimon is a choral song without anapaestic and trochaic
rhythms;[b] a kommos is a dirge shared between chorus
and actors. We spoke earlier of the components of
tragedy that must be used as basic elements, while its formal and discrete sections are the ones given.

II   Next, after the foregoing discussion, we must consider
what should be aimed at and avoided in the construction
of plots, and how tragedy's effect is to be achieved. Since,
then, the structure of the finest tragedy should be complex not simple,[c] as well as representing fearful and
pitiable events (for this is the special feature of such
mimesis), it is, to begin with, clear that neither should
decent men be shown changing from prosperity to adversity, as this is not fearful nor yet pitiable but repugnant,[d]
nor the depraved changing from adversity to prosperity,
because this is the least tragic of all, possessing none
of the necessary qualities, since it arouses neither
fellow-feeling[e] nor pity nor fear. Nor, again, should
tragedy show the very wicked person falling from prosperity to adversity: such a pattern might arouse fellow-
feeling, but not pity or fear, since the one is felt

<hr />

[b] Both do in fact occur in stasima; Ar. may be thinking of
"recitative" units, such as the marching anapaests of choral paro-
doi, or trochaic tetrameters (see on 49a21).

[c] In the senses defined in ch. X.   [d] Cf. 53b39, 54a3.

[e] *Philanthrōpia*: a disputed concept; it may entail either a
broadly humane sympathy (even with some forms of merited suffering), or a basic sense of justice. Cf. 56a21.

ἀλλ' οὔτε ἔλεον οὔτε φόβον, ὁ μὲν γὰρ περὶ τὸν ἀνά-
ξιόν ἐστιν δυστυχοῦντα, ὁ δὲ περὶ τὸν ὅμοιον
5 (ἔλεος[1] μὲν περὶ τὸν ἀνάξιον, φόβος δὲ περὶ τὸν
ὅμοιον), ὥστε οὔτε ἐλεεινὸν οὔτε φοβερὸν ἔσται τὸ
συμβαῖνον. ὁ μεταξὺ ἄρα τούτων λοιπός. ἔστι δὲ
τοιοῦτος ὁ μήτε ἀρετῇ διαφέρων καὶ δικαιοσύνῃ
μήτε διὰ κακίαν καὶ μοχθηρίαν μεταβάλλων εἰς τὴν
δυστυχίαν ἀλλὰ δι' ἁμαρτίαν τινά, τῶν ἐν μεγάλῃ
10 δόξῃ ὄντων καὶ εὐτυχίᾳ, οἷον Οἰδίπους καὶ Θυέστης
καὶ οἱ ἐκ τῶν τοιούτων γενῶν ἐπιφανεῖς ἄνδρες.
ἀνάγκη ἄρα τὸν καλῶς ἔχοντα μῦθον ἁπλοῦν εἶναι
μᾶλλον ἢ διπλοῦν, ὥσπερ τινές φασι, καὶ μεταβάλλειν οὐκ εἰς εὐτυχίαν ἐκ δυστυχίας ἀλλὰ τοὐναντίον
ἐξ εὐτυχίας εἰς δυστυχίαν μὴ διὰ μοχθηρίαν ἀλλὰ
15 δι' ἁμαρτίαν μεγάλην ἢ οἵου εἴρηται ἢ βελτίονος
μᾶλλον ἢ χείρονος. (σημεῖον δὲ καὶ τὸ γιγνόμενον·
πρῶτον μὲν γὰρ οἱ ποιηταὶ τοὺς τυχόντας μύθους
ἀπηρίθμουν, νῦν δὲ περὶ ὀλίγας οἰκίας αἱ κάλλισται
τραγῳδίαι συντίθενται, οἷον περὶ Ἀλκμέωνα καὶ
20 Οἰδίπουν καὶ Ὀρέστην καὶ Μελέαγρον καὶ Θυέστην
καὶ Τήλεφον καὶ ὅσοις ἄλλοις συμβέβηκεν ἢ παθεῖν
δεινὰ ἢ ποιῆσαι.) ἡ μὲν οὖν κατὰ τὴν τέχνην καλλίστη τραγῳδία ἐκ ταύτης τῆς συστάσεώς ἐστι. διὸ
καὶ οἱ Εὐριπίδῃ ἐγκαλοῦντες τὸ αὐτὸ ἁμαρτάνουσιν

---

[1] ἔλεος . . . ὅμοιον om. B

[a] *Hamartia*: the term, repeated at 53a16, could cover a range
of possible factors in tragic agency. See the Introduction.

for the undeserving victim of adversity, the other for one
like ourselves (pity for the undeserving, fear for one like
ourselves); so the outcome will be neither pitiable nor
fearful. This leaves, then, the person in-between these
cases. Such a person is someone not preeminent in virtue
and justice, and one who falls into adversity not through
evil and depravity, but through some kind of error;[a] and
one belonging to the class of those who enjoy great
renown and prosperity, such as Oedipus, Thyestes,[b] and
eminent men from such lineages. The well made plot,
then, ought to be single[c] rather than double, as some
maintain, with a change not to prosperity from adversity,
but on the contrary from prosperity to adversity, caused
not by depravity but by a great error of a character either
like that stated, or better rather than worse. (Actual practice too points to this. Originally, the poets recounted any
and every story, but nowadays the finest tragedies are
composed about only a few families, such as Alcmaeon,
Oedipus, Orestes, Meleager, Thyestes, Telephus,[d] and as
many others as have suffered or perpetrated terrible
things.) So the finest tragedy of which the art permits follows this structure. Which is why the same mistake[e] is

---

[b] T., King of Mycenae, was deceived by his brother, Atreus,
into eating his own children; he also committed unwitting incest
with his daughter, Pelopia. Cf. *OCD* s.v. Atreus.

[c] The same Greek adj. as "simple" in ch. X; but the context
dictates a separate sense here.   [d] Alcmaeon: see on 53b24.
Oedipus and Orestes: see e.g. ch. XI. Meleager: killed by the
agency of his mother, Althaea, after he had killed her brother(s).
Thyestes: see on 53a11. Telephus: Ar. may have in mind his
unwitting killing of his uncles; cf. *OCD* s.v.

[e] As made by those who prefer double plots (53a13).

25 ὅτι τοῦτο δρᾷ ἐν ταῖς τραγῳδίαις καὶ¹ αἱ πολλαὶ
αὐτοῦ εἰς δυστυχίαν τελευτῶσιν. τοῦτο γάρ ἐστιν
ὥσπερ εἴρηται ὀρθόν· σημεῖον δὲ μέγιστον· ἐπὶ γὰρ
τῶν σκηνῶν καὶ τῶν ἀγώνων τραγικώταται αἱ τοιαῦται φαίνονται, ἂν κατορθωθῶσιν, καὶ ὁ Εὐριπίδης,
εἰ καὶ τὰ ἄλλα μὴ εὖ οἰκονομεῖ, ἀλλὰ τραγικώτατός
30 γε τῶν ποιητῶν φαίνεται. δευτέρα δ' ἡ πρώτη λεγομένη ὑπὸ τινῶν ἐστιν σύστασις, ἡ διπλῆν τε τὴν
σύστασιν ἔχουσα καθάπερ ἡ Ὀδύσσεια καὶ τελευ-
τῶσα ἐξ ἐναντίας τοῖς βελτίοσι καὶ χείροσιν. δοκεῖ
δὲ εἶναι πρώτη διὰ τὴν τῶν θεάτρων ἀσθένειαν· ἀκο-
λουθοῦσι γὰρ οἱ ποιηταὶ κατ' εὐχὴν ποιοῦντες τοῖς
35 θεαταῖς. ἔστιν δὲ οὐχ αὕτη ἀπὸ τραγῳδίας ἡδονὴ
ἀλλὰ μᾶλλον τῆς κωμῳδίας οἰκεία· ἐκεῖ γὰρ οἳ² ἂν
ἔχθιστοι ὦσιν ἐν τῷ μύθῳ, οἷον Ὀρέστης καὶ Αἴγι-
σθος, φίλοι γενόμενοι ἐπὶ τελευτῆς ἐξέρχονται, καὶ
ἀποθνήσκει οὐδεὶς ὑπ' οὐδενός.

1453b   Ἔστιν μὲν οὖν τὸ φοβερὸν καὶ ἐλεεινὸν ἐκ τῆς
XIV   ὄψεως γίνεσθαι, ἔστιν δὲ καὶ ἐξ αὐτῆς τῆς συστάσεως τῶν πραγμάτων, ὅπερ ἐστὶ πρότερον καὶ ποιητοῦ ἀμείνονος. δεῖ γὰρ καὶ ἄνευ τοῦ ὁρᾶν οὕτω συνεστάναι τὸν μῦθον ὥστε τὸν ἀκούοντα τὰ πράγματα
5   γινόμενα καὶ φρίττειν καὶ ἐλεεῖν ἐκ τῶν συμβαινόν-

¹ καὶ αἱ Knebel: καὶ Α: αἱ Β
² οἳ ἂν Bonitz: ἂν οἱ ΑΒ

made by those who complain that Euripides does this in his plays, and that most[a] end in adversity. For this, as explained, is the right way. And the greatest indication of this is that in theatrical contests such plays are found the most tragic, if successfully managed; and Euripides, even if he does not arrange other details well, is at least found the most tragic of the poets. Second-best is the structure held the best by some people: the kind with a double structure like the *Odyssey* and with opposite outcomes for good and bad characters. It is thought to be best because of the weakness of audiences: the poets follow, and pander to the taste of, the spectators. Yet this is not the pleasure to expect from tragedy, but is more appropriate to comedy, where those who are deadliest enemies in the plot, such as Orestes and Aegisthus,[b] exit at the end as new friends, and no one dies at anyone's hands.

XIV   Now, what is fearful and pitiable can result from spectacle,[c] but also from the actual structure of events, which is the higher priority and the aim of a superior poet. For the plot should be so structured that, even without seeing it performed, the person who hears the events that occur experiences horror[d] and pity at what

---

[a] Or, on a different textual reading, "many"; it is anyway unclear why Eur. should be singled out for such criticism.

[b] Lover of Clytemnestra, Orestes' mother, with whom she plotted to kill her husband, Agamemnon. Ar. envisages a burlesque treatment which avoids the usual revenge killing of Aegisthus by Orestes.

[c] See on 49b33.

[d] Here, and only here, Ar. uses a verb which literally means to "shudder" with fear.

των· ἅπερ ἂν πάθοι τις ἀκούων τὸν τοῦ Οἰδίπου
μῦθον. τὸ δὲ διὰ τῆς ὄψεως τοῦτο παρασκευάζειν
ἀτεχνότερον καὶ χορηγίας δεόμενόν ἐστιν. οἱ δὲ μὴ
τὸ φοβερὸν διὰ τῆς ὄψεως ἀλλὰ τὸ τερατῶδες μόνον
παρασκευάζοντες οὐδὲν τραγῳδίᾳ κοινωνοῦσιν· οὐ
10   γὰρ πᾶσαν δεῖ ζητεῖν ἡδονὴν ἀπὸ τραγῳδίας ἀλλὰ
τὴν οἰκείαν. ἐπεὶ δὲ τὴν ἀπὸ ἐλέου καὶ φόβου διὰ
μιμήσεως δεῖ ἡδονὴν παρασκευάζειν τὸν ποιητήν,
φανερὸν ὡς τοῦτο ἐν τοῖς πράγμασιν ἐμποιητέον.

ποῖα οὖν δεινὰ ἢ ποῖα οἰκτρὰ φαίνεται τῶν συμ-
πιπτόντων, λάβωμεν. ἀνάγκη δὴ[1] ἢ φίλων εἶναι
15   πρὸς ἀλλήλους τὰς τοιαύτας πράξεις ἢ ἐχθρῶν ἢ
μηδετέρων. ἂν μὲν οὖν ἐχθρὸς ἐχθρόν, οὐδὲν ἐλεεινὸν οὔτε ποιῶν οὔτε μέλλων, πλὴν κατ' αὐτὸ τὸ
πάθος· οὐδ' ἂν μηδετέρως ἔχοντες· ὅταν δ' ἐν ταῖς
φιλίαις ἐγγένηται τὰ πάθη, οἷον ἢ ἀδελφὸς ἀδελφὸν
20   ἢ υἱὸς πατέρα ἢ μήτηρ υἱὸν ἢ υἱὸς μητέρα ἀπο-
κτείνῃ ἢ μέλλῃ ἤ τι ἄλλο τοιοῦτον δρᾷ, ταῦτα ζητητέον. τοὺς μὲν οὖν παρειλημμένους μύθους λύειν
οὐκ ἔστιν, λέγω δὲ οἷον τὴν Κλυταιμήστραν ἀποθα-
νοῦσαν ὑπὸ τοῦ Ὀρέστου καὶ τὴν Ἐριφύλην ὑπὸ τοῦ
Ἀλκμέωνος, αὐτὸν δὲ εὑρίσκειν δεῖ καὶ τοῖς παραδε-
25   δομένοις χρῆσθαι καλῶς. τὸ δὲ καλῶς τί λέγομεν,
εἴπωμεν σαφέστερον. ἔστι μὲν γὰρ οὕτω γίνεσθαι
τὴν πρᾶξιν, ὥσπερ οἱ παλαιοὶ ἐποίουν εἰδότας καὶ

---

[1] δὴ Spengel: δὲ AB

---

[a] Soph. *OT*, as usual; Ar. may have in mind recitation (a common Greek practice), rather than mere plot summary.

comes about (as one would feel when hearing the plot of the *Oedipus*).[a] To create this effect through spectacle has little to do with the poet's art, and requires material resources.[b] Those who use spectacle to create an effect not of the fearful but only of the sensational have nothing at all in common with tragedy, as it is not every pleasure one should seek from tragedy, but the appropriate kind. And since the poet should create the pleasure which comes from pity and fear through mimesis, obviously this should be built into the events.

Let us, then, take up the question of what sorts of incidents strike us as terrible or pitiable. Now, such actions must occur between friends,[c] enemies, or neutrals. Well, if enemy acts towards enemy, there is nothing pitiable in either the deed or the prospect of it, except for the suffering[d] as such; nor if the parties are neutrals. What tragedy must seek are cases where the sufferings occur within relationships, such as brother and brother, son and father, mother and son, son and mother—when the one kills (or is about to kill) the other, or commits some other such deed. Now, one cannot break up the transmitted stories (I mean, e.g., Clytemnestra's death at Orestes' hands,[e] and Eriphyle's at Alcmaeon's),[f] but the poet should be inventive as well as making good use of traditional stories. Let me explain more clearly what I mean by "good use." First, the action can occur as in the early

[b] Cf. the final sentence of ch. VI.

[c] *Philoi*, "friends," here embraces all (esp. kin) who share strong personal or social ties.

[d] Defined at the end of ch. XI.

[e] See on 53a37.

[f] A. killed his mother (in different versions) either accidentally (in *Astydamas*, 53b33), or to avenge his father, Amphiaraus.

γιγνώσκοντας, καθάπερ καὶ Εὐριπίδης ἐποίησεν
ἀποκτείνουσαν τοὺς παῖδας τὴν Μήδειαν·[1] ἔστιν δὲ
πρᾶξαι μέν, ἀγνοοῦντας δὲ πρᾶξαι τὸ δεινόν, εἶθ᾽
30 ὕστερον ἀναγνωρίσαι τὴν φιλίαν, ὥσπερ ὁ Σοφοκλέους Οἰδίπους· τοῦτο μὲν οὖν ἔξω τοῦ δράματος,
ἐν δ᾽ αὐτῇ τῇ τραγῳδίᾳ οἷον ὁ Ἀλκμέων[2] ὁ Ἀστυ-
δάμαντος ἢ ὁ Τηλέγονος ὁ ἐν τῷ τραυματίᾳ Ὀδυσσεῖ. ἔτι δὲ τρίτον παρὰ ταῦτα τὸ[3] μέλλοντα ποιεῖν
35 τι τῶν ἀνηκέστων δι᾽ ἄγνοιαν ἀναγνωρίσαι πρὶν
ποιῆσαι. καὶ παρὰ ταῦτα οὐκ ἔστιν ἄλλως· ἢ γὰρ
πρᾶξαι ἀνάγκη ἢ μὴ καὶ εἰδότας ἢ μὴ εἰδότας. τούτων δὲ τὸ μὲν γινώσκοντα μελλῆσαι καὶ μὴ πρᾶξαι
χείριστον· τό τε γὰρ μιαρὸν ἔχει, καὶ οὐ τραγικόν·
ἀπαθὲς γάρ. διόπερ οὐδεὶς ποιεῖ ὁμοίως, εἰ μὴ ὀλι-
1454a γάκις, οἷον ἐν Ἀντιγόνῃ τὸν Κρέοντα ὁ Αἵμων. τὸ
δὲ πρᾶξαι δεύτερον. βέλτιον δὲ τὸ ἀγνοοῦντα μὲν
πρᾶξαι, πράξαντα δὲ ἀναγνωρίσαι· τό τε γὰρ μιαρὸν οὐ πρόσεστιν καὶ ἡ ἀναγνώρισις ἐκπληκτικόν.
κράτιστον δὲ τὸ τελευταῖον, λέγω δὲ οἷον ἐν τῷ

---

[1] post Μήδειαν lacunam stat. Gudeman (cf. "quod non faciat
. . . ubi cognoscunt," Arab.)
[2] Ἀλκμαίων ὁ Vettori: ἀλκμαίωνος AB
[3] τὸ Theod. Rentius, Bonitz: τὸν AB

---

[a] Medea's deliberate killing of her children, in Eur.'s play, was
probably an innovation in the myth.
[b] Astydamas junior, active 370s-340s; OCD s.v., TrGF I no.
60.
[c] Apparently a variant title of Soph.'s Odysseus Akanthoplēx,

poets who made the agents act in knowledge and cognisance (as Euripides too made Medea kill her children).[a] Alternatively, the agents can commit the terrible deed, but do so in ignorance, then subsequently recognise the relationship, as with Sophocles' Oedipus: here, of course, the deed is outside the play, but cases within the tragedy are, for instance, Alcmaeon in Astydamas,[b] or Telegonus in *Odysseus Wounded*.[c] This leaves a third[d] possibility, when the person is on the point of unwittingly committing something irremediable, but recognises it before doing so. These are the only patterns: either the action is or is not executed, and by agents who either know or do not know its nature. Of these, the worst is for someone to be about to act knowingly, and yet not do so: this is both repugnant[e] and untragic (since it lacks suffering). That is why no one makes such plots, or only rarely, for instance with Haemon and Creon in *Antigone*.[f] Next worst is execution of the deed.[g] Better is the act done in ignorance, and followed by recognition: there is nothing repugnant here, and the recognition is thrilling. But best is the last option:[h] I mean, for example, in *Cresphontes*[i] Merope is

[d] But Ar.'s first possibility, at 27–9, concealed another (about to act in ignorance, yet failing to do so: see 37–8), yielding four types altogether.   [e] Cf. 52b36.

[f] At Soph. *Ant.* 1226–34 the messenger relates Haemon's abortive attempt to kill his father.

[g] I.e. in full knowledge.

[h] Often thought to contradict ch. XIII; yet Ar. sees great scope for pity and fear in narrowly averted catastrophes.

[i] Eur.'s: M. recognised her son when on the very point of killing him in his sleep.

77

5 Κρεσφόντῃ ἡ Μερόπη μέλλει τὸν υἱὸν ἀποκτείνειν,
ἀποκτείνει δὲ οὔ, ἀλλ' ἀνεγνώρισε, καὶ ἐν τῇ Ἰφιγε-
νείᾳ ἡ ἀδελφὴ τὸν ἀδελφόν, καὶ ἐν τῇ Ἕλλῃ ὁ υἱὸς
τὴν μητέρα ἐκδιδόναι μέλλων ἀνεγνώρισεν. διὰ γὰρ
τοῦτο, ὅπερ πάλαι εἴρηται, οὐ περὶ πολλὰ γένη αἱ
10 τραγῳδίαι εἰσίν. ζητοῦντες γὰρ οὐκ ἀπὸ τέχνης
ἀλλ' ἀπὸ τύχης εὗρον τὸ τοιοῦτον παρασκευάζειν ἐν
τοῖς μύθοις· ἀναγκάζονται οὖν ἐπὶ ταύτας τὰς οἰκίας
ἀπαντᾶν ὅσαις τὰ τοιαῦτα συμβέβηκε πάθη. περὶ
μὲν οὖν τῆς τῶν πραγμάτων συστάσεως καὶ ποίους
15 τινὰς εἶναι δεῖ τοὺς μύθους εἴρηται ἱκανῶς.

XV   Περὶ δὲ τὰ ἤθη τέτταρά ἐστιν ὧν δεῖ στοχάζεσθαι, ἓν μὲν καὶ πρῶτον, ὅπως χρηστὰ ᾖ. ἕξει δὲ
ἦθος μὲν ἐὰν ὥσπερ ἐλέχθη ποιῇ φανερὸν ὁ λόγος ἢ
ἡ πρᾶξις προαίρεσίν τινα ᾖ[1] τις ἂν ᾖ, χρηστὸν δὲ
ἐὰν χρηστήν. ἔστιν δὲ ἐν ἑκάστῳ γένει· καὶ γὰρ
20 γυνή ἐστιν χρηστὴ καὶ δοῦλος, καίτοι γε ἴσως τούτων τὸ μὲν χεῖρον, τὸ δὲ ὅλως φαῦλόν ἐστιν. δεύτερον δὲ τὸ ἁρμόττοντα· ἔστιν γὰρ ἀνδρεῖον μὲν τὸ
ἦθος, ἀλλ' οὐχ ἁρμόττον γυναικὶ οὕτως[2] ἀνδρείαν ἢ
δεινὴν εἶναι. τρίτον δὲ τὸ ὅμοιον. τοῦτο γὰρ ἕτερον
τοῦ χρηστὸν τὸ ἦθος καὶ ἁρμόττον ποιῆσαι ὡς προ-
25 είρηται. τέταρτον δὲ τὸ ὁμαλόν. κἂν γὰρ ἀνώμαλός
τις ᾖ ὁ τὴν μίμησιν παρέχων καὶ τοιοῦτον ἦθος ὑποτεθῇ,[3] ὅμως ὁμαλῶς ἀνώμαλον δεῖ εἶναι. ἔστιν δὲ

[1] ᾖ τις ἂν add. Vahlen: om. AB
[2] οὕτως Vahlen: οὐ τῷ B: **τῶι A: τὸ rec.
[3] ὑποτεθῇ B: ὑποτιθεὶς A

78

about to kill her son, but recognises him in time; likewise
with sister and brother in *Iphigeneia*;[a] and in *Helle*[b] the
son recognises his mother when about to hand her over.
Hence, as I said previously, not many families provide
subjects for tragedies. In their experiments, it was not art
but chance that made the poets discover how to produce
such effects in their plots; thus they are now obliged to
turn to the families which such sufferings have befallen.
Enough, then, has now been said about the structure of
events and the required qualities of plots.

V   As regards characters, four things should be aimed
at—first and foremost, that they be good.[c] Characterisation appears when, as said earlier,[d] speech or action
reveals the nature of a moral choice; and good character
when the choice is good. Good character exists in each
class of person: there is a good woman and good slave,
even if the first of these is an inferior class, the other
wholly paltry. The second aim is appropriateness: there is
courage of character, but it is inappropriate for a woman
to be courageous or clever[e] in this way. The third aim is
likeness,[f] which is distinct from making the character
good and appropriate as indicated. Fourth is consistency:
even if the subject represented is someone inconsistent,
and such character is presupposed, he should still be con-

---

[a] Eur. *IT* 727 ff.   [b] Play unknown.

[c] Since "elevated" characters are a defining feature of
tragedy; cf. esp. 48a16–18.

[d] 50b8–10; in fact, the earlier definition was narrower, men-
tioning only "speech."

[e] Character encompasses intellectual virtues; cf. *Eth. Nic.* VI.

[f] As the rest of the sentence suggests, likeness in basic
humanity: cf. "like us" at e.g. 48a5–6.

παράδειγμα πονηρίας μὲν ἤθους μὴ ἀναγκαίας[1] οἷον
ὁ Μενέλαος ὁ ἐν τῷ Ὀρέστῃ, τοῦ δὲ ἀπρεποῦς καὶ
30 μὴ ἁρμόττοντος ὅ τε θρῆνος Ὀδυσσέως ἐν τῇ
Σκύλλῃ καὶ ἡ τῆς Μελανίππης ῥῆσις, τοῦ δὲ ἀνωμά-
λου ἡ ἐν Αὐλίδι Ἰφιγένεια· οὐδὲν γὰρ ἔοικεν ἡ ἱκε-
τεύουσα τῇ ὑστέρᾳ. χρὴ δὲ καὶ ἐν τοῖς ἤθεσιν
ὁμοίως ὥσπερ καὶ ἐν τῇ τῶν πραγμάτων συστάσει
ἀεὶ ζητεῖν ἢ τὸ ἀναγκαῖον ἢ τὸ εἰκός, ὥστε τὸν τοι-
35 οῦτον τὰ τοιαῦτα λέγειν ἢ πράττειν ἢ ἀναγκαῖον ἢ
εἰκὸς καὶ τοῦτο μετὰ τοῦτο γίνεσθαι ἢ ἀναγκαῖον ἢ
εἰκός. (φανερὸν οὖν ὅτι καὶ τὰς λύσεις τῶν μύθων ἐξ
αὐτοῦ δεῖ τοῦ μύθου[2] συμβαίνειν, καὶ μὴ ὥσπερ ἐν
1454b τῇ Μηδείᾳ ἀπὸ μηχανῆς καὶ ἐν τῇ Ἰλιάδι τὰ περὶ
τὸν ἀπόπλουν. ἀλλὰ μηχανῇ χρηστέον ἐπὶ τὰ ἔξω
τοῦ δράματος, ἢ ὅσα πρὸ τοῦ γέγονεν ἃ οὐχ οἷόν τε
ἄνθρωπον εἰδέναι, ἢ ὅσα ὕστερον, ἃ δεῖται προαγο-
5 ρεύσεως καὶ ἀγγελίας· ἅπαντα γὰρ ἀποδίδομεν τοῖς
θεοῖς ὁρᾶν. ἄλογον δὲ μηδὲν εἶναι ἐν τοῖς πράγμασιν, εἰ δὲ μή, ἔξω τῆς τραγῳδίας, οἷον τὸ ἐν τῷ
Οἰδίποδι τῷ Σοφοκλέους.) ἐπεὶ δὲ μίμησίς ἐστιν ἡ

---

[1] ἀναγκαίας Thurot: -αῖον AB
[2] μύθου AB: ἤθους Arab.

---

[a] Eur. Or. 356 ff, 1554 ff.
[b] A dithyramb by Timotheus (see on 48a15), on the theme of
Scylla the sea monster (Hom. Od. 12.85 ff); 61b32 may refer to
the same work.

sistently inconsistent. An example of unnecessary wickedness of character is Menelaus in *Orestes*;[a] of inapt and inappropriate character, Odysseus' dirge in *Scylla*,[b] and the speech of Melanippe;[c] of inconsistency, the *Iphigeneia at Aulis* (since the girl who beseeches bears no resemblance to her later self).[d] With character, precisely as in the structure of events, one should always seek necessity or probability—so that for such a person to say or do such things is necessary or probable, and the sequence of events is also necessary or probable. [e](Clearly the denouements[f] of plots should issue from the plot as such, and not from a deus ex machina as in *Medea*[g] and the scene of departure in the *Iliad*.[h] The deus ex machina should be employed for events outside the drama—preceding events beyond human knowledge, or subsequent events requiring prediction and announcement; for we ascribe to the gods the capacity to see all things. There should be nothing irrational[i] in the events; if there is, it should lie outside the play, as with Sophocles' *Oedipus*.[j]) Since tragedy is mimesis of those superior

---

[c] In Eur. *Melanippe the Wise*, frs. 480–88 Nauck; the heroine's speech showed knowledge of intellectual matters (cf. "clever," 54a24).   [d] Eur. *IA* 1211 ff, 1368 ff.

[e] I place in parenthesis some remarks which are, at the least, digressive, and perhaps misplaced.

[f] The term *lusis* will be technically defined in ch. XVIII; its use here is comparable, though perhaps not identical.

[g] Medea escapes in the Sun's chariot: Eur. *Med.* 1317 ff.

[h] *Il.* 2.155 ff: Athena's intervention prevents the Greeks from abandoning the war.

[i] I.e. grossly contrary to what is plausible or intelligible.

[j] Ar. alludes to Oedipus' ignorance about the death of Laius: cf. 60a29–30.

τραγῳδία βελτιόνων ἢ ἡμεῖς, δεῖ μιμεῖσθαι τοὺς
ἀγαθοὺς εἰκονογράφους· καὶ γὰρ ἐκεῖνοι ἀποδιδόν-
10 τες τὴν ἰδίαν μορφὴν ὁμοίους ποιοῦντες καλλίους
γράφουσιν· οὕτω καὶ τὸν ποιητὴν μιμούμενον καὶ
ὀργίλους καὶ ῥαθύμους καὶ τἆλλα τὰ τοιαῦτα ἔχοντας ἐπὶ τῶν ἠθῶν τοιούτους ὄντας ἐπιεικεῖς ποιεῖν,
οἷον τὸν Ἀχιλλέα ἀγαθὸν[1] καὶ παράδειγμα[2] σκλη-
15 ρότητος Ὅμηρος. ταῦτα δὴ διατηρεῖν, καὶ πρὸς
τούτοις τὰ[3] παρὰ τὰς ἐξ ἀνάγκης ἀκολουθούσας
αἰσθήσεις τῇ ποιητικῇ· καὶ γὰρ κατ' αὐτὰς ἔστιν
ἁμαρτάνειν πολλάκις· εἴρηται δὲ περὶ αὐτῶν ἐν τοῖς
ἐκδεδομένοις λόγοις ἱκανῶς.

XVI   Ἀναγνώρισις δὲ τί μέν ἐστιν, εἴρηται πρότερον·
εἴδη δὲ ἀναγνωρίσεως, πρώτη μὲν ἡ ἀτεχνοτάτη καὶ
20 ᾗ πλείστῃ χρῶνται δι' ἀπορίαν, ἡ διὰ τῶν σημείων.
τούτων δὲ τὰ μὲν σύμφυτα, οἷον "λόγχην ἣν
φοροῦσι Γηγενεῖς" ἢ ἀστέρας οἵους ἐν τῷ Θυέστῃ
Καρκίνος, τὰ δὲ ἐπίκτητα, καὶ τούτων τὰ μὲν ἐν τῷ
σώματι, οἷον οὐλαί, τὰ δὲ ἐκτός, οἷον τὰ περιδέραια
25 καὶ οἷον ἐν τῇ Τυροῖ διὰ τῆς σκάφης. ἔστιν δὲ καὶ
τούτοις χρῆσθαι ἢ βέλτιον ἢ χεῖρον, οἷον Ὀδυσ-

---

[1] ἀγαθὸν B: ἀγαθῶν A: Ἀγάθων rec.
[2] παράδειγμα σκληρ. ante οἷον habent AB: transpos. Lobel
[3] τὰ rec.: τὰς AB

---

[a] See 48a17–18.

to us,[a] poets should emulate good portrait painters, who render personal appearance and produce likenesses, yet enhance people's beauty. Likewise the poet, while showing irascible and indolent people and those with other such character traits, should make them nonetheless decent, as for example Homer made Achilles good though an epitome of harshness. These things are to be watched, as also are points arising from the perceptions necessarily attending the art of poetry:[b] one can commit many errors in respect of these; I have discussed them sufficiently in my published discourses.[c]

XVI The definition of recognition was stated earlier.[d] As for its kinds, first is the least artistic and the one used the most from uninventiveness: recognition through tokens. Some tokens are congenital, as with "the spear the Earth-born bear,"[e] or stars like those Carcinus[f] uses in *Thyestes*; others are acquired, and can be divided into the bodily, such as scars, and external, such as necklaces or the boat in *Tyro*.[g] Even these things can be put to better or worse

[b] The sense of this obscure clause has never been cogently elucidated; "points arising from" might alternatively mean "contraventions of."

[c] Presumably in the dialogue *On Poets*: cf. the Introduction.

[d] Ch. XI.

[e] Quotation from an unknown tragedy (fr. adesp. 84 Nauck): the "spear" is a birthmark of the "earthborn" men sown from dragon's teeth by Cadmus.

[f] The 4th-cent. tragedian of this name, *OCD* s.v. (2); the ref. may be to a play elsewhere called *Aërope*: *TrGF* I 210–11.

[g] In Soph.'s *Tyro*, T. identified her children by the boat in which they had been placed as infants.

σεὺς διὰ τῆς οὐλῆς ἄλλως ἀνεγνωρίσθη ὑπὸ τῆς
τροφοῦ καὶ ἄλλως ὑπὸ τῶν συβοτῶν· εἰσὶ γὰρ αἱ
μὲν πίστεως ἕνεκα ἀτεχνότεραι, καὶ αἱ τοιαῦται
πᾶσαι, αἱ δὲ ἐκ περιπετείας, ὥσπερ ἡ ἐν τοῖς
30 Νίπτροις, βελτίους. δεύτεραι δὲ αἱ πεποιημέναι ὑπὸ
τοῦ ποιητοῦ, διὸ ἄτεχνοι. οἷον Ὀρέστης[1] ἐν τῇ Ἰφι-
γενείᾳ ἀνεγνώρισεν ὅτι Ὀρέστης· ἐκείνη μὲν γὰρ
διὰ τῆς ἐπιστολῆς, ἐκεῖνος δὲ αὐτὸς λέγει ἃ βούλεται ὁ ποιητὴς ἀλλ' οὐχ ὁ μῦθος· διό τι ἐγγὺς τῆς
35 εἰρημένης ἁμαρτίας ἐστίν, ἐξῆν γὰρ ἂν ἔνια καὶ
ἐνεγκεῖν. καὶ ἐν τῷ Σοφοκλέους Τηρεῖ ἡ τῆς κερκί-
δος φωνή. ἡ[2] τρίτη διὰ μνήμης, τῷ αἰσθέσθαι τι
ἰδόντα, ὥσπερ ἡ ἐν Κυπρίοις τοῖς Δικαιογένους,
1455a ἰδὼν γὰρ τὴν γραφὴν ἔκλαυσεν, καὶ ἡ ἐν Ἀλκίνου
ἀπολόγῳ, ἀκούων γὰρ τοῦ κιθαριστοῦ καὶ μνησθεὶς
ἐδάκρυσεν, ὅθεν ἀνεγνωρίσθησαν. τετάρτη δὲ ἡ ἐκ
συλλογισμοῦ, οἷον ἐν Χοηφόροις, ὅτι ὅμοιός τις
5 ἐλήλυθεν, ὅμοιος δὲ οὐθεὶς ἀλλ' ἢ Ὀρέστης, οὗτος
ἄρα ἐλήλυθεν. καὶ ἡ Πολυίδου τοῦ σοφιστοῦ περὶ

----

[1] Ὀρέστης A: om. B
[2] ἡ τρίτη Spengel (τρίτη ἡ rec.): ἤτοι τῇ AB

----

[a] *Od.* 19.386 ff (Eurycleia sees the scar when washing Od.),
21.205 ff (Od. shows it to the swineherds for proof).

[b] I.e. the case of Odysseus and Eurycleia (last note); "Bath
Scene" was a standard title for this episode (cf. 60a26): the
Homeric poems were not yet divided into books.

[c] See on 52b6.

use (e.g. through his scar Odysseus was differently recognised by his nurse and the swineherds),[a] since recognitions for the sake of proof, and all of this type, are less artistic, but those linked to reversal, like the one in the Bath Scene,[b] are superior. The second kind are those contrived by the poet, and hence inartistic. For example, Orestes in *Iphigeneia* causes recognition of his identity; Iphigeneia reveals herself by the letter, but Orestes himself says what the poet, not the plot, wants him to:[c] so it is close to the fault I described, as he might even have carried some tokens. Also the voice of the shuttle in Sophocles' *Tereus*.[d] The third kind is through memory, when the sight of something brings awareness, like the case in Dicaeogenes'[e] *Cyprians* (on seeing the painting he cried), and the one in Odysseus' tale to Alcinous (on hearing the singer he was reminded and wept),[f] whence they were recognised. Fourth is recognition by reasoning — such as the inference in *Choephori* that someone like her has come, no one is like her except Orestes, therefore he has come.[g] And the recognition used by Polyidus[h] the

[d] Philomela used her weaving to reveal to her sister, Procne, that she had been raped by the latter's husband, Tereus.

[e] A late 5th cent. tragedian (*TrGF* I no. 52): work and context unknown.

[f] *Od.* 8.521 ff: Od. weeps on hearing Demodocus sing of the sack of Troy.

[g] Electra's reasoning at Aesch. *Cho.* 168 ff.

[h] Identity obscure; a dithyrambic or tragic poet of the same name is known (*TrGF* I 248–9). P.'s work may have been a showpiece oration discussing or fictionalising the reunion of Orestes and Iphigeneia; cf. 55b10–11.

τῆς Ἰφιγενείας· εἰκὸς γὰρ ἔφη[1] τὸν Ὀρέστην συλ-
λογίσασθαι ὅτι ἥ τ᾽ ἀδελφὴ ἐτύθη καὶ αὐτῷ συμβαίνει θύεσθαι. καὶ ἐν τῷ Θεοδέκτου Τυδεῖ, ὅτι
ἐλθὼν ὡς εὑρήσων τὸν υἱὸν αὐτὸς ἀπόλλυται. καὶ ἡ
10 ἐν τοῖς Φινείδαις· ἰδοῦσαι γὰρ τὸν τόπον συνελογί-
σαντο τὴν εἱμαρμένην ὅτι ἐν τούτῳ εἵμαρτο ἀποθανεῖν αὐταῖς, καὶ γὰρ ἐξετέθησαν ἐνταῦθα. ἔστιν δέ
τις καὶ συνθετὴ ἐκ παραλογισμοῦ τοῦ θεάτρου,[2] οἷον
ἐν τῷ Ὀδυσσεῖ τῷ ψευδαγγέλῳ· τὸ μὲν γὰρ τὸ τόξον
ἐντείνειν,[3] ἄλλον δὲ μηδένα, πεποιημένον ὑπὸ τοῦ
ποιητοῦ καὶ ὑπόθεσις, καὶ εἴ γε τὸ τόξον ἔφη γνώσεσθαι[4] ὃ οὐχ ἑωράκει· τὸ δὲ ὡς δι᾽[5] ἐκείνου ἀνα-
15 γνωριοῦντος διὰ τούτου ποιῆσαι παραλογισμός.
πασῶν δὲ βελτίστη ἀναγνώρισις ἡ ἐξ αὐτῶν τῶν
πραγμάτων, τῆς ἐκπλήξεως γιγνομένης δι᾽ εἰκότων,
οἷον ἐν τῷ Σοφοκλέους Οἰδίποδι καὶ τῇ Ἰφιγενείᾳ·
εἰκὸς γὰρ βούλεσθαι ἐπιθεῖναι γράμματα. αἱ γὰρ
τοιαῦται μόναι ἄνευ τῶν πεποιημένων σημείων καὶ
20 περιδεραίων. δεύτεραι δὲ αἱ ἐκ συλλογισμοῦ.
XVII Δεῖ δὲ τοὺς μύθους συνιστάναι καὶ τῇ λέξει συν-
απεργάζεσθαι ὅτι μάλιστα πρὸ ὀμμάτων τιθέμενον·
οὕτω γὰρ ἂν ἐναργέστατα ὁρῶν ὥσπερ παρ᾽ αὐτοῖς
γιγνόμενος τοῖς πραττομένοις εὑρίσκοι τὸ πρέπον

---

[1] ἔφη B Arab.: om. A
[2] θεάτρου AB: θατέρου Hermann
[3] ἐντείνειν . . . τόξον B: om. A
[4] γνώσεσθαι A: ἐντείνειν B
[5] δι᾽ AB: δὴ Tyrwhitt

sophist in Iphigeneia's case: it was probable, he said, that
Orestes should reason that his sister had been sacrificed,
and his fate was to be sacrificed too. Also in Theodectes'[a]
Tydeus, the reflection that having come to find his son he
was doomed himself. Again, the instance in the
Phineidae:[b] when the women saw the place, they inferred
it was their destiny to die there, where they had also been
exposed. There is also compound recognition which
depends on the audience's mistaken reasoning, as in
Odysseus the False Messenger:[c] that he and no one else
could bend the bow is contrived by the poet and a
premise, even if he said he would recognise the bow
which he had not seen; but to have him recognised by this
means, when he was expected to cause recognition in the
other way, involves false reasoning. Best of all is recognition ensuing from the events themselves, where the emotional impact comes from a probable sequence, as in
Sophocles' *Oedipus* and the *Iphigeneia* (where it is probable she should want to entrust a letter).[d] For only such
recognitions do without contrived tokens and necklaces.
Second-best are those by reasoning.

VII   One should construct plots, and work them out in diction, with the material as much as possible in the mind's
eye. In this way, by seeing things most vividly, as if present at the actual events, one will discover what is appo-

---

[a] Rhetorician, tragedian, and friend of Ar.'s; *OCD* s.v. Nothing is known of this play (*TrGF* I 233).

[b] I.e. the sons of Phineus (subject of tragedies by Aesch. and
Soph.); but the ref. is opaque (*TrGF* II 22), and we cannot identify the women mentioned.

[c] Apparently an unknown tragedy (*TrGF* II 15), related to the
events of Hom. *Od.* bk. 21; the following clauses are irredeemably dark.   [d] Eur. *IT* 578 ff.

25 καὶ ἥκιστα ἂν λανθάνοι τὰ ὑπεναντία. σημεῖον δὲ
τούτου ὃ ἐπετιμᾶτο Καρκίνῳ. ὁ γὰρ Ἀμφιάραος ἐξ
ἱεροῦ ἀνήει, ὃ μὴ ὁρῶντα[1] ἐλάνθανεν, ἐπὶ δὲ τῆς
σκηνῆς ἐξέπεσεν δυσχερανάντων τοῦτο τῶν θεατῶν.
ὅσα δὲ δυνατὸν καὶ τοῖς σχήμασιν συναπεργαζόμε-
30 νον· πιθανώτατοι γὰρ ἀπὸ τῆς[2] αὐτῆς φύσεως οἱ ἐν
τοῖς πάθεσίν εἰσιν, καὶ χειμαίνει ὁ χειμαζόμενος καὶ
χαλεπαίνει ὁ ὀργιζόμενος ἀληθινώτατα. διὸ εὐφυ-
οῦς ἡ ποιητική ἐστιν ἢ[3] μανικοῦ· τούτων γὰρ οἱ μὲν
εὔπλαστοι οἱ δὲ ἐκστατικοί εἰσιν. τούς τε λόγους
καὶ τοὺς πεποιημένους δεῖ καὶ αὐτὸν ποιοῦντα ἐκτί-
1455b θεσθαι καθόλου, εἶθ' οὕτως ἐπεισοδιοῦν καὶ παρα-
τείνειν. λέγω δὲ οὕτως ἂν θεωρεῖσθαι τὸ καθόλου,
οἷον τῆς Ἰφιγενείας· τυθείσης τινὸς κόρης καὶ ἀφα-
νισθείσης ἀδήλως τοῖς θύσασιν, ἱδρυνθείσης δὲ εἰς
ἄλλην χώραν, ἐν ᾗ νόμος ἦν τοὺς ξένους θύειν τῇ
5 θεῷ, ταύτην ἔσχε τὴν ἱερωσύνην· χρόνῳ δὲ ὕστερον
τῷ ἀδελφῷ συνέβη ἐλθεῖν τῆς ἱερείας, τὸ δὲ ὅτι
ἀνεῖλεν ὁ θεὸς[4] ἐλθεῖν ἐκεῖ καὶ ἐφ' ὅ τι δὲ ἔξω τοῦ

---

[1] ὁρῶντα τὸν θεατὴν AB: τὸν θ. secl. Butcher
[2] τῆς αὐτῆς AB: αὐτῆς τῆς Tyrwhitt
[3] ἢ AB: μᾶλλον ἢ Tyrwhitt
[4] post θεὸς seq. διά τινα αἰτίαν ἔξω τοῦ καθόλου in AB: διά
. . . καθ. secl. Christ

[a] See on 54b23. Both play and situation referred to are
unknown; *TrGF* I 211–12.
[b] The Greek verb implies that the work was hissed off stage;
cf. 56a18–19, 59b31.

site and not miss contradictions. An indication of this is
the criticism that was made of Carcinus:[a] Amphiaraus was
returning from a shrine, which was missed by one who
failed to visualise it; in performance the audience was
annoyed at this and the play foundered.[b] So far as possible, one should also work out the plot in gestures, since a
natural affinity makes those in the grip of emotions the
most convincing, and the truest distress or anger is conveyed by one who actually feels these things.[c] Hence
poetry is the work of a gifted person, or[d] of a manic: of
these types, the former have versatile imaginations, the
latter get carried away. With both ready-made stories and
his own inventions,[e] the poet should lay out the general[f]
structure, and only then develop the sequence of
episodes. For what I mean by contemplating the general
structure, take the *Iphigeneia*.[g] A girl was sacrificed, and
vanished without trace from her sacrificers; settled in a
different country, where it was a custom to sacrifice
strangers to the goddess, she became priestess of this rite.
Later, the priestess' brother happened to arrive there
(that the god's oracle told him to go there, and for what

[c] Ar. implies that acting out a role will help to induce the con-
comitant feelings.

[d] A textual emendation would make this "rather than," on the
grounds that "manic" sounds *too* passionate for the psychology of
composition posited by Ar.

[e] Cf. 51b15–26.

[f] *Katholou*, the same term as "universal" at 51b8–9: the sense
is not different here (it refers to the *kinds* of event), though its
emphasis is more limited than in ch. IX.

[g] Eur. *IT*.

μύθου· ἐλθὼν δὲ καὶ ληφθεὶς θύεσθαι μέλλων ἀνεγνώρισεν, εἴθ' ὡς Εὐριπίδης εἴθ' ὡς Πολύιδος ἐποίη-
10 σεν, κατὰ τὸ εἰκὸς εἰπὼν ὅτι οὐκ ἄρα μόνον τὴν
ἀδελφὴν ἀλλὰ καὶ αὐτὸν ἔδει τυθῆναι, καὶ ἐντεῦθεν
ἡ σωτηρία. μετὰ ταῦτα δὲ ἤδη ὑποθέντα τὰ ὀνόματα ἐπεισοδιοῦν· ὅπως δὲ ἔσται οἰκεῖα τὰ ἐπεισόδια, οἷον ἐν τῷ Ὀρέστῃ ἡ μανία δι' ἧς ἐλήφθη καὶ
15 ἡ σωτηρία διὰ τῆς καθάρσεως. ἐν μὲν οὖν τοῖς δρά-
μασιν τὰ ἐπεισόδια σύντομα, ἡ δ' ἐποποιία τούτοις
μηκύνεται. τῆς γὰρ Ὀδυσσείας οὐ[1] μακρὸς ὁ λόγος
ἐστίν· ἀποδημοῦντός τινος ἔτη πολλὰ καὶ παρα-
φυλαττομένου ὑπὸ τοῦ Ποσειδῶνος καὶ μόνου ὄντος,
ἔτι δὲ τῶν οἴκοι οὕτως ἐχόντων ὥστε τὰ χρήματα
20 ὑπὸ μνηστήρων ἀναλίσκεσθαι καὶ τὸν υἱὸν ἐπιβου-
λεύεσθαι, αὐτὸς δὲ ἀφικνεῖται χειμασθείς, καὶ ἀνα-
γνωρίσας τινὰς ἐπιθέμενος αὐτὸς μὲν ἐσώθη τοὺς δ'
ἐχθροὺς διέφθειρε. τὸ μὲν οὖν ἴδιον τοῦτο, τὰ δ'
ἄλλα ἐπεισόδια.

XVIII   Ἔστι δὲ πάσης τραγῳδίας τὸ μὲν δέσις τὸ δὲ
λύσις, τὰ μὲν ἔξωθεν καὶ ἔνια τῶν ἔσωθεν πολλάκις
25 ἡ δέσις, τὸ δὲ λοιπὸν ἡ λύσις· λέγω δὲ δέσιν μὲν
εἶναι τὴν ἀπ' ἀρχῆς μέχρι τούτου τοῦ μέρους ὃ
ἔσχατόν ἐστιν ἐξ οὗ μεταβαίνει εἰς εὐτυχίαν ἢ εἰς
ἀτυχίαν, λύσιν δὲ τὴν ἀπὸ τῆς ἀρχῆς τῆς μεταβά-
σεως μέχρι τέλους· ὥσπερ ἐν τῷ Λυγκεῖ τῷ Θεοδέκτου δέσις μὲν τά τε προπεπραγμένα καὶ ἡ τοῦ
30 παιδίου λῆψις καὶ πάλιν ἡ αὐτῶν * * * λύσις[2] δ' ἡ

[1] οὐ Arab.: om. AB

90

purpose, is outside the plot). Captured after his arrival, and on the point of being sacrificed, he caused his recognition—whether as in Euripides, or as Polyidus[a] designed it, by saying (as was probable) that it was not just his sister's but his own fate too to be sacrificed—and hence was rescued. The next stage is to supply names and devise the episodes; but care must be taken to keep the episodes integral: thus, in Orestes' case, the mad fit that caused his capture, and his rescue by purification.[b] Now, in plays the episodes are concise, but epic gains length from them. The *Odyssey*'s story is not long: a man is away from home many years; he is watched by Poseidon, and isolated; moreover, affairs at home are such that his property is consumed by suitors, and his son conspired against; but he returns after shipwreck, allows some people to recognise him, and launches an attack which brings his own survival and his enemies' destruction. That is the essential core; the rest is episodes.

Every tragedy has both a complication[c] and denouement: the complication comprises events outside the play, and often some of those within it; the remainder is the dénouement. I define the complication as extending from the beginning[d] to the furthest point before the transformation to prosperity or adversity; and the denouement as extending from the beginning of the transformation till the end. Thus, in Theodectes' *Lynceus*[e] the complication covers the preceding events, the

---

[a] See on 55a6.   [b] *IT* 281 ff, 1029 ff.

[c] Not to be confused with the "complex" plot of ch. X etc.

[d] Of the imagined "action," not necessarily of the play.

[e] *TrGF* I 232; cf. 52a27–9. Theodectes: see on 55a9.

---

² λύσις δ' ἡ rec., Arab.: δὴ (om. λύσις) AB

ἀπὸ τῆς αἰτιάσεως τοῦ θανάτου μέχρι τοῦ τέλους.
τραγῳδίας δὲ εἴδη εἰσὶ τέσσαρα (τοσαῦτα γὰρ καὶ
τὰ μέρη ἐλέχθη), ἡ μὲν πεπλεγμένη, ἧς τὸ ὅλον
ἐστὶν περιπέτεια καὶ ἀναγνώρισις, ἡ δὲ παθητική,
οἷον οἵ τε Αἴαντες καὶ οἱ Ἰξίονες, ἡ δὲ ἠθική, οἷον αἱ
1456a Φθιώτιδες καὶ ὁ Πηλεύς· τὸ δὲ τέταρτον ἡ[1] ἁπλῆ,
οἷον αἵ τε Φορκίδες καὶ ὁ Προμηθεὺς καὶ ὅσα ἐν
ᾅδου. μάλιστα μὲν οὖν ἅπαντα δεῖ πειρᾶσθαι ἔχειν,
εἰ δὲ μή, τὰ μέγιστα καὶ πλεῖστα, ἄλλως τε καὶ ὡς
νῦν συκοφαντοῦσιν τοὺς ποιητάς· γεγονότων γὰρ
5 καθ' ἕκαστον μέρος ἀγαθῶν ποιητῶν, ἑκάστου τοῦ
ἰδίου ἀγαθοῦ ἀξιοῦσι τὸν ἕνα ὑπερβάλλειν. δίκαιον
δὲ καὶ τραγῳδίαν ἄλλην καὶ τὴν αὐτὴν λέγειν
οὐδενὶ[2] ὡς τῷ μύθῳ· τοῦτο δέ, ὧν ἡ αὐτὴ πλοκὴ καὶ
λύσις. πολλοὶ δὲ πλέξαντες εὖ λύουσι κακῶς· δεῖ δὲ
10 ἄμφω[3] ἀεὶ κρατεῖσθαι. χρὴ δὲ ὅπερ εἴρηται πολλάκις μεμνῆσθαι καὶ μὴ ποιεῖν ἐποποιικὸν σύστημα
τραγῳδίαν—ἐποποιικὸν δὲ λέγω τὸ πολύμυθον—
οἷον εἴ τις τὸν τῆς Ἰλιάδος ὅλον ποιοῖ μῦθον. ἐκεῖ
μὲν γὰρ διὰ τὸ μῆκος λαμβάνει τὰ μέρη τὸ πρέπον

---

[1] ἡ ἁπλῆ Bursian: οης B: όης A: ὄψις Bywater
[2] οὐδενὶ ὡς Zeller: οὐδὲν ἴσως AB
[3] ἄμφω ἀεὶ κροτεῖσθαι A (κρατεῖσθαι Vahlen): ἀμφότερα
ἀντικροτεῖσθαι B: ἀμφότερα ἀρτικροτεῖσθαι Immisch

---

[a] This claim (perhaps spurious) does not match the enumera-
tion of components at 50a7–14. Cf. 59b8–9.

[b] "Suffering" as defined in ch. XI. Plays about Ajax, such as
Soph.'s, would centre on his suicide; those about Ixion, on his
punishment on the wheel in Hades.

seizure of the child, and again their * * *, while the
denouement runs from the accusation of murder to the
end. There are four types of tragedy (as that is the number of components we mentioned):[a] the complex, whose
essence is reversal and recognition; the kind rich in
suffering,[b] such as those about Ajax and Ixion; the character-based, such as *Phthiotides*[c] and *Peleus*;[d] and, fourth,
<the simple>,[e] such as *Phorcides*, *Prometheus*, and those
set in Hades. Now, ideally one should strive to have all
qualities, failing that, the best and the most, especially in
view of current censure of the poets: because there have
been poets good in various respects, people expect the
individual to surpass the special quality of each of them.
It is right to count plays as different or the same principally by plot: that is, "the same" means having the same
complication and denouement. Many poets handle the
complication well, the denouement badly: but constant
proficiency in both is needed. As noted several times, the
poet must remember to avoid turning a tragedy into an
epic structure (by "epic" I mean with a multiple plot), say
by dramatising the entire plot of the *Iliad*. In epic,
because of its length, the sections take on an apt magnitude, but in plays it[f] goes quite against expectation.

[c] *Women of Phthia*, perhaps Soph.'s play of this name: its subject is unknown; *TrGF* IV 481–2.

[d] Both Soph. and Eur. wrote plays about P., father of Achilles.

[e] The text is badly damaged here; the passage needs a ref. to
the "simple" tragedy (ch. X, cf. 59b9). *Phorcides*, "Daughters of
Phorcys" (guardians of the Gorgons), may be Aesch.'s work of
that name (*TrGF* III 361: a satyr play?), as may *Prometheus*: but
we cannot be sure.

[f] I.e. a plot of epic scope.

μέγεθος, ἐν δὲ τοῖς δράμασι πολὺ παρὰ τὴν ὑπόλη-
15 ψιν ἀποβαίνει. σημεῖον δέ, ὅσοι πέρσιν Ἰλίου ὅλην
ἐποίησαν καὶ μὴ κατὰ μέρος ὥσπερ Εὐριπίδης, ἢ[1]
Νιόβην καὶ μὴ ὥσπερ Αἰσχύλος, ἢ ἐκπίπτουσιν ἢ
κακῶς ἀγωνίζονται, ἐπεὶ καὶ Ἀγάθων ἐξέπεσεν ἐν
τούτῳ μόνῳ. ἐν δὲ ταῖς περιπετείαις καὶ ἐν τοῖς
ἁπλοῖς πράγμασι στοχάζονται ὧν βούλονται τῷ[2]
20 θαυμαστῷ· τραγικὸν γὰρ τοῦτο καὶ φιλάνθρωπον.
ἔστιν δὲ τοῦτο, ὅταν ὁ σοφὸς μὲν μετὰ πονηρίας δ᾽
ἐξαπατηθῇ, ὥσπερ Σίσυφος, καὶ ὁ ἀνδρεῖος μὲν ἄδι-
κος δὲ ἡττηθῇ. ἔστιν δὲ τοῦτο καὶ εἰκὸς ὥσπερ
Ἀγάθων λέγει, εἰκὸς γὰρ γίνεσθαι πολλὰ καὶ παρὰ
25 τὸ εἰκός. καὶ τὸν χορὸν δὲ ἕνα δεῖ ὑπολαμβάνειν
τῶν ὑποκριτῶν, καὶ μόριον εἶναι τοῦ ὅλου καὶ συν-
αγωνίζεσθαι μὴ ὥσπερ Εὐριπίδῃ ἀλλ᾽ ὥσπερ Σοφοκλεῖ. τοῖς δὲ λοιποῖς τὰ ᾀδόμενα[3] οὐδὲν[4] μᾶλλον
τοῦ μύθου ἢ ἄλλης τραγῳδίας ἐστίν· διὸ ἐμβόλιμα
ᾄδουσιν πρώτου ἄρξαντος Ἀγάθωνος τοῦ τοιούτου.
30 καίτοι τί διαφέρει ἢ ἐμβόλιμα ᾄδειν ἢ εἰ ῥῆσιν ἐξ
ἄλλου εἰς ἄλλο ἁρμόττοι ἢ ἐπεισόδιον ὅλον;
XIX Περὶ μὲν οὖν τῶν ἄλλων εἰδῶν[5] εἴρηται, λοιπὸν δὲ

---

[1] ἢ add. Vahlen
[2] τῷ θαυμαστῷ Castelvetro: θαυμαστῶς AB
[3] ᾀδόμενα Arab.: διδόμενα AB
[4] οὐδὲν Arab. (Vahlen): om. AB
[5] εἰδῶν B: ἠδ᾽ A

An indication of this is that those who have treated the entire fall of Troy, rather than part of it (like Euripides),[a] or Niobe's whole story (instead of what Aeschylus did),[b] either founder[c] or do badly in competition; even Agathon foundered through just this flaw.[d] In reversals and simple structures of events, poets aim for what they want by means of the awesome:[e] this is tragic and arouses fellow-feeling.[f] This occurs when an adroit but wicked person is deceived (like Sisyphus),[g] or a brave but unjust person is worsted. These things are even probable, as Agathon puts it,[h] since it is probable that many things should infringe probability. The chorus should be treated as one of the actors; it should be a part of the whole and should participate,[i] not as in Euripides but as in Sophocles. With the other poets, the songs are no more integral to the plot than to another tragedy—hence the practice, started by Agathon, of singing interlude odes. Yet what is the difference between singing interlude odes and transferring a speech or whole episode from one work to another?

The other components have now been discussed; it

[a] In *Trojan Women*.

[b] We do not know what was distinctive about Aesch.'s treatment of Niobe's suffering (cf. *OCD* s.v.); *TrGF* III 265–80.

[c] Cf. on 55a28.

[d] Ref. unknown; for Agathon, see 51b21.

[e] A difficult sentence; but Ar. apparently allows that "awe" (see on 52a4) can be achieved by simple as well as complex plots.

[f] Cf. on 52b38.

[g] We cannot identify the stories/plays about Sisyphus (*OCD* s.v.) which Ar. has in mind.

[h] Fr. 9 *TrGF* (I 164); see Ar.'s quotation at *Rh.* 1402a9–13.

[i] Sc. "in the action."

περὶ λέξεως καὶ[1] διανοίας εἰπεῖν. τὰ μὲν οὖν περὶ
τὴν διάνοιαν ἐν τοῖς περὶ ῥητορικῆς κείσθω· τοῦτο
35 γὰρ ἴδιον μᾶλλον ἐκείνης τῆς μεθόδου. ἔστι δὲ κατὰ
τὴν διάνοιαν ταῦτα, ὅσα ὑπὸ τοῦ λόγου δεῖ παρα-
σκευασθῆναι. μέρη δὲ τούτων τό τε ἀποδεικνύναι
καὶ τὸ λύειν καὶ τὸ πάθη παρασκευάζειν (οἷον ἔλεον
1456b ἢ φόβον ἢ ὀργὴν καὶ ὅσα τοιαῦτα) καὶ ἔτι μέγεθος
καὶ μικρότητας. δῆλον δὲ ὅτι καὶ ἐν τοῖς πράγμασιν
ἀπὸ τῶν αὐτῶν ἰδεῶν δεῖ χρῆσθαι ὅταν ἢ ἐλεεινὰ ἢ
δεινὰ ἢ μεγάλα ἢ εἰκότα δέῃ παρασκευάζειν· πλὴν
τοσοῦτον διαφέρει, ὅτι τὰ μὲν δεῖ φαίνεσθαι ἄνευ
5 διδασκαλίας, τὰ δὲ ἐν τῷ λόγῳ ὑπὸ τοῦ λέγοντος
παρασκευάζεσθαι καὶ παρὰ τὸν λόγον γίγνεσθαι.
τί γὰρ ἂν εἴη τοῦ λέγοντος ἔργον, εἰ φαίνοιτο ᾗ[2]
δέοι καὶ μὴ διὰ τὸν λόγον; τῶν δὲ περὶ τὴν λέξιν ἓν
μέν ἐστιν εἶδος θεωρίας τὰ σχήματα τῆς λέξεως, ἃ
ἐστιν εἰδέναι τῆς ὑποκριτικῆς καὶ τοῦ τὴν τοιαύτην
10 ἔχοντος ἀρχιτεκτονικήν, οἷον τί ἐντολὴ καὶ τί εὐχὴ
καὶ διήγησις καὶ ἀπειλὴ καὶ ἐρώτησις καὶ ἀπόκρισις
καὶ εἴ τι ἄλλο τοιοῦτον. παρὰ γὰρ τὴν τούτων γνῶσιν ἢ ἄγνοιαν οὐδὲν εἰς τὴν ποιητικὴν ἐπιτίμημα
φέρεται ὅ τι καὶ ἄξιον σπουδῆς. τί γὰρ ἄν τις ὑπο-
15 λάβοι ἡμαρτῆσθαι ἃ Πρωταγόρας ἐπιτιμᾷ, ὅτι εὔχε-
σθαι οἰόμενος ἐπιτάττει εἰπὼν "μῆνιν ἄειδε θεά"; τὸ
γὰρ κελεῦσαι, φησίν, ποιεῖν τι ἢ μὴ ἐπίταξίς ἐστιν.
διὸ παρείσθω ὡς ἄλλης καὶ οὐ τῆς ποιητικῆς ὂν
θεώρημα.

---

[1] καὶ Hermann: ἢ AB   [2] ᾗ δέοι Vahlen: ἡδέα AB

remains to speak about diction and thought. The discussion of thought can be left to my discourses on rhetoric,[a] for it is more integral to that enquiry. "Thought" covers all effects which need to be created by speech: their elements are proof, refutation, the conveying of emotions (pity, fear, anger, etc.), as well as enhancement and belittlement. It is clear that the same principles should also be used in the handling of events, when one needs to create impressions of what is pitiable, terrible, important, or probable—with this difference, that the latter effects must be evident without direct statement, while the former must be conveyed by the speaker in and through speech. For what would be the point of the speaker, if the required effects were evident even without speech? As for matters of diction, one type of study concerns forms of utterance (knowledge of which belongs to the art of delivery[b] and the person with this mastery)—namely, what is a command, prayer, narrative, threat, question, reply, and all the like. Knowledge or ignorance of these things can support no serious criticism of poetry. Why should anyone think it is a fault where Protagoras criticises Homer for purporting to pray but giving a command by saying "Sing, goddess, of the wrath ..."?[c] (To bid someone do or not do something, says Protagoras, is a command.) So, let this study be put aside as part of some other art, not poetry.

[a] Whether or not this means the surviving *Rhetoric*, "thought" (*dianoia*) certainly denotes the general sphere of argumentation in that work (*Rh.* 1403a36).

[b] The vocal art of the actor (*hupokritēs*) and orator: cf. 57a21, with *Rh.* III.1.

[c] We do not know where P. (c. 490–20) made his pedantic criticism of *Il.* 1.1.

ARISTOTLE

XX   Τῆς δὲ λέξεως ἁπάσης τάδ' ἐστὶ τὰ μέρη, στοι-
20 χεῖον συλλαβὴ σύνδεσμος ὄνομα ῥῆμα ἄρθρον
πτῶσις λόγος. στοιχεῖον μὲν οὖν ἐστιν φωνὴ ἀδιαί-
ρετος, οὐ πᾶσα δὲ ἀλλ' ἐξ ἧς πέφυκε συνθετὴ[1]
γίγνεσθαι φωνή· καὶ γὰρ τῶν θηρίων εἰσὶν ἀδιαίρε-
τοι φωναί, ὧν οὐδεμίαν λέγω στοιχεῖον. ταύτης δὲ
25 μέρη τό τε φωνῆεν καὶ τὸ ἡμίφωνον καὶ ἄφωνον.
ἔστιν δὲ ταῦτα φωνῆεν μὲν τὸ[2] ἄνευ προσβολῆς
ἔχον φωνὴν ἀκουστήν, ἡμίφωνον δὲ τὸ μετὰ προσβολῆς ἔχον φωνὴν ἀκουστήν, οἷον τὸ Σ καὶ τὸ Ρ,
ἄφωνον δὲ τὸ μετὰ προσβολῆς καθ' αὑτὸ μὲν οὐδεμίαν ἔχον φωνήν, μετὰ δὲ τῶν ἐχόντων τινὰ φωνὴν
30 γινόμενον ἀκουστόν, οἷον τὸ Γ καὶ τὸ Δ. ταῦτα δὲ
διαφέρει σχήμασί τε τοῦ στόματος καὶ τόποις καὶ
δασύτητι καὶ ψιλότητι καὶ μήκει καὶ βραχύτητι ἔτι
δὲ ὀξύτητι καὶ βαρύτητι καὶ τῷ μέσῳ· περὶ ὧν καθ'
ἕκαστον ἐν τοῖς μετρικοῖς προσήκει θεωρεῖν. συλ-
35 λαβὴ δέ ἐστι φωνὴ ἄσημος συνθετὴ ἐξ ἀφώνου καὶ
φωνὴν ἔχοντος· καὶ γὰρ τὸ ΓΡ ἄνευ τοῦ Α συλλαβὴ[3] καὶ μετὰ τοῦ Α, οἷον τὸ ΓΡΑ. ἀλλὰ καὶ τούτων θεωρῆσαι τὰς διαφορὰς τῆς μετρικῆς ἐστιν.
σύνδεσμος δέ ἐστιν φωνὴ ἄσημος ἣ οὔτε κωλύει

---

[1] συνθετὴ Arab.: συνετὴ AB
[2] τὸ add. Reiz
[3] συλλαβὴ καὶ AB: (?)οὐ συλλαβή, συλλαβὴ δὲ Arab.

---

[a] What follows, in chs. XX-XXI, is not "stylistics" but an outline of grammatical/linguistic categories.

98

The components of all diction are these:[a] element, syllable, connective, noun, verb, conjunction, inflection, statement. An element is an indivisible vocal sound, but only one from which a compound sound is naturally formed: for animals too produce indivisible sounds, none of which do I term an "element."[b] The classes of sound[c] are vowel, continuant,[d] and stop. A vowel is an audible[e] sound without oral contact; a continuant an audible sound *with* contact (e.g. *s* and *r*); while a stop[f] (e.g. *g* and *d*) involves contact but in itself produces no sound, and becomes audible by combination with elements that do produce a sound. Elements are distinguishable by the mouth shape and the points of contact; by aspiration and lack of it; by length and shortness,[g] and also by acute, grave, and intermediate accent:[h] detailed study of these things belongs to discourses on metre.[i] A syllable is a non-significant[j] sound, compounded of a stop and a voiced[k] element: *gr* is a syllable without *a*, and also with *a* (i.e. *gra*). But the study of these distinctions too belongs to metrics. A connective is a non-significant sound which neither prevents nor creates a single semantic utterance

[b] I.e. animals make some vocal sounds, but these do not combine to produce the syllables and words of language.

[c] From now on "sound," *phōnē*, denotes speech sounds.

[d] Sometimes termed "semi-vowel."

[e] Sc. in itself (unlike a stop).

[f] Also known as "mute."   [g] Of vowels.

[h] Pitch accent, not dynamic stress.

[i] Works which treated phonology within analysis of metrical patterns; cf. *Part. An.* 660a8.

[j] I.e. not a semantic unit.

[k] I.e. (apparently) vowel *or* continuant.

1457a οὔτε ποιεῖ φωνὴν μίαν σημαντικὴν ἐκ πλειόνων
φωνῶν, πεφυκυῖα[1] συντίθεσθαι καὶ ἐπὶ τῶν ἄκρων
καὶ ἐπὶ τοῦ μέσου, ἣν[2] μὴ ἁρμόττει ἐν ἀρχῇ λόγου
τιθέναι καθ' αὐτήν,[3] οἷον μέν δή[4] τοί δέ. ἢ φωνὴ
ἄσημος ἢ ἐκ πλειόνων μὲν φωνῶν μιᾶς σημαντικῶν[5]
5 δὲ ποιεῖν πέφυκεν μίαν σημαντικὴν φωνήν. ἄρθρον
δ' ἐστὶ φωνὴ ἄσημος ἢ λόγου ἀρχὴν ἢ τέλος ἢ διο-
ρισμὸν δηλοῖ. οἷον τὸ ἀμφί[6] καὶ τὸ περί καὶ τὰ
ἄλλα. ἢ φωνὴ ἄσημος ἢ οὔτε κωλύει οὔτε ποιεῖ
φωνὴν μίαν σημαντικὴν ἐκ πλειόνων φωνῶν, πεφυκυῖα τίθεσθαι καὶ ἐπὶ τῶν ἄκρων καὶ ἐπὶ τοῦ μέσου.
10 ὄνομα δέ ἐστι φωνὴ συνθετὴ σημαντικὴ ἄνευ χρόνου ἧς μέρος οὐδέν ἐστι καθ' αὐτὸ σημαντικόν· ἐν
γὰρ τοῖς διπλοῖς οὐ χρώμεθα ὡς καὶ αὐτὸ καθ' αὐτὸ
σημαῖνον, οἷον ἐν τῷ Θεόδωρος[7] τὸ δωρος οὐ σημαίνει. ῥῆμα δὲ φωνὴ συνθετὴ σημαντικὴ μετὰ χρόνου
ἧς οὐδὲν μέρος σημαίνει καθ' αὐτό, ὥσπερ καὶ ἐπὶ
15 τῶν ὀνομάτων· τὸ μὲν γὰρ ἄνθρωπος ἢ λευκόν οὐ
σημαίνει τὸ πότε, τὸ δὲ βαδίζει ἢ βεβάδικεν προσ-
σημαίνει τὸ μὲν τὸν παρόντα χρόνον τὸ δὲ τὸν

---

[1] πεφυκυῖα B: -αν A
[2] ἣν . . . μέσου (57a3–10) om. B
[3] αὐτήν Tyrwhitt (Lat.): αὐτόν A
[4] δή τοί Bywater: ἤτοι A
[5] σημαντικῶν Robortelli: -ὸν A
[6] ἀμφί Hartung: φ.μ.ι. A
[7] Θεόδωρος τὸ δωρος Ritter (Arab.): θεοδώρῳ τὸ δῶρον AB

[a] I.e. connective particles, though the definition is corrupt.
Cf. *Rh.* 1407a20 ff.

from a plurality of sounds, usually placed at the ends or in the middle of a statement, but not on its own at the start of one: e.g. *men, dē, toi, de.*[a] Or a nonsignificant sound which naturally produces a single semantic utterance from a plurality of sounds that have a single significance. A conjunction is a non-significant sound which indicates the beginning, end, or division of a statement: e.g. *amphi, peri,*[b] etc. Or a nonsignificant sound which neither prevents nor creates a single semantic utterance from a plurality of sounds, normally placed either at the ends or in the middle.[c] A noun[d] is a compound,[e] significant, non-temporal sound, no part of which is independently significant; for in double nouns[f] we do not employ any part as independently significant: e.g. in "Theodorus" the "-dorus" part has no meaning.[g] A verb is a compound, significant sound with a temporal force, but no part of which is independently significant (as with nouns): "man" or "white" does not signify time, but "is walking" or "has walked"[h] additionally signify present and past time,

[b] Exx. of prepositions, which do not at all fit the definition. This is one of several acute difficulties in the passage.

[c] The baffling replication of the first definition of "connective" points to further textual corruption.

[d] The term covers adjs. too; cf. 57a16.

[e] As in the following definitions of verb and statement, "compound" *qua* consisting of more than one phonological "element"; cf. 56b35.

[f] Cf. 57a32.

[g] I.e. no *functional* meaning (as opp. to etymology, from *dōron,* "gift") in the use of the name; cf. 57a33 f.

[h] In Greek, both verbs are single-word inflected forms.

101

παρεληλυθότα. πτῶσις δ' ἐστὶν ὀνόματος ἢ ῥήματος ἡ μὲν κατὰ[1] τὸ τούτου ἢ τούτῳ σημαῖνον καὶ
20 ὅσα τοιαῦτα, ἡ δὲ κατὰ τὸ ἑνὶ ἢ πολλοῖς, οἷον
ἄνθρωποι ἢ ἄνθρωπος, ἡ δὲ κατὰ τὰ ὑποκριτικά,
οἷον κατ' ἐρώτησιν ἢ ἐπίταξιν· τὸ γὰρ ἐβάδισεν; ἢ
βάδιζε πτῶσις ῥήματος κατὰ ταῦτα τὰ εἴδη ἐστίν.
λόγος δὲ φωνὴ συνθετὴ σημαντικὴ ἧς ἔνια μέρη
καθ' αὑτὰ σημαίνει τι· οὐ γὰρ ἅπας λόγος ἐκ ῥημά-
25 των καὶ ὀνομάτων σύγκειται, οἷον ὁ τοῦ ἀνθρώπου
ὁρισμός, ἀλλ' ἐνδέχεται ἄνευ ῥημάτων εἶναι λόγον,
μέρος μέντοι ἀεί τι σημαῖνον ἕξει, οἷον ἐν τῷ βαδίζει Κλέων ὁ Κλέων. εἷς δέ ἐστι λόγος διχῶς, ἢ γὰρ
ὁ ἓν σημαίνων, ἢ ὁ ἐκ πλειόνων συνδέσμῳ, οἷον ἡ
Ἰλιὰς μὲν συνδέσμῳ εἷς, ὁ δὲ τοῦ ἀνθρώπου τῷ ἓν
30 σημαίνειν.

XXI   Ὀνόματος δὲ εἴδη τὸ μὲν ἁπλοῦν, ἁπλοῦν δὲ
λέγω ὃ μὴ ἐκ σημαινόντων σύγκειται, οἷον γῆ, τὸ δὲ
διπλοῦν· τούτου δὲ τὸ μὲν ἐκ σημαίνοντος καὶ ἀσή-
μου, πλὴν οὐκ ἐν τῷ ὀνόματι[2] σημαίνοντος καὶ ἀσή-
μου, τὸ δὲ ἐκ σημαινόντων σύγκειται. εἴη δ' ἂν καὶ
τριπλοῦν καὶ τετραπλοῦν ὄνομα καὶ πολλαπλοῦν,
35 οἷον τὰ πολλὰ τῶν Μασσαλιωτῶν,[3] Ἑρμοκαϊκόξαν-
1457b θος * * *.[4] ἅπαν δὲ ὄνομά ἐστιν ἢ κύριον ἢ γλῶττα

---

[1] κατὰ τὸ Reiz: τὸ κατὰ AB
[2] ὀνόματι Vahlen: -τος AB
[3] Μασσαλιωτῶν Diels (ex Arab.): μεγαλιωτῶν AB
[4] lacunam stat. edd. (cf. Arab.: "supplicans domino caelo-
rum")

respectively. An inflection is the feature of a noun or verb which signifies case ("of him," "to him," etc.), or singular and plural (e.g. "man," "men"), or aspects of delivery,[a] such as question or command ("did he walk?" or "walk!" are verbal inflections in this classification).[b] A statement is a compound, significant utterance, some of whose parts do have independent significance. Not every statement consists of verbs and nouns, e.g. the definition of "man,"[c] but one can have a statement without verbs; yet it will always have a part with separate significance, e.g. "Cleon" in "Cleon is walking." A statement can be unitary in two ways, by signifying one thing or by being combined from a plurality: e.g. the *Iliad* is unitary by combination,[d] but the definition of "man" by signifying one thing.

XI Nouns can be classed as "single" (by which I mean those not comprising significant parts, e.g. *ge* ["earth"]) and "double." The latter can be subdivided into those formed from both significant and nonsignificant parts (though this is not their function within the noun),[e] and those comprising only significant parts. One could further distinguish "triple," "quadruple," and "polysyllabic" (e.g. most Massaliote[f] terms: Hermocaïcoxanthus * * *).

---

[a] See on 56b10. [b] All exx. in this para. again involve single-word inflected forms in Greek.

[c] I.e. a verbless phrase such as "rational, bipedal animal."

[d] "Combination," *sundesmos*, is the same term as "connective" at 56b38 ff: the word cannot have quite the same sense in both places, though the second use may imply the first.

[e] Cf. 57a11–14.

[f] Belonging to the dialect of Massilia (Marseilles): "Hermocaïcoxanthus" fuses the names of three rivers in the region of Phocaea, motherland of Massilia.

ἢ μεταφορὰ ἢ κόσμος ἢ πεποιημένον ἢ ἐπεκτεταμένον ἢ ὑφῃρημένον ἢ ἐξηλλαγμένον. λέγω δὲ κύριον
μὲν ᾧ χρῶνται ἕκαστοι, γλῶτταν δὲ ᾧ ἕτεροι· ὥστε
φανερὸν ὅτι καὶ γλῶτταν καὶ κύριον εἶναι δυνατὸν
5 τὸ αὐτό, μὴ τοῖς αὐτοῖς δέ· τὸ γὰρ σίγυννον Κυπρίοις
μὲν κύριον, ἡμῖν δὲ γλῶττα.

μεταφορὰ δέ ἐστιν ὀνόματος ἀλλοτρίου ἐπιφορὰ
ἢ ἀπὸ τοῦ γένους ἐπὶ εἶδος ἢ ἀπὸ τοῦ εἴδους ἐπὶ τὸ
γένος ἢ ἀπὸ τοῦ εἴδους ἐπὶ εἶδος ἢ κατὰ τὸ ἀνάλογον. λέγω δὲ ἀπὸ γένους μὲν ἐπὶ εἶδος οἷον "νηῦς
10 δέ μοι ἥδ' ἕστηκεν"· τὸ γὰρ ὁρμεῖν ἐστιν ἑστάναι τι.
ἀπ' εἴδους δὲ ἐπὶ γένος "ἦ δὴ μυρί' Ὀδυσσεὺς
ἐσθλὰ ἔοργεν"· τὸ γὰρ μυρίον πολύ ἐστιν, ᾧ νῦν
ἀντὶ τοῦ πολλοῦ κέχρηται. ἀπ' εἴδους δὲ ἐπὶ εἶδος
οἷον "χαλκῷ ἀπὸ ψυχὴν ἀρύσας"[1] καὶ "τεμὼν
15 ταναήκεϊ χαλκῷ"· ἐνταῦθα γὰρ τὸ μὲν ἀρύσαι
ταμεῖν, τὸ δὲ ταμεῖν ἀρύσαι εἴρηκεν· ἄμφω γὰρ
ἀφελεῖν τί ἐστιν. τὸ δὲ ἀνάλογον λέγω, ὅταν ὁμοίως
ἔχῃ τὸ δεύτερον πρὸς τὸ πρῶτον καὶ τὸ τέταρτον
πρὸς τὸ τρίτον· ἐρεῖ γὰρ ἀντὶ τοῦ δευτέρου τὸ τέταρτον ἢ ἀντὶ τοῦ τετάρτου τὸ δεύτερον. καὶ ἐνίοτε
προστιθέασιν ἀνθ' οὗ λέγει πρὸς ὅ ἐστι. λέγω δὲ
20 οἷον ὁμοίως ἔχει φιάλη πρὸς Διόνυσον καὶ ἀσπὶς
πρὸς Ἄρη· ἐρεῖ τοίνυν τὴν φιάλην ἀσπίδα Διονύ-

---

[1] ἀρύσας καὶ τεμών Tyrwhitt (rec.): ἀερύσασκετεμών A:
ἐρύσασκε τεμών B

---

[a] *Onoma*, used above for "noun," but here carrying the wider
sense; cf. e.g. 57b7, 25.

Every word[a] is either a standard term, loan word, metaphor, ornament, neologism, lengthening, contraction, or modification. By "standard term" I mean one used by a community, by "loan word" one used by outsiders; obviously, then, the same word can be both a loan word and a standard term, though not for the same groups: *sigunon* ["spear"] is standard for Cypriots, a loan word for us.[b]

A metaphor[c] is the application of a word that belongs to another thing: either from genus to species, species to genus, species to species, or by analogy. By "from genus to species" I mean, e.g., "my ship stands here":[d] mooring is a kind of standing. Species to genus: "ten thousand noble deeds has Odysseus accomplished";[e] ten thousand is many, and the poet has used it here instead of "many." Species to species: e.g. "drawing off the life with bronze,"[f] and "cutting with slender-edged bronze";[g] here he has used "drawing off" for "cutting" and *vice versa*, as both are kinds of removing. I call "by analogy" cases were *b* is to *a* as *d* is to *c*: one will then speak of *d* instead of *b*, or *b* instead of *d*. Sometimes people add that to which the replaced term is related. I mean, e.g., the wine bowl is to Dionysus as the shield to Ares: so one will call the wine

[b] For Ar. a "loan word" cannot be a naturalised borrowing, but must be perceived as exotic (cf. *Rh.* 1410b12–13).

[c] As definition and exx. reveal, "metaphor" includes things which might now be classed as synecdoche or metonymy. Cf. *Rh.* 1405a3 ff.

[d] Hom. *Od.* 1.185.   [e] Hom. *Il.* 2.272.

[f] Empedocles fr. 138 DK; image is the killing of an animal.

[g] Empedocles fr. 143 DK; the ref. is to filling a bronze vessel with water.

105

σου καὶ τὴν ἀσπίδα φιάλην "Αρεως. ἢ ὃ γῆρας
πρὸς βίον, καὶ ἑσπέρα πρὸς ἡμέραν· ἐρεῖ τοίνυν τὴν
ἑσπέραν γῆρας ἡμέρας, ἢ ὥσπερ Ἐμπεδοκλῆς καὶ
τὸ γῆρας ἑσπέραν βίου ἢ δυσμὰς βίου. ἐνίοις δ᾽
25 οὐκ ἔστιν ὄνομα κείμενον τῶν ἀνάλογον, ἀλλ᾽ οὐδὲν
ἧττον ὁμοίως λεχθήσεται· οἷον τὸ τὸν καρπὸν μὲν
ἀφιέναι σπείρειν, τὸ δὲ τὴν φλόγα ἀπὸ τοῦ ἡλίου
ἀνώνυμον· ἀλλ᾽ ὁμοίως ἔχει τοῦτο πρὸς τὸν ἥλιον
καὶ τὸ σπείρειν πρὸς τὸν καρπόν, διὸ εἴρηται "σπεί-
ρων θεόκτισταν φλόγα". ἔστι δὲ τῷ τρόπῳ τούτῳ
30 τῆς μεταφορᾶς χρῆσθαι καὶ ἄλλως, προσαγορεύ-
σαντα τὸ ἀλλότριον ἀποφῆσαι τῶν οἰκείων τι, οἷον
εἰ τὴν ἀσπίδα εἴποι φιάλην μὴ "Αρεως ἀλλ᾽[1] ἄοινον.
* * * πεποιημένον δ᾽ ἐστὶν ὃ ὅλως μὴ καλούμενον
ὑπὸ τινῶν αὐτὸς τίθεται ὁ ποιητής· δοκεῖ γὰρ ἔνια
εἶναι τοιαῦτα, οἷον τὰ κέρατα ἔρνυγας[2] καὶ τὸν ἱερέα
35 ἀρητῆρα. ἐπεκτεταμένον δέ ἐστιν ἢ ἀφῃρημένον τὸ
1458a μὲν ἐὰν φωνήεντι μακροτέρῳ κεχρημένον ᾖ τοῦ
οἰκείου ἢ συλλαβῇ ἐμβεβλημένῃ, τὸ δὲ ἂν ἀφῃρημένον τι ᾖ αὐτοῦ, ἐπεκτεταμένον μὲν οἷον τὸ πόλεως
πόληος καὶ τὸ Πηλείδου[3] Πηληιάδεω, ἀφῃρημένον
δὲ οἷον τὸ κρῖ καὶ τὸ δῶ καὶ "μία γίνεται ἀμφοτέρων

---

[1] ἀλλ᾽ ἄοινον Vettori: ἀλλὰ οἴνου AB
[2] ἔρνυγας Vettori: ἐρινύγας A: ἐρινύγας B
[3] πηλείδου rec.: πηλέος A: πηλέως B

---

[a] Fr. 152 DK, but it is disputed which phrase Ar. ascribes to
E.; for "evening of life" cf. Alexis fr. 230 *PCG*, "life's sunset" Pl.
Laws 770a6.

bowl "Dionysus' shield," and the shield "Ares' wine bowl."
Or old age is to life as evening to day: so one will call
evening "the day's old age," or, like Empedocles,[a] call old
age "the evening of life" or "life's sunset." In some cases
of analogy no current term exists, but the same form of
expression will still be used.[b] For instance, to release seed
is to "sow," while the sun's release of fire lacks a name; but
the latter stands to the sun as does sowing to the seed,[c]
hence the phrase "sowing his divine fire."[d] This type of
metaphor can further be used by predicating the bor-
rowed term while denying one of its attributes: suppose
one were to call the shield not "Ares' wine bowl" but "a
wineless wine bowl."

* * * *[e] A neologism is a term without existing usage but
coined by the poet himself; some words seem to be of this
kind, e.g. *ernuges* for *kerata* ["horns"] and *arētēr* for
hiereus ["priest"].[f] A lengthening uses a longer vowel than
the standard form, or an extra syllable; a contraction has
had some part removed: lengthenings are e.g. *poleōs* for
poleōs, and *Pēlēïadeō* for *Pēleidou*;[g] contractions, e.g. *kri*,
dō,[h] and "a single vision [*ops*] comes from both."[i] A

[b] A usage sometimes known as "catachresis": e.g. Quint. *Inst.*
8.6.34 b. [c] Strictly, to the sower.

[d] Unidentified quotation, from tragedy or lyric poetry.

[e] It is assumed that an explanation of "ornament," *kosmos*,
has dropped out here; see 57b2, and cf. *Rh.* 1408a14.

[f] The second occurs 3x in the *Iliad*; the first is not found in
extant literature.

[g] Genitive forms of, respectively, *polis* (city/citadel) and
Pēleidēs (son of Peleus, i.e. Achilles); the first form in each case is
epic.

[h] Shortened epic forms of *krithē* (barley) and *dōma* (house).

[i] Empedocles fr. 88 DK.

ARISTOTLE

5 ὄψ".[1] ἐξηλλαγμένον δ' ἐστὶν ὅταν τοῦ ὀνομαζομένου τὸ μὲν καταλείπῃ τὸ δὲ ποιῇ, οἷον τὸ "δεξιτερὸν κατὰ μαζόν" ἀντὶ τοῦ δεξιόν.

αὐτῶν δὲ τῶν ὀνομάτων τὰ μὲν ἄρρενα τὰ δὲ θήλεα τὰ δὲ μεταξύ, ἄρρενα μὲν ὅσα τελευτᾷ εἰς τὸ Ν καὶ Ρ καὶ Σ καὶ ὅσα ἐκ τούτου σύγκειται (ταῦτα
10 δ' ἐστὶν δύο, Ψ καὶ Ξ), θήλεα δὲ ὅσα ἐκ τῶν φωνηέντων εἴς τε τὰ ἀεὶ μακρά, οἷον εἰς Η καὶ Ω, καὶ τῶν ἐπεκτεινομένων εἰς Α· ὥστε ἴσα συμβαίνει πλήθει εἰς ὅσα τὰ ἄρρενα καὶ τὰ θήλεα· τὸ γὰρ Ψ καὶ τὸ Ξ σύνθετά[2] ἐστιν. εἰς δὲ ἄφωνον οὐδὲν ὄνομα τελευτᾷ,
15 οὐδὲ εἰς φωνῆεν βραχύ. εἰς δὲ τὸ Ι τρία μόνον, μέλι κόμμι πέπερι. εἰς δὲ τὸ Υ πέντε[3] * * *. τὰ δὲ μεταξὺ εἰς ταῦτα καὶ Ν καὶ Σ.

XXII Λέξεως δὲ ἀρετὴ σαφῆ καὶ μὴ ταπεινὴν εἶναι. σαφεστάτη μὲν οὖν ἐστιν ἡ ἐκ τῶν κυρίων ὀνομάτων, ἀλλὰ ταπεινή· παράδειγμα δὲ ἡ Κλεοφῶντος
20 ποίησις καὶ ἡ Σθενέλου. σεμνὴ δὲ καὶ ἐξαλλάττουσα τὸ ἰδιωτικὸν ἡ τοῖς ξενικοῖς κεχρημένη· ξενικὸν δὲ λέγω γλῶτταν καὶ μεταφορὰν καὶ ἐπέκτασιν καὶ πᾶν τὸ παρὰ τὸ κύριον. ἀλλ' ἄν τις ἄπαντα τοιαῦτα ποιήσῃ, ἢ αἴνιγμα ἔσται ἢ βαρβαρισμός· ἂν

---

[1] ὄψ Vettori: ὀης A: ὁης B
[2] σύνθετα Arab.: ταῦτα AB: ταὐτά rec., Lat.
[3] post πέντε add. nomina quinque Arab.

---

[a] Hom. Il. 5.393.
[b] Alpha, iota, upsilon.

modification is one where part of the form is kept, part added: e.g. "in his right [*dexiteron*] breast,"[a] instead of *dexion*.

Of nouns, some are masculine, some feminine, some neuter: masculine, those which terminate in nu, rho, sigma, or letters containing sigma (there are two: psi and xi); feminine, those which end in vowels that are always long (i.e. eta and omega), or in alpha (of the vowels that can be lengthened).[b] So the number of masculine and feminine terminations is the same[c] (as psi and xi are compound sounds). No noun terminates in a stop, nor in a short vowel. Three alone end in iota: *meli*, *kommi*, *peperi*.[d] Five end in upsilon * * *.[e] Neuter nouns have these endings,[f] as well as nu and sigma.

II   Excellence of diction means clarity and avoidance of banality. Now, clearest is the diction that uses standard terms, but this is banal: the poetry of Cleophon[g] and Sthenelus[h] exemplifies this. Impressive and above the ordinary is the diction that uses exotic language (by "exotic" I mean loan words, metaphors, lengthenings, and all divergence from the standard). But if one composes entirely in this vein, the result will be either a riddle or barbarism—a riddle, if metaphors predominate, bar-

[c] This ignores a number of feminine nouns which end in the same consonants as masculines.

[d] "Honey," "gum," "pepper"; there were in fact others, all of them rare.

[e] *astu*, *gonu*, *doru*, *napu*, *pōu*.

[f] Ar. may mean alpha as well as iota and upsilon; but he omits neuters ending in rho (e.g. *nektar*).

[g] See on 48a12.

[h] Tragedian of later 5th cent.; *TrGF* I no. 32.

ARISTOTLE

25 μὲν οὖν ἐκ μεταφορῶν, αἴνιγμα, ἐὰν δὲ ἐκ γλωττῶν,
βαρβαρισμός. αἰνίγματός τε γὰρ ἰδέα αὕτη ἐστί, τὸ
λέγοντα ὑπάρχοντα ἀδύνατα συνάψαι· κατὰ μὲν οὖν
τὴν τῶν ἄλλων[1] ὀνομάτων σύνθεσιν οὐχ οἷόν τε
τοῦτο ποιῆσαι, κατὰ δὲ τὴν μεταφορῶν[2] ἐνδέχεται,
οἷον "ἄνδρ' εἶδον πυρὶ χαλκὸν ἐπ' ἀνέρι κολλή-
30 σαντα", καὶ τὰ τοιαῦτα. τὰ δὲ ἐκ τῶν γλωττῶν βαρβαρισμός. δεῖ ἄρα κεκρᾶσθαί πως τούτοις· τὸ μὲν
γὰρ τὸ μὴ ἰδιωτικὸν ποιήσει μηδὲ ταπεινόν, οἷον ἡ
γλῶττα καὶ ἡ μεταφορὰ καὶ ὁ κόσμος καὶ τἆλλα τὰ
εἰρημένα εἴδη, τὸ δὲ κύριον τὴν σαφήνειαν. οὐκ
ἐλάχιστον δὲ μέρος συμβάλλεται εἰς τὸ σαφὲς τῆς
1458b λέξεως καὶ μὴ ἰδιωτικὸν αἱ ἐπεκτάσεις καὶ ἀποκοπαὶ
καὶ ἐξαλλαγαὶ τῶν ὀνομάτων· διὰ μὲν γὰρ τὸ ἄλλως
ἔχειν ἢ ὡς τὸ κύριον παρὰ τὸ εἰωθὸς γιγνόμενον τὸ
μὴ ἰδιωτικὸν ποιήσει, διὰ δὲ τὸ κοινωνεῖν τοῦ εἰωθό-
5 τος τὸ σαφὲς ἔσται. ὥστε οὐκ ὀρθῶς ψέγουσιν οἱ
ἐπιτιμῶντες τῷ τοιούτῳ τρόπῳ τῆς διαλέκτου καὶ
διακωμῳδοῦντες τὸν ποιητήν, οἷον Εὐκλείδης ὁ
ἀρχαῖος, ὡς ῥᾴδιον ὂν ποιεῖν εἴ τις δώσει ἐκτείνειν
ἐφ' ὁπόσον βούλεται, ἰαμβοποιήσας ἐν αὐτῇ τῇ
λέξει "Ἐπιχάρην[3] εἶδον Μαραθῶνάδε βαδίζοντα",
10 καὶ "οὐκ ἐγκεράμενος[4] τὸν ἐκείνου ἐλλέβορον". τὸ
μὲν οὖν φαίνεσθαί πως χρώμενον τούτῳ τῷ τρόπῳ

[1] ἄλλων Twining (Arab.): om. AB
[2] μεταφορῶν Bywater: -ὰν AB
[3] Ἐπιχάρην Bursian ('H- Tyrwhitt): ἢ ἐπιχαρην B: ἤτει χάριν A

110

barism, if loan words. For this is the nature of a riddle, to attach impossibilities to a description of real things. One cannot do this by composing with other terms, but one can with metaphors (e.g. "I saw a man welding bronze on a man with fire,"[a] and such things). Passages of loan words constitute barbarism. One needs, then, a certain blend of these components: one kind (loan words, metaphor, ornaments, and the other classes listed) will create an impression that is neither ordinary nor banal, while standard terms will ensure clarity. A major contribution to clarity and unusualness of diction is made by lengthenings, shortenings, and modifications of words: contrast with the standard, and divergence from the usual, will create an out-of-the-ordinary impression; but the presence of some usual forms will preserve clarity. So those who criticise such usage, and mock the poet for it, are wrong to carp—like Eucleides the elder,[b] who, supposing it easy to write poetry if one is allowed to lengthen words at whim, lampooned Homer in his very diction ("I saw Epichares walking to Marathon," and "not mixing his hellebore").[c] Now, the blatant use of such a manner is

---

[a] Cleobulina fr. 1 West, a hexameter. The ref. is to medical use of a cupping glass; cf. *Rh.* 1405b1–4.

[b] Otherwise unknown.

[c] Both quotations (the second very uncertain), using absurd vowel-lengthenings to satisfy hexameter rhythm, parody metrical licences in Homer. Epichares was a very common Athenian name; its choice here is probably arbitrary.

---

[4] ἐγκεράμενος coni. Kassel: ἂν γεράμενος A: ἄν γε ἀράμενος B

γελοῖον· τὸ δὲ μέτρον κοινὸν ἁπάντων ἐστὶ τῶν
μερῶν· καὶ γὰρ μεταφοραῖς καὶ γλώτταις καὶ τοῖς
ἄλλοις εἴδεσι χρώμενος ἀπρεπῶς καὶ ἐπίτηδες ἐπὶ τὰ
γελοῖα τὸ αὐτὸ ἂν ἀπεργάσαιτο. τὸ δὲ ἁρμόττον[1]
15 ὅσον διαφέρει ἐπὶ τῶν ἐπῶν θεωρείσθω ἐντιθεμένων
τῶν κυρίων[2] ὀνομάτων εἰς τὸ μέτρον. καὶ ἐπὶ τῆς
γλώττης δὲ καὶ ἐπὶ τῶν μεταφορῶν καὶ ἐπὶ τῶν
ἄλλων ἰδεῶν μετατιθεὶς ἄν τις τὰ κύρια ὀνόματα
κατίδοι ὅτι ἀληθῆ λέγομεν· οἷον τὸ αὐτὸ ποιήσαντος
ἰαμβεῖον Αἰσχύλου καὶ Εὐριπίδου, ἓν δὲ μόνον
20 ὄνομα μεταθέντος, ἀντὶ κυρίου εἰωθότος γλῶτταν, τὸ
μὲν φαίνεται καλὸν τὸ δ' εὐτελές. Αἰσχύλος μὲν
γὰρ ἐν τῷ Φιλοκτήτῃ ἐποίησε

δ.τ.τ. φαγέδαιναν[3] ἥ μου σάρκας ἐσθίει ποδός,
ὁ δὲ ἀντὶ τοῦ ἐσθίει τὸ θοινᾶται μετέθηκεν. καὶ
25 δ.τ.τ. νῦν δέ μ' ἐὼν ὀλίγος τε καὶ οὐτιδανὸς καὶ ἀεικής,
εἴ τις λέγοι τὰ κύρια μετατιθεὶς
δ.τ.τ. νῦν δέ μ' ἐὼν μικρός τε καὶ ἀσθενικὸς καὶ ἀειδής·
καὶ
δ.τ.τ. δίφρον ἀεικέλιον καταθεὶς ὀλίγην τε τράπεζαν,
30 δ.τ.τ. δίφρον μοχθηρὸν καταθεὶς μικράν τε τράπεζαν·
καὶ τὸ "ἠιόνες βοόωσιν", ἠιόνες κράζουσιν. ἔτι δὲ
'Αριφράδης τοὺς τραγῳδοὺς ἐκωμῴδει ὅτι ἃ οὐδεὶς
ἂν εἴπειεν ἐν τῇ διαλέκτῳ τούτοις χρῶνται, οἷον τὸ
δωμάτων ἄπο ἀλλὰ μὴ ἀπὸ δωμάτων, καὶ τὸ σέθεν

---

[1] ἁρμόττον rec.: ἁρμόττοντος A: ἁρμόττον πως B
[2] κυρίων add. Vahlen
[3] φαγέδαιναν Hermann: -α rec.: φαγάδαινα B: φαγάδενα A

ridiculous; moderation applies equally to all components.
By using metaphors, loan words, and the other classes
inaptly one could achieve the same result as by deliberate
comic distortion. But the difference it makes to use them
fittingly in epic should be studied by introducing the standard words into the verse. Likewise with loan words,
metaphors, and the other classes, one could observe the
truth of my argument by substituting the standard terms.
For instance, Aeschylus and Euripides composed the
same iambic line, but the latter replaced just one word,
using a loan word instead of the familiar standard term;
one of the lines strikes us as beautiful, the other as
tawdry. Aeschylus, in his *Philoctetes*,[a] wrote: ". . . the can-
cer which eats the flesh of my foot." Euripides changed
"eats" to "feasts on."[b] Likewise with "but now one lowly,
paltry, and unseemly . . . ,"[c] if one were to substitute the
standard terms, "but now one small, weak, and ugly . . ."
And compare "setting out an unsightly chair, and a lowly
table . . . ,"[d] with "setting out a bad chair, and a small table
. . ." Or "the headlands clamour"[e] with "the headlands
bawl." Again, Ariphrades[f] ridiculed the tragedians for
using expressions which no one would ever say in conversation, such as "the palace from" instead of "from

[a] Fr. 253 *TrGF* (III 357).

[b] Fr. 792 Nauck; here and below, translation cannot capture
the pertinent nuances of tone.

[c] Hom. *Od.* 9.515 (Cyclops' description of Odysseus); in mss.
of Homer the third adj. is different again (*akikus*, "feeble").

[d] Hom. *Od.* 20.259.

[e] Hom. *Il.* 17.265.

[f] Very likely, given the name's rarity, the comic poet mentioned several times by Aristophanes (e.g. *Knights* 1280 ff).

καὶ τὸ ἐγὼ δέ νιν καὶ τὸ Ἀχιλλέως πέρι ἀλλὰ μὴ

1459a περὶ Ἀχιλλέως, καὶ ὅσα ἄλλα τοιαῦτα. διὰ γὰρ τὸ
μὴ εἶναι ἐν τοῖς κυρίοις ποιεῖ τὸ μὴ ἰδιωτικὸν ἐν τῇ
λέξει ἅπαντα τὰ τοιαῦτα· ἐκεῖνος δὲ τοῦτο ἠγνόει.
ἔστιν δὲ μέγα μὲν τὸ ἑκάστῳ τῶν εἰρημένων πρεπόντως χρῆσθαι, καὶ διπλοῖς ὀνόμασι καὶ γλώτταις,
5 πολὺ δὲ μέγιστον τὸ μεταφορικὸν εἶναι. μόνον γὰρ
τοῦτο οὔτε παρ' ἄλλου ἔστι λαβεῖν εὐφυΐας τε
σημεῖόν ἐστι· τὸ γὰρ εὖ μεταφέρειν τὸ τὸ ὅμοιον
θεωρεῖν ἐστιν. τῶν δ' ὀνομάτων τὰ μὲν διπλᾶ
μάλιστα ἁρμόττει τοῖς διθυράμβοις, αἱ δὲ γλῶτται
10 τοῖς ἡρωικοῖς, αἱ δὲ μεταφοραὶ τοῖς ἰαμβείοις. καὶ
ἐν μὲν τοῖς ἡρωικοῖς ἅπαντα χρήσιμα τὰ εἰρημένα,
ἐν δὲ τοῖς ἰαμβείοις διὰ τὸ ὅτι μάλιστα λέξιν μιμεῖσθαι ταῦτα ἁρμόττει τῶν ὀνομάτων ὅσοις κἂν ἐν
λόγοις τις χρήσαιτο· ἔστι δὲ τὰ τοιαῦτα τὸ κύριον
καὶ μεταφορὰ καὶ κόσμος.

περὶ μὲν οὖν τραγῳδίας καὶ τῆς ἐν τῷ πράττειν
15 μιμήσεως ἔστω ἡμῖν ἱκανὰ τὰ εἰρημένα.

XXIII Περὶ δὲ τῆς διηγηματικῆς καὶ ἐν μέτρῳ μιμητικῆς, ὅτι δεῖ τοὺς μύθους καθάπερ ἐν ταῖς τραγῳδίαις
συνιστάναι δραματικοὺς καὶ περὶ μίαν πρᾶξιν ὅλην
καὶ τελείαν ἔχουσαν ἀρχὴν καὶ μέσα καὶ τέλος, ἵν'
20 ὥσπερ ζῷον ἓν ὅλον ποιῇ τὴν οἰκείαν ἡδονήν, δῆλον,

---

^a Two of Ar.'s exx. are of anastrophe (placing of a preposition
after its noun), and two of predominantly poetic pronominal
forms.

the palace," and "of thee," and "I him . . . ," and "Achilles round" instead of "round Achilles," etc.[a] Because absent from standard speech, all such expressions make an out-of-the-ordinary impression; but Ariphrades failed to realise that. It is important to use aptly each of the features mentioned, including double nouns and loan words; but much the greatest asset is a capacity for metaphor. This alone cannot be acquired from another, and is a sign of natural gifts: because to use metaphor well is to discern similarities.[b] Of word types, double forms particularly suit dithyramb,[c] loan words suit epic, and metaphors suit iambic verse.[d] In epic, everything mentioned has some use, but in iambic verse, because of the very close relation to ordinary speech,[e] suitable words are those one would also use in prose—namely, standard terms, metaphors, ornaments.

Let that, then, count as sufficient discussion of tragedy and enactive[f] mimesis.

XIII As regards narrative mimesis in verse,[g] it is clear that plots, as in tragedy, should be constructed dramatically, that is, around a single, whole, and complete action, with beginning, middle, and end, so that epic, like a single and whole animal, may produce the pleasure proper to it. Its

[b] Cf. *Rh.* 1405a8–10, *Top.* 140a8–11.

[c] Because dithyramb tends towards linguistic virtuosity: cf. *Rh.* 1406b1–2.

[d] See on 47b11.

[e] Cf. 49a23–8.

[f] Cf. ch. III's third mode of mimesis, 48a24–5.

[g] The periphrasis places epic (loosely) in Ar.'s scheme of media and modes (chs. I, III).

καὶ μὴ ὁμοίας ἱστορίαις[1] τὰς συνθέσεις εἶναι, ἐν αἷς
ἀνάγκη οὐχὶ μιᾶς πράξεως ποιεῖσθαι δήλωσιν ἀλλ'
ἑνὸς χρόνου, ὅσα ἐν τούτῳ συνέβη περὶ ἕνα ἢ πλείους, ὧν ἕκαστον ὡς ἔτυχεν ἔχει πρὸς ἄλληλα.
ὥσπερ γὰρ κατὰ τοὺς αὐτοὺς χρόνους ἥ τ' ἐν Σαλα-
25 μῖνι ἐγένετο ναυμαχία καὶ ἡ ἐν Σικελίᾳ Καρχηδο-
νίων μάχη οὐδὲν πρὸς τὸ αὐτὸ συντείνουσαι τέλος,
οὕτω καὶ ἐν τοῖς ἐφεξῆς χρόνοις ἐνίοτε γίνεται θάτερον μετὰ θάτερον, ἐξ ὧν ἐν οὐδὲν γίνεται τέλος.
σχεδὸν δὲ οἱ πολλοὶ τῶν ποιητῶν τοῦτο δρῶσι. διὸ
30 ὥσπερ εἴπομεν ἤδη καὶ ταύτῃ θεσπέσιος ἂν φανείη
Ὅμηρος παρὰ τοὺς ἄλλους, τῷ μηδὲ τὸν πόλεμον
καίπερ ἔχοντα ἀρχὴν καὶ τέλος ἐπιχειρῆσαι ποιεῖν
ὅλον· λίαν γὰρ ἂν μέγας καὶ οὐκ εὐσύνοπτος ἔμελ-
λεν ἔσεσθαι ὁ[2] μῦθος, ἢ τῷ μεγέθει μετριάζοντα
καταπεπλεγμένον τῇ ποικιλίᾳ. νῦν δ' ἐν μέρος ἀπο-
35 λαβὼν ἐπεισοδίοις κέχρηται αὐτῶν πολλοῖς, οἷον
νεῶν καταλόγῳ καὶ ἄλλοις ἐπεισοδίοις οἷς[3] διαλαμ-
βάνει τὴν ποίησιν. οἱ δ' ἄλλοι περὶ ἕνα ποιοῦσι καὶ
περὶ ἕνα χρόνον καὶ μίαν πρᾶξιν πολυμερῆ, οἷον ὁ
1459b τὰ Κύπρια[4] ποιήσας καὶ τὴν μικρὰν Ἰλιάδα. τοιγα-
ροῦν ἐκ μὲν Ἰλιάδος καὶ Ὀδυσσείας μία τραγῳδία
ποιεῖται ἑκατέρας ἢ δύο μόναι, ἐκ δὲ Κυπρίων πολ-

---

[1] ἱστορίαις τὰς συνθέσεις Sophianus, Dacier (ἱ. τ. συνθή-
σεις B): ἱστορίας τὰς συνήθεις A
[2] ὁ μῦθος B: om. A
[3] οἷς rec.: δἱσ (sed erasum) A: om. B
[4] Κύπρια Castelvetro: κυπρικὰ AB

116

structures should not be like histories, which require an exposition not of a single action but of a single period, with all the events (in their contingent relationships) that happened to one person or more during it.[a] For just as there was chronological coincidence between the sea battle at Salamis and the battle against the Carthaginians in Sicily,[b] though they in no way converged on the same goal, so in a continuous stretch of time event sometimes follows event without yielding any single goal. Yet probably most poets do this. That is why, as I said earlier,[c] Homer's inspired[d] superiority over the rest can be seen here too: though the war had beginning and end, he did not try to treat its entirety, for the plot was bound to be too large and incoherent, or else, if kept within moderate scope, too complex in its variety. Instead, he has selected one section, but has used many others as episodes, such as the catalogue of ships and other episodes by which he diversifies the composition. But the others build their works round a single figure or single period, hence an action of many parts, as with the author of the *Cypria* and the *Little Iliad*.[e] Accordingly, with the *Iliad* and the *Odyssey* a single tragedy, or at most two, can be made from each; but many can be made from the *Cypria*, and

[a] Cf. 51a38–b11; Ar. reductively equates history with a chronicle narrative.

[b] The battles of Salamis and Himera took place on the same day in 480 (Hdt. 7.166).

[c] 51a22–30.

[d] The term *thespesios* is itself Homeric—a deliberate allusion. [e] Two poems from the so-called Epic Cycle (*OCD* s.v.), dealing respectively with antecedents to the Trojan War and its earlier years, and with its later parts and aftermath.

117

λαὶ καὶ τῆς μικρᾶς Ἰλιάδος πλέον ἢ ὀκτώ, οἷον
5 ὅπλων κρίσις, Φιλοκτήτης, Νεοπτόλεμος, Εὐρύπυ-
λος, πτωχεία, Λάκαιναι, Ἰλίου πέρσις καὶ ἀπόπλους,
καὶ Σίνων καὶ Τρωάδες.

XXIV   Ἔτι δὲ τὰ εἴδη ταὐτὰ δεῖ ἔχειν τὴν ἐποποιίαν τῇ
τραγῳδίᾳ, ἢ γὰρ ἁπλῆν ἢ πεπλεγμένην ἢ ἠθικὴν ἢ
10 παθητικήν· καὶ τὰ μέρη ἔξω μελοποιίας καὶ ὄψεως
ταὐτά· καὶ γὰρ περιπετειῶν δεῖ καὶ ἀναγνωρίσεων
καὶ παθημάτων· ἔτι τὰς διανοίας καὶ τὴν λέξιν ἔχειν
καλῶς. οἷς ἅπασιν Ὅμηρος κέχρηται καὶ πρῶτος
καὶ ἱκανῶς. καὶ γὰρ τῶν ποιημάτων ἑκάτερον συνέστηκεν ἡ μὲν Ἰλιὰς ἁπλοῦν καὶ παθητικόν, ἡ δὲ
15 Ὀδύσσεια πεπλεγμένον (ἀναγνώρισις γὰρ διόλου)
καὶ ἠθική· πρὸς δὲ [1] τούτοις λέξει καὶ διανοίᾳ πάντα
ὑπερβέβληκεν.

    Διαφέρει δὲ κατά τε τῆς συστάσεως τὸ μῆκος ἡ
ἐποποιία καὶ τὸ μέτρον. τοῦ μὲν οὖν μήκους ὅρος
ἱκανὸς ὁ εἰρημένος· δύνασθαι γὰρ δεῖ συνορᾶσθαι
τὴν ἀρχὴν καὶ τὸ τέλος. εἴη δ' ἂν τοῦτο, εἰ τῶν μὲν
20 ἀρχαίων ἐλάττους αἱ συστάσεις εἶεν, πρὸς δὲ τὸ
πλῆθος τραγῳδιῶν τῶν εἰς μίαν ἀκρόασιν τιθεμένων

---

[1] δὲ rec.: γὰρ AB

---

[a] Aesch. wrote a play with this title, on the contested award of
Achilles' arms, after his death, to Odysseus rather than Ajax
(*TrGF* III 288).   [b] P. was fetched from Lemnos to Troy, for
the sake of his bow (once Heracles'); cf. Soph. *Phil.*

[c] N., son of Achilles, was brought to fight at Troy after his
father's death.

more than eight from the *Little Iliad*—namely, *Judgement of Arms*,[a] *Philoctetes*,[b] *Neoptolemus*,[c] *Eurypylus*,[d] *Begging Episode*,[e] *Spartan Women*,[f] *Sack of Troy*, and *The Fleet's Departure*, as well as *Sinon*[g] and *Trojan Women*.[h]

XIV   Moreover, epic should encompass the same types as tragedy,[i] namely simple, complex, character-based, rich in suffering; it has the same components, except for lyric poetry and spectacle, for it requires reversals, recognitions, and scenes of suffering, as well as effective thought and diction. All of which Homer was the first to employ, and employed proficiently. Of his poems, the *Iliad*'s structure is simple and rich in suffering, while the *Odyssey* is complex (it is pervaded by recognition) and character-based. In addition, each excels all epics in diction and thought.

Epic is distinct in its size of structure and its metre. As for length, the definition already given[j] is adequate, since it should be possible for beginning and end to be held in a coherent view. This will be feasible with plot structures shorter than the early epics, but equivalent to the length

---

[d] A Trojan ally killed by Neoptolemus; possibly a Sophoclean subject (*TrGF* IV 195).

[e] Odysseus entered Troy disguised as a beggar; cf. Hom. *Od.* 4.244 ff.

[f] Helen and her maids, who helped Odysseus and Diomedes steal the Palladium from Troy; a Sophoclean title (*TrGF* IV 328).

[g] S. was the Greek who tricked the Trojans into taking the Wooden Horse into the city; Soph. wrote a *Sinon* (*TrGF* IV 413).

[h] Cf. Eur. *Tro.*

[i] Cf. 55b32–56a3, with nn.

[j] See ch. VII, esp. 51a9–15.

παρήκοιεν. ἔχει δὲ πρὸς τὸ ἐπεκτείνεσθαι τὸ μέγεθος πολύ τι ἡ ἐποποιία ἴδιον διὰ τὸ ἐν μὲν τῇ τραγῳδίᾳ μὴ ἐνδέχεσθαι ἅμα πραττόμενα πολλὰ μέρη
25 μιμεῖσθαι ἀλλὰ τὸ ἐπὶ τῆς σκηνῆς καὶ τῶν ὑποκριτῶν μέρος μόνον· ἐν δὲ τῇ ἐποποιίᾳ διὰ τὸ διήγησιν
εἶναι ἔστι πολλὰ μέρη ἅμα ποιεῖν περαινόμενα, ὑφ'
ὧν οἰκείων ὄντων αὔξεται ὁ τοῦ ποιήματος ὄγκος.
ὥστε τοῦτ' ἔχει τὸ ἀγαθὸν εἰς μεγαλοπρέπειαν καὶ
τὸ μεταβάλλειν τὸν ἀκούοντα καὶ ἐπεισοδιοῦν ἀνο-
30 μοίοις ἐπεισοδίοις· τὸ γὰρ ὅμοιον ταχὺ πληροῦν
ἐκπίπτειν ποιεῖ τὰς τραγῳδίας. τὸ δὲ μέτρον τὸ
ἡρωικὸν ἀπὸ τῆς πείρας ἥρμοκεν. εἰ γάρ τις ἐν
ἄλλῳ τινὶ μέτρῳ διηγηματικὴν μίμησιν ποιοῖτο ἢ ἐν
πολλοῖς, ἀπρεπὲς ἂν φαίνοιτο· τὸ γὰρ ἡρωικὸν στα-
35 σιμώτατον καὶ ὀγκωδέστατον τῶν μέτρων ἐστίν (διὸ
καὶ γλώττας καὶ μεταφορὰς δέχεται μάλιστα·
περιττὴ γὰρ καὶ ταύτῃ[1] ἡ διηγηματικὴ μίμησις τῶν
ἄλλων), τὸ δὲ ἰαμβεῖον καὶ τετράμετρον κινητικὰ
καὶ τὸ μὲν ὀρχηστικὸν τὸ δὲ πρακτικόν. ἔτι δὲ ἀτο-
1460a πώτερον εἰ μιγνύοι τις αὐτά, ὥσπερ Χαιρήμων. διὸ
οὐδεὶς μακρὰν σύστασιν ἐν ἄλλῳ πεποίηκεν ἢ τῷ
ἡρῴῳ, ἀλλ' ὥσπερ εἴπομεν αὐτὴ ἡ φύσις διδάσκει
τὸ ἁρμόττον αὐτῇ αἱρεῖσθαι.[2]
5   Ὅμηρος δὲ ἄλλα τε πολλὰ ἄξιος ἐπαινεῖσθαι καὶ
δὴ καὶ ὅτι μόνος τῶν ποιητῶν οὐκ ἀγνοεῖ ὃ δεῖ ποι-

---

[1] ταύτῃ add. Twining
[2] αἱρεῖσθαι Bonitz: διαιρ- AB

of a group of tragedies offered at one hearing.[a] But epic has special scope for substantial extension of size, because tragedy does not allow multiple sections of action to be represented as they occur, but only the one on stage involving the actors; whereas in epic, given the narrative mode, it is possible for the poem to include many simultaneous sections, which, if integral, enhance the poem's dignity. So this gives epic an asset for the development of grandeur, variety for the hearer, and diversity of episodes, whereas sameness soon cloys and causes tragedies to founder.[b] As for metre, the hexameter has proved apt by experience. If one were to compose a narrative mimesis in some other metre, or in several, the incongruity would be plain, since the hexameter is the most stately and dignified of metres (hence its great receptivity to loan words and metaphors:[c] in this respect too narrative mimesis is exceptional), while the iambic trimeter and trochaic tetrameter are rhythms for movement, the latter suiting dancing, the former action.[d] Still more absurd would be a mixture of these metres, as in Chairemon.[e] This is why no one has composed a long epic structure other than in the hexameter; but as I said,[f] the genre's own nature teaches poets to choose what is apt for it.

Homer deserves praise for many other qualities, but especially for realising, alone among epic poets, the place

---

[a] This suggests an epic of about 4,500 lines, much shorter than the Homeric poems, which must be meant by "early epics."

[b] See on 55a28.   [c] Cf. 59a9–11.

[d] Cf. 49a21–7.   [e] See 47b21–2.

[f] The point was made for tragedy's metre at 49a24; "experience" at 59b32 above may imply the same point.

εἶν αὐτόν. αὐτὸν γὰρ δεῖ τὸν ποιητὴν ἐλάχιστα
λέγειν· οὐ γάρ ἐστι κατὰ ταῦτα μιμητής. οἱ μὲν οὖν
ἄλλοι αὐτοὶ μὲν δι' ὅλου ἀγωνίζονται, μιμοῦνται δὲ
ὀλίγα καὶ ὀλιγάκις· ὁ δὲ ὀλίγα φροιμιασάμενος
10 εὐθὺς εἰσάγει ἄνδρα ἢ γυναῖκα ἢ ἄλλο τι ἦθος, καὶ
οὐδέν' ἀήθη ἀλλ' ἔχοντα ἦθος. δεῖ μὲν οὖν ἐν ταῖς
τραγῳδίαις ποιεῖν τὸ θαυμαστόν, μᾶλλον δ' ἐνδέχεται ἐν τῇ ἐποποιίᾳ τὸ ἄλογον,[1] δι' ὃ συμβαίνει
μάλιστα τὸ θαυμαστόν, διὰ τὸ μὴ ὁρᾶν εἰς τὸν
πράττοντα· ἐπεὶ τὰ περὶ τὴν Ἕκτορος δίωξιν ἐπὶ
15 σκηνῆς ὄντα γελοῖα ἂν φανείη, οἱ μὲν ἑστῶτες καὶ
οὐ διώκοντες, ὁ δὲ ἀνανεύων, ἐν δὲ τοῖς ἔπεσιν λανθάνει. τὸ δὲ θαυμαστὸν ἡδύ· σημεῖον δέ, πάντες
γὰρ προστιθέντες ἀπαγγέλλουσιν ὡς χαριζόμενοι.
δεδίδαχεν δὲ μάλιστα Ὅμηρος καὶ τοὺς ἄλλους
ψευδῆ λέγειν ὡς δεῖ. ἔστι δὲ τοῦτο παραλογισμός.
20 οἴονται γὰρ οἱ ἄνθρωποι, ὅταν τουδὶ ὄντος τοδὶ ᾖ ἢ
γινομένου γίνηται, εἰ τὸ ὕστερον ἔστιν, καὶ τὸ πρότερον εἶναι ἢ γίνεσθαι· τοῦτο δέ ἐστι ψεῦδος. διὸ
δεῖ, ἂν τὸ πρῶτον ψεῦδος, ἄλλο[2] δὲ τούτου ὄντος
ἀνάγκη εἶναι ἢ γενέσθαι ᾖ,[3] προσθεῖναι· διὰ γὰρ τὸ
τοῦτο εἰδέναι ἀληθὲς ὂν παραλογίζεται ἡμῶν ἡ ψυχὴ
25 καὶ τὸ πρῶτον ὡς ὄν. παράδειγμα δὲ τούτου τὸ ἐκ
τῶν Νίπτρων. προαιρεῖσθαί τε δεῖ ἀδύνατα εἰκότα

---

[1] ἄλογον Vettori: ἀνάλογον AB
[2] ἄλλο δὲ cod. Robortelli: ἄλλου δὲ A: ἀλλ' οὐδὲ BA²
[3] ᾖ Jortin: ἢ AB

of the poet's own voice. For the poet should say as little as possible in his own voice, as it is not this that makes him a mimetic artist.[a] The others participate in their own voice throughout, and engage in mimesis only briefly and occasionally, whereas Homer, after a brief introduction, at once "brings onto stage"[b] a man, woman, or other figure (all of them rich in character). In tragedy one needs to create a sense of awe, but epic has more scope for the irrational (the chief cause of awe), because we do not actually see the agent. The entire pursuit of Hector,[c] if put on stage, would strike us as ludicrous—with the men standing and refraining from pursuit, and Achilles forbidding them—but in epic this goes unnoticed. Awe is pleasurable: witness the fact that all men exaggerate when relating stories, to give delight. It is above all Homer who has taught other poets the right way to purvey falsehoods: that is, by false inference. When the existence or occurrence of b follows from that of a, people suppose that, if b is the case, a too must exist or be occurrent; but this is false. So, if the antecedent is false, but were it true some further fact would necessarily exist or occur, the poet should supply the latter: because it knows the truth of the consequent, our mind falsely infers the truth of the antecedent too. One example of this comes from the Bath Scene.[d] Things probable though impossible should

[a] This passage appears, through overstatement, to deny (*contra* 48a22–3) that narrative is a mode of mimesis.

[b] Ar. uses a theatrical term to highlight Homer's "dramatic" quality; cf. 48b35–6.   [c] *Il.* 22.131 ff (esp. 205–6).

[d] Cf. on 54b30; Ar. may mean Penelope's false inference, at *Od.* 19.249–50 (cf. 215–19), that the stranger had really seen Odysseus.

μᾶλλον ἢ δυνατὰ ἀπίθανα· τούς τε λόγους μὴ συνίστασθαι ἐκ μερῶν ἀλόγων, ἀλλὰ μάλιστα μὲν
μηδὲν ἔχειν ἄλογον, εἰ δὲ μή, ἔξω τοῦ μυθεύματος,
ὥσπερ Οἰδίπους τὸ μὴ εἰδέναι πῶς ὁ Λάιος ἀπέθα-
30   νεν, ἀλλὰ μὴ ἐν τῷ δράματι, ὥσπερ ἐν Ἠλέκτρᾳ οἱ
τὰ Πύθια ἀπαγγέλλοντες ἢ ἐν Μυσοῖς ὁ ἄφωνος ἐκ
Τεγέας εἰς τὴν Μυσίαν ἥκων. ὥστε τὸ λέγειν ὅτι
ἀνῄρητο ἂν ὁ μῦθος γελοῖον· ἐξ ἀρχῆς γὰρ οὐ δεῖ
συνίστασθαι τοιούτους. ἂν δὲ[1] θῇ καὶ φαίνηται
35   εὐλογωτέρως ἐνδέχεσθαι, καὶ ἄτοπον· ἐπεὶ καὶ τὰ ἐν
Ὀδυσσείᾳ ἄλογα τὰ περὶ τὴν ἔκθεσιν ὡς οὐκ ἂν ἦν
ἀνεκτὰ δῆλον ἂν γένοιτο, εἰ αὐτὰ φαῦλος ποιητὴς
1460b   ποιήσειε· νῦν δὲ τοῖς ἄλλοις ἀγαθοῖς ὁ ποιητὴς
ἀφανίζει ἡδύνων τὸ ἄτοπον. τῇ δὲ λέξει δεῖ διαπο-
νεῖν ἐν τοῖς ἀργοῖς μέρεσιν καὶ μήτε ἠθικοῖς μήτε
διανοητικοῖς· ἀποκρύπτει γὰρ πάλιν ἡ λίαν λαμπρὰ
5   λέξις τά τε ἤθη καὶ τὰς διανοίας.
XXV   Περὶ δὲ προβλημάτων καὶ λύσεων, ἐκ πόσων τε
καὶ ποίων εἰδῶν ἐστιν, ὧδ' ἂν θεωροῦσιν γένοιτ' ἂν
φανερόν. ἐπεὶ γάρ ἐστι μιμητὴς ὁ ποιητὴς ὡσπερα-
νεὶ ζωγράφος ἤ τις ἄλλος εἰκονοποιός, ἀνάγκη
μιμεῖσθαι τριῶν ὄντων τὸν ἀριθμὸν ἕν τι ἀεί, ἢ γὰρ
10   οἷα ἦν ἢ ἔστιν, ἢ οἷά φασιν καὶ δοκεῖ, ἢ οἷα εἶναι

[1] δὲ θῇ ΒΑ[2]: δεθῇ Α: δὲ τεθῇ cod. Robortelli

---

[a] *OT* 112–13; cf. 54b6–8.
[b] Soph. *El.* 680 ff; the objection may be to the anachronism of
Pythian Games in the mythological setting.

be preferred to the possible but implausible. Stories should not comprise irrational components; ideally there should be no irrationality, or, failing that, it should lie outside the plot (as with Oedipus' ignorance of how Laius died),[a] not inside the drama (as with those who report events at Delphi in *Electra*,[b] or the silent figure who comes from Tegea to Mysia in the *Mysians*).[c] The excuse that the plot would have been ruined[d] is ridiculous; one should not construct plots like this in the first place. If a poet posits an irrationality, and a more rational alternative is apparent, this is an absurdity. Even the irrational details in the *Odyssey* about the putting ashore[e] would patently be intolerable if an inferior poet were to handle them; as it is, Homer uses his other qualities to soften and disguise the absurdity. The poet should elaborate his diction especially in quieter passages which involve no characterisation or thought; a highly brilliant diction, on the other hand, obscures character and thought.

With problems[f] and their solutions, the following considerations will clarify their number and their types. Since the poet, like a painter or any other image-maker, is a mimetic artist, he must represent, in any instance, one of three objects: the kind of things which were or are the case; the kind of things that people say and think; the kind

[c] A ref. to the long period of silence endured by Telephus in the *Mysians* of either Aesch. or Soph.

[d] Sc. without one of these elements.

[e] Of Odysseus by the Phaeacians: 13.116 ff.

[f] Ch. XXV may summarise points from Ar.'s (lost) *Homeric Problems* in six books.

δεῖ. ταῦτα δ᾽ ἐξαγγέλλεται λέξει ἐν¹ ᾗ καὶ γλῶτται²
καὶ μεταφοραὶ καὶ πολλὰ πάθη τῆς λέξεώς ἐστι·
δίδομεν γὰρ ταῦτα τοῖς ποιηταῖς. πρὸς δὲ τούτοις
οὐχ ἡ αὐτὴ ὀρθότης ἐστὶν τῆς πολιτικῆς καὶ τῆς
ποιητικῆς οὐδὲ ἄλλης τέχνης καὶ ποιητικῆς. αὐτῆς
15   δὲ τῆς ποιητικῆς διττὴ ἁμαρτία, ἡ μὲν γὰρ καθ᾽
αὑτήν, ἡ δὲ κατὰ συμβεβηκός. εἰ μὲν γὰρ προείλετο
μιμήσασθαι * * *³ ἀδυναμίαν, αὐτῆς ἡ ἁμαρτία· εἰ
δὲ τὸ προελέσθαι μὴ ὀρθῶς, ἀλλὰ τὸν ἵππον ἄμφω
τὰ δεξιὰ προβεβληκότα, ἢ τὸ καθ᾽ ἑκάστην τέχνην
20   ἁμάρτημα, οἷον τὸ κατ᾽ ἰατρικὴν ἢ ἄλλην τέχνην⁴
ὁποιανοῦν, οὐ καθ᾽ ἑαυτήν. ὥστε δεῖ τὰ ἐπιτιμήματα
ἐν τοῖς προβλήμασιν ἐκ τούτων ἐπισκοποῦντα λύειν.

πρῶτον μὲν τὰ πρὸς αὐτὴν τὴν τέχνην· ἀδύνατα
πεποίηται, ἡμάρτηται· ἀλλ᾽ ὀρθῶς ἔχει, εἰ τυγχάνει
τοῦ τέλους τοῦ αὑτῆς (τὸ γὰρ τέλος εἴρηται), εἰ
25   οὕτως ἐκπληκτικώτερον ἢ αὐτὸ ἢ ἄλλο ποιεῖ μέρος.
παράδειγμα ἡ τοῦ Ἕκτορος δίωξις. εἰ μέντοι τὸ
τέλος ἢ μᾶλλον⁵ ἢ μὴ ἧττον ἐνεδέχετο ὑπάρχειν καὶ

¹ ἐν ᾗ B: ἢ A
² γλῶτται καὶ μεταφοραὶ Menardos: -ὰ καὶ -ὰ B: γλώτταις
καὶ μεταφοραῖς A
³ lacunam stat. et ὀρθῶς, ἥμαρτε δ᾽ ἐν τῷ μιμήσασθαι
suppl. Vahlen
⁴ post τέχνην seq. ἢ ἀδύνατα πεποίηται in AB: secl. Duentzer (ἢ ἀδύνατα non vertit Lat.)
⁵ μᾶλλον ἢ μὴ ἧττον Ueberweg: μᾶλλον ἂν ἢ ἧττον B:
μᾶλλον ἧττον A

of things that ought[a] to be the case. These are conveyed in a diction which includes loan words, metaphors, and many stylistic abnormalities: we allow poets these. Moreover, poetry does not have the same standard of correctness as politics,[b] or as any other art. In poetry as such, there are two kinds of fault: one intrinsic, the other incidental. If the poet chose to represent <correctly, but failed through>[c] incapacity, the fault lies in his art. But if the choice is not correct, but (say) to show the horse with both right legs thrown forward,[d] or a technical mistake (e.g. in medicine or any other art), the fault is not intrinsic.[e] So it is on these principles that one should examine and resolve the criticisms contained in problems.

First, cases involving the art itself. Say a poem contains impossibilities: this is a fault. But it is acceptable if the poetry achieves its goal (which has been stated),[f] that is, if it makes this or some other part of the work more thrilling. An example is the pursuit of Hector.[g] But if the goal could be achieved better, or no less well, without

[a] In moral or ideal terms; cf. 60b33 ff.

[b] *Politikē*, Ar.'s general term for the ethics of both public and private life; cf. 50b6-7.

[c] Without some such supplement, the passage's sense is lost.

[d] Not, in fact, a physical impossibility, ctr. Ar. *De incessu anim.* 712a24–30.

[e] Contrast Pl. *Ion* 537a ff.

[f] Ar. probably means various remarks about plot-construction (e.g. 50a22–3) and emotional qualities of both tragedy and epic.

[g] I.e. the scene (cf. 60a14–16) is dramatically thrilling, despite allegedly "irrational" elements.

κατὰ τὴν περὶ τούτων τέχνην, οὐκ[1] ὀρθῶς· δεῖ γὰρ εἰ
ἐνδέχεται ὅλως μηδαμῇ ἡμαρτῆσθαι. ἔτι ποτέρων
ἐστὶ τὸ ἁμάρτημα, τῶν κατὰ τὴν τέχνην ἢ κατ᾽ ἄλλο
30 συμβεβηκός; ἔλαττον γὰρ εἰ μὴ ᾔδει ὅτι ἔλαφος
θήλεια κέρατα οὐκ ἔχει ἢ εἰ ἀμιμήτως ἔγραψεν.
πρὸς δὲ τούτοις ἐὰν ἐπιτιμᾶται ὅτι οὐκ ἀληθῆ, ἀλλ᾽
ἴσως ὡς[2] δεῖ, οἷον καὶ Σοφοκλῆς ἔφη αὐτὸς μὲν
οἵους δεῖ ποιεῖν, Εὐριπίδην[3] δὲ οἷοι εἰσίν, ταύτῃ
35 λυτέον. εἰ δὲ μηδετέρως, ὅτι οὕτω φασίν, οἷον τὰ
περὶ θεῶν· ἴσως γὰρ οὔτε βέλτιον οὕτω λέγειν οὔτ᾽
ἀληθῆ, ἀλλ᾽ εἰ ἔτυχεν ὥσπερ Ξενοφάνει· ἀλλ᾽ οὖν[4]
1461a φασι. τὰ δὲ ἴσως οὐ βέλτιον μέν, ἀλλ᾽ οὕτως εἶχεν,
οἷον τὰ περὶ τῶν ὅπλων, "ἔγχεα δέ σφιν ὀρθ᾽ ἐπὶ
σαυρωτῆρος"· οὕτω γὰρ τότ᾽ ἐνόμιζον, ὥσπερ καὶ
νῦν Ἰλλυριοί. περὶ δὲ τοῦ καλῶς ἢ μὴ καλῶς εἰ[5]
εἴρηταί τινι ἢ πέπρακται, οὐ μόνον σκεπτέον εἰς
5 αὐτὸ τὸ πεπραγμένον ἢ εἰρημένον βλέποντα εἰ
σπουδαῖον ἢ φαῦλον, ἀλλὰ καὶ εἰς τὸν πράττοντα ἢ
λέγοντα πρὸς ὃν ἢ ὅτε ἢ ὅτῳ ἢ οὗ ἕνεκεν, οἷον εἰ
μείζονος ἀγαθοῦ, ἵνα γένηται, ἢ μείζονος κακοῦ, ἵνα
ἀπογένηται.

[1] ante οὐκ habent ἡμαρτῆσθαι (τήμ- B, μαρτ- A[1]) AB: del.
Ussing
[2] ὡς add. Vahlen
[3] Εὐριπίδην Heinsius: -δης AB
[4] οὖν Tyrwhitt: οὔ AB
[5] εἰ Spengel: ἢ A: om. B

infringing the relevant art, it *does* matter: since, if possible, there should be no faults. Next, ask what the fault pertains to—the realm of poetic art, or something incidental? For it is less serious not to know that a female deer has no horns, than to depict one unconvincingly.[a] In addition, if the criticism is that something is false, well perhaps it is as it ought[b] to be, just as Sophocles said[c] he created characters as they ought to be, Euripides as they really are. If neither solution fits, there remains the principle that people say such things,[d] for example in religion: perhaps it is neither ideal nor true to say such things, but maybe it is as Xenophanes[e] thought; no matter, people do say them. Other details may not be ideal, but were once like this; for instance, in the case of the weapons, "their spears stood erect on the butt-spike":[f] this was then their custom, as it still is among Illyrians. When the question is whether or not someone has spoken or acted well, one should examine not only whether the actual deed or utterance is good or bad, but also the identity of the agent or speaker, to whom he acted or spoke, when, with what means, and for what end—namely, whether to occasion greater good, or avert greater evil.

[a] Lit. "unmimetically," which implies (again) that mimetic standards are irreducible to factual fidelity.

[b] See 60b11.

[c] Where or when is unknown.

[d] Cf. 60b10.

[e] Polemical philosopher-poet, c. 570–475: see frs. 11–16 DK for satire of anthropomorphic beliefs, fr. 30 for denial of religious knowledge.

[f] Hom. *Il.* 10.152; cf. Ar. fr. 383 Gigon/160 Rose.

τὰ δὲ πρὸς τὴν λέξιν ὁρῶντα δεῖ διαλύειν, οἷον
10 γλώττῃ τὸ "οὐρῆας μὲν πρῶτον"· ἴσως γὰρ οὐ τοὺς
ἡμιόνους λέγει ἀλλὰ τοὺς φύλακας· καὶ τὸν Δόλωνα,
"ὅς ῥ᾽ ἦ τοι εἶδος μὲν ἔην κακός", οὐ τὸ σῶμα ἀσύμ-
μετρον ἀλλὰ τὸ πρόσωπον αἰσχρόν, τὸ γὰρ εὐειδὲς
οἱ Κρῆτες τὸ εὐπρόσωπον καλοῦσι· καὶ τὸ "ζωρότε-
15 ρον δὲ κέραιε" οὐ τὸ ἄκρατον ὡς οἰνόφλυξιν ἀλλὰ τὸ
θᾶττον. τὸ δὲ κατὰ μεταφορὰν εἴρηται, οἷον "πάντες[1] μέν ῥα θεοί τε καὶ ἀνέρες[2] εὗδον παννύχιοι"·
ἅμα δέ φησιν "ἦ τοι ὅτ᾽ ἐς πεδίον τὸ Τρωικὸν ἀθρή-
σειεν, αὐλῶν συρίγγων τε ὅμαδον"· τὸ γὰρ πάντες
ἀντὶ τοῦ πολλοί κατὰ μεταφορὰν εἴρηται, τὸ γὰρ
20 πᾶν πολύ τι. καὶ τὸ "οἴη δ᾽ ἄμμορος" κατὰ μεταφοράν, τὸ γὰρ γνωριμώτατον μόνον. κατὰ δὲ προσῳ-
δίαν, ὥσπερ Ἱππίας ἔλυεν ὁ Θάσιος, τὸ "δίδομεν δέ
οἱ εὖχος ἀρέσθαι" καὶ "τὸ μὲν οὖ καταπύθεται
ὄμβρῳ". τὰ δὲ διαιρέσει, οἷον Ἐμπεδοκλῆς "αἶψα
δὲ θνήτ᾽ ἐφύοντο τὰ πρὶν μάθον ἀθάνατ᾽ εἶναι,

---

[1] πάντες Graefenhan: ἄλλοι AB
[2] ἀνέρες AB: ἀν. ἱπποκορυσταὶ Arab., Lat.

---

[a] Hom. *Il.* 1.50; the issue was why Apollo would have sent the plague first upon animals. But *oureis*, unlike *ouroi*, does mean "mules," as also at 10.84.

[b] Hom. *Il.* 10.316; the "problem" stemmed from the continuation, "but was swift of foot."

[c] Hom. *Il.* 9.203; Greeks rarely drank undiluted wine.

[d] Hom. *Il.* 10.1–2, garbled (but cf. 2.1–2), and 10.11, 13: "he marvelled at" is in Homer but not Ar.'s quotation.

Some problems should be resolved by reference to diction, such as the use of a loan word in "first against the *oureis* ...":[a] perhaps he does not mean the mules, but the guards. And with Dolon, "who in form [*eidos*] was poor,"[b] perhaps he does not mean his body was misshapen, but his face was ugly, since the Cretans call facial beauty *eueides*. And "mix it stronger"[c] may not imply neat wine for topers, but mixing faster. Other points involve metaphor; for instance, "all gods and men slept through the night," yet at the same time he says "whenever he gazed at the Trojan plain, he marvelled at the din of reed pipes and panpipes":[d] "all" has been said metaphorically for "many," as all is a kind of multiplicity.[e] Likewise "alone without a share"[f] is metaphorical, since "alone" means "best known."[g] Accentuation, as in Hippias of Thasus' solutions, affects "we grant him to achieve his prayer,"[h] and "the part rotted by rain."[i] Others are solved by punctuation, such as Empedocles' "at once things became mortal

[e] Cf. 57b11–13, metaphor from species to genus."

[f] Hom. *Il.* 18.489, *Od.* 5.275 (the Bear constellation, which "alone" never sets).

[g] Metaphor from species ("unique") to genus ("notable"); cf. 57b11–13

[h] Cf. Hom. *Il.* 21.297, but the ref. is to 2.15 (see *Soph. El.* 166b6–8); a change of accent makes "we grant" into (imperative) "grant": the (tortuous) aim is to exculpate Zeus of deception at *Il.* 2.15. Hippias cannot be identified with confidence.

[i] Hom. *Il.* 23.328: change of accent (and breathing) produces a preferable negative, "which is not rotted by rain"; cf. *Soph. El.* 166b3–6.

25 ζωρά[1] τε πρὶν κέκρητο".[2] τὰ δὲ ἀμφιβολίᾳ, "παρώ-
χηκεν δὲ πλέω νύξ"· τὸ γὰρ πλείω ἀμφίβολόν ἐστιν.
τὰ δὲ κατὰ τὸ ἔθος τῆς λέξεως· τὸν κεκραμένον
οἶνόν φασιν εἶναι, ὅθεν πεποίηται "κνημὶς νεοτεύ-
κτου κασσιτέροιο"· καὶ χαλκέας τοὺς τὸν σίδηρον
ἐργαζομένους, ὅθεν εἴρηται ὁ Γανυμήδης Διὶ οἰνοχο-
30 εύειν, οὐ πινόντων οἶνον. εἴη δ' ἂν τοῦτό γε καὶ [3]
κατὰ μεταφοράν.

δεῖ δὲ καὶ ὅταν ὄνομά τι ὑπεναντίωμά τι δοκῇ
σημαίνειν, ἐπισκοπεῖν ποσαχῶς ἂν σημήνειε τοῦτο
ἐν τῷ εἰρημένῳ, οἷον τῷ[4] "τῇ ῥ' ἔσχετο χάλκεον
ἔγχος" τὸ ταύτῃ κωλυθῆναι ποσαχῶς ἐνδέχεται,
ὡδὶ ἢ ὡδί, ὡς μάλιστ' ἄν τις ὑπολάβοι· κατὰ τὴν
35 καταντικρὺ ἢ ὡς Γλαύκων λέγει, ὅτι ἔνιοι[5] ἀλόγως
1461b προϋπολαμβάνουσί τι καὶ αὐτοὶ καταψηφισάμενοι
συλλογίζονται, καὶ ὡς εἰρηκότος ὅ τι δοκεῖ ἐπιτιμῶ-
σιν, ἂν ὑπεναντίον ᾖ τῇ αὑτῶν οἰήσει. τοῦτο δὲ
πέπονθε τὰ περὶ Ἰκάριον. οἴονται γὰρ αὐτὸν
Λάκωνα εἶναι· ἄτοπον οὖν τὸ μὴ ἐντυχεῖν τὸν Τηλέ-
5 μαχον αὐτῷ εἰς Λακεδαίμονα ἐλθόντα. τὸ δ' ἴσως

---

[1] ζωρά Vettori ex Athen. 423F: ζῷα AB
[2] κέκρητο A: κέκριτο BA[2]
[3] καὶ add. Heinsius (Arab.)   [4] τῷ Bywater: τὸ AB
[5] ἔνιοι Vettori (Arab.): ἔνια AB

---

[a] Fr. 35.14–15 DK (text disputed): the ambiguity is between
taking "previously" with "unmixed" or the verb.

[b] Hom. Il. 10.252; the context is "more . . . than two thirds,
but a third is still left": it is uncertain whether Ar. wished "more

that previously had known immortality, and unmixed previously were mixed."[a] Others by ambiguity: in "more of the night has passed,"[b] "more" is ambiguous. Others involve usage of diction. People still speak of "wine" when it is mixed; so too with the phrase "a greave of new-forged tin."[c] And as we call iron workers "bronzesmiths," so too Ganymede is described as "pouring wine for Zeus,"[d] even though gods do not drink wine. The last could also be a case of metaphor.[e]

When the sense of a word seems to entail a contradiction, one should consider how many senses it could have in the context: as in "by which the bronze spear was stopped,"[f] how many senses are possible for its being blocked at this point, choosing the best assumption between alternatives. This is the reverse of what Glaucon[g] describes, that some people adopt an unreasonable premise, base inferences on their prejudgement, and, if something contradicts their opinion, blame the poet as though he had said what they merely suppose. The issue of Icarius is a case in point: people think he was a Laconian, so it is absurd Telemachus did not encounter him when he went to Sparta.[h] But perhaps it is as the

than" to mean "the greater part of" or "full"; cf. fr. 385 Gigon/161 Rose.

[c] Hom. *Il.* 21.592: i.e. "tin" means "tin alloyed with copper."

[d] Cf. Hom. *Il.* 20.234; gods drink nectar.

[e] "By analogy": 57b16 ff.

[f] Hom. *Il.* 20.272; the problem is how a spear, having penetrated two layers of bronze, could be stopped by a presumably outer layer of gold. Ar. gives no solution.

[g] Unidentifiable, but cf. Pl. *Ion* 530d.   [h] In Hom. *Od.* bk. 4, where Icarius (Penelope's father) does not appear.

ἔχει ὥσπερ οἱ Κεφαλλῆνές φασι· παρ' αὐτῶν γὰρ
γῆμαι λέγουσι τὸν Ὀδυσσέα καὶ εἶναι Ἰκάδιον ἀλλ'
οὐκ Ἰκάριον· δι'[1] ἁμάρτημα δὲ τὸ πρόβλημα εἰκός
ἐστιν. ὅλως δὲ τὸ ἀδύνατον μὲν πρὸς τὴν ποίησιν ἢ
10 πρὸς τὸ βέλτιον ἢ πρὸς τὴν δόξαν δεῖ ἀνάγειν.
πρός τε γὰρ τὴν ποίησιν αἱρετώτερον πιθανὸν ἀδύνατον ἢ ἀπίθανον καὶ δυνατόν· * * *[2] τοιούτους
εἶναι οἷον Ζεῦξις ἔγραφεν, ἀλλὰ βέλτιον· τὸ γὰρ
παράδειγμα δεῖ ὑπερέχειν. πρὸς ἅ φασιν τἄλογα·
15 οὕτω τε καὶ ὅτι ποτὲ οὐκ ἄλογόν ἐστιν· εἰκὸς γὰρ
καὶ παρὰ τὸ εἰκὸς γίνεσθαι. τὰ δ' ὑπεναντίως[3] εἰρημένα οὕτω σκοπεῖν ὥσπερ οἱ ἐν τοῖς λόγοις ἔλεγχοι
εἰ τὸ αὐτὸ καὶ πρὸς τὸ αὐτὸ καὶ ὡσαύτως, ὥστε καὶ
αὐτὸν[4] ἢ πρὸς ἃ αὐτὸς λέγει ἢ ὃ ἂν φρόνιμος ὑπο-
θῆται. ὀρθὴ δ' ἐπιτίμησις καὶ ἀλογίᾳ[5] καὶ μοχθη-
20 ρίᾳ, ὅταν μὴ ἀνάγκης οὔσης μηθὲν χρήσηται τῷ
ἀλόγῳ, ὥσπερ Εὐριπίδης τῷ Αἰγεῖ, ἢ τῇ πονηρίᾳ,
ὥσπερ ἐν Ὀρέστῃ τῇ[6] τοῦ Μενελάου. τὰ μὲν οὖν
ἐπιτιμήματα ἐκ πέντε εἰδῶν φέρουσιν· ἢ γὰρ ὡς
ἀδύνατα ἢ ὡς ἄλογα ἢ ὡς βλαβερὰ ἢ ὡς ὑπεναντία
ἢ ὡς παρὰ τὴν ὀρθότητα τὴν κατὰ τέχνην. αἱ δὲ

---

[1] δι' ἁμάρτημα Maggi (Lat.): διαμάρτημα A
[2] lacunam stat. Vahlen: καὶ ἴσως ἀδύνατον suppl. Gomperz
(ex Arab.)
[3] ὑπεναντίως Twining: ὑπεναντία ὡς A
[4] αὐτὸν AB: λυτέον M. Schmidt
[5] ἀλογίᾳ καὶ μοχθηρίᾳ Vahlen: -α . . . -α A
[6] τῇ add. Vahlen

Cephallenians[a] maintain: they say it was one of *their* people Odysseus married, and the father's name was Icadius not Icarius. That the problem is due to a mistake seems likely. In general, impossibility should be referred to poetic needs, to the ideal, or to popular belief. Poetic needs make something plausible though impossible preferable to what is possible but implausible. <It may be impossible> that people should be as Zeuxis[b] painted them, but it is ideal, since a paragon should be of higher stature. Refer irrationalities to what people say;[c] and there is also the defence that they are sometimes *not* irrational, since it is probable that improbable things occur.[d] Contradictions should be scrutinised as with refutations in argument,[e] to see whether the same is meant, in the same relation, and in the same respect, so that the poet himself contradicts either his own words or what an intelligent person would assume. But criticism of both irrationality and depravity is right when they are unnecessary and no purpose is served by the irrationality (as with Aegeus in Euripides)[f] or the wickedness (as with Menelaus' in *Orestes*).[g] So then, people make criticisms of five types: that things are impossible, irrational, harmful,[h] contradictory, or contrary to artistic stan-

[a] Cephallenia: island s.w. of (Odysseus') Ithaca.

[b] See on 50a27.

[c] Cf. 60b10.

[d] Cf. 56a24–5.

[e] The subject of Ar.'s *Sophistici Elenchi*.

[f] Eur. *Med.* 663 ff.

[g] Eur. *Or.* 356 ff, 1554 ff; cf. 54a29.

[h] This was implicit at 61a4–9; cf. e.g. Pl. *Rep.* 3.391b4.

λύσεις ἐκ τῶν εἰρημένων ἀριθμῶν σκεπτέαι. εἰσὶν
25 δὲ δώδεκα.

XXVI   Πότερον δὲ βελτίων ἡ ἐποποιικὴ μίμησις ἢ ἡ
τραγική, διαπορήσειεν ἄν τις. εἰ γὰρ ἡ ἧττον φορ-
τικὴ βελτίων, τοιαύτη δ' ἡ πρὸς βελτίους θεατάς
ἐστιν ἀεί,[1] λίαν δῆλον ὅτι ἡ ἅπαντα μιμουμένη φορ-
τική· ὡς γὰρ οὐκ αἰσθανομένων ἂν μὴ αὐτὸς
30 προσθῇ, πολλὴν κίνησιν κινοῦνται, οἷον οἱ φαῦλοι
αὐληταὶ κυλιόμενοι ἂν δίσκον δέῃ μιμεῖσθαι, καὶ
ἕλκοντες τὸν κορυφαῖον ἂν Σκύλλαν αὐλῶσιν. ἡ μὲν
οὖν τραγῳδία τοιαύτη ἐστίν, ὡς καὶ οἱ πρότερον
τοὺς ὑστέρους αὐτῶν ᾤοντο ὑποκριτάς· ὡς λίαν γὰρ
ὑπερβάλλοντα πίθηκον ὁ Μυννίσκος τὸν Καλλιππί-
35 δην ἐκάλει, τοιαύτη δὲ δόξα καὶ περὶ Πινδάρου ἦν·
ὡς δ' οὗτοι ἔχουσι πρὸς αὐτούς, ἡ ὅλη τέχνη πρὸς
1462a τὴν ἐποποιίαν ἔχει. τὴν μὲν οὖν πρὸς θεατὰς ἐπιεικεῖς φασιν εἶναι οἳ[2] οὐδὲν δέονται τῶν σχημάτων,
τὴν δὲ τραγικὴν πρὸς φαύλους· εἰ οὖν φορτική, χεί-
ρων δῆλον ὅτι ἂν εἴη. πρῶτον μὲν οὐ τῆς ποιητικῆς
5 ἡ κατηγορία ἀλλὰ τῆς ὑποκριτικῆς, ἐπεὶ ἔστι περι-
εργάζεσθαι τοῖς σημείοις καὶ ῥαψῳδοῦντα, ὅπερ[3]
Σωσίστρατος, καὶ διάδοντα, ὅπερ ἐποίει Μνασίθεος
ὁ Ὀπούντιος. εἶτα οὐδὲ κίνησις ἅπασα ἀποδοκιμα-

---

[1] ἀεί, λίαν Vahlen: δειλίαν A
[2] οἳ Vettori (Arab.): om. A
[3] ὅπερ ἐστὶ A: ἐστὶ del. Duentzer

ᵃ Attempts to make sense of this number have proved incon-
clusive.

dards. Solutions should be sought from the categories set out, of which there are twelve.[a]

XVI One might reasonably ask whether epic or tragic mimesis is superior. If the less vulgar art is superior, and if this is always the one addressed to a superior audience, evidently the art which represents[b] everything is utterly vulgar: here, in the belief that the spectators do not notice anything unless the performer stresses it, they engage in profuse movement (e.g. crude aulos players[c] rolling round to represent a discus, and mauling the chorus leader if their music concerns Scylla).[d] Well, tragedy is like this, just as with the earlier actors' views of their successors: it was for an excessive style that Mynniscus dubbed Callippides an "ape," and the same opinion was also held about Pindarus.[e] As the later actors stand to the earlier, so does tragic art as a whole to epic. People say that the latter is addressed to decent spectators who have no need of gestures, but tragedy to crude spectators; if, then, tragedy is vulgar, it will evidently be inferior. Now, in the first place, this charge applies not to poetry but to acting, since one can overdo visual signals both in an epic recital, like Sosistratus,[f] and in a singing display, as Mnasitheus[g] the Opountian used to do. Secondly, not all

[b] *Mimeisthai* here implies full enactment; cf. Pl. *Rep.* 3.397a.

[c] See on 47a15.

[d] The musicians elaborate poetic themes with grotesque movements; Scylla: see on 54a31.

[e] Mynniscus acted for Aesch., but also as late as 422 (*DFA*[2] pp. 93, 105, 112); Callippides belongs to the later 5th cent. (Xen. *Symp.* 3.11, *DFA*[2] p. 94), as probably does Pindarus.

[f] An unknown rhapsode.

[g] Unknown.

στέα, εἴπερ μηδ' ὄρχησις, ἀλλ' ἡ φαύλων, ὅπερ καὶ
Καλλιππίδῃ ἐπετιμᾶτο καὶ νῦν ἄλλοις ὡς οὐκ ἐλευ-
10   θέρας γυναῖκας μιμουμένων. ἔτι ἡ τραγῳδία καὶ
ἄνευ κινήσεως ποιεῖ τὸ αὑτῆς, ὥσπερ ἡ ἐποποιία·
διὰ γὰρ τοῦ ἀναγινώσκειν φανερὰ ὁποία τίς ἐστιν·
εἰ οὖν ἐστι τά γ' ἄλλα κρείττων, τοῦτό γε οὐκ
ἀναγκαῖον αὐτῇ ὑπάρχειν. ἔπειτα διότι πάντ' ἔχει
15   ὅσαπερ ἡ ἐποποιία (καὶ γὰρ τῷ μέτρῳ ἔξεστι χρῆσθαι), καὶ ἔτι οὐ μικρὸν μέρος τὴν μουσικὴν καὶ τὰς
ὄψεις, δι' ἃς[1] αἱ ἡδοναὶ συνίστανται ἐναργέστατα·
εἶτα καὶ τὸ ἐναργὲς ἔχει καὶ ἐν τῇ ἀναγνώσει[2] καὶ
ἐπὶ τῶν ἔργων· ἔτι τῷ ἐν ἐλάττονι μήκει τὸ τέλος τῆς
μιμήσεως εἶναι (τὸ γὰρ ἀθροώτερον ἥδιον[3] ἢ πολλῷ
1462b   κεκραμένον τῷ χρόνῳ, λέγω δ' οἷον εἴ τις τὸν Οἰδίπουν θείη τὸν Σοφοκλέους ἐν ἔπεσιν ὅσοις ἡ Ἰλιάς)·
ἔτι ἧττον μία[4] ἡ μίμησις ἡ τῶν ἐποποιῶν (σημεῖον
δέ, ἐκ γὰρ ὁποιασοῦν μιμήσεως πλείους τραγῳδίαι
5   γίνονται), ὥστε ἐὰν μὲν ἕνα μῦθον ποιῶσιν, ἢ βραχέως δεικνύμενον μύουρον φαίνεσθαι, ἢ ἀκολου-
θοῦντα τῷ τοῦ μέτρου μήκει ὑδαρῆ· λέγω δὲ οἷον ἐὰν
ἐκ πλειόνων πράξεων ᾖ συγκειμένη, ὥσπερ ἡ Ἰλιὰς

[1] ἃς coni. Vahlen: ἧς A
[2] ἀναγνώσει Maggi: ἀναγνωρίσει A
[3] ἥδιον ἢ Maggi: ἴδιον ἢ B: ἡδονὴ A
[4] μία ἡ Spengel: ἡ μία AB

[a] The point concerns acting style, not choice of roles; Callippides: see 61b35.
[b] Ar. probably thinks of reading aloud; cf. 50b18–19, 53b3–6.

movement (any more than all dancing) should be eschewed, but only that of crude performers, as with the complaint levelled against Callippides and now other actors, regarding portrayals of low women.[a] Besides, tragedy achieves its effect even without actors' movements, just like epic; reading makes its qualities clear.[b] So if tragedy is otherwise superior, this defect[c] need not adhere to it. Add the fact that tragedy possesses all epic's resources (it can even use its metre),[d] as well as having a substantial role for music[e] and spectacle, which engender the most vivid pleasures.[f] Again, tragedy has vividness in both reading and performance. Also, tragedy excels by achieving the goal of its mimesis in a shorter scope; greater concentration is more pleasurable than dilution over a long period: suppose someone were to arrange Sophocles' *Oedipus* in as many hexameters as the *Iliad*. Also, the mimesis of epic poets is less unified (a sign of this is that any epic yields several tragedies),[g] so that if they compose a single plot, it will seem either truncated (if its exposition is brief) or diluted (if it comports with the length that suits epic metre).[h] By the latter I mean a structure of multiple actions,[i] in the way that the *Iliad*

[a] I.e. vulgar performance practices.

[d] Hexameters are in fact infrequent in tragedy.

[e] *Mousikē* must here be equivalent to *melos*, "melody," at 47b25, and to *melopoiïa*, "lyric poetry," at 49b33 etc.; epic recitals were accompanied by music of a plainer kind.

[f] Cf. and contrast 50b15–20.

[g] But cf. 59b2–7.

[h] Epic's hexameter suits its nature, incl. its length: cf. 59b30–60a5.

[i] Cf. 59b1.

ἔχει πολλὰ τοιαῦτα μέρη καὶ ἡ Ὀδύσσεια ἃ καὶ
καθ' ἑαυτὰ ἔχει μέγεθος· καίτοι ταῦτα τὰ ποιήματα
10 συνέστηκεν ὡς ἐνδέχεται ἄριστα καὶ ὅτι μάλιστα
μιᾶς πράξεως μίμησις. εἰ οὖν τούτοις τε διαφέρει
πᾶσιν καὶ ἔτι τῷ τῆς τέχνης ἔργῳ (δεῖ γὰρ οὐ τὴν
τυχοῦσαν ἡδονὴν ποιεῖν αὐτὰς ἀλλὰ τὴν εἰρημένην),
φανερὸν ὅτι κρείττων ἂν εἴη μᾶλλον τοῦ τέλους
15 τυγχάνουσα τῆς ἐποποιίας.

περὶ μὲν οὖν τραγῳδίας καὶ ἐποποιίας, καὶ αὐτῶν
καὶ τῶν εἰδῶν καὶ τῶν μερῶν, καὶ πόσα καὶ τί διαφέρει, καὶ τοῦ εὖ ἢ μὴ τίνες αἰτίαι, καὶ περὶ ἐπιτιμή-
σεων καὶ λύσεων, εἰρήσθω τοσαῦτα.[1] * * *

---

[1] seq. vestigia obscura in B, unde περὶ δὲ (?)ἰάμβων καὶ
κωμῳδίας restitui potest

and *Odyssey* have many such parts of individual magnitude. Yet these poems are structured as well as could be, and are as close as possible to mimesis of a single action. If, then, tragedy excels in all these respects, as well as in the function of the art (for these genres should produce no ordinary pleasure, but the one stated),[a] it will evidently be superior to epic through greater success in achieving its goal.

As regards tragedy and epic, the number and distinguishing features of their variation and components, the reasons for success and failure in them, and criticisms and their solutions, let this count as sufficient discussion. * * *[b]

---

[a] At 53b10–13 (for tragedy).

[b] There originally followed a discussion of comedy in the work's "second book"; cf. 49b21–2.

LONGINUS
ON THE SUBLIME

EDITED AND TRANSLATED BY
W. HAMILTON FYFE

REVISED BY
DONALD RUSSELL

INTRODUCTION

Date and authorship

Both date and authorship of this famous and important book remain a matter of controversy. The only evidence for the author's name is given by the conflicting statements of the tenth-century manuscript (Parisinus 2036, hereafter P) on which alone our text depends. P has, in the title, Διονυσίου Λογγίνου; in the table of contents, Διονυσίου ἢ Λογγίνου. Which represents ancient tradition? If the ἢ ("or") is original, and its omission in the title an accident, we clearly have two guesses at the author, presumably by Byzantine scholars: he was either the Augustan Dionysius of Halicarnassus or the third-century Cassius Longinus, a pupil of Plotinus, but a scholar and statesman rather than a philosopher. Neither guess is at all probable. Dionysius' numerous works are quite different from our book in style and in general approach. It is true that both he and our author (39.1) wrote on word arrangement (σύνθεσις), but Dionysius' treatise is in one book, and our author says he has written two.

Cassius Longinus has been a much more popular choice; indeed, this identification was undisputed until the early nineteenth century, and the lofty tone of *On the Sublime* was seen as the natural reflection of the heroic temper of the minister of Queen Zenobia, who was put to death after the fall of Palmyra in A.D. 273 (Gibbon, ch. xi). Moreover, there are actually some overlaps between *On the Sublime* and the fragments of Cassius Longinus' rhetorical treatise (conveniently printed in A. O. Prickard's edition of *On the Sublime*, Oxford 1906, as in many early editions); and the eleventh-century rhetorician John of Sicily (*Rhetores graeci* 6.211, 6.225 Walz) actually refers to Longinus' Φιλόλογοι ὁμιλίαι for opinions which coincide with points made in *On the Sublime* 3.1 and 9.9 (see now G. Mazzucchi, *Aevum* 64 (1990) 153–63). But there is no reason why any of this should be taken as proving Longinian authorship. Indeed there are even differences in the details of style and language, which surely make identification impossible: to take a small but notable matter, *On the Sublime* regularly has πάντες ἑξῆς for "absolutely all," whereas Longinus has ἐφεξῆς in the same idiom (Russell, 1964, xxv n.1). There are powerful arguments also in matters of content. In *On the Sublime*, no writer later than Cicero, Caecilius, and Theodorus is named; the real Longinus—if these fragmentary texts are to be trusted—spoke favourably of Aelius Aristides. Again, our author is an admirer of Plato, and much of his argument is directed to defending Plato against unappreciative critics like Caecilius; Longinus himself seems to have criticized Plato's "poetic" style in terms very like those of our author's opponents (R 7–10, S 23–25 Prickard).

The principal argument against Cassius Longinus is also a general argument against any date later than about A.D. 100, namely that derived from the closing chapter (44). Here, a "philosopher" presents the view that the

INTRODUCTION

"decline" of oratory is due to the loss of free speech and
political liberty, while the author represents himself as
countering this by attributing the decline to a moral collapse rather than external circumstances. There are
indeed a lot of ambiguities and difficulties in this little
dialogue; it is not easy to be sure whether the author is
thinking of the contrast between the free cities of Greece
in the age of Demosthenes and their subsequent subjec-
tion to Macedon and later to Rome, or of the contrast
between Cicero's republican liberty and the principate of
Augustus and his successors. The setting and tone of the
book, however, suggest that it is primarily this second set
of circumstances that is meant. After all, the addressee,
Postumius Terentianus, is a young Roman of some standing; and our author is prepared to venture an opinion
about Cicero. It is all relevant to Rome. But if this is so,
parallels in other authors—the two Senecas, Tacitus,
Pliny—strongly suggest a date in the first century A.D. It
is harder to be more precise. Good arguments have been
advanced for an Augustan date (G. P. Goold, *American
Journal of Philology* 92 (1961) 168–192), the age of
Tiberius (H. Selb, "Probleme der Schrift περὶ ὕψους"
diss. Heidelberg 1957), and the end of the century (e.g.
K. Heldmann, *Antike Theorien über Entwicklung und
Verfall der Redekunst*, Munich 1982, 286–293, making
the book a response to Tacitus' *Dialogus*). The third-
century date still has advocates (G. W. Williams, *Change
and Decline*, Berkeley 1978, 17–25; G. Luck, *Arctos* 5
(1967) 97–113; and, tentatively, G. M. A. Grube, *Greek
and Roman Critics*, Toronto 1965, 340–352), but the case
is not strong.

So what are we to call the author? He is either anonymous, the Great Unknown, or, if we assume that the title of P has authority, he is Dionysius Longinus; the name is not impossible after all. It is tantalizing that his addressee, Postumius Terentianus, cannot be identified; he *may*, of course, be the Terentianus who served in Egypt A.D. 85/6 (Martial 1.86), or the man whose name is on a lead water pipe of the second century (*C.I.L.* XV.2.7373). But who these people were, and what circle they moved in, are less important questions than what the book says, and what place it holds in the history of criticism.

Analysis

Analysis of the treatise is rendered difficult by the damage which P has suffered; there are six long lacunae, and something missing at the end. We have lost about a third of the book. Nevertheless, we can see the author's plan clearly enough, except in one important respect, the treatment given to πάθος. We can also see that some of his central theses are presented not in the course of the argument as he advertises it in chapter 8, but in the eloquent and powerful digressions. He is a sophisticated artist, both in his style and in his economy. This has always been recognized. Pope's famous remark (*Essay on Criticism* 675–680) that he is "himself the great sublime he draws" has antecedents in the earliest period of Longinian criticism: Francesco Porto (1569) says of him: "non solum docet sed etiam rapit, et quodammodo vim affert lectoribus"—exactly what "Longinus" says himself of the writers he admires.

Let us set out the analysis as far as we can.

1–2: A formal preface, in which Caecilius of Caleacte (a friend of Dionysius, it seems: *ad Pompeium* 3) is criticized, Terentianus flattered, the subject defined, and the objection that ὕψος is a matter of nature, not art, raised and answered.

3–5: Following the first lacuna, we find ourselves in the midst of a discussion of faults consequent on inadequate or misconceived attempts to achieve sublimity: turgidity, frigid conceits, inappropriate emotiveness. This helps to define the subject by contrast.

6–7: A positive account of the true sublime follows, but in very general terms. It is something which stands repeated reading, and makes a powerful and lasting impression on readers of different backgrounds. It will endure.

8: There are five sources of sublimity: (i) great thoughts (9–15); (ii) strong emotion—something Caecilius left out; (iii) certain figures of thought and speech (16–29); (iv) noble diction (30–38, 43); (v) dignified word arrangement (39–42).

But where is emotion (ii) discussed? This is the problem that has most exercised critics; see, for a good discussion, J. Bompaire, *REG* 86 (1973) 323–343. We are told at the very end (44.12) that πάθη are to be the subject of a special treatment to follow next; on the other hand, there are many references throughout the book to emotion, seen as an integral element in sublimity, and associated with all the other four sources. The safest conclusion is that some explanation of this procedure was given in the long passage lost following 9.4.

INTRODUCTION

150

23–24: Polyptoton, singular for plural, plural for singular.

25: Historic present.

26–27: Vivid second person; abrupt introduction of direct speech.

28–29: Periphrasis.

29.2: Summary, emphasizing again the close links between emotion and sublimity.

(iv)

30: Introduction to the section on language. A lacuna follows.

31: The discussion is now about metaphor, and especially vivid and idiomatic examples.

32: Criticism of Caecilius' rule that one should not use more than two or three metaphors on any one theme: examples from Demosthenes, Xenophon, and Plato's *Timaeus*. Caecilius' criticism of Plato and excessive enthusiasm for Lysias are seen to be motivated by contentiousness.

33–35: A "digression," to which Wilamowitz gave the title *Regel und Genie*. (It is the most eloquent part of the book, and central to its message.) Genius, even when it makes mistakes, is preferable to impeccable mediocrity. Mechanical criticism would prefer Hyperides to Demosthenes, and we see this to be absurd; the gap between Plato and Lysias is infinitely wider. Our admiration goes to the greatest works of nature, not to mere prettiness, and hence also to the products of natural genius, which all ages admire.

37: Beginning of a discussion of similes. A lacuna follows.

38: Hyperbole.

(v)

39–42: Word arrangement: examples of the ways in which rhythm is decisive in producing sublime effects, and common words can be given grandeur by skilful placing. Dangers of excessive rhythmization and brevity.

43.1–5: seems to belong under "choice of words" not under "arrangement." We have a lengthy discussion of a passage of Theopompus, in which the effect of a grand situation is marred by the intrusion of commonplace words and details.

43.6: In general, the opposites of the devices that produce sublimity will produce its opposite, lowness of style.

44.1–11: The deeper causes of failure are examined in a dialogue, in which an unnamed philosopher makes the case that it is loss of liberty that produces the current dearth of lofty writing, and the author attributes it rather to moral decline.

44.12: Transition to the promised discussion of πάθη, broken off short in our text.

A little about the background

"The appearance of this unknown Greek ... has something miraculous about it." Ernst Curtius (*Latin Literature and the European Middle Ages*, 399 [E.T.]), in company with many, exaggerates. It is Longinus' eloquence, and the fact that no similar work survives, that have led people to think him more mysterious than he really is. In fact he represents a tradition.

The basic division between grand and ordinary styles goes back a long way in Greek thinking: the ἀγών between Aeschylus and Euripides in Aristophanes' *Frogs* is a classical expression of the contrast. Indeed, later rhetoricians even found it in Homer, who contrasts Menelaus' rapid, clear speech with Odysseus' "winter snows" (*Iliad* 3.214). A third manner—the smoothness of Isocrates, or the honeyed words of Nestor (*Iliad* 1.243)—was, it seems, added later; and the resulting three-style theory is canonical in Cicero, Quintilian, and much later criticism. This development is not really relevant to Longinus, who is concerned only to identify the characteristics that mark out the emotionally intense and elevated from the merely pleasing and soothing. Nor is it precisely a style—a χαρακτήρ or *genus dicendi*—that is his subject; this is better described as a tone of writing, attainable only as a consequence of a developed intellectual and emotional response to life. This is not to say that his ὕψος is conceptually unique in ancient criticism; but it resembles not so much the *genera dicendi* as what Dionysius calls "additional virtues" (*epithetoi aretai*), the possession of which lends a particular character to writers who already possess the "necessary virtues" of purity, clarity, and brevity. Even closer, perhaps, are certain of the *ideai*—forms or tones of speech—identified by the second-century rhetor Hermogenes and others of the same period. According to Hermogenes, all these *ideai* could be found in Demosthenes; but once detected and isolated, they could become patterns for imitation. Among these *ideai* were σεμνότης and σφοδρότης, solemnity and vehemence; and these, and others like them, were sharply opposed to the *ideai* of charm and delicacy, in a general contrast very like that which Longinus draws between Hyperides and Demosthenes. (The

153

translation of Hermogenes by Cecil Wooten, Chapel Hill, 1988, may be consulted to form a notion of this theory and its implications.) But not even in Hermogenes is there so detailed, comprehensive, and enthusiastic a discussion of the high tone as in our treatise. Moreover, it is sharply distinguished from anything Hermogenes wrote by its firm moral basis. For Hermogenes, anyone could choose to write grandly if he selected his subject appropriately and followed the suggestions laid down about vocabulary, figures, sentence structure, and rhythm; for our author, it is only possible if you really develop your intellect and your emotions, by the study of the classics, to the point when high thoughts and their due expression come more or less instinctively to mind. This kind of attitude is quite common in the imperial period, and seems to have appealed especially to Romans. It is primarily a response on the part of teachers of rhetoric to accusations made by philosophers that their art was amoral, and could be used indifferently for good or bad ends. Longinus' warm defence of Plato against Caecilius (and indeed Dionysius) and his assignment of the moral argument in chapter 44 to himself rather than to any philosopher point in the same direction; he wishes to commend himself to Terentianus not only as a technical teacher but as a guide to right attitudes in life. Only thus can his concern with Homer and classical poetry and his insistence on the need to look to posterity be seen to be "useful to public men," ἀνδράσι πολιτικοῖς χρήσιμον, as he puts it in the preface (1.2).

INTRODUCTION

Influence

Parisinus 2036 was copied for Bessarion in 1468, and at least once again later in the century. Other copies of these copies were also made, and Latin translations circulated in manuscript before the first printed editions (1554–5) and printed Latin translations (1566, 1572). But the work made little impact on the literary world at large until much later. The Italian translation of Niccolo da Falgano (1560) remained in manuscript; the first published English version is by John Hall (1652). All was changed in 1674 by Boileau's *Traité du sublime ou du merveilleux dans le discours, truduit du grec de Longin*. This made "Longinus" a central text in European criticism throughout the eighteenth century. In England, its influence was first advanced by John Dennis' *Advancement and Reformation of Poetry* (1701), and *Grounds of Criticism in Poetry* (1704). No doubt the book's moral stance was congenial to a thinker who regarded religion and "enthusiastic passion" as the natural subjects of poetry. But Dryden and Addison were also familiar with it, Sir Joshua Reynolds' *Discourses on Painting* adapt many of its ideas, Gibbon and Dr. Johnson both admired it, and Burke at least used it as a starting point of speculation, though the main contentions of *The Sublime and the Beautiful* go far beyond Longinus' scope. This eighteenth-century admiration faded with the coming of Romanticism, when that liberty of thought and comparative freedom from rule which Longinus authorized came to be taken for granted and no longer needed special defence. The eloquence of the book, however, has always continued to earn it enthusiastic readers and a wide

response; the wealth of learned work on its text and interpretation, and the special place it always holds in histories
of criticism, are testimony to its enduring significance.

Text

The text rests on Parisinus 2036 (P), supplemented by the
apographa in two places where P was damaged after the
primary copies were taken (viz. ὡς κἂν . . . ἠρκέσθην
[8.1–9.4] and τὸ ἐπ᾽ οὐρανόν . . . ἰδέσθαι [9.4–9.10])
and also by two miscellanies (Parisinus 985 and its copy
Vaticanus 285) which alone preserve the "fragmentum
Tollianum," viz. φύσις . . . θεωρίαν (2.3). Our brief and
very selective apparatus mentions also (as "K marg.")
some variants (conjectures, no doubt) in the margin of
Cantabrigiensis KK.VI.34, a copy of Bessarion's copy,
made by Francesco Porto, apparently in connection with
the preparation of the Aldine edition of 1555.

Translation

This is a revision of W. Hamilton Fyfe's version, and I
have tried not to tamper with it where it did not seem
positively misleading. Thus I have left the poetical quotations for the most part as they were, though their style is
now very dated, and made even more artificial by Fyfe's
attempt to render Greek hexameters into English hexameters. I have also left some of Fyfe's notes, but have
replaced or supplied others. The text and punctuation
have also been revised.

BIBLIOGRAPHY

The literature on *On the Sublime* is vast. Apart from the bibliographies in the principal editions (see below), there are bibliographies by D. S. Marin (*Bibliography of the Essay on The Sublime*, privately printed, 1967) and by D. Tavani (*La filologia recente di fronte al Peri Hypsous*, Rome 1971), and a survey article by G. Martano in *ANRW* II, 32.1 (1984), 364–403.

Of older editions, those of J. Toll (Utrecht 1694), J. Toup (Oxford 1778), B. Weiske (Leipzig 1809, Oxford 1820) are especially worth consulting. The fullest apparatus and list of conjectures is to be found in O. Jahn–J. Vahlen, *Dionysii Longini de sublimitate liber*, 4th ed. (1910), re-issued with index by H. D. Blume (1967).

The principal modern editions with commentary are those of W. Rhys Roberts (Cambridge, 2nd ed. 1907, contains also a translation), D. A. Russell (Oxford 1964), and C. M. Mazzucchi (Milan 1992; especially useful for its study of the Renaissance tradition of the text). A. Rostagni's edition (Milan 1947) is also of importance.

Translations are innumerable. Boileau's was well edited by C.-H. Boudhors (Paris 1942). Contemporary English versions include those by G. M. A. Grube (New York 1957), T. S. Dorsch (in Penguin *Classical Literary Criticism* 1965), D. A. Russell (in *Ancient Literary Criticism*, Oxford 1972, and World's Classics *Classical Literary Criticism*, Oxford 1985). The version of W. Smith (London 1739) is a good example of an eighteenth-century rendering.

Brief general interpretations are to be found in most manuals of the history of criticism: e.g. G. M. A. Grube,

The Greek and Roman Critics, London 1965, 340–353; G. A. Kennedy, *The Art of Rhetoric in the Roman World*, Princeton 1972, 369–377; D. A. Russell in G. A. Kennedy (ed.), *Cambridge History of Literary Criticism* i (1990) 306–311.

Other contributions to interpretation which should be specially noted are: W. Bühler, *Beiträge zur Erklärung der Schrift vom Erhabenen*, 1964; J. Bompaire, "Le pathos dans le traité du Sublime," *Revue des Etudes Grecques* 86 (1973) 323–343; D. A. Russell, "Longinus Revisited," *Mnemosyne* IV.34 (1981) 72–86; E. Matelli, "Struttura e Stile del περὶ ὕψους," *Aevum* 61 (1987) 137–207.

On Longinus' influence, see especially: S. H. Monk, *The Sublime*, New York 1935; M. H. Abrams, *The Mirror and the Lamp*, New York and London 1953; T. R. Henn, *Longinus and English Criticism*, Cambridge 1934; A. Rosenberg, *Longinus in England bis zum Ende des 18. Jahrhunderts*, diss. Berlin, 1917; J. Brody, *Boileau and Longinus*, Geneva 1958; K. Maurer, "Boileaus Uebersetzung" in *Le Classicisme à Rome"* (*Entretiens Hardt* XXV, 1979) 213–257.

ΠΕΡΙ ΥΨΟΥΣ

ΠΕΡΙ ΥΨΟΥΣ

1. Τὸ μὲν τοῦ Καικιλίου συγγραμμάτιον, ὃ περὶ ὕψους συνετάξατο, ἀνασκοπουμένοις ἡμῖν ὡς οἶσθα κοινῇ, Ποστούμιε Τερεντιανὲ[1] φίλτατε, ταπεινότερον ἐφάνη τῆς ὅλης ὑποθέσεως, καὶ ἥκιστα τῶν καιρίων ἐφαπτόμενον οὐ πολλήν τε ὠφέλειαν, ἧς μάλιστα δεῖ στοχάζεσθαι τὸν γράφοντα, περιποιοῦν τοῖς ἐντυγχάνουσιν, εἴγ'[2] ἐπὶ πάσης τεχνολογίας δυεῖν ἀπαιτουμένων, προτέρου μὲν τοῦ δεῖξαι τί τὸ ὑποκείμενον, δευτέρου δὲ τῇ τάξει, τῇ δυνάμει δὲ κυριωτέρου, πῶς ἂν ἡμῖν αὐτὸ τοῦτο καὶ δι' ὧντινων μεθόδων κτητὸν γένοιτο, ὅμως ὁ Καικίλιος ποῖον μέν τι ὑπάρχει τὸ ὑψηλὸν διὰ μυρίων ὅσων ὡς ἀγνοοῦσι πειρᾶται δεικνύναι, τὸ δὲ δι' ὅτου τρόπου τὰς ἑαυτῶν φύσεις προάγειν ἰσχύοιμεν ἂν εἰς ποσὴν μεγέθους ἐπίδοσιν, οὐκ οἶδ' ὅπως ὡς οὐκ ἀναγκαῖον παρέλι-
2 πεν· πλὴν ἴσως τουτονὶ μὲν τὸν ἄνδρα οὐχ οὕτως αἰτιᾶσθαι τῶν ἐκλελειμμένων ὡς αὐτῆς τῆς ἐπινοίας καὶ σπουδῆς ἄξιον ἐπαινεῖν. ἐπεὶ δ' ἐνεκελεύσω καὶ ἡμᾶς τι περὶ ὕψους πάντως εἰς σὴν ὑπομνηματίσα-

---

[1] Φλωρεντιανὲ P, corr. Manutius.
[2] εἴγ' Spengel: εἴτ'.

ON THE SUBLIME

1. You know, my dear Postumius Terentianus, that when we were studying together Caecilius'[a] little treatise on the Sublime it appeared to us to fall below the level of the subject and to fail to address the main points, or render its readers very much of that assistance which should be an author's chief aim, seeing that there are two requisites in every systematic treatise: the author must first define his subject, and secondly, though this is really more important, he must show us how and by what means we may reach the goal ourselves. Caecilius, however, endeavouring by a thousand instances to demonstrate the nature of the sublime, as though we know nothing about it, apparently thought it unnecessary to deal with the means by which we may be enabled to develop our natures to some degree of grandeur. Still, we ought perhaps rather to praise our author for the mere conception of such a treatise and the trouble spent upon it than to blame him for his omissions. But since you have now asked me in my turn to prepare some notes on the sublime for your own sake, let us then see whether my

[a] Caecilius of Caleacte in Sicily was a noted rhetorician and historian, contemporary with Dionysius of Halicarnassus, and said to have been a Jew. See E. Ofenloch, *Caecilii Fragmenta* (1907) for a full (but uncritical) collection of material.

σθαι χάριν, φέρε, εἴ τι δὴ δοκοῦμεν ἀνδράσι πολιτικοῖς τεθεωρηκέναι χρήσιμον ἐπισκεψώμεθα. αὐτὸς
δ᾽ ἡμῖν, ἑταῖρε, τὰ ἐπὶ μέρους, ὡς πέφυκας καὶ
καθήκει, συνεπικρινεῖς ἀληθέστατα· εὖ γὰρ δὴ ὁ
ἀποφηνάμενος, τί θεοῖς ὅμοιον ἔχομεν, "εὐεργεσίαν"
3 εἴπας "καὶ ἀλήθειαν." γράφων δὲ πρὸς σέ, φίλτατε,
τὸν παιδείας ἐπιστήμονα, σχεδὸν ἀπήλλαγμαι καὶ
τοῦ διὰ πλειόνων προϋποτίθεσθαι, ὡς ἀκρότης καὶ
ἐξοχή τις λόγων ἐστὶ τὰ ὕψη, καὶ ποιητῶν τε οἱ
μέγιστοι καὶ συγγραφέων οὐκ ἄλλοθεν ἢ ἐνθένδε
ποθὲν ἐπρώτευσαν καὶ ταῖς ἑαυτῶν περιέβαλον εὐ-
4 κλείαις τὸν αἰῶνα. οὐ γὰρ εἰς πειθὼ τοὺς ἀκροωμέ-
νους ἀλλ᾽ εἰς ἔκστασιν ἄγει τὰ ὑπερφυᾶ· πάντη δέ
γε σὺν ἐκπλήξει τοῦ πιθανοῦ καὶ τοῦ πρὸς χάριν ἀεὶ
κρατεῖ τὸ θαυμάσιον, εἴγε τὸ μὲν πιθανὸν ὡς τὰ
πολλὰ ἐφ᾽ ἡμῖν, ταῦτα δὲ δυναστείαν καὶ βίαν ἄμαχον προσφέροντα παντὸς ἐπάνω τοῦ ἀκροωμένου
καθίσταται· καὶ τὴν μὲν ἐμπειρίαν τῆς εὑρέσεως καὶ
τὴν τῶν πραγμάτων τάξιν καὶ οἰκονομίαν οὐκ ἐξ
ἑνὸς οὐδ᾽ ἐκ δυεῖν, ἐκ δὲ τοῦ ὅλου τῶν λόγων ὕφους
μόλις ἐκφαινομένην ὁρῶμεν, ὕψος δέ που καιρίως
ἐξενεχθὲν τά τε πράγματα δίκην σκηπτοῦ πάντα
διεφόρησεν καὶ τὴν τοῦ ῥήτορος εὐθὺς ἀθρόαν ἐνε-
δείξατο δύναμιν. ταῦτα γὰρ[1] οἶμαι καὶ τὰ παρα-

---

[1] δὲ Faber, perhaps rightly.

observations have any value for public speakers; and you yourself, my friend, will, I am sure, do what duty and your heart alike dictate and give me the benefit of your unbiased judgement in detail. For he spoke well who, in answer to the question, "What have we in common with the gods?" said "Beneficence and Truth."[a] Further, writing for a man of such education as yourself, dear friend, I almost feel freed from the need of a lengthy preface showing how the Sublime consists in a consummate excellence and distinction of language, and that this alone gave to the greatest poets and prose writers their preeminence and clothed them with immortal fame. For the effect of genius is not to persuade the audience but rather to transport them out of themselves. Invariably what inspires wonder, with its power of amazing us, always prevails over what is merely convincing and pleasing. For our persuasions are usually under our own control, while these things exercise an irresistible power and mastery, and get the better of every listener.[b] Again, experience in invention and the due disposal and marshalling of facts do not show themselves in one or two touches but emerge gradually from the whole tissue of the composition, while, on the other hand, a well-timed flash of sublimity shatters everything like a bolt of lightning and reveals the full

[a] This saying is attributed to Pythagoras (Aelian, *VH* 12.59) but also to Aristotle and Demosthenes and others (see *Gnomologium Vaticanum*, p. 25 Sternbach).

[b] A listener is also a reader; ancient literary criticism often favours the vocabulary of listening and speaking over that of reading and writing, because the literature was thought of as primarily oral, and the sense of speeches and poems as auditory experiences was never lost.

πλήσια, Τερεντιανὲ ἥδιστε, κἂν αὐτὸς ἐκ πείρας ὑφηγήσαιο.

2. Ἡμῖν δ' ἐκεῖνο διαπορητέον ἐν ἀρχῇ, εἰ ἔστιν ὕψους τις ἢ πάθους[1] τέχνη, ἐπεί τινες ὅλως οἴονται διηπατῆσθαι τοὺς τὰ τοιαῦτα ἄγοντας εἰς τεχνικὰ παραγγέλματα. γεννᾶται γάρ, φησί, τὰ μεγαλοφυῆ καὶ οὐ διδακτὰ παραγίνεται, καὶ μία τέχνη πρὸς αὐτὰ τὸ πεφυκέναι· χείρω τε τὰ φυσικὰ ἔργα, ὡς οἴονται, καὶ τῷ παντὶ δειλότερα καθίσταται ταῖς
2 τεχνολογίαις κατασκελετευόμενα. ἐγὼ δὲ ἐλεγχθή-σεσθαι τοῦθ' ἑτέρως ἔχον φημί, εἰ ἐπισκέψαιτό τις ὅτι ἡ φύσις, ὥσπερ τὰ πολλὰ ἐν τοῖς παθητικοῖς καὶ διηρμένοις αὐτόνομον, οὕτως οὐκ εἰκαῖόν τι κἀκ παντὸς ἀμέθοδον εἶναι φιλεῖ· καὶ ὅτι αὐτὴ μὲν πρῶ-τόν τι καὶ ἀρχέτυπον γενέσεως στοιχεῖον ἐπὶ πάν-των ὑφέστηκεν, τὰς δὲ ποσότητας καὶ τὸν ἐφ' ἑκάστου καιρὸν ἔτι δὲ τὴν ἀπλανεστάτην ἄσκησίν τε καὶ χρῆσιν ἱκανὴ πορίσαι[2] καὶ συνενεγκεῖν ἡ μέθοδος· καὶ ὡς ἐπικινδυνότερα αὐτὰ ἐφ' αὑτῶν δίχα ἐπιστήμης ἀστήρικτα καὶ ἀνερμάτιστα ἐαθέντα τὰ μεγάλα, ἐπὶ μόνῃ τῇ φορᾷ καὶ ἀμαθεῖ τόλμῃ λειπό-μενα· δεῖ γὰρ αὐτοῖς ὡς κέντρου πολλάκις, οὕτω δὲ
3 καὶ χαλινοῦ· ὅπερ γὰρ ὁ Δημοσθένης ἐπὶ τοῦ κοινοῦ τῶν ἀνθρώπων ἀποφαίνεται βίου, μέγιστον μὲν εἶναι τῶν ἀγαθῶν τὸ εὐτυχεῖν, δεύτερον δὲ καὶ οὐκ

---

[1] πάθους is an old conjecture, presupposed by the translation of G. da Falgano (1575) and found in many later editions: P has βάθους.

[2] πορίσαι P marg., for παρορίσαι.

power of the speaker at a single stroke. But, as I say, my dear Terentianus, these and other such hints you with your experience could supply yourself.

2. We must begin now by raising the question whether there is an art of sublimity or emotion,[a] for some think those are wholly at fault who try to bring such matters under systematic rules. Genius, it is said, is born and does not come of teaching, and the only art for producing it is nature. Works of natural genius, so people think, are spoiled and utterly demeaned by being reduced to the dry bones of rule and precept. For my part I hold that the opposite may be proved, if we consider that while in matters of elevation and emotion Nature for the most part knows no law, yet it is not the way of Nature to work at random and wholly without system. In all production Nature is the first and primary element; but all matters of degree, of the happy moment in each case, and again of the safest rules of practice and use, are adequately provided and contributed by system. We must remember also that mere grandeur runs the greatest risk if left to itself without the stay and ballast of scientific method and abandoned to the impetus of uninstructed temerity. For genius needs the curb as often as the spur. Speaking of the common life of men Demosthenes[b] declares that the greatest of all blessings is good fortune, and that next

---

[a] This translates the emendation *pathous* for the manuscript reading *bathous*, which has been interpreted as "profundity" or "bathos."

[b] *Oration* 23.113.

ἔλαττον τὸ εὖ βουλεύεσθαι, ὅπερ οἷς ἂν μὴ παρῇ
συναναιρεῖ πάντως καὶ θάτερον, τοῦτ' ἂν καὶ ἐπὶ τῶν
λόγων εἴποιμεν, ὡς ἡ μὲν[1] φύσις τὴν τῆς εὐτυχίας
τάξιν ἐπέχει, ἡ τέχνη δὲ τὴν τῆς εὐβουλίας· τὸ δὲ
κυριώτατον, ὅτι καὶ αὐτὸ τὸ εἶναί τινα τῶν ἐν λόγοις
ἐπὶ μόνῃ τῇ φύσει οὐκ ἄλλοθεν ἡμᾶς ἢ παρὰ τῆς
τέχνης ἐκμαθεῖν δεῖ· εἰ ταῦθ', ὡς ἔφην, ἐπιλογίσαιτο
καθ' ἑαυτὸν ὁ τοῖς χρηστομαθοῦσιν ἐπιτιμῶν, οὐκ
ἂν ἔτι, μοὶ δοκῶ, περιττὴν καὶ ἄχρηστον τὴν ἐπὶ τῶν
προκειμένων ἡγήσαιτο θεωρίαν.

3. . . . καὶ καμίνου σχῶσι μάκιστον σέλας.
 εἰ γάρ τιν' ἑστιοῦχον ὄψομαι μόνον,
 μίαν παρείρας πλεκτάνην χειμάρροον,
 στέγην πυρώσω καὶ κατανθρακώσομαι·
 νῦν δ' οὐ κέκραγά πω τὸ γενναῖον μέλος.

οὐ τραγικὰ ἔτι ταῦτα, ἀλλὰ παρατράγῳδα, αἱ
πλεκτάναι καὶ τὸ πρὸς οὐρανὸν ἐξεμεῖν καὶ τὸ τὸν
Βορέαν αὐλητὴν ποιεῖν, καὶ τὰ ἄλλα ἑξῆς· τεθόλω-
ται γὰρ τῇ φράσει καὶ τεθορύβηται ταῖς φαντασίαις
μᾶλλον ἢ δεδείνωται, κἂν ἕκαστον αὐτῶν πρὸς
αὐγὰς ἀνασκοπῇς, ἐκ τοῦ φοβεροῦ κατ' ὀλίγον ὑπο-
νοστεῖ πρὸς τὸ εὐκαταφρόνητον. ὅπου δ' ἐν τραγῳδίᾳ, πράγματι ὀγκηρῷ φύσει καὶ ἐπιδεχομένῳ στόμφον, ὅμως τὸ παρὰ μέλος οἰδεῖν ἀσύγγνωστον,
σχολῇ γ' ἂν οἶμαι λόγοις ἀληθινοῖς ἁρμόσειεν.

[1] At this point, two pages of P have been lost; two of the later
manuscripts (A and B) preserve the passage φύσις . . . θεωρίαν.

comes good judgement, which is indeed quite as important, since the lack of it often completely cancels the
advantage of the former. We may apply this to literature
and say that Nature fills the place of good fortune, Art
that of good judgement. And above all we must remember this: the very fact that in literature some effects come
of natural genius alone can only be learned from art. If
then, as I said, those who censure students of this subject
would lay these considerations to heart, they would not, I
fancy, be any longer inclined to consider the investigation
of our present topic superfluous and useless.

[*Two pages of the manuscript are missing here.*]

3. . . . and they check the chimney's towering blaze.
> For if I see one hearthholder alone,
> I'll weave one torrent coronal of flame
> And fire his homestead to a heap of ash.
> But not yet have I blown the noble strain,[a]

All this has lost the tone of tragedy: it is pseudo-tragic
the "coronals" and "spewing to heaven" and making
Boreas a piper and all the rest of it. The phrasing is tur-
bid, while the images make for confusion rather than
forcefulness. Examine each in the light of day and it
gradually sinks from the terrible to the ridiculous. Now
seeing that in tragedy, which is essentially a majestic matter and admits of bombast, misplaced tumidity is none
the less unpardonable, it is even less likely to suit real

[a] Probably from Aeschylus' *Oritthyia* (fr. 281 Radt). The
speaker is Boreas.

ταύτῃ καὶ τὰ τοῦ Λεοντίνου Γοργίου γελᾶται γράφοντος "Ξέρξης ὁ τῶν Περσῶν Ζεύς," καί "γῦπες
ἔμψυχοι τάφοι," καί τινα τῶν Καλλισθένους ὄντα
οὐχ ὑψηλὰ ἀλλὰ μετέωρα, καὶ ἔτι μᾶλλον τὰ Κλει-
τάρχου· φλοιώδης γὰρ ἀνὴρ καὶ φυσῶν κατὰ τὸν
Σοφοκλέα "μικροῖς μὲν αὐλίσκοισι, φορβειᾶς δ'
ἄτερ"· τά γε μὴν 'Αμφικράτους τοιαῦτα καὶ 'Ηγη-
σίου καὶ Μάτριδος· πολλαχοῦ γὰρ ἐνθουσιᾶν ἑαυτοῖς δοκοῦντες οὐ βακχεύουσιν ἀλλὰ παίζουσιν.

3 ὅλως δ' ἔοικεν εἶναι τὸ οἰδεῖν ἐν τοῖς μάλιστα
δυσφυλακτότατον. φύσει γὰρ ἅπαντες οἱ μεγέθους
ἐφιέμενοι, φεύγοντες ἀσθενείας καὶ ξηρότητος κατά-
γνωσιν, οὐκ οἶδ' ὅπως ἐπὶ τοῦθ' ὑποφέρονται, πειθό-
μενοι τῷ "μεγάλων ἀπολισθαίνειν ὅμως εὐγενὲς
4 ἁμάρτημα." κακοὶ δὲ ὄγκοι καὶ ἐπὶ σωμάτων καὶ
λόγων οἱ χαῦνοι καὶ ἀναλήθεις καὶ μήποτε περι-
ιστάντες ἡμᾶς εἰς τοὐναντίον· οὐδὲν γάρ, φασί,
ξηρότερον ὑδρωπικοῦ.

'Αλλὰ τὸ μὲν οἰδοῦν ὑπεραίρειν βούλεται τὰ ὕψη,
τὸ δὲ μειρακιῶδες ἄντικρυς ὑπεναντίον τοῖς μεγέ-
θεσι· ταπεινὸν γὰρ ἐξ ὅλου καὶ μικρόψυχον καὶ τῷ
ὄντι κακὸν ἀγεννέστατον. τί ποτ' οὖν τὸ μειρακιῶ-
δές ἐστιν; ἢ δῆλον ὡς σχολαστικὴ νόησις, ὑπὸ
περιεργίας λήγουσα εἰς ψυχρότητα; ὀλισθαίνουσι δ'

---

[a] Gorgias fr. B 5a Diels-Kranz (*Fragmente der Vorsokratiker*[6]).　　[b] Nephew of Aristotle and historian of Alexander.
[c] Historian of Alexander, writing in the reign of Ptolemy II
(285–246 B.C.).

speeches. Thus it is that people laugh at Gorgias of Leontini for calling Xerxes "the Persian Zeus," and vultures "living sepulchres";[a] also at certain phrases of Callisthenes[b] which are not sublime but highfalutin, and still more at some of Clitarchus's[c] efforts, an affected creature, blowing, as Sophocles says, "on scrannel pipes, yet wasting all his wind."[d] You find the same sort of thing in Amphicrates too, and in Hegesias and Matris.[e] For often when they think themselves inspired, their supposed ecstasy is merely childish folly. Speaking generally, tumidity seems one of the hardest faults to guard against. For all who aim at grandeur, in trying to avoid the charge of being feeble and arid, fall somehow into this fault, pinning their faith to the maxim that "to miss a high aim is to fail without shame." Tumours are bad things whether in books or bodies, those empty inflations, void of sincerity, as likely as not producing the opposite to the effect intended. For, as they say, "there's naught so dry as dropsy."

But, while tumidity seeks to outdo the sublime, puerility is the exact opposite of grandeur; utterly abject, mean spirited, and in fact the most ignoble of faults. What then is puerility? Is it not obviously an idea born in the classroom, whose overelaboration ends in frigid failure? Writ-

[d] Cicero (*Ad Atticum* 2.16.2) quotes a different version of this passage (= fr. 768 Radt), and Longinus perhaps adapts it to his own purpose.

[e] These Hellenistic writers were all despised by classicizing critics of the Augustan and later periods. Amphicrates fled from Athens to Seleucia in 86 B.C. Hegesias of Magnesia dates from the third century B.C. Matris of Thebes wrote hymns and encomia. For Hegesias' style, see E. Norden, *Antike Kunstprosa* 134ff.

εἰς τοῦτο τὸ γένος ὀρεγόμενοι μὲν τοῦ περιττοῦ καὶ
πεποιημένου καὶ μάλιστα τοῦ ἡδέος, ἐξοκέλλοντες[1]
δὲ εἰς τὸ ῥωπικὸν καὶ κακόζηλον. τούτῳ παράκειται
τρίτον τι κακίας εἶδος ἐν τοῖς παθητικοῖς, ὅπερ ὁ
Θεόδωρος παρένθυρσον ἐκάλει. ἔστι δὲ πάθος ἄκαιρον καὶ κενὸν ἔνθα μὴ δεῖ πάθους, ἢ ἄμετρον ἔνθα
μετρίου δεῖ. πολλὰ γὰρ ὥσπερ ἐκ μέθης τινὲς εἰς τὰ
μηκέτι τοῦ πράγματος, ἴδια <δ᾽>[2] ἑαυτῶν καὶ σχο-
λικὰ παραφέρονται πάθη, εἶτα πρὸς οὐδὲν πεπονθό-
τας ἀκροατὰς ἀσχημονοῦσιν εἰκότως, ἐξεστηκότες
πρὸς οὐκ ἐξεστηκότας. πλὴν περὶ μὲν τῶν παθητι-
κῶν ἄλλος ἡμῖν ἀπόκειται τόπος.

4. Θατέρου δὲ ὧν εἴπομεν, λέγω δὲ τοῦ ψυχροῦ,
πλήρης ὁ Τίμαιος, ἀνὴρ τὰ μὲν ἄλλα ἱκανὸς καὶ
πρὸς λόγων ἐνίοτε μέγεθος οὐκ ἄφορος, πολυΐστωρ,
ἐπινοητικός, πλὴν ἀλλοτρίων μὲν ἐλεγκτικώτατος
ἁμαρτημάτων, ἀνεπαίσθητος δὲ ἰδίων, ὑπὸ δὲ ἔρωτος τοῦ ξένας νοήσεις ἀεὶ κινεῖν πολλάκις ἐκπίπτων
εἰς τὸ παιδαριωδέστατον. παραθήσομαι δὲ τἀνδρὸς
ἓν ἢ δύο, ἐπειδὴ τὰ πλείω προέλαβεν ὁ Καικίλιος.
ἐπαινῶν ᾽Αλέξανδρον τὸν μέγαν "ὃς τὴν ᾽Ασίαν

---

[1] ἐξοκέλλοντες Wilamowitz, for ἐποκέλλοντες.
[2] <δ᾽> add. Faber.

[a] Probably a rhetorician from Gadara, one of whose pupils
was the emperor Tiberius, and who taught that, so long as the
argumentation of a case was sound, the orator need not hold

ers fall into this fault through trying to be uncommon and exquisite, and above all to please, and founder instead upon the rock of cheap affectation. Closely allied to this is a third kind of fault peculiar to emotional passages, what Theodorus[a] used to call the pseudo-bacchanalian. This is emotion misplaced and pointless where none is needed, or unrestrained where restraint is required. For writers often behave as if they were drunk and give way to outbursts of emotion which the subject no longer warrants, but which are private to themselves and consequently tedious, so that to an audience which feels none of it their behaviour looks unseemly. And naturally so, for while they are in ecstasy, the audience is not. However we have reserved another place in which to treat of emotional subjects.[b]

4. The second fault of which we spoke above is Frigidity, of which there are many examples in Timaeus, in other respects a capable writer and sometimes not at all badly endowed for greatness of style, learned, and full of ideas. Yet while keenly critical of others' faults, he is blind and deaf to his own, and his insatiable passion for starting strange conceits often lands him in the most puerile effects. I will quote only one or two examples from Timaeus,[c] as Caecilius has forestalled me with most of them. In his eulogy of Alexander the Great he speaks

religiously to the traditional arrangement of prooemium, narrative, argument, counterargument, and peroration.

[b] If this refers to the present treatise, and not to a separate work (see Introd.), it must be to a passage now lost.

[c] A Sicilian historian (from Tauromenium), who died c. 260 B.C.; he is adversely criticized by Polybius for inaccuracy and bad taste.

ὅλην" φησίν "ἐν ἐλάττοσι<ν ἔτεσι>[1] παρέλαβεν ἢ
ὅσοις τὸν ὑπὲρ τοῦ πρὸς Πέρσας πολέμου πανηγυρικὸν λόγον Ἰσοκράτους ἔγραψεν." θαυμαστή γε
τοῦ Μακεδόνος ἡ πρὸς τὸν σοφιστὴν σύγκρισις·
δῆλον γάρ, ὦ Τίμαιε, ὡς οἱ Λακεδαιμόνιοι διὰ τοῦτο
πολὺ τοῦ Ἰσοκράτους κατ' ἀνδρείαν ἐλείποντο,
ἐπειδὴ οἱ μὲν τριάκοντα[2] ἔτεσι Μεσσήνην παρέλα-
βον, ὁ δὲ τὸν πανηγυρικὸν ἐν μόνοις δέκα συνετά-
3 ξατο. τοῖς δὲ Ἀθηναίοις ἁλοῦσιν περὶ Σικελίαν τίνα
τρόπον ἐπιφωνεῖ; ὅτι "εἰς τὸν Ἑρμῆν ἀσεβήσαντες
καὶ περικόψαντες αὐτοῦ τὰ ἀγάλματα, διὰ τοῦτ' ἔδω-
καν δίκην οὐχ ἥκιστα δι' ἕνα ἄνδρα, ὃς ἀπὸ τοῦ
παρανομηθέντος διὰ πατέρων ἦν, Ἑρμοκράτη τὸν
Ἕρμωνος." ὥστε θαυμάζειν με, Τερεντιανὲ ἥδιστε,
πῶς οὐ καὶ εἰς Διονύσιον γράφει τὸν τύραννον· "ἐπεὶ
γὰρ εἰς τὸν Δία καὶ τὸν Ἡρακλέα δυσσεβὴς ἐγένετο, διὰ τοῦτ' αὐτὸν Δίων καὶ Ἡρακλείδης τῆς
4 τυραννίδος ἀφείλοντο." <καὶ>[3] τί δεῖ περὶ Τιμαίου
λέγειν, ὅπου γε καὶ οἱ ἥρωες ἐκεῖνοι, Ξενοφῶντα
λέγω καὶ Πλάτωνα, καίτοιγε ἐκ τῆς Σωκράτους ὄντες
παλαίστρας, ὅμως διὰ τὰ οὕτως μικροχαρῆ ποτε
ἑαυτῶν ἐπιλανθάνονται; ὁ μέν γε ἐν τῇ Λακεδαιμονίων γράφει πολιτείᾳ· "ἐκείνων γοῦν[4] ἧττον μὲν ἂν

[1] add. Spengel.

[2] εἴκοσι Faber.

[3] <καὶ> added by early editors.

[4] P has μὲν before γοῦν, but this is incorrect Greek, and is
not in our text of Xenophon (*Resp. Laced.* 3.5).

of "one who subdued the whole of Asia in fewer years than Isocrates took to write his *Panegyric* urging war on Persia."[a] Surely this is an odd comparison of the Macedonian to the sophist, for it is obvious, friend Timaeus, that on this showing Isocrates was a far better man than the Spartans, since they spent thirty years in subduing Messene,[b] while he composed his *Panegyric* in no more than ten! Again, take his final comment on the Athenian prisoners in Sicily: "Having committed sacrilege against Hermes and mutilated his statues they were therefore punished, mainly owing to the action of a single man, who was kin on his father's side to the injured deity, Hermocrates the son of Hermon."[c] This makes me wonder, my dear Terentianus, why he does not write of the tyrant Dionysius that "Having shown impiety towards Zeus and Heracles, he was therefore deprived of his tyranny by Dion and Heracleides."[d] But why speak of Timaeus when those very demi-gods, Xenophon and Plato, for all their training in the school of Socrates, yet sometimes forgot themselves in their fondness for such cheap effects? In his *Constitution of Sparta* Xenophon says, "Certainly you would hear as little speech from these

[a] Isocrates is said to have spent the decade c. 390–380 B.C. working over this famous speech.

[b] The Spartan war of conquest in the eighth century B.C. is usually said to have taken 20 years, but there were later conflicts also. It is unsafe to emend Longinus' figure.

[c] See Plutarch, *Nicias* 1.

[d] The conceit depends on the fact that the oblique cases of *Zeus* are *Dia, Dios, Dii,* so that a pun similar to that on Hermes/Hermocrates is produced.

φωνὴν ἀκούσαις ἢ τῶν λιθίνων, ἧττον δ' ἂν ὄμματα
στρέψαις ἢ τῶν χαλκῶν, αἰδημονεστέρους δ' ἂν
αὐτοὺς ἡγήσαιο καὶ αὐτῶν τῶν ἐν τοῖς ὀφθαλμοῖς
παρθένων." Ἀμφικράτει καὶ οὐ Ξενοφῶντι ἔπρεπε
τὰς ἐν τοῖς ὀφθαλμοῖς ἡμῶν κόρας λέγειν παρθέ-
νους αἰδήμονας· οἷον δὲ Ἡράκλεις τὸ τὰς ἁπάντων
ἑξῆς κόρας αἰσχυντηλὰς εἶναι πεπεῖσθαι, ὅπου
φασὶν οὐδενὶ οὕτως ἐνσημαίνεσθαι τήν τινων ἀναί-
δειαν ὡς ἐν τοῖς ὀφθαλμοῖς· ἰταμὸν "οἰνοβαρές,
5   κυνὸς ὄμματ' ἔχων" φησίν.[1] ὁ μέντοι Τίμαιος, ὡς
φωρίου τινὸς ἐφαπτόμενος, οὐδὲ τοῦτο Ξενοφῶντι τὸ
ψυχρὸν κατέλιπεν. φησὶ γοῦν ἐπὶ τοῦ Ἀγαθοκλέους
κατὰ[2] τὸ τὴν ἀνεψιὰν ἑτέρῳ δεδομένην ἐκ τῶν ἀνα-
καλυπτηρίων ἁρπάσαντα ἀπελθεῖν, "ὃ τίς ἂν ἐποίη-
6   σεν ἐν ὀφθαλμοῖς κόρας, μὴ πόρνας ἔχων;" τί δὲ ὁ
τἆλλα θεῖος Πλάτων; τὰς δέλτους θέλων εἰπεῖν
"γράψαντες" φησίν "ἐν τοῖς ἱεροῖς θήσουσιν κυπα-
ριττίνας μνήμας"· καὶ πάλιν "περὶ δὲ τειχῶν, ὦ
Μέγιλλε, ἐγὼ ξυμφεροίμην ἂν τῇ Σπάρτῃ τὸ καθεύ-
7   δειν ἐᾶν ἐν τῇ γῇ κατακείμενα τὰ τείχη καὶ μὴ
ἐπανίστασθαι." καὶ τὸ Ἡροδότειον οὐ πόρρω, τὸ

---

[1] Kayser deleted ἰταμὸν . . . φησίν. The introduction of the
Homeric parallel is very abrupt.

[2] κατὰ Reiske, for καί.

Spartans as from marble statues, and could as easily catch the eye of a bronze figure; indeed you might well think them as modest as the maidens in their eyes."[a] It would have better suited Amphicrates than Xenophon to speak of the pupils in our eyes as modest maidens. And fancy believing that every single man of them had modest pupils, when they say that people show their immodesty in nothing so much as their eyes! Why, a violent man is called "Heavy with wine, with the eyes of a dog."[b] However, Timaeus, laying hands as it were on stolen goods, could not leave even this frigid conceit to Xenophon. For example, speaking of Agathocles when he carried off his cousin from the unveiling ceremony[c] although she had been given in marriage to another, he says, "Who could have done such a thing, had he not harlots instead of maidens in his eyes?" And what of the otherwise divine Plato? "They will inscribe and store in the temples," he says, "cypress memorials," meaning wooden tablets: and again, "As for walls, Megillus, I would consent with Sparta to let the walls lie slumbering on the ground and never rise again."[d] Herodotus' phrase for fair women

[a] The manuscript tradition of Xenophon, *Resp. Lac.* 3.5 has maidens in their chambers" (τῶν ἐν τοῖς θαλάμοις παρθένων), but Stobaeus (*Flor.* CXLIV.2.23 Hense) has the same reading as Longinus, which involves a pun on the two meanings of κόρη, "girl," and "pupil of the eye" (*pupula*)—a sense presumably derived from the fact that, if you look into someone's pupil closely, you see a doll-like image of yourself.   [b] Achilles to Agamemnon, *Iliad* 1.225.   [c] I.e. on the third day after the marriage, when the bride first appeared unveiled. Agathocles ruled Syracuse, 317–287 B.C.; this story is not mentioned elsewhere.   [d] *Laws* 5.741C, 6.778D, freely quoted.

φάναι τὰς καλὰς γυναῖκας "ἀλγηδόνας ὀφθαλμῶν."
καίτοιγε ἔχει τινὰ παραμυθίαν, οἱ γὰρ παρ' αὐτῷ
ταυτὶ λέγοντές εἰσιν οἱ βάρβαροι καὶ ἐν μέθῃ, ἀλλ'
οὐδ' ἐκ τοιούτων προσώπων διὰ μικροψυχίαν καλὸν
ἀσχημονεῖν πρὸς τὸν αἰῶνα.

5. Ἅπαντα μέντοι τὰ οὕτως ἄσεμνα διὰ μίαν
ἐμφύεται τοῖς λόγοις αἰτίαν, διὰ τὸ περὶ τὰς νοήσεις
καινόσπουδον, περὶ ὃ δὴ μάλιστα κορυβαντιῶσιν οἱ
νῦν. ἀφ' ὧν γὰρ ἡμῖν τἀγαθά, σχεδὸν ἀπ' αὐτῶν
τούτων καὶ τὰ κακὰ γεννᾶσθαι φιλεῖ. ὅθεν ἐπίφορον
εἰς συνταγμάτων κατόρθωσιν τά τε κάλλη τῆς ἑρμηνείας καὶ τὰ ὕψη καὶ πρὸς τούτοις αἱ ἡδοναί, καὶ
αὐτὰ ταῦτα, καθάπερ τῆς ἐπιτυχίας, οὕτως ἀρχαὶ
καὶ ὑποθέσεις καὶ τῶν ἐναντίων καθίστανται. τοιοῦτόν πως καὶ αἱ μεταβολαὶ[1] καὶ ὑπερβολαὶ καὶ τὰ
πληθυντικά· δείξομεν δ' ἐν τοῖς ἔπειτα τὸν κίνδυνον,
ὃν ἔχειν ἐοίκασιν. διόπερ ἀναγκαῖον ἤδη διαπορεῖν
καὶ ὑποτίθεσθαι, δι' ὅτου τρόπου τὰς ἀνακεκραμένας
κακίας τοῖς ὑψηλοῖς ἐκφεύγειν δυνάμεθα.

6. Ἔστι δέ, ὦ φίλος, εἴ τινα περιποιησαίμεθ' ἐν
πρώτοις καθαρὰν τοῦ κατ' ἀλήθειαν ὕψους ἐπιστήμην καὶ ἐπίκρισιν. καίτοι τὸ πρᾶγμα δύσληπτον· ἡ
γὰρ τῶν λόγων κρίσις πολλῆς ἐστι πείρας τελευταῖον ἐπιγέννημα· οὐ μὴν ἀλλ', ὡς εἰπεῖν ἐν παραγ-
γέλματι, ἐντεῦθέν ποθεν ἴσως τὴν διάγνωσιν αὐτῶν
οὐκ ἀδύνατον πορίζεσθαι.

---

[1] μεταφοραὶ Wilamowitz

is not much better: "torments for eyes" he calls them.[a] Yet he has some excuse, for in Herodotus this is said by the barbarians, who are, moreover, in their cups. Yet even in the mouths of such characters as these it is not right to display the triviality of one's mind before an audience of all the ages.

5. However, all these lapses from dignity in literature spring from the same cause, namely that passion for novelty of thought which is the particular craze of the present day. For our virtues and vices spring from much the same sources. And so while beauty of style, sublimity, yes, and charm too, all contribute to successful composition, yet these same things are the source and groundwork no less of failure than of success. And we must say the same, I suppose, about variety of construction, hyperbole, and the use of plurals for singulars. We will show later[b] the danger which they seem to us to involve. We are thus bound at this stage to raise and propose the answer to the question how we can avoid the faults that go so closely with the elevated style.

6. And this, my friend, is the way: first of all to obtain a clear knowledge and appreciation of what is really sublime. But this is not an easy thing to grasp. Judgement in literature is the ultimate fruit of ripe experience. However, if I must speak of precept, it is perhaps not impossible that a true discernment in such matters may be derived from some such considerations as the following.

[a] Herodotus 5.18, in an amusing account of the way the Macedonians entertained the Persian invaders of Greece.

[b] In chapters 23 and 38.

7. Εἰδέναι χρή, φίλτατε, διότι, καθάπερ κἀν τῷ κοινῷ βίῳ οὐδὲν ὑπάρχει μέγα, οὗ τὸ καταφρονεῖν ἐστιν μέγα, οἷον πλοῦτοι τιμαὶ δόξαι τυραννίδες καὶ ὅσα δὴ ἄλλα ἔχει πολὺ τὸ ἔξωθεν προστραγῳδούμενον οὐδ'[1] ἂν τῷ γε φρονίμῳ δόξειεν ἀγαθὰ ὑπερβάλλοντα, ὧν αὐτὸ τὸ περιφρονεῖν ἀγαθὸν οὐ μέτριον—θαυμάζουσι γοῦν τῶν ἐχόντων αὐτὰ μᾶλλον τοὺς δυναμένους ἔχειν καὶ διὰ μεγαλοψυχίαν ὑπερορῶντας—τῇδέ που καὶ ἐπὶ τῶν διηρμένων ἐν ποιήμασι καὶ λόγοις ἐπισκεπτέον, μή τινα μεγέθους φαντασίαν ἔχοι τοιαύτην ᾗ πολὺ πρόσκειται τὸ εἰκῆ προσαναπλαττόμενον, ἀναπτυττόμενα δὲ ἄλλως εὑρίσκοιτο χαῦνα, ὧν τοῦ θαυμάζειν τὸ περιφρονεῖν

2 εὐγενέστερον. φύσει γάρ πως ὑπὸ τἀληθοῦς ὕψους ἐπαίρεταί τε ἡμῶν ἡ ψυχὴ καὶ γαῦρόν τι παράστημα[2] λαμβάνουσα πληροῦται χαρᾶς καὶ μεγα-

3 λαυχίας, ὡς αὐτὴ γεννήσασα ὅπερ ἤκουσεν. ὅταν οὖν ὑπ' ἀνδρὸς ἔμφρονος καὶ ἐμπείρου λόγων πολλάκις ἀκουόμενόν τι πρὸς μεγαλοφροσύνην τὴν ψυχὴν μὴ συνδιατιθῇ μηδ' ἐγκαταλείπῃ τῇ διανοίᾳ πλεῖον τοῦ λεγομένου τὸ ἀναθεωρούμενον, πίπτῃ δ', ἂν αὐτὸ[3] συνεχὲς ἐπισκοπῇς, εἰς ἀπαύξησιν, οὐκ ἂν ἔτ' ἀληθὲς ὕψος εἴη μέχρι μόνης τῆς ἀκοῆς σῳζόμενον. τοῦτο γὰρ τῷ ὄντι μέγα, οὗ πολλὴ μὲν ἡ ἀναθεώρησις, δύσκολος δέ, μᾶλλον δ' ἀδύνατος ἡ κατεξανάστασις, ἰσχυρὰ δὲ ἡ μνήμη καὶ δυσεξάλει-

---

[1] οὐδ' Reiske, for οὐκ.

7. We must realize, dear friend, that as in our every-day life nothing is really great which it is a mark of greatness to despise, I mean, for instance, wealth, position, reputation, sovereignty, and all the other things which possess a very grand exterior, nor would a wise man think things supremely good, contempt for which is itself eminently good—certainly men feel less admiration for those who have these things than for those who could have them but are big enough to slight them—well, so it is with the lofty style in poetry and prose. We must consider whether some of these passages have merely some such outward show of grandeur with a rich layer of casual accretions, and whether, if all this is peeled off, they may not turn out to be empty bombast which it is more noble to despise than to admire. For the true sublime naturally elevates us: uplifted with a sense of proud exaltation, we are filled iwth joy and pride, as if we had ourselves produced the very thing we heard. If, then, a man of sense, well-versed in literature, after hearing a passage several times finds that it does not affect him with a sense of sublimity, and does not leave behind in his mind more food for thought than the words at first suggest, but rather that on consideration it sinks into the bathetic, then it cannot really be the true sublime, if its effect does not outlast the moment of utterance. For what is truly great bears repeated consideration; it is difficult, nay, impossible, to resist its effect; and the memory of it is stubborn and

---

[2] παράστημα Manutius, for ἀνάστημα.
[3] ἂν αὐτὸ Pearce, for ἄνευ τό.

4 πτος. ὅλως δὲ καλὰ νόμιζε ὕψη καὶ ἀληθινὰ τὰ διὰ
παντὸς ἀρέσκοντα καὶ πᾶσιν. ὅταν γὰρ τοῖς ἀπὸ
διαφόρων ἐπιτηδευμάτων βίων ζήλων ἡλικιῶν
λόγων[1] ἕν τι καὶ ταὐτὸν ἅμα περὶ τῶν αὐτῶν ἅπασιν
δοκῇ, τόθ᾽ ἡ ἐξ ἀσυμφώνων ὡς κρίσις καὶ συγκατά-
θεσις τὴν ἐπὶ τῷ θαυμαζομένῳ πίστιν ἰσχυρὰν λαμβάνει καὶ ἀναμφίλεκτον.

8. Ἐπεὶ δὲ πέντε, ὡς ἂν εἴποι τις, πηγαί τινές
εἰσιν αἱ τῆς ὑψηγορίας γονιμώταται, προϋποκειμέ-
νης ὥσπερ ἐδάφους τινὸς κοινοῦ ταῖς πέντε ταύταις
ἰδέαις τῆς ἐν τῷ λέγειν δυνάμεως, ἧς ὅλως χωρὶς
οὐδέν, πρῶτον μὲν καὶ κράτιστον τὸ περὶ τὰς νοήσεις ἁδρεπήβολον, ὡς κἀν τοῖς περὶ Ξενοφῶντος
ὡρισάμεθα· δεύτερον δὲ τὸ σφοδρὸν καὶ ἐνθουσια-
στικὸν πάθος· ἀλλ᾽ αἱ μὲν δύο αὗται τοῦ ὕψους κατὰ
τὸ πλέον αὐθιγενεῖς συστάσεις, αἱ λοιπαὶ δ᾽ ἤδη καὶ
διὰ τέχνης, ἥ τε ποιὰ τῶν σχημάτων πλά-
σις—δισσὰ δέ που ταῦτα, τὰ μὲν νοήσεως, θάτερα
δὲ λέξεως—ἐπὶ δὲ τούτοις ἡ γενναία φράσις, ἧς
μέρη πάλιν ὀνομάτων τε ἐκλογὴ καὶ ἡ τροπικὴ καὶ
πεποιημένη λέξις· πέμπτη δὲ μεγέθους αἰτία καὶ
συγκλείουσα τὰ πρὸ ἑαυτῆς ἅπαντα, ἡ ἐν ἀξιώματι
καὶ διάρσει σύνθεσις· φέρε δὴ τὰ ἐμπεριεχόμενα
καθ᾽ ἑκάστην ἰδέαν τούτων ἐπισκεψώμεθα, τοσοῦτον
προειπόντες, ὅτι τῶν πέντε μορίων ὁ Καικίλιος ἔστιν

---

[1] χρόνων Richards, τρόπων Morus.

indelible. To speak generally, you should consider that to be beautifully and truly sublime which pleases all people at all times. For when men who differ in their pursuits, their lives, their tastes, their ages, their languages,[a] all agree together in holding one and the same view about the same writings, then the unanimous verdict, as it were, of such discordant judges makes our faith in the admired passage strong and indisputable.

8. There are, one may say, some five most productive sources of the sublime in literature, the common groundwork, as it were, of all five being competence in speaking, without which nothing can be done. The first and most powerful is the power of grand conceptions—I have defined this in my book on Xenophon[b]—and the second is the inspiration of vehement emotion. These two constituents of the sublime are for the most part congenital. But the other three come partly from art, namely the proper construction of figures—these being of course of two kinds, figures of thought and figures of speech—and, over and above these, nobility of language, which again may be resolved into choice of words and the use of metaphor and elaborated diction. The fifth cause of grandeur, which gives form to all those already mentioned, is dignified and elevated word-arrangement. Let us then consider all that is involved under each of these heads, merely prefacing this, that Caecilius has omitted

[a] Text unsure: the suggested emendations mean "dates" or "manners."

[b] This book is lost.

2 ἃ παρέλιπεν, ὡς καὶ τὸ πάθος ἀμέλει. ἀλλ᾽ εἰ μὲν ὡς
ἕν τι ταῦτ᾽ ἄμφω, τό τε ὕψος καὶ τὸ παθητικόν, καὶ
ἔδοξεν αὐτῷ πάντη συνυπάρχειν τε ἀλλήλοις καὶ
συμπεφυκέναι, διαμαρτάνει· καὶ γὰρ πάθη τινὰ διε-
στῶτα ὕψους καὶ ταπεινὰ εὑρίσκεται, καθάπερ οἶκτοι
λῦπαι φόβοι, καὶ ἔμπαλιν πολλὰ ὕψη δίχα πάθους,
ὡς πρὸς μυρίοις ἄλλοις καὶ τὰ περὶ τοὺς Ἀλωάδας
τῷ ποιητῇ παρατετολμημένα·

> Ὄσσαν ἐπ᾽ Οὐλύμπῳ μέμασαν θέμεν· αὐτὰρ
>   ἐπ᾽ Ὄσσῃ
> Πήλιον εἰνοσίφυλλον, ἵν᾽ οὐρανὸς ἄμβατος
>   εἴη·

καὶ τὸ τούτοις ἔτι μεῖζον ἐπιφερόμενον

> καί νύ κεν ἐξετέλεσσαν.

3 παρά γε μὴν τοῖς ῥήτορσι τὰ ἐγκώμια καὶ τὰ πομ-
πικὰ καὶ ἐπιδεικτικὰ τὸν μὲν ὄγκον καὶ τὸ ὑψηλὸν ἐξ
ἅπαντος περιέχει, πάθους δὲ χηρεύει κατὰ τὸ πλεῖ-
στον· ὅθεν ἥκιστα τῶν ῥητόρων οἱ περιπαθεῖς ἐγκω-
4 μιαστικοὶ ἢ ἔμπαλιν οἱ ἐπαινετικοὶ περιπαθεῖς. εἰ δ᾽
αὖ πάλιν ἐξ ὅλου μὴ ἐνόμισεν <ὁ>[1] Καικίλιος τὸ
ἐμπαθὲς <εἰς>[2] τὰ ὕψη ποτὲ συντελεῖν καὶ διὰ τοῦτ᾽
οὐχ ἡγήσατο μνήμης ἄξιον, πάνυ διηπάτηται· θαρ-
ρῶν γὰρ ἀφορισαίμην ἄν, ὡς μεγαλήγορον, ὥσπερ
ὑπὸ μανίας τινὸς καὶ πνεύματος ἐνθουσιαστικῶς
ἐπιπνέον[3] καὶ οἱονεὶ φοιβάζον τοὺς λόγους.

9. Οὐ μὴν ἀλλ᾽ ἐπεὶ τὴν κρατίστην μοῖραν ἐπ-

---

[1] <ὁ> add. Manutius.   [2] add. Faber.

some of these five classes, one obvious omission being that of emotion. Now if he thought that sublimity and emotion were the same thing, and that one always essentially involved the other, he is wrong. For one can find emotions that are mean and devoid of sublimity, for instance feelings of pity, grief, and fear. On the other hand, many sublime passages are quite without emotion. Examples are countless: take for instance the poet's daring lies about the Aloadae:[a]

> Ossa then up on Olympus they strove to set, then upon Ossa
> Pelion, ashiver with leaves, to build them a ladder to Heaven;

and the still greater exaggeration that follows,

> And they would have done it as well.

Then again in the orators their eulogies and ceremonial speeches and show pieces always include touches of dignity and sublimity, yet are usually void of emotion. The result is that emotional orators excel least in eulogy, while panegyrists equally lack emotional power. If, on the other hand, it never entered Caecilius' head that emotion sometimes contributes towards sublimity, and he therefore omitted it as undeserving of mention, then great indeed is his mistake. I would confidently lay it down that nothing makes so much for grandeur as genuine emotion in the right place. It inspires the words as it were with a fine frenzy and fills them with divine spirit.

9. Now, since the first, I mean natural, greatness plays

[a] *Odyssey* 11.315.

[3] Morus, for ἐκπνέον.

ἔχει τῶν ἄλλων τὸ πρῶτον, λέγω δὲ τὸ μεγαλοφυές,
χρὴ κἀνταῦθα, καὶ εἰ δωρητὸν τὸ πρᾶγμα μᾶλλον ἢ
κτητόν, ὅμως καθ' ὅσον οἷόν τε τὰς ψυχὰς ἀνατρέ-
2 φειν πρὸς τὰ μεγέθη καὶ ὥσπερ ἐγκύμονας ἀεὶ ποιεῖν γενναίου παραστήματος. τίνα, φήσεις, τρόπον;
γέγραφά που καὶ ἑτέρωθι τὸ τοιοῦτον· ὕψος μεγαλοφροσύνης ἀπήχημα. ὅθεν καὶ φωνῆς δίχα θαυμάζε-
ταί ποτε ψιλὴ καθ' ἑαυτὴν ἔννοια δι' αὐτὸ τὸ μεγα-
λόφρον, ὡς ἡ τοῦ Αἴαντος ἐν Νεκυίᾳ σιωπὴ μέγα
3 καὶ παντὸς ὑψηλότερον λόγου. πρῶτον οὖν τὸ ἐξ οὗ
γίνεται προϋποτίθεσθαι πάντως ἀναγκαῖον, ὡς ἔχειν
δεῖ τὸν ἀληθῆ ῥήτορα μὴ ταπεινὸν φρόνημα καὶ
ἀγεννές. οὐδὲ γὰρ οἷόν τε μικρὰ καὶ δουλοπρεπῆ
φρονοῦντας καὶ ἐπιτηδεύοντας παρ' ὅλον τὸν βίον
θαυμαστόν τι καὶ τοῦ παντὸς αἰῶνος ἐξενεγκεῖν
ἄξιον· μεγάλοι δὲ οἱ λόγοι τούτων κατὰ τὸ εἰκὸς ὧν
4 ἂν ἐμβριθεῖς ὦσιν αἱ ἔννοιαι. ταύτῃ καὶ εἰς τοὺς
μάλιστα φρονηματίας ἐμπίπτει τὰ ὑπερφυᾶ· ὁ γὰρ
τῷ Παρμενίωνι φήσαντι "ἐγὼ μὲν ἠρκέσθην . . .[1]

. . . τὸ ἐπ' οὐρανὸν ἀπὸ γῆς διάστημα· καὶ τοῦτ'
ἂν εἴποι τις οὐ μᾶλλον τῆς Ἔριδος ἢ Ὁμήρου

---

[1] P lost a whole quaternion (8 pages) after ἀδρεπηβόλον
(above, 8.1); but the two outer pages are preserved in copies
made when the damage was less; these however fail us at this
point. P resumes at ἐν δὲ φάει καὶ ὄλεσσον (9.10).

[a] *Odyssey* 11.543–67. Ajax, summoned from Hades, refuses

184

a greater part than all the others, here too, even if it is
rather a gift than an acquired quality, we should still do
our utmost to train our minds into sympathy with what is
noble and, as it were, impregnate them again and again
with lofty thoughts. "How?" you will ask. Well, elsewhere I have written something like this, "Sublimity is the
echo of a noble mind." And so even without being spoken
the bare idea often of itself wins admiration for its inherent grandeur. How grand, for instance, is the silence of
Ajax in the Summoning of the Ghosts,[a] more sublime
than any speech! In the first place, then, it is absolutely
necessary to state whence greatness comes, and to show
that the thought of the genuine orator must be neither
small nor ignoble. For it is impossible that those whose
thoughts and habits all their lives long are petty and
servile should produce anything wonderful, worthy of
immortal life. No, a grand style is the natural product of
those whose ideas are weighty. This is why splendid
remarks come particularly to men of high spirit. Alexander's answer to Parmenio when he said "For my part I had
been content . . ."[b]

[*Six pages are lost here.*]

. . . the distance between earth and heaven. One
might say too that this measured the stature not of Strife

---

to speak to Odysseus, because he is still angry at the award of
Achilles' armour to Odysseus rather than to himself.

[b] The story (told in most of the historians of Alexander: see
e.g. Plutarch, *Alexander* 29), and perhaps derived from Callisthenes, is that Darius offered Alexander territory and one of his
daughters in marriage; Parmenio said "If I were Alexander, I
should have accepted," and Alexander replied "If I were Parmenio, so should I."

5 μέτρον. ᾧ ἀνόμοιόν γε τὸ Ἡσιόδειον ἐπὶ τῆς Ἀχλύος, εἴγε Ἡσιόδου καὶ τὴν Ἀσπίδα θετέον,

> τῆς ἐκ μὲν ῥινῶν μύξαι ῥέον·

οὐ γὰρ δεινὸν ἐποίησε τὸ εἴδωλον, ἀλλὰ μισητόν. ὁ δὲ πῶς μεγεθύνει τὰ δαιμόνια;

> ὅσσον δ' ἠεροειδὲς ἀνὴρ ἴδεν ὀφθαλμοῖσιν,
> ἥμενος ἐν σκοπιῇ, λεύσσων ἐπὶ οἴνοπα πόντον,
> τόσσον ἐπιθρώσκουσι θεῶν ὑψηχέες ἵπποι.

τὴν ὁρμὴν αὐτῶν κοσμικῷ διαστήματι καταμετρεῖ. τίς οὖν οὐκ ἂν εἰκότως διὰ τὴν ὑπερβολὴν τοῦ μεγέθους ἐπιφθέγξαιτο, ὅτι ἂν δὶς ἑξῆς ὀφορμήσωσιν οἱ τῶν θεῶν ἵπποι, οὐκέθ' εὑρήσουσιν ἐν κόσμῳ τόπον;

6 ὑπερφυᾶ καὶ τὰ ἐπὶ τῆς θεομαχίας φαντάσματα·

> ἀμφὶ δὲ σάλπιγξεν μέγας οὐρανὸς Οὔλυμπός
> τε.
>
> ἔδδεισεν δ' ὑπένερθεν ἄναξ ἐνέρων Ἀϊδωνεύς,
> δείσας δ' ἐκ θρόνου ἆλτο καὶ ἴαχε, μή οἱ
> ἔπειτα

---

[a] Evidently *Iliad* 4.442:

> Small is the crest that she rears at the first, but behold her thereafter
> Planting her head in the skies, while she treads with her feet on the earth.

so much as of Homer.[a] Quite unlike this is Hesiod's description of Gloom, if indeed we are right in adding the *Shield* to the list of Hesiod's works:[b]

> Mucus from her nostrils was running.

He has made the image not terrible, but repulsive. But see how Homer magnifies the powers of heaven:

> Far as a man can see with his eyes in the shadowy
> distance,
> Keeping his watch on a hilltop, agaze o'er the wine-
> dark ocean,
> So far leap at a bound the high-neighing horses of
> heaven.[c]

He uses a cosmic interval to measure their stride. So supreme is the grandeur of this, one might well say that if the horses of heaven take two consecutive strides there will then be no place found for them in the world. Marvellous too is the imaginative picture of his Battle of the Gods:

> Blared round about like a trumpet the firmament
> vast and Olympus;
> Shuddering down in the depths, the king of the
> dead, Aïdoneus,

[b] *Shield of Heracles* 267. Aristophanes of Byzantium was among the ancient scholars who regarded the *Shield* as perhaps not Hesiod's, but Apollonius and others took it to be genuine.
[c] *Iliad* 5.770–2.

γαῖαν ἀναρρήξειε Ποσειδάων ἐνοσίχθων,
οἰκία δὲ θνητοῖσι καὶ ἀθανάτοισι φανείη,
σμερδαλέ᾽ εὐρώεντα, τά τε στυγέουσι θεοί περ.

ἐπιβλέπεις, ἑταῖρε, ὡς ἀναρρηγνυμένης μὲν ἐκ
βάθρων γῆς, αὐτοῦ δὲ γυμνουμένου ταρτάρου, ἀνα-
τροπὴν δὲ ὅλου καὶ διάστασιν τοῦ κόσμου λαμβά-
νοντος, πάνθ᾽ ἅμα, οὐρανὸς ᾅδης, τὰ θνητὰ τὰ ἀθά-
νατα, ἅμα τῇ τότε συμπολεμεῖ καὶ συγκινδυνεύει
7 μάχῃ; ἀλλὰ ταῦτα φοβερὰ μέν, πλὴν ἄλλως, εἰ μὴ
κατ᾽ ἀλληγορίαν λαμβάνοιτο, παντάπασιν ἄθεα καὶ
οὐ σῴζοντα τὸ πρέπον. Ὅμηρος γάρ μοι δοκεῖ
παραδιδοὺς τραύματα θεῶν στάσεις τιμωρίας
δάκρυα δεσμὰ πάθη πάμφυρτα τοὺς μὲν ἐπὶ τῶν
Ἰλιακῶν ἀνθρώπους ὅσον ἐπὶ τῇ δυνάμει θεοὺς
πεοιηκέναι, τοὺς θεοὺς δὲ ἀνθρώπους. ἀλλ᾽ ἡμῖν μὲν
δυσδαιμονοῦσιν ἀπόκειται λιμὴν κακῶν ὁ θάνατος,
τῶν θεῶν δ᾽ οὐ τὴν φύσιν, ἀλλὰ τὴν ἀτυχίαν ἐποίη-
8 σεν αἰώνιον. πολὺ δὲ τῶν περὶ τὴν θεομαχίαν
ἀμείνω τὰ ὅσα ἄχραντόν τι καὶ μέγα τὸ δαιμόνιον
ὡς ἀληθῶς καὶ ἄκρατον παρίστησιν, οἷα (πολλοῖς
δὲ πρὸ ἡμῶν ὁ τόπος ἐξείργασται) τὰ ἐπὶ τοῦ
Ποσειδῶνος·

τρέμε δ᾽ οὔρεα μακρὰ καὶ ὕλη
καὶ κορυφαὶ Τρώων τε πόλις καὶ νῆες Ἀχαιῶν

---

[a] A conflation of *Iliad* 21.388 and 20.61–5.

[b] A proverbial image, cf. (e.g.) [Plutarch] *Consolation to Apollonius* 10, Epictetus 4.10.27, Seneca, *Agamemnon* 592 (with R. J. Tarrant's note).

> Sprang from his throne with a shuddering cry, for
>   fear the earthshaker, Poseidon,
> Might soon splinter asunder the earth, and his
>   mansions lie open,
> Clear to the eyes of immortals and mortals alike all
>   uncovered,
> Grim and dreary and dank, which the very gods see
>   with abhorrence.[a]

You see, friend, how the earth is split to its foundations, hell itself laid bare, the whole universe sundered and turned upside down; and meanwhile everything, heaven and hell, mortal and immortal alike, shares in the conflict and danger of that battle. Terrible as these passages are, they are utterly irreligious and breach the canons of propriety unless one takes them allegorically. I feel indeed that in recording as he does the wounding of the gods, their quarrels, vengeance, tears, imprisonment, and all their manifold passions Homer has done his best to make the men in the *Iliad* gods and the gods men. Yet, if we mortals are unhappy, death is the "harbour from our troubles,"[b] whereas Homer has given the gods not only immortal natures but immortal sorrows. The Battle of the Gods, however, is far surpassed by those passages which represent the divine nature as truly uncontaminated, majestic, and pure. Take, for instance, the lines about Poseidon, though they have been treated fully enough by others before us:

> Trembled the woods, and trembled the long-lying
>   ranges
> Yes, and the peaks and the city of Troy and the
>   ships of Achaia

ποσσὶν ὑπ᾽ ἀθανάτοισι Ποσειδάωνος ἰόντος.
βῆ δ᾽ ἐλάαν ἐπὶ κύματ᾽, ἄταλλε δὲ κήτε᾽ ὑπ᾽
αὐτοῦ
πάντοθεν ἐκ κευθμῶν, οὐδ᾽ ἠγνοίησεν ἄνακτα·
γηθοσύνῃ δὲ θάλασσα διίστατο, τοὶ δὲ
πέτοντο.

9   ταύτῃ καὶ ὁ τῶν Ἰουδαίων θεσμοθέτης, οὐχ ὁ τυχὼν
ἀνήρ, ἐπειδὴ τὴν τοῦ θείου δύναμιν κατὰ τὴν ἀξίαν
ἐχώρησε κἀξέφηνεν, εὐθὺς ἐν τῇ εἰσβολῇ γράψας
τῶν νόμων "εἶπεν ὁ θεός," φησί· τί; "γενέσθω φῶς,
καὶ ἐγένετο· γενέσθω γῆ, καὶ ἐγένετο."

10   Οὐκ ὀχληρὸς ἂν ἴσως, ἑταῖρε, δόξαιμι, ἐν ἔτι τοῦ
ποιητοῦ καὶ τῶν ἀνθρωπίνων παραθέμενος τοῦ
μαθεῖν χάριν, ὡς εἰς τὰ ἡρωϊκὰ μεγέθη συνεμβαί-
νειν ἐθίζει. ἀχλὺς ἄφνω καὶ νὺξ ἄπορος αὐτῷ τὴν
τῶν Ἑλλήνων ἐπέχει μάχην· ἔνθα δὴ ὁ Αἴας ἀμηχα-
νῶν

"Ζεῦ πάτερ," φησίν, "ἀλλὰ σὺ ῥῦσαι ὑπ᾽
ἠέρος οἵας Ἀχαιῶν,
ποίησον δ᾽ αἴθρην, δὸς δ᾽ ὀφθαλμοῖσιν
ἰδέσθαι·
ἐν δὲ φάει καὶ ὄλεσσον."

---

[a] Another conflation: *Iliad* 13.18, 20.60, 13.19, 27–9. In view of Longinus' comment, the passage was perhaps put together by earlier critics, and is not simply a confused quotation from memory.

[b] This loose quotation of *Genesis* 1.3–9 has often been suspected of being an interpolation, and indeed the argument runs on without it perfectly well. But there is no reason why Longinus

190

Under the feet immortal and the oncoming march
    of Poseidon.
He set him to drive o'er the swell of the sea, and
    the whales at his coming
Capering leapt from the deep and greeted the
    voice of their master.
Then the sea parted her waves for joy, and they
    flew on the journey.[a]

Soo, too, the lawgiver of the Jews, no ordinary man, having formed a worthy conception of divine power and given expression to it, writes at the very beginning of his *Laws*: "God said"—what? 'let there be light,' and there was light, 'Let there be earth,' and there was earth."[b]

Perhaps you will not think me boring, my friend, if I insert here another passage from the poet, one that treats of human affairs, to show you his habit of entering into the sublimity of his heroic theme. Darkness and helpless night suddenly descend upon his Greek army. At his wits' end Ajax cries:

Zeus Father, rescue from out of the mist the sons of
    Achaia,
Brighten the heaven with sunshine, grant us the
    sight of our eyes.
Just so it be in daylight, destroy us.[c]

should not have known it; and the tradition that Caecilius may have been a Jew suggests a possible source. The syntax of the sentence is controversial; see now Mazzucchi, pp. 172–4. For the considerable influence of the passage in the eighteenth century, see esp. Boileau, *Réflexions sur le Sublime X*, and Robert Louth's Oxford lectures *De sacra poesi Hebraeorum* (1753).

[c] *Iliad* 17.645–7.

ἔστιν ὡς ἀληθῶς τὸ πάθος Αἴαντος, οὐ γὰρ ζῆν
εὔχεται (ἦν γὰρ τὸ αἴτημα τοῦ ἥρωος ταπεινότερον),
ἀλλ' ἐπειδὴ ἐν ἀπράκτῳ σκότει τὴν ἀνδρείαν εἰς
οὐδὲν γενναῖον εἶχε διαθέσθαι, διὰ ταῦτ' ἀγανακτῶν
ὅτι πρὸς τὴν μάχην ἀργεῖ, φῶς ὅτι τάχιστα αἰτεῖται,
ὡς πάντως τῆς ἀρετῆς εὑρήσων ἐντάφιον ἄξιον, κἂν
11   αὐτῷ Ζεὺς ἀντιτάττηται. ἀλλὰ γὰρ Ὅμηρος μὲν
ἐνθάδε οὔριος συνεμπνεῖ τοῖς ἀγῶσιν καὶ οὐκ ἄλλο
τι αὐτὸς πέπονθεν ἢ

> μαίνεται, ὡς ὅτ' Ἄρης ἐγχέσπαλος ἢ ὀλοὸν
> πῦρ
> οὔρεσι μαίνηται, βαθέης ἐν τάρφεσιν ὕλης,
> ἀφλοισμὸς δὲ περὶ στόμα γίγνεται·

δείκνυσι δ' ὅμως διὰ τῆς Ὀδυσσείας (καὶ γὰρ ταῦτα
πολλῶν ἕνεκα προσεπιθεωρητέον), ὅτι μεγάλης
φύσεως ὑποφερομένης ἤδη ἴδιόν ἐστιν ἐν γήρᾳ τὸ
12   φιλόμυθον. δῆλος γὰρ ἐκ πολλῶν τε ἄλλων συντε-
θεικὼς ταύτην δευτέραν τὴν ὑπόθεσιν, ἀτὰρ δὴ κἀκ
τοῦ λείψανα τῶν Ἰλιακῶν παθημάτων διὰ τῆς
Ὀδυσσείας ὡς ἐπεισόδιά τινα[1] προσεπεισφέρειν καὶ
νὴ Δί' ἐκ τοῦ τὰς ὀλοφύρσεις καὶ τοὺς οἴκτους ὡς
πάλαι που προεγνωσμένους[2] τοῖς ἥρωσιν ἐνταῦθα
προσαποδιδόναι· οὐ γὰρ ἀλλ' ἢ τῆς Ἰλιάδος ἐπί-
λογός ἐστιν ἡ Ὀδυσσεια·

---

[1] The manuscripts here add τοῦ Τρωϊκοῦ πολέμου, but these
words spoil the sense, and are perhaps a gloss on τῶν Ἰλιακῶν
παθημάτων.

These are the true feelings of an Ajax. He does not plead for his life: such a prayer would demean the hero: but since the disabling darkness robbed his courage of all noble use, therefore, distressed to be idle in battle, he prays for light on the instant, hoping thus at the worst to find a burial worthy of his courage, even though Zeus be ranged against him. Here indeed the battle is blown along by the force of Homer's writing, and he himself

> Stormily raves, as the spear-wielding War-god, or
> Fire, the destroyer,
> Stormily raves on the hills in the deep-lying thick-
> ets of woodland;
> Fringed are his lips with the foam-froth.[a]

Yet throughout the *Odyssey*, which for many reasons we must not exclude from our consideration, Homer shows that, as genius ebbs, it is the love of storytelling that characterizes old age. There are indeed many indications that he composed this tale after the *Iliad*, for example, throughout the *Odyssey* he introduces as episodes remnants of the adventures at Ilium; yes, and does he not in this poem render to his heroes their meed of lamentation as if it were something long known? In fact the *Odyssey* is simply an epilogue to the *Iliad*:

[a] *Iliad* 15.605.

---

[2] προεγνωσμένοις Reiske (i.e. it is the heroes, not the lamentations, which are "long known").

ἔνθα μὲν Αἴας κεῖται ἀρήϊος, ἔνθα δ᾽
Ἀχιλλεύς,
ἔνθα δὲ Πάτροκλος, θεόφιν μήστωρ
ἀτάλαντος,
ἔνθα δ᾽ ἐμὸς φίλος υἱός.

13 ἀπὸ δὲ τῆς αὐτῆς αἰτίας, οἶμαι, τῆς μὲν Ἰλιάδος
γραφομένης ἐν ἀκμῇ πνεύματος ὅλον τὸ σωμάτιον
δραματικὸν ὑπεστήσατο καὶ ἐναγώνιον, τῆς δὲ
Ὀδυσσείας τὸ πλέον διηγηματικόν, ὅπερ ἴδιον
γήρως. ὅθεν ἐν τῇ Ὀδυσσείᾳ παρεικάσαι τις ἂν
καταδυομένῳ τὸν Ὅμηρον ἡλίῳ, οὗ δίχα τῆς σφο-
δρότητος παραμένει τὸ μέγεθος. οὐ γὰρ ἔτι τοῖς
Ἰλιακοῖς ἐκείνοις ποιήμασιν ἴσον ἐνταῦθα σῴζει τὸν
τόνον, οὐδ᾽ ἐξωμαλισμένα τὰ ὕψη καὶ ἱζήματα
μηδαμοῦ λαμβάνοντα, οὐδὲ τὴν πρόχυσιν ὁμοίαν
τῶν ἐπαλλήλων παθῶν, οὐδὲ τὸ ἀγχίστροφον καὶ
πολιτικὸν καὶ ταῖς ἐκ τῆς ἀληθείας φαντασίαις
καταπεπυκνωμένον, ἀλλ᾽ οἷον ὑποχωροῦντος εἰς ἑαυτὸν Ὠκεανοῦ καὶ περὶ τὰ ἴδια μέτρα ἡμερουμένου[1]
τὸ λοιπὸν φαίνονται τοῦ μεγέθους ἀμπώτιδες κἂν
14 τοῖς μυθώδεσι καὶ ἀπίστοις πλάνος. λέγων δὲ ταῦτ᾽
οὐκ ἐπιλέλησμαι τῶν ἐν τῇ Ὀδυσσείᾳ χειμώνων καὶ
τῶν περὶ τὸν Κύκλωπα καί τινων ἄλλων, ἀλλὰ
γῆρας διηγοῦμαι, γῆρας δ᾽ ὅμως Ὁμήρου· πλὴν ἐν

---

[1] So John Price (a seventeenth-century scholar, professor at
Pisa: quoted by Toup) for P's ἐρημουμένου ("made desolate").

There then Ajax lies, great warrior; there lies
    Achilles;
There, too, Patroclus lies, the peer of the gods in
    counsel;
There, too, my own dear son.[a]

It was, I imagine, for the same reason that, writing the
Iliad in the heyday of his genius he made the whole piece
lively with dramatic action, whereas in the *Odyssey* narrative predominates, the characteristic of old age. So in the
Odyssey one may liken Homer to the setting sun; the
grandeur remains without the intensity. For no longer
does he preserve the sustained energy of the great *Iliad*
lays, the consistent sublimity which never sinks into flat-
ness, the flood of moving incidents in quick succession,
the versatile rapidity and actuality, dense with images
drawn from real life. It is rather as though the Ocean had
retreated into itself and lay quiet within its own confines.
Henceforth we see the ebbing tide of Homer's greatness,
as he wanders in the realm of the fabulous and incredible.
In saying this I have not forgotten the storms in the
Odyssey and such incidents as that of the Cyclops—I am
describing old age, but the old age of a Homer— yet the

[a] *Odyssey* 3.109–11. Both opinions about the order of *Iliad*
and *Odyssey* were held in antiquity: Seneca (*De brevitate vitae*
13) regards it as a typical example of the useless questions raised
by literary scholars.

Other possibilities include Toup's ἠπειρουμένου ("becoming dry
land") and, e.g., ἠρέμα κεχυμένου ("quietly flowing").

ἅπασι τούτοις ἑξῆς τοῦ πρακτικοῦ κρατεῖ τὸ μυθικόν.

Παρεξέβην δ᾽ εἰς ταῦθ᾽, ὡς ἔφην, ἵνα δείξαιμι ὡς εἰς λῆρον ἐνίοτε ῥᾷστον κατὰ τὴν ἀπακμὴν[1] τὰ μεγαλοφυῆ παρατρέπεται, οἷα τὰ περὶ τὸν ἀσκὸν καὶ τοὺς ἐκ Κίρκης συομορφουμένους, οὓς ὁ Ζωΐλος ἔφη χοιρίδια κλαίοντα, καὶ τὸν ὑπὸ τῶν πελειάδων ὡς νεοσσὸν παρατρεφόμενον Δία καὶ τὸν ἐπὶ τοῦ ναυαγίου δέχ᾽ ἡμέρας ἄσιτον τά τε περὶ τὴν μνη- στηροφονίαν ἀπίθανα. τί γὰρ ἂν ἄλλο φήσαιμεν ταῦτα ἢ τῷ ὄντι τοῦ Διὸς ἐνύπνια;

15 Δευτέρου δὲ εἵνεκα προσιστορείσθω τὰ κατὰ τὴν Ὀδύσσειαν, ὅπως ᾖ σοι γνώριμον, ὡς ἡ ἀπακμὴ τοῦ πάθους ἐν τοῖς μεγάλοις συγγραφεῦσι καὶ ποιηταῖς εἰς ἦθος ἐκλύεται. τοιαῦτα γάρ που τὰ περὶ τὴν τοῦ Ὀδυσσέως ἠθικῶς αὐτῷ βιολογούμενα οἰκίαν, οἱονεὶ κωμῳδία τίς ἐστιν ἠθολογουμένη.

10. Φέρε νῦν, εἴ τι καὶ ἕτερον ἔχοιμεν ὑψηλοὺς ποιεῖν τοὺς λόγους δυνάμενον, ἐπισκεψώμεθα. οὐκοῦν ἐπειδὴ πᾶσι τοῖς πράγμασι φύσει συνεδρεύει τινὰ μόρια ταῖς ὕλαις συνυπάρχοντα, ἐξ ἀνάγκης γένοιτ᾽ ἂν ἡμῖν ὕψους αἴτιον τὸ τῶν ἐμφερομένων[2]

---

[1] Manutius, for P's ἀκμήν.
[2] So Toll for P's ἐκφερομένων.

---

[a] Aeolus imprisoned the winds in a wineskin: *Odyssey* 10.19–22.

fact is that in every one of these passages the mythical element predominates over the real.

I have been led into this digression to show you, as I said, that great genius with the decline of vigour often lapses very easily into nonsense—there is the story of the wineskin[a] and the men whom Circe turned into swine[b]—Zoilus called them "porkers in tears"—there is the nurturing of Zeus like a nestling by the doves,[c] Odysseus' ten days without food on the wrecked ship,[d] and the incredible story of the suitors' slaying.[e] Can one call these things anything but veritable dreams of Zeus?[f]

There is another justification for our considering the *Odyssey* as well as the *Iliad*. I wanted you to realize how, in great writers and poets, declining emotional power passes into character portrayals. For instance, his character sketches of the daily life in Odysseus' household constitute a sort of comedy of character.

10. Well, then, let us see whether we can find anything else that can make style sublime. Since with all things there are associated certain elements, inherent in their substance, it follows of necessity that we shall find

[b] *Odyssey* 10.237. Zoilus of Amphipolis nicknamed *Homeromastix*, Scourge of Homer—was a fourth-century sophist and moralist who criticized improbable and inappropriate features in the epic.

[c] Zeus supplied with ambrosia by doves: *Odyssey* 12.62.

[d] *Odyssey* 12.447.

[e] *Odyssey* 22.

[f] An obscure phrase, probably suggesting that, Homer being Zeus of poets (cf. Quintilian 10.1.46), he sometimes dozes and dreams (*bonus dormitat Homerus*, Horace, *Ars Poetica* 359).

ἐκλέγειν ἀεὶ τὰ καιριώτατα καὶ ταῦτα τῇ πρὸς
ἄλληλα ἐπισυνθέσει καθάπερ ἕν τι σῶμα ποιεῖν
δύνασθαι· ὁ[1] μὲν γὰρ τῇ ἐκλογῇ τὸν ἀκροατὴν τῶν
λημμάτων, ὁ[1] δὲ τῇ πυκνώσει τῶν ἐκλελεγμένων
προσάγεται. οἷον ἡ Σαπφὼ τὰ συμβαίνοντα ταῖς
ἐρωτικαῖς μανίαις παθήματα ἐκ τῶν παρεπομένων
καὶ ἐκ τῆς ἀληθείας αὐτῆς ἑκάστοτε λαμβάνει. ποῦ
δὲ τὴν ἀρετὴν ἀποδείκνυται; ὅτε τὰ ἄκρα αὐτῶν καὶ
ὑπερτεταμένα δεινὴ καὶ ἐκλέξαι καὶ εἰς ἄλληλα συν-
δῆσαι.

2   φαίνεταί μοι κῆνος ἴσος θέοισιν
    ἔμμεν' ὤνηρ, ὅττις ἐνάντιός τοι
    ἰζάνει καὶ πλάσιον ἆδυ φωνεί-
        σας ὑπακούει

    καὶ γελαίσας ἰμερόεν, τό μ' ἦ μὰν
    καρδίαν ἐν στήθεσιν ἐπτόαισεν.
    ὡς γὰρ <ἐς> σ' ἴδω βρόχε' ὥς με φώνας
        οὐδὲν ἔτ' εἴκει·

    ἀλλὰ κὰμ μὲν γλῶσσα ἔαγε· λέπτον δ'
    αὐτίκα χρῷ πῦρ ὑποδεδρόμακεν
    ὀππάτεσσι δ' οὐδὲν ὄρημμ', ἐπιρόμ-
        βεισι δ' ἄκουαι·

    ἀ δέ μ' ἴδρως[2] κακχέεται, τρόμος δὲ
    παῖσαν ἄγρει, χλωροτέρα δὲ ποίας
    ἔμμι· τεθνάκην δ' ὀλίγω 'πιδεύης
        φαίνομ' <ἐμαυτᾷ>·

    ἀλλὰ πᾶν τόλματον, ἐπεὶ †καὶ πένητα†[3]

one factor of sublimity in a consistently happy choice of these constituent elements, and in the power of combining them together as it were into an organic whole. The first procedure attracts the reader by the selection of ideas, the second by the density of those selected. Sappho, for instance, never fails to take the emotions incident to the passion of love from its attendant symptoms and from real life. And wherein does she show her excellence? In the skill with which she selects and combines the most striking and intense of those symptoms.

> I think him God's peer that sits near you face to
>   face, and listens to your sweet speech and
>   lovely laughter.
> It's this that makes my heart flutter in my breast. If
>   I see you but for a little, my voice comes no
>   more and my tongue is broken.
> At once a delicate flame runs through my limbs; I
>   see nothing with my eyes, and my ears thun-
>   der.
> The sweat pours down. shivers grip me all over. I
>   am grown paler than grass, and seem to
>   myself to be very near to death.
> But all must be endured, since . . .

ᵃ Sappho fr. 31, in D. A. Campbell (ed.), *Greek Lyric* I (Loeb Classical Library).

---

[1] So Pearce for P's ὁ in both places.
[2] P has ψυχρὸς after ἱδρῶς (so accented).
[3] We have not sought to reproduce P's text here in detail.

3 οὐ θαυμάζεις, ὡς, ὑπ<ὸ τὸ>¹ αὐτὸ τὴν ψυχὴν τὸ
σῶμα τὰς ἀκοὰς τὴν γλῶσσαν τὰς ὄψεις τὴν χρόαν,
πάνθ᾽ ὡς ἀλλότρια διοιχόμενα ἐπιζητεῖ καὶ καθ᾽
ὑπεναντιώσεις ἅμα ψύχεται κάεται, ἀλογιστεῖ φρο-
νεῖ [ἢ γὰρ φοβεῖται ἢ παρ᾽ ὀλίγον τέθνηκεν]² ἵνα
μὴ ἕν τι περὶ αὐτὴν πάθος φαίνηται, παθῶν δὲ σύνοδος. πάντα μὲν τοιαῦτα γίνεται περὶ τοὺς ἐρῶντας,
ἡ λῆψις δ᾽ ὡς ἔφην τῶν ἄκρων καὶ ἡ εἰς ταὐτὸ συν-
αίρεσις ἀπειργάσατο τὴν ἐξοχήν. ὅνπερ οἶμαι καὶ
ἐπὶ τῶν χειμώνων τρόπον ὁ ποιητὴς ἐκλαμβάνει τῶν
4 παρακοκουθούντων τὰ χαλεπώτατα. ὁ μὲν γὰρ τὰ
Ἀριμάσπεια ποιήσας ἐκεῖνα οἴεται δεινά·

θαῦμ᾽ ἡμῖν καὶ τοῦτο μέγα φρεσὶν ἡμετέρῃσιν.
ἄνδρες ὕδωρ ναίουσιν ἀπὸ χθονὸς ἐν πελάγεσσι·
δύστηνοί τινές εἰσιν, ἔχουσι γὰρ ἔργα πονηρά,
ὄμματ᾽ ἐν ἄστροισι, ψυχὴν δ᾽ ἐνὶ πόντῳ ἔχουσιν.
ἦ που πολλὰ θεοῖσι φίλας ἀνὰ χεῖρας ἔχοντες
εὔχονται σπλάγχνοισι κακῶς ἀναβαλλομένοισι.

5 παντὶ οἶμαι δῆλον, ὡς πλέον ἄνθος ἔχει τὰ λεγόμενα
ἢ δέος. ὁ δὲ Ὅμηρος πῶς; ἓν γὰρ ἀπὸ πολλῶν

---

¹ Toll: P has ὑπ᾽ αὐτὸ.
² [ἢ ... τέθνηκεν] ("she is either afraid or at the point of
death") deleted by Weiske. Fyfe conjectured ἢ γὰρ φοιβᾶται ἢ
... τέθνηκεν ("she who is at the point of death is surely beside
herself").

Is it not wonderful how she summons at the same time, soul, body, hearing, tongue, sight, skin, all as though they had wandered off apart from herself? She feels contradictory sensations, freezes, burns, raves, reasons, so that she displays not a single emotion, but a whole congeries of emotions. Lovers show all such symptoms, but what gives supreme merit to her art is, as I said, the skill with which she takes up the most striking and combines them into a single whole. It is, I fancy, much in the same way that the poet in describing storms picks out the most alarming circumstances. The author of the *Arimaspeia*,[a] to be sure, thinks these lines awe-inspiring:

> Here is another thing also that fills us with feelings of wonder,
> Men that dwell on the water, away from the earth, on the ocean.
> Sorrowful wretches they are, and theirs is a grievous employment:
> Fixing their eyes on the stars, their lives they entrust to the waters.
> Often, I think, to the gods they lift up their hands and they pray,
> Ever their innermost parts are terribly tossed to and fro.

Anyone can see, I fancy, that this is more elegant than awe-inspiring. But how does Homer do it? Let us take

[a] Aristeas of Proconnesus (see J. D. P. Bolton, *Aristeas of Proconnesus*, Oxford 1962, 8–15) wrote an epic description of the peoples of the far North: Herodotus (4.27) interprets *Arimaspi* as derived from Scythian words meaning one-eyed. This passage is fr. 1 Kinkel, fr. 7 Bolton, fr. 11 Bernabé.

λεγέσθω·

> ἐν δ' ἔπεσ', ὡς ὅτε κῦμα θοῇ ἐν νηῒ πέσῃσι
> λάβρον ὑπαὶ νεφέων ἀνεμοτρεφές, ἡ δέ τε
> πᾶσα
> ἄχνῃ ὑπεκρύφθη, ἀνέμοιο δὲ δεινὸς ἀήτης
> ἱστίῳ ἐμβρέμεται, τρομέουσι δέ τε φρένα
> ναῦται
> δειδιότες· τυτθὸν γὰρ ὑπὲκ θανάτοιο φέρονται.

6 ἐπεχείρησεν καὶ ὁ Ἄρατος τὸ αὐτὸ τοῦτο μετενεγκεῖν·

> ὀλίγον δὲ διὰ ξύλον ἄϊδ' ἐρύκει·

πλὴν μικρὸν αὐτὸ καὶ γλαφυρὸν ἐποίησεν ἀντὶ φοβεροῦ· ἔτι δὲ παρώρισε τὸν κίνδυνον εἰπών "ξύλον ἄϊδ' ἐρύκει[1]." οὐκοῦν ἀπείργει·[2] ὁ δὲ ποιητὴς οὐκ εἰς ἅπαξ παρορίζει τὸ δεινόν, ἀλλὰ τοὺς ἀεὶ καὶ μονονουχὶ κατὰ πᾶν κῦμα πολλάκις ἀπολλυμένους εἰκονογραφεῖ. καὶ μὴν τὰς προθέσεις ἀσυνθέτους οὔσας συναναγκάσας παρὰ φύσιν καὶ εἰς ἀλλήλας συμβιασάμενος [ὑπὲκ θανάτοιο][3] τῷ μὲν συνεμπίπτοντι πάθει τὸ ἔπος ὁμοίως ἐβασάνισεν, τῇ δὲ τοῦ ἔπους συνθλίψει τὸ πάθος ἄκρως ἀπεπλάσατο

---

[1] Manutius: P has ἀπείργει.

[2] οὐκοῦν ἀπείργει (omitted by Robortello) may be a gloss on ἐρύκει (so Ruhnken, Mazzucchi).

[3] [ὑπὲκ θανάτοιο] deleted by "G.S.A." (1811).

one example of many:

> He fell on the host as a wave of the sea on a hurry-
>   ing vessel,
> Rising up under the clouds, a boisterous son of the
>   storm-wind.
> The good ship is lost in the shroud of the foam, and
>   the breath of the tempest
> Terribly roars in the sails; and in their heart trem-
>   ble the sailors,
> By the breadth of a hand swept out from under the
>   jaws of destruction.[a]

Aratus, too, tried to adapt this same idea:

> Only the tiniest plank now bars them from bitter
>   destruction.[b]

But he has demeaned the idea and made it pretty instead of awe-inspiring. Moreover, he dismisses the danger when he says, "The plank bars them from destruction." Why then, it keeps it off. Homer, on the other hand, instead of dismissing the danger once and for all, depicts the sailors as being all the time, again and again, with every wave on the very brink of death. Moreover, by forcing into an abnormal union prepositions not usually compounded[c] he has tortured his language into conformity with the impending disaster, magnificently figured the disaster by the compression of his language, and

---

[a] *Iliad* 15.624–8.
[b] Aratus, *Phaenomena* 299.
[c] I.e. ὑπέκ is a compound of ὑπό ('under') and ἐκ ('from').

καὶ μόνον οὐκ ἐνετύπωσεν τῇ λέξει τοῦ κινδύνου τὸ
7 ἰδίωμα "ὑπὲκ θανάτοιο φέρονται." οὐκ ἄλλως ὁ
Ἀρχίλοχος ἐπὶ τοῦ ναυαγίου, καὶ ἐπὶ τῇ προσαγγε-
λίᾳ ὁ Δημοσθένης· "ἑσπέρα μὲν γὰρ ἦν" φησίν.
ἀλλὰ τὰς ἐξοχὰς ὡς <ἂν>[1] εἴποι τις ἀριστίνδην
ἐκκαθήραντες ἐπισυνέθηκαν, οὐδὲν φλοιῶδες ἢ
ἄσεμνον ἢ σχολικὸν ἐγκατατάττοντες διὰ μέσου.
λυμαίνεται γὰρ ταῦτα τὸ ὅλον, ὡσανεὶ ψύγματα ἢ
ἀραιώματα ἐμποιοῦντα <εἰς>[2] μεγέθη συνοικοδομούμενα[3] τῇ πρὸς ἄλληλα σχέσει συντετειχισμένα.

11. Σύνεδρός ἐστι ταῖς προεκκειμέναις ἀρετὴ καὶ
ἣν καλοῦσιν αὔξησιν, ὅταν δεχομένων τῶν πραγμάτων καὶ ἀγώνων κατὰ περιόδους ἀρχάς τε πολλὰς
καὶ ἀναπαύλας ἕτερα ἑτέροις ἐπεισκυκλούμενα
2 μεγέθη συνεχῶς ἐπεισάγηται κατὰ ἐπίτασιν.[4] τοῦτο
δὲ εἴτε διὰ τοπηγορίαν, εἴτε δείνωσιν, ἢ πραγμάτων
ἢ κατασκευῶν ἐπίρρωσιν, εἴτ᾽ ἐποικοδομίαν[5] ἔργων
ἢ παθῶν (μυρίαι γὰρ ἰδέαι τῶν αὐξήσεων) γίνοιτο,
χρὴ γινώσκειν ὅμως τὸν ῥήτορα, ὡς οὐδὲν ἂν τούτων καθ᾽ αὑτὸ συσταίη χωρὶς ὕψους τέλειον, πλὴν εἰ
μὴ ἐν οἴκτοις ἄρα νὴ Δία ἢ ἐν εὐτελισμοῖς, τῶν δ᾽

---

[1] <ἂν> add. Ruhnken.
[2] <εἰς> add. Roberts.
[3] συνοικοδομούμενα K marg., Manutius: P has συνοικονο-
μούμενα.
[4] ἐπίτασιν Wilamowitz, for ἐπίβασιν.
[5] ἐποικοδομίαν K marg., Portus: P has ἐποικονομίαν.

almost stamped on the diction the precise form of the danger—"swept out from under the jaws of destruction." Comparable to this is the passage of Archilochus about the shipwreck[a] and the description of the arrival of the news in Demosthenes. "Now it was evening," etc.[b] What they have done is to clean up, as it were, the very best of the main points, and to fit them together, allowing nothing affected or undignified or pedantic to intervene. These things ruin the whole, by introducing, as it were, gaps and crevices into masses which are built together, walled in by their mutual relationships.

11. Closely allied to the merits set out above is what is called amplification. Whenever the subject matter and the issues admit of several fresh starts and halting-places from section to section, then one great phrase after another is wheeled into place with increasing force. This may be done either by the development of a commonplace, or by exaggeration, or by laying stress on facts or arguments, or by careful build-up of actions or feelings. There are indeed countless kinds of amplification. Still the speaker must recognize that none of these methods can achieve its goal on its own, without sublimity. One may indeed very well make an exception where the effect required is one of commiseration or depreciation, but in

[a] Archilochus frr. 105–6 West.

[b] *De corona* 169: "Now it was evening, and there came one with a message for the *prytaneis*, that Elatea had fallen"; there follows a vivid description of the ensuing panic at Athens. Elatea fell to Philip late in 339.

ἄλλων αὐξητικῶν ὅτου περ ἂν τὸ ὑψηλὸν ἀφέλῃς, ὡς
ψυχὴν ἐξαιρήσεις σώματος· εὐθὺς γὰρ ἀτονεῖ καὶ
κενοῦται τὸ ἔμπρακτον αὐτῶν μὴ τοῖς ὕψεσι συν-
3 επιρρωννύμενον. ἦ μέντοι διαφέρει τοῦ ἀρτίως εἰρη-
μένου τὰ νῦν παραγγελλόμενα (περιγραφὴ γάρ τις
ἦν ἐκεῖνο τῶν ἄκρων λημμάτων καὶ εἰς ἑνότητα σύν-
ταξις) καὶ τίνι καθόλου τῶν αὐξήσεων παραλλάττει
τὰ ὕψη, τῆς σαφηνείας αὐτῆς ἕνεκα συντόμως διορι-
στέον.

12. Ὁ μὲν οὖν τῶν τεχνογράφων ὅρος ἔμοιγ' οὐκ
ἀρεστός. αὔξησίς ἐστι, φασί, λόγος μέγεθος περι-
τιθεὶς τοῖς ὑποκειμένοις· δύναται γὰρ ἀμέλει καὶ
ὕψους καὶ πάθους καὶ τρόπων εἶναι κοινὸς οὗτος
ὅρος, ἐπειδὴ κἀκεῖνα τῷ λόγῳ περιτίθησι ποιόν τι
μέγεθος. ἐμοὶ δὲ φαίνεται ταῦτα ἀλλήλων παραλ-
λάττειν, ᾗ κεῖται τὸ μὲν ὕψος ἐν διάρματι, ἡ δ' αὔξησις καὶ ἐν πλήθει· δι' ὃ κεῖνο μὲν κἂν νοήματι ἑνὶ
πολλάκις, ἡ δὲ πάντως μετὰ ποσότητος καὶ περιου-
2 σίας τινὸς ὑφίσταται. καὶ ἔστιν ἡ αὔξησις, ὡς
τύπῳ περιλαβεῖν, συμπλήρωσις ἀπὸ πάντων τῶν
ἐμφερομένων τοῖς πράγμασι μορίων καὶ τόπων,
ἰσχυροποιοῦσα τῇ ἐπιμονῇ τὸ κατεσκευασμένον,
ταύτῃ τῆς πίστεως διεστῶσα, ὅτι ἡ μὲν τὸ ζητούμενον ἀποδεί<κνυσιν>[1] . . .

---

[1] The completion of the word is due to Manutius.

all other forms of amplification to remove the touch of sublimity is like taking soul from body. For their practical effect instantly loses its vigour and substance if it is not reinforced by the strength of the sublime. But what is the difference between this topic of advice and what we discussed just now, namely the delimitation and unifying arrangement of vital points? What in general is the distinction between instances of amplification and those of sublimity? I must define these matters briefly in order to make my position clear.

12. The definition given by writers on the art of rhetoric does not satisfy me. Amplification, they say, is language which invests the subject with grandeur.[a] Now that definition could obviously serve just as well for the sublime, the emotional, and the metaphorical style, since these also invest the language with some quality of grandeur. But in my view they are each distinct. Sublimity lies in elevation, amplification rather in amount; and so you often find sublimity in a single idea, whereas amplification always goes with quantity and a certain degree of redundance. To give a rough definition, amplification consists in accumulating all the aspects and topics inherent in the subject and thus strengthening the argument by dwelling upon it. Therein it differs from proof, which demonstrates the required point . . .

[*Two pages are lost here.*]

---

[a] Aristotle (*Rhetoric* 1.9.1368a27) makes the point that amplification is most appropriate to epideictic speeches, because the facts are already admitted, and what remains as the speaker's task is to add grandeur and beauty.

3   ... πλουσιώτατα, καθάπερ τι πέλαγος, εἰς ἀνα-
πεπταμένον κέχυται πολλαχῇ μέγεθος. ὅθεν οἶμαι
κατὰ λόγον ὁ μὲν ῥήτωρ ἅτε παθητικώτερος πολὺ τὸ
διάπυρον ἔχει καὶ θυμικῶς ἐκφλεγόμενον, ὁ δὲ καθε-
στὼς ἐν ὄγκῳ καὶ μεγαλοπρεπεῖ σεμνότητι οὐκ
4   ἔψυκται μέν, ἀλλ' οὐχ οὕτως ἐπέστραπται.[1] οὐ κατ'
ἄλλα δέ τινα ἢ ταῦτα, ἐμοὶ δοκεῖ, φίλτατε Τερεν-
τιανέ, (λέγω δέ, <εἰ>[2] καὶ ἡμῖν ὡς Ἕλλησιν ἐφεῖταί
τι γινώσκειν) καὶ ὁ Κικέρων τοῦ Δημοσθένους ἐν
τοῖς μεγέθεσι παραλλάττει. ὁ μὲν γὰρ ἐν ὕψει τὸ
πλέον ἀποτόμῳ, ὁ δὲ Κικέρων ἐν χύσει· καὶ ὁ μὲν
ἡμέτερος διὰ τὸ μετὰ βίας ἕκαστα ἔτι δὲ τάχους
ῥώμης δεινότητος οἷον καίειν τε ἅμα καὶ διαρπάζειν
σκηπρῷ τινι παρεικάζοιτ' ἂν ἢ κεραυνῷ· ὁ δὲ Κικέρων ὡς ἀμφιλαφής τις ἐμπρησμὸς οἶμαι πάντη
νέμεται καὶ ἀνειλεῖται, πολὺ ἔχων καὶ ἐπίμονον ἀεὶ
τὸ καῖον καὶ διακληρονομούμενον ἄλλοτ' ἀλλοίως ἐν
5   αὐτῷ καὶ κατὰ διαδοχὰς ἀνατρεφόμενον. ἀλλὰ
ταῦτα μὲν ὑμεῖς ἂν ἄμεινον ἐπικρίνοιτε, καιρὸς δὲ
τοῦ Δημοσθενικοῦ μὲν ὕψους καὶ ὑπερτεταμένου ἔν
τε ταῖς δεινώσεσι καὶ τοῖς σφοδροῖς πάθεσι καὶ
ἔνθα δεῖ τὸν ἀκροατὴν τὸ σύνολον ἐκπλῆξαι, τῆς δὲ
χύσεως ὅπου χρὴ καταντλῆσαι· τοπηγορίαις τε γὰρ
καὶ ἐπιλόγοις κατὰ τὸ πλέον καὶ παρεκβάσεσι καὶ
τοῖς φραστικοῖς ἅπασι καὶ ἐπιδεικτικοῖς, ἱστορίαις
τε καὶ φυσιολογίαις, καὶ οὐκ ὀλίγοις ἄλλοις μέρεσιν
ἁρμόδιος.

13. Ὅτι μέντοι ὁ Πλάτων (ἐπάνειμι γάρ) τοιούτῳ

... very rich indeed: like a sea, often flooding a vast expanse of grandeur. I should say then that in point of style the orator, being more emotional, has abundant warmth and passionate glow, whereas Plato, steady in his majestic and stately dignity, is less intense, though of course by no means frigid. It is in the very same respect—so I feel, my dear Terentianus, if indeed we Greeks may be allowed an opinion—that Cicero differs from Demosthenes in his grand effects. Demosthenes' strength is usually in rugged sublimity, Cicero's in diffusion. Our countryman with his violence, yes, and his speed, his force, his terrific power of rhetoric, burns, as it were, and scatters everything before him, and may therefore be compared to a flash of lightning or a thunderbolt. Cicero seems to me like a widespread conflagration, rolling along and devouring all around it: his is a strong and steady fire, its flames duly distributed, now here, now there, and fed by fresh supplies of fuel. You Romans, of course, can form a better judgement on this question, but clearly the opportunity for Demosthenes' sublimity and nervous force comes in his intensity and violent emotion, and in passages where it is necessary to amaze the audience; whereas diffuseness is in place when you need to overwhelm them with a flood of rhetoric. The latter then mostly suits the treatment of a commonplace, a peroration, a digression, and all descriptive and epideictic passages, as well as historical and scientific contexts, and many other types of writing.

13. However, to return to Plato, though the stream of

---

[1] Bentley conjectured ἀπαστράπτει, "flashes like lightning."

[2] <εἰ> add. K marg., Manutius.

τινὶ χεύματι ἀψοφητὶ ῥέων οὐδὲν ἧττον μεγεθύνεται,
ἀνεγνωκὼς τὰ ἐν τῇ Πολιτείᾳ τὸν τύπον οὐκ ἀγνοεῖς.
"οἱ ἄρα φρονήσεως," φησί, "καὶ ἀρετῆς ἄπειροι
εὐωχίαις δὲ καὶ τοῖς τοιούτοις ἀεὶ συνόντες κάτω ὡς
ἔοικε φέρονται καὶ ταύτῃ πλανῶνται διὰ βίου, πρὸς
δὲ τὸ ἀληθὲς ἄνω οὔτ' ἀνέβλεψαν πώποτε οὔτ' ἀνη-
νέχθησαν οὐδὲ βεβαίου τε καὶ καθαρᾶς ἡδονῆς
ἐγεύσαντο, ἀλλὰ βοσκημάτων δίκην κάτω ἀεὶ βλέ-
ποντες καὶ κεκυφότες εἰς γῆν καὶ εἰς τραπέζας
βόσκονται χορταζόμενοι καὶ ὀχεύοντες, καὶ ἕνεκα
τῆς τούτων πλεονεξίας λακτίζοντες καὶ κυρίττοντες
ἀλλήλους σιδηροῖς κέρασι καὶ ὁπλαῖς ἀποκτιννύ-
ουσι δι' ἀπληστίαν."

2   Ἐνδείκνυται δ' ἡμῖν οὗτος ἀνήρ, εἰ βουλοίμεθα
μὴ κατολιγωρεῖν, ὡς καὶ ἄλλη τις παρὰ τὰ εἰρημένα
ὁδὸς ἐπὶ τὰ ὑψηλὰ τείνει. ποία δὲ καὶ τίς αὕτη; τῶν
ἔμπροσθεν μεγάλων συγγραφέων καὶ ποιητῶν
μίμησίς τε καὶ ζήλωσις. καί γε τούτου, φίλτατε,
ἀπρὶξ ἐχώμεθα τοῦ σκοποῦ· πολλοὶ γὰρ ἀλλοτρίῳ
θεοφοροῦνται πνεύματι τὸν αὐτὸν τρόπον, ὃν καὶ τὴν
Πυθίαν λόγος ἔχει τρίποδι πλησιάζουσαν, ἔνθα
ῥῆγμά ἐστι γῆς ἀναπνέον[1] ὥς φασιν ἀτμὸν ἔνθεον,
αὐτόθεν ἐγκύμονα τῆς δαιμονίου καθισταμένην
δυνάμεως παραυτίκα χρησμῳδεῖν κατ' ἐπίπνοιαν·
οὕτως ἀπὸ τῆς τῶν ἀρχαίων μεγαλοφυΐας εἰς τὰς

---

[1] ἀναπνέον Manutius for ἀναπνεῖν P.

[a] *Theaetetus* 144B.

his words flows as noiselessly as oil,[a] he none the less attains sublimity. You have read the *Republic* and you know the sort of thing. "Those who have then no experience," he says, "of wisdom or of goodness, living always amid banquets and other such festivities, are seemingly borne downwards and there they wander all their lives. They have never yet raised their eyes to the truth, never been carried upwards, never tasted true, abiding pleasure. They are like so many cattle, stooping downwards, with their eyes always bent on the earth and on their dinner tables, they feed and fatten and breed, and so greedy are they for these enjoyments that they kick and butt with hooves and horns of iron and kill each other for insatiate desire."[b]

Here is an author who shows us, if we will condescend to see, that there is another road, besides those we have mentioned, which leads to sublimity. What and what manner of road is this? Zealous imitation of the great prose writers and poets of the past. That is the aim, dear friend; let us hold to it with all our might. For many are carried away by the inspiration of another, just as the story runs that the Pythian priestess on approaching the tripod where there is, they say, a rift in the earth, exhaling divine vapour,[c] thereby becomes impregnated with the divine power and is at once inspired to utter oracles; so, too, from the natural genius of those old writers there

[b] *Republic* 9.586A, with some changes and omissions.

[c] The theory that the prophetic power of Delphi was due to such an intoxicating vapour or *pneuma* was widely held in antiquity, but the geology of Delphi lends it no support and no "rift in the earth" has been identified.

τῶν ζηλούντων ἐκείνους ψυχὰς ὡς ἀπὸ ἱερῶν στο-
μίων ἀπόρροιαί τινες φέρονται, ὑφ᾽ ὧν ἐπιπνεόμενοι
καὶ οἱ μὴ λίαν φοιβαστικοὶ τῷ ἑτέρων συνενθου-
3 σιῶσι μεγέθει. μόνος Ἡρόδοτος Ὁμηρικώτατος
ἐγένετο; Στησίχορος ἔτι πρότερον ὅ τε Ἀρχίλοχος,
πάντων δὲ τούτων μάλιστα ὁ Πλάτων, ἀπὸ τοῦ
Ὁμηρικοῦ κείνου νάματος εἰς αὑτὸν μυρίας ὅσας
παρατροπὰς ἀποχετευσάμενος. καὶ ἴσως ἡμῖν ἀπο-
δείξεων ἔδει, εἰ μὴ τὰ ἐπ᾽ εἴδους καὶ οἱ περὶ Ἀμμώ-
4 νιον ἐκλέξαντες ἀνέγραψαν. ἔστιν δ᾽ οὐ κλοπὴ τὸ
πρᾶγμα, ἀλλ᾽ ὡς ἀπὸ καλῶν ἠθῶν[1] ἢ[2] πλασμάτων ἢ
δημιουργημάτων ἀποτύπωσις. καὶ οὐδ᾽ ἂν ἐπακμά-
σαι[3] μοι δοκεῖ τηλικαῦτά τινα τοῖς τῆς φιλοσοφίας
δόγμασι καὶ εἰς ποιητικὰς ὕλας πολλαχοῦ συνεμβῆ-
ναι καὶ φράσεις, εἰ μὴ περὶ πρωτείων νὴ Δία παντὶ
θυμῷ πρὸς Ὅμηρον, ὡς ἀνταγωνιστὴς νέος πρὸς
ἤδη τεθαυμασμένον, ἴσως μὲν φιλονεικότερον καὶ
οἱονεὶ διαδορατιζόμενος, οὐκ ἀνωφελῶς δ᾽ ὅμως διη-
ριστεύετο. "ἀγαθὴ" γὰρ κατὰ τὸν Ἡσίοδον "ἔρις
ἥδε βροτοῖσι." καὶ τῷ ὄντι καλὸς οὗτος καὶ ἀξιονι-
κότατος εὐκλείας ἀγών τε καὶ στέφανος, ἐν ᾧ καὶ τὸ
ἡττᾶσθαι τῶν προγενεστέρων οὐκ ἄδοξον.

[1] εἰδῶν Toll.   [2] ἡ Jahn: ἢ P: ᾗ Fyfe.
[3] ἐπανθίσαι Bühler.

---

[a] Stesichorus' lyrics were largely epic in theme and language,
while Archilochus' vigorous iambics had been compared with
Homer by earlier critics (Heraclides Ponticus wrote on "Homer
and Archilochus," but the contents of the book are not known).

flows into the hearts of their admirers as it were an ema-
nation from those holy mouths. Inspired by this, even
those who are not easily moved to prophecy share the
enthusiasm of these others' grandeur. Was Herodotus
alone Homeric in the highest degree? No, there was
Stesichorus at a still earlier date and Archilochus too,[a]
and above all others Plato,[b] who drew off for his own use
ten thousand runnels from the great Homeric spring. We
might need to give instances, had not people like
Ammonius[c] drawn up a collection. Such borrowing is no
theft; it is rather like the reproduction of good character
by sculptures or other works of art.[d] So many of these
qualities would never have flourished among Plato's
philosophic tenets, nor would he have entered so often
into the subjects and language of poetry, had he not
striven, with heart and soul, to contest the prize with
Homer, like a young antagonist with one who had already
won his spurs, perhaps in too keen emulation, longing as
it were to break a lance, and yet always to good purpose;
for, as Hesiod says, "Good is this strife for mankind."[e]
Fair indeed is the crown, and the fight for fame well
worth the winning, where even to be worsted by our fore-
runners is not without glory.

[b] Ancient critics saw resemblances between Plato and Homer
in grandeur, character drawing, and psychological theory. It is
curious that the third-century Longinus (F15 Prickard) actually
says: "Plato is the first who best transferred Homeric grandeur
(ὄγκον) into prose." Cf. Introduction.

[c] A pupil of Aristarchus, who wrote on Plato's debt to Homer.

[d] Or (reading ἤ for ἤ): "an impression taken from good characters, sculptures, or other works of art."

[e] Hesiod, *Works and Days* 24.

14. Οὐκοῦν καὶ ἡμᾶς, ἡνίκ' ἂν διαπονῶμεν ὑψηγορίας τι καὶ μεγαλοφροσύνης δεόμενον, καλὸν ἀναπλάττεσθαι ταῖς ψυχαῖς, πῶς ἂν εἰ τύχοι ταὐτὸ τοῦθ' Ὅμηρος εἶπεν, πῶς δ' ἂν Πλάτων ἢ Δημοσθένης ὕψωσαν ἢ ἐν ἱστορίᾳ Θουκυδίδης. προσπίπτοντα γὰρ ἡμῖν κατὰ ζῆλον ἐκεῖνα τὰ πρόσωπα καὶ οἷον διαπρέποντα τὰς ψυχὰς ἀνοίσει πως πρὸς
2 τὰ ἀνειδωλοποιούμενα μέτρα· ἔτι δὲ μᾶλλον, εἰ κἀκεῖνο τῇ διανοίᾳ προσυπογράφοιμεν, πῶς ἂν τόδε τι ὑπ' ἐμοῦ λεγόμενον παρὼν Ὅμηρος ἤκουσεν ἢ Δημοσθένης, ἢ πῶς ἂν ἐπὶ τούτῳ διετέθησαν; τῷ γὰρ ὄντι μέγα τὸ ἀγώνισμα, τοιοῦτον ὑποτίθεσθαι τῶν ἰδίων λόγων δικαστήριον καὶ θέατρον καὶ ἐν τηλικούτοις ἥρωσι κριταῖς τε καὶ μάρτυσιν ὑπέχειν
3 τῶν γραφομένων εὐθύνας πεπαῖχθαι.[1] πλέον δὲ τούτων παρορμητικόν, εἰ προστιθείης πῶς ἂν ἐμοῦ ταῦτα γράψαντος ὁ μετ' ἐμὲ πᾶς ἀκούσειεν αἰών; εἰ δέ τις αὐτόθεν φοβοῖτο, μὴ τοῦ ἰδίου βίου καὶ χρόνου φθέγξαιτό τι ὑπερήμερον, ἀνάγκη καὶ τὰ συλλαμβανόμενα ὑπὸ τῆς τούτου ψυχῆς ἀτελῆ καὶ τυφλὰ ὥσπερ ἀμβλοῦσθαι, πρὸς τὸν τῆς ὑστεροφημίας ὅλως μὴ τελεσφορούμενα χρόνον.

15. Ὄγκου καὶ μεγαληγορίας καὶ ἀγῶνος ἐπὶ τούτοις, ὦ νεανία, καὶ αἱ φαντασίαι παρασκευαστικώταται· οὕτω γοῦν <ἡμεῖς>[2] εἰδωλοποιίας <δ'>[3] αὐτὰς ἔνιοι λέγουσι. καλεῖται μὲν γὰρ κοινῶς φαντασία πᾶν τὸ ὁπωσοῦν ἐννόημα γεννητικὸν λόγου παριστάμενον, ἤδη δ' ἐπὶ τούτων κεκράτηκεν τοῦ-

14. We too, then, when we are working at some passage that demands sublimity of thought and expression, should do well to form in our hearts the question, "How might Homer have said this same thing, how would Plato or Demosthenes or (in history) Thucydides have made it sublime?" Emulation will bring those great characters before our eyes, and their shining presence will lead our thoughts to the ideal standards of perfection. Still more will this be so, if we also try to imagine to ourselves: "How would Homer or Demosthenes, had either been present, have listened to this passage of mine? How would that passage have affected them?" Great indeed is the ordeal, if we suppose such a jury and audience as this to listen to our own utterances and make believe that we are submitting our work to the scrutiny of such heroes as witnesses and judges. Even more stimulating would it be to add, "If I write this, how would all posterity receive it?" But if a man shrinks at the very thought of saying anything that is going to outlast his own life and time, then must all the conceptions of that man's mind be like some blind, half-formed embryo, all too abortive for the life of posthumous fame.

15. Weight, grandeur, and urgency in writing are very largely produced, dear young friend, by the use of "visualizations" (*phantasiai*). That at least is what I call them; others call them "image productions." For the term *phantasia* is applied in general to an idea which enters the mind from any source and engenders speech, but the word has now come to be used predominantly of

---

[1] πεπεῖσθαι Reiske.

[2,3] These changes are by Russell (1964).

νομα, ὅταν ἃ λέγεις ὑπ' ἐνθουασιασμοῦ καὶ πάθους
βλέπειν δοκῇς καὶ ὑπ' ὄψιν τιθῇς τοῖς ἀκούουσιν.

2 ὡς δ' ἕτερόν τι ἡ ῥητορικὴ φαντασία βούλεται καὶ
ἕτερον ἡ παρὰ ποιηταῖς, οὐκ ἂν λάθοι σε, οὐδ' ὅτι
τῆς μὲν ἐν ποιήσει τέλος ἐστὶν ἔκπληξις, τῆς δ' ἐν
λόγοις ἐνάργεια, ἀμφότεραι δ' ὅμως τό τε <παθητι-
κὸν>[1] ἐπιζητοῦσι καὶ τὸ συγκεκινημένον.

> ὦ μῆτερ, ἱκετεύω σε, μὴ 'πίσειέ μοι
> τὰς αἱματωποὺς καὶ δρακοντώδεις κόρας·
> αὗται γάρ, αὗται πλησίον θρώσκουσί μου.

καὶ

> οἴμοι, κτανεῖ με· ποῖ φύγω;

ἐνταῦθ' ὁ ποιητὴς αὐτὸς[2] εἶδεν Ἐρινύας, ὃ δὲ ἐφαντάσθη μικροῦ δεῖν θεάσασθαι καὶ τοὺς ἀκούοντας
3 ἠνάγκασεν. ἔστι μὲν οὖν φιλοπονώτατος ὁ Εὐριπίδης δύο ταυτὶ πάθη, μανίας τε καὶ ἔρωτας, ἐκτραγω-
δῆσαι, κἀν τούτοις ὡς οὐκ οἶδ' εἴ τισιν ἑτέροις
ἐπιτυχέστατος, οὐ μὴν ἀλλὰ καὶ ταῖς ἄλλαις ἐπιτί-
θεσθαι φαντασίαις οὐκ ἄτολμος. ἥκιστά γέ τοι
μεγαλοφυὴς ὢν ὅμως τὴν αὐτὸς αὐτοῦ φύσιν ἐν
πολλοῖς γενέσθαι τραγικὴν προσηνάγκασεν καὶ
παρ' ἕκαστα ἐπὶ τῶν μεγεθῶν, ὡς ὁ ποιητής,

---

[1] add. Kayser.
[2] Manutius added <οὐκ>: "the poet did *not* see Furies."

---

[a] Euripides, *Orestes* 255–7, from the classic scene in which

passages where, inspired by strong emotion, you seem to see what you describe and bring it vividly before the eyes of your audience. That *phantasia* means one thing in oratory and another in poetry you will yourself detect, and also that the object of the poetical form of it is to enthral, and that of the prose form to present things vividly, though both indeed aim at the emotional and the excited.

> Mother, I beg you, do not drive against me
> These snake-like women with blood-reddened
> eyes.
> See there! See there! They leap upon me close.[a]

And

> Ah, she will slay me, whither shall I flee?[b]

In these passages the poet himself saw Furies and compelled the audience almost to see what he had visualized. Now Euripides makes his greatest efforts in presenting these two emotions, madness and love, in tragic guise, and succeeds more brilliantly with these emotions than, I think, with any others; not that he lacks enterprise to attack other forms of visualization as well. While his natural genius is certainly not sublime, yet in many places he forces it into the tragic mould and invariably in his grand passages, as the poet says,

Orestes has a madman's vision of Clytemnestra sending the Erinyes against him.

[b] Euripides, *Iphigenia in Tauris* 291: a herdsman describes to Iphigenia the mad behaviour and words of the man he has seen on the beach, who turns out to be Orestes, who is experiencing the same delusion of attack by the Erinyes avenging his mother.

οὐρῇ δὲ πλευράς τε καὶ ἰσχίον ἀμφοτέρωθεν
μαστίεται, ἑὲ δ' αὐτὸν ἐποτρύνει μαχέσασθαι.

4   τῷ γοῦν Φαέθοντι παραδιδοὺς τὰς ἡνίας ὁ Ἥλιος

ἔλα δὲ μήτε Λιβυκὸν αἰθέρ' εἰσβαλών·
κρᾶσιν γὰρ ὑγρὰν οὐκ ἔχων ἁψῖδα σὴν
καίων[1] διήσει . . .

φησίν, εἶθ' ἑξῆς

ἵει δ' ἐφ' ἑπτὰ Πλειάδων ἔχων δρόμον.
τοσαῦτ' ἀκούσας παῖς ἔμαρψεν ἡνίας·
κρούσας δὲ πλευρὰ πτεροφόρων ὀχημάτων
μεθῆκεν, αἱ δ' ἔπταντ' ἐπ' αἰθέρος πτύχας.
πατὴρ δ' ὄπισθε νῶτα σειρίου βεβὼς
ἵππευε παῖδα νουθετῶν· ἐκεῖσ' ἔλα,
τῇδε στρέφ' ἅρμα, τῇδε.

ἆρ' οὐκ ἂν εἴποις, ὅτι ἡ ψυχὴ τοῦ γράφοντος συν-
επιβαίνει τοῦ ἅρματος καὶ συγκινδυνεύουσα τοῖς
ἵπποις συνεπτέρωται; οὐ γὰρ ἄν, εἰ μὴ τοῖς οὐρανί-
οις ἐκείνοις ἔργοις ἰσοδρομοῦσα ἐφέρετο, τοιαῦτ' ἂν
ποτε ἐφαντάσθη. ὅμοια καὶ τὰ ἐπὶ τῆς Κασσάνδρας
αὐτῷ

----

[1] Richards, for P's κάτω.

His tail at his ribs and his flanks now lashes on this,
　　now on that side,
Ever he spurs himself on to share in the joys of the
　　battle.[a]

For instance, when Helios hands over the reins to
Phaethon:[b]

"And do not drive into the Libyan sky.
Its torrid air with no damp humour tempered
Will burn your wheel and melt it."

And he goes on,

"But toward the seven Pleiads hold your course."
This heard, young Phaethon caught up the reins,
Slashed at the flanks of his wing-wafted team,
And launched them flying to the cloudy vales.
Behind, his sire, astride the Dog star's back,
Rode, schooling thus his son. "Now, drive on there,
Now this way wheel your car, this way."

Would you not say that the writer's soul is aboard the car,
and takes wing to share the horses' peril? Never could it
have visualized such things, had it not run beside those
heavenly bodies. You find the same sort of thing in his
Cassandra's speech:

[a] *Iliad* 20.170, describing a wounded lion.

[b] The following passages are from Euripides' *Phaethon* (fr.
779 Nauck[2], see J. Diggle, *Euripides' Phaethon*, Cambridge
1970, lines 168–77). They come from a messenger's speech
relating Phaethon's fatal ride in the Sun god's chariot.

ἀλλ᾽ ὦ φίλιπποι Τρῶες.

5 τοῦ δ᾽ Αἰσχύλου φαντασίαις ἐπιτολμῶντος ἡρωϊκω
τάταις, ὥσπερ καὶ <οἱ>[1] Ἑπτὰ ἐπὶ Θήβας παρ᾽
αὐτῷ

> ἄνδρες (φησίν) ἑπτὰ θούριοι λοχαγέται,
> ταυροσφαγοῦντες εἰς μελάνδετον σάκος
> καὶ θιγγάνοντες χερσὶ ταυρείου φόνου
> Ἄρη τ᾽ Ἐννὼ καὶ φιλαίματον Φόβον
> ὁρκωμότησαν

τὸν ἴδιον αὐτῶν[2] πρὸς ἀλλήλους δίχα οἴκτου συν
ομνύμενοι θάνατον, ἐνίοτε μέντοι ἀκατεργάστους καὶ
οἰονεὶ ποκοειδεῖς τὰς ἐννοίας καὶ ἀμαλάκτους φέρον
τος, ὅμως ἑαυτὸν ὁ Εὐριπίδης κἀκείνοις ὑπὸ φιλοτι
6 μίας τοῖς κινδύνοις προσβιβάζει. καὶ παρὰ μὲν
Αἰσχύλῳ παραδόξως τὰ τοῦ Λυκούργου βασίλεια
κατὰ τὴν ἐπιφάνειαν τοῦ Διονύσου θεοφορεῖται,

> ἐνθουσιᾷ δὴ δῶμα, βακχεύει στέγη·

ὁ δ᾽ Εὐριπίδης τὸ αὐτὸ τοῦθ᾽ ἑτέρως ἐφηδύνας ἐξε
φώνησε,

> πᾶν δὲ συνεβάκχευ᾽ ὄρος.

---

[1] add. Morus; K marg. has ὥσπερ οἱ.
[2] Faber: P has αὐτῶν.

[a] Euripides fr. 935 Nauck[2]. This may come from the *Alexandros*, and may have to do with Cassandra's warning against the

O you horse-loving Trojans[a]

And whereas when Aeschylus ventures upon heroic imaginings, he is like his own "Seven against Thebes," where

> Seven resistless captains o'er a shield
> Black-bound with hide have slit a bullock's throat,
> And dipped their fingers in the bullock's blood,
> Swearing a mighty oath by War and Havoc
> And Panic, bloodshed's lover   [b]

and all pledge themselves to each other to die "apart from pity," and though he sometimes introduces unworked ideas, all woolly, as it were, and tangled, Euripides' competitiveness leads him also to embark on the same perilous path. Aeschylus uses a startling phrase of Lycurgus's palace, magically possessed at the appearance of Dionysus,

> The palace is possessed, the roof turns bacchanal.[c]

Euripides expressed the same idea differently, softening it down,

> And all the mountain
> Turned bacchanal with them.[d]

Trojan Horse; if so, "horse-loving" is an apt taunt. Presumably Longinus means us to recall more of the speech than these opening words.   [b] *Seven against Thebes* 42–6: "apart from pity" comes from the same passage (51).   [c] Aeschylus fr. 58 Radt, from the *Lycurgeia*, the trilogy dealing with Lycurgus' resistance to the cult of Dionysus in Thrace, a parallel theme to that of Euripides' *Bacchae*, where Pentheus of Thebes vainly resists the god.   [d] Euripides, *Bacchae* 726.

7 ἄκρως δὲ καὶ ὁ Σοφοκλῆς ἐπὶ τοῦ θνήσκοντος Οἰδίπου καὶ ἑαυτὸν μετὰ διοσημείας τινὸς θάπτοντος
πεφάντασται, καὶ κατὰ τὸν ἀπόπλουν τῶν Ἑλλήνων
ἐπὶ τἀχιλλέως προφαινομένου τοῖς ἀναγομένοις
ὑπὲρ τοῦ τάφου, ἣν οὐκ οἶδ' εἴ τις ὄψιν ἐναργέστερον εἰδωλοποίησε Σιμωνίδου· πάντα δ' ἀμήχανον
8 παρατίθεσθαι. οὐ μὴν ἀλλὰ τὰ μὲν παρὰ τοῖς ποιηταῖς μυθικωτέραν ἔχει τὴν ὑπερέκπτωσιν, ὡς ἔφην,
καὶ πάντῃ τὸ πιστὸν ὑπεραίρουσαν, τῆς δὲ ῥητορικῆς φαντασίας κάλλιστον ἀεὶ τὸ ἔμπρακτον καὶ ἐνά-
ληθες. δειναὶ δὲ καὶ ἔκφυλοι αἱ παραβάσεις, ἡνίκ'
ἂν ᾖ ποιητικὸν τοῦ λόγου καὶ μυθῶδες τὸ πλάσμα
καὶ εἰς πᾶν προεκπῖπτον[1] τὸ ἀδύνατον, ὡς ἤδη νὴ
Δία καὶ οἱ καθ' ἡμᾶς δεινοὶ ῥήτορες, καθάπερ οἱ
τραγῳδοί, βλέπουσιν Ἐρινύας καὶ οὐδὲ ἐκεῖνο
μαθεῖν οἱ γενναῖοι δύνανται, ὅτι ὁ λέγων Ὀρέστης

μέθες· μί' οὖσα τῶν ἐμῶν Ἐρινύων
μέσον μ' ὀχμάζεις, ὡς βάλῃς ἐς τάρταρον

φαντάζεται ταῦθ' ὅτι μαίνεται.

9 Τί οὖν ἡ ῥητορικὴ φαντασία δύναται; πολλὰ μὲν
ἴσως καὶ ἄλλα τοῖς λόγοις ἐναγώνια καὶ ἐμπαθῆ
προσεισφέρειν, κατακιρναμένη μέντοι ταῖς πραγμα-
τικαῖς ἐπιχειρήσεσιν οὐ πείθει τὸν ἀκροατὴν μόνον
ἀλλὰ καὶ δουλοῦται. "καὶ μὴν εἴ τις," φησίν,
"αὐτίκα δὴ μάλα κραυγῆς ἀκούσειε πρὸ τῶν δικα-

---

[1] So Morus, for προσεκπῖπτον

[a] *Oedipus at Colonus* 1586–1666.

Sophocles too describes with superb visualization the dying Oedipus conducting his own burial amid strange portents in the sky;[a] and Achilles at the departure of the Greeks, when he appears above his tomb to those embarking,[b] a scene which nobody perhaps has depicted so vividly as Simonides.[c] But to give all the instances would be endless. However, as I said, these examples from poetry show an exaggeration which belongs to fable and far exceeds the limits of credibility, whereas the most perfect effect of visualization in oratory is always one of reality and truth. Transgressions of this rule have a strange, outlandish air, when the texture of the speech is poetical and fabulous and deviates into all sorts of impossibilities. For instance, our wonderful modern orators—god help us!—are like so many tragedians in seeing Furies, and the fine fellows cannot even understand that when Orestes says,

> Let go! Of my own Furies you are one
> And grip my waist to cast me down to Hell,[d]

he only imagines that, because he is mad.

What then is the use of visualization in oratory? It may be said generally to introduce a great deal of excitement and emotion into one's speeches, but when combined with factual arguments it not only convinces the audience, it positively masters them. Take Demosthenes: "And yet, suppose that at this very moment we were to hear an uproar in front of the law courts and someone

[b] In *Polyxena*, fr. 523 Radt.
[c] D. A. Campbell (ed.), *Greek Lyric* III (Loeb Classical Library) Simonides fr. 557 (= fr. 52 Page).
[d] Euyripides, *Orestes* 264–5.

στηρίων, εἶτ᾽ εἴποι τις, ὡς ἀνέῳκται τὸ δεσμωτήριον,
οἱ δὲ δεσμῶται φεύγουσιν, οὐθεὶς οὕτως οὔτε γέρων
οὔτε νέος ὀλίγωρός ἐστιν, ὃς οὐχὶ βοηθήσει καθ᾽
ὅσον δύναται· εἰ δὲ δή τις εἴποι παρελθών, ὡς ὁ τούτους ἀφεὶς οὗτός ἐστιν, οὐδὲ λόγου τυχὼν παραυτίκ᾽
10 ἂν ἀπόλοιτο." ὡς νὴ Δία καὶ ὁ Ὑπερείδης κατηγο-
ρούμενος, ἐπειδὴ τοὺς δούλους μετὰ τὴν ἧτταν ἐλευ-
θέρους ἐψηφίσατο, "τοῦτο τὸ ψήφισμα," εἶπεν, "οὐχ
ὁ ῥήτωρ ἔγραψεν ἀλλ᾽ ἡ ἐν Χαιρωνείᾳ μάχη." ἅμα
γὰρ τῷ πραγματικῶς ἐπιχειρεῖν ὁ ῥήτωρ πεφάντασται, διὸ καὶ τὸν τοῦ πείθειν ὅρον ὑπερβέβηκεν τῷ
11 λήμματι. φύσει δέ πως ἐν τοῖς τοιούτοις ἅπασιν ἀεὶ
τοῦ κρείττονος ἀκούομεν, ὅθεν ἀπὸ τοῦ ἀποδεικτικοῦ
περιελκόμεθα εἰς τὸ κατὰ φαντασίαν ἐκπληκτικόν, ᾧ
τὸ πραγματικὸν ἐγκρύπτεται περιλαμπόμενον. καὶ
τοῦτ᾽ οὐκ ἀπεικότως πάσχομεν· δυεῖν γὰρ συνταττο-
μένων ὑφ᾽ ἓν ἀεὶ τὸ κρεῖττον εἰς ἑαυτὸ τὴν θατέρου
δύναμιν περισπᾷ.

12   Τοσαῦτα περὶ τῶν κατὰ τὰς νοήσεις ὑψηλῶν καὶ
ὑπὸ μεγαλοφροσύνης <ἢ>[1] μιμήσεως ἢ φαντασίας
ἀπογεννωμένων ἀρκέσει.

16. Αὐτόθι μέντοι καὶ ὁ περὶ σχημάτων ἐφεξῆς
τέτακται τόπος· καὶ γὰρ ταῦτ᾽, ἂν ὃν δεῖ σκευάζηται
τρόπον, ὡς ἔφην, οὐκ ἂν ἡ τυχοῦσα μεγέθους εἴη
μερίς. οὐ μὴν ἀλλ᾽ ἐπεὶ τὸ πάντα διακριβοῦν πολὺ
ἔργον[2] ἐν τῷ παρόντι, μᾶλλον δ᾽ ἀπεριόριστον,

---

[1] add. Manutius: <ἢ διὰ> Vahlen.
[2] Bühler, for πολύεργον.

were to tell us, 'The prison has been broken open and the prisoners are escaping,' there is no man, old or young, so unheeding that he would not run to give all the assistance in his power. But suppose someone were to come and actually tell us that this was the man who set them free, he would be killed on the moment without a hearing."[a] And then, to be sure, there is Hyperides on his trial, when he had moved the enfranchisement of the slaves after the Athenian reverse. "It was not the speaker that framed this measure, but the battle of Chaeronea."[b] There, besides developing his factual argument the orator has visualized the event and consequently his conception far exceeds the limits of mere persuasion. In all such cases the stronger element seems naturally to catch our ears, so that our attention is drawn from the reasoning to the enthralling effect of the imagination, and the reality is concealed in a halo of brilliance. And this effect on us is natural enough; set two forces side by side and the stronger always absorbs the virtues of the other.

This must suffice for our treatment of sublimity in ideas, as produced by nobility of mind or imitation or visualization.[c]

16. The topic of figures comes next, for these too, if rightly handled, may be, as I said,[d] an important element in the sublime. However, since it would be a long, and indeed an interminable task to treat them all in detail

---

[a] Demosthenes, *Oration* 24.208.   [b] After Philip's victory at Chaeronea (338 B.C.), Hyperides proposed the enfranchisement of slaves, and defended this panic measure, it is said, in these terms: see Rutilius Lupus 1.19, [Plutarch] *Lives of the Ten Orators*, 849A.   [c] This summary is puzzling: it omits the contents of chap. 10.   [d] In chap. 8.

ὀλίγα τῶν ὅσα μεγαληγορίας ἀποτελεστικὰ τοῦ
πιστώσασθαι τὸ προκείμενον ἕνεκα καὶ δὴ διέξιμεν.

2 ἀπόδειξιν ὁ Δημοσθένης ὑπὲρ τῶν πεπολιτευμένων
εἰσφέρει. τίς δ' ἦν ἡ κατὰ φύσιν χρῆσις αὐτῆς;
"οὐχ ἡμάρτετε, ὦ τὸν ὑπὲρ τῆς τῶν Ἑλλήνων ἐλευ-
θερίας ἀγῶνα ἀράμενοι· ἔχετε δὲ οἰκεῖα τούτου
παραδείγματα· οὐδὲ γὰρ οἱ ἐν Μαραθῶνι ἥμαρτον
οὐδ' οἱ ἐν Σαλαμῖνι οὐδ' οἱ ἐν Πλαταιαῖς." ἀλλ'
ἐπειδὴ καθάπερ ἐμπνευσθεὶς ἐξαίφνης ὑπὸ θεοῦ καὶ
οἱονεὶ φοιβόληπτος γενόμενος τὸν τῶν ἀριστέων τῆς
Ἑλλάδος ὅρκον ἐξεφώνησεν "οὐκ ἔστιν ὅπως ἡμάρτετε, μὰ τοὺς ἐν Μαραθῶνι προκινδυνεύσαντας,"
φαίνεται δι' ἑνὸς τοῦ ὀμοτικοῦ σχήματος, ὅπερ
ἐνθάδε ἀποστροφὴν ἐγὼ καλῶ, τοὺς μὲν προγόνους
ἀποθεώσας, ὅτι δεῖ τοὺς οὕτως ἀποθανόντας ὡς
θεοὺς ὀμνύναι παριστάνων, τοῖς δὲ κρίνουσι τὸ τῶν
ἐκεῖ προκινδυνευσάντων ἐντιθεὶς φρόνημα, τὴν δὲ
τῆς ἀποδείξεως φύσιν μεθεστακὼς εἰς ὑπερβάλλον
ὕψος καὶ πάθος καὶ ξένων καὶ ὑπερφυῶν ὅρκων
ἀξιοπιστίαν, καὶ ἅμα παιώνειόν τινα καὶ ἀλεξιφάρ-
μακον εἰς τὰς ψυχὰς τῶν ἀκουόντων καθιεὶς λόγον,
ὡς κουφιζομένους ὑπὸ τῶν ἐγκωμίων μηδὲν ἔλαττον
τῇ μάχῃ τῇ πρὸς Φίλιππον ἢ ἐπὶ τοῖς κατὰ Μαρα-
θῶνα καὶ Σαλαμῖνα νικητηρίοις παρίστασθαι φρο-

3 νεῖν· οἷς πᾶσι τοὺς ἀκροατὰς διὰ τοῦ σχηματισμοῦ
συναρπάσας ᾤχετο. καίτοι παρὰ τῷ Εὐπόλιδι τοῦ
ὅρκου τὸ σπέρμα φασὶν εὑρῆσθαι·

at this point, we will by way of confirmation of our thesis merely run through a few of those which make for grandeur. Demosthenes is producing an argument in defence of his political career. What was the natural way to treat it? "You were not wrong, you who undertook that struggle for the freedom of Greece, and you have proof of this at home, for neither were the men at Marathon misguided nor those at Salamis nor those at Plataea."[a] But when in a sudden moment of inspiration, as if possessed by the divine, he utters his great oath by the champions of Greece, "It cannot be that you were wrong; no, by those who risked their lives at Marathon," then you feel that by employing the single figure of adjuration—which I here call apostrophe—he has deified the ancestors by suggesting that one should swear by men who met such a death, as if they were gods; he has filled his judges with the spirit of those who risked their lives there; he has transformed a demonstrative argument into a passage of transcendent sublimity and emotion, giving it the power of conviction that lies in so strange and startling an oath; and at the same time his words have administered to his hearers a healing medicine, with the result that, relieved by his eulogy, they come to feel as proud of the war with Philip as of their victories at Marathon and Salamis. In all this he is enabled to carry the audience away with him by the use of the figure. True, the germ of the oath is said to have been found in Eupolis:

[a] *De corona* 208. The passage was much admired in antiquity (Quintil. 9.2.62; 12.10.24; Hermogenes, *De ideis* p. 267 Rabe), and Longinus' discussion was highly praised by Dr. Johnson (*Life of Dryden* p. 299, World's Classics edition).

οὐ γὰρ μὰ τὴν Μαραθῶνι τὴν ἐμὴν μάχην
χαίρων τις αὐτῶν τοὐμὸν ἀλγυνεῖ κέαρ.

ἔστι δ' οὐ τὸ ὁπωσοῦν τινὰ ὀμόσαι μέγα, τὸ δὲ ποῦ
καὶ πῶς καὶ ἐφ' ὧν καιρῶν καὶ τίνος ἕνεκα. ἀλλ'
ἐκεῖ μὲν οὐδέν ἐστ' εἰ μὴ ὅρκος, καὶ πρὸς εὐτυχοῦν-
τας ἔτι καὶ οὐ δεομένους παρηγορίας τοὺς Ἀθηναί-
ους· ἔτι δ' οὐχὶ τοὺς ἄνδρας ἀπαθανατίσας ὁ ποιητὴς ὤμοσεν, ἵνα τῆς ἐκείνων ἀρετῆς τοῖς ἀκούουσιν
ἐντέκῃ λόγον ἄξιον, ἀλλ' ἀπὸ τῶν προκινδυνευσάντων ἐπὶ τὸ ἄψυχον ἀπεπλανήθη, τὴν μάχην. παρὰ
δὲ τῷ Δημοσθένει πεπραγμάτευται πρὸς ἡττημένους
ὁ ὅρκος, ὡς μὴ Χαιρώνειαν ἔτ' Ἀθηναίοις ἀτύχημα
φαίνεσθαι, καὶ ταὐτόν, ὡς ἔφην, ἅμα ἀπόδειξίς ἐστι
τοῦ μηδὲν ἡμαρτηκέναι, παράδειγμα, ὅρκων[1] πίστις,
4   ἐγκώμιον, προτροπή. κἀπειδήπερ ὑπήντα τῷ ῥήτορι
"λέγεις ἧτταν πολιτευσάμενος, εἶτα νίκας ὀμνύεις;"
διὰ ταῦθ' ἑξῆς κανονίζει καὶ δι' ἀσφαλείας ἄγει καὶ[2]
ὀνόματα, διδάσκων ὅτι κἂν βακχεύμασι νήφειν ἀναγκαῖον. "τοὺς προκινδυνεύσαντας," φησί, "Μαραθῶνι καὶ τοὺς Σαλαμῖνι καὶ ἐπ' Ἀρτεμισίῳ ναυμα-
χήσαντας καὶ τοὺς ἐν Πλαταιαῖς παραταξαμένους."
οὐδαμοῦ "νικήσαντας" εἶπεν, ἀλλὰ πάντη τὸ τοῦ
τέλους διακέκλοφεν ὄνομα, ἐπειδήπερ ἦν εὐτυχὲς καὶ
τοῖς κατὰ Χαιρώνειαν ὑπεναντίον. διόπερ καὶ τὸν
ἀκροατὴν φθάνων εὐθὺς ὑποφέρει· "οὓς ἅπαντας

[1] ὅρκων deleted by Kayser.
[2] καὶ <κατ'> Mazzucchi.

228

> No, by the fight I fought at Marathon,
> No one of them shall vex me and go free.[a]

But the mere swearing of an oath is not sublime: we must consider the place, the manner, the circumstances, the motive. In Eupolis there is nothing but an oath, and that addressed to Athens, when still in prosperity and needing no consolation. Moreover, the poet's oath does not immortalize the men so as to beget in the audience a true opinion of their worth, but instead he wanders from those who risked their lives to an inanimate object, namely the fight. In Demosthenes the oath is carefully designed to suit the feelings of defeated men, so that the Athenians should no longer regard Chaeronea as a disaster; and it is, as I said, at the same time a proof that no mistake has been made, an example, a sworn confirmation, an encomium, and an exhortation. The orator was faced with the objection, "You are speaking of a reverse due to your policy and then you go swearing by victories," and therefore in the sequel he measures his every word and keeps on the safe side, inculcating the lesson that "in the wildest rite" you must stay sober[b] "Those who risked their lives," he says, "at Marathon and those who fought on shipboard at Salamis and Artemisium and those who stood in the line at Plataea"—never "those who won the victory." Throughout he cunningly avoids naming the result, because it was a happy one, and the opposite of what happened at Chaeronea. So before his hearers can raise the objection he promptly adds, "To all of these the

[a] From the *Demes* (fr. 106 Kassel-Austin).
[b] A reminiscence of Euripides, *Bacchae* 317.

ἔθαψε δημοσίᾳ" φησίν "ἡ πόλις, Αἰσχίνη, οὐχὶ τοὺς κατορθώσαντας μόνους."

17. Οὐκ ἄξιον ἐπὶ τούτου τοῦ τόπου παραλιπεῖν ἔν τι τῶν ἡμῖν τεθεωρημένων, φίλτατε, ἔσται δὲ πάνυ σύντομον, ὅτι φύσει πως συμμαχεῖ τε τῷ ὕψει τὰ σχήματα καὶ πάλιν ἀντισυμμαχεῖται θαυμαστῶς ὑπ' αὐτοῦ. πῇ δὲ καὶ πῶς; ἐγὼ φράσω. ὕποπτόν ἐστιν ἰδίως τὸ διὰ σχημάτων πανουργεῖν καὶ προσβάλλον ὑπόνοιαν ἐνέδρας ἐπιβουλῆς παραλογισμοῦ, καὶ ταῦθ' ὅταν ᾖ πρὸς κριτὴν κύριον ὁ λόγος, μάλιστα δὲ πρὸς τυράννους βασιλέας ἡγεμόνας ἐν ὑπεροχαῖς· ἀγανακτεῖ γὰρ εὐθύς, εἰ ὡς παῖς ἄφρων ὑπὸ τεχνίτου ῥήτορος σχηματίοις κατασοφίζεται, καὶ εἰς καταφρόνησιν ἑαυτοῦ λαμβάνων τὸν παραλογισμὸν ἐνίοτε μὲν ἀποθηριοῦται τὸ σύνολον, κἂν ἐπικρατήσῃ δὲ τοῦ θυμοῦ, πρὸς τὴν πειθὼ τῶν λόγων πάντως ἀντιδιατίθεται. διόπερ καὶ τότε ἄριστον δοκεῖ τὸ σχῆμα, ὅταν αὐτὸ τοῦτο διαλανθάνῃ ὅτι σχῆμά ἐστιν. τὸ τοίνυν ὕψος καὶ πάθος τῆς ἐπὶ τῷ σχηματίζειν ὑπονοίας ἀλέξημα καὶ θαυμαστή τις ἐπικουρία καθίσταται, καί πως περιλαμφθεῖσ' ἡ[1] τοῦ πανουργεῖν τέχνη τοῖς κάλλεσι καὶ μεγέθεσι τὸ λοιπὸν δέδυκεν καὶ πᾶσαν ὑποψίαν ἐκπέφευγεν. ἱκανὸν δὲ τεκμήριον τὸ προειρημένον "μὰ τοὺς ἐν Μαραθῶνι." τίνι γὰρ ἐνταῦθ' ὁ ῥήτωρ ἀπέκρυψε τὸ σχῆμα; δῆλον ὅτι τῷ φωτὶ αὐτῷ. σχεδὸν γὰρ ὥσπερ καὶ τἀμυδρὰ φέγγη ἐναφανίζεται τῷ ἡλίῳ περιαυγούμενα, οὕτω τὰ τῆς ῥητορικῆς σοφίσματα

country gave a public funeral, Aeschines, not only to those who were successful."

17. While on this topic I must not omit to mention a view of my own, dear friend, which I will state, however, quite concisely. Figures seem to be natural allies of the sublime and to draw in turn marvellous reinforcement from the alliance. Where and how? I will tell you. There is an inevitable suspicion attaching to the sophisticated use of figures. It gives a suggestion of treachery, craft, fallacy, especially when your speech is addressed to a judge with absolute authority, or still more to a despot, a king, or a ruler in high place. He is promptly indignant that he is being treated like a silly child and outwitted by the figures of a skilled speaker. Construing the fallacy as a personal affront, he sometimes turns downright savage; and even if he controls his feelings, he becomes conditioned against being persuaded by the speech. So we find that a figure is always most effective when it conceals the very fact of its being a figure. Sublimity and emotional intensity are a wonderfully helpful antidote against the suspicion that accompanies the use of figures. The artfulness of the trick is no longer obvious in its brilliant setting of beauty and grandeur, and thus avoids all suspicion. A sufficient instance is that mentioned above, "By those at Marathon." In that case how did the orator conceal the figure? By its very brilliance, of course. Much in the same way that dimmer lights vanish in the surrounding radiance of the sun, so an all-embracing atmosphere of grandeur obscures the rhetorical devices. We see some-

---

[1] περιλαμφθεῖσ' ἡ Bury for παραληφθεῖσαν P.

3 ἐξαμαυροῖ περιχυθὲν πάντοθεν τὸ μέγεθος. οὐ
πόρρω δ᾽ ἴσως τούτου καὶ ἐπὶ τῆς ζωγραφίας τι
συμβαίνει· ἐπὶ γὰρ τοῦ αὐτοῦ κειμένων ἐπιπέδου
παραλλήλων ἐν χρώμασι τῆς σκιᾶς τε καὶ τοῦ
φωτός, ὅμως προϋπαντᾷ τε τὸ φῶς ταῖς ὄψεσι καὶ οὐ
μόνον ἔξοχον ἀλλὰ καὶ ἐγγυτέρω παρὰ πολὺ φαίνεται. οὐκοῦν καὶ τῶν λόγων τὰ πάθη καὶ τὰ ὕψη,
ταῖς ψυχαῖς ἡμῶν ἐγγυτέρω κείμενα, διά τε φυσικήν
τινα συγγένειαν καὶ διὰ λαμπρότητα ἀεὶ τῶν σχημάτων προεμφανίζεται καὶ τὴν τέχνην αὐτῶν ἀπο-
σκιάζει καὶ οἷον ἐν κατακαλύψει τηρεῖ.

18. Τί δ᾽ ἐκεῖνα φῶμεν, τὰς πεύσεις τε καὶ ἐρωτή-
σεις; ἆρα οὐκ αὐταῖς ταῖς τῶν σχημάτων εἰδοποιίαις
παρὰ πολὺ ἐμπρακτότερα καὶ σοβαρώτερα συντείνει
τὰ λεγόμενα; "ἢ βούλεσθε, εἰπέ μοι, περιϊόντες
ἀλλήλων πυνθάνεσθαι· λέγεταί τι καινόν; τί γὰρ ἂν
γένοιτο τούτου καινότερον ἢ Μακεδὼν ἀνὴρ καταπο-
λεμῶν τὴν Ἑλλάδα; τέθνηκε Φίλιππος; οὐ μὰ Δί᾽
ἀλλ᾽ ἀσθενεῖ. τί δ᾽ ὑμῖν διαφέρει; καὶ γὰρ ἂν οὗτός
τι πάθῃ, ταχέως ὑμεῖς ἕτερον Φίλιππον ποιήσετε."
καὶ πάλιν "πλέωμεν ἐπὶ Μακεδονίαν," φησί. "ποῖ
δὴ προσορμιούμεθα; ἤρετό τις. εὑρήσει τὰ σαθρὰ
τῶν Φιλίππου πραγμάτων αὐτὸς ὁ πόλεμος." ἦν δὲ
ἁπλῶς ῥηθὲν τὸ πρᾶγμα τῷ παντὶ καταδεέστερον,
νυνὶ δὲ τὸ ἔνθουν καὶ ὀξύρροπον τῆς πεύσεως καὶ
ἀποκρίσεως καὶ τὸ πρὸς ἑαυτὸν ὡς πρὸς ἕτερον
ἀνθυπαντᾶν οὐ μόνον ὑψηλότερον ἐποίησε τῷ σχη-
2 ματισμῷ τὸ ῥηθὲν ἀλλὰ καὶ πιστότερον. ἄγει γὰρ
τὰ παθητικὰ τότε μᾶλλον, ὅταν αὐτὰ φαίνηται μὴ

thing of the same kind in painting. Though the highlights and shadows lie side by side in the same plane, yet the highlights spring to the eye and seem not only to stand out but to be actually much nearer. So it is in writing. What is sublime and moving lies nearer to our hearts, and thus, partly from a natural affinity, partly from brilliance of effect, it always strikes the eye long before the figures, thus throwing their art into the shade and keeping it hid as it were under a bushel.

18. Now what are we to say of our next subject, the figures of inquiry and interrogation? Is it not just the specific character of these figures which gives the language much greater realism, vigour and tension? "Tell me, my friend, do you all want to go round asking each other 'Is there any news?'[a] For what stranger news could there be than this of a Macedonian conquering Greece? 'Is Philip dead?' 'No, not dead but ill.' What difference does it make to you? Whatever happens to him, you will soon manufacture another Philip for yourselves." Or again: "Let us sail to Macedon. Someone asks me, 'Where on earth shall we land?' Why, the mere course of the war will find out the weak spots in Philip's situation." Here a bare statement would have been utterly inadequate. As it is, the inspiration and quick play of the question and answer, and his way of confronting his own words as if they were someone else's, make the passage, through his use of the figure, not only loftier but also more convincing. For emotion is always more telling when it seems not to be

[a] This and the following passage are loose quotations from the *First Philippic* (Demosthenes, *Oration* 4.10 and 44).

ἐπιτηδεύειν αὐτὸς ὁ λέγων ἀλλὰ γεννᾶν ὁ καιρός, ἡ
δ' ἐρώτησις ἡ εἰς ἑαυτὸν καὶ ἀπόκρισις μιμεῖται τοῦ
πάθους τὸ ἐπίκαιρον. σχεδὸν γὰρ ὡς οἱ ὑφ' ἑτέρων
ἐρωτώμενοι παροξυνθέντες ἐκ τοῦ παραχρῆμα πρὸς
τὸ λεχθὲν ἐναγωνίως καὶ ἀπ' αὐτῆς τῆς ἀληθείας
ἀνθυπαντῶσιν, οὕτως τὸ σχῆμα τῆς πεύσεως καὶ
ἀποκρίσεως εἰς τὸ δοκεῖν ἕκαστον τῶν ἐσκεμμένων
ἐξ ὑπογύου κεκινῆσθαί τε καὶ λέγεσθαι τὸν ἀκροατὴν ἀπάγον καὶ παραλογίζεται. ἔτι τοίνυν (ἐν γάρ
τι τῶν ὑψηλοτάτων τὸ Ἡροδότειον πεπίστευται) εἰ
οὕτως ἔ . . .[1]

19. . . . <ἀσύμ>πλοκα[2] ἐκπίπτει καὶ οἱονεὶ προ-
χεῖται τὰ λεγόμενα, ὀλίγου δεῖν φθάνοντα καὶ αὐτὸν
τὸν λέγοντα. "καὶ συμβαλόντες," φησὶν ὁ Ξενοφῶν,
"τὰς ἀσπίδας ἐωθοῦντο ἐμάχοντο ἀπέκτεινον ἀπέ-
2   θνῃσκον." καὶ τὰ τοῦ Εὐρυλόχου

> ἤλθομεν, ὡς ἐκέλευες, ἀνὰ δρυμά, φαίδιμ'
>   Ὀδυσσεῦ.
> εἴδομεν ἐν βήσσῃσι τετυγμένα δώματα καλά.

τὰ γὰρ ἀλλήλων διακεκομμένα καὶ οὐδὲν ἧσσον
κατεσπευσμένα φέρει τῆς ἀγωνίας ἔμφασιν ἅμα καὶ
ἐμποδιζούσης τι καὶ συνδιωκούσης.[3] τοιαῦθ' ὁ ποιη-

---

[1] Perhaps ἔ<γραψε>, if Longinus was about to compare
Herodotus' actual use of the figure with the ineffective alternative of doing without it. Cf. chap. 21.
[2] So K marg., Manutius.
[3] So Faber for P's συνδιοικούσης.

premeditated by the speaker but to be born of the moment; and this way of questioning and answering one's self counterfeits spontaneous emotion. People who are cross-questioned by others in the heat of the moment reply to the point forcibly and with utter candour; and in much the same way the figure of question and answer actually misleads the audience, by encouraging it to suppose that each carefully premeditated argument has been aroused in the mind and put into words on the spur of the moment. Moreover— for this passage of Herodotus has always been reckoned one of the most sublime—if in this way . . .[a]

[Two pages are missing here.]

19.[b] . . . the phrases tumble out unconnected in a sort of spate, almost too quick for the speaker himself. "And locking their shields," says Xenophon, "they pushed, fought, slew, fell."[c] And take the words of Eurylochus,

> We came, as you told us to come, through the oak
> coppice, shining Odysseus.
> Built in the glades we beheld habitations of wonderful beauty.[d]

The phrases being disconnected, and yet none the less rapid, give the idea of an agitation which both checks the utterance and at the same time drives it on. This is the

---

[a] The passage of Herodotus cannot be identified, but may be 7.21, which has notable rhetorical questions.

[b] The subject is now asyndeton, i.e. the omission of conjunctions.

[c] Xenophon, *Hellenica* 4.3.19 (= *Agesilaus* 2.12).

[d] *Odyssey* 10.251–2.

LONGINUS

τῆς ἐξήνεγκε διὰ τῶν ἀσυνδέτων.

20. Ἄκρως δὲ καὶ ἡ ἐπὶ ταὐτὸ σύνοδος τῶν σχημάτων εἴωθε κινεῖν, ὅταν δύο ἢ τρία οἷον κατὰ συμ-
μορίαν ἀνακιρνάμενα ἀλλήλοις ἐρανίζῃ τὴν ἰσχὺν
τὴν πειθὼ τὸ κάλλος, ὁποῖα καὶ τὰ εἰς τὸν Μειδίαν,
ταῖς ἀναφοραῖς ὁμοῦ καὶ τῇ διατυπώσει συναναπε-
πλεγμένα τὰ ἀσύνδετα. "πολλὰ γὰρ ἂν ποιήσειεν ὁ
τύπτων, ὧν ὁ παθὼν ἔνια οὐδ᾽ ἂν ἀπαγγεῖλαι
δύναιτο ἑτέρῳ, τῷ σχήματι, τῷ βλέμματι, τῇ φωνῇ."
2 εἶθ᾽ ἵνα μὴ ἐπὶ τῶν αὐτῶν ὁ λόγος ἰὼν στῇ (ἐν στά-
σει γὰρ τὸ ἠρεμοῦν, ἐν ἀταξίᾳ δὲ τὸ πάθος, ἐπεὶ
φορὰ ψυχῆς καὶ συγκίνησίς ἐστιν), εὐθὺς ἐπ᾽ ἄλλα
μεθήλατο ἀσύνδετα καὶ ἐπαναφοράς· "τῷ σχήματι,
τῷ βλέμματι, τῇ φωνῇ, ὅταν ὡς ὑβρίζων, ὅταν ὡς
ἐχθρός, ὅταν κονδύλοις, ὅταν ὡς δοῦλον." οὐδὲν
ἄλλο διὰ τούτων ὁ ῥήτωρ ἢ ὅπερ ὁ τύπτων ἐργάζεται, τὴν διάνοιαν τῶν δικαστῶν τῇ ἐπαλλήλῳ πλήτ-
3 τει φορᾷ. εἶτ᾽ ἐντεῦθεν πάλιν ὡς αἱ καταιγίδες
ἄλλην ποιούμενος ἐμβολήν "ὅταν κονδύλοις, ὅταν
ἐπὶ κόρρης" φησί· "ταῦτα κινεῖ, ταῦτα ἐξίστησιν
ἀνθρώπους, ἀήθεις ὄντας τοῦ προπηλακίζεσθαι·
οὐδεὶς ἂν ταῦτα ἀπαγγέλλων δύναιτο τὸ δεινὸν
παραστῆσαι." οὐκοῦν τὴν μὲν φύσιν τῶν ἐπαναφο-
ρῶν καὶ ἀσυνδέτων πάντη φυλάττει τῇ συνεχεῖ
μεταβολῇ· οὕτως αὐτῷ καὶ ἡ τάξις ἄτακτον καὶ
ἔμπαλιν ἡ ἀταξία ποιὰν περιλαμβάνει τάξιν.

effect the poet has achieved by his use of asyndeton.

20. The combination of several figures often has an exceptionally powerful effect, when two or three combined cooperate, as it were, to contribute force, conviction, beauty. Thus, for instance, in the speech against Midias the asyndeta are interwoven with the figures of repetition and vivid presentation.[a] "For the aggressor may do many injuries, some of which the victim could not even describe to anyone else—by his manner, his look, his voice." Then to prevent the speech coming to a halt by running over the same ground—for immobility expresses inertia, while emotion, being a violent movement of the soul, demands disorder—he leaps at once into further asyndeta and anaphoras. "By his manner, his looks, his voice, when he strikes with insult, when he strikes like an enemy, when he strikes with his knuckles, when he strikes you like a slave." Here the orator does just the same as the aggressor, he belabours the minds of the jury with blow after blow. Then at this point he proceeds to make another onslaught, like a tornado. "When it's with his knuckles, when it's a slap on the face," he says, "this rouses, this maddens a man who is not accustomed to insult. Nobody could convey the horror of it simply by reporting it." Thus all the time he preserves the essence of his repetitions and asyndeta through continual variation, so that his very order is disordered and equally his disorder involves a certain element of order.

[a] Demosthenes, *Oration* 21.72 (with some variations from our text).

21. Φέρε οὖν, πρόσθες τοὺς συνδέσμους, εἰ
θέλοις, ὡς ποιοῦσιν οἱ Ἰσοκράτειοι "καὶ μὴν οὐδὲ
τοῦτο χρὴ παραλιπεῖν, ὡς πολλὰ ἂν ποιήσειεν ὁ
τύπτων, πρῶτον μὲν τῷ σχήματι, εἶτα δὲ τῷ βλέμματι, εἶτά γε μὴν αὐτῇ τῇ φωνῇ," καὶ εἴσῃ κατὰ
τὸ ἑξῆς οὕτως παραγράφων, ὡς τοῦ πάθους τὸ
συνδεδιωγμένον καὶ ἀποτραχυνόμενον, ἐὰν τοῖς
συνδέσμοις ἐξομαλίσῃς εἰς λειότητα, ἄκεντρόν τε
2 προσπίπτει καὶ εὐθὺς ἔσβεσται. ὥσπερ γὰρ εἴ τις
συνδήσειε τῶν θεόντων τὰ σώματα τὴν φορὰν αὐτῶν
ἀφῄρηται, οὕτως καὶ τὸ πάθος ὑπὸ τῶν συνδέσμων
καὶ τῶν ἄλλων προσθηκῶν ἐμποδιζόμενον ἀγα-
νακτεῖ· τὴν γὰρ ἐλευθερίαν ἀπολλύει[1] τοῦ δρόμου
καὶ τὸ ὡς ἀπ᾽ ὀργάνου τινὸς ἀφίεσθαι.

22. Τῆς δὲ αὐτῆς ἰδέας καὶ τὰ ὑπερβατὰ θετέον.
ἔστιν δὲ λέξεων ἢ νοήσεων ἐκ τοῦ κατ᾽ ἀκολουθίαν
κεκινημένη τάξις καὶ οἱονεὶ χαρακτὴρ ἐναγωνίου
πάθους ἀληθέστατος. ὡς γὰρ οἱ τῷ ὄντι ὀργιζόμε-
νοι ἢ φοβούμενοι ἢ ἀγανακτοῦντες ἢ ὑπὸ ζηλοτυ-
πίας ἢ ὑπὸ ἄλλου τινός (πολλὰ γὰρ καὶ ἀναρίθμητα
πάθη καὶ οὐδ᾽ ἂν εἰπεῖν τις ὁπόσα δύναιτο) ἑκάστοτε
παραπίπτοντες ἄλλα προθέμενοι πολλάκις ἐπ᾽ ἄλλα
μεταπηδῶσι, μέσα τινὰ παρεμβαλόντες ἀλόγως, εἶτ᾽
αὖθις ἐπὶ τὰ πρῶτα ἀνακυκλοῦντες καὶ πάντη πρὸς
τῆς ἀγωνίας, ὡς ὑπ᾽ ἀστάτου πνεύματος, τῇδε
κἀκεῖσε ἀγχιστρόφως ἀντισπώμενοι τὰς λέξεις τὰς

---

[1] So Finck for P's ἀπολύει.

21. Now insert the connecting particles, if you care to do so, in the style of Isocrates[a] and his school. "And yet one must not overlook this too, that the aggressor may do much, first by his manner, then by his looks, and then again by his mere voice." If you thus paraphrase it sentence by sentence you will see that if the rush and ruggedness of the emotion is levelled and smoothed out by the use of connecting particles,[b] it loses its sting and its fire is quickly put out. For just as you deprive runners of their speed if you bind them up, emotion equally resents being hampered by connecting particles and other appendages. It loses its freedom of motion and the sense of being, as it were, catapulted out.

22. In the same category we must place hyperbaton. This figure consists in arranging words and thoughts out of the natural sequence, and is, as it were, the truest mark of vehement emotion. Just as people who are really angry or frightened or indignant, or are carried away by jealousy or some other feeling —there are countless emotions, no one can say how many—often put forward one point and then spring off to another with various illogical interpolations, and then wheel round again to their original position, while, under the stress of their excitement, like a ship before a veering wind, they lay their words and

[a] Isocrates was the principal proponent and model of the periodic style which articulates every clause carefully and avoids hiatus.

[b] The word for "conjunction" or "connecting particle," *sundesmos*, literally means "bond."

νοήσεις τὴν ἐκ τοῦ κατὰ φύσιν εἱρμοῦ παντοίως
πρὸς μυρίας τροπὰς ἐναλλάττουσι τάξιν, οὕτω παρὰ
τοῖς ἀρίστοις συγγραφεῦσι διὰ τῶν ὑπερβατῶν ἡ
μίμησις ἐπὶ τὰ τῆς φύσεως ἔργα φέρεται. τότε γὰρ
ἡ τέχνη τέλειος, ἡνίκ' ἂν φύσις εἶναι δοκῇ, ἡ δ' αὖ
φύσις ἐπιτυχής, ὅταν λανθάνουσαν περιέχῃ τὴν
τέχνην. ὥσπερ λέγει ὁ Φωκαεὺς Διονύσιος παρὰ τῷ
Ἡροδότῳ· "ἐπὶ ξυροῦ γὰρ ἀκμῆς ἔχεται ἡμῖν τὰ
πράγματα, ἄνδρες Ἴωνες, εἶναι ἐλευθέροις ἢ δού-
λοις καὶ τούτοις ὡς δραπέτῃσιν. νῦν ὦν ὑμεῖς ἢν
μὲν βούλησθε ταλαιπωρίας ἐνδέχεσθαι, παραχρῆμα
μὲν πόνος ὑμῖν, οἷοί τε δὲ ἔσεσθε ὑπερβαλέσθαι
2   τοὺς πολεμίους." ἐνταῦθ' ἦν τὸ κατὰ τάξιν· "ὦ
ἄνδρες Ἴωνες, νῦν καιρός ἐστιν ὑμῖν πόνους ἐπιδέ-
χεσθαι· ἐπὶ ξυροῦ γὰρ ἀκμῆς ἔχεται ἡμῖν τὰ πράγματα." ὁ δὲ τὸ μὲν "ἄνδρες Ἴωνες" ὑπερεβίβασεν·
προεισέβαλεν οὖν[1] εὐθὺς ἀπὸ τοῦ φόβου, ὡς μηδ'
ἀρχὴν φθάνων πρὸς τὸ ἐφεστὼς δέος προσαγορεῦ-
σαι τοὺς ἀκούοντας· ἔπειτα δὲ τὴν τῶν νοημάτων
ἀπέστρεψε τάξιν· πρὸ γὰρ τοῦ φῆσαι ὅτι αὐτοὺς δεῖ
πονεῖν (τοῦτο γάρ ἐστιν ὃ παρακελεύεται) ἔμπροσθεν ἀποδίδωσι τὴν αἰτίαν δι' ἣν πονεῖν δεῖ,
"ἐπὶ ξυροῦ ἀκμῆς" φήσας "ἔχεται ἡμῖν τὰ πράγματα," ὡς μὴ δοκεῖν ἐσκεμμένα λέγειν ἀλλ'
3   ἠναγκασμένα. ἔτι δὲ μᾶλλον ὁ Θουκυδίδης καὶ τὰ
φύσει πάντως ἡνωμένα καὶ ἀδιανέμητα ὅμως ταῖς
ὑπερβάσεσιν ἀπ' ἀλλήλων ἄγειν δεινότατος. ὁ δὲ
Δημοσθένης οὐχ οὕτως μὲν αὐθάδης ὥσπερ οὗτος,

thoughts first on one tack then another, and keep altering
the natural order of sequence into innumerable variations—so, too, in the best prose writers the use of hyperbata allows imitation to approach the effects of nature.
For art is only perfect when it looks like nature and
Nature succeeds only when she conceals latent art. Take
the speech of Dionysius the Phocaean, in Herodotus.[a]
"Our fortunes stand upon a razor's edge, men of Ionia,
whether we be free men or slaves, aye, and runaway
slaves. Now, therefore if you are willing to endure hard-
ship, at the moment there is toil for you, but you will be
able to overcome your enemies." Here the natural order
was, "O men of Ionia, now is the time for you to endure
toil, for our fortunes stand upon a razor's edge." He has
transposed "men of Ionia" and started at once with his
fears, as though the terror was so immediate that he could
not even address the audience first. He has, moreover,
inverted the order of ideas. Before saying that they must
toil—for that is the point of his exhortation—he first gives
the reason why they must toil, by saying, "Our fortunes
stand upon a razor's edge." The result is that his words do
not seem premeditated but rather wrung from him.
Thucydides is even more a master in the use of hyperbata
to separate ideas which are naturally one and indivisible.
Demosthenes, though not indeed so wilful as Thucydides,

[a] Herodotus 6.11.

[1] γὰρ Spengel.

πάντων δ' ἐν τῷ γένει τούτῳ κατακορέστατος καὶ
πολὺ τὸ ἀγωνιστικὸν ἐκ τοῦ ὑπερβιβάζειν καὶ ἔτι νὴ
Δία τὸ ἐξ ὑπογύου λέγειν συνεμφαίνων καὶ πρὸς
τούτοις εἰς τὸν κίνδυνον τῶν μακρῶν ὑπερβατῶν
4 τοὺς ἀκούοντας συνεπισπώμενος· πολλάκις γὰρ τὸν
νοῦν ὃν ὥρμησεν εἰπεῖν ἀνακρεμάσας καὶ μεταξύ
πως[1] εἰς ἀλλόφυλον καὶ ἀπεοικυῖαν τάξιν ἄλλ' ἐπ'
ἄλλοις διὰ μέσου καὶ ἔξωθέν ποθεν ἐπεισκυκλῶν εἰς
φόβον ἐμβαλὼν τὸν ἀκροατὴν ὡς ἐπὶ παντελεῖ τοῦ
λόγου διαπτώσει καὶ συναποκινδυνεύειν ὑπ' ἀγωνίας
τῷ λέγοντι συναναγκάσας, εἶτα παραλόγως διὰ
μακροῦ τὸ πάλαι ζητούμενον εὐκαίρως ἐπὶ τέλει που
προσαποδούς, αὐτῷ τῷ κατὰ τὰς ὑπερβάσεις παρα-
βόλῳ καὶ ἀκροσφαλεῖ πολὺ μᾶλλον ἐκπλήττει.
φειδὼ δὲ τῶν παραδειγμάτων ἔστω διὰ τὸ πλῆθος.

23. Τά γε μὴν πολύπτωτα λεγόμενα, ἀθροισμοὶ
καὶ μεταβολαὶ καὶ κλίμακες, πάνυ ἀγωνιστικά, ὡς
οἶσθα, κόσμου τε καὶ παντὸς ὕψους καὶ πάθους συν-
εργά. τί δὲ αἱ τῶν πτώσεων χρόνων προσώπων
ἀριθμῶν γενῶν ἐναλλάξεις, πῶς ποτε καταποικίλ-
2 λουσι καὶ ἐπεγείρουσι τὰ ἑρμηνευτικά; φημὶ δὲ τῶν
κατὰ τοὺς ἀριθμοὺς οὐ μόνα ταῦτα κοσμεῖν, ὁπόσα
τοῖς τύποις ἑνικὰ ὄντα τῇ δυνάμει κατὰ τὴν ἀναθεώ-
ρησιν πληθυντικὰ εὑρίσκεται·

αὐτίκα (φησί) λαὸς ἀπείρων
θύννον[2] ἐπ' ἠιόνεσσι διστάμενοι κελάδησαν·

[1] So Wilamowitz, for P's μεταξὺ ὡς.
[2] θύννον Vahlen for P's θύννων.

is the most lavish of all in this kind of use and not only employs hyperbata to give a great effect of vehemence, and indeed of improvisation, but also drags his audience along with him to share the perils of these long hyperbata. For he often suspends the sense which he has begun to express, and in the interval manages to bring forward one extraneous idea after another in a strange and unlikely order, making the audience terrified of a total collapse of the sentence, and compelling them from sheer excitement to share the speaker's risk; then unexpectedly, after a great interval, the long-lost phrase turns up pat at the end, so that he astounds them all the more by the very recklessness and audacity of the transpositions. But there are so many examples that I must stay my hand.

23. Again, accumulation, variation, and climax, the so-called "polyptota," are, as you know, very powerful, and contribute to ornament and to sublimity and emotion of all kinds. And consider, too, what variety and liveliness is lent to the exposition by changes of case, tense, person, number, or gender. In the category of number, for example, not only are those uses ornamental where the singular in form is found on consideration to signify a plural— take the lines:

> And straightway a numberless people
> Scatter the length of the beaches and thunder, "the
> Tunny, the Tunny!"[a]

[a] The source of this quotation is not known. If the text here printed is right, the reference is to tunny-fishing, when the approach of a shoal is watched for and eagerly announced to the fishermen.

ἀλλ' ἐκεῖνα μᾶλλον παρατηρήσεως ἄξια, ὅτι ἔσθ'
ὅπου προσπίπτει τὰ πληθυντικὰ μεγαλορρημονέ-
στερα καὶ αὐτῷ δοξοκοποῦντα τῷ ὄχλῳ τοῦ ἀριθμοῦ.

3   τοιαῦτα παρὰ τῷ Σοφοκλεῖ τὰ ἐπὶ τοῦ Οἰδίπου·

> ὦ γάμοι, γάμοι,
> ἐφύσαθ' ἡμᾶς καὶ φυτεύσαντες πάλιν
> ἀνεῖτε ταὐτὸ σπέρμα κἀπεδείξατε
> πατέρας ἀδελφοὺς παῖδας, αἷμ' ἐμφύλιον,
> νύμφας γυναῖκας μητέρας τε χὠπόσα
> αἴσχιστ' ἐν ἀνθρώποισιν ἔργα γίγνεται.

πάντα γὰρ ταῦτα ἓν ὄνομά ἐστιν, Οἰδίπους, ἐπὶ δὲ
θατέρου Ἰοκάστη, ἀλλ' ὅμως χυθεὶς εἰς τὰ πληθυντικὰ ὁ ἀριθμὸς συνεπλήθυσε καὶ τὰς ἀτυχίας· καὶ
ὡς ἐκεῖνα πεπλεόνασται,

> ἐξῆλθον Ἕκτορές τε καὶ Σαρπηδόνες·

4   καὶ τὸ Πλατωνικόν, ὃ καὶ ἑτέρωθι παρετεθείμεθα, ἐπὶ
τῶν Ἀθηναίων· "οὐ γὰρ Πέλοπες οὐδὲ Κάδμοι οὐδ'
Αἴγυπτοί τε καὶ Δαναοὶ οὐδ' ἄλλοι πολλοὶ φύσει
βάρβαροι συνοικοῦσιν ἡμῖν, ἀλλ' αὐτοὶ Ἕλληνες,
οὐ μιξοβάρβαροι οἰκοῦμεν" καὶ τὰ ἑξῆς. φύσει γὰρ
ἐξακούεται τὰ πράγματα κομπωδέστερα ἀγεληδὸν
οὕτως τῶν ὀνομάτων ἐπισυντιθεμένων. οὐ μέντοι δεῖ
ποιεῖν αὐτὸ ἐπ' ἄλλων εἰ μὴ ἐφ' ὧν δέχεται τὰ ὑποκείμενα[1] αὔξησιν ἢ πληθὺν ἢ ὑπερβολὴν ἢ πάθος,

---

[1] ὑποκείμενα Petra for ὑπερκείμενα.

—but it is still more worthy of notice that plurals sometimes make a grander impression, courting favour by the
sense of multitude given by the grammatical number.
This is the case with Sophocles' lines about Oedipus:

> Curse on the marriages
> That gave us birth and having given birth
> Flung forth the selfsame seed again and showed
> Fathers and sons and brothers all blood-kin,
> And brides and wives and mothers, all the shame
> Of all the foulest deeds that men have done.[a]

These all mean one person, Oedipus, and on the other
side Jocasta, but the expansion into the plural serves to
make the misfortunes plural as well. There is the same
sense of multiplication in "Forth came Hectors and
Sarpedons too,"[b] and in the passage of Plato about the
Athenians, which we have also quoted elsewhere: "For no
Pelopses nor Cadmuses nor Aegyptuses and Danauses
nor any other hordes of born barbarians share our home,
but we are pure Greeks here, no semi-barbarians,"[c] and
so on. The facts naturally sound more imposing from the
accumulation of names in groups. This device should not,
however, be employed except where the subject invites

[a] *Oedipus Tyrannus* 1403–8.
[b] Source unknown: see Kannicht-Snell, *Tragicorum Graecorum Fragmenta* II (Adespota 1 fr. 289).
[c] Plato, *Menexenus* 245D. "Elsewhere" presumably refers to
another book.

ἔν τι τούτων ἢ τὰ πλείονα, ἐπεί τοι τὸ πανταχοῦ
κώδωνας ἐξῆφθαι λίαν σοφιστικόν.

24. Ἀλλὰ μὴν καὶ τοὐναντίον τὰ ἐκ τῶν πληθυν-
τικῶν εἰς τὰ ἑνικὰ ἐπισυναγόμενα ἐνίοτε ὑψηλοφανέ-
στατα. "ἔπειθ᾽ ἡ Πελοπόννησος ἅπασα διειστήκει"
φησί. "καὶ δὴ Φρυνίχῳ δρᾶμα Μιλήτου ἅλωσιν
διδάξαντι εἰς δάκρυα ἔπεσε τὸ θέητρον."[1] τὸ ἐκ τῶν
διῃρημένων εἰς τὰ ἡνωμένα ἐπισυστρέψαι τὸν ἀριθμὸν σωματοειδέστερον. αἴτιον δ᾽ ἐπ᾽ ἀμφοῖν τοῦ
κόσμου ταὐτὸν οἶμαι· ὅπου τε γὰρ ἑνικὰ ὑπάρχει τὰ
ὀνόματα, τὸ πολλὰ ποιεῖν αὐτὰ παρὰ δόξαν ἐμπα-
θοῦς, ὅπου τε πληθυντικά, τὸ εἰς ἕν τι εὔηχον
συγκορυφοῦν τὰ πλείονα διὰ τὴν εἰς τοὐναντίον
μεταμόρφωσιν τῶν πραγμάτων ἐν τῷ παραλόγῳ.

25. Ὅταν γε μὴν τὰ παρεληλυθότα τοῖς χρόνοις
εἰσάγῃς ὡς γινόμενα καὶ παρόντα, οὐ διήγησιν ἔτι
τὸν λόγον ἀλλ᾽ ἐναγώνιον πρᾶγμα ποιήσεις. "πε-
πτωκὼς δέ τις," φησὶν ὁ Ξενοφῶν, "ὑπὸ τῷ Κύρου
ἵππῳ καὶ πατούμενος παίει τῇ μαχαίρᾳ εἰς τὴν
γαστέρα τὸν ἵππον· ὁ δὲ σφαδᾴζων ἀποσείεται τὸν
Κῦρον, ὁ δὲ πίπτει." τοιοῦτος ἐν τοῖς πλείστοις ὁ
Θουκυδίδης.

26. Ἐναγώνιος δ᾽ ὁμοίως καὶ ἡ τῶν προσώπων
ἀντιμετάθεσις καὶ πολλάκις ἐν μέσοις τοῖς κινδύνοις
ποιοῦσα τὸν ἀκροατὴν δοκεῖν στρέφεσθαι.

---

[1] ἔπεσε τὸ θέητρον Toll for ἔπεσον οἱ θεώμενοι.

amplification or redundance or exaggeration or emotion, either one or more of these. To have bells hung all over you is the mark of a sophist.

24. Yet again, the converse of this, the contraction of plurals to singulars, sometimes gives a great effect of sublimity. "Moreover, the whole Peloponnese was split," says Demosthenes.[a] Again, "when Phrynichus produced his *Capture of Miletus* the theatre burst into tears."[b] To compress the number of separate individuals into a unified whole gives more sense of solidity. The ornamental effect in both is due to the same cause. Where the words are singular, to make them unexpectedly plural suggests emotion: where they are plural and you combine a number of things into a well-sounding singular, then this opposite change of the facts gives an effect of surprise.

25. Again, if you introduce events in past time as happening at the present moment, the passage will be transformed from a narrative into a vivid actuality. "Someone has fallen," says Xenophon, "under Cyrus' horse and, as he is trodden under foot, is striking the horse's belly with his dagger. The horse, rearing, throws Cyrus, and he falls."[c] Thucydides uses such effects very often.

26. Change of person gives an equally powerful effect, and often makes the audience feel themselves set in the thick of the danger.

[a] *De corona (Oration* 18) 18.
[b] Herodotus 6.21.
[c] Xenophon, *Cyropaedia* 7.1.37.

φαίης κ' ἀκμῆτας καὶ ἀτειρέας
ἄντεσθ' ἐν πολέμῳ· ὡς ἐσσυμένως ἐμάχοντο.

καὶ ὁ Ἄρατος

μὴ κείνῳ ἐνὶ μηνὶ περικλύζοιο θαλάσσῃ.

2 ὧδέ που καὶ ὁ Ἡρόδοτος· "ἀπὸ δὲ Ἐλεφαντίνης
πόλεως ἄνω πλεύσεαι, καὶ ἔπειτα ἀφίξῃ ἐς πεδίον
λεῖον· διεξελθὼν δὲ τοῦτο τὸ χωρίον αὖθις εἰς ἕτερον
πλοῖον ἐμβὰς πλεύσεαι δύ' ἡμέρας, ἔπειτα ἥξεις ἐς
πόλιν μεγάλην, ᾗ ὄνομα Μερόη." ὁρᾷς, ὦ ἑταῖρε, ὡς
παραλαβών σου τὴν ψυχὴν διὰ τῶν τόπων ἄγει τὴν
ἀκοὴν ὄψιν ποιῶν; πάντα δὲ τὰ τοιαῦτα πρὸς αὐτὰ
ἀπερειδόμενα τὰ πρόσωπα ἐπ' αὐτῶν ἵστησι τὸν
3 ἀκροατὴν τῶν ἐνεργουμένων. καὶ ὅταν ὡς οὐ πρὸς
ἅπαντας ἀλλ' ὡς πρὸς μόνον τινὰ λαλῇς,

Τυδείδην δ' οὐκ ἂν γνοίης ποτέροισι μετείη,

ἐμπαθέστερόν τε αὐτὸν ἅμα καὶ προσεκτικώτερον
καὶ ἀγῶνος ἔμπλεων ἀποτελέσεις, ταῖς εἰς ἑαυτὸν
προσφωνήσεσιν ἐξεγειρόμενον.

27. Ἔτι γε μὴν ἔσθ' ὅτε περὶ προσώπου διηγού-
μενος ὁ συγγραφεὺς ἐξαίφνης παρενεχθεὶς εἰς τὸ
αὐτοπρόσωπον ἀντιμεθίσταται, καὶ ἔστι τὸ τοιοῦτον
εἶδος ἐκβολή τις πάθους.

---

[a] *Iliad* 15.697–8.
[b] Aratus, *Phaenomena* 287.

> . . . You would say that unworn and
> with temper undaunted
> Each met the other in war, so headlong the rush of
> their battle.[a]

And Aratus' line:

> In that month may you never be found where the
> sea surges round you.[b]

Herodotus does much the same: "You will sail up from the city of Elephantine and there come to a smooth plain. And when you have passed through that place you will board again another ship and sail two days and then you will come to a great city, the name of which is Meroe."[c] Do you see, friend, how he takes you along with him through the country and turns hearing into sight? All such passages with a direct personal address put the hearer in the presence of the action itself. By appearing to address not the whole audience but a single individual—

> Of Tydeus' son you could not have known with
> which of the hosts he was fighting—[d]

you will move him more and make him more attentive and full of active interest, because he is roused by the appeals to him in person.

27. Again sometimes a writer, while speaking about a person suddenly turns and changes into the person himself. A figure of this kind is a sort of outbreak of emotion:

[c] Herodotus 2.29.
[d] *Iliad* 5.85.

Ἕκτωρ δὲ Τρώεσσιν ἐκέκλετο μακρὸν ἀΰσας
νηυσὶν ἐπισσεύεσθαι, ἐᾶν δ᾽ ἔναρα βροτόεντα·
ὃν δ᾽ ἂν ἐγὼν ἀπάνευθε νεῶν ἐθέλοντα νοήσω,
αὐτοῦ οἱ θάνατον μητίσομαι.

οὐκοῦν τὴν μὲν διήγησιν ἅτε πρέπουσαν ὁ ποιητὴς
προσῆψεν ἑαυτῷ, τὴν δ᾽ ἀπότομον ἀπειλὴν τῷ θυμῷ
τοῦ ἡγεμόνος ἐξαπίνης οὐδὲν προδηλώσας περιέθη-
κεν· ἐψύχετο γάρ, εἰ παρενετίθει "ἔλεγεν δὲ τοιά τινα
καὶ τοια ὁ Ἕκτωρ," νυνὶ δ᾽ ἔφθακεν ἄφνω τὸν μετα-
2 βαίνοντα ἡ τοῦ λόγου μετάβασις. διὸ καὶ ἡ
πρόσχρησις[1] τοῦ σχήματος τότε, ἡνίκ᾽ ἂν ὀξὺς ὁ
καιρὸς ὢν διαμέλλειν τῷ γράφοντι μὴ διδῷ ἀλλ᾽
εὐθὺς ἐπαναγκάζῃ μεταβαίνειν ἐκ προσώπων εἰς
πρόσωπα· ὡς καὶ παρὰ τῷ Ἑκαταίῳ· "Κῆϋξ δὲ
ταῦτα δεινὰ ποιούμενος αὐτίκα ἐκέλευε τοὺς [Ἡρα-
κλείδας][2] ἐπιγόνους ἐκχωρεῖν· οὐ γὰρ ὑμῖν δυνατός
εἰμι ἀρήγειν. ὡς μὴ ὦν αὐτοί τε ἀπολέεσθε κἀμὲ
3 τρώσετε, ἐς ἄλλον τινὰ δῆμον ἀποίχεσθε." ὁ μὲν
γὰρ Δημοσθένης κατ᾽ ἄλλον τινὰ τρόπον ἐπὶ τοῦ
Ἀριστογείτονος ἐμπαθὲς τὸ πολυπρόσωπον καὶ
ἀγχίστροφον παρέστακεν. "καὶ οὐδεὶς ὑμῶν χο-
λήν," φησίν, "οὐδ᾽ ὀργὴν ἔχων εὑρεθήσεται ἐφ᾽ οἷς
ὁ βδελυρὸς οὗτος καὶ ἀναιδὴς βιάζεται, ὅς, ὦ μιαρώτατε ἁπάντων, κεκλεισμένης σοι τῆς παρρησίας
οὐ κιγκλίσιν οὐδὲ θύραις, ἃ καὶ παρανοίξειεν ἄν τις
..." ἐν ἀτελεῖ τῷ νῷ ταχὺ διαλλάξας καὶ μόνον

---

[1] πρόσχρησις Manutius for πρόχρησις P.
[2] [Ἡρακλείδας] del. Russell (1964).

Hector lifted his voice and cried afar to the Trojans
To rush back now to the galleys and leave the
     blood-spattered booty.
Whomsoever I see of his own will afar from the
     galleys,
Death for him there will I plan.[a]

There the poet has assigned the narrative to himself as his
proper share, and then suddenly without any warning
attached the abrupt threat to the angry champion. To
insert "Hector said so and so" would have been frigid. As
it is, the change of construction has suddenly run ahead of
the change of speaker. So this figure is useful, when a
sudden crisis will not let the writer wait, and forces him to
change at once from one character to another. There is
an instance in Hecataeus: "Ceyx took this ill and immediately bade the descendants be gone. For I cannot help
you. So to prevent perishing yourselves and hurting me,
away with you to some other people."[b] By a somewhat
different method Demosthenes in the *Aristogeiton* has
used variety of person to suggest rapid shifts of emotion.
"And will none of you," he says, "be found to feel anger
and indignation at the violence of this shameless rascal,
who—oh you most accursed of villains, who are cut off
from free speech not by gates and doors which one might
very well open . . ."[c] Leaving his sense incomplete he has

[a] *Iliad* 15.346–9.

[b] Hecataeus fr 30 (*FGrHist* 1). By descendants, Hecataeus
means the descendants of Heracles, as the intrusive gloss indicates: Ceyx, king of Trachis, is unable to help them, and so sends
them away. See Diodorus Siculus 4.57.2.

[c] [Demosthenes] *Or.* 25.27–8.

LONGINUS

οὐ μίαν λέξιν διὰ τὸν θυμὸν εἰς δύο διασπάσας
πρόσωπα "ὅς, ὦ μιαρώτατε" εἶτα πρὸς τὸν Ἀριστογείτονα τὸν λόγον[1] ἀποστρέψας καὶ ἀπολιπεῖν
δοκῶν, ὅμως διὰ τοῦ πάθους πολὺ πλέον ἐπέστρεψεν.
4 οὐκ ἄλλως ἡ Πηνελόπη·

κῆρυξ, τίπτε δέ σε πρόεσαν μνηστῆρες
ἀγαυοί;
εἰπέμεναι δμωῇσιν Ὀδυσσῆος θείοιο
ἔργων παύσασθαι, σφίσι δ' αὐτοῖς δαῖτα
πένεσθαι;
μὴ μνηστεύσαντες, μηδ' ἄλλοθ' ὁμιλήσαντες,
ὕστατα καὶ πύματα νῦν ἐνθάδε δειπνήσειαν,
οἳ θάμ' ἀγειρόμενοι βίοτον κατακείρετε πολλόν,
. . . οὐδέ τι πατρῶν
ὑμετέρων τῶν πρόσθεν ἀκούετε, παῖδες ἐόντες,
οἷος Ὀδυσσεὺς ἔσκε.

28. Καὶ μέντοι περίφρασις ὡς οὐχ ὑψηλοποιόν,
οὐδεὶς ἂν οἶμαι διστάσειεν. ὡς γὰρ ἐν μουσικῇ διὰ
τῶν παραφώνων καλουμένων ὁ κύριος φθόγγος
ἡδίων ἀποτελεῖται, οὕτως ἡ περίφρασις πολλάκις
συμφθέγγεται τῇ κυριολογίᾳ καὶ εἰς κόσμον ἐπὶ
πολὺ συνηχεῖ, καὶ μάλιστ', ἂν μὴ ἔχῃ φυσῶδές τι
2 καὶ ἄμουσον ἀλλ' ἡδέως κεκραμένον. ἱκανὸς δὲ
τοῦτο τεκμηριῶσαι καὶ Πλάτων κατὰ τὴν εἰσβολὴν

[1] So Weiske, for τὸν πρὸς τὸν Ἀριστογείτονα λόγον. Editors have also proposed a lacuna before ἀπολιπεῖν, supplying,

252

made a sudden change and in his indignation almost a split a single phrase between two persons—"who—oh you most accursed"— and thus, while swinging his speech round on to Aristogeiton and appearing to abandon the jury, he has yet by means of the emotion made his appeal to them much more intense. Penelope does the same:

> Herald, oh why have they sent you hither, those
> high-born suitors?
> Is it to tell the hand-maidens that serve in the
> house of Odysseus
> Now to desist from their tasks and make ready a
> feast for the suitors?
> Would that they never had wooed me nor ever met
> here in our halls,
> Would they might make in my house their last and
> latest of banquets,
> You that meet often together and utterly ravage our
> substance!
>   ... Nor yet from your fathers
> Heard you ever at home long ago in the days of
> your childhood
> What manner of man was Odysseus [a]

28. That periphrasis can contribute to the sublime, no one, I fancy, would question. Just as in music what we call accompaniment enhances the beauty of the melody, so periphrasis often chimes in with the literal expression and gives it a far richer note, especially if it is not bombastic or tasteless but agreeably blended. A sufficient proof of this

[a] *Odyssey* 4.681–9.

---

e.g., $<\tau o\grave{v}\varsigma\ \kappa\rho\iota\tau\grave{a}\varsigma>$. The translation assumes this sense. See Bühler (1964), 130.

τοῦ ἐπιταφίου· "ἔργῳ μὲν ὑμῖν οἶδ' ἔχουσι τὰ
προσήκοντα σφίσιν αὐτοῖς, ὧν τυχόντες πορεύονται
τὴν εἱμαρμένην πορείαν, προπεμφθέντες κοινῇ μὲν
ὑπὸ τῆς πόλεως, ἰδίᾳ δὲ ἕκαστος ὑπὸ τῶν προσηκόν-
των." οὐκοῦν τὸν θάνατον εἶπεν εἱμαρμένην
πορείαν, τὸ δὲ τετυχηκέναι τῶν νομιζομένων προ-
πομπήν τινα δημοσίαν ὑπὸ τῆς πατρίδος. ἆρα δὴ
τούτοις μετρίως ὤγκωσε τὴν νόησιν, ἢ ψιλὴν λαβὼν
τὴν λέξιν ἐμελοποίησε καθάπερ ἁρμονίαν τινὰ τὴν
3 ἐκ τῆς περιφράσεως περιχεάμενος εὐμέλειαν; καὶ
Ξενοφῶν "πόνον δὲ τοῦ ζῆν ἡδέως ἡγεμόνα νομίζετε,
κάλλιστον δὲ πάντων καὶ πολεμικώτατον κτῆμα εἰς
τὰς ψυχὰς συγκεκόμισθε· ἐπαινούμενοι γὰρ μᾶλλον
ἢ τοῖς ἄλλοις πᾶσι χαίρετε" ἀντὶ τοῦ "πονεῖν
θέλετε" "πόνον ἡγεμόνα τοῦ ζῆν ἡδέως ποιεῖσθε"
εἰπὼν καὶ τἆλλ' ὁμοίως ἐπεκτείνας μεγάλην τινὰ
4 ἔννοιαν τῷ ἐπαίνῳ προσπεριωρίσατο. καὶ τὸ ἀμίμητον ἐκεῖνο τοῦ Ἡροδότου· "τῶν δὲ Σκυθέων τοῖς
συλήσασιν τὸ ἱερὸν ἐνέβαλεν ἡ θεὸς θήλειαν
νοῦσον."

29. Ἐπίκηρον μέντοι τὸ πρᾶγμα, ἡ περίφρασις,
τῶν ἄλλων πλέον, εἰ μὴ σὺν μέτρῳ[1] τινὶ λαμβά-
νοιτο· εὐθὺς γὰρ ἀβλεμὲς προσπίπτει, κουφολογίας
τε ὄζον καὶ παχύτητος.[2] ὅθεν καὶ τὸν Πλάτωνα (δεινὸς γὰρ ἀεὶ περὶ σχῆμα κἄν τισιν ἀκαίρως) ἐν τοῖς

---

[1] σὺν μέτρῳ Morus for συμμέτρως.
[2] παχύτητος Manutius, for παχύτατον.

is the opening of Plato's Funeral Oration: "First then in deeds we have given them their due reward, and, this won, they travel now their destined journey, escorted all in common by their country and each man severally by his kinsmen."[a] Here he calls death a destined journey and their enjoyment of due rites a sort of public escort by their country. Is it a trivial dignity that he thus gives to the thought, or has he rather taken the literal expression and made it musical, wrapping it, as it were, in the tuneful harmonies of his periphrasis? Again Xenophon says, "You hold that hard work is a guide to the pleasures of life and you have stored in your hearts the noblest and most warrior-like of all treasures. For nothing pleases you so much as praise."[b] By saying "You make hard work a guide to living with pleasure" instead of "You are willing to work hard," and by similarly expanding the rest of his sentence, he has invested the eulogy with a further grand idea. Then there is that inimitable phrase in Herodotus: "Upon those Scythians that sacked her temple the goddess sent a female malady."[c]

29. However it is a risky business, periphrasis, more so than any of the other figures, unless used with a due sense of proportion. For it soon falls flat, smacking of triviality and grossness. So that critics have even made fun of Plato—always so clever at a figure, sometimes

[a] Plato, *Menexenus* 236D.
[b] Xenophon, *Cyropaedia* 1.5.12.
[c] Herodotus 1.105.4.

Νόμοις λέγοντα "ὡς οὔτε ἀργυροῦν δεῖ πλοῦτον οὔτε χρυσοῦν ἐν πόλει ἱδρυμένον ἐᾶν οἰκεῖν" διαχλευάζουσιν, ὡς εἰ πρόβατα, φησίν, ἐκώλυε κεκτῆσθαι, δῆλον ὅτι προβάτειον ἂν καὶ βόειον πλοῦτον ἔλεγεν.

2 Ἀλλὰ γὰρ ἅλις ὑπὲρ τῆς εἰς τὰ ὑψηλὰ τῶν σχημάτων χρήσεως ἐκ παρενθήκης τοσαῦτα πεφιλολογῆσθαι, Τερεντιανὲ φίλτατε· πάντα γὰρ ταῦτα παθητικωτέρους καὶ συγκεκινημένους ἀποτελεῖ τοὺς λόγους· πάθος δὲ ὕψους μετέχει τοσοῦτον, ὁπόσον ἦθος ἡδονῆς.

30. Ἐπειδὴ μέντοι ἡ τοῦ λόγου νόησις ἥ τε φράσις τὰ πλείω δι' ἑκατέρου διέπτυκται, ἴθι δή, [ἂν][1] τοῦ φραστικοῦ μέρους εἴ[2] τινα λοιπὰ ἔτι, προσεπιθεασώμεθα. ὅτι μὲν τοίνυν ἡ τῶν κυρίων καὶ μεγαλοπρεπῶν ὀνομάτων ἐκλογὴ θαυμαστῶς ἄγει καὶ κατακηλεῖ τοὺς ἀκούοντας καὶ ὡς πᾶσι τοῖς ῥήτορσι καὶ συγγραφεῦσι κατ' ἄκρον ἐπιτήδευμα, μέγεθος ἅμα κάλλος εὐπίνειαν βάρος ἰσχὺν κράτος ἔτι δὲ γάνωσίν τινα τοῖς λόγοις ὥσπερ ἀγάλμασι καλλίστοις δι' αὐτῆς ἐπανθεῖν παρασκευάζουσα καὶ οἱονεὶ ψυχήν τινα τοῖς πράγμασι φωνητικὴν ἐντιθεῖσα, μὴ καὶ περιττὸν ᾖ πρὸς εἰδότας διεξιέναι. φῶς γὰρ τῷ

2 ὄντι ἴδιον τοῦ νοῦ τὰ καλὰ ὀνόματα. ὁ μέντοι γε ὄγκος αὐτῶν οὐ πάντη χρειώδης, ἐπεὶ τοῖς μικροῖς πραγματίοις περιτιθέναι μεγάλα καὶ σεμνὰ ὀνόματα ταὐτὸν ἂν φαίνοιτο, ὡς εἴ τις τραγικὸν προσωπεῖον

[1] [ἂν] del. Russell (1964).

unseasonably so—for saying in his *Laws* "that we should
not let silvern treasure nor golden settle and make a home
in a city."[a] Had he been forbidding people to possess
sheep, says the critic, he would clearly have said "ovine
and bovine treasure."

But, my dear Terentianus, this digression must suffice
for our discussion of the use of figures as factors in the
sublime. They all serve to lend emotion and excitement
to the style. But emotion is as much an element of the
sublime, as characterization is of charm.[b]

30. Now, since thought and diction are generally
closely involved with each other we must further consider
whether there are any elements of diction still left
untouched. It is probably superfluous to explain at length
to someone who knows, how the choice of the right word
and the fine word has a marvellously moving and seduc-
tive effect upon an audience and how all orators and
prose writers make this their supreme object. For this of
itself gives to the style at once grandeur, beauty, old
world charm, weight, force, strength, and a sort of lustre,
like the bloom on the surface of the most beautiful
bronzes, and endows the facts as it were with a living
voice. Truly, beautiful words are the very light of thought.
However, their majesty is not for common use, since to
attach great and stately words to trivial things would be

[a] Plato, *Laws* 7.801B

[b] Cf. the comparison between *Iliad* and *Odyssey*, above
9.11-15.

---

[2] Spengel reads $\hat{\eta}$, retaining $\mathring{\alpha}\nu$.

μέγα παιδὶ περιθείη νηπίῳ. πλὴν ἐν μὲν ποιήσει
καὶ ἱ . . .[1]

31. . . . θρεπτικώτατον καὶ γόνιμον, τὸ δ᾽[2]
Ἀνακρέοντος "οὐκέτι Θρηικίης <πώλου>[3] ἐπιστρέ-
φομαι." ταύτῃ καὶ τὸ τοῦ Θεοπόμπου καινὸν
ἐπαινετόν[4]—διὰ τὸ ἀνάλογον ἔμοι γε σημαντικώ-
τατα ἔχειν δοκεῖ—ὅπερ ὁ Καικίλιος οὐκ οἶδ᾽ ὅπως
καταμέμφεται. "δεινὸς ὤν," φησίν, "ὁ Φίλιππος
ἀναγκοφαγῆσαι πράγματα." ἔστιν ἄρ᾽ ὁ ἰδιωτι-
σμὸς ἐνίοτε τοῦ κόσμου παρὰ πολὺ ἐμφανιστικώτε-
ρον· ἐπιγινώσκεται γὰρ αὐτόθεν ἐκ τοῦ κοινοῦ βίου,
τὸ δὲ σύνηθες ἤδη πιστότερον. οὐκοῦν ἐπὶ τοῦ τὰ
αἰσχρὰ καὶ ῥυπαρὰ τλημόνως καὶ μεθ᾽ ἡδονῆς ἕνεκα
2 πλεονεξίας καρτεροῦντος τὸ ἀναγκοφαγεῖν τὰ
πράγματα ἐναργέστατα παρείληπται. ὧδέ πως ἔχει
καὶ τὰ Ἡροδότεια· "ὁ Κλεομένης," φησί, "μανεὶς
τὰς ἑαυτοῦ σάρκας ξιφιδίῳ κατέτεμεν εἰς λεπτά,
ἕως ὅλον καταχορδεύων ἑαυτὸν διέφθειρεν," καί "ὁ
Πύθης ἕως τοῦδε ἐπὶ τῆς νεὼς ἐμάχετο, ἕως ἅπας
κατεκρεουργήθη." ταῦτα γὰρ ἐγγὺς παραξύει τὸν
ἰδιώτην, ἀλλ᾽ οὐκ ἰδιωτεύει τῷ σημαντικῶς.

---

[1] ἱστορίᾳ (Toll) must be the word that is broken off.

[2] Perhaps τὸ τἀνακρέοντος (Russell 1964); but it is possible
that οὐκέτι is not part of the quotation, and that the writer means
that Anacreon's phrase (by contrast with something just mentioned, and lost to us) is *not* admirable.

[3] <πώλου> supplied by Bergk.

[4] So Vahlen; καὶ τὸν ἐπήνετον P.

like fastening a great tragic mask on a little child. However in poetry and history . . .

[*Four pages are lost here.*]

31. . . . is most nourishing and productive; so, too, with Anacreon's "No more care I for the Thracian filly."[a] In the same way the novel phrase used by Theopompus is commendable; it seems to me extremely expressive because of the analogy, though Caecilius for some reason finds fault with it. "Philip," he says, "had a wonderful faculty of stomaching things."[b] Thus a common expression sometimes proves far more vivid than elegant language. Being taken from our common life it is immediately recognized, and what is familiar is thereby the more convincing. Applied to one whose greedy ambition makes him glad to endure with patience what is shameful and sordid, "stomaching things" forms a very vivid phrase. It is much the same with Herodotus' phrases: "In his madness," he says, "Cleomenes cut his own flesh into strips with a dagger, until he made mincemeat of himself and perished," and "Pythes went on fighting in the ship until he was chopped to pieces."[c] These come perilously near to vulgarity, but are not vulgar because they are so expressive.

[a] Anacreon, fr. eleg. 5 (D. A. Campbell, *Greek Lyric* II p. 148).

[b] Theopompus fr. 262 (*FGrHist* 115 F 262).

[c] Herodotus 6.75, 7.181.

32. Περὶ δὲ πλήθους [καὶ]¹ μεταφορῶν ὁ μὲν
Καικίλιος ἔοικε συγκατατίθεσθαι τοῖς δύο ἢ τὸ
πλεῖστον τρεῖς ἐπὶ ταὐτοῦ νομοθετοῦσι τάττεσθαι· ὁ
γὰρ Δημοσθένης ὅρος καὶ τῶν τοιούτων· ὁ τῆς
χρείας δὲ καιρός, ἔνθα τὰ πάθη χειμάρρου δίκην
ἐλαύνεται, καὶ τὴν πολυπλήθειαν αὐτῶν ὡς ἀναγ-
2 καίαν ἐνταῦθα συνεφέλκεται. "ἄνθρωποι," φησί
"μιαροὶ καὶ κόλακες, ἠκρωτηριασμένοι τὰς ἑαυτῶν
ἕκαστοι πατρίδας, τὴν ἐλευθερίαν προπεπωκότες
πρότερον Φιλίππῳ, νυνὶ δὲ Ἀλεξάνδρῳ, τῇ γαστρὶ
μετροῦντες καὶ τοῖς αἰσχίστοις τὴν εὐδαιμονίαν, τὴν
δ' ἐλευθερίαν καὶ τὸ μηδένα ἔχειν δεσπότην, ἃ τοῖς
πρότερον Ἕλλησιν ὅροι τῶν ἀγαθῶν ἦσαν καὶ
κανόνες, ἀνατετροφότες." ἐνταῦθα τῷ πλήθει τῶν
τροπικῶν ὁ κατὰ τῶν προδοτῶν ἐπιπροσθεῖ τοῦ ῥή-
3 τορος θυμός. διόπερ ὁ μὲν Ἀριστοτέλης καὶ ὁ Θεόφραστος μειλίγματά φασί τινα τῶν θρασειῶν εἶναι
ταῦτα μεταφορῶν, τὸ "ὡσπερεί" φάναι καί "οἱονεί"
καί "εἰ χρὴ τοῦτον εἰπεῖν τὸν τρόπον" καί "εἰ δεῖ
παρακινδυνευτικώτερον λέξαι." ἡ γὰρ ὑποτίμησις,
4 φασίν, ἰᾶται τὰ τολμηρά· ἐγὼ δὲ καὶ ταῦτα μὲν ἀπο-
δέχομαι, ὅμως δὲ πλήθους καὶ τόλμης μεταφορῶν,
ὅπερ ἔφην κἀπὶ² τῶν σχημάτων, τὰ εὔκαιρα καὶ
σφοδρὰ πάθη καὶ τὸ γενναῖον ὕψος εἶναί φημι ἴδιά
τινα ἀλεξιφάρμακα, ὅτι τῷ ῥοθίῳ τῆς φορᾶς ταυτὶ

---

¹ καὶ deleted by Robortelli.
² κἀπὶ Pearce for κἄπειτα.

32. As to the proper number of metaphors, Caecilius seems on the side of those who rule that not more than two or at the most three may be used together. Demosthenes assuredly is the canon in these matters too. And the occasion for their use is when emotion sweeps on like a flood and carries the multitude of metaphors along as an inevitable consequence. "Men," he says, "of evil life, flatterers, who have each foully mutilated their own country and toasted away their liberty first to Philip and now to Alexander, men who measure happiness by their bellies and their basest appetites, and have overthrown that liberty and freedom from despotism which to Greeks of older days was the canon and standard of all that was good."[a] Here it is the orator's indignation against the traitors which screens the multitude of metaphors. Accordingly, Aristotle and Theophrastus say that bold metaphors are softened by inserting "as if" or "as it were" or "if one may say so" or "if one may risk the expression."[b] The apology, they tell us, mitigates the audacity of the language. I accept this, but at the same time, as I said in speaking of figures, the proper antidote for a multitude of daring metaphors is strong and timely emotion and genuine sublimity. These by their nature sweep everything

[a] *De corona* (= *Or.* 18) 296.
[b] See Aristotle fr. 131 Rose, with *Rhet.* 3.7.1408b2, Cicero, *De oratore* 3.165, Theophrastus fr. 690 Fortenbaugh.

πέφυκεν ἅπαντα τἆλλα παρασύρειν καὶ προωθεῖν,
μᾶλλον δὲ καὶ ὡς ἀναγκαῖα πάντως εἰσπράττεσθαι
τὰ παράβολα, καὶ οὐκ ἐᾷ τὸν ἀκροατὴν σχολάζειν
περὶ τὸν τοῦ πλήθους ἔλεγχον διὰ τὸ συνενθουσιᾶν
τῷ λέγοντι.

5   Ἀλλὰ μὴν ἔν γε ταῖς τοπηγορίαις καὶ διαγρα-
φαῖς οὐκ ἄλλο τι οὕτως κατασημαντικὸν ὡς οἱ συνεχεῖς καὶ ἐπάλληλοι τρόποι. δι' ὧν καὶ παρὰ Ξενοφῶντι ἡ τἀνθρωπίνου σκήνους ἀνατομὴ πομπικῶς
καὶ ἔτι μᾶλλον ἀναζωγραφεῖται θείως παρὰ τῷ
Πλάτωνι. τὴν μὲν κεφαλὴν αὐτοῦ φησιν ἀκρόπολιν,
ἰσθμὸν δὲ μέσον διῳκοδομῆσθαι μεταξὺ τοῦ στή-
θους τὸν αὐχένα, σφονδύλους τε ὑπεστηρίχθαι
φησιν οἷον στρόφιγγας καὶ τὴν μὲν ἡδονὴν ἀνθρώποις εἶναι κακῶν[1] δέλεαρ, γλῶσσαν δὲ γεύσεως
δοκίμιον· ἄναμμα δὲ τῶν φλεβῶν τὴν καρδίαν καὶ
πηγὴν τοῦ περιφερομένου σφοδρῶς αἵματος, εἰς τὴν
δορυφορικὴν οἴκησιν κατατεταγμένην· τὰς δὲ δια-
δρομὰς τῶν πόρων ὀνομάζει στενωπούς· "τῇ δὲ
πηδήσει τῆς καρδίας ἐν τῇ τῶν δεινῶν προσδοκίᾳ
καὶ τῇ τοῦ θυμοῦ ἐπεγέρσει, ἐπειδὴ διάπυρος ἦν,
ἐπικουρίαν μηχανώμενοι," φησί, "τὴν τοῦ πλεύμονος
ἰδέαν ἐνεφύτευσαν, μαλακὴν καὶ ἄναιμον καὶ
σήραγγας ἐντὸς ἔχουσαν οἷον μάλαγμα, ἵν' ὁ
θυμὸς ὁπότ' ἐν αὐτῇ ζέσῃ, πηδῶσα εἰς ὑπεῖκον μὴ
λυμαίνηται." καὶ τὴν μὲν τῶν ἐπιθυμιῶν οἴκησιν
προσεῖπεν ὡς γυναικωνῖτιν, τὴν τοῦ θυμοῦ δὲ ὥσπερ
ἀνδρωνῖτιν· τόν γε μὴν σπλῆνα τῶν ἐντὸς μαγεῖον,

along in the forward surge of their current, or rather they positively demand bold imagery as essential to their effect, and do not give the hearer time to examine how many metaphors there are, because he shares the excitement of the speaker.

Moreover in the treatment of a commonplace and in descriptions there is nothing so expressive as a sustained series of metaphors. It is thus that in Xenophon[a] the anatomy of the human tabernacle is magnificently depicted, and still more divinely in Plato.[b] The head he calls the citadel of the body, the neck is an isthmus built between the head and chest, and the vertebrae, he says, are planted beneath like hinges; pleasure is evil's bait for man, and the tongue is the touchstone of taste. The heart is a knot of veins and the source whence the blood runs vigorously round, and it has its station in the guardhouse of the body. The passageways of the body he calls alleys, and "for the leaping of the heart in the expectation of danger or the arising of wrath, since this was due to fire, the gods devised a support by implanting the lungs, making them a sort of buffer, soft and bloodless and full of pores inside, so that when anger boiled up in the heart it might throb against a yielding surface and suffer no damage." The seat of the desires he compares to the women's apartments and the seat of anger to the men's. The spleen

[a] Xenophon, *Memorabilia* 1.4.5.
[b] Plato, *Timaeus* 65C–85E, quoted selectively and with considerable freedom; see Russell (1964) pp. 153–5.

---

[1] κακῶν K marg., Manutius (cf. Cicero *de Senectute* 44, *escam malorum*): κακὸν P.

"ὅθεν πληρούμενος τῶν ἀποκαθαιρομένων μέγας καὶ
ὕπουλος αὔξεται." "μετὰ δὲ ταῦτα σαρξὶ πάντα,"
φησί, "κατεσκίασαν, προβολὴν τῶν ἔξωθεν τὴν
σάρκα, οἷον τὰ πιλήματα,[1] προθέμενοι." νομὴν δὲ
σαρκῶν ἔφη τὸ αἷμα· "τῆς δὲ τροφῆς ἕνεκα," φησί,
"διωχέτευσαν τὸ σῶμα, τέμνοντες ὥσπερ ἐν κήποις
ὀχετούς, ὡς ἔκ τινος νάματος ἐπιόντος, ἀραιοῦ ὄντος
αὐλῶνος τοῦ σώματος, τὰ τῶν φλεβῶν ῥέοι νάματα."
ἡνίκα δὲ ἡ τελευτὴ παραστῇ, λύεσθαί φησι τὰ τῆς
ψυχῆς οἱονεὶ νεὼς πείσματα, μεθεῖσθαί τε αὐτὴν
6   ἐλευθέραν. ταῦτα καὶ τὰ παραπλήσια μυρί' ἄττα
ἐστὶν ἑξῆς· ἀπόχρη δὲ τὰ δεδηλωμένα, ὡς μεγάλαι
τε φύσιν εἰσὶν αἱ τροπικαί, καὶ ὡς ὑψηλοποιὸν αἱ
μεταφοραί, καὶ ὅτι οἱ παθητικοὶ καὶ φραστικοὶ κατὰ
7   τὸ πλεῖστον αὐταῖς χαίρουσι τόποι. ὅτι μέντοι καὶ
ἡ χρῆσις τῶν τρόπων, ὥσπερ τἆλλα πάντα καλὰ ἐν
λόγοις, προαγωγὸν ἀεὶ πρὸς τὸ ἄμετρον, δῆλον ἤδη,
κἂν ἐγὼ μὴ λέγω. ἐπὶ γὰρ τούτοις καὶ τὸν Πλάτωνα
οὐχ ἥκιστα διασύρουσι, πολλάκις ὥσπερ ὑπὸ
βακχείας τινὸς τῶν λόγων εἰς ἀκράτους καὶ ἀπηνεῖς
μεταφορὰς καὶ εἰς ἀλληγορικὸν στόμφον ἐκφερόμε-
νον. "οὐ γὰρ ῥᾴδιον ἐπινοεῖν," φησίν, "ὅτι πόλιν
εἶναι <δεῖ>[2] δίκην κρατῆρος κεκερασμένην, οὗ μαι-
νόμενος μὲν οἶνος ἐγκεχυμένος ζεῖ, κολαζόμενος δ'
ὑπὸ νήφοντος ἑτέρου θεοῦ καλὴν κοινωνίαν λαβὼν
ἀγαθὸν πόμα καὶ μέτριον ἀπεργάζεται." νήφοντα

---

[1] πιλήματα Toup for πηδήματα.

again is the towel for the entrails, "with whose off scourings it is filled and becomes swollen and fetid." "After this," he goes on, "they shrouded the whole in a covering of flesh, like felt, to shield it from the outer world." Blood he calls the fodder of the flesh, and adds, "For purposes of nutriment they irrigated the body, cutting channels as one does in a garden, and thus, the body being a conduit full of passages, the streams in the veins were able to flow as it were from a running stream." And when the end comes, the soul, he says, is loosed like a ship from its moorings and set free. These and thousands of similar metaphors occur throughout. Those we have pointed out suffice to show that figurative writing[a] has a natural grandeur and that metaphors make for sublimity: also that emotional and descriptive passages are most glad of them. However, it is obvious without my stating it, that the use of metaphor, like all the other beauties of style, always tempts writers to excess. Indeed it is for these passages in particular that critics pull Plato to pieces, on the ground that he is often carried away by a sort of Bacchic possession in his writing into harsh and intemperate metaphor and allegorical bombast. "It is by no means easy to see," he says, "that a city needs mixing like a wine bowl, where the mad wine seethes as it is poured in, but is chastened by another and a sober god and finding good company makes an excellent and temperate drink."[b]

[a] This translation understands λέξεις with τροπικαί.
[b] Plato, *Laws* 6.773C.

---

[2] add. K marg., Manutius.

γάρ, φασί, θεὸν τὸ ὕδωρ λέγειν, κόλασιν δὲ τὴν
κρᾶσιν, ποιητοῦ τινος τῷ ὄντι οὐχὶ νήφοντός ἐστι.

8   Τοῖς τοιούτοις ἐλαττώμασιν ἐπιχειρῶν ὅμως αὐτὸ
καὶ ὁ Καικίλιος ἐν τοῖς ὑπὲρ Λυσίου συγγράμμασιν
ἀπεθάρρησεν τῷ παντὶ Λυσίαν ἀμείνω Πλάτωνος
ἀποφήνασθαι, δυσὶ πάθεσι χρησάμενος ἀκρίτοις·
φιλῶν γὰρ τὸν Λυσίαν ὡς οὐδ’ αὐτὸς αὑτόν, ὅμως
μᾶλλον μισεῖ τῷ παντὶ Πλάτωνα ἢ Λυσίαν φιλεῖ.
πλὴν οὗτος μὲν ὑπὸ φιλονεικίας οὐδὲ τὰ θέματα
ὁμολογούμενα, καθάπερ ᾠήθη. ὡς γὰρ ἀναμάρτη-
τον καὶ καθαρὸν τὸν ῥήτορα προφέρει πολλαχῇ
διημαρτημένου τοῦ Πλάτωνος· τὸ δ’ ἦν ἄρα οὐχὶ
τοιοῦτον, οὐδὲ ὀλίγου δεῖ.

33.   Φέρε δή, λάβωμεν τῷ ὄντι καθαρόν τινα
συγγραφέα καὶ ἀνέγκλητον. ἆρ’ οὐκ ἄξιόν ἐστι
διαπορῆσαι περὶ αὐτοῦ τούτου καθολικῶς, πότερόν
ποτε κρεῖττον ἐν ποιήμασι καὶ λόγοις μέγεθος ἐν
ἐνίοις διημαρτημένον[1] ἢ τὸ σύμμετρον μὲν ἐν τοῖς
κατορθώμασιν ὑγιὲς δὲ πάντη καὶ ἀδιάπτωτον; καὶ
ἔτι νὴ Δία, πότερόν ποτε αἱ πλείους ἀρεταὶ τὸ πρω-
τεῖον ἐν λόγοις ἢ αἱ μείζους δικαίως ἂν φέροιντο;

2   ἔστι γὰρ ταῦτ’ οἰκεῖα τοῖς περὶ ὕψους σκέμματα καὶ
ἐπικρίσεως ἐξ ἅπαντος δεόμενα. ἐγὼ δ’ οἶδα μέν, ὡς
αἱ ὑπερμεγέθεις φύσεις ἥκιστα καθαραί· τὸ γὰρ ἐν
παντὶ ἀκριβὲς κίνδυνος μικρότητος, ἐν δὲ τοῖς μεγέθεσιν, ὥσπερ ἐν τοῖς ἄγαν πλούτοις, εἶναί τι χρὴ

---

[1] διημαρτημένον K marg., Manutius: διημαρτημένοις P.

To call water "a sober god" and mixing "chastisement," say the critics, is the language of a poet who is far from sober.

Caecilius too, in attacking like defects, has actually had the face to declare in his book on Lysias that Lysias is altogether superior to Plato. Here he has given way to two confused emotions: for though he loves Lysias even better than himself, yet his hatred for Plato altogether outweighs his love for Lysias. However he is moved by a spirit of contentiousness and even his premises are not agreed, as he supposed. For he prefers his orator on the ground that he is immaculate[a] and never makes a mistake, whereas Plato is full of mistakes. But the truth, we find, is different, very different indeed.

33. Suppose we illustrate this by taking some altogether immaculate and unimpeachable writer, must we not in this very connection raise the general question: Which is the better in poetry and in prose, grandeur flawed in some respects, or moderate achievement accompanied by perfect soundness and impeccability? And again: is the first place in literature rightly due to the largest number of excellences or to the excellences that are greatest in themselves? These inquiries are proper to a treatise on the sublime and on every ground demand decision. Now I am well aware that the greatest natures are least immaculate. Perfect precision runs the risk of triviality, whereas in great writing as in great wealth there

[a] *Katharos*, i.e. "pure," in language, possessing one of the basic stylistic virtues.

καὶ παρολιγωρούμενον· μήποτε δὲ τοῦτο καὶ ἀναγκαῖον ᾖ, τὸ τὰς μὲν ταπεινὰς καὶ μέσας φύσεις διὰ
τὸ μηδαμῇ παρακινδυνεύειν μηδὲ ἐφίεσθαι τῶν
ἄκρων ἀναμαρτήτους ὡς ἐπὶ τὸ πολὺ καὶ ἀσφαλε-
στέρας διαμένειν, τὰ δὲ μεγάλα ἐπισφαλῆ δι᾽ αὐτὸ
3 γίνεσθαι τὸ μέγεθος. ἀλλὰ μὴν οὐδὲ ἐκεῖνο ἀγνοῶ
τὸ δεύτερον, ὅτι φύσει πάντα τὰ ἀνθρώπεια ἀπὸ τοῦ
χείρονος ἀεὶ μᾶλλον ἐπιγινώσκεται καὶ τῶν μὲν
ἁμαρτημάτων ἀνεξάλειπτος ἡ μνήμη παραμένει, τῶν
4 καλῶν δὲ ταχέως ἀπορρεῖ. παρατεθειμένος δ᾽ οὐκ
ὀλίγα καὶ αὐτὸς ἁμαρτήματα καὶ Ὁμήρου καὶ τῶν
ἄλλων ὅσοι μέγιστοι, καὶ ἥκιστα τοῖς πταίσμασιν
ἀρεσκόμενος, ὅμως δὲ οὐχ ἁμαρτήματα μᾶλλον
αὐτὰ ἑκούσια καλῶν ἢ παροράματα δι᾽ ἀμέλειαν
εἰκῆ που καὶ ὡς ἔτυχεν ὑπὸ μεγαλοφυΐας ἀνεπιστά-
τως παρενηνεγμένα, οὐδὲν ἧττον οἶμαι τὰς μείζονας
ἀρετάς,[1] εἰ καὶ μὴ ἐν πᾶσι διομαλίζοιεν, τὴν τοῦ
πρωτείου ψῆφον μᾶλλον ἀεὶ φέρεσθαι, κἂν εἰ μὴ δι᾽
ἑνὸς ἑτέρου, τῆς μεγαλοφροσύνης αὐτῆς ἕνεκα· ἐπείτοιγε καὶ ἄπτωτος ὁ Ἀπολλώνιος ἐν τοῖς Ἀργοναύ-
ταις ποιητὴς κἀν τοῖς βουκολικοῖς πλὴν ὀλίγων τῶν
ἔξωθεν ὁ Θεόκριτος ἐπιτυχέστατος· ἆρ᾽ οὖν Ὅμηρος
5 ἂν μᾶλλον ἢ Ἀπολλώνιος ἐθέλοις γενέσθαι; τί δέ;
Ἐρατοσθένης ἐν τῇ Ἠριγόνῃ (διὰ πάντων γὰρ ἀμώ-
μητον τὸ ποιημάτιον) Ἀρχιλόχου πολλὰ καὶ ἀνοικο-
νόμητα παρασύροντος, κἀκείνης τῆς ἐκβολῆς τοῦ

---

[1] ἀρετάς Petra, for αἰτίας.

must needs be something overlooked. Perhaps it is inevitable that humble, mediocre natures, because they never run any risks and never aid at the heights, should remain to a large extent safe from error, while in great natures their very greatness spells danger. Not indeed that I am ignorant of the second point, that whatever men do is always inevitably regarded from the worst side: faults make an ineradicable impression, but beauties soon slip from our memory. I have myself cited a good many faults in Homer[a] and the other greatest authors, and though these slips certainly offend my taste, yet I prefer to call them not wilful mistakes but careless oversights, let in casually almost and at random by the heedlessness of genius. In spite, then, of these faults I still think that the greatest excellences, even if they are not sustained throughout at the same level, should always be voted the first place, if for nothing else, for the greatness of mind they reveal. Apollonius, for instance, is an impeccable poet in the *Argonautica*, and Theocritus—except in a few extraneous matters[b]—is supremely successful in his pastorals. Yet would you not rather be Homer than Apollonius? And what of Eratosthenes in his *Erigone*?[c] Wholly blameless as the little poem is, do you therefore think him a greater poet than Archilochus with all his disorganized flood and those outbursts of divine inspiration, which are

---

[a] Presumably in other works.   [b] This refers either to the parts of Theocritus which are not pastoral or (more probably) to slips of factual detail noted by grammarians.

[c] A learned elegiac poem by the astronomer-poet (third century B.C.), in which was related the Attic myth of the death of Icarius and the suicide by hanging of his daughter Erigone, the principal characters being all translated into stars. See J. U. Powell, *Collectanea Alexandrina* 64ff.

δαιμονίου πνεύματος ἦν ὑπὸ νόμον τάξαι δύσκολον,
ἆρα δὴ μείζων ποιητής; τί δέ; ἐν μέλεσι μᾶλλον ἂν
εἶναι Βακχυλίδης ἕλοιο ἢ Πίνδαρος καὶ ἐν τραγῳδίᾳ
Ἴων ὁ Χῖος ἢ Δία Σοφοκλῆς; ἐπειδὴ οἱ μὲν ἀδιά-
πτωτοι καὶ ἐν τῷ γλαφυρῷ πάντη κεκαλλιγραφημέ-
νοι, ὁ δὲ Πίνδαρος καὶ ὁ Σοφοκλῆς ὁτὲ μὲν οἷον
πάντα ἐπιφλέγουσι τῇ φορᾷ, σβέννυνται δ' ἀλόγως
πολλάκις καὶ πίπτουσιν ἀτυχέστατα. ἢ οὐδεὶς ἂν εὖ
φρονῶν ἑνὸς δράματος, τοῦ Οἰδίποδος, εἰς ταὐτὸ
συνθεὶς τὰ Ἴωνος <ἅπαντα>[1] ἀντιτιμήσαιτο ἑξῆς.

34. Εἰ δ' ἀριθμῷ, μὴ τῷ μεγέθει κρίνοιτο τὰ
κατορθώματα, οὕτως ἂν καὶ Ὑπερείδης τῷ παντὶ
προέχοι Δημοσθένους. ἔστι γὰρ αὐτοῦ πολυφωνό-
τερος καὶ πλείους ἀρετὰς ἔχων, καὶ σχεδὸν ὕπακρος
ἐν πᾶσιν ὡς ὁ πένταθλος, ὥστε τῶν μὲν πρωτείων ἐν
ἅπασι τῶν ἄλλων ἀγωνιστῶν λείπεσθαι, πρωτεύειν
δὲ τῶν ἰδιωτῶν. ὁ μέν γε Ὑπερείδης πρὸς τῷ πάντα
ἔξω γε τῆς συνθέσεως μιμεῖσθαι τὰ Δημοσθένεια
κατορθώματα καὶ τὰς Λυσιακὰς ἐκ περιττοῦ περιεί-
ληφεν ἀρετάς τε καὶ χάριτας· καὶ γὰρ λαλεῖ μετὰ
ἀφελείας, ἔνθα χρή, καὶ οὐ πάντα ἑξῆς [καὶ]² μονο-
τόνως, ὡς ὁ Δημοσθένης λέγεται, τό τε ἠθικὸν ἔχει
μετὰ γλυκύτητος [ἡδὺ]³ λιτῶς ἐφηδυνόμενον· ἄφατοί
τε περὶ αὐτόν εἰσιν ἀστεϊσμοί, μυκτὴρ πολιτικώτα-
τος, εὐγένεια, τὸ κατὰ τὰς εἰρωνείας εὐπάλαιστρον,

[1] add. Toup.
[2] del. Schurzfleisch.
[3] del. Weiske: νὴ Δία Richards.

so troublesome to bring under any rule? In lyrics, again, would you choose to be Bacchylides rather than Pindar, or in tragedy Ion of Chios[a] rather than Sophocles? In both pairs the first named is impeccable and a master of elegance in the smooth style, while Pindar and Sophocles sometimes seem to fire the whole landscape as they sweep across it, though often their fire is unaccountably quenched and they fall miserably flat. The truth is rather that no one in his senses would give the single tragedy of *Oedipus* for all the works of Ion together.

34. If achievements were to be judged by the number of excellences and not by their greatness, Hyperides would then be altogether superior to Demosthenes. He has greater variety of voice and his excellences are more numerous. He may almost be said to come a good second in every competition, like the winner of the Pentathlon.[b] In each contest he loses to the professional champion, but comes first of the amateurs. Besides reproducing all the virtues of Demosthenes, except his skill in word arrangement, Hyperides has embraced all the excellences and graces of Lysias. He talks plainly, where necessary, does not speak always in the same tone, as Demosthenes is said to do, and has the power of characterization, seasoned moreover by simplicity and charm. Then he has an untold store of polished wit, urbane sarcasm, well-bred

[a] Ion of Chios (mid-fifth century B.C.) was better known for his prose works ("Memoirs" and "Visits of Famous Men"), but a number of his tragedies were known in Hellenistic times (*TGF* i pp. 95ff; A. von Blumenthal, *Ion von Chios* (1939)).

[b] The best result in all five contests taken together—jumping, running, discus, javelin, wrestling—would doubtless be achieved by an athlete who was not an outstanding performer in any one.

σκώμματα οὐκ ἄμουσα οὐδ' ἀνάγωγα, κατὰ τοὺς
Ἀττικοὺς ἐκείνους ἅλας[1] ἐπικείμενα, διασυρμός τε
ἐπιδέξιος καὶ πολὺ τὸ κωμικὸν καὶ μετὰ παιδιᾶς
εὐστόχου κέντρον, ἀμίμητον δὲ εἰπεῖν τὸ ἐν πᾶσι
τούτοις ἐπαφρόδιτον· οἰκτίσασθαί τε προσφυέστα-
τος, ἔτι δὲ μυθολογῆσαι κεχυμένως[2] καὶ ἐν ὑγρῷ
πνεύματι διεξοδεῦσαί τι[3] εὐκαμπὴς ἄκρως, ὥσπερ
ἀμέλει τὰ μὲν περὶ τὴν Λητὼ ποιητικώτερα, τὸν δ'
3   ἐπιτάφιον ἐπιδεικτικῶς, ὡς οὐκ οἶδ' εἴ τις ἄλλος, διέ-
θετο. ὁ δὲ Δημοσθένης ἀνηθοποίητος ἀδιάχυτος,
ἥκιστα ὑγρὸς ἢ ἐπιδεικτικός, ἁπάντων ἑξῆς τῶν
προειρημένων κατὰ τὸ πλέον ἄμοιρος, ἔνθα μὲν
γελοῖος εἶναι βιάζεται καὶ ἀστεῖος, οὐ γέλωτα κινεῖ
μᾶλλον ἢ καταγελᾶται, ὅταν δὲ ἐγγίζειν θέλῃ τῷ
ἐπίχαρις εἶναι, τότε πλέον ἀφίσταται. τό γέ τοι
περὶ Φρύνης ἢ Ἀθηνογένους λογίδιον ἐπιχειρήσας
4   γράφειν ἔτι μᾶλλον ἂν Ὑπερείδην συνέστησεν.
ἀλλ' ἐπειδήπερ, οἶμαι, τὰ μὲν θατέρου καλά, καὶ εἰ
πολλὰ ὅμως ἀμεγέθη, καρδίῃ νήφοντος ἀργὰ καὶ

---

[1] ἅλας Tucker for ἀλλά.
[2] κεχυμένως Blass, for κεχυμένος.
[3] τι Buecheler, for ἔτι.

---

[a] Hyperides' lost *Deliacus* (frr. 67–75 Kenyon; the date is
about 343 B.C.) upheld the Athenian claim to the presidency of
the temple at Delos, where Leto gave birth to Apollo and
Artemis.

[b] The *Funeral Oration* (*Oration* 6) 322 B.C., on those who fell
in the Lamian War, is extant on a papyrus first published in 1858.

elegance, supple turns of irony, jests neither tasteless nor
ill-bred, well-dressed with wit like the Attic masters,
clever satire, plenty of pointed ridicule and well-directed
fun, and in all this a quite indescribable charm. Nature
endowed him fully with the power of evoking pity and
also with a superb flexibility in narrating myths copiously,
and pursuing a theme with fluency. His story of Leto,[a] for
instance, is in a more poetical vein, while his Funeral
Oration[b] is as good a piece of epideictic composition as
anyone could produce. Demosthenes, on the other hand,
has no gift of characterization or of fluency, is far from
facile, and no epideictic orator. In fact he has no part in
any one of the qualities we have just mentioned. When
he is forced into attempting a jest or a witty passage, he
rather raises the laugh against himself; and when he tries
to approximate charm, he is farther from it than ever. If
he had tried to write the little speech on Phryne[c] or
Athenogenes,[d] he would have been an even better adver-
tisement for Hyperides. But nevertheless I feel that the
beauties of Hyperides, many as they are, yet lack
grandeur; "inert in the heart of a sober man,"[e] they

[c] Hyperides' defence of the courtesan Phryne (frr. 171–80
Kenyon) is lost, but was famous for the peroration, in which
Phryne's charms were displayed to the court (Athenaeus
13.590E).

[d] *Against Athenogenes* (*Oration* 3, a large part of which survives in a papyrus published in 1892) concerns a contract for the
purchase of slaves; it is lively and full of character, but the case is
a complicated one.

[e] Proverbial and perhaps a verse quotation.

τὸν ἀκροατὴν ἠρεμεῖν ἐῶντα (οὐδεὶς γοῦν Ὑπερείδην
ἀναγινώσκων φοβεῖται), ὁ δὲ ἔνθεν ἑλὼν τοῦ μεγα-
λοφυεστάτου καὶ ἐπ' ἄκρον ἀρετὰς συντετελεσμένας,
ὑψηγορίας τόνον, ἔμψυχα πάθη, περιουσίαν ἀγχί-
νοιαν τάχος, ἔνθα δὴ καίριον,[1] τὴν ἅπασιν ἀπρόσι-
τον δεινότητα καὶ δύναμιν, ἐπειδὴ ταῦτα, φημί, ὡς
θεόπεμπτά τινα[2] δωρήματα (οὐ γὰρ εἰπεῖν θεμιτὸν
ἀνθρώπινα) ἀθρόα ἐς ἑαυτὸν ἔσπασεν, διὰ τοῦτο οἷς
ἔχει καλοῖς ἅπαντας ἀεὶ νικᾷ καὶ ὑπὲρ ὧν οὐκ ἔχει
καὶ ὡσπερεὶ καταβροντᾷ καὶ καταφέγγει τοὺς ἀπ'
αἰῶνος ῥήτορας· καὶ θᾶττον ἄν τις κεραυνοῖς φερο-
μένοις ἀντανοῖξαι τὰ ὄμματα δύναιτο ἢ ἀντοφθαλ-
μῆσαι τοῖς ἐπαλλήλοις ἐκείνου πάθεσιν.

35. Ἐπὶ μέντοι τοῦ Πλάτωνος καὶ ἄλλη τίς ἐστιν,
ὡς ἔφην, διαφορά. οὐ γὰρ μεγέθει τῶν ἀρετῶν ἀλλὰ
καὶ τῷ πλήθει πολὺ λειπόμενος αὐτοῦ Λυσίας ὅμως[3]
πλεῖον ἔτι τοῖς ἁμαρτήμασιν περιττεύει ἢ ταῖς ἀρε-
ταῖς λείπεται. τί ποτ' οὖν εἶδον οἱ ἰσόθεοι ἐκεῖνοι
καὶ τῶν μεγίστων ἐπορεξάμενοι τῆς συγγραφῆς, τῆς
δ' ἐν ἅπασιν ἀκριβείας ὑπερφρονήσαντες; πρὸς
πολλοῖς ἄλλοις ἐκεῖνο, ὅτι ἡ φύσις οὐ ταπεινὸν ἡμᾶς
ζῷον οὐδ' ἀγεννὲς ἔκρινε[4] τὸν ἄνθρωπον, ἀλλ' ὡς εἰς
μεγάλην τινὰ πανήγυριν εἰς τὸν βίον καὶ εἰς τὸν
σύμπαντα κόσμον ἐπάγουσα θεατάς τινας τῶν

---

[1] καίριον Richards for κύριον: εἶθ', ὁ δὴ κύριον Rohde.
[2] τινα Manutius for δεινὰ.
[3] ὅμως Toup for ὁ μὲν.
[4] ἔκτισε Seager.

do not trouble the peace of the audience. No one feels frightened while reading Hyperides. But Demosthenes no sooner "takes up the tale"[a] than he shows the merits of great genius in their most consummate form, sublime intensity, living emotion, redundance, readiness, speed— where speed is in season—and his own unapproachable vehemence and power: concentrating in himself all these heaven-sent gifts—it would be impious to call them human—he thus uses the beauties he possesses to win a victory over all others that even compensates for his weaknesses, and out-thunders, as it were, and outshines orators of every age. You could sooner open your eyes to the descent of a thunderbolt than face his repeated outbursts of emotion without blinking.

35. There is, as I said,[b] a further point of difference as compared with Plato. Lysias is far inferior to him both in the greatness and number of his excellences; yet the abundance of his faults is still greater than his deficiency in excellences. What then was the vision of those demigods who aimed only at what is greatest in writing and scorned detailed accuracy? This above all: that Nature has judged man[c] a creature of no mean or ignoble quality, but, as if she were inviting us to some great gathering, she has called us into life, into the whole universe, there to be spectators of her games and eager competi-

[a] A Homeric phrase (*Odyssey* 8.500).

[b] In chap. 32.

[c] If this reading is right, Nature "admits" men as spectators and competitors in the games of life: but Seager's conjecture—"created"—may well be right.

ἄθλων[1] αὐτῆς ἐσομένους καὶ φιλοτιμοτάτους ἀγωνι-
στάς, εὐθὺς ἄμαχον ἔρωτα ἐνέφυσεν ἡμῶν ταῖς
ψυχαῖς παντὸς ἀεὶ τοῦ μεγάλου καὶ ὡς πρὸς ἡμᾶς
3 δαιμονιωτέρου. διόπερ τῇ θεωρίᾳ καὶ διανοίᾳ τῆς
ἀνθρωπίνης ἐπιβολῆς οὐδ᾽ ὁ σύμπας κόσμος ἀρκεῖ,
ἀλλὰ καὶ τοὺς τοῦ περιέχοντος πολλάκις ὅρους ἐκ-
βαίνουσιν αἱ ἐπίνοιαι· καὶ εἴ τις περιβλέψαιτο ἐν
κύκλῳ τὸν βίον, ὅσῳ πλέον ἔχει τὸ περιττὸν ἐν πᾶσι
καὶ μέγα καὶ καλόν, ταχέως εἴσεται πρὸς ἃ γεγόνα-
4 μεν. ἔνθεν φυσικῶς πως ἀγόμενοι μὰ Δί᾽ οὐ τὰ
μικρὰ ῥεῖθρα θαυμάζομεν, εἰ καὶ διαυγῆ καὶ χρήσιμα, ἀλλὰ τὸν Νεῖλον καὶ Ἴστρον ἢ Ῥῆνον, πολὺ
δ᾽ ἔτι μᾶλλον τὸν Ὠκεανόν, οὐδέ γε τὸ ὑφ᾽ ἡμῶν
τουτὶ φλογίον ἀνακαιόμενον, ἐπεὶ καθαρὸν σῴζει τὸ
φέγγος, ἐκπληττόμεθα τῶν οὐρανίων μᾶλλον, καίτοι
πολλάκις ἐπισκοτουμένων, οὐδὲ τῶν τῆς Αἴτνης
κρατήρων ἀξιοθαυμαστότερον νομίζομεν, ἧς αἱ ἀνα-
χοαὶ πέτρους τε ἐκ βυθοῦ καὶ ὅλους ὄχθους ἀναφέ-
ρουσι καὶ ποταμοὺς ἐνίοτε τοῦ γηγενοῦς[2] ἐκείνου καὶ
5 αὐτομάτου[3] προχέουσιν πυρός. ἀλλ᾽ ἐπὶ τῶν τοιούτων ἁπάντων ἐκεῖν᾽ ἂν εἴποιμεν, ὡς εὐπόριστον μὲν
ἀνθρώποις τὸ χρειῶδες ἢ καὶ ἀναγκαῖον, θαυμαστὸν
δ᾽ ὅμως ἀεὶ τὸ παράδοξον.

36. Οὐκοῦν ἐπί γε τῶν ἐν λόγοις μεγαλοφυῶν,
ἐφ᾽ ὧν οὐκέτ᾽ ἔξω τῆς χρείας καὶ ὠφελείας πίπτει τὸ
μέγεθος, προσήκει συνθεωρεῖν αὐτόθεν, ὅτι τοῦ ἀνα-
μαρτήτου πολὺ ἀφεστῶτες οἱ τηλικοῦτοι ὅμως παντός[4] εἰσιν ἐπάνω τοῦ θνητοῦ· καὶ τὰ μὲν ἄλλα τοὺς

tors; and she therefore from the first breathed into our hearts an unconquerable passion for whatever is great and more divine than ourselves. Thus the whole universe is not enough to satisfy the speculative intelligence of human thought; our ideas often pass beyond the limits that confine us. Look at life from all sides and see how in all things the extraordinary, the great, the beautiful stand supreme, and you will soon realize what we were born for. So it is by some natural instinct that we admire, not the small streams, clear and useful as they are, but the Nile, the Danube, the Rhine, and above all the Ocean. The little fire we kindle for ourselves keeps clear and steady, yet we do not therefore regard it with more amazement than the fires of Heaven, which are often darkened, or think it more wonderful than the craters of Etna in eruption, hurling up rocks and whole hills from their depths and sometimes shooting forth rivers of that earthborn, spontaneous fire. But on all such matters I would only say this, that what is useful or necessary is easily obtained by man; it is always the unusual which wins our wonder.

36. In dealing, then, with writers of genius, whose grandeur is of a kind that comes within the limits of use and profit, we must at the outset observe that, while they are far from unerring, yet they are above all mortal range.

---

[1] ἄθλων Reiske for ὅλων.

[2] γηγενοῦς Markland, for γένους.

[3] αὐτομάτου Haupt, for αὐτοῦ μόνου.

[4] παντός Pearce, for πάντες.

χρωμένους ἀνθρώπους ἐλέγχει, τὸ δ' ὕψος ἐγγὺς
αἴρει μεγαλοφροσύνης θεοῦ. καὶ τὸ μὲν ἄπταιστον
2 οὐ ψέγεται, τὸ μέγα δὲ καὶ θαυμάζεται. τί χρὴ πρὸς
τούτοις ἔτι λέγειν ὡς ἐκείνων τῶν ἀνδρῶν ἕκαστος
ἅπαντα τὰ σφάλματα ἑνὶ ἐξωνεῖται πολλάκις ὕψει
καὶ κατορθώματι, καὶ τὸ κυριώτατον, ὡς, εἴ τις[1] ἐκ-
λέξας τὰ Ὁμήρου, τὰ Δημοσθένους, τὰ Πλάτωνος,
τῶν ἄλλων ὅσοι δὴ μέγιστοι, παραπτώματα πάντα
ὁμόσε συναθροίσειεν, ἐλάχιστον ἄν τι, μᾶλλον δ'
οὐδὲ πολλοστημόριον ἂν εὑρεθείη τῶν ἐκείνοις τοῖς
ἥρωσι πάντη κατορθουμένων. διὰ ταῦθ' ὁ πᾶς
αὐτοῖς αἰὼν καὶ βίος, οὐ δυνάμενος ὑπὸ τοῦ φθόνου
παρανοίας ἁλῶναι, φέρων ἀπέδωκεν τὰ νικητήρια
καὶ ἄχρι νῦν ἀναφαίρετα φυλάττει καὶ ἔοικε τηρή-
σειν,

> ἔστ' ἂν ὕδωρ τε ῥέῃ καὶ δένδρεα μακρὰ
> τεθήλῃ.

3 πρὸς μέντοι γε τὸν γράφοντα, ὡς ὁ κολοσσὸς ὁ
ἡμαρτημένος οὐ κρείττων ἢ ὁ Πολυκλείτου δορυφό-
ρος, παράκειται πρὸς πολλοῖς εἰπεῖν, ὅτι ἐπὶ μὲν
τέχνης θαυμάζεται τὸ ἀκριβέστατον, ἐπὶ δὲ τῶν
φυσικῶν ἔργων τὸ μέγεθος, φύσει δὲ λογικὸν ὁ
ἄνθρωπος· κἀπὶ μὲν ἀνδριάντων ζητεῖται τὸ ὅμοιον
ἀνθρώπῳ, ἐπὶ δὲ τοῦ λόγου τὸ ὑπεραῖρον, ὡς ἔφην,

---

[1] τις K marg., Manutius for γε.

[a] Quoted in Plato (*Phaedrus* 264C) as part of an epitaph said

278

Other qualities prove their possessors men, sublimity lifts them near the mighty mind of God. Correctness escapes censure: greatness earns admiration as well. We need hardly add that each of these great men again and again redeems all his mistakes by a single touch of sublimity and true excellence; and, what is finally decisive, if we were to pick out all the faults in Homer, Demosthenes, Plato, and all the other greatest authors and put them together, we should find them a tiny part, not the smallest fraction, of the true successes to be found everywhere in the work of these heroes. That is why the judgement of all ages, which no jealousy can convict of mental incompetence, has awarded them the crown of victory, guards it as their irremovable possession, and is likely to preserve it,

> So long as the rivers run and the tall trees flourish
> and grow.[a]

As to the statement that the faulty Colossus[b] is no better than the Doryphorus of Polyclitus,[c] there are many obvious answers to that. For one thing, we admire accuracy in art, grandeur in nature; and it is Nature that has given man the power of using words. Also we expect a statue to resemble a man, but in literature, as I said before, we

to have been written for Midas. See *Anthologia Palatina* 7.153.

[b] Perhaps the Colossus of Rhodes, damaged in an earthquake when it had stood for sixty years; but more probably any colossal statue: cf. Strabo 1.1.23, who speaks of *kolossoi* in which the total effect is all-important, and the accuracy of the detail insignificant.

[c] The statue of the boy with a lance by Polyclitus of Argos was regarded as a model of beautiful proportions (Pliny, *Natural History* 34.55).

4 τὰ ἀνθρώπινα. προσήκει δ᾽ ὅμως (ἀνακάμπτει γὰρ
ἐπὶ τὴν ἀρχὴν ἡμῖν τοῦ ὑπομνήματος ἡ παραίνεσις),
ἐπειδὴ τὸ μὲν ἀδιάπτωτον ὡς ἐπὶ τὸ πολὺ τέχνης
ἐστὶ κατόρθωμα, τὸ δ᾽ ἐν ὑπεροχῇ πλὴν οὐχ ὁμότο-
νον μεγαλοφυΐας, βοήθημα τῇ φύσει πάντη πορίζεσθαι τὴν τέχνην· ἡ γὰρ ἀλληλουχία τούτων ἴσως
γένοιτ᾽ ἂν τὸ τέλειον. τοσαῦτα ἦν ἀναγκαῖον ὑπὲρ
τῶν προτεθέντων ἐπικρῖναι σκεμμάτων· χαιρέτω δ᾽
ἕκαστος οἷς ἥδεται.

37. Ταῖς δὲ μεταφοραῖς γειτνιῶσιν (ἐπανιτέον
γάρ) αἱ παραβολαὶ καὶ εἰκόνες, ἐκείνῃ μόνον παραλ-
λάττουσαι . . .

38. <καταγελα>στοὶ[1] καὶ αἱ τοιαῦται· "εἰ μὴ τὸν
ἐγκέφαλον ἐν ταῖς πτέρναις καταπεπατημένον
φορεῖτε." διόπερ εἰδέναι χρὴ τὸ μέχρι ποῦ παρορι-
στέον ἕκαστον· τὸ γὰρ ἐνίοτε περαιτέρω προεκπί-
πτειν ἀναιρεῖ τὴν ὑπερβολὴν καὶ τὰ τοιαῦτα ὑπερ-
τεινόμενα χαλᾶται, ἔσθ᾽ ὅτε δὲ καὶ εἰς ὑπεναντιώσεις
2 ἀντιπεριΐσταται. ὁ γοῦν Ἰσοκράτης οὐκ οἶδ᾽ ὅπως
παιδὸς πρᾶγμα ἔπαθεν διὰ τὴν τοῦ πάντα αὐξητικῶς
ἐθέλειν λέγειν φιλοτιμίαν. ἔστι μὲν γὰρ ὑπόθεσις
αὐτῷ τοῦ πανηγυρικοῦ λόγου, ὡς ἡ Ἀθηναίων πόλις
ταῖς εἰς τοὺς Ἕλληνας εὐεργεσίαις ὑπερβάλλει τὴν
Λακεδαιμονίων, ὁ δ᾽ εὐθὺς ἐν τῇ εἰσβολῇ ταῦτα
τίθησιν· "ἔπειθ᾽ οἱ λόγοι τοσαύτην ἔχουσι δύναμιν,
ὥσθ᾽ οἷόν τ᾽ εἶναι καὶ τὰ μεγάλα ταπεινὰ ποιῆσαι
καὶ τοῖς μικροῖς περιθεῖναι μέγεθος καὶ τὰ παλαιὰ
καινῶς εἰπεῖν καὶ περὶ τῶν νεωστὶ γεγενημένων

look for something greater than human. However (this advice reverts to something with which we began our treatise), since impeccable correctness is, generally speaking, due to art, and the height of excellence, even if erratic, to genius, it is proper that art should always assist Nature. Their cooperation may well result in perfection. This much had to be said to decide the questions before us. But everyone is welcome to his own taste.

37. Closely akin to metaphors (to return to them) are comparisons and similes. The only difference is . . .

[Two pages are lost here.]

38. . . . Laughable[a] also are such things as "If you do not carry your brains trodden down in your heels."[b] One must know, then, where to draw the line in each case. The hyperbole is sometimes ruined by overshooting the mark. Overdo the strain and the thing sags, and often produces the opposite effect to that intended. For instance, Isocrates fell into unaccountable puerility through his ambition to amplify everything. The theme of his *Panegyric* is that Athens surpasses Sparta in her benefits to Greece. But at the very outset he puts this: "Moreover words have such power that they can make great things humble and endue small things with greatness, give a new guise to what is old, and describe recent

[a] This assumes Reiske's supplement.
[b] [Demosthenes] *Oration* 7.45.

---

[1] Reiske.

ἀρχαίως διελθεῖν"—οὐκοῦν, φησί τις, Ἰσόκρατες,
οὕτως μέλλεις καὶ τὰ περὶ Λακεδαιμονίων καὶ Ἀθηναίων ἐναλλάττειν; σχεδὸν γὰρ τὸ τῶν λόγων ἐγκώμιον ἀπιστίας τῆς καθ' αὑτοῦ τοῖς ἀκούουσι παράγ-
3 γελμα καὶ προοίμιον ἐξέθηκεν. μήποτ' οὖν ἄρισται
τῶν ὑπερβολῶν, ὡς καὶ ἐπὶ τῶν σχημάτων προείπο-
μεν, αἱ αὐτὸ τοῦτο διαλανθάνουσαι ὅτι εἰσὶν ὑπερ-
βολαί. γίνεται δὲ τὸ τοιόνδε, ἐπειδὰν ὑπὸ ἐκπαθείας
μεγέθει τινὶ συνεκφωνῶνται περιστάσεως, ὅπερ ὁ
Θουκυδίδης ἐπὶ τῶν ἐν Σικελίᾳ φθειρομένων ποιεῖ.
"οἵ τε γὰρ Συρακούσιοι," φησίν, "ἐπικαταβάντες
τοὺς ἐν τῷ ποταμῷ μάλιστα ἔσφαζον, καὶ τὸ ὕδωρ
εὐθὺς διέφθαρτο, ἀλλ' οὐδὲν ἧσσον ἐπίνετο ὁμοῦ τῷ
πηλῷ ᾑματωμένον καὶ τοῖς πολλοῖς ἔτι ἦν περιμά-
χητον." αἷμα καὶ πηλὸν πινόμενα ὅμως εἶναι περι-
μάχητα ἔτι ποιεῖ πιστὸν ἡ τοῦ πάθους ὑπεροχὴ καὶ
4 περίστασις. καὶ τὸ Ἡροδότειον ἐπὶ τῶν ἐν Θερμο-
πύλαις ὅμοιον. "ἐν τούτῳ" φησίν "ἀλεξομένους
μαχαίρῃσιν, ὅσοις αὐτῶν ἔτι ἐτύγχανον περιοῦσαι,
καὶ χερσὶ καὶ στόμασι κατέχωσαν οἱ βάρβαροι
<βάλλοντες>[1]." ἐνταῦθ', οἷόν ἐστι τὸ καὶ στόμασι
μάχεσθαι πρὸς ὡπλισμένους καὶ ὁποῖόν τι τὸ κατα-
κεχῶσθαι βέλεσιν, ἐρεῖς, πλὴν ὁμοίως ἔχει πίστιν·
οὐ γὰρ τὸ πρᾶγμα ἕνεκα τῆς ὑπερβολῆς παραλαμ-
βάνεσθαι δοκεῖ, ἡ ὑπερβολὴ δ' εὐλόγως γεννᾶσθαι
5 πρὸς τοῦ πράγματος. ἔστι γάρ, ὡς οὐ διαλείπω
λέγων, παντὸς τολμήματος λεκτικοῦ λύσις καὶ παν-

---

[1] Add. Manutius, from Herodotus.

events in the style of long ago"[a]—"Why, Isocrates," one may say, "do you intend by this means to reverse the positions of the Spartans and the Athenians?" For his praise of the power of words has all but issued a prefatory warning to the audience that he himself is not to be believed. Perhaps then, as we said above of figures,[b] the best hyperbole is the one which conceals the very fact of its being a hyperbole. And this happens when it is uttered under stress of emotion to suit the circumstances of a great crisis. This is what Thucydides does in speaking of those who were killed in Sicily. "For the Syracusans went down and began to slaughter chiefly those in the river. The water was immediately tainted but none the less they kept on drinking it, foul though it was with mud and gore, and most of them were still ready to fight for it."[c] That a drink of mud and gore should yet still be worth fighting for is made credible only by the height of the emotion which the circumstances arouse. It is the same with Herodotus' description of those who fought at Thermopylae. "On this spot," he says, "while they defended themselves with daggers, such as still had daggers left, and with hands and teeth, the barbarians buried them under a shower of missiles."[d] Here you may well ask what is meant by actually "fighting with teeth" against armed men or being "buried" with missiles; yet it carries credence in the same way, because Herodotus does not seem to have introduced the incident to justify the hyperbole, but the hyperbole for the sake of the incident. As I am never tired of saying, to atone for a daring phrase the universal

[a] Isocrates, *Panegyricus* 8.
[b] See chap. 17.   [c] Thucydides 7.84.
[d] Herodotus 7.225.

ἀκειά τις τὰ ἐγγὺς ἐκστάσεως ἔργα καὶ πάθη. ὅθεν
καὶ τὰ κωμικὰ καίτοιγ᾽ εἰς ἀπιστίαν ἐκπίπτοντα
πιθανὰ διὰ τὸ γελοῖον·

ἀγρὸν
ἔσχ᾽ ἐλάττω γῆν ἔχοντ᾽ ἐπιστολῆς
<Λακωνικῆς>[1]

6 καὶ γὰρ ὁ γέλως πάθος ἐν ἡδονῇ. αἱ δ᾽ ὑπερβολαὶ
καθάπερ ἐπὶ τὸ μεῖζον, οὕτως καὶ ἐπὶ τοὔλαττον,
ἐπειδὴ κοινὸν ἀμφοῖν ἡ ἐπίτασις· καί πως ὁ διασυρ-
μὸς ταπεινότητός ἐστιν αὔξησις.

39. Ἡ πέμπτη μοῖρα τῶν συντελουσῶν εἰς τὸ
ὕψος, ὧν γε ἐν ἀρχῇ προὐθέμεθα, ἔθ᾽ ἡμῖν λείπεται,
κράτιστε, ἣν δὲ[2] τῶν λόγων αὕτη ποιὰ σύνθεσις.
ὑπὲρ ἧς ἐν δυσὶν ἀποχρώντως ἀποδεδωκότες συν-
τάγμασιν, ὅσα γε τῆς θεωρίας ἦν ἡμῖν ἐφικτά,
τοσοῦτον ἐξ ἀνάγκης προσθείημεν ἂν εἰς τὴν
παροῦσαν ὑπόθεσιν, ὡς οὐ μόνον ἐστὶ πειθοῦς καὶ
ἡδονῆς ἡ ἁρμονία φυσικὸν ἀνθρώποις ἀλλὰ καὶ
μεγαληγορίας καὶ πάθους θαυμαστόν τι ὄργανον.
2 οὐ γὰρ αὐλὸς μὲν ἐντίθησίν τινα πάθη τοῖς ἀκροω-
μένοις καὶ οἷον ἔκφρονας καὶ κορυβαντιασμοῦ πλή-
ρεις ἀποτελεῖ, καὶ βάσιν ἐνδούς τινα ῥυθμοῦ πρὸς
ταύτην ἀναγκάζει[3] βαίνειν ἐν ῥυθμῷ καὶ συνεξομοι-
οῦσθαι τῷ μέλει τὸν ἀκροατήν, κἂν ἄμουσος ᾖ παν-
τάπασι, καὶ νὴ Δία φθόγγοι κιθάρας, οὐδὲν ἁπλῶς

[1] Add. Portus (1569).

specific is found in actions and feelings that almost make one beside oneself. Thus, too, comic expressions, even if they result in the incredible, yet sound convincing because they are laughable:

His field was shorter than a Spartan letter.[a]

Laughter indeed is an emotion based on pleasure. Hyperbole may tend to belittle as well as to magnify: the common element in both is a strain on the facts. In a sense too vilification is an amplification of the low and trivial.

39. Of those factors of sublimity which we specified at the beginning,[b] the fifth one still remains, good friend— this was the arrangement of the words themselves in a certain order. On this question I have in two books given a sufficient account of such conclusions as I could reach, and for our present purpose I need only add this, that men find in melody not only a natural instrument of persuasion and pleasure, but also a marvellous instrument of grandeur and emotion. The flute, for instance, induces certain emotions in those who hear it. It seems to carry them away and fill them with divine frenzy. It sets a particular rhythmic movement and forces them to move in rhythm. The hearer has to conform to the tune, though he may be utterly unmusical. Why, the very tones of the

---

[a] The brevity of Spartan messages was proverbial. The line is perhaps from comedy (cf. fr. adesp. 417–19 Kock).

[b] In chap. 8.

---

[2] Russell (1964), for ἡ διὰ.

[3] ἀναγκάζει Manutius, for ἀναγκάσει.

σημαίνοντες, ταῖς τῶν ἤχων μεταβολαῖς καὶ τῇ
πρὸς ἀλλήλους κράσει[1] καὶ μίξει τῆς συμφωνίας
3 θαυμαστὸν ἐπάγουσι πολλάκις, ὡς ἐπίστασαι,
θέλγητρον (καίτοι ταῦτα εἴδωλα καὶ μιμήματα νόθα
ἐστὶ πειθοῦς, οὐχὶ τῆς ἀνθρωπείας φύσεως, ὡς ἔφην,
ἐνεργήματα γνήσια), οὐκ οἰόμεθα δ' ἄρα τὴν σύνθεσιν, ἁρμονίαν τινὰ οὖσαν λόγων ἀνθρώποις ἐμφύ-
των καὶ τῆς ψυχῆς αὐτῆς, οὐχὶ τῆς ἀκοῆς μόνης
ἐφαπτομένων, ποικίλας κινοῦσαν ἰδέας ὀνομάτων
νοήσεων πραγμάτων κάλλους εὐμελείας, πάντων
ἡμῖν ἐντρόφων καὶ συγγενῶν, καὶ ἅμα τῇ μίξει καὶ
πολυμορφίᾳ τῶν ἑαυτῆς φθόγγων τὸ παρεστὼς τῷ
λέγοντι πάθος εἰς τὰς ψυχὰς τῶν πέλας παρεισ-
άγουσαν καὶ εἰς μετουσίαν αὐτοῦ τοὺς ἀκούοντας ἀεὶ
παθιστᾶσαν, τῇ τε τῶν λέξεων ἐποικοδομήσει τὰ
μεγέθη συναρμόζουσαν, δι' αὐτῶν τούτων κηλεῖν[2] τε
ὁμοῦ καὶ πρὸς ὄγκον τε καὶ ἀξίωμα καὶ ὕψος καὶ
πᾶν ὃ ἐν αὐτῇ[3] περιλαμβάνει καὶ ἡμᾶς ἑκάστοτε
συνδιατιθέναι, παντοίως ἡμῶν τῆς διανοίας ἐπικρα-
4 τοῦσαν; ἀλλ' εἰ καὶ μανία τὸ περὶ τῶν οὕτως ὁμολο-
γουμένων διαπορεῖν (ἀποχρῶσα γὰρ ἡ πεῖρα
πίστις), ὑψηλόν γέ που δοκεῖ[4] νόημα καὶ ἔστι τῷ
ὄντι θαυμάσιον, ὃ τῷ ψηφίσματι ὁ Δημοσθένης ἐπι-
φέρει "τοῦτο τὸ ψήφισμα τὸν τότε τῇ πόλει περι-
στάντα κίνδυνον παρελθεῖν ἐποίησεν ὥσπερ νέφος,"
ἀλλ' αὐτῆς τῆς διανοίας οὐκ ἔλαττον τῇ ἁρμονίᾳ
πεφώνηται. ὅλον τε γὰρ ἐπὶ τῶν δακτυλικῶν εἴρηται
ῥυθμῶν, εὐγενέστατοι δ' οὗτοι καὶ μεγεθοποιοί, διὸ

harp, themselves meaningless, by the variety of their sounds and by their combination and harmonious blending often exercise, as you know, a marvellous spell. (Yet these are only a bastard counterfeit of persuasion, not, as I said above, a genuine activity of human nature.) Must we not think, then, that composition, which is a kind of melody in words—words which are part of man's nature and reach not his ears only but his very soul— stirring as it does myriad ideas of words, thoughts, things, beauty, musical charm, all of which are born and bred in us, and by the blending of its own manifold tones, bringing into the hearts of the bystanders the speaker's actual emotion so that all who hear him share in it, and by piling phrase on phrase builds up one majestic whole—must we not think, I say, that by these very means it casts a spell on us and always turns *our* thoughts towards what is majestic and dignified and sublime and all else that it embraces, winning a complete mastery over our minds? Now it may indeed seem lunacy to raise any question on matters of such agreement, since experience is a sufficient test, yet surely the idea which Demosthenes applies to his decree strikes one as sublime and truly marvellous: "This decree made the peril at that time encompassing the country pass away like as a cloud."[a] But its effect is due no less to the harmony than to the thought. Its delivery rests wholly on the dactyls, which are the noblest of rhythms and

---

[a] *De corona* 188.

---

[1] K marg., Pearce, for κρούσει.

[2] κηλεῖν K marg., Manutius, for καλεῖν.

[3] αὐτῇ Toll, for αὐτῆ.

[4] που δοκεῖ Reiske, for τοῦ δοκεῖν.

καὶ τὸ ἡρῷον ὧν ἴσμεν κάλλιστον μέτρον συν-
ιστᾶσι· [τό τε]¹ ἐπείτοιγε ἐκ τῆς ἰδίας αὐτὸ χώρας
μετάθες ὅποι δὴ ἐθέλεις "τοῦτο τὸ ψήφισμα ὥσπερ
νέφος ἐποίησε τὸν τότε κίνδυνον παρελθεῖν," ἢ νὴ
Δία μίαν ἀπόκοψον συλλαβὴν μόνον "ἐποίησε
παρελθεῖν ὡς νέφος," καὶ εἴσῃ, πόσον ἡ ἁρμονία τῷ
ὕψει συνηχεῖ. αὐτὸ γὰρ τὸ "ὥσπερ νέφος" ἐπὶ
μακροῦ τοῦ πρώτου ῥυθμοῦ βέβηκε, τέτρασι κατα-
μετρουμένου² χρόνοις· ἐξαιρεθείσης δὲ τῆς μιᾶς
συλλαβῆς "ὡς νέφος" εὐθὺς ἀκρωτηριάζει τῇ συγ-
κοπῇ τὸ μέγεθος, ὡς ἔμπαλιν, ἐὰν ἐπεκτείνῃς
"παρελθεῖν ἐποίησεν ὡσπερεὶ³ νέφος," τὸ αὐτὸ
σημαίνει, οὐ τὸ αὐτὸ δὲ ἔτι προσπίπτει, ὅτι τῷ μήκει
τῶν ἄκρων χρόνων συνεκλύεται καὶ διαχαλᾶται τὸ
ὕψος τὸ ἀπότομον.

40. Ἐν δὲ τοῖς μάλιστα μεγεθοποιεῖ τὰ λεγόμενα, καθάπερ τὰ σώματα ἡ τῶν μελῶν ἐπισύνθεσις,
ὧν ἓν μὲν οὐδὲν τμηθὲν ἀφ' ἑτέρου καθ' ἑαυτὸ ἀξιό-
λογον ἔχει, πάντα δὲ μετ' ἀλλήλων ἐκπληροῖ τέλειον
σύστημα· οὕτως τὰ μεγάλα σκεδασθέντα μὲν ἀπ'
ἀλλήλων ἄλλοσ' ἄλλῃ ἅμα ἑαυτοῖς συνδιαφορεῖ καὶ
τὸ ὕψος, σωματοποιούμενα δὲ τῇ κοινωνίᾳ καὶ ἔτι
δεσμῷ τῆς ἁρμονίας περικλειόμενα, αὐτῷ τῷ κύκλῳ
φωνήεντα γίνεται· καὶ σχεδὸν ἐν ταῖς περιόδοις ἔρα-
νός ἐστι πλήθους τὰ μεγέθη. ἀλλὰ μὴν ὅτι γε πολ-

¹ Manutius omitted τό τε; Pearce and others propose a
lacuna to follow it, e.g. τό τε <τελευταῖον κόμμα θαυμαστῶς
συντέτακται> Mazzucchi.

make for grandeur—and that is why the most beautiful of all known metres, the heroic, is composed of dactyls. Change the position of the phrase[a] to any place you like— τοῦτο τὸ ψήφισμα ὥσπερ νέφος ἐποίησε τὸν τότε κίνδυνον παρελθεῖν—or simply cut off a single syllable—ἐποίησε παρελθεῖν ὡς νέφος— and you will realize how truly the harmony chimes in with the sublimity. Indeed the actual phrase ὥσπερ νέφος rests on its long first rhythmical element, equivalent to four beats. Cut out the one syllable—ὡς νέφος—and the curtailment at once mutilates the grandeur. So again if you lengthen it—παρελθεῖν ἐποίησεν ὡσπερεὶ νέφος— the meaning is the same, but it does not strike the same upon the ear, because the sheer sublimity is broken up and loosened by the breaking up of the longs in the final syllables.[b]

40. Nothing is of greater service in giving grandeur to what is said than the organization of the various members. It is the same with the human body. None of the members has any value by itself apart from the others, yet one with another they all constitute a perfect system. Similarly if these effects of grandeur are separated, the sublimity is scattered with them: but if they are united into a single whole and embraced by the bonds of rhythm, then they gain a living voice just by being merely rounded into a period. In a period, one might say, the grandeur

[a] I.e. the words ὥσπερ νέφος.

[b] I.e. both the proposed changes involve losing the effect of ὥσπερ as two longs.

---

[2] καταμετρουμένου Toll for καταμετρούμενον.

[3] ὡσπερεὶ K marg. for ὥσπερ.

λοὶ καὶ συγγραφέων καὶ ποιητῶν οὐκ ὄντες ὑψηλοὶ
φύσει, μήποτε δὲ καὶ ἀμεγέθεις, ὅμως κοινοῖς καὶ
δημώδεσι τοῖς ὀνόμασι καὶ οὐδὲν ἐπαγομένοις
περιττὸν ὡς τὰ πολλὰ συγχρώμενοι, διὰ μόνου τοῦ
συνθεῖναι καὶ ἁρμόσαι ταῦτα δεόντως[1] ὄγκον καὶ
διάστημα καὶ τὸ μὴ ταπεινοὶ δοκεῖν εἶναι περιεβά-
λοντο, καθάπερ ἄλλοι τε πολλοὶ καὶ Φίλιστος, Ἀριστοφάνης ἔν τισιν, ἐν τοῖς πλείστοις Εὐριπίδης,
3   ἱκανῶς ἡμῖν δεδήλωται. μετά γέ τοι τὴν τεκνοκτο-
νίαν Ἡρακλῆς φησι

> γέμω κακῶν δὴ κοὐκέτ' ἔσθ' ὅποι τεθῇ.

σφόδρα δημῶδες τὸ λεγόμενον, ἀλλὰ γέγονεν ὑψηλὸν τῇ πλάσει ἀναλογοῦν· εἰ δ' ἄλλως αὐτὸ συναρ-
μόσεις, φανήσεταί σοι, διότι τῆς συνθέσεως ποιητὴς
4   ὁ Εὐριπίδης μᾶλλόν ἐστιν ἢ τοῦ νοῦ. ἐπὶ δὲ τῆς
συρομένης ὑπὸ τοῦ ταύρου Δίρκης,

> εἰ δέ που τύχοι
> πέριξ ἑλίξας, εἷλκε <πάνθ'>[2] ὁμοῦ λαβὼν
> γυναῖκα πέτραν δρῦν μεταλλάσσων ἀεί,

ἔστι μὲν γενναῖον καὶ τὸ λῆμμα, ἁδρότερον δὲ
γέγονε τῷ τὴν ἁρμονίαν μὴ κατεσπεῦσθαι μηδ' οἷον
ἐν ἀποκυλίσματι φέρεσθαι, ἀλλὰ στηριγμούς τε

---

[1] δεόντως von Arnim for δ' ὅμως; but it may be best to make
a lacuna after δ' (Mazzucchi).
[2] Add. Bergk.

comes from the multitude of contributors. We have indeed abundantly shown[a] that many writers both in prose and poetry, who are not by nature sublime, perhaps even the very opposite, while using for the most part current vulgar words, which suggests nothing out of the common, yet by the mere arrangement and fitting together of these properly have achieved dignity and distinction and a reputation for grandeur; Philistus,[b] for instance, among many others, Aristophanes occasionally, Euripides almost always. After the slaughter of his children Heracles says:

I am loaded with woes and have no room for more.[c]

The phrase is exceedingly ordinary, yet becomes sublime by being apt to the situation. If you put the passage together in any other way, you will realize that Euripides is a poet of word arrangement more than of ideas. Speaking of Dirce being torn apart by the bull, he says,

And if perchance it happened
To twist itself around, It dragged them all,
Woman and rock and oak, and juggled with them.[d]

The idea itself is a fine one, but it gains additional force from the fact that the rhythm is not hurried along or, as it

[a] Presumably in the (lost) work in two books referred to at 39.1.

[b] Sicilian historian of the fourth century, imitator of Thucydides: *FGrHist* 556.

[c] Euripides, *Hercules Furens* 1245.

[d] From *Antiope* (fr. 221 Nauck²): Amphion and Zethus, having discovered that Antiope was their mother, inflict on the cruel queen Dirce the punishment she had intended for Antiope.

ἔχειν πρὸς ἄλληλα τὰ ὀνόματα καὶ ἐξερείσματα τῶν
χρόνων πρὸς ἑδραῖον διαβεβηκότα μέγεθος.

41. Μικροποιοῦν δ' οὐδὲν οὕτως ἐν τοῖς ὑψηλοῖς
ὡς ῥυθμὸς κεκλασμένος λόγων καὶ σεσοβημένος,
οἷον δὴ πυρρίχιοι καὶ τροχαῖοι καὶ διχόρειοι, τέλεον
εἰς ὀρχηστικὸν συνεκπίπτοντες. εὐθὺς γὰρ πάντα
φαίνεται τὰ κατάρρυθμα κομψὰ καὶ μικροχαρῆ
2 [καὶ]¹ ἀπαθέστατα διὰ τῆς ὁμοειδείας ἐπιπολάζοντα·
καὶ ἔτι τούτων τὸ χείριστον ὅτι, ὥσπερ τὰ ᾠδάρια
τοὺς ἀκροατὰς ἀπὸ τοῦ πράγματος ἀφέλκει καὶ ἐφ'
αὑτὰ βιάζεται, οὕτως καὶ τὰ κατερρυθμισμένα τῶν
λεγομένων οὐ τὸ τοῦ λόγου πάθος ἐνδίδωσι τοῖς
ἀκούουσι, τὸ δὲ τοῦ ῥυθμοῦ, ὡς ἐνίοτε προειδότας
τὰς ὀφειλομένας καταλήξεις αὐτοὺς ὑποκρούειν τοῖς
λέγουσι καὶ φθάνοντας ὡς ἐν χορῷ τινι προαποδιδό-
3 ναι τὴν βάσιν. ὁμοίως δὲ ἀμεγέθη καὶ τὰ λίαν
συγκείμενα καὶ εἰς μικρὰ καὶ βραχυσύλλαβα
συγκεκομμένα καὶ ὡσανεὶ γόμφοις τισὶν ἐπαλλήλοις
κατ' ἐγκοπὰς καὶ σκληρότητας ἐπισυνδεδεμένα.

42. Ἔτι γε μὴν ὕψους μειωτικὸν καὶ ἡ ἄγαν τῆς
φράσεως συγκοπή· πηροῖ γὰρ τὸ μέγεθος, ὅταν εἰς
λίαν συνάγηται βραχύ· ἀκουέσθω δὲ νῦν μὴ τὰ
[οὐ]² δεόντως συνεστραμμένα, ἀλλ' ὅσα ἄντικρυς
μικρὰ καὶ κατακεκερματισμένα· συγκοπὴ μὲν γὰρ
2 κολούει τὸν νοῦν, συντομία δ' ἐπ' εὐθύ. δῆλον δ' ὡς

---

¹ [καὶ] del. Russell (1964).
² Manutius omitted οὐ.

were, running on rollers, but the words prop one another up and are separated by intervals, so that they stand firm and give the impression of stable grandeur.[a]

41. Nothing damages an elevated passage so much as effeminate and agitated rhythm, pyrrhics ($\smile\smile$), for instance, and trochees ($-\smile$ or $\smile\smile\smile$), and dichorees ($-\smile-\smile$), which fall into a regular dance rhythm. For all over-rhythmical passages at once become merely pretty and cheap, recurring monotonously without producing the slightest emotional effect. Moreover, the worst of it is that, just as songs divert the attention of the audience from the action and forcibly claim it for themselves, so, too, over-rhythmical prose gives the audience the effect not of the words but of the rhythm. Thus they sometimes foresee the due ending themselves and keep time with their feet, anticipating the speaker and setting the step as if it were a dance. Equally deficient in grandeur are those passages which are too close-packed and concise, broken up into tiny fragments and short syllables. They give the impression of being bolted together, as it were, at frequent intervals with rough and uneven joins.

42. Extreme conciseness of expression also tends to diminish sublimity. The grandeur is mutilated by being too closely compressed. You must understand here not proper compression, but sentences which are, in absolute terms, small and fragmented. For extreme conciseness cripples the sense: true brevity goes straight to the point.

[a] The point is that combinations of consonants delay the smooth running of the words: note especially *perix helixas* and *petran drun* in the passage just quoted.

ἔμπαλιν τὰ ἐκτάδην ἀπόψυχα τὰ παρ᾽[1] ἄκαιρον
μῆκος ἀναχαλώμενα.[2]

43. Δεινὴ δ᾽ αἰσχῦναι τὰ μεγέθη καὶ ἡ μικρότης
τῶν ὀνομάτων. παρὰ γοῦν τῷ Ἡροδότῳ κατὰ μὲν τὰ
λήμματα δαιμονίως ὁ χειμὼν πέφρασται, τινὰ δὲ νὴ
Δία περιέχει τῆς ὕλης ἀδοξότερα· καὶ τοῦτο μὲν
ἴσως "ζεσάσης δὲ τῆς θαλάσσης," ὡς τὸ "ζεσάσης"
πολὺ τὸ ὕψος περισπᾷ, διὰ τὸ κακόστομον· ἀλλ᾽
"ὁ ἄνεμος" φησίν "ἐκοπίασεν," καί "τοὺς περὶ τὸ
ναυάγιον δρασσομένους ἐξεδέχετο τέλος ἄχαρι."
ἄσεμνον γὰρ τὸ κοπιάσαι ἰδιωτικὸν <ὄν,>[3] τὸ δ᾽
2 ἀχάριστον τηλικούτου πάθους ἀνοίκειον. ὁμοίως
καὶ ὁ Θεόπομπος ὑπερφυῶς σκευάσας τὴν τοῦ Πέρ-
σου κατάβασιν ἐπ᾽ Αἴγυπτον ὀνοματίοις τισὶ τὰ ὅλα
διέβαλεν. "ποία γὰρ πόλις ἢ ποῖον ἔθνος τῶν κατὰ
τὴν Ἀσίαν οὐκ ἐπρεσβεύετο πρὸς βασιλέα; τί δὲ
τῶν ἐκ τῆς γῆς γεννωμένων ἢ τῶν κατὰ τέχνην ἐπι-
τελουμένων καλῶν ἢ τιμίων οὐκ ἐκομίσθη δῶρον ὡς
αὐτόν; οὐ πολλαὶ μὲν καὶ πολυτελεῖς στρωμναὶ καὶ
χλανίδες, τὰ μὲν ἁλουργῆ, τὰ δὲ ποικιλτά, τὰ δὲ
λευκά, πολλαὶ δὲ σκηναὶ χρυσαῖ κατεσκευασμέναι
πᾶσι τοῖς χρησίμοις, πολλαὶ δὲ καὶ ξυστίδες καὶ
κλῖναι πολυτελεῖς; ἔτι δὲ καὶ κοῖλος ἄργυρος καὶ
χρυσὸς ἀπειργασμένος καὶ ἐκπώματα καὶ κρατῆρες,

---

[1] παρ᾽ ἄκαιρον Pearce, for γὰρ ἄκαιρον.
[2] ἀναχαλώμενα Toup, for ἀνακαλούμενα.
[3] <ὄν> add. Wilamowitz.

It is plain that the opposite holds of fully extended expressions; what is relaxed by unseasonable length is dead.

43. The use of trivial words also has a terribly debasing effect on a grand passage. The storm in Herodotus, for instance, is, as far as the ideas go, wonderfully described, but it includes certain things which are beneath the dignity of the subject. One might instance perhaps "the sea seething":[a] the word seething is so cacophonous that it takes off a great deal of the sublimity. But he does worse. "The wind," he says, "flagged," and "For those who were clinging to the wreck there awaited an unpleasant end."[b] "Flagged" is too colloquial a word to be dignified, and "unpleasant" ill befits so terrible a disaster. Similarly Theopompus,[c] after fitting out the Persian king's descent into Egypt in the most marvellous manner, discredited the whole description by the use of some paltry words. "For what city or what people of those in Asia did not send envoys to the king? What was there of beauty or of value whether born of the earth or perfected by art that was not brought as an offering to him? Were there not many costly coverlets and cloaks, some purple, some embroidered, some white; many pavilions of gold furnished with all things needful, many robes of state and costly couches? Then, moreover, there was plate of beaten silver and wrought gold, cups, and

[a] Herodotus 7.188.

[b] Herodotus 7.191, 8.13.

[c] Fr. 263a (*FGrHist*): the passage is quoted by Athenaeus (2.67F), but somewhat differently. It refers to the expedition of Artaxerxes Ochus against Egypt in the middle of the fourth century (cf. Diod. Sic. 16.44ff).

LONGINUS

ὧν τοὺς μὲν λιθοκολλήτους, τοὺς δ᾽ ἄλλως ἀκριβῶς
καὶ πολυτελῶς εἶδες ἂν ἐκπεπονημένους. πρὸς δὲ
τούτοις ἀναρίθμητοι μὲν ὅπλων μυριάδες τῶν μὲν
Ἑλληνικῶν, τῶν δὲ βαρβαρικῶν, ὑπερβάλλοντα δὲ
τὸ πλῆθος ὑποζύγια καὶ πρὸς κατακοπὴν ἱερεῖα
σιτευτά, καὶ πολλοὶ μὲν ἀρτυμάτων μέδιμνοι, πολλοὶ
δὲ θύλακοι καὶ σάκκοι καὶ χύτραι βυβλίων¹ καὶ τῶν
ἄλλων ἁπάντων χρησίμων· τοσαῦτα δὲ κρέα τεταρι-
χευμένα παντοδαπῶν ἱερείων, ὡς σωροὺς αὐτῶν
γενέσθαι τηλικούτους, ὥστε τοὺς προσιόντας πόρρωθεν ὑπολαμβάνειν ὄχθους εἶναι καὶ λόφους ἀντω-
3 θουμένους." ἐκ τῶν ὑψηλοτέρων εἰς τὰ ταπεινότερα
ἀποδιδράσκει, δέον ποιήσασθαι τὴν αὔξησιν ἔμπα-
λιν· ἀλλὰ τῇ θαυμαστῇ τῆς ὅλης παρασκευῆς ἀγγελίᾳ παραμίξας τοὺς θυλάκους καὶ τὰ ἀρτύματα καὶ
τὰ σακκία μαγειρείου τινὰ φαντασίαν ἐποίησεν.
ὥσπερ γὰρ εἴ τις ἐπ᾽ αὐτῶν ἐκείνων τῶν προκοσμη-
μάτων μεταξὺ τῶν χρυσίων καὶ λιθοκολλήτων κρατήρων καὶ ἀργύρου κοίλου σκηνῶν τε ὁλοχρύσων
καὶ ἐκπωμάτων φέρων μέσα ἔθηκεν θυλάκια καὶ
σακκία ἀπρεπὲς ἂν ἦν τῇ προσόψει τὸ ἔργον, οὕτω
καὶ τῆς ἑρμηνείας τὰ τοιαῦτα ὀνόματα αἴσχη καὶ
οἱονεὶ στίγματα καθίσταται παρὰ καιρὸν ἐγκατα-
4 ταττόμενα. παρέκειτο δ᾽ ὡς ὁλοσχερῶς ἐπελθεῖν καὶ
οὓς ὄχθους λέγει συμβεβλῆσθαι καὶ περὶ τῆς ἄλλης
παρασκευῆς οὕτως ἀλλάξας εἰπεῖν καμήλους καὶ
πλῆθος ὑποζυγίων φορταγωγούντων πάντα τὰ πρὸς
τρυφὴν καὶ ἀπόλαυσιν τραπεζῶν χορηγήματα, ἢ

296

bowls, some of which you might have seen studded with
jewels and others embellished by some other means both
cunning and costly. Besides these there were countless
myriads of weapons, some Greek, some barbarian; baggage animals beyond number, and victims fatted for
slaughter; many bushels of spice, and many bags and
sacks and pots of papyrus[a] and of all other things needful;
and such a store of salted meat of every kind that it lay in
heaps so large that those who approached from a distance
took them for mounds and hills confronting them." He
descends from the sublime to the trivial, where he needs
rather a crescendo. As it is, by introducing bags and
spices and sacks in the middle of his wonderful description of the whole equipage he has almost given the effect
of a cook shop. Suppose that in all this show itself someone had brought bags and sacks and set them in the middle of the gold and jewelled bowls, the beaten silver, the
pavilions of solid gold and the drinking cups—that would
have presented an unseemly sight. In the same way the
untimely introduction of such words as these disfigures
the style, and puts a brand on it, as it were. He might
have given a comprehensive description both of what he
calls the heaped-up mounds and of the rest of the
equipage by altering his description thus: "camels and a
multitude of baggage animals laden with all that serves
the luxury and pleasure of the table"; or he might

[a] Or onions, if we accept Toup's conjecture.

---

[1] Athenaeus (2.67f) has πολλοὶ δὲ σάκκοι καὶ θύλακοι βι-
βλίων; P has πολλοὶ δ' οἱ θύλακοι καὶ σάκκοι καὶ χάρται
βυβλίων. Toup proposed χύτραι βολβῶν, "jars of onions," and
the reference below to μαγειρεῖον perhaps supports this.

LONGINUS

σωροὺς ὀνομάσαι παντοίων σπερμάτων καὶ τῶν
ἅπερ διαφέρει πρὸς ὀψοποιίας καὶ ἡδυπαθείας, ἢ
εἴπερ πάντως ἐβούλετο αὐτὰ καὶ ῥητῶς[1] θεῖναι, καὶ
ὅσα τραπεζοκόμων εἰπεῖν καὶ ὀψοποιῶν ἡδύσματα.
5 οὐ γὰρ δεῖ κατανταν ἐν τοῖς ὕψεσιν εἰς τὰ ῥυπαρὰ
καὶ ἐξυβρισμένα, ἂν μὴ σφόδρα ὑπό τινος ἀνάγκης
συνδιωκώμεθα, ἀλλὰ τῶν πραγμάτων πρέποι ἂν καὶ
τὰς φωνὰς ἔχειν ἀξίας καὶ μιμεῖσθαι τὴν δημιουρ-
γήσασαν φύσιν τὸν ἄνθρωπον, ἥτις ἐν ἡμῖν τὰ μέρη
τὰ ἀπόρρητα οὐκ ἔθηκεν ἐν προσώπῳ οὐδὲ τὰ τοῦ
παντὸς ὄγκου περιηθήματα,[2] ἀπεκρύψατο δὲ ὡς ἐνῆν
καὶ κατὰ τὸν Ξενοφῶντα τοὺς τούτων ὅτι πορρωτάτω
ὀχετοὺς ἀπέστρεψεν, οὐδαμῇ καταισχύνασα τὸ τοῦ
6 ὅλου ζῴου κάλλος. ἀλλὰ γὰρ οὐκ ἐπ᾽ εἴδους[3] ἐπείγει
τὰ μικροποιὰ διαριθμεῖν· προϋποδεδειγμένων γὰρ
τῶν ὅσα εὐγενεῖς καὶ ὑψηλοὺς ἐργάζεται τοὺς
λόγους, δῆλον ὡς τὰ ἐναντία τούτων ταπεινοὺς ποιήσει κατὰ τὸ πλεῖστον καὶ ἀσχήμονας.

44. Ἐκεῖνο μέντοι λοιπὸν ἕνεκα τῆς σῆς χρηστο-
μαθείας οὐκ ὀκνήσομεν ἐπιπροσθεῖναι[4] <καὶ>[5] δια-
σαφῆσαι, Τερεντιανὲ φίλτατε, ὅπερ ἐζήτησέ τις τῶν
φιλοσόφων πρὸς <ἐμὲ> ἔναγχος,[6] "θαῦμά μ᾽ ἔχει,"
λέγων, "ὡς ἀμέλει καὶ ἑτέρους πολλούς, πῶς ποτε
κατὰ τὸν ἡμέτερον αἰῶνα πιθαναὶ μὲν ἐπ᾽ ἄκρον καὶ
πολιτικαί, δριμεῖαί τε καὶ ἐντρεχεῖς καὶ μάλιστα
πρὸς ἡδονὰς λόγων εὔφοροι, ὑψηλαὶ δὲ λίαν καὶ

---

[1] So Richards for αὐτάρκη οὕτως P; perhaps αὐτὰ ἀκριβῶς
(cf. ταῦτα ἀκριβῆ οὕτως, Mazzucchi).

298

have called them "heaps of every kind of grain and of all known aids to cookery and good living"; or, if he must at all hazards be explicit, "all the dainties known to caterers and cooks." One ought not in elevated passages to descend to what is sordid and contemptible, except under the severe pressure of necessity, but the proper course is to suit the words to the dignity of the subject and thus imitate Nature, the artist that created man. Nature did not place in full view our dishonourable parts nor the drains that purge our whole frame, but as far as possible concealed them and, as Xenophon says,[a] thrust their channels into the furthest background, for fear of spoiling the beauty of the whole creature. There is, however, no immediate need for enumerating and classifying the factors of mean style in detail. As we have already laid down all the qualities that make our utterance noble and sublime, it obviously follows that the opposite of these will generally make it trivial and ungainly.

44. One problem now remains for solution, my dear Terentianus, and knowing your love of learning I will not hesitate to append it—a problem which a certain philosopher recently put to me. "It surprises me," he said, "as it doubtless surprises many others too, how it is that in this age of ours we find natures that are supremely persuasive and suited for public life, shrewd and versatile and especially rich in literary charm, yet really sublime and tran-

---

[a] *Memorabilia* 1.4.6.

---

[2] περιηθήματα Pearce, for περιθήματα.

[3] ἐπ᾽ εἴδους Toll, for ἐπιδούς.

[4] ἐπιπροσθεῖναι Manutius for ἐπιπροσθῆναι.

[5] ‹καὶ› add. K marg., Manutius.

[6] πρὸς ‹ἐμὲ› ἔναγχος Cobet, for προσέναγχος.

ὑπερμεγέθεις, πλὴν εἰ μή τι σπάνιον, οὐκέτι γεννῶν-
ται φύσεις. τοσαύτη λόγων κοσμική τις ἐπέχει τὸν
2 βίον ἀφορία. ἢ νὴ Δί'" ἔφη "πιστευτέον ἐκείνῳ τῷ
θρυλουμένῳ, ὡς ἡ δημοκρατία τῶν μεγάλων ἀγαθὴ
τιθηνός, ᾗ μόνῃ σχεδὸν καὶ συνήκμασαν οἱ περὶ
λόγους δεινοὶ καὶ συναπέθανον; θρέψαι τε γάρ,
φασίν, ἱκανὴ τὰ φρονήματα τῶν μεγαλοφρόνων ἡ
ἐλευθερία καὶ ἐπελπίσαι καὶ ἅμα διεγείρειν¹ τὸ πρό-
θυμον τῆς πρὸς ἀλλήλους ἔριδος καὶ τῆς περὶ τὰ
3 πρωτεῖα φιλοτιμίας. ἔτι γε μὴν διὰ τὰ προκείμενα
ἐν ταῖς πολιτείαις ἔπαθλα ἑκάστοτε τὰ ψυχικὰ προ-
τερήματα τῶν ῥητόρων μελετώμενα ἀκονᾶται καὶ
οἷον ἐκτρίβεται καὶ τοῖς πράγμασι κατὰ τὸ εἰκὸς
ἐλεύθερα συνεκλάμπει. οἱ δὲ νῦν ἐοίκαμεν" ἔφη
"παιδομαθεῖς εἶναι δουλείας δικαίας, τοῖς αὐτοῖς
ἔθεσι καὶ ἐπιτηδεύμασιν ἐξ ἁπαλῶν ἔτι φρονημάτων
μόνον οὐκ ἐνεσπαργανωμένοι καὶ ἄγευστοι καλλί-
στου καὶ γονιμωτάτου λόγων νάματος, τὴν ἐλευθερίαν" ἔφη "λέγω, διόπερ οὐδὲν ὅτι μὴ κόλακες ἐκ-
4 βαίνομεν μεγαλοφυεῖς." διὰ τοῦτο τὰς μὲν ἄλλας
ἕξεις καὶ εἰς οἰκέτας πίπτειν ἔφασκεν, δοῦλον δὲ μηδένα γίνεσθαι ῥήτορα· εὐθὺς γὰρ ἀναζεῖν² τὸ ἀπαρ-
ρησίαστον καὶ οἷον ἔμφρουρον ὑπὸ συνηθείας ἀεὶ
κεκονδυλισμένον· "ἥμισυ γάρ τ' ἀρετῆς" κατὰ τὸν
5 Ὅμηρον "ἀποαίνυται δούλιον ἦμαρ." "ὥσπερ οὖν,
εἴ γε" φησί "τοῦτο πιστόν ἐστιν <ὃ>³ ἀκούω, τὰ

¹ Morus, for διελθεῖν.
² ἀναζεῖν Weiske, for ἀναζεῖ.

scendent natures are no longer, or only very rarely, now produced. Such is the universal dearth of literature that besets our times. Are we really to believe the hackneyed view that democracy is the kindly nurse of genius and that—speaking generally—the great men of letters flourished only with democracy and perished with it? Freedom, they say, has the power to foster noble minds and to fill them with high hopes, and at the same time to rouse our spirit of mutual rivalry and eager competition for the foremost place. Moreover, thanks to the prizes which a republic offers, an orator's intellectual gifts are whetted by practice, burnished, so to speak, by friction, and share, as is only natural, the light of freedom which illuminates the state. But in these days we seem to be schooled from childhood in an equitable slavery, swaddled, I might say, from the tender infancy of our minds in the same servile ways and practices. We never drink from the fairest and most fertile source of eloquence, which is freedom, and therefore we turn out to be nothing but flatterers on a grand scale." This is the reason, he alleged, that, while all other faculties are granted even to slaves, no slave ever becomes an orator. According to him, the inability to speak freely, and the sense of being as it were in prison, immediately assert themselves, the product of the repeated beating of habit. As Homer says: "Surely half of our manhood is robbed by the day of enslavement."[a] "And so," he adds, "if what I hear is true that not only do the

[a] *Odyssey* 17.322.

---

[3] <ὁ> add. Pearce.

γλωττόκομα, ἐν οἷς οἱ πυγμαῖοι, καλούμενοι δὲ
νᾶνοι, τρέφονται, οὐ μόνον κωλύει τῶν ἐγκεκλεσμέ-
νων τὰς αὐξήσεις ἀλλὰ καὶ συναραιοῖ[1] διὰ τὸν περι-
κείμενον τοῖς σώμασι δεσμόν, οὕτως ἅπασαν δου-
λείαν, κἂν ᾖ δικαιοτάτη, ψυχῆς γλωττόκομον καὶ
6   κοινὸν ἄν τις ἀποφήναιτο δεσμωτήριον." ἐγὼ μέντοι
γε ὑπολαβών[2] "ῥᾴδιον," ἔφην "ὦ βέλτιστε, καὶ ἴδιον
ἀνθρώπου τὸ καταμέμφεσθαι τὰ ἀεὶ παρόντα· ὅρα
δὲ μή ποτε οὐχ ἡ τῆς οἰκουμένης εἰρήνη διαφθείρει
τὰς μεγάλας φύσεις, πολὺ δὲ μᾶλλον ὁ κατέχων
ἡμῶν τὰς ἐπιθυμίας ἀπεριόριστος οὑτοσὶ πόλεμος,
καὶ νὴ Δία πρὸς τούτῳ τὰ φρουροῦντα τὸν νῦν βίον
καὶ κατ' ἄκρας ἄγοντα καὶ φέροντα ταυτὶ πάθη. ἡ
γὰρ φιλοχρηματία, πρὸς ἣν ἅπαντες ἀπλήστως ἤδη
νοσοῦμεν, καὶ ἡ φιληδονία δουλαγωγοῦσι, μᾶλλον
δέ, ὡς ἂν εἴποι τις, καταβυθίζουσιν αὐτάνδρους ἤδη
τοὺς βίους· φιλαργυρία μὲν <γὰρ>[3] νόσημα μικρο-
7   ποιόν, φιληδονία δ' ἀγεννέστατον. οὐ δὴ ἔχω λογι-
ζόμενος εὑρεῖν, ὡς οἷόν τε πλοῦτον ἀόριστον ἐκτιμή-
σαντας, τὸ δ' ἀληθέστερον εἰπεῖν, ἐκθειάσαντας, τὰ
συμφυῆ τούτῳ κακὰ εἰς τὰς ψυχὰς ἡμῶν ἐπεισιόντα
μὴ παραδέχεσθαι. ἀκολουθεῖ γὰρ τῷ ἀμέτρῳ
πλούτῳ καὶ ἀκολάστῳ συνημμένη καὶ ἴσα, φασί,
βαίνουσα πολυτέλεια, καὶ ἅμα ἀνοίγοντος ἐκείνου
τῶν πόλεων καὶ οἴκων τὰς εἰσόδους εὐθὺς[4] ἐμβαίνει
καὶ συνοικίζεται. χρονίσαντα δὲ ταῦτα ἐν τοῖς βίοις

---

[1] συναραιοῖ Schmidt for συνάροι.

cages in which they keep the pygmies or dwarfs, as they are called, stunt the growth of their prisoners, but enfeeble them by the bonds applied to their bodies, on the same principle all slavery, however equitable, might well be described as a cage for the soul, a common prison." However I took him up and said, "It is easy, my good friend, and it is characteristic of human nature always to find fault with things as they are at the moment. But consider. Perhaps it is not the world's peace that corrupts great natures but much rather this endless warfare which besets our hearts, yes, and these passions that garrison our lives in present days and make utter havoc of them. It is the love of money, that insatiable sickness from which we all now suffer, and the love of pleasure, that enslave us, or rather one might say, sink our ship of life with all hands; for love of gold is a withering sickness, and love of pleasure utterly ignoble. Indeed, I cannot discover on consideration how, if we value boundless wealth, or to speak more truly, make a god of it, we can possibly keep our minds safe from the intrusion of the evils that accompany it. In close company with vast and unconscionable Wealth there follows, 'step for step,' as they say,[a] Extravagance: and no sooner has the one opened the gates of cities or houses, than the other comes and makes a home there too. And when they have spent some time in our

---

[a] Cf. Demosthenes, *Oration* 19.314.

---

[2] ὑπολαβών Bühler, for ὑπολαμβάνω.

[3] <γὰρ> add. Spengel.

[4] εὐθὺς Mathews, for εἰς ἃς.

νεοττοποιεῖται κατὰ τοὺς σοφοὺς καὶ ταχέως γενόμενα περὶ τεκνοποιΐαν ἀλαζόνειάν τε γεννῶσι καὶ
τῦφον καὶ τρυφήν, οὐ νόθα ἑαυτῶν γεννήματα ἀλλὰ
καὶ πάνυ γνήσια. ἐὰν δὲ καὶ τούτους τις τοῦ πλούτου τοὺς ἐκγόνους εἰς ἡλικίαν ἐλθεῖν ἐάσῃ, ταχέως
δεσπότας ταῖς ψυχαῖς ἐντίκτουσιν ἀπαραιτήτους,
8 ὕβριν καὶ παρανομίαν καὶ ἀναισχυντίαν. ταῦτα γὰρ
οὕτως ἀνάγκη γίνεσθαι καὶ μηκέτι τοὺς ἀνθρώπους
ἀναβλέπειν μηδ' ὑστεροφημίας[1] τελεσιουργεῖσθαι
κατ' ὀλίγον τὴν τῶν βίων διαφθοράν, φθίνειν δὲ καὶ
καταμαραίνεσθαι τὰ ψυχικὰ μεγέθη καὶ ἄζηλα γίνεσθαι, ἡνίκα τὰ θνητὰ ἑαυτῶν μέρη καὶ ἀνόητα[2] ἐκ-
9 θαυμάζοιεν, παρέντες αὔξειν τἀθάνατα. οὐ γὰρ ἐπὶ
κρίσει μέν τις δεκασθεὶς οὐκ ἂν ἔτι τῶν δικαίων καὶ
καλῶν ἐλεύθερος καὶ ὑγιὴς ἂν κριτὴς γένοιτο
(ἀνάγκη γὰρ τῷ δωροδόκῳ τὰ οἰκεῖα μὲν φαίνεσθαι
καλὰ καὶ δίκαια[3]), ὅπου δὲ ἡμῶν ἑκάστου τοὺς
ὅλους ἤδη βίους δεκασμοὶ βραβεύουσι καὶ ἀλλοτρίων θῆραι θανάτων καὶ ἐνέδραι διαθηκῶν, τὸ δ' ἐκ
τοῦ παντὸς κερδαίνειν ὠνούμεθα τῆς ψυχῆς ἕκαστος
πρὸς τῆς <φιλοχρηματίας>[4] ἠνδραποδισμένοι, ἆρα
δὴ ἐν τῇ τοσαύτῃ λοιμικῇ τοῦ βίου διαφθορᾷ δοκοῦμεν ἔτι ἐλεύθερόν τινα κριτὴν τῶν μεγάλων ἢ διη-
κόντων πρὸς τὸν αἰῶνα κἀδέκαστον[5] ἀπολελεῖφθαι
καὶ μὴ καταρχαιρεσιάζεσθαι πρὸς τῆς τοῦ πλεονε-
10 κτεῖν ἐπιθυμίας; ἀλλὰ μήποτε τοιούτοις, οἷοί περ

---

[1] μηδ' ὑστεροφημίας Reiske, for μηδ' ἕτερα φήμης.

lives, philosophers tell us, they build a nest there[a] and promptly set about begetting children; these are Swagger and Conceit and Luxury, no bastards but their trueborn issue. And if these offspring of wealth are allowed to grow to maturity, they soon breed in our hearts inexorable tyrants, Insolence and Disorder and Shamelessness. This must inevitably happen, and men no longer then look upwards nor take any further thought for future fame. Little by little the ruin of their lives is completed in the cycle of such vices, their greatness of soul wastes away and dies and is no longer something to strive for, since they value that part of them which is mortal and foolish, and neglect the development of their immortal part. A man who has been bribed for his verdict can no longer give an unbiased and sound judgement on what is just and fair (for the corrupt judge inevitably regards his own interest as fair and just). So, seeing that the whole life of each one of us is now governed wholly by bribery and by hunting after other people's deaths and laying traps for legacies, and we have sold our souls for profit at any price, slaves that we all are to our greed, can we then expect in such pestilential ruin of our lives that there is left a single free and unbribed judge of the things that are great and last to all eternity? Are we not all corrupted by our passion for gain? Nay, for such as we are perhaps it is better

[a] Cf. Plato, *Republic* 9.573C.

---

[2] καὶ ἀνόητα Toup, for καπανητα.

[3] Spengel, with reason, suspected a lacuna here: the sense of the missing words would be "but other people's interests improper." [4] <φιλοχρηματίας> add. Toll.

[5] κἀδέκαστον Toll, for καθέκαστον

ἐσμὲν ἡμεῖς, ἄμεινον ἄρχεσθαι ἢ ἐλευθέροις εἶναι·
ἐπείτοιγε ἀφεθεῖσαι τὸ σύνολον, ὡς ἐξ εἱρκτῆς ἄφε-
τοι, κατὰ τῶν πλησίον αἱ πλεονεξίαι κἂν ἐπικλύ-
11 σειαν[1] τοῖς κακοῖς τὴν οἰκουμένην. ὅλως δὲ δάπανον[2] ἔφην εἶναι τῶν νῦν γεννωμένων φύσεων τὴν
ῥᾳθυμίαν, ᾗ πλὴν ὀλίγων πάντες ἐγκαταβιοῦμεν,
οὐκ ἄλλως πονοῦντες ἢ ἀναλαμβάνοντες εἰ μὴ ἐπαίνου καὶ ἡδονῆς ἕνεκα, ἀλλὰ μὴ τῆς ζήλου καὶ τιμῆς
12 ἀξίας ποτὲ ὠφελείας." "κράτιστον εἰκῇ ταῦτ' ἐᾶν,"
ἐπὶ δὲ τὰ συνεχῆ χωρεῖν· ἦν δὲ ταῦτα τὰ πάθη, περὶ
ὧν ἐν ἰδίῳ προηγουμένως ὑπεσχόμεθα γράψειν ὑπο-
μνήματι, ἅτε[3] τήν τε τοῦ ἄλλου λόγου καὶ αὐτοῦ τοῦ
ὕψους μοῖραν ἐπεχόντων, ὡς ἡμῖν. . . .[4]

---

[1] ἐπικλύσειαν Markland, for ἐπικαύσειαν
[2] δάπανον Toll, for δαπανῶν
[3] ἅτε Mazzucchi for ὅ.
[4] The next few words can only be guessed; perhaps εἴρηται,
κρατίστην . . .

to have a master than to be free. Were it given complete liberty, like released prisoners, as it were, to prey on our neighbours, greed would swamp the world in a deluge of evils. In fact," I said, "what wastes the talents of the present generation is the idleness in which all but a few of us pass our lives, only exerting ourselves or showing any enterprise for the sake of getting praise or pleasure out of it, never from the honourable and admirable motive of doing good to the world." "It's best to let this be"[a] and pass on to the next question, which is that of the Emotions, a topic on which I previously undertook to write a separate treatise, for they seem to me to form part of the general subject of literature and especially of sublimity . . .

[*The rest is lost.*]

[a] Euripides, *Electra* 379.

DEMETRIUS
ON STYLE

EDITED AND TRANSLATED BY
DOREEN C. INNES

BASED ON THE TRANSLATION BY
W. RHYS ROBERTS

INTRODUCTION

On Style may well be the earliest post-Aristotelian treatise on literary theory to survive complete; and even if it is not, it is an important early source on an exceptionally wide range of topics. In contrast to the more stimulating but idiosyncratic Aristotle's *Poetics* and Longinus' *On the Sublime*, it is not likely to be highly innovative,[1] but that in itself makes *On Style* a particularly useful introduction and guide to our understanding of the strengths and weaknesses of classical literary criticism.

The author gives us our most extensive surviving account of the theory of styles, a particularly popular framework for critical analysis and judgment, and he does so in a complex theory of four styles for which we have no exact parallel. He also gives succinct, clear, and usually perceptive accounts of standard topics such as sentence theory and metaphor, and shows a more personal interest

---

NOTE. I thank Donald Russell and Rudolf Kassel for their benevolent and helpful comments on this introduction and the text respectively.

[1] See § 179, where Demetrius is "forced" to be original because no one else has treated the subject before; he also fails to integrate some of his disparate sources, especially in the elegant style. His strength is in analysis of individual topics and examples.

311

in less usual topics, such as the letter, music, and acting, and in less usual authors, such as Sophron, Ctesias, and Demades. Theory is consistently illustrated with typically brief and well-chosen examples, and in contrast to many of our other sources, particularly in Latin, there is no bias towards oratory.

Date and authorship

The author of *On Style* is conventionally called Demetrius. The most famous critic by this name is Demetrius of Phaleron (ca. 360–280 B.C.), the student of Aristotle who governed Athens 317–307 B.C. and wrote on a number of literary and rhetorical subjects,[2] and *On Style* is mistakenly attributed to him in the superscription of the tenth-century manuscript P.[3] But this attribution is a later addition, as we can see from the simpler version in the subscription of the same manuscript, "Demetrius On Style" (Δημητρίου περὶ ἑρμηνείας). This will be the original text. Demetrius is also the form in the few earlier references to name the author of *On Style*.[4] The eventual

---

[2] The fragments are edited by F. Wehrli, *Die Schule des Aristoteles* vol. 4 [Basel 1968]).

[3] Δημητρίου Φαληρέως περὶ ἑρμηνείας, ὅ ἐστι περὶ φράσεως (so also N and H; on the manuscripts see below). Manuscript attributions are in any case unreliable, as we can see from P's misattribution of Aristotle's *Rhetoric* to Dionysius and the similar problem of "Longinus".

[4] Probably first in the fourth to fifth centuries in Syrianus, *In Hermog. comm.* 1.99–100 Rabe; then in the sixth century by Ammonius' commentary on Aristotle's *De Interpretatione* (*Comm. in Arist. Graeca* 4.5), p. 4 Busse, and Phoebammon,

identification of a Demetrius with the most famous critic by that name was probably inevitable (and may well have ensured the work's survival), but it has no authority, and seems in any case inconsistent with the way in which Demetrius of Phaleron is cited in § 289. We cannot even be sure that the author was called Demetrius; if so, it was a common name, and no identification with any specific Demetrius is possible.

The date of the work is equally uncertain, and controversy continues. For much of this century scholars favoured a date in the first century A.D. (especially Roberts and Radermacher), but more recently scholars have argued for an earlier date; so ca. 270 B.C. (Grube), second century B.C. (Morpurgo Tagliabue), late second or early first century B.C. (Chiron), and a reworking in the first century A.D. of contents reflecting the second or early first century B.C. (Schenkeveld). I would agree with this growing consensus that the contents at least do not preclude and may best reflect the second century B.C. Firm evidence is, however, hard to find since we have no complete texts and only fragmentary knowledge of literary and rhetorical theory between Aristotle and authors of the first century B.C., a period including Theophrastus' On Style (περὶ λέξεως) and the development of the theories of styles, tropes, and figures which we see in the

---

Proleg. Syll. 377 Rabe. More frequently authorship is vaguely ascribed to "the ancients". Grube 53–54 suggests that the report of Demetrius of Phaleron's criticism of the long periods of Isocrates' followers in Philodemus, *Rhet.* 1.198 Sudhaus = F 169 Wehrli refers to *On Style* § 303, but Isocrates is not mentioned there, and we have similar contexts in other surviving fragments of Demetrius of Phaleron (cf. F 161–68 Wehrli).

313

works of Cicero and his contemporaries.[5] Textbooks are also prone to conservatism, so that early material may not prove early date, and "updating" revisions[6] may produce isolated later references which prove nothing about the rest of the work.

The latest known persons[7] to be named in *On Style* are roughly of the first half of the third century B.C.: Praxiphanes, Sotades, Demetrius of Phaleron, and Clitarchus (§§ 57, 189, 289, and 304), and the references to Demetrius and Sotades both suggest a date after their deaths. Grube stresses the number of quotations from authors of the fourth and early third century B.C., but we may compare two other texts with an unusual range, the Antiatticist and Rutilius Lupus.[8] Equally striking, and to be

---

[5] Particularly *Ad Herennium* IV (probably 86–82 B.C.), and Cicero, especially *De Oratore* (54 B.C.) and *Orator* (46 B.C.).

[6] A possible example: § 38 ὅνπερ νῦν λόγιον ὀνομάζουσιν. On λόγιος see note 22.

[7] But likely to be somewhat later are Archedemus and Artemon (§§ 34–35, 223), both perhaps second century B.C.; see Chiron, p. xxxii and J. M. Rist, "Demetrius the Stylist and Artemon the Compiler," *Phoenix* 18 (1964) 2–8. Reference to the Augustan critic Theodorus of Gadara, in § 237, is very doubtful, and the context suggests a historian, not a critic. Chronological deductions in general depend also on whether Demetrius cited contemporaries, as Aristotle did, or followed the usual later practice of citing earlier authors.

[8] Text of the former in *Anecdota Graeca* 1.77–116 Bekker (Berlin 1814) and of the latter in *Rhetores Latini Minores* 3–21 Halm (Leipzig 1863), also ed. E. Brooks (Leiden 1970); Rutilius based his treatise on figures of speech on the Greek critic Gorgias the Younger, who lived in the late first century B.C. and early first century A.D.

explained by Demetrius' Peripatetic sympathies, is the focus on examples from the circles of Socrates, Plato, and Aristotle.[9]

The claim in § 179 to be the first to discuss elegant composition, γλαφυρὰ σύνθεσις, implies ignorance of the treatment of this topic in Dionysius, *De Comp. Verb.* 23, written some time after 30 B.C. This fits the absence of other standard later material. In particular, there is no mention of a three-style theory in the defence of four styles against those who allow only two (§§ 36–37);[10] and Demosthenes is virtually restricted to the forceful style in contrast to his later preeminence as the master of all styles, a position generally acknowledged by the time of Cicero (e.g. *De Or.* 3.199; cf. e.g. DH. *Dem.* 8). This partly results from Demetrius' recognition of independent grand and forceful styles and the parallel virtual restriction of political oratory to the forceful style, but even there Demosthenes is given no special praise comparable to that of Thucydides for the grand style, the "divine" Sappho for charm, and Aristotle for the letter (§§ 40, 127, and 230).

Perhaps most tantalising of all is the question of Demetrius' relationship to Aristotle and the early Peripatos. Is it exceptionally close, does it have implications for the

[9] Cf. §§ 296–98 with the choice of three philosophical styles from Aristippus, Xenophon, and Socrates in contrast to Zeno, Diogenes, and Socrates in Epictetus 3.21.19 and 23.33; and perhaps the interest in Demades (§§ 282–86, cf. Theophr. F 706 Fortenbaugh).

[10] See further below. But conversely the silence about four styles in Cicero, Dionysius, and others proves nothing, since they also ignore the (different) four-style theory mentioned in Philodemus, *Rhet.* 1.165 Sudhaus.

date, and did Demetrius know Aristotle's writings directly, or through intermediaries? A Peripatetic debt is to
some extent inevitable, since the early Peripatos, especially Aristotle and Theophrastus, was exceptionally influential in the development of critical theory;[11] but it is
striking that the only critics named in *On Style* are either
Peripatetics (Aristotle, Theophrastus, and Praxiphanes),
or appear in contexts closely linked to Aristotle (Archedemus and Artemon). It seems also a sign of special admiration that the Peripatetics head the authors praised for
elegance (§ 181), while Aristotle himself is supreme at
letter-writing (§ 230), and, if the text is sound, heads the
authors illustrating comic charm (§ 126). Yet the reference to the Peripatetics also suggests that Demetrius was
not himself one, and could look back on the *early* Peripatos as an identifiable group with a shared elegance of
style (cf. Cic. *Orator* 127).

Aristotle's influence is particularly strong in the discussion of the clause and period (§§ 1–35), prose rhythm
(§§ 38–43), metaphor (§§ 78ff), frigidity (§ 116, where the
text of the *Rhetoric* even allows us to fill a lacuna), and
clarity (§§ 191ff, including the distinction between writing and oral delivery). But it is not clear that Demetrius
had read Aristotle. None of the four apparently direct
quotations (§§ 11, 34, 38, 116) is verbally exact, and
though the usual practice of quotation from memory and
adaptation to the new context may explain the discrepan-
cies, it is troubling that the quotation in § 38 distorts Ar.
Rhet. 1408b32ff in a way that implies later theory on the

[11] E.g. Cic. *De Or.* 1.43. See F. Solmsen, "The Aristotelian
Tradition in Ancient Rhetoric," *American Journal of Philology* 62
(1941) 35–50 and 169–90 (on style especially 43ff and 181ff).

grandeur of the paean (cf. Cic. *Orator* 197, a contrast of the iamb of the plain style with the grander paean, "paean autem in amplioribus").

Demetrius has been accused of a fundamental misunderstanding of Aristotle's theory of the period (§§ 10ff), but this depends on a doubtful and controversial interpretation of Aristotle. More plausibly, Demetrius may confuse a detail (see on § 12, a confusion of terminology), but he rightly interprets Aristotle,[12] while also following later theory. There is agreement on the fundamental point, that a period is a unit of thought, a structured whole where thought and form end together. The differences are that Aristotle confined the period to one or two clauses (a restriction Demetrius explicitly rejects in § 34), and favoured periods with antithesis and/or assonance, typically illustrated from Isocrates. Demetrius first defines and illustrates the period in accordance with post-Aristotelian theory (§ 10),[13] with focus on the ending and an example which is from Demosthenes and shows con-

---

[12] See R. A. Fowler, "Aristotle on the Period," *Classical Quarterly* 32 (1982) 89–99, and D. C. Innes, "Period and Colon: Theory and Example in Demetrius and Longinus," *Rutgers University Studies in Classical Humanities* VI, New Brunswick (1994). For a contrary view, that for Aristotle it is not the thought but prose-rhythm that shapes a period, see J. Zehetmeier, "Die Periodenlehre des Aristoteles," *Philologus* 83 (1930) 192–208, 255–84, 414–36, and Schenkeveld, Ch. II, especially pp. 28ff.

[13] E.g. Hermogenes 178 Rabe, "A period is an independent (αὐτοτελές) shaping of a whole thought in verbal form, succinctly brought to a conclusion (συντόμως ἀπηρτισμένον), and succinct hyperbata in it shape periods well."

spicuous hyperbaton. Only then does he bring in Aristotle (§ 11). Aristotelian influence is then seen particularly in periods with parallelism of structure (§§ 22ff), in some of the terminology (e.g. § 12 κατεστραμμένη) and in the inclusion of the one-clause period (§ 17).[14] Yet other vocabulary is post-Aristotelian (e.g. ἀπηρτισμένος, κύκλος, περιαγωγή), as is the upper limit of four clauses, and the three types of period (§§ 16 and 19–21).[15] So too "enthymeme" in §§ 30–33 has the Aristotelian meaning, but some of the terminology is later, as is the possible confusion with the epiphoneme in § 109 (we may compare Quint. 8.5.11, where the enthymeme may be used for decorative purpose, added "epiphonematis modo"). Demetrius also gives strong personal endorsement in § 15 to a moderate use of periods, a formulation which suggests the Peripatetic mean but is not in Aristotle.

This combination of material from Aristotle modified by later theory is typical. In §§ 78ff, for example, the theory of metaphor[16] shows strong Aristotelian influence,

[14] A type unimportant in later theory, but cf. Quint. 9.4.124, with the same criteria of length and rounding, "simplex, cum sensus unus longiore ambitu circumducitur." See also Hermogenes in the next note.

[15] In itself a triad found only here, but compare the looser style of philosophy and the distinction of periods for history and rhetoric in Cic. *Orator* 62ff. For the number of clauses, cf. Hermogenes 180 Rabe, "There are single-clause periods; there are also two-clause and three-clause periods, formed from <two or> three clauses, and a four-clause period formed from four clauses; and a clause is a thought brought to a conclusion." Cic. *Orator* 221 and Quint. 9.4.125 allow more than four.

[16] For a more detailed analysis see Schenkeveld, Ch. IV; D. C. Innes, "Cicero On Tropes," *Rhetorica* 6 (1988) 307–25;

but adds material which is found elsewhere in later theory, especially on the simile and dead metaphors; and metaphor from adding a privative adjective (§ 85) is unimportant in later theory and so likely to reflect a special interest in Aristotle, who provides the example: yet Demetrius adds the author's name, Theognis. In similar minor modifications Aristotle provides the theory and some but not all the examples in §§ 22ff and 116.

Some of these adaptations may derive from Theophrastus, for example the grandeur of the paean (cf § 41). There are four explicit references to him (§§ 41, 114, 173, and 222). He is also the likely source for the analysis of wit and charm in the elegant style, and he or other early Peripatetics for the interest in delivery, and the recurrent sequences of topics analysed under diction and composition.[17]

The theory of figures and tropes in *On Style* is less developed than that found in *Ad Herennium* and in Cicero, who dismissively assumes a familiarity with endless lists of figures (*De Or.* 3.200). Some specifically Stoic influence is likely here, perhaps especially in the figures in the forceful style, the only style in which Demetrius distinguishes figures of speech and thought, §§ 263ff)[18]

Marsh McCall, *Ancient Rhetorical Theories of the Simile and Comparison*, Cambridge, Mass. 1969. For an interesting Peripatetic fragment of ca. 200 B.C. see Pap. Hamburg 128, discussed by D. M. Schenkeveld, *Zeitschrift für Papyrologie und Epigraphik* 97 (1993) 67–80.

[17] See F. Solmsen, "Demetrios περὶ ἑρμηνείας und sein peripatetisches Quellenmaterial," *Hermes* 66 (1931) 241–67; Schenkeveld, pp. 21ff.

[18] See Schenkeveld, Chs. V and VI. Given the Stoic praise of

The Stoics also influence his theory of neologism, the vocabulary for some terms of grammar in §§ 60, 201, and 214, and possibly the use of ἀστεῖος = "good" in § 114 and μεταφορὰ πλεονάζουσα, the definition of the simile in § 80.[19] Archedemus (§ 34) may well be the Stoic Archedemus, and Chrysippus (280–207 B.C.) may be the source of the proverbs in § 172. But these Stoic traces are superficial or in language theory, an area where the Stoics influenced all later theory. What we have, then, in *On Style* is a work showing unusually strong and evident Peripatetic influence, but an influence often adapted and supplemented to fit standard later theory. As we shall see, it is also set into a very different conceptual framework of four styles.

Finally, there is linguistic evidence, an uncertain guide since we know too little about standard, educated Hellenistic prose, in particular the beginnings of linguistic Atticism, the conscious imitation of classical Attic Greek. But in terms of our current state of knowledge such Atticism is less likely as early as the second century B.C.; yet some signs of it are to be seen in Demetrius, as in

---

brevity, Stoic origin may also lie behind the second series of items on arrangement in §§ 103–5 and 253–58, brevity, aposiopesis, and cacophony. But much about Stoic theory of style remains obscure and controversial: see C. Atherton, "Hand over Fist: the Failure of Stoic Rhetoric," *Classical Quarterly* 38 (1988) 392–427.

[19] On grammar see Schenkeveld, p. 137 (but Peripatetic interest in connectives is seen in Theophr. F 683 Fortenbaugh and Praxiphanes, quoted in § 55). For ἀστεῖος, cf. e.g. SVF iii.674 (Chrysippus), and for the definition of the simile, cf. ὁρμὴ πλεονάζουσα, the Stoic definition of emotion, e.g. SVF iii.130.

the use of the dual for forms other than δύο and ἄμφω,[20] and the preposition ἀμφί[21] in § 288. Vocabularly, however, is in general not decisive, since many forms which used to be thought "late" have been found to have early instances or comparable forms (see the valuable lists in Grube, Appendix I; Schenkeveld, p. 145, n. 1). The most interesting are the few terms specifically said to be recent usages, λόγιος of grandeur in § 38,[22] and the group κακόζηλος, κακοζηλία, and (§ 239) ξηροκακοζηλία. The last is attested only here, and it is tempting to relate it to the "novum genus cacozeliae" which a hostile contemporary attributes to Virgil (Donatus, *Vit. Virg.* 44), a new affectation said to be neither swollen nor arid but produced from ordinary words and so less obvious. There may then be a few points of language to suggest a date of composition as late as the early first century B.C.

[20] Particularly striking in Demetrius are the examples in §§ 36 (two verbs) and 235 (genitives); see Chiron, p. xxiii, Schenkeveld, p. 140. Aristotle has only one dual involving a verb, Polybius has none, and seems the last to use the genitive dual. Later use of the dual was a choice artificial revival, to our knowledge first in the second half of the first century B.C. There are two examples of τὼ χεῖρε in the scholarly Parthenius, verbs and genitives seem to occur first in Dionysius, and verbal forms are rare even in Atticist authors.

[21] See Schenkeveld, p. 144. It has disappeared already from Aristotle, Parthenius has one example, Dionysius about thirty.

[22] See E. Orth, *Logios*, Leipzig, 1926; Grube, p. 150. It is first securely used meaning "eloquent" in Philo, and linked with grandeur perhaps first in the period of Plutarch, e.g. *Mor.* 350c. But see also note 6.

Structure

The overall structure of *On Style* is clear and methodical, a preliminary account of sentence theory (§§ 1–35), followed by analysis of four styles: the grand, elegant, plain, and forceful (§§ 36–304). In the absence of any formal introduction or conclusion, these may seem two independent accounts, but there are links and cross references (e.g. §§ 6 and 121, §§ 7–9 and 241–42), and the first, a useful preliminary to a topic common to all the styles in the second part, is too long to fit within any one style: contrast, for example, the inclusion of general remarks on prose rhythm, metaphor, and neologism on their first occurrence within the grand style (§§ 38 and 78ff), clarity and vividness within the plain style (§§ 191 and 209ff), and forms of open and oblique rebuke in the forceful style (§§ 287ff).

Clauses and periods are analysed in an orderly textbook progression of topics (§§ 1–35).[23] The unusually detailed account of the clause (§§ 1–9) moves from origin and definition to appropriate use of long and short clauses, while the period is analysed under definition, origin and history, length, and subtypes, with remarks interspersed on use. Finally, there are two appendices, reverting to definition (§§ 34–35), just as additional topics tend to follow the main analysis in the individual styles.

After a preliminary defence of the four-style theory, Demetrius analyses each of the four styles in turn. Each ends with a brief discussion of its faulty counterpart, the

---

[23] Cf. e.g. Cic. *Orator* 174. The sequence of definition and use is natural and common, cf. §§ 22–29, M. Fuhrmann, *Das systematische Lehrbuch*, Göttingen 1960.

frigid, affected, arid, and unpleasant, and, with the partial exception of the elegant style, each is analysed under the same three aspects of diction, composition, and content.[24] This basic structure is seen at its simplest in the brief accounts of the faulty styles, in the grand style, and, if we remove the digressions, the plain style (§§ 190–91 and 204–8). In the forceful style the three headings are covered in §§ 240–76, but then comes a ragbag of extras: further figures of speech, Demades, forms of rebuke, and disapproval of hiatus. The elegant style is more complicated and in part confused by the immediate subdivision of two types of charm, the gracefully poetic and the wittily comic (§§ 128–31), and—an intrusion from traditional accounts of wit—analysis under two headings of style and content (§§ 132–62, cf. Cic. *De Or.* 2.248). Λέξις, normally diction, now includes some topics of arrangement (and then in §§ 142–45 is confusingly restricted to single words). At this point the main discussion seems concluded, since appendices follow on the differences between charm and laughter, appropriate and inappropriate use of gibes (§§ 163–72), and on Theophrastus' definition of beautiful words and musical theory (§§ 173–78).[25] But then we find elegant arrangement, γλαφυρὰ σύνθεσις (§§ 179–85), as if Demetrius had noticed a gap and wished to complete his usual structure of three aspects.

[24] The three headings are traditional, and all appear in the context of the styles in *Ad Herennium* 4.8.11 and Cic. *Orator* 20. Further use of traditional material appears in the recurrent series of items found under diction and arrangement, where at least the opening items show Peripatetic influence (see note 17).

[25] This amplifies the reference to beautiful words in § 164, a good example of how appendices would often be footnotes in modern texts.

This final section apologises for originality, and reintroduces the generic term for the style, γλαφυρός, which with one exception (§ 138) had been ousted by χάρις and cognates. Taken together with the other structural peculiarities, it confirms that Demetrius adopted and modified an account of χάρις because he had no detailed model for his elegant style.

The four styles

The early history of the theory of styles, χαρακτῆρες, is obscure and controversial, particularly the contribution of Theophrastus, but the fundamental criterion is propriety, τὸ πρέπον: certain subjects fit certain styles, and violation of this is normally a fault (e.g. § 120). A division into two styles, grand and plain, is found already in Aristophanes' *Frogs*, where Euripides is accused of using an unsuitably plain style, though "great ideas and thoughts must father equally great words" (1058–59, ἀνάγκη μεγάλων γνωμῶν καὶ διανοιῶν ἴσα καὶ τὰ ῥήματα τίκτειν). This match of content and form is why the theory of styles regularly gives content an integral place, as in Cicero, *Orator* 100, an example of a three-style theory, the standard number in the Roman period: "the true orator can express humble subjects in a plain style, elevated subjects in a weighty style, and intermediate subjects in a middle style." The emphasis is however on style, and Demetrius' discussion of suitable subject matter is always brief. Since the choice of style depends on appropriate context, all the styles are equally valid, and though he rather scorns the plain style (§ 207), Demetrius expresses no preference (nor does *Ad Herennium* 4.8.11ff; contrast

the supremacy of the grand style for the orator in Cic.
Orator 97).

The analysis of styles has two functions: to evaluate
existing writers and to instruct the future writer. Both are
normally present, though one may predominate. Demetrius is primarily prescriptive (he uses many imperatives
and futures), whereas, for example, Dionysius' *Demosthenes* is analytic. Individual authors may also be classi-
fied under a specific style, as Demetrius may implicitly
classify Thucydides under the grand style, while other
authors such as Homer and Plato will control and mix
more than one style (§ 37; compare Demosthenes' mastery of all three styles in Cic. *Orator* 26). But these two
functions are difficult to disentangle when past authors
are analysed to provide models for the present.
Demetrius' formulation of four styles is in itself unusual,
but its nature and use are not essentially different from
the formulations of other critics.[26]

We can distinguish various strands in the development
of the styles found in Demetrius. The theory of two
styles, grand and plain, remained influential (e.g. Cic.
Brutus 201), and as he almost admits in §§ 36–37, this is
where Demetrius derives his four styles, by subdividing
grand into grand and forceful, and plain into plain and
elegant. He ignores the three-style theory, first securely
attested in *Ad Herennium* 4.8.11ff and Cicero, *De Or.*
3.177, 199, 210–12 (cf. *Orator* 20ff), and it concerns us
here only because this silence is very curious if it was
known to Theophrastus.[27] Probably, however, Theo-

[26] Contrast the view of Schenkeveld, Ch. III.

[27] Cf. D. C. Innes, "Theophrastus and the Theory of Style,"
Rutgers University Studies in Classical Humanities II, New

phrastus recognised only one good style (or diction), a mean between excessive plainness and elaboration, while defining this mean with vocabulary which was later associated with a specifically grand style. This at any rate fits the few surviving fragments: he recognised three types of diction, recommending as a mean the type blended from the other two, he discussed grandeur in diction, τὸ μέγα καὶ σεμνὸν καὶ περιττόν (DH. *Dem.* 3 and *Isoc.* 3 = F 685 and 691 Fortenbaugh), and he defined frigidity as what exceeds (τὸ ὑπερβάλλον) the appropriate form of expression (§ 114), a definition suggesting a single fault of excess. If so, Theophrastus developed what was in essence already in Aristotle, who advised appropriate diction, neither low nor too elaborate, and illustrated excess diction under τὸ ψυχρόν (*Rhet.* 1404b3–4 and 1405b35ff).

Another strand in the Demetrian styles is the theory of qualities or virtues (ἀρεταί). To simplify yet another controversial issue,[28] Aristotle's one good style or diction, a single virtue blending clarity and distinction, was turned by Theophrastus into a list of four necessary virtues, purity, clarity, propriety, and pleasing stylistic elabora-

---

Brunswick 1985, pp. 251–67; and G. M. A. Grube, "Theophrastus as a Literary Critic," *Transactions of the American Philological Association* 83 (1952) 172–83.

[28] See previous note; add D. A. Russell, *Criticism in Antiquity*, London 1981, Ch. IX; S. F. Bonner, *The Literary Treatises of Dionysius of Halicarnassus*, Cambridge 1939; and on the later and more elaborate theory of Hermogenes, Περὶ Ἰδεῶν, C. Wooten, *Hermogenes on Types of Style*, Chapel Hill 1987 (with translation). This theory of qualities also influenced Longinus' concept of the sublime.

INTRODUCTION

tion, "ornatum illud suave et affluens" (Cic. *Orator* 79).
But later critics added to the list and already by the time
of Cicero and Dionysius (who notes in *Thuc.* 22 that others had elaborated the theory before him), it is divided
into necessary and additional virtues. The latter no
longer allow a single pack of simultaneously required
qualities, and an author may be strong in one and weak in
another. Distinctions between styles and qualities now
become inevitably blurred, since any style, for example
the grand style, is speech shaped to embody a specific
quality, for example grandeur, and Demetrius, like other
later critics, moves freely between vocabulary of styles
and qualities (e.g. § 240, "forcefulness . . , like all the previous styles"). But the list of qualities also provides our
closest parallel for the stylistic categories which
Demetrius distinguishes as separate styles, since for
Dionysius the additional virtues form three groups,
grandeur, force, and charm (cf. DH. *Imit.* 3, *Thuc.* 22, *Ad
Pomp.* 3). The plain style can then be seen to use only the
necessary virtues, while the grand, forceful, and elegant
styles show the qualities of grandeur, force, and charm.

The grand style is appropriate for great battles and big
natural phenomena (§ 75),[29] and the examples show a
preference for epic and history, Homer and Thucydides,
figures such as Ajax (e.g. § 48) and set pieces of historical
narrative and description, such as the plague at Athens,
the river Achelous, and the sea battle at Pylos (§§ 39,
45–46, and 65); this is very much Cicero's view of history
as literature, "et narratur ornate et regio saepe aut pugna
describitur" (*Orator* 66). Oratory is absent, save for an

[29] Cf. Cic. *Part. Or.* 56, Hermogenes 242–46 Rabe.

327

atypical descriptive passage from Antiphon (§ 53) and a metaphor from Demosthenes (§ 80), which is cited more aptly in § 272 for its force. Oratorical grandeur will often mix force and grandeur, and it would seem that Demetrius prefers to concentrate on what is basic to the style. This at least would explain why emotion is in general almost excluded. Allegory (§§ 99–102) evokes awe and τὸ φοβερόν, but this aspect,[30] usually prominent in theories of grandeur, is not developed, probably because of the overlap with the forceful style where the same examples reappear (§§ 241–43).

The elegant style has a much less satisfactory unity, as is clear from the initial division into two types, dignified charm and comic gibes. Homer's simile of Artemis and Lysias' toothless hag seem to have little in common (§ 128–29). These are, however, the two extremes, where charm edges into the grand and forceful styles respectively, and in practice Demetrius moves the main focus to a more unified area, the elegant wit of a Sappho or Xenophon. As we have seen, Demetrius probably lacked any better source and tried to modify an account of wit, χάρις. Thus this section has its own unity and perceptive comments, and shares a common tradition with Cicero and Quintilian.[31] But though χάρις means both charm

---

[30] In §§ 57–58 particles are said to evoke emotion as well as grandeur: this is a digression, and emotion is distinct from grandeur.

[31] Cf. Cic. *De Or.* 2.216–90, Quint. 6.3. The common source is probably Theophrastus. Cf. E. Arndt, *De ridiculi doctrina rhetorica*, Bonn 1904, M. A. Grant, *The Ancient Rhetorical Theories of the Laughable in the Greek Rhetoricians and Cicero*, Madison, 1924, and especially the commentary on Cicero's *De*

and wit, and both concepts are part of ἡδονή, the pleasurable, in contrast to grandeur and force,[32] they do not always coincide, and it is charm, not wit, that is suggested by the subject matter recommended in §§ 132–33, gardens of the nymphs, wedding songs, love, birds, and spring.

Within Demetrius the elegant style has closest links with the plain style (note how "small" birds and flowers contrast great battles in § 76), and classification of it as part of the plain style, its probable origin (cf. § 36), may be compared to Cicero, *Orator* 20, where the plain style has two subdivisions, the first deliberately like ordinary speech (cf. Demetrius § 207), but the second "more elegant and witty, even given a brightness and modest ornamentation." Yet when exemplified by the smoothly euphonious Isocratean type of sentences, elegance may also both be in polar contrast to forcefulness (§§ 258, 300–301) and combine with grandeur (§ 29). Since Demetrius is struggling to express this style, parallels in other authors are hard to find, but we find a more unified concept of charm in the later quality of sweetness, γλυκύτης, with its beautiful landscapes and themes of love (Hermogenes 330–39 Rabe), and the importance of charm as an independent element of style is already clear in the first century B.C. from its place in the theory of qualities and from the varying attempts to add it to the theory of styles, as part of the middle style (Cic. *Orator*

Oratore, Vol. III, ed. A. D. Leeman, H. Pinkster, and E. Rabbie, Heidelberg 1989.

[32] As in the theory of qualities. Compare Longinus 34.3, where Demosthenes lacks both charm and wit.

69), or as an independent style, γλαφυρότης (Philodemus, *Rhet.* 1.165 Sudhaus).

The account of *the plain style* is brief and traditional: simple subjects, diction, and arrangement. To judge from the few examples, it fits private speeches and domestic scenes (as in Lysias) and Socratic dialogues, and we can compare the similar range of subjects which the plain style illustrates in Dionysius, *Demosthenes* 2 and *Ad Herennium* 4.10.14 (an incident in a bathhouse, a forensic narrative, with dialogue), and Ps.Plutarch, *Vit. Hom.* 72 (the domestic scene of Hector and his son in Hom. *Il.* 6.466ff). Since he has little to say, Demetrius adds more general discussions of clarity, vividness, and persuasiveness. He is here adapting the virtues of narrative (these were traditionally clarity, brevity, and persuasiveness, but some added vividness, Quint. 4.2.63–64), and much is standard later theory: compare on clarity e.g. Cic. *De Or.* 3.49 and Quint. 8.2; on vividness Quint. 8.3.61–71; and on persuasiveness Quint. 4.2.52–60. Demetrius also has the same two types of vividness which Quintilian recognises, the use of every detail and good circumstantial detail ("tota rerum imago," "etiam ex accidentibus"), but originality is seen in the examples, where quick allusion to familiar passages of Homer is followed by a more detailed excursus on the much less usual figure of the historian Ctesias (§§ 212–16), including a powerful analysis of the dramatic tension as a mother is told of her son's death.

Demetrius concludes the plain style with an example of a mixed style, the combination of charm and simplicity suited to the letter. This is our earliest extant analysis of letter-writing, and perceptively explores the differences between the letter and dialogue and letters to friends and kings, emphasising the importance of character in the letter of friendship, since the letter mirrors the writer's soul. In terms of classical prose theory this is a rare extension beyond the usual limits of history, philosophy, and oratory.[33]

The forceful style fits the expression of strong emotion, particularly anger and invective,[34] and the main source of examples is oratory, especially Demosthenes and, in an appendix, Demades (§§ 282–86). Appendices continue the focus on accusation but dilute the unity of the style by including milder forms of oblique and even tactful censure. In the three-style theory such force falls under the grand style, and in *Ad Herennium* 4.8.12 it is an invective passage which illustrates the grand style. But independent concepts of force and grandeur were recognised in the theory of qualities (see above), and forcefulness already interested the early Peripatetics, particularly the distinction between a smooth unemotional epideictic style and a more vigorous forensic style of oral delivery. note the λέξις ἀγωνιστική in Ar. *Rhet.* 1413b3ff, the recognition of Demosthenes' boldness (Dem. Phal. F 163 Wehrli), and Isocrates' lack of such vigour (Hieronymus F 52 Wehrli).

The faulty styles. each style has a neighbouring faulty

---

[33] But much was probably traditional, if we compare the brief remarks in e.g. Cic. *Ad Fam.* 2.4.1, Quint. 9.4.19, Theon, RG 2.115. See H. Koskenniemi, *Studien zur Idee und Phraseologie des griechischen Briefes bis 400 n. Chr.*, Helsinki 1956; K. Thraede, *Grundzüge griechisch-römischer Brieftopik*, Munich 1970.

[34] But not the softer emotions of pity and lament, cf. § 28, and Russell (ed. 1964) on Longinus 8.2.

counterpart. This is a familiar theory, e.g. *Ad Herennium*
4.10.15–11.16 and Longinus 3–5. Yet despite their traditional nature, Demetrius' faulty styles are not entirely
convincing. The affected and unpleasant styles seem an
agglomerate of points derived from their correct styles,
and though the frigid and arid styles have more unity,
they complement each other rather than their corresponding correct style. The arid style is a great theme
given trivial language, the frigid style a trivial theme
given rich language (§§ 114, 119, and 237). The arid style
is also not a fault of excess like the other faults—we
should expect something like the excessively plain style of
the bathhouse quarrel in *Ad Herennium* 4.10.16. It is
then an attractive deduction that there were originally
faults for only the grand and plain styles, and that the
nature of the arid style in Demetrius reflects an earlier
stage when good style was a Peripatetic mean located
between faults of excess and deficiency (ὑπερβολή and
ἔλλειψις), frigidity and aridity.[35]

Text and manuscripts

The text is based on Parisinus gr. 1741 (P), a manuscript
of the tenth century which is of great importance for
other texts, including Aristotle's *Poetics*.[36] Corrections in

[35] Compare Aristotle's ethical theory of μεγαλοψυχία as a
mean between χαυνότης and μικροψυχία (*Eth. Nic.* 1125a17–
18), and see Russell (ed. 1964) on Longinus 3.4. Use of the term
ψυχρός may itself suggest Peripatetic influence since the usual
term is the swollen, τὸ οἰδοῦν, "tumidus," "sufflatus."

[36] D. Harlfinger, D. Reinsch, "Die Aristotelica des Parisinus
Gr. 1741," *Philologus* 114 (1970) 28–50.

a later hand (P[2]) seem to show in at least some cases access to a second (lost) manuscript.[37] There are a further forty-four manuscripts, some of them fragmentary,[38] but virtually all derive from P, and where the reading in P is not followed, the *apparatus criticus* reports significant differences

For the very beginning, §§ 1–3 μέν, two manuscripts of the fourteenth century, Matritensis 4684 (H) and Neapolitanus II E 2 (N), give some readings independent of P.[39]

Closely resembling P is Marcianus gr. 508 (M), of ca. 1330–1380. Chiron argues that it is independent of P and cites its readings fully in his *apparatus criticus*. M offers various linguistically more "correct" readings (e.g. ἀπο-κατέστησεν and ἀνέμνησεν in §§ 196 and 298 eliminate the only two examples in P of the double augment), and it includes some more accurate and fuller versions of passages quoted (e.g. §§ 4, 21, 61, 199, and 250). Most strikingly, it adds one extra lengthy quotation, but, quite independently of the question of the relationship of M to P, this addition seems to derive from a scribal marginal annotation (see note on § 53). In various places M seems to aim to improve the faulty text in P (not always successfully, e.g. § 287 διαπλεύσαντας <ἰδεῖν>), and I suspect M is ultimately an idiosyncratic descendant of P,[40] subse-

---

[37] Radermacher, pp. vff.

[38] Chiron, p. cviii.

[39] For H as copy of N in the text of the Alexander Rhetoric, see M. Fuhrmann, *Untersuchungen zur Textgeschichte der pseudoaristotelischen Alexander-Rhetorik*, Mainz, 1965.

[40] This is also the view of H. Gärtner and R. Kassel (private correspondence). For M as a copy of P for the text of Dionysius

quent to the corrections in P² (examples of readings shared with P²: §§ 28, 66, 89, 122, 194, 229, 237, 288, and 291). In the *apparatus criticus* I give some of the more interesting readings, and I also give it precedence for readings accepted in the text but conjectured previously by various scholars. Collations of other manuscripts might well produce further conjectures or reattributions.[41]

There is also a thirteenth-century medieval Latin translation (Lat.) published by Wall in 1937.[42] It is often more of a paraphrase, and it omits many passages, in particular the less usual material (especially all mention of the fourth style, since it conflicted with the medieval tradition of a theory of three styles; much of the discussion of wit; and poetic examples). It is close to P, but has a few "better" readings which may suggest independence (e.g. § 194).

Finally, in the indirect tradition,[43] there are some sub-

---

of Halicarnassus, see G. Aujac, "Recherches sur la tradition du περὶ συνθέσεως de Denys d'Halicarnasse," *Revue d'Histoire des Textes* 4 (1974) 1–44.

[41] H. Gärtner gives a few examples in "Demetriana Varia," *Hermes* 118 (1990) 213–36. See especially p. 214, n. 6 (on conjectures wrongly attributed to Victorius); p. 216, n. 12 for Vaticanus gr. 1904, of the early fifteenth century and the oldest known descendant of P; and p. 221, n. 29 for Dresdensis Da 4, of the earlier fifteenth century.

[42] B. V. Wall, *A Medieval Latin Version of Demetrius' De elocutione*, Washington 1937.

[43] H. Gärtner, "Zur byzantinischen Nebenüberlieferung von Demetrios, Περὶ ἑρμηνείας," *Kyklos, Festschrift Rudolf Keydell*, ed. H. G. Beck, A. Kambylis, and P. Moraux, Berlin, 1978.

stantial quotations in the commentaries on Hermogenes by Gregory of Corinth (Greg.), Byzantine scholar of ca. 1070–1156. No excerpt is verbally exact, some are paraphrases, but their common archetype seems a close but independent relative of P.

SYNOPSIS

BIBLIOGRAPHY

Select editions

Aldus Manutius, Venice 1508 (*editio princeps*)
Victorius, P., Florence 1552 (with Latin translation and commentary, 1562)
Gale, T., Oxford 1676 (ed. Glasg. = revised reprint, Glasgow, 1743)
Schneider, J. G., Altenburg 1799
Goeller, F., Leipzig 1837

Spengel, L., Leipzig 1856

Radermacher, L., Leipzig 1901

Roberts, W. Rhys, Cambridge 1902

Roberts, W. Rhys, 1927 (Loeb, based on 1902 edition)

Wall, B. V., Washington 1937 (*editio princeps* of medieval Latin translation)

Grube, G. M. A., Toronto 1961 (English translation with substantial introduction, notes and appendices)

Chiron, P., Paris 1993 (Budé edition)

Books and articles

Brief general interpretations are to be found in most surveys of classical criticism, e.g. G. A. Kennedy, *Cambridge History of Literary Criticism,* Vol. I, Cambridge 1990, pp. 196–98; G. M. A. Grube, *The Greek and Roman Critics,* Toronto 1965; and D. A. Russell, *Criticism in Antiquity,* London 1981, pp. 129–47. See also:

Gärtner, H., "Demetriana varia," *Hermes* 118 (1990) 213–36

Grant, M. A., *The Ancient Rhetorical Theories of the Laughable in the Greek Rhetoricians and Cicero,* Univ. of Wisconsin Studies 21, Madison 1924

Grube, G. M. A., "Theophrastus as a Literary Critic," *Transactions of the American Philological Society* 83 (1952) 172–83

Hendrickson, G. L., "The Peripatetic Mean of Style and the Three Stylistic Characters" and "The Origins and Meaning of the Ancient Characters of Style," *American Journal of Philology* 25 (1904) 125–46 and 26 (1905) 249–70

Innes, D. C., "Theophrastus and the Theory of Style,"

Rutgers University Studies in Classical Humanities II, New Brunswick 1985, pp. 251–67

Innes, D. C., "Period and Colon: Theory and Example in Demetrius and Longinus," *Rutgers University Studies in Classical Humanities* VI, New Brunswick 1994, pp. 36–53

Kroll, W., RE. Suppl. VII, *Rhetorik*, coll. 1039–1138, Stuttgart 1940

Morpurgo-Tagliabue, G., *Demetrio: dello stile*, Rome 1980

Schenkeveld, D. M., *Studies in Demetrius On Style*, Amsterdam 1964

Solmsen, F., "Demetrios περὶ ἑρμηνείας und sein peripatetisches Quellenmaterial," *Hermes* 66 (1931) 241–67

Solmsen, F., "The Aristotelian Tradition in Ancient Rhetoric," *American Journal of Philology* 62 (1941) 35–50 and 169–90

ABBREVIATIONS

Ar.	Aristotle
Art. Scr.	*Artium Scriptores* (Reste der voraristotelischen Rhetorik), ed. L. Radermacher, Vienna 1951
DH.	Dionysius of Halicarnassus (*CV = On Composition of Words*)
D–K	*Die Fragmente der Vorsokratiker*, ed. H. Diels, W. Kranz, revised edition, Berlin 1951–52
EGF	*Epicorum Graecorum Fragmenta*, ed. M. Davies, Göttingen 1988

FGrHist	*Die Fragmente der Griechischen Historiker*, ed. F. Jacoby, Berlin 1923–30, Leiden 1940–58
Giannantoni	*Socraticorum reliquiae*, ed. G. Giannantoni, Naples 1983–85
Kaibel	*Comicorum Graecorum Fragmenta*, Vol. I (Doriensium comoedia), ed. G. Kaibel, Berlin 1899
Kock	*Comicorum Atticorum Fragmenta*, ed. T. Kock, Leipzig 1880–88
L–P	*Poetarum Lesbiorum Fragmenta*, ed. E. Lobel, D. Page, Oxford 1955
Overbeck	*Die antiken Schriftquellen zur Geschichte der bildenden Kunst bei den Griechen*, ed. J. Overbeck, Leipzig 1868
Paroem. Gr.	*Corpus Paroemiographorum Graecorum*, ed. E. L. Leutsch, F. G. Schneidewin, Göttingen 1839–51
PCG	*Poetae Comici Graeci*, ed. R. Kassel, C. Austin, Berlin 1983
PLG	*Poetae Lyrici Graeci*, ed. T. Bergk, revised edition Leipzig 1882
PMG	*Poetae melici Graeci*, ed. D. Page, Oxford 1962
P.Oxy.	The Oxyrhynchus Papyri
Powell	*Collectanea Alexandrina*, ed. J. U. Powell, Oxford 1925
RE	*Real-Encyclopädie der classischen Altertumswissenschaft*, ed. A. Pauly, G. Wissowa, Stuttgart/Munich, 1894–1978

RG	*Rhetores Graeci*, ed. L. Spengel, Leipzig 1853–56 (Sp.–H. = Vol. 1.2, revised edition, 1894, L. Spengel, C. Hammer)
Sauppe	*Oratorum Atticorum Fragmenta*, ed. H. Sauppe, Turici 1845
Supp. Com.	*Supplementum comicum*, ed. J. Demiańczuk, Cracow 1912
SVF	*Stoicorum Veterum Fragmenta*, ed. J. von Arnim, Leipzig 1905
TGF	*Tragicorum Graecorum Fragmenta*, ed. A. Nauck, 2d ed., Leipzig 1889
TrGF	*Tragicorum Graecorum Fragmenta*, ed. B. Snell, R. Kannicht, S. Radt, Göttingen 1971–
Wehrli	*Die Schule des Aristoteles*, ed. F. Wehrli, Basel 1967–78
West	*Iambi et Elegi Graeci*, ed. M. L. West, Oxford 1971–72

ΠΕΡΙ ΕΡΜΗΝΕΙΑΣ

ΠΕΡΙ ΕΡΜΗΝΕΙΑΣ

(1) Ὥσπερ ἡ ποίησις διαιρεῖται τοῖς μέτροις, οἷον ἡμιμέτροις ἢ ἑξαμέτροις ἢ τοῖς ἄλλοις, οὕτω καὶ τὴν ἑρμηνείαν τὴν λογικὴν διαιρεῖ καὶ διακρίνει τὰ καλούμενα κῶλα, καθάπερ ἀναπαύοντα τὸν λέγοντά τε καὶ τὰ λεγόμενα[1] αὐτά, καὶ ἐν πολλοῖς ὅροις ὁρίζοντα τὸν λόγον, ἐπεί τοι μακρὸς ἂν εἴη καὶ ἄπειρος καὶ ἀτεχνῶς πνίγων τὸν λέγοντα. (2) βούλεται μέντοι διάνοιαν ἀπαρτίζειν τὰ κῶλα ταῦτα, ποτὲ μὲν ὅλην διάνοιαν, οἷον[2] ὡς Ἑκαταῖός φησιν ἐν τῇ ἀρχῇ τῆς ἱστορίας, ''Ἑκαταῖος Μιλήσιος ὧδε μυθεῖται''· συνείληπται γὰρ διάνοια τῷ κώλῳ ὅλῳ ὅλη, καὶ ἄμφω συγκαταλήγουσιν. ἐνίοτε μέντοι τὸ κῶλον ὅλην[3] μὲν οὐ συμπεραιοῖ διάνοιαν, μέρος δὲ ὅλης ὅλον· ὡς γὰρ τῆς χειρὸς οὔσης ὅλου τινὸς μέρη αὐτῆς ὅλα ὅλης[4] ἐστίν, οἷον δάκτυλοι[5] καὶ πῆχυς[6] (ἰδίαν γὰρ περιγραφὴν ἔχει τούτων τῶν

---

[1] λεγόμενά τε καὶ τὰ λεγόμενα Finckh: λόγον τά τε καταλεγόμενα PNH.

[2] οἷον om. NH.

[3] ὅλην P: ὅλον NH (totum Lat.).

[4] ὅλης Hp.c.: ὅλη PNHa.c.

[5] δάκτυλοι PN (digiti Lat.): δάκτυλος H.

ON STYLE

(1) Just as poetry is organised by metres (such as half-lines,[a] hexameters, and the like), so too prose[b] is organised and divided by what are called clauses. Clauses give a sort of rest to both the speaker and what is actually being said; and they mark out its boundaries at frequent points, since it would otherwise continue at length without limit and simply run the speaker out of breath. (2) But the proper function of such clauses is to conclude a thought. Sometimes a clause is a complete thought, for example Hecataeus at the beginning of his *History*: "Hecataeus of Miletus speaks as follows."[c] Here a complete clause coincides with a complete thought and both end together. Sometimes, however, the clause marks off not a complete thought, but a complete part of one. For just as the arm[d] is a whole, yet has parts such as fingers and forearm which are themselves each a whole, since

[a] For half-lines cf. § 180, and see note on § 5 where a half-hexameter illustrates short metres.

[b] More literally "prose expression," implying formal prose. Elsewhere "style" most often translates ἑρμηνεία.

[c] FGrHist 264 Hecataeus, F 1A (cf. § 12).

[d] Since *kôlon* or clause is literally a limb of the body (cf. Latin *membrum*), comparisons from the body are common.

[6] πῆχυς H: πήχεις PN (*cubiti* Lat.).

DEMETRIUS

μερῶν ἕκαστον, καὶ ἴδια μέρη), οὕτω καὶ διανοίας[1]
τινὸς ὅλης οὔσης μεγάλης ἐμπεριλαμβάνοιτ᾽ ἂν
μέρη τινὰ αὐτῆς ὁλόκληρα ὄντα καὶ αὐτά· (3) ὥσπερ
ἐν τῇ ἀρχῇ τῆς Ἀναβάσεως τῆς[2] Ξενοφῶντος τὸ
τοιοῦτον, "Δαρείου καὶ Παρυσάτιδος" μέχρι τοῦ
"νεώτερος δὲ Κῦρος," συντετελεσμένη πᾶσα διάνοιά
ἐστιν· τὰ δ᾽ ἐν αὐτῇ κῶλα δύο μέρη μὲν αὐτῆς ἑκάτε-
ρόν ἐστι, διάνοια δὲ ἐν ἑκατέρῳ πληροῦταί τις,[3]
ἴδιον ἔχουσα πέρας, οἷον "Δαρείου καὶ Παρυσάτιδος
γίνονται παῖδες."[4] ἔχει γάρ τινα ὁλοκληρίαν ἡ διάνοια αὐτὴ καθ᾽ αὑτήν, ὅτι ἐγένοντο Δαρείῳ καὶ
Παρυσάτιδι παῖδες. καὶ[5] ὡσαύτως τὸ ἕτερον κῶλον,
ὅτι "πρεσβύτερος μὲν[6] Ἀρταξέρξης, νεώτερος δὲ
Κῦρος." ὥστε τὸ μὲν κῶλον, ὡς φημί, διάνοιαν
περιέξει τινὰ πάντη πάντως, ἤτοι ὅλην ἢ μέρος ὅλης
ὅλον.

(4) Δεῖ δὲ οὔτε πάνυ μακρὰ ποιεῖν τὰ κῶλα, ἐπεί
τοι γίνεται ἄμετρος ἡ σύνθεσις ἢ δυσπαρακολούθη-
τος· οὐδὲ γὰρ ἡ ποιητικὴ ὑπὲρ ἑξάμετρον ἦλθεν, εἰ
μή που ἐν ὀλίγοις· γελοῖον γὰρ τὸ μέτρον ἄμετρον
εἶναι, καὶ καταλήγοντος τοῦ μέτρου ἐπιλελῆσθαι
ἡμᾶς πότε ἤρξατο. οὔτε δὴ[7] τὸ μῆκος τῶν κώλων
πρέπον τοῖς λόγοις διὰ τὴν ἀμετρίαν, οὔτε ἡ μικρότης, ἐπεί τοι γίνοιτ᾽ ἂν ἡ λεγομένη ξηρὰ σύνθεσις,
οἷον ἡ τοιάδε "ὁ βίος βραχύς, ἡ τέχνη μακρά, ὁ

---

[1] διανοίας P: διάνοιαν NH.   [2] τῆς PN: τοῦ H.
[3] τις P: τῆς N: τὸ H.   [4] δύο add. M, codd. Xen.

each of these has its own shape and indeed its own parts,[a] so too a complete thought, when it is extensive, may subsume within it parts which are themselves whole, (3) as at the beginning of Xenophon's *Anabasis* in the words "Darius and Parysatis" down to "the younger Cyrus."[b] This is a fully completed thought, yet it contains two clauses, each is a part of it, and in each part a thought is completed within its own limits. Take the words "Darius and Parysatis had sons": the thought that Darius and Parysatis had sons has its own completeness. In the same way the second clause has the complete thought, "the elder was Artaxerxes, the younger Cyrus." So a clause will, I maintain, in all cases and circumstances form a thought, either a complete one or a complete part of a whole one.

(4) You should not produce very long clauses; otherwise the composition has no limits[c] and is hard to follow. Even poetry only rarely goes beyond the length of the hexameter, since it would be absurd if metre had no limits, and by the end of the line we had forgotten when it began. But if long clauses are out of place in prose because they have no limit, so too are brief clauses, since their use would produce what is called arid composition, as in the words "life is short, art long, opportunity

---

[a] I.e. sub-parts, such as fingernails, cf. Quint. 7.10.7. Clauses may similarly contain sub-clauses or phrases, as in the bipartite second clause of the Xenophon example in § 3.

[b] Xen. *Anab.* 1.1 (cf. § 19).

[c] The Greek is more pointed, since *metron*/metre means also limit or measure.

---

[5] καὶ om. NH.   [6] post μὲν des. NH.
[7] δὴ Victorius: δὲ P.

καιρὸς ὀξύς."[1] κατακεκομμένη γὰρ ἔοικεν ἡ σύνθεσις καὶ κεκερματισμένη, καὶ εὐκαταφρόνητος διὰ τὸ
μικρὰ σύμπαντα ἔχειν. (5) γίνεται μὲν οὖν ποτε καὶ
μακροῦ κώλου καιρός, οἷον ἐν τοῖς μεγέθεσιν, ὡς ὁ
Πλάτων φησί, "τὸ γὰρ δὴ πᾶν τόδε τοτὲ μὲν[2] αὐτὸς
ὁ θεὸς πορευόμενον συμποδηγεῖ[3] καὶ συγκυκλεῖ."
σχεδὸν γὰρ τῷ μεγέθει τοῦ κώλου συνεξῆρται καὶ ὁ
λόγος. διὰ τοῦτο καὶ <τὸ>[4] ἑξάμετρον ἡρῷόν τε
ὀνομάζεται ὑπὸ τοῦ μήκους καὶ πρέπον ἥρωσιν, καὶ
οὐκ ἂν τὴν Ὁμήρου Ἰλιάδα πρεπόντως τις γράψειεν[5] τοῖς Ἀρχιλόχου βραχέσιν, οἷον "ἀχνυμένη
σκυτάλη" καὶ "τίς σὰς παρήειρε φρένας;" οὐδὲ τοῖς
Ἀνακρέοντος, <ὡς>[6] τὸ "φέρ' ὕδωρ, φέρ' οἶνον, ὦ
παῖ"· μεθύοντος γὰρ ὁ ῥυθμὸς ἀτεχνῶς γέροντος, οὐ
μαχομένου ἥρωος.

(6) Μακροῦ μὲν δὴ κώλου καιρὸς γίνοιτ' ἄν ποτε
διὰ ταῦτα· γίνοιτο δ' ἄν ποτε καὶ βραχέος, οἷον ἤτοι
μικρόν τι ἡμῶν λεγόντων, ὡς ὁ Ξενοφῶν φησιν, ὅτι
ἀφίκοντο οἱ Ἕλληνες ἐπὶ τὸν Τηλεβόαν ποταμόν·
"οὗτος δὲ ἦν μέγας μὲν οὔ, καλὸς δέ." τῇ γὰρ

---

[1] ἡ δὲ πεῖρα σφαλερή add. M (cf. § 238).
[2] τοτὲ μὲν codd. Plat.: τὸ μὲν P.
[3] πορευόμενον συμποδηγεῖ codd. Plat.: πορευόμενος ποδη-
γεῖ P.
[4] τὸ add. Radermacher.
[5] γράψειεν Victorius: scriberet Lat.: γράψει ἐν P.
[6] ὡς add. Roberts.

fleeting."[a] For the composition here seems chopped up
and minced fine, and it fails to impress because all its
parts are minute. (5) Occasionally, however, a long clause
is appropriate, for example in elevated passages, such as
Plato's sentence, "Sometimes God himself helps to escort
and revolve this whole universe on its circling way."[b] The
elevation of the language virtually corresponds to the size
of the clause. That is why the hexameter is called heroic,[c]
because its length suits heroes. Homer's *Iliad* could not
be suitably written in the brief lines of Archilochus, for
example "staff of grief"[d] or "who stole away your mind?"[e]
nor in those of Anacreon, for example "bring water, bring
wine, boy."[f] That is plainly the rhythm for a drunk old
man, not for a hero in battle.

(6) Sometimes, then, a long clause may be appropriate
for the reasons given, at other times a short one, for
instance when our subject is small, as in Xenophon's
account of the Greeks' arrival at the river Teleboas, "this
river was not large, it was beautiful however."[g] The short,

[a] Hippocr. *Aphorism.* 1.1. In §238 the quotation continues
with a further clause, which appears here in M but not P.

[b] Pl. *Pol.* 269c.   [c] See on §42.

[d] Archil. 185.2 West. The staff is the Spartan staff used for
messages in cipher, and the phrase became proverbial for a message of grief, e.g. Plu. *Mor.* 152e (cf. Paroem. Gr. ii.323). It is
half a hexameter, and the other two examples are dimeters: short
clauses or phrases are similarly like half-lines and less than a
trimeter (§§ 1, 205).

[e] Archil. 172.2 West.

[f] PMG 396 Anacreon 51.1.

[g] Xen. *Anab.* 4.4.3 καλὸς μέν, μέγας δ' οὔ. Here and in
§ 121 Demetrius misquotes, but retains the abruptness.

μικρότητι καὶ ἀποκοπῇ τοῦ ῥυθμοῦ συνανεφάνη καὶ ἡ μικρότης τοῦ ποταμοῦ καὶ χάρις· εἰ δὲ οὕτως ἐκτείνας αὐτὸ εἶπεν, "οὗτος δὲ μεγέθει μὲν ἦν ἐλάττων τῶν πολλῶν, κάλλει δὲ ὑπερεβάλλετο πάντας," τοῦ πρέποντος ἀπετύγχανεν ἄν, καὶ ἐγίγνετο ὁ λεγόμενος ψυχρός· ἀλλὰ περὶ ψυχρότητος μὲν ὕστερον λεκτέον.

(7) Τῶν δὲ μικρῶν κώλων κἂν δεινότητι χρῆσίς ἐστι· δεινότερον γὰρ τὸ ἐν ὀλίγῳ πολὺ ἐμφαινόμενον καὶ σφοδρότερον, διὸ καὶ οἱ Λάκωνες βραχυλόγοι ὑπὸ δεινότητος· καὶ τὸ μὲν ἐπιτάσσειν σύντομον καὶ βραχύ, καὶ πᾶς δεσπότης δούλῳ μονοσύλλαβος, τὸ δὲ ἱκετεύειν μακρὸν καὶ τὸ ὀδύρεσθαι. <καὶ γὰρ>[1] αἱ Λιταὶ καθ' Ὅμηρον καὶ χωλαὶ καὶ ῥυσαὶ ὑπὸ βραδυτῆτος, τουτέστιν ὑπὸ μακρολογίας, καὶ οἱ γέροντες μακρολόγοι διὰ τὴν ἀσθένειαν. (8) παράδειγμα δὲ βραχείας συνθέσεως τὸ "Λακεδαιμόνιοι Φιλίππῳ· Διονύσιος ἐν Κορίνθῳ." πολὺ γὰρ δεινότερον φαίνε-

---

[1] καὶ γάρ addidi (καὶ iam Richards).

---

[a] In §§ 114–27.

[b] §§ 241–42 repeat the same advice and the example in § 8. For Spartan brevity cf. e.g. Hdt. 3.46.

[c] Strongly iambic, perhaps from comedy (*Adesp.* 538 Kock). Later citation as a proverb derives from Demetrius (Paroem. Gr. ii.606).

broken rhythm brings into relief both the smallness of the river and its charm. If Xenophon had expanded the idea to say, "this river was in size inferior to most rivers, but in beauty it surpassed them all," he would have failed in propriety, and would have become what is called the frigid writer—but frigidity is to be discussed later.[a]

(7) Short clauses should also be used in forceful passages,[b] for there is a greater force and vehemence when a lot of meaning is packed into a few words. So it is because of this forcefulness that the Spartans are brief in speech. Commands too are always terse and brief, and every master is monosyllabic to his slave,[c] but supplication and lament are lengthy. For the Prayers in Homer[d] are represented as wrinkled and lame in allusion to their slowness—that is, their length in speech. Old men too speak at length, because they are weak. (8) Take this instance of brevity in composition, "The Spartans to Philip: Dionysius in Corinth."[e] These brief words have a

[d] Hom. *Il.* 9.502–3:

καὶ γάρ τε Λιταί εἰσι Διὸς κοῦραι μεγάλοιο,
χωλαί τε ῥυσαί τε παραβλῶπές τ' ὀφθαλμώ.

Allegorical interpretation of the Prayers refers elsewhere to the physical appearance of suppliants, not their speech, e.g. Ps. Heraclitus, *Hom. Alleg.* 37. The sequence of examples suggests that Demetrius intends the aged Phoenix, whose long suppliant speech in *Iliad* 9 includes the Prayers passage.

[e] Cf. §§ 102, 241. It is a stock tag (e.g. Plu. *Mor.* 511e). The tyrant Dionysius was expelled in 344 B.C., and his retirement into private life in Corinth attracted apocryphal detail, such as the version in § 241 that poverty forced him to become a schoolmaster, cf. Ovid, *Ex Pont.* 4.3.39–40 (for an alternative motive, the wish to rule, see e.g. Cic. *Ad Att.* ix.9).

ται ῥηθὲν οὕτω βραχέως, ἢ εἴπερ αὐτὸ μακρῶς ἐκτείναντες εἶπον, ὅτι ὁ Διονύσιός ποτε μέγας ὢν τύραννος ὥσπερ σὺ ὅμως νῦν ἰδιωτεύων οἰκεῖ Κόρινθον. οὐ γὰρ ἔτι διὰ πολλῶν ῥηθὲν ἐπιπλήξει ἐῴκει ἀλλὰ διηγήματι, καὶ μᾶλλόν τινι διδάσκοντι, οὐκ ἐκφοβοῦντι· οὕτως ἐκτεινόμενον ἐκλύεται τοῦ λόγου τὸ θυμικὸν καὶ σφοδρόν. ὥσπερ <γὰρ>¹ τὰ θηρία συστρέψαντα ἑαυτὰ μάχεται, τοιαύτη τις ἂν εἴη συστροφὴ καὶ λόγου καθάπερ ἐσπειραμένου πρὸς δεινότητα. (9) ἡ δὲ τοιαύτη βραχύτης κατὰ τὴν σύνθεσιν κόμμα ὀνομάζεται. ὁρίζονται δ᾽ αὐτὸ ὧδε, κόμμα ἐστὶν τὸ κώλου ἔλαττον, οἷον τὸ προειρημένον, τὸ [τε]² "Διονύσιος ἐν Κορίνθῳ," καὶ τὸ "γνῶθι σεαυτόν," καὶ τὸ "ἕπου θεῷ," τὰ τῶν σοφῶν. ἔστι γὰρ καὶ ἀποφθεγματικὸν ἡ βραχύτης καὶ γνωμολογικόν, καὶ σοφώτερον τὸ ἐν ὀλίγῳ πολλὴν διάνοιαν ἠθροῖσθαι, καθάπερ ἐν τοῖς σπέρμασιν δένδρων ὅλων δυνάμεις· εἰ δ᾽ ἐκτείνοιτό τις τὴν γνώμην ἐν μακροῖς, διδασκαλία γίνεταί τις καὶ ῥητορεία ἀντὶ γνώμης.

(10) Τῶν μέντοι κώλων καὶ κομμάτων τοιούτων συντιθεμένων πρὸς ἄλληλα συνίστανται αἱ περίοδοι ὀνομαζόμεναι. ἔστιν γὰρ ἡ περίοδος σύστημα ἐκ κώλων ἢ κομμάτων εὐκαταστρόφως πρὸς τὴν διάνοιαν τὴν ὑποκειμένην ἀπηρτισμένον, οἷον "μάλιστα

---

¹ γὰρ add. Markland.
² τε del. Hahne.

much more forceful impact than if the Spartans had expanded the sentence at great length to say "Although once a mighty tyrant like yourself, Dionysius now lives in Corinth as an ordinary citizen." This lengthened version no longer seems a rebuke but a piece of narrative, and it suggests a wish to instruct rather than intimidate. With this expansion the passion and vehemence of the words are dissipated, and just as a wild beast gathers itself together for an attack, speech should similarly gather itself together as if in a coil to increase its force. (9) Such brevity in composition is called a phrase.[a] A phrase is generally defined as "what is less than a clause," for example the words already quoted, "Dionysius in Corinth," and the sayings of the sages, "know yourself" and "follow God,"[b] For brevity characterises proverbs and maxims; and the compression of a lot of meaning into a small space shows more skill, just as seeds contain the potential for whole trees. Expand a maxim at great length and it becomes a piece of instruction or rhetoric.

(10) From the combination of such clauses and phrases are formed what are called periods. The period is a combination of clauses and phrases arranged to conclude the underlying thought with a well-turned ending. For example: "Chiefly because I thought it was in the

[a] Literally a cut segment or chip (cf. Latin *incisum*), the *komma* or phrase is a short clause, independent, as here, or part of a complex (§ 10). On its length see note on § 5.

[b] Cf. e.g. Cic. *De Fin.* 3.73, Paroem. Gr. ii.19 and 40.

DEMETRIUS

μὲν εἴνεκα τοῦ νομίζειν συμφέρειν τῇ πόλει λελύσθαι τὸν νόμον, εἶτα καὶ τοῦ παιδὸς εἴνεκα τοῦ
Χαβρίου, ὡμολόγησα τούτοις, ὡς ἂν οἷός τε ὦ, συνερεῖν"· αὕτη γὰρ ἡ περίοδος ἐκ τριῶν κώλων οὖσα
καμπήν τέ τινα καὶ συστροφὴν ἔχει κατὰ τὸ τέλος.
(11) Ἀριστοτέλης δὲ ὁρίζεται τὴν περίοδον οὕτως,
"περίοδός ἐστι λέξις ἀρχὴν ἔχουσα καὶ τελευτήν,"
μάλα καλῶς καὶ πρεπόντως ὁρισάμενος· εὐθὺς γὰρ ὁ
τὴν περίοδον λέγων ἐμφαίνει, ὅτι ἦρκταί ποθεν καὶ
ἀποτελευτήσει ποι καὶ[1] ἐπείγεται εἴς τι τέλος, ὥσπερ
οἱ δρομεῖς ἀφεθέντες· καὶ γὰρ ἐκείνων συνεμφαίνε-
ται τῇ ἀρχῇ τοῦ δρόμου τὸ τέλος. ἔνθεν καὶ περίοδος ὠνομάσθη, ἀπεικασθεῖσα ταῖς ὁδοῖς ταῖς
κυκλοειδέσι καὶ περιωδευμέναις. καὶ καθόλου[2] οὐδὲν
ἡ περίοδός ἐστι πλὴν ποιὰ σύνθεσις. εἰ γοῦν λυθείη
αὐτῆς τὸ περιωδευμένον καὶ μετασυντεθείη, τὰ μὲν
πράγματα μένει τὰ αὐτά, περίοδος δὲ οὐκ ἔσται,
οἷον εἰ τὴν προειρημένην τις τοῦ Δημοσθένους περίοδον ἀναστρέψας εἴποι ὡδέ πως, "συνερῶ τούτοις,
ὦ ἄνδρες Ἀθηναῖοι· φίλος γάρ μοί ἐστιν ὁ υἱὸς
Χαβρίου, πολὺ δὲ μᾶλλον τούτου ἡ πόλις, ᾗ συνει-
πεῖν με δίκαιόν ἐστιν." οὐ γὰρ ἔτι οὐδαμοῦ ἡ περίοδος εὑρίσκεται.

[1] ἀποτελευτήσει ποι καὶ H. Stephanus: ἀποτελευτῆσαι
ποιεῖ καὶ P.
[2] καὶ καθόλου Radermacher: καθόλου P.

354

interest of the state for the law to be repealed, but also for the sake of Chabrias' boy, I have agreed to speak to the best of my ability in their support."[a] This three-clause period has a sort of backward bend and compactness at the end. (11) Aristotle gives this definition of the period, "a period is a portion of speech that has a beginning and an end."[b] His definition is excellent and apt. For the very use of the word "period" implies that it has had a beginning at one point, will end at another, and is speeding towards a definite goal, like runners sprinting from the starting place. For at the very beginning of their race the end of the course is already before their eyes.[c] Hence the name "period," an image drawn from paths which go round and are in a circle. In general terms, a period is nothing more nor less than a particular arrangement of words. If its circular form should be destroyed and the arrangement changed, the subject matter remains the same, but there will be no period. Suppose, for example, you were to invert the period I have quoted from Demosthenes to say something like this, "I will speak in their support, men of Athens. For Chabrias' son is dear to me, and much more so is the state, whose cause it is right for me to support."[d] No longer is there any trace of the period.

[a] Dem. *Lept.* 1 (cf. §§ 11, 20, 245).

[b] Ar. *Rhet.* 1409a35–b1.

[c] Demetrius intends the *diaulos*, the two-lap race where the runner ran back along the same or parallel track to the starting point. The period is literally a path which goes round (cf. Latin *ambitus, circuitus*), and so at its end returns us to its beginning, just as the period bends back on itself by hyperbaton or the completion of some pattern such as antithesis. [d] Cf. § 10.

DEMETRIUS

(12) Γένεσις δ' αὐτῆς ἥδε· τῆς ἑρμηνείας ἡ μὲν ὀνομάζεται κατεστραμμένη, οἷον ἡ κατὰ περιόδους ἔχουσα, ὡς ἡ τῶν Ἰσοκρατείων ῥητορειῶν[1] καὶ Γοργίου καὶ Ἀλκιδάμαντος· ὅλαι γὰρ διὰ περιόδων εἰσὶν συνεχῶν οὐδέν τι ἔλαττον ἤπερ ἡ Ὁμήρου ποίησις δι' ἑξαμέτρων· ἡ δέ τις διῃρημένη ἑρμηνεία καλεῖται, ἡ εἰς κῶλα λελυμένη οὐ μάλα ἀλλήλοις συνηρτημένα, ὡς ἡ Ἑκαταίου καὶ τὰ πλεῖστα τῶν Ἡροδότου καὶ ὅλως ἡ ἀρχαία πᾶσα. παράδειγμα αὐτῆς, "Ἑκαταῖος Μιλήσιος ὧδε μυθεῖται· τάδε γράφω, ὥς μοι δοκεῖ ἀληθέα εἶναι· οἱ γὰρ Ἑλλήνων λόγοι πολλοί τε καὶ γελοῖοι, ὡς ἐμοὶ φαίνονται, εἰσίν." ὥσπερ γὰρ σεσωρευμένοις ἐπ' ἀλλήλοις τὰ κῶλα ἔοικεν καὶ ἐπερριμμένοις καὶ οὐκ ἔχουσιν σύνδεσιν οὐδ' ἀντέρεισιν, οὐδὲ βοηθοῦντα ἀλλήλοις ὥσπερ ἐν ταῖς περιόδοις. (13) ἔοικε γοῦν τὰ μὲν περιοδικὰ κῶλα τοῖς λίθοις τοῖς ἀντερείδουσι τὰς περιφερεῖς στέγας καὶ συνέχουσι, τὰ δὲ τῆς διαλελυμένης ἑρμηνείας διερριμμένοις πλησίον λίθοις μόνον καὶ οὐ συγκειμένοις. (14) διὸ καὶ περιεξεσμένον ἔχει τι ἡ ἑρμηνεία ἡ πρὶν καὶ εὐσταλές, ὥσπερ καὶ τὰ ἀρχαῖα ἀγάλματα, ὧν τέχνη ἐδόκει ἡ συστολὴ καὶ ἰσχνότης, ἡ δὲ τῶν μετὰ ταῦτα ἑρμηνεία τοῖς Φειδίου ἔργοις ἤδη ἔοικεν ἔχουσά τι καὶ μεγα-

---

[1] ῥητορειῶν Weil: ῥητῶν P.

---

[a] The source is Aristotle (see *Rhet.* 1409a26ff), but the term

(12) The origin of the period is as follows. There are two types of style. The first is called the compact style,[a] namely that which consists of periods, as in the rhetorical displays of Isocrates, Gorgias, and Alcidamas,[b] where period succeeds period no less regularly than the hexameters in Homer's poetry. The second style is called the disjointed style, since it is divided into clauses which are not closely attached to each other, as in Hecataeus, Herodotus for the most part, and the older writers in general. Here is an example: "Hecataeus of Miletus speaks as follows. I write these things as they seem to me to be true. For the stories told by the Greeks are, as it appears to me, many and absurd."[c] Here the clauses seem thrown one on top of the other in a heap without the connections or buttressing or mutual support which we find in periods. (13) The clauses in the periodic style may in fact be compared to the stones which support and hold together the roof which encircles them, and the clauses of the disjointed style to stones which are simply thrown about near one another and not built into a structure.[d] (14) So the older style has something of the sharp, clean lines of early statues[e] where the skill was thought to lie in their succinctness and spareness, and the style of those who followed is like the works of Phidias, since it already to

for the nonperiodic style, the "disjointed," seems a confused memory of *Rhet.* 1409b32 where it refers to the nonantithetical form of period.

[b] For Alcidamas, pupil of Gorgias, cf. § 116.

[c] FGrHist 264 Hecataeus F 1A (cf. § 2).

[d] A traditional comparison, cf. DH. *CV* 22.

[e] For comparisons to the parallel development of style and sculpture, cf. DH. *Isoc.* 3, Quint. 12.10.7–9.

λεῖον καὶ ἀκριβὲς ἅμα. (15) δοκιμάζω γὰρ δὴ ἔγωγε
μήτε περιόδοις ὅλον τὸν λόγον συνείρεσθαι, ὡς ὁ
Γοργίου, μήτε διαλελύσθαι ὅλον, ὡς τὰ ἀρχαῖα,
ἀλλὰ μεμῖχθαι μᾶλλον δι' ἀμφοτέρων· οὕτω γὰρ καὶ
ἐγκατάσκευος ἔσται καὶ ἁπλοῦς ἅμα, καὶ ἐξ ἀμφοῖν
ἡδύς, καὶ οὔτε μάλα ἰδιωτικός οὔτε μάλα σοφιστι-
κός. τῶν δὲ[1] τὰς πυκνὰς περιόδους λεγόντων οὐδ' αἱ
κεφαλαὶ ῥᾳδίως ἑστᾶσιν, ὡς ἐπὶ τῶν οἰνωμένων, οἵ
τε ἀκούοντες ναυτιῶσι διὰ τὸ ἀπίθανον, τοτὲ δὲ καὶ
ἐκφωνοῦσι τὰ τέλη τῶν περιόδων προειδότες καὶ
προαναβοῶσι.

(16) Τῶν δὲ περιόδων αἱ μικρότεραι μὲν ἐκ δυοῖν
κώλοιν συντίθενται, αἱ μέγισται δὲ ἐκ τεττάρων· τὸ
δ' ὑπὲρ τέτταρα οὐκέτ' ἂν ἐντὸς εἴη περιοδικῆς συμ-
μετρίας. (17) γίνονται δὲ καὶ τρίκωλοί τινες· καὶ
μονόκωλοι δέ, ἃς καλοῦσιν ἁπλᾶς περιόδους. ὅταν
γὰρ τὸ κῶλον μῆκός τε ἔχῃ καὶ καμπὴν κατὰ τὸ
τέλος, τότε μονόκωλος περίοδος γίνεται, καθάπερ ἡ
τοιάδε, "Ἡροδότου Ἁλικαρνασῆος ἱστορίης ἀπόδεξις ἥδε"· καὶ πάλιν, "ἡ γὰρ σαφὴς φράσις πολὺ
φῶς παρέχεται ταῖς τῶν ἀκουόντων διανοίαις." ὑπ'
ἀμφοῖν μέντοι συνίσταται ἡ ἁπλῆ περίοδος, καὶ ὑπὸ
τοῦ μήκους καὶ ὑπὸ τῆς καμπῆς τῆς περὶ τὸ τέλος,
ὑπὸ δὲ θατέρου οὐδέ ποτε. (18) ἐν δὲ ταῖς συνθέτοις
περιόδοις τὸ τελευταῖον κῶλον μακρότερον χρὴ
εἶναι, καὶ ὥσπερ περιέχον καὶ περιειληφὸς τἆλλα.
οὕτω γὰρ μεγαλοπρεπὴς ἔσται καὶ σεμνὴ περίοδος,

some degree unites grandeur and finish. (15) My own personal view is that speech should neither, like that of Gorgias, consist wholly of a series of periods, nor be wholly disconnected like the older style, but should rather combine the two methods. It will then be simultaneously elaborate and simple, and draw charm from the presence of both, being neither too ordinary nor too artificial. Those who crowd periods together are as light-headed as those who are drunk, and their listeners are nauseated by the implausibility; and sometimes they even foresee and, loudly declaiming, shout out in advance the endings of the periods.

(16) The smaller periods consist of two clauses, the largest of four. Anything beyond four would transgress the boundaries for a period. (17) There are also periods of three clauses, and others of one clause, which are called simple periods. Any clause which has length and also bends back at the end forms the one-clause period, as in this example, "The History of Herodotus of Halicarnassus is here set out,"[a] and again "Clear expression sheds much light on the listeners' thoughts."[b] For the simple period these are the two essentials, the length of the clause and the bending back at the end. In the absence of either there is no period. (18) In compound periods the last clause should be longer than the rest, and should as it were contain and envelop them all. This is how a period

[a] Hdt. 1.1 (cf. § 44).

[b] Author unknown. The "bend" is probably the completion of the antithesis of word and thought provided by the first and last word-groups.

---

[1] δὲ Schneider: τε P.

εἰς σεμνὸν καὶ μακρὸν λήγουσα κῶλον· εἰ δὲ μή,
ἀποκεκομμένη καὶ χωλῇ ὁμοία. παράδειγμα δ᾽
αὐτῆς τὸ τοιοῦτον, "οὐ γὰρ τὸ εἰπεῖν καλῶς καλόν,
ἀλλὰ τὸ εἰπόντα δρᾶσαι τὰ εἰρημένα."

(19) Τρία δὲ γένη περιόδων ἐστίν, ἱστορική, δια-
λογική, ῥητορική. ἱστορικὴ μὲν ἡ μήτε περιηγμένη
μήτ᾽ ἀνειμένη σφόδρα, ἀλλὰ μεταξὺ ἀμφοῖν, ὡς
μήτε ῥητορικὴ δόξειεν καὶ ἀπίθανος διὰ τὴν περι-
αγωγήν, τὸ σεμνόν τε ἔχουσα καὶ ἱστορικὸν ἐκ τῆς
ἁπλότητος, οἷον ἡ τοιάδε, "Δαρείου καὶ Παρυσάτιδος γίγνονται" μέχρι τοῦ "νεώτερος δὲ Κῦρος."
ἑδραίᾳ γάρ τινι καὶ ἀσφαλεῖ καταλήξει ἔοικεν αὐτῆς
ἡ ἀπόθεσις. (20) τῆς δὲ ῥητορικῆς περιόδου συνεστραμμένον τὸ εἶδος καὶ κυκλικὸν καὶ δεόμενον
στρογγύλου στόματος καὶ χειρὸς συμπεριαγομένης
τῷ ῥυθμῷ, οἷον τῆς "μάλιστα μὲν εἵνεκα τοῦ νομίζειν συμφέρειν τῇ πόλει λελύσθαι τὸν νόμον, εἶτα
καὶ τοῦ παιδὸς εἵνεκα τοῦ Χαβρίου, ὡμολόγησα
τούτοις, ὡς ἂν οἷός τε ὦ, συνερεῖν." σχεδὸν γὰρ
εὐθὺς ἐκ τῆς ἀρχῆς ἡ περίοδος ἡ τοιάδε συνεστραμμένον τι ἔχει καὶ ἐμφαῖνον ὅτι οὐκ ἂν ἀπολήξειεν εἰς
ἁπλοῦν τέλος. (21) διαλογικὴ δέ ἐστι περίοδος ἡ ἔτι
<μᾶλλον>[1] ἀνειμένη καὶ ἁπλουστέρα τῆς ἱστορι-
κῆς,[2] καὶ μόλις ἐμφαίνουσα, ὅτι περίοδός ἐστιν,
ὥσπερ ἡ τοιάδε, "κατέβην χθὲς εἰς [τὸν][3] Πειραιᾶ"

[1] μᾶλλον add. Goeller.
[2] ἱστορικῆς Victorius: ῥητορικῆς P.
[3] τὸν add. P: om. M Plat. codd.

will be imposing and impressive, if it ends on an imposing, long clause; otherwise it will break off abruptly and seem to limp. Here is an example: "For it is not to speak nobly that is noble, but after speaking to perform what has been spoken."[a]

(19) There are three kinds of period, the historical, the dialogue, and the rhetorical. The historical period should be neither too carefully rounded nor too loose, but between the two, in such a way that it is not thought rhetorical and unconvincing because of its rounding, but has the dignity and aptness for history from its simplicity, as in the period "Darius and Parysatis" down to "the younger Cyrus."[b] Its closing words resemble a firm and securely based ending. (20) The form of the rhetorical period is compact and circular; and it needs a well-rounded mouth and hand gestures to follow each movement of the rhythm. For example: "Chiefly because I thought it was in the interest of the state for the law to be repealed, but also for the sake of Chabrias' boy, I have agreed to speak to the best of my ability in their support."[c] Almost right from the very beginning such a period has compactness, and shows that it will not stop on a simple ending. (21) The dialogue period is one which is still looser and simpler than the historical period, and scarcely shows that it is a period. For instance: "I went down yesterday to Piraeus" as far as the words "since they

[a] Author unknown.

[b] Xen. *Anab.* 1.1 (cf. § 3).

[c] Dem. *Lept.* 1 (cf. §§ 10–11, 245).

DEMETRIUS

μέχρι τοῦ "ἅτε νῦν πρῶτον ἄγοντες." ἐπέρριπται
γὰρ ἀλλήλοις τὰ κῶλα ἐφ' ἑτέρῳ[1] ἕτερον, ὥσπερ ἐν
τοῖς διαλελυμένοις λόγοις, καὶ ἀπολήξαντες μόλις
ἂν ἐννοηθεῖμεν[2] κατὰ τὸ τέλος, ὅτι τὸ λεγόμενον
περίοδος ἦν. δεῖ γὰρ μεταξὺ διῃρημένης τε καὶ
κατεστραμμένης λέξεως τὴν διαλογικὴν περίοδον
γράφεσθαι, καὶ μεμιγμένην ὁμοίαν ἀμφοτέροις.
περιόδων μὲν εἴδη τοσάδε.

(22) Γίνονται δὲ καὶ ἐξ ἀντικειμένων κώλων περίοδοι, ἀντικειμένων δὲ ἤτοι τοῖς πράγμασιν, οἷον
"πλέων μὲν διὰ τῆς ἠπείρου, πεζεύων[3] δὲ διὰ τῆς
θαλάσσης," ἢ ἀμφοτέροις, τῇ τε λέξει καὶ τοῖς
πράγμασιν, ὥσπερ ἡ αὐτὴ περίοδος ὧδε ἔχει. (23)
κατὰ δὲ τὰ ὀνόματα μόνον ἀντικείμενα κῶλα τοιάδε
ἐστίν, οἷον ὡς ὁ τὴν Ἑλένην παραβαλὼν τῷ Ἡρα-
κλεῖ φησιν, ὅτι "τοῦ[4] μὲν ἐπίπονον καὶ πολυκίνδυνον
τὸν βίον ἐποίησεν, τῆς δὲ περίβλεπτον καὶ περιμά-
χητον τὴν φύσιν κατέστησεν." ἀντίκειται γὰρ καὶ
ἄρθρον ἄρθρῳ, καὶ σύνδεσμος συνδέσμῳ, ὅμοια
ὁμοίοις, καὶ τἆλλα δὲ κατὰ τὸν αὐτὸν τρόπον, τῷ μὲν
"ἐποίησεν" τὸ "κατέστησεν," τῷ δὲ "ἐπίπονον" τὸ
"περίβλεπτον," τῷ δὲ "πολυκίνδυνον" τὸ "περιμάχη-
τον," καὶ ὅλως ἓν πρὸς ἕν, ὅμοιον παρ' ὅμοιον, ἡ
ἀνταπόδοσις. (24) ἔστι δὲ κῶλα, ἃ μὴ ἀντικείμενα

[1] ἑτέρῳ edd.: ἑκατέρω P.
[2] ἐννοηθεῖμεν Spengel: ἐννοηθῶμεν P.
[3] πλεῦσαι . . . πεζεῦσαι codd. Isoc.

362

were now celebrating it for the first time."[a] The clauses
are flung one on top of the other, as in the disjointed style,
and when we reach the end we can hardly realise that the
words formed a period. For the dialogue period should
be a form of writing midway between the disconnected
and the compact style, compounded of both and resembling both. This concludes my account of the different
kinds of period.

(22) Periods are also formed from antithetical clauses.
The antithesis may lie in the content, for example "sailing
across the mainland and marching across the sea,"[b] or it
may be twofold, in content and language, as in this same
period. (23) There are also clauses which have only verbal antithesis, as in the comparison drawn between Heracles and Helen, "The man's life he created for labours and
dangers, the woman's beauty he formed for admiration
and strife."[c] Here article is in antithesis to article, connective to connective, like to like, everything in parallel,
"formed" to "created," "admiration" to "labours," and
"strife" to "dangers." There is correspondence throughout of each detail, like with like. (24) There are some

---

[a] Pl. *Rep.* 327a (cf. §§ 205–6): κατέβην χθὲς εἰς Πειραιᾶ
μετὰ Γλαύκωνος τοῦ Ἀρίστωνος προσευξόμενός τε τῇ θεῷ
καὶ ἅμα <u>τὴν ἑορτὴν</u> βουλόμενος <u>θεάσασθαι</u> τίνα τρόπον
<u>ποιήσουσιν</u> ἅτε νῦν πρῶτον ἄγοντες. The last three verbs all
take the same object, returning us to the festival (all underlined).

[b] Isoc. *Panegyr.* 89. Xerxes bridges the Hellespont and digs a
canal through Mount Athos.

[c] Isoc. *Helen* 17.

---

[4] τοῦ scripsi, cum codd. Isoc.: τῷ P.

ἐμφαίνει τινὰ ἀντίθεσιν διὰ τὸ τῷ σχήματι ἀντιθέ-
τως γεγράφθαι, καθάπερ τὸ παρ' Ἐπιχάρμῳ τῷ
ποιητῇ πεπαιγμένον, ὅτι "τόκα μὲν ἐν τήνοις ἐγὼν
ἦν, τόκα δὲ παρὰ τήνοις ἐγών." τὸ αὐτὸ μὲν γὰρ
εἴρηται, καὶ οὐδὲν ἐναντίον· ὁ δὲ τρόπος τῆς ἑρμηνείας μεμιμημένος[1] ἀντίθεσίν τινα πλανῶντι ἔοικεν.
ἀλλ' οὗτος μὲν ἴσως γελωτοποιῶν οὕτως ἀντέθηκεν,
καὶ ἅμα σκώπτων τοὺς ῥήτορας.

(25) Ἔστι δὲ καὶ παρόμοια κῶλα, ἅτινα παρόμοια ἤτοι[2] τοῖς ἐπ' ἀρχῆς, οἷον "δωρητοί τε πέλοντο,
παράρρητοί τ' ἐπέεσσιν"· ἢ ὡς ἐπὶ τέλους, ὡς ἡ τοῦ
Πανηγυρικοῦ ἀρχή, "πολλάκις ἐθαύμασα τῶν τὰς
πανηγύρεις συναγαγόντων καὶ τοὺς γυμνικοὺς ἀγῶνας καταστησάντων." εἶδος δὲ τοῦ παρομοίου τὸ
ἰσόκωλον, ἐπὰν ἴσας ἔχῃ τὰ κῶλα τὰς συλλαβάς,
ὥσπερ Θουκυδίδῃ, "ὡς οὔτε ὧν πυνθάνονται ἀπα-
ξιούντων τὸ ἔργον, οἷς τε[3] ἐπιμελὲς εἴη εἰδέναι οὐκ
ὀνειδιζόντων"· ἰσόκωλον μὲν δὴ τοῦτο. (26) ὁμοιοτέ-
λευτα δέ ἐστι τὰ εἰς ὅμοια καταλήγοντα, ἤτοι εἰς
ὀνόματα ταὐτά,[4] ὥσπερ ἔχει ἐπὶ τοῦ "σὺ δ' αὐτὸν
καὶ ζῶντα ἔλεγες κακῶς, καὶ νῦν ἀποθανόντα[5] γράφεις κακῶς"· ἢ ὅταν εἰς συλλαβὴν καταλήγῃ τὴν
αὐτήν, ὥσπερ τὰ ἐκ τοῦ Πανηγυρικοῦ προειρημένα.

---

[1] μεμιμημένος Muretus: μεμιγμένος P.
[2] ἤτοι Lockwood: δὴ P.
[3] τε M, Thuc.: το (sic) P.   [4] ταῦτα P: corr. edd.
[5] ἀποθανόντα Orth (cf. § 211): θανόντα P: omittitur apud Ar.
Rhet. 1410a34–35.

clauses which are not really antithetical but suggest an antithesis because of the antithetical form in which they are written, like the playful joke in the poet Epicharmus, "at one time I was among them, at another time with them."[a] The same idea is repeated, and there is no contrast. But the stylistic manner, with its imitation of an antithesis, suggests an intent to deceive. Epicharmus probably used the antithesis to raise a laugh, and also to mock the rhetoricians.

(25) There are also clauses with assonance. The assonance is either at the beginning, for example "giving gifts could win them, making pleas could move them,"[b] or at the end, as in the opening passage of the *Panegyric*: "I have often wondered at those who convened the assemblies and instituted the athletic contests."[c] Another form of assonance is the isocolon, which is when the clauses have an equal number of syllables, as in this sentence of Thucydides: "since neither do those who are questioned disown the deed, nor do those who are concerned to know censure it."[d] This then is isocolon. (26) Homoeoteleuton is when clauses end similarly, either with the same word, as in the sentence, "you are the man who when he was alive spoke to his discredit, and now that he is dead write to his discredit,"[e] or with the same syllable, as in the passage I have already quoted from Isocrates' *Panegyric*.

---

[a] Epicharmus 147 Kaibel, an unusual example, deriving from Ar. *Rhet.* 1410b3 5. Aristotle strongly influences both theory and examples in §§ 22–26.

[b] Hom. *Il.* 9.526, with assonance of -*rêtoi*.

[c] Isoc. *Panegyr.* 1, with assonance of -*ontôn/-antôn*.

[d] Th. 1.5.2.

[e] Author unknown (cf. § 211, Ar. *Rhet.* 1410a34–35).

(27) Χρῆσις δὲ τῶν τοιούτων κώλων ἐπισφαλής.
οὔτε γὰρ δεινῶς λέγοντι ἐπιτήδεια· ἐκλύει γὰρ τὴν
δεινότητα ἡ περὶ αὐτὰ τερθρεία καὶ φροντίς. δῆλον
δ' ἡμῖν τοῦτο ποιεῖ Θεόπομπος. κατηγορῶν γὰρ τῶν
Φιλίππου φίλων φησίν, "ἀνδροφόνοι δὲ τὴν φύσιν
ὄντες, ἀνδροπόρνοι τὸν τρόπον ἦσαν· καὶ ἐκαλοῦντο
μὲν ἑταῖροι, ἦσαν δὲ ἑταῖραι." ἡ γὰρ ὁμοιότης ἡ
περὶ τὰ κῶλα καὶ ἀντίθεσις ἐκλύει τὴν δεινότητα διὰ
τὴν κακοτεχνίαν. θυμὸς γὰρ τέχνης οὐ δεῖται, ἀλλὰ
δεῖ τρόπον τινὰ αὐτοφυᾶ εἶναι ἐπὶ τῶν τοιούτων
κατηγοριῶν καὶ ἁπλᾶ τὰ λεγόμενα. (28) οὔτε δῆτα ἐν
δεινότητι χρήσιμα τὰ τοιαῦτα, ὡς ἔδειξα,[1] οὔτε ἐν
πάθεσι καὶ ἤθεσιν· ἁπλοῦν γὰρ εἶναι βούλεται καὶ
ἀποίητον τὸ πάθος, ὁμοίως δὲ καὶ τὸ ἦθος. ἐν γοῦν
τοῖς Ἀριστοτέλους περὶ δικαιοσύνης ὁ τὴν Ἀθηναίων πόλιν ὀδυρόμενος εἰ μὲν οὕτως εἴποι ὅτι
"ποίαν τοιαύτην πόλιν εἷλον τῶν ἐχθρῶν, οἵαν τὴν
ἰδίαν πόλιν ἀπώλεσαν," ἐμπαθῶς ἂν εἰρηκὼς εἴη καὶ
ὀδυρτικῶς· εἰ δὲ παρόμοιον αὐτὸ ποιήσει· "ποίαν
γὰρ πόλιν τῶν ἐχθρῶν τοιαύτην ἔλαβον, ὁποίαν τὴν
ἰδίαν ἀπέβαλον," οὐ μὰ τὸν Δία πάθος κινήσει οὐδὲ
ἔλεον, ἀλλὰ τὸν καλούμενον κλαυσιγέλωτα. τὸ γὰρ
ἐν πενθοῦσι παίζειν, κατὰ τὴν παροιμίαν, τὸ τὰ τοιαῦτα ἐν τοῖς πάθεσι κακοτεχνεῖν ἐστι. (29) γίνεται
μέντοι γε χρήσιμά ποτε, ὡς Ἀριστοτέλης φησίν,
"ἐγὼ ἐκ μὲν Ἀθηνῶν εἰς Στάγειρα ἦλθον διὰ

---

[1] ὡς ἔδειξα P[2] in mg.: om. P[1].

(27) The use of such clauses is full of risk. They do not suit the forceful speaker, since their studied artifice dissipates the force. Theopompus proves our point in his invective against the friends of Philip when he says, "men-slayers by nature, they were men-harlots in behaviour; they were called companions but were concubines."[a] The assonance and antithesis of the clauses dissipate the force by their artificiality. For anger needs no artifice; in such invectives what is said should be, in a way, spontaneous and simple. (28) Such clauses are of no use for force, as I have shown, nor yet for the expression of emotion or character. For emotion is properly simple and unforced, and the same is true of character. In Aristotle's dialogue *On Justice*, for instance, a speaker weeps for the city of Athens. If he were to say, "what city had they taken from their enemies as great as their own city which they had lost,"[b] he would have spoken with emotion and grief; but if he creates assonance, "what city from their enemies had they taken as great as their own city which they had forsaken," he will certainly not evoke emotion or pity, but rather the so-called "tears of laughter."[c] For artificiality of this kind in emotional contexts is no better than the proverbial "fun at a funeral." (29) Assonance is however sometimes useful, as in the following passage of Aristotle: "I went from Athens to

---

[a] FGrHist 185 Theopompus F 225(c) (cf. §§ 247, 250).

[b] Ar. *fr.* 82 Rose.

[c] Xen. *Hell.* 7.2.9. Demetrius' glossing proverb is otherwise unknown.

τὸν βασιλέα τὸν μέγαν, ἐκ δὲ Σταγείρων εἰς Ἀθή
νας διὰ τὸν χειμῶνα τὸν μέγαν"· εἰ γοῦν ἀφέλοις τὸ
ἕτερον "μέγαν,"[1] συναφαιρήσῃ καὶ τὴν χάριν· τῇ
δὲ[2] μεγαληγορίᾳ συνεργοῖ ἂν[3] τὰ τοιαῦτα κῶλα,
ὁποῖα τῶν Γοργίου τὰ πολλὰ ἀντίθετα καὶ τῶν Ἰσο
κράτους. περὶ μὲν δὴ τῶν παρομοίων ταῦτα.

(30) Διαφέρει δὲ ἐνθύμημα περιόδου τῇδε, ὅτι ἡ
μὲν περίοδος σύνθεσίς τίς ἐστι περιηγμένη, ἀφ᾽ ἧς
καὶ ὠνόμασται, τὸ δὲ ἐνθύμημα ἐν τῷ διανοήματι
ἔχει τὴν δύναμιν καὶ σύστασιν· καὶ ἔστιν ἡ μὲν
περίοδος κύκλος τοῦ ἐνθυμήματος, ὥσπερ καὶ τῶν
ἄλλων πραγμάτων, τὸ δ᾽ ἐνθύμημα διάνοιά τις ἤτοι
ἐκ μάχης λεγομένη <ἢ>[4] ἐν ἀκολουθίας σχήματι.
(31) σημεῖον δέ· εἰ γὰρ διαλύσειας τὴν σύνθεσιν τοῦ
ἐνθυμήματος, τὴν μὲν περίοδον ἠφάνισας, τὸ δ᾽
ἐνθύμημα ταὐτὸν μένει, οἷον εἴ τις τὸ παρὰ Δημο
σθένει διαλύσειεν ἐνθύμημα τὸ τοιοῦτον, "ὥσπερ
γὰρ εἴ τις ἐκείνων ἑάλω, σὺ τάδ᾽ οὐκ ἂν ἔγραψας·
οὕτως ἂν σὺ νῦν ἁλῷς, ἄλλος οὐ γράψει"· διαλύ
σειεν δὲ οὕτω· "μὴ ἐπιτρέπετε τοῖς τὰ παράνομα
γράφουσιν· εἰ γὰρ ἐκωλύοντο, οὐκ ἂν νῦν οὗτος
ταῦτα ἔγραφεν, οὐδ᾽ ἕτερος ἔτι γράψει τούτου νῦν
ἁλόντος." ἐνταῦθα τῆς περιόδου μὲν ὁ κύκλος ἐκλέ
λυται, τὸ δ᾽ ἐνθύμημα ἐν ταὐτῷ μένει. (32) καὶ καθ
όλου δὲ τὸ μὲν ἐνθύμημα συλλογισμός τίς ἐστι

---

[1] τὸ ἕτερον μέγα P: corr. edd.   [2] δὲ Solmsen: γὰρ P.
[3] συνεργοῖ ἂν Goeller: συνεργοῖεν P.   [4] ἢ add. Finckh.

Stagira because of the great king, and from Stagira to Athens because of the great storm."[a] If you take away the second "great," you will at the same time take away the charm. Such clauses may also contribute towards an imposing grandeur, like the many antitheses of Gorgias and Isocrates. This concludes my discussion of assonance.

(30) The enthymeme differs from the period. The latter is a rounded structure (hence its name in fact), the former has its meaning and constitution in the thought. The period circumscribes the enthymeme in the same way as any other subject matter, the enthymeme is a thought, expressed either controversially or in the form of a logical consequence.[b] (31) In proof of this, if you were to break up the verbal structure of the enthymeme, you have got rid of the period but the enthymeme remains intact. Suppose, for instance, the following enthymeme in Demosthenes were broken up: "Just as you would not have made this proposal if any of them had been convicted, so if you are convicted now, no one will make it in future."[c] Let it be broken up: "Show no leniency to those who make illegal proposals, for if they were regularly checked, the defendant would not be making these proposals now, nor will anyone make them in future if he is convicted now." Here the rounded form of the period has been destroyed, but the enthymeme remains where it was. (32) In general, the enthymeme is a rhetorical syllogism, while the

[a] Ar. *fr.* 669 Rose = 14 Plezia (cf. § 154).

[b] For the two types of syllogism, refutation of an opponent and demonstration of a point off agreed premisses, see Ar. *Rhet.* 1396b23ff. The terminology is later, e.g. Quint. 5.10.2, RG 1.285 Sp–H.   [c] Dem. *Aristocr.* 99 (cf. § 248).

ῥητορικός, ἡ περίοδος δὲ συλλογίζεται μὲν οὐδέν,
σύγκειται δὲ μόνον· καὶ περιόδους μὲν ἐν παντὶ
μέρει τοῦ λόγου τίθεμεν, οἷον ἐν τοῖς προοιμίοις,
ἐνθυμήματα δὲ οὐκ ἐν παντί· καὶ τὸ μὲν ὥσπερ ἐπιλέγεται, τὸ ἐνθύμημα, ἡ περίοδος δὲ αὐτόθεν λέγε-
ται· καὶ τὸ μὲν οἷον συλλογισμός ἐστιν ἀτελής, ἡ δὲ
οὔτε ὅλον τι οὔτε ἀτελὲς συλλογίζεται. (33) συμβέβηκε μὲν οὖν τῷ ἐνθυμήματι καὶ περιόδῳ εἶναι, διότι
περιοδικῶς σύγκειται, περίοδος δ᾽ οὐκ ἔστι, ὥσπερ
τῷ οἰκοδομουμένῳ συμβέβηκε μὲν καὶ λευκῷ εἶναι,
ἂν λευκὸν ᾖ, τὸ οἰκοδομούμενον δ᾽ οὐκ ἔστι λευκόν.
περὶ μὲν δὴ διαφορᾶς ἐνθυμήματος καὶ περιόδου
εἴρηται.

(34) Τὸ δὲ κῶλον Ἀριστοτέλης οὕτως ὁρίζεται,
"κῶλόν ἐστι τὸ ἕτερον μέρος περιόδου"· εἶτα ἐπιφέ-
ρει· "γίνεται δὲ καὶ ἁπλῆ περίοδος." οὕτως ὁρισά-
μενος, "τὸ ἕτερον μέρος," δίκωλον ἐβούλετο εἶναι
τὴν περίοδον δηλονότι. ὁ δ᾽ Ἀρχέδημος, συλλαβὼν
τὸν ὅρον τοῦ Ἀριστοτέλους καὶ τὸ ἐπιφερόμενον τῷ
ὅρῳ, σαφέστερον καὶ τελεώτερον οὕτως ὡρίσατο,
"κῶλόν ἐστιν ἤτοι ἁπλῆ περίοδος, ἢ συνθέτου περιόδου μέρος." (35) τί μὲν οὖν ἁπλῆ περίοδος, εἴρηται·
συνθέτου δὲ φήσας αὐτὸ περιόδου μέρος, οὐ δυσὶ
κώλοις τὴν περίοδον ὁρίζειν ἔοικεν ἀλλὰ καὶ τρισὶ
καὶ πλείοσιν· ἡμεῖς δὲ μέτρον μὲν περιόδου ἐκτεθεί-
μεθα, νῦν δὲ περὶ τῶν χαρακτήρων τῆς ἑρμηνείας
λέγωμεν.[1]

---

[1] λέγομεν P: corr. edd.

370

period is not a form of reasoning but purely a combination of words. Moreover, we use periods in every part of a speech, for example in introductions, but we do not use enthymemes everywhere. The enthymeme is, as it were, added to the verbal form, the period is exclusively verbal. The former is a sort of imperfect syllogism, the latter is no syllogism at all, perfect or imperfect. (33) Sometimes the enthymeme has the accidental property of periodicity, because its construction is periodic, but it is not a period, just as a building, if it is white, has the accidental property of whiteness, but a building is not by definition white. This concludes my account of the difference between the enthymeme and the period.

(34) This is Aristotle's definition of the clause, "a clause is one of the two parts of a period." He then adds, "a period may also be simple."[a] The reference in his definition to "one of the two parts" makes it clear that he preferred the period to have two clauses. Archedemus combines Aristotle's definition and its supplement, and produces his own clearer and fuller definition, "a clause is either a simple period or part of a compound period."[b] (35) The simple period has already been described. In saying that a clause may be part of a compound period, he seems to limit the period not to two clauses but to three or more. We have now set out the limits of the period; let us now describe the types of style.

[a] Ar. *Rhet.* 1409b16–17 (but his term for simple is $\dot{a}\phi\epsilon\lambda\dot{\eta}s$).

[b] Unknown, often identified with the second-century Stoic Archedemus of Tarsus (see SVF iii. Archedemus 7) or the rhetorician Archedemus of Quint. 3.6.31–33.

(36) Εἰσὶ δὲ τέτταρες οἱ ἁπλοῖ χαρακτῆρες, ἰσχνός, μεγαλοπρεπής, γλαφυρός, δεινός, καὶ λοιπὸν οἱ ἐκ τούτων μιγνύμενοι. μίγνυνται δὲ οὐ πᾶς παντί, ἀλλ' ὁ γλαφυρὸς μὲν καὶ τῷ ἰσχνῷ καὶ τῷ μεγαλοπρεπεῖ, καὶ ὁ δεινὸς δὲ ὁμοίως ἀμφοτέροις· μόνος δὲ ὁ μεγαλοπρεπὴς τῷ ἰσχνῷ οὐ μίγνυται, ἀλλ' ὥσπερ ἀνθέστατον καὶ ἀντίκεισθον ἐναντιωτάτω. διὸ[1] δὴ καὶ μόνους δύο χαρακτῆράς τινες ἀξιοῦσιν εἶναι τούτους, τοὺς δὲ λοιποὺς δύο μεταξὺ τούτων, τὸν μὲν γλαφυρὸν τῷ ἰσχνῷ προσνέμοντες μᾶλλον, τῷ δὲ μεγαλοπρεπεῖ τὸν δεινόν, ὡς τοῦ γλαφυροῦ μὲν μικρότητά τινα καὶ κομψείαν ἔχοντος, τοῦ δεινοῦ δὲ ὄγκον καὶ μέγεθος. (37) γελοῖος δ' ὁ τοιοῦτος λόγος. ὁρῶμεν γὰρ πλὴν τῶν εἰρημένων[2] χαρακτήρων ἐναντίων πάντας μιγνυμένους πᾶσιν, οἷον τὰ Ὁμήρου τε ἔπη καὶ τοὺς Πλάτωνος λόγους καὶ Ξενοφῶντος καὶ Ἡροδότου καὶ ἄλλων πολλῶν πολλὴν μὲν μεγαλοπρέπειαν καταμεμιγμένην ἔχοντας, πολλὴν δὲ δεινότητά τε καὶ χάριν, ὥστε τὸ μὲν πλῆθος τῶν χαρακτήρων τοσοῦτον ἂν εἴη ὅσον λέλεκται. ἑρμηνεία δ' ἑκάστῳ πρέπουσα γένοιτ' ἂν τοιάδε τις·

(38) Ἄρξομαι δὲ ἀπὸ τοῦ μεγαλοπρεποῦς, ὅνπερ νῦν λόγιον ὀνομάζουσιν. ἐν τρισὶ δὴ τὸ μεγαλοπρεπές, διανοίᾳ, λέξει, τῷ συγκεῖσθαι προσφόρως. σύνθεσις δὲ μεγαλοπρεπής, ὥς φησιν Ἀριστοτέλης, ἡ παιωνική. παίωνος δὲ εἴδη δύο, τὸ μὲν προκαταρκτικόν, οὗ ἄρχει μὲν μακρά, λήγουσι δὲ τρεῖς βραχεῖαι, οἷον τὸ τοιόνδε, "ἤρξατὄ δέ," τὸ δὲ καταληκτι-

(36) There are four simple styles, the plain, the grand, the elegant, and the forceful. In addition there are their various combinations, though not every style can combine with every other. The elegant combines with the plain and the grand, and the forceful similarly with both. Only the grand and the plain cannot combine, but the pair stand, as it were, in polar opposition and conflict. For this reason some writers maintain that only these two styles exist, and the other two are subsumed within them; and instead they assimilate the elegant to the plain, and the forceful to the grand, as though the first contained something slight and refined, the second something massive and imposing. (37) Such a theory is absurd. We can see for ourselves that, with the exception I have mentioned of the two polar opposites, any style may combine with any other. In the poetry of Homer, for example, as well as in the prose of Plato, Xenophon, Herodotus, and many other authors, considerable grandeur is combined with considerable forcefulness and charm. Consequently the number of the styles is as I have already indicated. The form of expression appropriate to each will be as follows.

(38) I shall begin with grandeur, which men today identify with true eloquence. Grandeur has three aspects, thought, diction, and composition in the appropriate way. According to Aristotle[a] composition with paeans is grand. There are two kinds of paean, the initial paean, beginning with a long syllable and ending with three shorts (e.g. *êrxato de*, "it originated"[b]), and the final

---

[a] Cf. Ar. *Rhet.* 1408b32ff. [b] Th. 2.48.1.

---

[1] διὸ Victorius: δὲ ὁ P.

[2] εἰρημένων Victorius: ὁρωμένων P.

DEMETRIUS

κὸν θατέρῳ ἀντίστροφον, οὗ τρεῖς μὲν βραχεῖαι
ἄρχουσιν, λήγει δὲ μία μακρά, ὥσπερ τὸ
"᾿Αρᾰβῐᾱ." (39) δεῖ δὲ ἐν τοῖς κώλοις τοῦ μεγαλοπρεποῦς λόγου τὸν προκαταρκτικὸν μὲν παίωνα
ἄρχειν τῶν κώλων, τὸν καταληκτικὸν δὲ ἕπεσθαι.
παράδειγμα δ᾽ αὐτῶν τὸ Θουκυδίδειον τόδε, "ἦρξᾰτὸ
δὲ τὸ κἀκὸν ἐξ Αἰθῐὸπῐᾱς." τί ποτ᾽ οὖν ᾿Αριστοτέλης
οὕτω διετάξατο; ὅτι δεῖ καὶ τὴν ἐμβολὴν τοῦ κώλου
καὶ ἀρχὴν μεγαλοπρεπῆ εὐθὺς εἶναι καὶ <τὸ>¹
τέλος, τοῦτο δ᾽ ἔσται, ἐὰν ἀπὸ μακρᾶς ἀρχώμεθα
καὶ εἰς μακρὰν λήγωμεν. φύσει γὰρ μεγαλεῖον ἡ
μακρά, καὶ προλεγομένη τε πλήσσει εὐθὺς καὶ ἀπο-
λήγουσα ἐν μεγάλῳ τινὶ καταλείπει τὸν ἀκούοντα.
πάντες γοῦν ἰδίως τῶν τε πρώτων μνημονεύομεν καὶ
τῶν ὑστάτων, καὶ ὑπὸ τούτων κινούμεθα, ὑπὸ δὲ τῶν
μεταξὺ ἔλαττον ὥσπερ ἐγκρυπτομένων ἢ ἐναφανιζο-
μένων. (40) δῆλον δὲ τοῦτο ἐν τοῖς Θουκυδίδου· σχεδὸν γὰρ ὅλως τὸ μεγαλοπρεπὲς ἐν πᾶσιν αὐτῷ ποιεῖ
ἡ τοῦ ῥυθμοῦ μακρότης, καὶ κινδυνεύει τῷ ἀνδρὶ
τούτῳ παντοδαποῦ ὄντος τοῦ μεγαλοπρεποῦς αὕτη ἡ
σύνθεσις μόνη ἢ μάλιστα περιποιεῖν τὸ μέγιστον.

(41) Δεῖ μέντοι λογίζεσθαι, ὅτι κἂν μὴ ἀκριβῶς
δυνώμεθα τοῖς κώλοις περιτιθέναι τοὺς παίωνας
ἔνθεν καὶ ἔνθεν ἀμφοτέρους, παιωνικήν γε πάντως
ποιησόμεθα τὴν σύνθεσιν, οἷον ἐκ μακρῶν ἀρχόμε-
νοι καὶ εἰς μακρὰς καταλήγοντες. τοῦτο γὰρ καὶ
᾿Αριστοτέλης παραγγέλλειν ἔοικεν, ἄλλως δὲ τὸ δικ-
τὸν τοῦ παίωνος τετεχνολογηκέναι ἀκριβείας ἕνεκα.

374

paean, the converse of the other, beginning with three shorts and ending with one long (e.g. *Arabiā*). (39) In the grand style the clauses should begin with an initial paean and be followed by a final paean, as in this passage of Thucydides, *êrrato de to kakon ex Aithiopiâs* ("Ethiopia was where the evil originated"[a]). Why then did Aristotle give this advice? It was because the opening and beginning of a clause should be instantly impressive, and so should its close; and this will result if we begin with a long syllable and end with a long syllable. For a long syllable has in its very nature something grand, and its use at the beginning is immediately striking, while as a conclusion it leaves the listener with a sense of grandeur. Certainly we all uniquely remember and are stirred by words which come first and last, while those in the middle have less impact, as though they were obscured or hidden among the others. (40) This is clearly seen in the case of Thucydides, whose verbal dignity is in every instance almost entirely due to the long syllables in his rhythms. While he has the full range of grandeur, it is perhaps this power of organisation which alone or chiefly secures his greatest grandeur.

(41) We must, however, bear in mind that even if we cannot position the two paeans with precision at either end of each clause, we can at least make the composition roughly paeonic, by beginning and ending with long syllables. This seems to be what Aristotle recommends,[b] and it was only to be precise that he went into technical detail

---

[a] Th. 2.48.1; "the evil" is the plague of 430 B.C.
[b] Cf. Ar. *Rhet.* 1408b31.

---

[1] τὸ M: om. P.

διόπερ Θεόφραστος παράδειγμα ἐκτέθειται μεγαλοπρεπείας τὸ τοιοῦτον κῶλον, "τῶν μὲν περὶ τὰ μηδε-
νὸς ἄξια φιλοσοφούντων·" οὐ γὰρ ἐκ παιώνων ἀκριβῶς, ἀλλὰ παιωνικόν τί ἐστι. παραλάβωμεν[1] μέντοι
τὸν παίωνα εἰς τοὺς λόγους, ἐπειδὴ μικτός τίς ἐστι
καὶ ἀσφαλέστερος, τὸ μεγαλοπρεπὲς μὲν ἐκ τῆς
μακρᾶς λαμβάνων, τὸ λογικὸν δὲ ἐκ τῶν βραχειῶν.
(42) οἱ δ' ἄλλοι, ὁ μὲν ἥρωος σεμνὸς καὶ οὐ λογικός,
ἀλλ' ἠχώδης· <. . .>[2] οὐδὲ εὔρυθμος,[3] ἀλλ' ἄρυθμος,[4] ὥσπερ ὁ τοιόσδε ἔχει,[5] "ἥκων ἡμῶν εἰς τὴν
χώραν·" ἡ γὰρ πυκνότης τῶν μακρῶν ὑπερπίπτει
τοῦ λογικοῦ μέτρου. (43) ὁ δὲ ἴαμβος εὐτελὴς καὶ τῇ
τῶν πολλῶν λέξει ὅμοιος. πολλοὶ γοῦν μέτρα ἰαμ-
βικὰ λαλοῦσιν οὐκ εἰδότες. ὁ δὲ παίων ἀμφοῖν
μέσος καὶ μέτριος, καὶ ὁποῖος συγκεκραμένος. ἡ
μὲν δὴ παιωνικὴ ἐν τοῖς μεγαλοπρεπέσι σύνθεσις
ὧδ' ἄν πως λαμβάνοιτο.

(44) Ποιεῖ δὲ καὶ τὰ μήκη τῶν κώλων μέγεθος,
οἷον "Θουκυδίδης Ἀθηναῖος ξυνέγραψε τὸν πόλεμον

---

[1] παραλάβωμέν τοι iam Victorius: παραλαβὼν P (λα supra
versum scripto).
[2] lacunam mihi iam statuenti prop. Kassel <εἰ δὲ διὰ πάντων
μακρὰν (vel μακρὰς) ἔχει,> (cf. § 117).
[3] εὔρυθμος edd.: ἔνρυθμος P.
[4] ἄρυθμος Victorius: ἀνάρυθμος P.
[5] ἔχει Radermacher: ἐκεῖ P.

on the two sorts of paean. On the same principle Theophrastus[a] illustrated grandeur with the following clause, *tôn men peri ta mêdenos axia philosophountôn* ("those who are philosophers about what is worthless."[b] It is not formed from paeans with any precision, yet it is roughly paeonic. Let us then adopt the paean in prose, since it is a mix of long and short, and so safer, deriving grandeur from the long syllable and suitability for prose from the shorts. (42) As for the other rhythms, the heroic is solemn and not suitable for prose. It is too sonorous, nor is it even a good rhythm but it has no rhythm < . . .>,[c] as in the following words, *hêkôn hêmôn eis tên chôrân* ("arriving inside our land"),[d] Here the accumulation of long syllables goes beyond the limits of prose. (43) The iamb by contrast is ordinary and like normal speech. In fact, many people speak in iambics without knowing it.[e] The paean is a mean between the two extremes and a sort of composite. Paeonic composition may then be used in elevated passages in this sort of way.

(44) Long clauses also produce grandeur, for example "Thucydides the Athenian wrote the history of the war

[a] Theophr. F 703 Fortenbaugh.

[b] Author unknown. Runs of short syllables give a paeonic effect.

[c] Since *hêrous* describes the heroic hexameter (§§ 5 and 204), it regularly includes the dactyl, as in e.g. Ar. *Rhet.* 1408b32ff, which Demetrius closely follows. The transmitted text anomalously restricts it to the spondee, and I posit a lacuna, e.g. <"if it is wholly spondaic">, a supplement suggested by R. Kassel.

[d] Author unknown (cf. § 117).

[e] Cf. Ar. *Rhet.* 1408b33, *Po.* 1449a24, and often later, e.g. Quint. 9.4.88.

377

τῶν Πελοποννησίων καὶ Ἀθηναίων," καὶ "Ἡροδότου
Ἁλικαρνασέως ἱστορίης ἀπόδεξις ἥδε." τὸ γὰρ
ταχέως ἀποσιωπᾶν εἰς κῶλον βραχὺ κατασμικρύνει
τὴν τοῦ λόγου σεμνότητα, κἂν ἡ ὑποκειμένη διάνοια
μεγαλοπρεπὴς ᾖ, κἂν τὰ ὀνόματα. (45) μεγαλοπρεπὲς δὲ καὶ τὸ ἐκ περιαγωγῆς τῇ συνθέσει λέγειν,
οἷον ὡς Θουκυδίδης· "ὁ γὰρ Ἀχελῷος ποταμὸς ῥέων
ἐκ Πίνδου ὄρους διὰ Δολοπίας καὶ Ἀγριανῶν[1] καὶ
Ἀμφιλόχων, ἄνωθεν <μὲν>[2] παρὰ Στράτον πόλιν ἐς
θάλασσαν διεξιεὶς[3] παρ' Οἰνιάδας, καὶ τὴν πόλιν
αὐτοῖς περιλιμνάζων ἄπορον ποιεῖ ὑπὸ τοῦ ὕδατος ἐν
χειμῶνι στρατεύεσθαι." σύμπασα γὰρ ἡ τοιαύτη
μεγαλοπρέπεια ἐκ τῆς περιαγωγῆς γέγονεν, καὶ ἐκ
τοῦ μόγις ἀναπαῦσαι αὐτόν τε καὶ τὸν ἀκούοντα.
(46) εἰ δ' οὕτω διαλύσας αὐτὸ εἴποι τις· "ὁ γὰρ
Ἀχελῷος ποταμὸς ῥεῖ μὲν ἐκ Πίνδου ὄρους, ἐκβάλ-
λει δὲ παρ' Οἰνιάδας ἐς θάλασσαν· πρὸ δὲ τῆς ἐκβολῆς τὸ Οἰνιαδῶν πεδίον λίμνην ποιεῖ, ὥστ' αὐτοῖς
πρὸς τὰς χειμερινὰς ἐφόδους τῶν πολεμίων ἔρυμα
καὶ πρόβλημα γίνεσθαι τὸ ὕδωρ"· εἰ δή τις οὕτω
μεταβαλὼν ἑρμηνεύσειεν αὐτό, πολλὰς μὲν ἀναπαύλας παρέξει τῷ λόγῳ, τὸ μέγεθος δ' ἀφαιρήσεται.
(47) καθάπερ γὰρ τὰς μακρὰς ὁδοὺς αἱ συνεχεῖς
καταγωγαὶ μικρὰς ποιοῦσιν, αἱ δ' ἐρημίαι κἂν ταῖς
μικραῖς ὁδοῖς ἔμφασίν τινα ἔχουσι μήκους, ταὐτὸ
δὴ κἀπὶ τῶν κώλων ἂν γίγνοιτο.

[1] Ἀγραῶν Thuc.

378

between the Peloponnesians and the Athenians"[a] and "The History of Herodotus of Halicarnassus is here set out."[b] A sudden drop into silence on a short clause lessens the dignity of a passage, despite any grandeur in the underlying thought or vocabulary. (45) The use of periodic form is also impressive, as in the following passage of Thucydides: "For the river Achelous, flowing from Mount Pindus through Dolopia and the land of the Agrianians and Amphilochians, passing inland by the city of Stratus on the way into the sea near Oeniadae, and surrounding that town with a marsh, by its floods makes a winter expedition impossible."[c] All this impressiveness has come from the periodic form, and from the fact that Thucydides hardly allows any pause to himself and the reader. (46) If you were to break the sentence up to say, "For the river Achelous flows from Mount Pindus and makes its way into the sea near Oeniadae; but before reaching its outlet it turns the plain of Oeniadae into a marsh, so that the floods form a defence and protection against enemy attack in winter," if you vary and rephrase it in this way, you will give the passage many pauses but destroy its grandeur. (47) Inns at frequent intervals make long journeys shorter, while desolate roads, even when the distances are short, give the impression of length.[d] The same principle applies to clauses.

[a] Th. 1.1.1.
[b] Hdt. 1.1 (cf. § 17).
[c] Th. 2.102.2 (cf. §§ 202, 206).
[d] See on § 202.

---

2 μὲν addidi ex § 202, Thuc.
3 διεξιεὶς Thuc.: διεξίεισι P.

DEMETRIUS

(48) Ποιεῖ δὲ καὶ δυσφωνία συνθέσεως ἐν πολλοῖς μέγεθος, οἷον τὸ "Αἴας δ᾽ ὁ μέγας αἰὲν ἐφ᾽ Ἕκτορι χαλκοκορυστῇ." ἄλλως μὲν γὰρ ἴσως δυσήκοος ἡ τῶν γραμμάτων σύμπληξις, ὑπερβολὴ[1] δ᾽ ἐμφαίνουσα τὸ μέγεθος τοῦ ἥρωος· λειότης γὰρ καὶ τὸ εὐήκοον οὐ πάνυ ἐν μεγαλοπρεπείᾳ χώραν ἔχουσιν, εἰ μή που ἐν ὀλίγοις. καὶ ὁ Θουκυδίδης δὲ πανταχοῦ σχεδὸν φεύγει τὸ λεῖον καὶ ὁμαλὲς τῆς συνθέσεως, καὶ ἀεὶ μᾶλλόν τι προσκρούοντι ἔοικεν, ὥσπερ οἱ τὰς τραχείας ὁδοὺς πορευόμενοι, ἐπὰν λέγῃ, "ὅτι τὸ μὲν δὴ ἔτος, ὡς ὡμολόγητο, ἄνοσον ἐς τὰς ἄλλας ἀσθενείας ἐτύγχανεν ὄν." ῥᾷον μὲν γὰρ καὶ ἥδιον ὧδ᾽ ἄν τις εἶπεν, ὅτι "ἄνοσον ἐς τὰς ἄλλας ἀσθενείας ὂν ἐτύγχανεν," ἀφῄρητο δ᾽ αὐτοῦ τὴν μεγαλοπρέπειαν. (49) ὥσπερ γὰρ ὄνομα τραχὺ μέγεθος ἐργάζεται, οὕτω σύνθεσις. ὀνόματα δὲ τραχέα τό τε "κεκραγὼς" ἀντὶ τοῦ "βοῶν," καὶ τὸ "ῥηγνύμενον" ἀντὶ τοῦ "φερόμενον," οἷος πᾶσιν[2] ὁ Θουκυδίδης χρῆται, ὅμοια λαμβάνων τά τε ὀνόματα τῇ συνθέσει, τοῖς τε ὀνόμασι τὴν σύνθεσιν.

(50) Τάσσειν δὲ τὰ ὀνόματα χρὴ τόνδε τὸν τρόπον· πρῶτα μὲν τιθέναι τὰ μὴ μάλα ἐναργῆ, δεύτερα δὲ καὶ ὕστατα τὰ ἐναργέστερα. οὕτω γὰρ καὶ τοῦ

---

[1] ὑπερβολῇ Gale: ὑπερβολὴ P.
[2] οἷος πᾶσιν Hammer: οἷον σπᾶσιν P.

380

(48) In many passages grandeur is produced by a series of ugly sounds, for example by the line, "mighty Ajax aimed always at bronze-helmeted Hector" (*Aiâs d' ho megas aien eph' Hektori chalkokorustêi*).[a] In other respects the ugly clash of sounds is perhaps unpleasant to the ear, but by its very excess it brings out the greatness of the hero, since in the grand style smoothness and euphony find only an occasional place. Thucydides almost invariably avoids a smooth, even structure. He seems rather to be for ever stumbling, like men going along rough roads, as when he says: "this year from other diseases, by common consent, was as it happened free" (... *etunchanon on*).[b] It would have been easier and more euphonious to say, "from other diseases happened to be free" (... *on etunchanen*). But this would have destroyed the grandeur. (49) Harsh composition creates grandeur, just as a harsh word does. Instances of harsh words are "shrieking" instead of "crying out" (*kekragôs* and *boôn*), and "bursting out" instead of "charging" (*rhêgnumenon* and *pheromenon*). They are the sort of words Thucydides[c] uses everywhere, matching the words to the composition and the composition to the words.

(50) Word order should be as follows: place first those that are not specially vivid, next or last the more vivid. In this way what comes first will sound vivid to us, and what

---

[a] Hom. *Il.* 16.358. The whole line is harsh, but the focus is on Ajax and § 105 specifies a clash of two sounds, so note either *Aias* and *aien*, with their internal hiatus, or the "irregular" lengthening of *ho mmegas* (see note on *opphin* in § 255).

[b] Th. 2.49.1. It ends on a monosyllable.

[c] He does not in fact use these particular examples.

πρώτου ἀκουσόμεθα ὡς ἐναργοῦς, καὶ τοῦ μετ᾽ αὐτὸ
ὡς ἐναργεστέρου. εἰ δὲ μή, δόξομεν ἐξησθενηκέναι
[οἷον καταπεπτωκέναι ἀπὸ ἰσχυροτέρου ἐπὶ ἀσθε-
νές].[1] (51) παράδειγμα δὲ τὸ παρὰ τῷ Πλάτωνι
λεγόμενον, ὅτι "ἐπὰν[2] μέν τις μουσικῇ παρέχῃ
καταυλεῖν καὶ καταχεῖν[3] διὰ τῶν ὤτων"· πολὺ γὰρ
τὸ δεύτερον ἐναργέστερον τοῦ προτέρου· καὶ πάλιν
προϊὼν φησιν, "ὅταν δὲ καταχέων[4] μὴ ἀνῇ, ἀλλὰ
κηλῇ, τὸ δὴ μετὰ τοῦτο ἤδη τήκει καὶ λείβει." τὸ
γὰρ "λείβει" τοῦ "τήκει" ἐμφατικώτερον καὶ ἐγγυτέρω ποιήματος. εἰ δὲ προεξήνεγκεν αὐτό, ἀσθενέ-
στερον ἂν τὸ "τήκει" ἐπιφερόμενον ἐφάνη. (52) καὶ
Ὅμηρος δὲ ἐπὶ τοῦ Κύκλωπος ἀεὶ ἐπαύξει τὴν ὑπερ-
βολήν, καὶ ἐπανιόντι ἐπ᾽ αὐτῆς <ἔοικεν>,[5] οἷον

 οὐ γὰρ ἐῴκει
ἀνδρί γε σιτοφάγῳ, ἀλλὰ ῥίῳ ὑλήεντι,

καὶ προσέτι ὑψηλοῦ ὄρους καὶ ὑπερφαινομένου τῶν
ἄλλων ὀρῶν. ἀεὶ γὰρ καίτοι μεγάλα ὄντα τὰ πρότερον ἥττονα φαίνεται, μειζόνων αὐτοῖς τῶν μετὰ
ταῦτα ἐπιφερομένων.

(53) Χρὴ δὲ καὶ τοὺς συνδέσμους μὴ μάλα ἀντα-
ποδίδοσθαι ἀκριβῶς, οἷον τῷ "μὲν" συνδέσμῳ τὸν
"δέ"· μικροπρεπὲς γὰρ ἡ ἀκρίβεια· ἀλλὰ καὶ ἀτα-
κτοτέρως πως χρῆσθαι, καθάπερ που ὁ Ἀντιφῶν

---

[1] del. Radermacher.   [2] ὅταν Plat. codd.
[3] καταχεῖν τῆς ψυχῆς Plat.   [4] καταχέων P: ἐπέχων Plat.
[5] ἔοικεν edd.: om. P.

follows more vivid still. Otherwise we will seem to have lost vigour.[a] (51) An example is this passage from Plato, "when a man lets music play over him and flood through his ears."[b] Here the second verb is far more vivid than the first. And further on he says, "but when the flood fails to stop and enchants him, at that point he melts and liquefies." The word "liquefies" is more striking than the word "melts," and is closer to poetry.[c] If he had reversed the order, the verb "melts," coming later, would have appeared weaker. (52) Homer similarly, in describing the Cyclops, keeps augmenting his hyperbole and seems to climb higher and higher with it: "for he was not like men who eat bread but like a wooded summit," and what is more, the summit of a high mountain, one towering above all the others.[d] For however big they are, things which come first always seem less big when bigger things follow.

(53) Connectives[e] should not correspond too precisely (e.g. *men* and *de*, "on the one hand" and "on the other hand"), since there is something trivial about exact precision. Use them with rather more freedom, as in Antiphon

---

[a] Here the transmitted text adds "and as it were collapsed from strength into weakness."

[b] Pl. *Rep.* 411a.

[c] Pl. *Rep.* 411b (cf. §§ 183–85, from the same passage). The verb λείβει is poetic and rare in prose.

[d] Hom. *Od.* 9.190–92, with paraphrase of the last line, ὑψη-λῶν ὀρέων, ὅ τε φαίνεται οἷον ἀπ᾽ ἄλλων.

[e] Since it covers both, I translate σύνδεσμος as connective or particle as fits each case.

λέγει· "ἡ <μὲν>[1] γὰρ νῆσος ἦν ἔχομεν[2] δήλη μὲν
καὶ πόρρωθεν <ὅτι>[3] ἐστιν ὑψηλὴ καὶ τραχεῖα· καὶ
τὰ μὲν χρήσιμα καὶ ἐργάσιμα μικρὰ αὐτῆς ἐστι, τὰ
δὲ ἀργὰ πολλὰ σμικρᾶς αὐτῆς οὔσης." τρισὶ γὰρ
τοῖς "μὲν" συνδέσμοις εἷς ὁ "δὲ" ἀνταποδίδοται.[4]
(54) πολλάκις μέντοι τεθέντες πως ἐφεξῆς σύνδεσμοι καὶ τὰ μικρὰ μεγάλα ποιοῦσιν, ὡς παρ'
Ὁμήρῳ τῶν Βοιωτιακῶν πόλεων τὰ ὀνόματα εὐτελῆ
ὄντα καὶ μικρὰ ὄγκον τινὰ ἔχει καὶ μέγεθος διὰ τοὺς
συνδέσμους ἐφεξῆς τοσούτους τεθέντας, οἷον ἐν τῷ
"Σχοῖνόν τε Σκῶλόν τε, πολύκνημόν τ' Ἐτεωνόν."

(55) Τοῖς δὲ παραπληρωματικοῖς συνδέσμοις
χρηστέον, οὐχ ὡς προσθήκαις κεναῖς καὶ οἷον
προσφύμασιν ἢ παραξύσμασιν, ὥσπερ τινὲς τῷ
"δὴ" χρῶνται πρὸς οὐδὲν καὶ τῷ "νυ" καὶ τῷ "†πρό-
τερον†,"[5] ἀλλ' ἂν συμβάλλωνταί τι τῷ μεγέθει τοῦ
λόγου, (56) καθάπερ παρὰ Πλάτωνι, "ὁ μὲν δὴ

[1] μὲν add. Capperonerius: *quidem* Lat.
[2] ἐχομένη edd.: ἔχομεν P.
[3] ὅτι add. Sauppe.
[4] longum exemplum Platonis (*Grg.* 465e2–466a3) praebet M
(crucibus inclusum), suspicor ex margine in textum deductum.
[5] πρότερον P, vix recte: περ Roshdestwenski.

---

[a] Antiph. *fr.* 50 Blass.

somewhere: "For on the one hand the island which we inhabit is clearly on the one hand even from a distance high and rugged; and the part of it which is on the one hand cultivated and useful is small, on the other hand the uncultivated part is large, though the island itself is small."[a] There is only one "on the other hand" to answer the three examples of "on the one hand."[b] (54) Yet an unbroken chain of connectives can often make even small things great, like the names of the Boeotian towns in Homer: they are ordinary and small, but they acquire a certain dignity and greatness from the long chain of connectives, for example "and Schoenus and Scolus and mountainous Eteonus."[c]

(55) Expletive particles[d] should not be used as superfluous extras and, as it were, excrescences or fillings, as "indeed" and "now" and "†earlier†" are sometimes aimlessly used. Use them only if they contribute to the grandeur of what is being said, (56) as in Plato, "and

[b] M adds a passage, enclosed within cruces and probably an intrusion from a marginal annotation: "Another example is Plato in the *Gorgias* [465c 466a]: 'Perhaps on the one hand I have done something extraordinary in not allowing you to make long speeches, while I myself have spoken at length. It is on the one hand right to excuse me; for when I was speaking briefly, you did not understand me, nor were you able to follow the reply I gave you, but you needed an explanation. So on the one hand, if I too am unable to follow your reply, deliver a long speech yourself in turn. But otherwise let me use one, for that is only fair.'"

[c] Hom. *Il.* 2.497 (cf. § 257).

[d] These were a recognised grammatical category of particles added for reasons of rhythm or style (e.g. Dion. Thrax, *Ars Gramm.* p. 96 Ühlig). The third example is corrupt, concealing e.g. the intensifier $\pi\epsilon\rho$, "truly."

μέγας[1] ἐν οὐρανῷ Ζεύς"· καὶ παρ' Ὁμήρῳ, "ἀλλ' ὅτε
δὴ πόρον ἷξον ἐϋρρεῖος ποταμοῖο." ἀρκτικὸς γὰρ
τεθεὶς ὁ σύνδεσμος καὶ ἀποσπάσας[2] τῶν προτέρων
τὰ ἐχόμενα μεγαλεῖόν τι εἰργάσατο· αἱ γὰρ πολλαὶ
ἀρχαὶ σεμνότητα ἐργάζονται. εἰ δ' ὧδε εἶπεν, "ἀλλ'
ὅτε ἐπὶ τὸν πόρον ἀφίκοντο τοῦ ποταμοῦ," μικρολο-
γοῦντι ἐῴκει καὶ ἔτι ὡς περὶ ἑνὸς πράγματος
λέγοντι.

(57) Λαμβάνεται δὲ καὶ παθητικῶς[3] πολλάκις ὁ
σύνδεσμος οὗτος, ὥσπερ ἐπὶ τῆς Καλυψοῦς πρὸς τὸν
Ὀδυσσέα,

> Διογενὲς Λαερτιάδη, πολυμήχαν' Ὀδυσσεῦ,
> οὕτω δὴ οἰκόνδε φίλην ἐς πατρίδα γαῖαν;

εἰ γοῦν τὸν σύνδεσμον ἐξέλοις, συνεξαιρήσεις καὶ
τὸ πάθος. καθόλου γάρ, ὥσπερ ὁ Πραξιφάνης
φησίν, ἀντὶ μυγμῶν παρελαμβάνοντο οἱ τοιοῦτοι
σύνδεσμοι καὶ στεναγμῶν, ὥσπερ τὸ "αἳ αἵ," καὶ τὸ
"φεῦ," καὶ "†ποῖόν τί ἐστιν†,"[4] ὡς αὐτός φησι, τὸ
"καί νύ κ' ὀδυρομένοισιν" ἔπρεψεν, ἔμφασίν τινα
ἔχον οἴκτρου ὀνόματος. (58) οἱ δὲ πρὸς οὐδὲν ἀνα-
πληροῦντες, φησί, τὸν σύνδεσμον ἐοίκασιν τοῖς

---

[1] μέγας ἡγεμὼν Plat. codd.
[2] ἀποσπάσας Finckh: ἀποσπασθεὶς P.
[3] παθητικῶς Greg.: παθητικοῖς P.
[4] locus corruptissimus, e.g. ὡς γὰρ pro ὥσπερ et ὡσαύτως
pro ὡς αὐτός Radermacher

indeed mighty Zeus in his heaven,"[a] and in Homer, "but
when indeed they came to the ford of the fair-flowing
river."[b] Placed near the beginning and severing what follows from what precedes, the particle makes a dignified
impression. For the use of many opening words has an
imposing effect. If Homer had said, "but when they ar-
rived at the ford of the river," he would have seemed to be
using trivial language and speaking of only one particular
event.

(57) The particle "indeed" is also frequently used to
add emotion, as in Calypso's words to Odysseus,

> "Born of Zeus, son of Laertes, Odysseus of the
> many wiles,
> do you indeed wish so much to go home to your
> own dear land?[c]

Remove the particle, and you will simultaneously remove
the emotion. In general, as Praxiphanes says,[d] such particles were used as substitutes for moans and laments, like
"ah ah" and "alas" and †in the sort of way†, as he himself
says, "and so now grieving"[e] was appropriate, since to
some degree it suggests a word of mourning. (58) But
those who use expletive particles aimlessly are, as Praxi-

[a] Pl. *Phdr.* 246e.   [b] Hom. *Il.* 14.433, 21.1.

[c] Hom. *Od.* 5.203–4; and cf. *Od.* 16.220, 21.226.

[d] Praxiphanes 13 Wehrli.

[e] The text is corrupt, but particles and interjections are presumably compared, as in § 58, and the particle νυ (or the cluster
καί νύ κε) is said to have the same piteous effect as "ah ah" and
"alas." For the last phrase, illustrating how καί νύ κε emphasises
a verb of mourning, cf. e.g. Hom. *Il.* 23.154 "and as indeed they
mourned the sun set on them."

ὑποκριταῖς τοῖς τὸ καὶ τὸ ἐπιλέγουσιν[1] λέγουσιν, οἷον εἴ τις ὧδε λέγοι,

Καλυδὼν μὲν ἥδε γαῖα Πελοπίας[2] χθονός, φεῦ. ἐν ἀντιπόρθμοις πεδί' ἔχουσ' εὐδαίμονα, αἲ, αἴ.

ὡς γὰρ παρέλκει τὸ αἲ αἲ καὶ τὸ φεῦ ἐνθάδε, οὕτω καὶ ὁ πανταχοῦ μάτην ἐμβαλλόμενος σύνδεσμος.[3]

(59) Οἱ μὲν δὴ σύνδεσμοι τὴν σύνθεσιν μεγαλοπρεπῆ ποιοῦσιν, ὡς εἴρηται, τὰ δὲ σχήματα τῆς λέξεώς ἐστι μὲν καὶ αὐτὰ συνθέσεώς τι εἶδος· τὸ[4] γὰρ δὴ τὰ αὐτὰ λέγειν δὶς ἀναδιπλοῦντα[5] ἢ ἐπαναφέροντα ἢ ἀνθυπαλλάσσοντα διαταττομένῳ καὶ μετασυντιθέντι ἔοικεν. διατακτέον δὲ τὰ πρόσφορα αὐτῶν χαρακτῆρι ἑκάστῳ, οἷον τῷ μεγαλοπρεπεῖ μὲν περὶ οὗ πρόκειται, ταῦτα· (60) πρῶτον μὲν τὴν ἀνθυπαλλαγήν, ὡς Ὅμηρος, "οἱ δὲ δύο σκόπελοι ὁ μὲν οὐρανὸν εὐρὺν ἱκάνει"· πολὺ γὰρ οὕτω μεγαλειότερον ἐναλλαγείσης ⟨τῆς⟩[6] πτώσεως, ἢ εἴπερ οὕτως ἔφη, "τῶν δὲ δύο σκοπέλων ὁ μὲν οὐρανὸν εὐρύν"· συνήθως γὰρ ἐλέγετο. πᾶν δὲ τὸ σύνηθες μικροπρεπές, διὸ καὶ ἀθαύμαστον.

(61) Τὸν δὲ Νιρέα, αὐτόν τε ὄντα μικρὸν καὶ τὰ πράγματα αὐτοῦ μικρότερα, τρεῖς ναῦς καὶ ὀλίγους

[1] ἐπιλέγουσιν Nauck: ἔπος λέγουσιν P
[2] Πελοπίας (cf. Ar. *Rhet.* 1409b10): Πελοπείας P
[3] σύνδεσμος Greg.: om. P
[4] τὸ Dresd.: τῶν P
[5] ἀναδιπλοῦντα Solmsen: διπλοῦντα P

388

phanes says, like actors who add this or that exclamation without purpose, as though you were to say,

> "This land of Calydon, of the land of Pelops (alas!)
> the facing shore, with its fertile plains (ah! ah!)."[a]

For just as in this passage the "ah! ah!" and the "alas!" are superfluous, so is any particle which is inserted indiscriminately and without reason.

(59) Connectives then, as has been said, give grandeur to the composition. Next, figures of speech: these are themselves a form of composition, since it is practically a matter of rearrangement and redistribution when you say the same thing twice, through repetition or anaphora or anthypallage.[b] Each style must be assigned its appropriate figures, in the case of the grand style, our present concern, the following: (60) First, anthypallage, as in Homer's line, "the two rocks, one of them reaches up to the wide heaven."[c] With this change from the normal genitive, the line is far more imposing than if he had said, "of the two rocks one reaches up to the wide heaven." That would have been the usual construction, but anything usual is trivial and so fails to impress.

(61) Again, take Nireus, who is personally insignificant and his contingent still more so, three ships and a few

[a] TCF Eur. *Meleager fr.* 515. The interjections make it seem that Calydon is in the Peloponnese.

[b] Anthypallage is a change of grammatical case, subdividing a plural into its parts (a type of διλογία, cf. § 103).

[c] Hom. *Od.* 12.73.

---

[6] τῆς add. Kroll.

ἄνδρας, μέγαν[1] καὶ μεγάλα ἐποίησεν καὶ πολλὰ ἀντ'
ὀλίγων, τῷ σχήματι διπλῷ καὶ μικτῷ χρησάμενος
ἐξ ἐπαναφορᾶς τε καὶ διαλύσεως. "Νιρεὺς γάρ,"
φησι, "τρεῖς νῆας ἄγεν, Νιρεὺς Ἀγλαΐης υἱός,
Νιρεύς, ὃς κάλλιστος ἀνήρ".[2] ἥ τε γὰρ ἐπαναφορὰ
τῆς λέξεως ἐπὶ τὸ αὐτὸ ὄνομα τὸν Νιρέα καὶ ἡ διά-
λυσις πλῆθός τι ἐμφαίνει πραγμάτων, καίτοι δύο ἢ
τριῶν ὄντων. (62) καὶ σχεδὸν ἅπαξ τοῦ Νιρέως ὀνο-
μασθέντος ἐν τῷ δράματι μεμνήμεθα οὐδὲν ἧττον ἢ
τοῦ Ἀχιλλέως καὶ τοῦ Ὀδυσσέως, καίτοι κατ' ἔπος
ἕκαστον[3] λαλουμένων σχεδόν. αἰτία δ' ἡ τοῦ σχήματος δύναμις· εἰ δ' οὕτως εἶπεν, "Νιρεὺς ὁ
Ἀγλαΐας υἱὸς ἐκ Σύμης τρεῖς νῆας ἦγεν," παρασε-
σιωπηκότι ἐῴκει τὸν Νιρέα· ὥσπερ γὰρ ἐν ταῖς
ἑστιάσεσι τὰ ὀλίγα διαταχθέντα πως πολλὰ φαίνεται, οὕτω κἂν τοῖς λόγοις. (63) πολλαχοῦ μέντοι τὸ
ἐναντίον τῇ λύσει, ἡ συνάφεια, μεγέθους αἴτιον
γίνεται μᾶλλον, οἷον ὅτι "ἐστρατεύοντο Ἕλληνές τε
καὶ Κᾶρες καὶ Λύκιοι καὶ Πάμφυλοι καὶ Φρύγες." ἡ
γὰρ τοῦ αὐτοῦ συνδέσμου θέσις ἐμφαίνει τι ἄπειρον
πλῆθος. (64) τὸ δὲ τοιοῦτο "κυρτά, φαληριόωντα,"
τῇ ἐξαιρέσει τοῦ "καὶ" συνδέσμου μεγαλειότερον

---

[1] μέγαν edd.: μέγα P.
[2] ὑπὸ Ἴλιον ἦλθεν add. Greg. M.
[3] ἕκαστον edd. ἑκάστων P.

men. But Homer has made him and it impressive, and has multiplied the small contingent by using the two combined figures of anaphora and absence of connectives. "Nireus," he says, "brought three ships, Nireus, son of Aglaia, Nireus the most handsome man...."[a] The verbal anaphora of the same word, Nireus, and the absence of connectives give an impression of a huge contingent, even though it is only two or three ships. (62) Nireus is mentioned barely once in the course of the action,[b] but we remember him no less than Achilles and Odysseus, the subjects of almost every line. The impact of the figure is the cause. If Homer had said, "Nireus, the son of Aglaia, brought three ships from Syme," he might just as well have passed over Nireus in silence. Speech is like a banquet: a few dishes may be arranged to seem many. (63) In many passages, however, linking with connectives, the opposite of asyndeton, tends to increase the grandeur, for example "to the war marched Greeks and Carians and Lycians and Pamphylians and Phrygians."[c] The use of the same connective suggests infinite numbers. (64) But in a phrase such as "high-arched, foam-crested"[d] the omission of the connective "and" makes the language more impres-

---

[a] Hom. Il. 2.671ff, a traditional example, e.g. Ar. Rhet. 1414a2–7 and Ps.Plu. Vit. Hom. 33. The name Nireus begins three successive lines:

Νιρεὺς αὖ Σύμηθεν ἄγε τρεῖς νῆας ἐΐσας,
Νιρεὺς Ἀγλαΐης υἱὸς Χαρόποιό τ' ἄνακτος,
Νιρεὺς ὃς κάλλιστος ἀνὴρ ὑπὸ Ἴλιον ἦλθεν.

[b] For δρᾶμα of nondramatic genres, compare the mimes of Sophron in § 156, and Plato's Menexenus in § 266 (in both because of the use of direct speech).

[c] Author unknown.   [d] Hom. Il. 13.799 (cf. § 81).

ἀπέβη μᾶλλον, ἢ <εἴπερ>[1] εἶπεν, "κυρτὰ καὶ φαληριόωντα."

(65) [Τὸ][2] μεγαλεῖον μέντοι ἐν τοῖς σχήμασιν τὸ
μηδὲ ἐπὶ τῆς αὐτῆς μένειν πτώσεως, ὡς Θουκυδίδης,
"καὶ πρῶτος ἀποβαίνων ἐπὶ τὴν ἀποβάθραν ἐλειπο-
ψύχησέ τε, καὶ πεσόντος αὐτοῦ ἐς τὴν παρεξειρεσίαν
. . ." πολὺ γὰρ οὕτως μεγαλειότερον, ἢ εἴπερ ἐπὶ τῆς
αὐτῆς πτώσεως οὕτως ἔφη, ὅτι "ἔπεσεν ἐς τὴν
παρεξειρεσίαν καὶ ἀπέβαλε τὴν ἀσπίδα." (66) καὶ
ἀναδίπλωσις δ' ἔπους[3] εἰργάσατο μέγεθος, ὡς Ἡρόδοτος[4] "δράκοντες δέ που," φησίν, "ἦσαν ἐν τῶ
Καυκάσω <. . .>[5] μέγεθος, καὶ μέγεθος καὶ πλῆθος." δὶς ῥηθὲν τὸ "μέγεθος" ὄγκον τινὰ τῇ ἑρμηνείᾳ
παρέσχεν. (67) χρῆσθαι μέντοι τοῖς σχήμασι μὴ
πυκνοῖς· ἀπειρόκαλον γὰρ καὶ παρεμφαῖνόν τινα τοῦ
λόγου ἀνωμαλίαν. οἱ γοῦν ἀρχαῖοι πολλὰ σχήματα
ἐν τοῖς λόγοις τιθέντες συνηθέστεροι τῶν ἀσχηματί-
στων εἰσίν, διὰ τὸ ἐντέχνως τιθέναι.

(68) Περὶ δὲ συγκρούσεως φωνηέντων ὑπέλαβον
ἄλλοι ἄλλως. Ἰσοκράτης μὲν γὰρ ἐφυλάττετο συμ-
πλήσσειν αὐτά, καὶ οἱ ἀπ' αὐτοῦ, ἄλλοι δέ τινες ὡς
ἔτυχε συνέκρουσαν καὶ παντάπασι· δεῖ δὲ οὔτε
ἠχώδη ποιεῖν τὴν σύνθεσιν, ἀτέχνως αὐτὰ συμ-
πλήσσοντα καὶ ὡς ἔτυχε· διασπασμῷ γὰρ τοῦ
λόγου τὸ τοιοῦτον καὶ διαρρίψει ἔοικεν· οὔτε μὴν

---

[1] εἴπερ Radermacher: εἰ Greg.: om. P.
[2] τὸ del. Radermacher et Roberts.
[3] ἀναδίπλωσις δ' ἔπους P[2]: ἀναδιπλώσας δ' ἔπος P[1].

sive than if Homer had said "high-arched and foam-crested."

(65) Grandeur in figures is also produced from variety in the use of cases, as in Thucydides, "the first to step on the gangway, he fainted, and in his falling on the oars, his shield . . ."[a] This is far more striking than if he had kept to the same case and said, "he fell on the oars and dropped his shield." (66) Repetition of a word is also imposing, as in this passage of Herodotus, "there were serpents in the Caucasus, <vast> in size, yes in size and number."[b] The repetition of the word "size" adds weight to the style. (67) Do not, however, crowd figures together. That is tasteless and suggests an uneven style. The early writers, it is true, use many figures in their works, but they position them so skilfully that they seem less unusual than those who avoid figures altogether.

(68) Next, hiatus, on which opinions have differed. Isocrates and his school avoided any clash of vowels, while others admitted it wholesale wherever it happened to occur. You should, however, neither make your composition too sonorous by a random and unskilful use of hiatus (for that produces a jerky and disjointed style), nor yet

---

[a] Th. 4.12.1. The sentence continues, ἡ ἀσπὶς περιερρύη ἐς τὴν θάλασσαν, "his shield slipped off into the sea."

[b] Text uncertain and perhaps a memory of Hdt. 1.203.1, ἐὸν ὀρέων καὶ πλήθει μέγιστον καὶ μεγέθει ὑψηλότατον. But the parallel is not close, there are no snakes, and Orth, *Philologische Wochenschrift* 45 (1925) 778–83, attractively suggests Herodorus of Heraclea (FGrHist 31 F 63 addenda, p.*12 Jacoby).

---

4 Ἡρόδοτος P: Ἡρόδωρος Orth.
5 lacuna subest, e.g. <θαυμαστοὶ τὸ> Kroll.

παντελῶς φυλάσσεσθαι τὴν συνέχειαν τῶν γραμμά-
των· λειοτέρα μὲν γὰρ οὕτως ἔσται ἴσως ἡ σύνθεσις, ἀμουσοτέρα δὲ καὶ κωφὴ ἀτεχνῶς, πολλὴν
εὐφωνίαν ἀφαιρεθεῖσα τὴν γινομένην ἐκ τῆς
συγκρούσεως. (69) σκεπτέον δὲ πρῶτον μέν, ὅτι καὶ
ἡ συνήθεια αὐτὴ συμπλήττει τὰ γράμματα τὰ ἐν[1]
τοῖς ὀνόμασιν, καίτοι στοχαζομένη μάλιστα εὐφωνίας, οἷον ἐν τῷ Αἰακὸς καὶ χιών. πολλὰ δὲ καὶ διὰ
μόνων τῶν φωνηέντων συντίθησιν ὀνόματα, οἷον
Αἰαίη καὶ Εὔιος, οὐδέν τε δυσφωνότερα τῶν ἄλλων
ἐστὶ ταῦτα, ἀλλ' ἴσως καὶ μουσικώτερα. (70) τά γε
μὴν ποιητικά, οἷον τὸ ἠέλιος, διῃρημένον καὶ
συγκρουόμενον ἐπίτηδες, εὐφωνότερόν ἐστι τοῦ
ἥλιος καὶ τὸ ὀρέων τοῦ ὀρῶν. ἔχει γάρ τινα ἡ λύσις
καὶ ἡ σύγκρουσις οἷον ᾠδὴν ἐπιγινομένη. πολλὰ
δὲ καὶ ἄλλα ἐν συναλιφῇ μὲν λεγόμενα δύσφωνα[2]
ἦν, διαιρεθέντα δὲ καὶ συγκρουσθέντα εὐφωνότερα,
ὡς τὸ "πάντα μὲν τὰ νέα καὶ καλά ἐστιν." εἰ δὲ
συναλείψας εἴποις "καλ' ἐστίν,"[3] δυσφωνότερον
ἔσται τὸ λεγόμενον καὶ εὐτελέστερον. (71) ἐν
Αἰγύπτῳ δὲ καὶ τοὺς θεοὺς ὑμνοῦσι διὰ τῶν ἑπτὰ
φωνηέντων οἱ ἱερεῖς, ἐφεξῆς ἠχοῦντες αὐτά, καὶ ἀντὶ
αὐλοῦ καὶ ἀντὶ κιθάρας τῶν γραμμάτων τούτων ὁ
ἦχος ἀκούεται ὑπ' εὐφωνίας, ὥστε ὁ ἐξαιρῶν τὴν

[1] τὰ ἐν Roshdestwenski: ταῦτα P.
[2] δύσφωνα edd., δύσφορα P.
[3] καλ' ἐστίν (sic) Ahrens: καλά 'στιν P.

avoid hiatus altogether, since your composition will then perhaps be smoother but it will be less musical and quite flat when robbed of much of the euphony produced by hiatus. (69) Note first that ordinary usage itself aims above all at euphony, yet it has a clash of vowels within such words as *Aiakos* and *chiôn* ("snow"), and it even forms many words exclusively from vowels, e.g. *Aiaiê* and *Euios*,[a] and these words are no less pleasant than any others and possibly even more musical. (70) Poetic forms[b] where the resolution and hiatus are deliberate have more euphony, for example *êelios* for *hêlios* ("sun") and *oreôn* for *orôn* ("mountains"), since the separate sounds produced by the hiatus add a sort of singing effect. Many other words would be harsh if the sounds were run together, but are more melodious when they are separated in hiatus, for example *kala estin* (at the end of the sentence "all that is young is beautiful"[c]). Running the vowels together, *kal' estin*, will make the phrase harsher and more ordinary. (71) In Egypt when the priests sing hymns to the gods, they sing the seven vowels in succession,[d] and the sound of these vowels has such euphony that men listen to it instead of the flute and the lyre. The removal here of hiatus simply removes the

---

[a] I.e. god of the bacchant cry, *euoi* (Dionysus).

[b] Both examples (the first recurs in § 207) show epic forms, as do those in § 73.

[c] Author unknown (cf. § 207).

[d] The seven vowels are a e ê i o u ô. Such vowel songs appear in Egyptian/Greek magical texts. See H. D. Betz, *The Greek Magical Papyri in Translation*, Chicago 1986, e.g. pp. 172–95.

σύγκρουσιν οὐδὲν ἄλλο ἢ μέλος ἀτεχνῶς ἐξαιρεῖ τοῦ
λόγου καὶ μοῦσαν. ἀλλὰ περὶ τούτων μὲν οὐ καιρὸς
μηκύνειν ἴσως.

(72) Ἐν δὲ τῷ μεγαλοπρεπεῖ χαρακτῆρι σύγκρουσις παραλαμβάνοιτ' ἂν πρέπουσα ἤτοι διὰ μακρῶν,
ὡς τὸ "λᾶαν ἄνω ὤθεσκε"· καὶ γὰρ ὁ στίχος μῆκός
τι ἔσχεν ἐκ τῆς συγκρούσεως, καὶ μεμίμηται τοῦ
λίθου τὴν ἀναφορὰν καὶ βίαν· ὡσαύτως καὶ τὸ "μὴ
ἤπειρος εἶναι" τὸ Θουκυδίδειον. συγκρούονται καὶ
δίφθογγοι διφθόγγοις, "ταύτην κατῴκησαν μὲν
Κερκυραῖοι· οἰκιστὴς δὲ ἐγένετο. . . ." (73) ποιεῖ μὲν
οὖν καὶ τὰ αὐτὰ μακρὰ συγκρουόμενα μέγεθος καὶ
αἱ αὐταὶ δίφθογγοι. αἱ δὲ ἐκ διαφερόντων συγκρού-
σεις ὁμοῦ καὶ μέγεθος ποιοῦσιν καὶ ποικιλίαν ἐκ τῆς
πολυηχίας,[1] οἷον "ἠώς," ἐν δὲ τῷ "οἴην" οὐ μόνον
διαφέροντα τὰ γράμματά ἐστιν, ἀλλὰ καὶ οἱ ἦχοι ὁ
μὲν δασύς, ὁ δὲ ψιλός, ὥστε πολλὰ ἀνόμοια εἶναι.
(74) καὶ ἐν ᾠδαῖς δὲ τὰ μελίσματα ἐπὶ [τοῦ][2] ἑνὸς
γίνεται <καὶ>[3] τοῦ αὐτοῦ μακροῦ γράμματος, οἷον
ᾠδῶν ἐπεμβαλλομένων ᾠδαῖς, ὥστε ἡ τῶν ὁμοίων
σύγκρουσις μικρὸν ἔσται τι ᾠδῆς μέρος καὶ
μέλισμα. περὶ μὲν δὴ συγκρούσεως, καὶ ὡς γίνοιτ'
ἂν μεγαλοπρεπὴς σύνθεσις, λελέχθω τοσαῦτα.

(75) Ἔστι δὲ καὶ ἐν πράγμασι τὸ μεγαλοπρεπές,

---

[1] τῆς οὐ P: οὐ del. Victorius.
[2] ἐπὶ [τοῦ] edd.: ἀπὸ vel ἀπὸ τοῦ codd. rec.: ἀπὸ τοῦ vel
fort. κατὰ P.
[3] καὶ add. Gärtner.

music and harmony of the song. But perhaps this is not the time to enlarge on this subject.

(72) In the grand style the appropriate hiatus to use would be between long vowels, for example "ô" + "ô" in *lâan anô ôtheske* ("he kept pushing the stone up").[a] The line has been lengthened by the hiatus and has reproduced the stone's upward movement and the effort needed. Thucydides has a similar example, "ê" + "ê" in *mê ēpeiros oinai* ("not to be mainland").[b] Diphthongs too may clash with diphthongs, for example "oi" + "oi" in *Kerkuraioi oikistês* ("its colonists were Corcyrean, its founder was   ").[c] (73) Hiatus then between the same long syllables and the same diphthongs creates grandeur. Yet so does hiatus between different vowels, producing variety as well as grandeur from the change of sound, for example *eôs* ("dawn"); and in the case of *hoiên* ("such") not only are the vowels different but also the breathings, rough followed by smooth, so there is considerable variety. (74) In songs, too, a note can be prolonged on one and the same long vowel,[d] a sort of song within a song, so that hiatus from similar vowels will produce a tiny part of a song, a prolonged note. But let this be enough on hiatus and the kind of composition appropriate to the grand style.

(75) Grandeur also comes from the subject, for exam-

[a] Hom. *Od.* 11.596. It is given detailed and sensitive analysis in DH. *CV* 20.

[b] Th. 6.1.2.

[c] Th. 1.24.2.

[d] On the text and meaning (a prolonged note, not a trill), see H. Gärtner, *Hermes* 118 (1990) 214–19.

ἂν μεγάλη καὶ διαπρεπὴς πεζομαχία ἢ ναυμαχία, ἢ
περὶ οὐρανοῦ ἢ περὶ γῆς λόγος· ὁ γὰρ τοῦ μεγάλου
ἀκούων πράγματος εὐθὺς καὶ <τὸν>[1] λέγοντα οἴεται
μεγάλως λέγειν, πλανώμενος· δεῖ γὰρ οὐ τὰ λεγόμενα σκοπεῖν, ἀλλὰ πῶς λέγεται· ἔστι γὰρ καὶ
μεγάλα μικρῶς λέγοντα ἀπρεπές <τι>[2] ποιεῖν τῷ
πράγματι. διὸ καὶ δεινούς τινάς φασιν, ὥσπερ καὶ
Θεόπομπον, δεινὰ οὐ δεινῶς λέγοντας.[3] (76) Νικίας
δ᾽ ὁ ζωγράφος καὶ τοῦτο εὐθὺς ἔλεγεν εἶναι τῆς
γραφικῆς τέχνης οὐ μικρὸν μέρος τὸ λαβόντα ὕλην
εὐμεγέθη γράφειν, καὶ μὴ κατακερματίζειν τὴν
τέχνην εἰς μικρά, οἷον ὀρνίθια ἢ ἄνθη, ἀλλ᾽ ἱππομα-
χίας καὶ ναυμαχίας, ἔνθα πολλὰ μὲν σχήματα δεί-
ξειεν ἄν τις ἵππων τῶν μὲν θεόντων, τῶν δὲ ἀνθιστα-
μένων ὀρθῶν, ἄλλων δὲ ὀκλαζόντων, πολλοὺς δ᾽
ἀκοντίζοντας, πολλοὺς δὲ καταπίπτοντας τῶν
ἱππέων· ᾤετο γὰρ καὶ τὴν ὑπόθεσιν αὐτὴν μέρος
εἶναι τῆς ζωγραφικῆς τέχνης, ὥσπερ τοὺς μύθους
τῶν ποιητῶν. οὐδὲν οὖν θαυμαστόν, εἰ καὶ ἐν τοῖς
λόγοις [καὶ][4] ἐκ πραγμάτων μεγάλων[5] μεγαλοπρέπεια γένηται.

(77) Τὴν δὲ λέξιν ἐν τῷ χαρακτῆρι τούτῳ περιττὴν εἶναι δεῖ καὶ ἐξηλλαγμένην καὶ ἀσυνήθη μᾶλ-
λον· οὕτω γὰρ ἕξει τὸν ὄγκον, ἡ δὲ κυρία καὶ συνή-
θης σαφὴς μέν ἀεί, τῇ[6] δὲ καὶ εὐκαταφρόνητος. (78)
πρῶτα μὲν οὖν μεταφοραῖς χρηστέον· αὗται γὰρ

[1] τὸν add. edd.   [2] τι add. Goeller.
[3] λέγοντας Hammer: λέγοντα P.

398

ple when the subject is a great and famous battle on land
or sea, or when earth or heaven is the theme. For the
man who listens to an impressive subject immediately
supposes that the speaker too is impressive—mistakenly,
for we must consider not what but how he says it, since an
unimpressive treatment of an impressive topic produces
inappropriateness. Hence some writers like Theopompus are said to be forceful, but it is their subject, not their
style that is forceful. (76) The painter Nicias[a] used to
maintain that no small part of the painter's skill was the
choice at the outset to paint an imposing subject, and
instead of frittering away his skill on minor subjects, such
as little birds or flowers, he should paint naval battles and
cavalry charges where he could represent horses in many
different poses, charging, or rearing up, or crouching low,
and many riders hurling javelins or being thrown. He
held that the theme itself was a part of the painter's skill,
just as plot was part of the poet's. So it is no surprise that
in prose similarly grandeur comes from grandeur in the
subject.

(77) The diction in the grand style should be distinguished, distinctive and the less usual. It will then have
weight, while the normal, usual words may always be
clear but are in certain cases unimpressive. (78) In the
first place, we should use metaphors, for they more than

---

[a] Nicias 1825 Overbeck, an Athenian painter of the later
fourth century. No cavalry battle is attested for him, but he was
famed for his paintings of animals, e.g. Pliny, *Nat. Hist.* 35.133.

---

[4] καὶ del. Spengel.

[5] μεγάλων M: *magnis* Lat.: μεγάλη P.

[6] ἀεὶ τῇ P: *semper et* Lat.: λειτῇ Spengel.

μάλιστα καὶ ἡδονὴν συμβάλλονται τοῖς λόγοις καὶ
μέγεθος, μὴ μέντοι πυκναῖς, ἐπεί τοι διθύραμβον
ἀντὶ λόγου γράφομεν· μήτε μὴν πόρρωθεν μετενη-
νεγμέναις, ἀλλ' αὐτόθεν καὶ ἐκ τοῦ ὁμοίου, οἷον
ἔοικεν ἀλλήλοις στρατηγός, κυβερνήτης, ἡνίοχος·
πάντες γὰρ οὗτοι ἄρχοντές εἰσιν. ἀσφαλῶς οὖν ἐρεῖ
καὶ ὁ τὸν στρατηγὸν κυβερνήτην λέγων τῆς πόλεως,
καὶ ἀνάπαλιν ὁ τὸν κυβερνήτην ἡνίοχον[1] τῆς νηός.
(79) οὐ πᾶσαι μέντοι ἀνταποδίδονται, ὥσπερ αἱ
προειρημέναι, ἐπεὶ τὴν ὑπώρειαν μὲν τῆς Ἴδης πόδα
ἐξῆν εἰπεῖν τὸν ποιητήν, τὸν δὲ τοῦ ἀνθρώπου πόδα
οὐκέτι ὑπώρειαν εἰπεῖν.

(80) Ἐπὰν μέντοι κινδυνώδης ἡ μεταφορὰ δοκῇ,
μεταλαμβανέσθω εἰς εἰκασίαν· οὕτω γὰρ ἀσφα-
λεστέρα γίγνοιτ' ἄν. εἰκασία δ'[2] ἐστὶ μεταφορὰ
πλεονάζουσα, οἷον εἴ τις <τῷ>[3] "τότε τῷ Πύθωνι τῷ
ῥήτορι ῥέοντι καθ' ὑμῶν" προσθεὶς εἴποι, "ὥσπερ
ῥέοντι καθ' ὑμῶν." οὕτω μὲν γὰρ εἰκασία γέγονεν
καὶ ἀσφαλέστερος ὁ λόγος, ἐκείνως δὲ μεταφορὰ καὶ
κινδυνωδέστερος. διὸ καὶ Πλάτων ἐπισφαλές τι
δοκεῖ ποιεῖν μεταφοραῖς μᾶλλον χρώμενος ἢ εἰκασίαις, ὁ μέντοι Ξενοφῶν εἰκασίαις μᾶλλον.

(81) Ἀρίστη δὲ δοκεῖ μεταφορὰ τῷ Ἀριστοτέλει
ἡ κατὰ ἐνέργειαν καλουμένη, ὅταν τὰ ἄψυχα ἐνερ-
γοῦντα εἰσάγηται καθάπερ ἔμψυχα, ὡς τὸ ἐπὶ τοῦ
βέλους·

[1] ἡνίοχον Finckh: ἄρχοντα P.   [2] δ' Victorius: ἀλλ' P.
[3] τῷ add. Gale.

anything make prose attractive and impressive, but they should not be crowded together (or we write a dithyramb instead of prose), nor yet far-fetched but from the same general area and based on a true analogy. For instance, general, pilot, and charioteer are similar in ruling over something. So it will be safe to say that a general is "the city's pilot" and conversely a pilot "the ship's charioteer."[a] (79) But not all metaphors are reciprocal, like the above. Homer could call the lower slope of Ida its foot[b] but never a man's foot his slope.

(80) When a metaphor seems bold, convert it into a simile for greater safety. A simile is an expanded metaphor. For example instead of saying "the orator Python was then a rushing torrent against you,"[c] expand it and say "was like a rushing torrent against you." The result is a simile and a less risky form of expression, while the former was a metaphor and more dangerous. This is why Plato's use of metaphor in preference to simile is thought risky. Xenophon by contrast prefers the simile.

(81) Aristotle[d] thought that what is called the personifying metaphor is the best, in which the inanimate is introduced personified as animate, for example in the

[a] For "charioteer of the ship" cf. EGF 'Homerus' F19 and 20 (= Ps.Plu. Vit. Hom. 2.20, RG 3.228). The change of text from "ruler" to "charioteer" provides a traditional example of metaphor, and preserves the focus on analogical metaphor (on which cf. Ar. Po. 1457b6ff).

[b] Cf. Hom. Il. 2.824; 20.59 and 218. Like other later critics, e.g. RG 3.228, he rejects Aristotle's advice that metaphors should always be reciprocal (Rhet. 1407a14–15).

[c] Dem. De Cor. 136 (cf. § 272).

[d] Nowhere explicitly, but cf. Ar. Rhet. 1410b35, 1411b32ff, which includes both the examples here.

ὀξυβελὴς καθ᾽ ὅμιλον ἐπιπτέσθαι μενεαίνων,

καὶ τὸ "κυρτὰ φαληριόωντα." πάντα γὰρ ταῦτα, τὸ
"φαληριόωντα" καὶ τὸ "μενεαίνων," ζωτικαῖς ἐνερ-
γείαις ἔοικεν. (82) ἔνια μέντοι σαφέστερον ἐν ταῖς
μεταφοραῖς λέγεται καὶ κυριώτερον ἤπερ[1] ἐν αὐτοῖς
τοῖς κυρίοις, ὡς τὸ "ἔφριξεν δὲ μάχη." οὐ γὰρ ἄν
τις αὐτὸ μεταβαλὼν διὰ κυρίων οὔτ᾽ ἀληθέστερον
εἴποι οὔτε σαφέστερον. τὸν γὰρ ἐκ τῶν δοράτων
κλόνον <καὶ τὸν>[2] γινόμενον τούτοις ἠρέμα ἦχον
συνεχῶς φρίσσουσαν μάχην προσηγόρευσεν, καὶ
ἅμα ἐπείληπταί πως τῆς κατ᾽ ἐνέργειαν μεταφορᾶς
τῆς προειρημένης, τὴν μάχην φρίσσειν εἰπὼν ὥσπερ
ζῷον.

(83) Δεῖ μέντοι μὴ λανθάνειν, ὅτι ἔνιαι μεταφοραὶ
μικροπρέπειαν ποιοῦσι μᾶλλον ἢ μέγεθος, καίτοι
τῆς μεταφορᾶς πρὸς ὄγκον λαμβανομένης, ὡς τὸ
"ἀμφὶ δ᾽ ἐσάλπιγξεν μέγας οὐρανός"· οὐρανὸν γὰρ
ὅλον ἠχοῦντα οὐκ ἐχρῆν προσεικάσαι ἠχούσῃ σάλ-
πιγγι, πλὴν εἰ μή τις ἄρα[3] ἀπολογοῖτο ὑπὲρ τοῦ
Ὁμήρου λέγων, ὡς οὕτως[4] ἤχησεν μέγας οὐρανός,
ὡς ἂν ἠχήσειεν σαλπίζων ὅλος οὐρανός. (84) ἑτέραν
οὖν ἐπινοήσωμεν μεταφορὰν μικρότητος αἰτίαν
γινομένην μᾶλλον ἢ μεγέθους· δεῖ γὰρ ἐκ τῶν μειζόνων μεταφέρειν εἰς τὰ μικρά, οὐ τὸ ἐναντίον, οἷον ὡς
ὁ Ξενοφῶν φησιν, "ἐπεὶ δὲ πορευομένων ἐξεκύμηνέ

---

[1] ἤπερ edd.: εἴπερ P.   [2] καὶ τὸν add. Spengel.
[3] ἄρα edd.: ἅμα P.   [4] ὡς οὕτως Greg.: ὡσαύτως P.

passage describing the arrow, "sharp-pointed, eager to
shoot into the crowd" and in the words "high-arched,
foam-crested."[a] All such expressions as "foam-crested"
and "eager" activate a personification. (82) Some things
are, however, expressed more clearly and properly by
metaphor than by the actual proper terms, for example
"the battle shuddered."[b] No change of phrasing to introduce the proper terms could convey the meaning with
greater truth or clarity. Homer has renamed as "shuddering battle" the clash of spears and the low, continuous
sound they make. In so doing he has simultaneously
exploited the personifying metaphor of our earlier discussion when he represents the battle shuddering as if alive.

(83) We must, however, keep in mind that some
metaphors produce triviality rather than grandeur, even
though the metaphor is intended to impress, for example
"all around the mighty heaven trumpeted."[c] The whole
heaven resounding ought not to have been compared
to a resounding trumpet— unless perhaps a defence of
Homer could be made that the mighty heaven resounded
in the way in which the whole heaven would resound if it
were trumpeting. (84) So let us consider a second example of metaphor which has a trivial rather than grand
effect. Metaphors should compare the smaller to the
greater, not the reverse. Xenophon, for example, says,

[a] Hom. *Il.* 4.126 and 13.799 (cf. § 64, illustrating asyndeton).

[b] Hom. *Il.* 13.339.

[c] Hom. *Il.* 21.388, a controversial metaphor, cf. Longinus 9.6,
Pliny, *Epist.* 9.26.6. Since it may be defended, Demetrius adds a
second example, which incontrovertibly trivialises.

τι τῆς[1] φάλαγγος." τὴν γὰρ τῆς τάξεως παρεκτρο-
πὴν ἐκκυμαινούσῃ θαλάσσῃ εἴκασεν καὶ προσωνό-
μασεν. εἰ δέ τις μεταβαλὼν εἴποι ἐκφαλαγγίσασαν
τὴν θάλασσαν, τάχα μὲν οὐδὲ οἰκείως μετοίσει,
πάντῃ δὲ πάντως μικροπρεπῶς.

(85) Ἔνιοι δὲ καὶ ἀσφαλίζονται τὰς μεταφορὰς
ἐπιθέτοις ἐπιφερομένοις, ὅταν αὐτοῖς κινδυνώδεις
δοκῶσιν, ὡς ὁ Θέογνις παρατίθεται τῷ τόξῳ "φόρμιγγα[2] ἄχορδον" ἐπὶ τοῦ τῷ τόξῳ βάλλοντος· ἡ μὲν
γὰρ φόρμιγξ κινδυνῶδες ἐπὶ τοῦ τόξου, τῷ δὲ[3]
ἀχόρδῳ ἠσφάλισται.

(86) Πάντων δὲ καὶ τῶν ἄλλων ἡ συνήθεια καὶ
μάλιστα μεταφορῶν διδάσκαλος· μικροῦ γὰρ [σχε-
δὸν][4] πάντα μεταφέρουσα λανθάνει διὰ τὸ ἀσφαλῶς
μεταφέρειν, λευκήν τε φωνὴν λέγουσα καὶ ὀξὺν
ἄνθρωπον καὶ τραχὺ ἦθος καὶ μακρὸν ῥήτορα καὶ
τἆλλα, ὅσα οὕτω μεταφέρεται μουσικῶς, ὥστε ὅμοια
δοκεῖν τοῖς κυρίοις. (87) τοῦτον <οὖν>[5] ἐγὼ κανόνα
τίθεμαι τῆς ἐν λόγοις μεταφορᾶς, τὴν τῆς συνηθείας
τέχνην εἴτε φύσιν. οὕτω γοῦν ἔνια μετήνεγκεν ἡ
συνήθεια καλῶς, ὥστε οὐδὲ κυρίων ἔτι ἐδεήθημεν,
ἀλλὰ μεμένηκεν ἡ μεταφορὰ κατέχουσα τὸν τοῦ

---

[1] τι Greg., Xen. codd.: om. P.
[2] τῷ τόξῳ φόρμιγγα Nauck: τὸν τοξοφόρμιγγα P.
[3] τῷ M: τὸ P.
[4] σχεδὸν del. Roberts.
[5] οὖν addidi: *autem* Lat.

"on the march a part of the phalanx surged out."[a] He compared a swerve from the line of march to a surging of the sea, and gave it that name. But if conversely you were to say that the sea swerved from its line of march, the metaphor would possibly not even fit; in any case it would be utterly and completely trivial.

(85) When they consider their metaphors risky, some writers try to make them safe by adding epithets; for example Theognis refers to the bow as a "lyre with tuneless strings,"[b] when describing an archer in the act of shooting. The image of the bow as lyre is bold, but it is made safe by the qualification "with tuneless strings."

(86) Usage[c] is our teacher everywhere, but particularly in the case of metaphors. Usage, in fact, expresses almost everything in metaphors, but they are so safe that we hardly notice them. It calls a voice pure, a man sharp, a character harsh, a speaker long, and so on. All are applied so harmoniously that they pass for the proper terms. (87) So my own rule for the use of metaphor is the art—or natural instinct—of usage. Metaphors have in some cases been so well established by usage that we no longer need the proper terms, and the metaphor has usurped the

[a] Xen. *Anab.* 1.8.18.

[b] TrGF i. Theognis F 1; cf. Ar. *Rhet.* 1413a1.

[c] For appeal to usage, cf. §§ 69, 91, and 96; for its role as διδάσκαλος or κανών, cf. Quint. 1.6.3 *loquendi magistra*, Hor. *Ars Po.* 72 *norma loquendi*.

§§ 86–87 discuss metaphors of ordinary speech, examples of usage so apt that we no longer try to find a proper term. Compare the necessary metaphor in Cic. *De Or.* 3.155 and Quint. 8.6.6, both with similar examples, e.g. *durum hominem* and *gemmare vites*.

DEMETRIUS

κυρίου τόπον, ὡς "ὁ τῆς ἀμπέλου ὀφθαλμὸς" καὶ εἴ
τι ἕτερον τοιοῦτον. (88) σφόνδυλος μέντοι καὶ κλεὶς
τὰ ἐπὶ τοῦ σώματος καὶ κτένες οὐ κατὰ μεταφορὰν
ὠνόμασται, ἀλλὰ καθ' ὁμοιότητα διὰ τὸ ἐοικέναι τὸ
μὲν κτενὶ μέρος, τὸ δὲ κλειδί, τὸ δὲ σφονδύλῳ.

(89) Ἐπὰν μέντοι εἰκασίαν ποιῶμεν τὴν μεταφοράν, ὡς προλέλεκται, στοχαστέον τοῦ συντόμου, καὶ
τοῦ μηδὲν πλέον τοῦ[1] "ὥσπερ" προτιθέναι, ἐπεί τοι
ἀντ' εἰκασίας παραβολὴ ἔσται ποιητική, οἷον τὸ τοῦ
Ξενοφῶντος, "ὥσπερ δὲ κύων γενναῖος ἀπρονοήτως
ἐπὶ κάπρον φέρεται," καὶ "ὥσπερ ἵππος λυθεὶς διὰ
πεδίου γαυριῶν καὶ ἀπολακτίζων"· ταῦτα γὰρ οὐκ
εἰκασίαις ἔτι ἔοικεν, ἀλλὰ παραβολαῖς ποιητικαῖς.
(90) τὰς δὲ παραβολὰς ταύτας οὔτε ῥᾳδίως ἐν τοῖς
πεζοῖς λόγοις τιθέναι δεῖ, οὔτε ἄνευ πλείστης φυλα-
κῆς. καὶ περὶ μεταφορᾶς μὲν <τοσαῦτα>[2] ὡς τύπῳ
εἰπεῖν.

(91) Ληπτέον δὲ καὶ σύνθετα ὀνόματα, οὐ τὰ
διθυραμβικῶς συγκείμενα, οἷον "θεοτεράτους πλά-
νας," οὐδὲ "ἄστρων δορύπυρον στρατόν," ἀλλ' ἐοικότα τοῖς ὑπὸ τῆς συνηθείας[3] συγκειμένοις· καθόλου
γὰρ ταύτην κανόνα ποιοῦμαι πάσης ὀνομασίας,

[1] τοῦ μηδὲ τὸ P[1]: μηδὲν πλέον τοῦ P[2] in mg.
[2] τοσαῦτα add. Schneider.
[3] συνηθείας Finckh: ἀληθείας P.

[a] The eye is normal Greek for the bud of a plant or tree, e.g.
Xen. *Oeconomicus* 19.10.

406

place of the proper term, for example the eye of the vine,[a] and so forth. (88) The parts of the body,[b] however, which are called the "disk" (vertebra), the "key" (collarbone), and the "combs" (back of the hand) derive their names not from metaphor but from the physical resemblance.

(89) When we turn a metaphor into a simile in the way I described,[c] we must aim at conciseness, and do no more than prefix "like," or else we shall have a poetic comparison instead of a simile. Take, for example, "like a gallant hound which recklessly charges a boar" (from Xenophon)[d] and "like a horse let loose, kicking and proudly prancing over the plain."[e] Such descriptions no longer seem similes but poetic comparisons, (90) and poetic comparisons should not be used freely in prose nor without the greatest caution. This concludes my outline on the subject of metaphor.

(91) Next, we should use compound words, but not those in dithyrambic formations, for example "god-prodigied wanderings" or "the fiery-speared army of the stars."[f] They should be like those formed by usage. In general, in all word formation I regard usage as the

[b] The connection of thought is unclear, but the term metaphor is now restricted to analogical metaphor (cf. § 78).

[c] See § 80.

[d] Xen. *Cyrop.* 1.4.21 (cf. § 274).

[e] Author unknown, an imitation of a famous simile in Hom. *Il.* 6.506ff.

> ὡς δ' ὅτε τις στατὸς ἵππος, ἀκοστήσας ἐπὶ φάτνῃ,
> δεσμὸν ἀπορρήξας θείῃ πεδίοιο κροαίνων . . .
> κυδιόων.

[f] PMG *Adesp.* 962(a) and (b).

νομοθέτας λέγουσαν καὶ ἀρχιτέκτονας, καὶ τοιάδε
πολλὰ ἔτερα ἀσφαλῶς συντιθεῖσαν. (92) ἔξει μέντοι
τὸ σύνθετον ὄνομα ὁμοῦ καὶ ποικιλίαν τινὰ ἐκ τῆς
συνθέσεως καὶ μέγεθος, καὶ ἅμα καὶ συντομίαν
τινά. ὄνομα γὰρ τεθήσεται ἀντὶ ὅλου τοῦ λόγου,
οἷον ἂν τὴν τοῦ σίτου κομιδὴν σιτοπομπίαν λέγῃς·
πολὺ γὰρ οὕτω μεῖζον. τάχα δ' ἂν καὶ λυθέντος
ὀνόματος εἰς λόγον ἕτερον τρόπον μεῖζον γένοιτο,
οἷον σίτου πομπὴ ἀντὶ σιτοπομπίας. (93) ὄνομα δ'
ἀντὶ λόγου τίθεται, οἷον ὡς ὁ Ξενοφῶν φησιν ὅτι
οὐκ ἦν λαβεῖν ὄνον ἄγριον, εἰ μὴ οἱ ἱππεῖς διαστάν-
τες θηρῷεν διαδεχόμενοι, ὀνόματι δηλῶν[1] ὅτι οἱ μὲν
ὄπισθεν ἐδίωκον, οἱ δ' ἀπήντων ὑπελαύνοντες
πρόσω, ὥστε τὸν ὄνον ἐν μέσῳ ἀπολαμβάνεσθαι.
φυλάττεσθαι μέντοι δεῖ πολλὰ[2] τιθέναι τὰ διπλᾶ
ὀνόματα· τοῦτο γὰρ ἔξεισι[3] λόγου πεζοῦ τὸ εἶδος.

(94) Τὰ δὲ πεποιημένα ὀνόματα ὁρίζονται μὲν τὰ
κατὰ μίμησιν ἐκφερόμενα πάθους ἢ πράγματος,
οἷον ὡς τὸ "σίζε" καὶ τὸ "λάπτοντες," (95) ποιεῖ δὲ
[μάλιστα][4] μεγαλοπρέπειαν διὰ τὸ οἷον ψόφοις ἐοικέναι καὶ μάλιστα τῷ ξένῳ· οὐ γὰρ ὄντα ὀνόματα
λέγει ἀλλὰ τότε γινόμενα, καὶ ἅμα σοφόν τι φαίνεται ὀνόματος καινοῦ γένεσις, οἷον συνηθείας· ἔοικεν

---

[1] δηλῶν Roberts: οἷον P.   [2] δεῖ πολλὰ Spengel: διπλᾶ P.
[3] ἔξεισι Victorius: ἔξει P.   [4] μάλιστα del. Richards.

---

[a] A rare meaning of πομπή, e.g. Th. 4.108.1.
[b] Xen. Anab. 1.5.2. The text is uncertain but concerns the
terse effect of the compound verb, διαδεχόμενοι, "in relays."

arbiter, usage which speaks of "lawgivers" and "master builders," and forms many other such safe compounds. (92) A compound word will usually, from the very fact that it is composite, have variety, grandeur, and simultaneously conciseness. One word will stand for an entire phrase. For instance, you might speak of "grain convoy" instead of "the transport of grain," using a much more striking expression. Still, the greater impact may sometimes result from the converse process of resolving a word into a phrase, "convoy[a] of grain," for instance, instead of "grain convoy." (93) An example of a word replacing a phrase is Xenophon's sentence: "It was not possible to capture a wild ass unless the mounted men separated and hunted in relays."[b] By the single word "relays" he says that some horsemen gave chase from behind, while others rode forward to meet them, so that the wild ass was caught in the middle. The use, however, of many compounds[c] should be avoided, since it oversteps the limits of prose.

(94) Onomatopoeic words are defined as those which are uttered in imitation of an emotion or action, for example "hissed" and "lapping" (*size* and *laptontes*).[d] (95) They create grandeur by their resemblance to inarticulate sounds, and above all by their novelty. The speaker is not using existing words but words which are only then coming into existence, and at the same time the creation of a new word is thought clever, as though it were the creation

[c] Cf. e.g. Ar. *Rhet.* 1404b23. Less probably, keeping the text of the mss, translate "The doubling of double compounds . . . ," a warning against triple compounds, cf. Ar. *Po.* 1457a34.

[d] Hom. *Od.* 9.394; *Il.* 16.161 (cf. § 220).

γοῦν <ὁ>[1] ὀνοματουργῶν τοῖς πρώτοις θεμένοις τὰ
ὀνόματα. <. . .>[2]

(96) Στοχαστέον <οὖν>[3] πρῶτον μὲν τοῦ σαφοῦς
ἐν τῷ ποιουμένῳ ὀνόματι καὶ συνήθους, ἔπειτα τῆς
ὁμοιότητος πρὸς τὰ κείμενα ὀνόματα, ὡς μὴ φρυγί-
ζειν ἢ σκυθίζειν τις δόξει μεταξὺ ἑλληνίζων τοῖς
ὀνόμασι.[4] (97) ποιητέον μέντοι ἤτοι τὰ μὴ ὠνομασ-
μένα, οἷον ὁ τὰ τύμπανα καὶ τἆλλα τῶν μαλθακῶν
ὄργανα κιναιδίας[5] εἰπὼν καὶ Ἀριστοτέλης τὸν ἐλε-
φαντιστήν· ἢ παρὰ τὰ κείμενα παρονομάζοντα
αὑτόν, οἷον ὡς τὸν σκαφίτην τις ἔφη τὸν τὴν σκά-
φην ἐρέσσοντα, καὶ Ἀριστοτέλης τὸν αὑτίτην οἷον
τὸν μόνον αὑτὸν ὄντα. (98) Ξενοφῶν δὲ "ἠλέλιξέ"[6]
φησιν "ὁ στρατός,"[7] τὴν τοῦ ἐλελεῦ ἀναβόησιν ἣν
ἀνεβόα ὁ στρατὸς[8] συνεχῶς παραποιήσας ὀνόματι.

[1] ὁ add. Rutherford.
[2] lacunam statui, ut transeamus ad conficta et declinata, cf.
etiam § 98 ὡς ἔφην.
[3] οὖν addidi.
[4] ἑλληνίζων τοῖς ὀνόμασι Lockwood: ἑλληνικοῖς ὀνόμασι
P: ἑλληνικῶν ὀνομάτων Dresd.
[5] an κιναίδια?
[6] ἠλέλιξε Victorius: ἤλλαξεν P.
[7] στρατός Victorius: στρατηγός P.
[8] στρατός Victorius: στρατηγός P.

[a] §§ 94–95 recognise only onomatopoeic neologism, §§ 97–98

of a new usage. So the creator of new words is like those who originally created language. <...>[a]

(96) The first aim in the formation of neologisms is to be clear and fit usage; the next, to follow the analogy of established words, in order to avoid the appearance of introducing Phrygian or Scythian speech in our Greek. (97) Neologisms should be either newly invented forms, as was done by the person who described the drums and other musical instruments of the effeminate priests as "lecheries,"[b] or by Aristotle when he invented "ele-phanteer";[c] or the writer may create secondary meanings from existing words, for example when someone gave the name "boatman"[d] to someone rowing a boat, and Aristotle called a man who lived alone by himself "selfish."[e] (98) Xenophon similarly says, "the army hurrah'd,"[f] denoting by the derivative the shout "hurrah" which the army

---

abruptly introduce neologism from compounds and derivatives, and in § 98 "as I said" lacks reference. I posit a lacuna, with the general sense, "There are also derivative neologisms; they are full of risk, even in poetry." For the three types, cf. *fingere, confingere, declinare* in Varro, *Ling. Lat.* 5.7, a classification of the Alexandrians.

[b] Author unknown.

[c] Ar. *Hist. Anim.* 497b28.

[d] Author unknown, cf. Strabo 17.1.49. The form could alternatively (though it is not attested) have the meaning "digger" (cf. σκαφεύς).

[e] Ar. *fr.* 668 Rose (cf. §§ 144, 164). The translation attempts a similar pun on self(ish)/being by one's self. Elsewhere αὐτίτης refers to homemade wine, i.e. wine made by one's self.

[f] Xen. *Anab.* 5.2.14. Here (also *Anab.* 1.8.18) it refers to the cry *eleleu*, but normally it means "to whirl around, cause to vibrate."

ἐπισφαλὲς μέντοι τοὖργον, ὡς[1] ἔφην, καὶ αὐτοῖς τοῖς
ποιηταῖς. καὶ τὸ διπλοῦν μέντοι ὄνομα εἶδος ἂν εἴη
πεποιημένου ὀνόματος· πᾶν γὰρ τὸ συντιθέμενον ἔκ
τινων γέγονεν δηλονότι.

(99) Μεγαλεῖον δέ τί ἐστι καὶ ἡ ἀλληγορία, καὶ
μάλιστα ἐν ταῖς ἀπειλαῖς, οἷον ὡς ὁ Διονύσιος, ὅτι
"οἱ τέττιγες αὐτοῖς ᾄσονται[2] χαμόθεν."[3] (100) εἰ δ'
οὕτως ἁπλῶς εἶπεν, ὅτι τεμεῖ τὴν Λοκρίδα χώραν,
καὶ ὀργιλώτερος ἂν ἐφάνη καὶ εὐτελέστερος. νῦν δὲ
ὥσπερ συγκαλύμματι τοῦ λόγου τῇ ἀλληγορίᾳ
κέχρηται· πᾶν γὰρ τὸ ὑπονοούμενον φοβερώτερον,
καὶ ἄλλος εἰκάζει ἄλλο τι· ὃ δὲ σαφὲς καὶ φανερόν,[4]
καταφρονεῖσθαι εἰκός, ὥσπερ τοὺς ἀποδεδυμένους.
(101) διὸ καὶ τὰ μυστήρια ἐν ἀλληγορίαις λέγεται
πρὸς ἔκπληξιν καὶ φρίκην, ὥσπερ ἐν σκότῳ[5] καὶ
νυκτί. ἔοικε δὲ καὶ ἡ ἀλληγορία τῷ σκότῳ[6] καὶ τῇ
νυκτί. (102) φυλάττεσθαι μέντοι κἀπὶ ταύτης τὸ
συνεχές, ὡς μὴ αἴνιγμα ὁ λόγος ἡμῖν γένηται, οἷον
τὸ ἐπὶ τῆς σικύας τῆς ἰατρικῆς· "ἄνδρ' εἶδον πυρὶ
χαλκὸν ἐπ' ἀνέρι κολλήσαντα." καὶ οἱ Λάκωνες
πολλὰ ἐν ἀλληγορίαις ἔλεγον ἐκφοβοῦντες, οἷον τὸ
"Διονύσιος ἐν Κορίνθῳ" πρὸς Φίλιππον, καὶ ἄλλα
τοιαῦτα οὐκ ὀλίγα.

---

[1] ὡς Victorius: καὶ ὡς P.
[2] ᾄσονται edd.: ἀρῶνται P.
[3] χαμόθεν M (cf. § 243): χαμάθεν P.
[4] φανερὸν Goeller: φοβερὸν P.

kept continuously shouting. The practice is, however, as I said,[a] full of risk even for the poets themselves. Note too that any compound is a form of neologism, for anything which is composite must, of course, derive from preexisting parts.

(99) Allegory is also impressive, particularly in threats, for example that of Dionysius, "their cicadas will sing from the ground."[b] (100) If he had said openly that he would ravage the land of Locris, he would have shown more anger but less dignity. As it is, he has shrouded his words, as it were, in allegory. What is implied always strikes more terror, since its meaning is open to different interpretations, whereas what is clear and plain is apt to be despised, like men who are stripped of their clothes. (101) This is why the mysteries are revealed in allegories, to inspire the shuddering and awe associated with darkness and night. In fact allegory is not unlike darkness and night. (102) Here again in the case of allegory we should avoid a succession of them, or our words become a riddle, as in the description of the surgeon's cupping glass: "I saw a man who had with fire welded bronze to a man."[c] The Spartans too often spoke in allegory to evoke fear, as in the message to Philip, "Dionysius in Corinth,"[d] and many other similar threats.

[a] See note on § 95.
[b] Stesichorus according to Ar. *Rhet.* 1395a1–2 and 1412a22–23 (= PMG 281(b)); cf. § 243.
[c] Cleobulina 1.1 West; cf. Ar. *Rhet.* 1405b1.
[d] Cf. §§ 8, 241.

---

[5] σκότῳ Victorius: αὐτῷ P.
[6] σκότῳ Victorius: αυτῷ (sic) P.

(103) Ἡ συντομία δὲ πῆ μὲν μεγαλοπρεπής, καὶ μάλιστα ἡ ἀποσιώπησις· ἔνια γὰρ μὴ ῥηθέντα μείζονα φαίνεται καὶ ὑπονοηθέντα μᾶλλον· πῆ δὲ μικροπρεπής. καὶ γὰρ ἐν διλογίαις γίνεται μέγεθος, οἷον ὡς Ξενοφῶν, "τὰ δὲ ἅρματα ἐφέρετο," φησί, "τὰ μὲν δι᾽ αὐτῶν τῶν φιλίων, τὰ δὲ καὶ δι᾽ αὐτῶν τῶν πολεμίων." πολὺ γὰρ οὕτω μεῖζον, ἢ εἴπερ ὧδ᾽ εἶπεν, "καὶ διὰ τῶν φιλίων καὶ διὰ τῶν πολεμίων αὐτῶν." (104) πολλαχοῦ δὲ καὶ τὸ πλάγιον μεῖζον τοῦ εὐθέος, οἷον "ἡ δὲ γνώμη ἦν, ὡς εἰς τὰς τάξεις τῶν Ἑλλήνων ἐλώντων¹ καὶ διακοψόντων" ἀντὶ τοῦ "διενοοῦντο ἐλάσαι καὶ διακόψαι." (105) συμβέβληται δὲ καὶ ἡ ὁμοιότης τῶν ὀνομάτων καὶ ἡ δυσφωνία ἡ φαινομένη· καὶ γὰρ τὸ δύσφωνον πολλαχοῦ ὀγκηρόν, ὥσπερ "Αἴας δ᾽ ὁ μέγας αἰὲν ἐφ᾽ Ἕκτορι." πολὺ γὰρ μᾶλλον τὸν Αἴαντα μέγαν ἐνέφηνεν ἡ τῶν δύο σύμπληξις τῆς ἑπταβοείου ἀσπίδος.

(106) Τὸ δὲ ἐπιφώνημα καλούμενον ὁρίζοιτο μὲν ἄν τις λέξιν ἐπικοσμοῦσαν, ἔστι δὲ τὸ μεγαλοπρεπέστατον ἐν τοῖς λόγοις. τῆς γὰρ λέξεως ἡ μὲν ὑπηρετεῖ, ἡ δὲ ἐπικοσμεῖ. ὑπηρετεῖ μὲν ἡ τοιάδε,

οἵαν τὰν ὑάκινθον ἐν οὔρεσι ποιμένες ἄνδρες
ποσσὶ καταστείβουσιν,

ἐπικοσμεῖ δὲ τὸ ἐπιφερόμενον τὸ "χαμαὶ δέ τε πόρ-

---

¹ ἐλώντων Xen. codd.: ἐλθόντων P.

ᵃ Xen. *Anab.* 1.8.20. Compare anthypallage in § 60.

(103) In certain cases conciseness, and especially aposiopesis, produce grandeur, since some things seem more
significant when they are not openly expressed but only
implied. In other cases, however, triviality is the result.
In fact, grandeur may result from repeating words, as in
Xenophon, "The chariots rushed on, some of them right
through the ranks of their friends, some right through the
ranks of their enemies."[a] This wording is far more striking
than if he had said, "right through the ranks of both
friends and enemies alike." (104) Often too an indirect
construction is more impressive than the direct, for example "the intention was that of charging the ranks of the
Greeks and cutting their way through,"[b] rather than "they
intended to charge and cut their way through." (105) The
assonance of the words and a conspicuous lack of
euphony have also contributed to its impact. For
cacophony is often impressive, as in the words, "mighty
Ajax aimed always at Hector,"[c] where the clash of the two
sounds brings out the greatness of Ajax more vividly than
his famous shield with its seven layers of oxhide.

(106) What is called the epiphoneme may be defined
as additional decorative detail. It is the most imposing
kind of verbal grandeur. Language can be functional; it
can also be decorative. It is functional in a passage like
this, "as the hyacinth in the mountains is by shepherds
trampled underfoot," but what comes next adds decora-

[b] Xen. *Anab.* 1.8.10. Indirect construction is at least primarily the use of subordinate participial constructions, cf. § 198.
The example (so § 105) also illustrates assonance (from the endings, *-on/-on/-ontôn/-ontôn*, cf. § 25) and clashing sounds (including hiatus of long syllables, cf. § 72).

[c] Hom. *Il.* 16.358 (cf. § 48).

φυρον ἄνθος"· ἐπενήνεκται γὰρ τοῦτο τοῖς προεξ-
ενηνεγμένοις[1] κόσμος σαφῶς καὶ κάλλος. (107)
μεστὴ δὲ τούτων καὶ ἡ Ὁμήρου ποίησις, οἷον

ἐκ καπνοῦ κατέθηκ', ἐπεὶ οὐκέτι τοῖσιν ἐῴκει,
οἷς τὸ πάρος Τροίηνδε κιὼν κατέλειπεν
                Ὀδυσσεύς.
πρὸς δ' ἔτι καὶ τόδε μεῖζον ἐπὶ φρεσὶν ἔμβαλε
                δαίμων,
μήπως οἰνωθέντες, ἔριν στήσαντες ἐν ὑμῖν,
ἀλλήλους τρώσητε.

εἶτα ἐπιφωνεῖ, "αὐτὸς γὰρ ἐφέλκεται ἄνδρα σίδη-
ρος." (108) καὶ καθόλου τὸ ἐπιφώνημα τοῖς τῶν
πλουσίων ἔοικεν ἐπιδείγμασιν, γείσοις λέγω καὶ
τριγλύφοις καὶ πορφύραις πλατείαις· οἷον γάρ τι
καὶ αὐτὸ τοῦ ἐν λόγοις πλούτου σημεῖόν ἐστιν.

(109) Δόξειεν δ' ἂν καὶ τὸ ἐνθύμημα ἐπιφωνήματος εἶδός τι εἶναι, οὐκ ὂν μέν (οὐ γὰρ κόσμου
ἕνεκεν, ἀλλὰ ἀποδείξεως παραλαμβάνεται), πλὴν
ἐπιλεγόμενόν γε ἐπιφωνηματικῶς. (110) ὡσαύτως δὲ
καὶ ἡ γνώμη ἐπιφωνουμένῳ τινὶ ἔοικεν ἐπὶ προειρη-
μένοις, ἀλλ' οὐδ' αὕτη ἐπιφώνημά ἐστι· καὶ γὰρ
προλέγεται πολλάκις, λαμβάνει μέντοι χώραν ποτὲ
ἐπιφωνήματος. (111) τὸ δέ, "νήπιος οὐδ' ἄρ' ἔμελλε
κακὰς ὑπὸ κῆρας ἀλύξειν," οὐδ' αὐτὸ ἐπιφώνημα ἂν

---

[1] προεξηνεγμένοις Lockwood: προενηνεγμένοις P.

[a] Sappho 105(c) L–P.

tive detail, "and on the ground the purple flower. . . ."[a]
For this addition to the preceding lines clearly adds decoration and beauty. (107) Homer's poetry is full of examples, for example

> "I have put the weapons away, out of the smoke,
> since they no longer look
> like those which Odysseus left behind earlier when
> he went to Troy.
> Moreover a god has put this yet greater fear in my
> heart,
> that you may become drunk, start up a quarrel
> and wound each other."

Then he adds the detail, "for iron of itself draws men to
fight."[b] (108) In general, the epiphoneme resembles the
things which only the rich display—cornices, triglyphs,
and broad bands of purple.[c] For it is in itself a sort of rich-
ness in speech.

(109) The enthymeme might be thought to be a kind
of epiphoneme. But it is not, since it is used for proof, not
decoration—though admittedly it may come last in the
manner of an epiphoneme. (110) Similarly a maxim
resembles in some ways a detail added to a previous statement, but it in its turn is not an epiphoneme, since it
often comes first and only sometimes takes the final position of an epiphoneme. (111) Again, take the line "the
fool! he was not going to escape hard fate";[d] that would

---

[b] Hom. *Od.* 16.288–94 = 19.7–13 (with omissions).

[c] In juxtaposition to cornices and triglyphs, the broad bands
of purple will be an architectural feature, such as bands of paint
on metopes or walls. Less probably, it is purple cloth, as in the
"purple patch" of Hor. *Ars Po.* 15–16.   [d] Hom. *Il.* 12.113.

εἴη· οὐ γὰρ ἐπιλέγεται οὐδὲ ἐπικοσμεῖ, οὐδ' ὅλως
ἐπιφωνήματι ἔοικεν ἀλλὰ προσφωνήματι ἢ ἐπικερ-
τομήματι.

(112) Τὸ δὲ ποιητικὸν ἐν λόγοις ὅτι μὲν μεγαλοπρεπές, καὶ τυφλῷ δῆλόν φασι, πλὴν οἱ μὲν γυμνῇ
πάνυ χρῶνται τῇ μιμήσει τῶν ποιητῶν, μᾶλλον δὲ
οὐ μιμήσει ἀλλὰ μεταθέσει, καθάπερ Ἡρόδοτος.
(113) Θουκυδίδης μέντοι κἂν λάβῃ παρὰ ποιητοῦ τι,
ἰδίως αὐτῷ χρώμενος ἴδιον τὸ ληφθὲν ποιεῖ, οἷον ὁ
μὲν ποιητὴς ἐπὶ τῆς Κρήτης ἔφη,

Κρήτη τις γαῖ' ἔστι[1] μέσῳ ἐνὶ οἴνοπι πόντῳ,
καλὴ καὶ πίειρα, περίρρυτος.

ὁ μὲν δὴ ἐπὶ τοῦ μεγέθους ἐχρήσατο τῷ "περίρρυτος," ὁ δὲ Θουκυδίδης ὁμονοεῖν τοὺς Σικελιώτας
καλὸν οἴεται εἶναι, γῆς ὄντας μιᾶς καὶ περιρρύτου,
καὶ ταῦτα[2] πάντα εἰπών, γῆν τε ἀντὶ νήσου καὶ
περίρρυτον ὡσαύτως, ὅμως ἕτερα λέγειν δοκεῖ, διότι
οὐχ ὡς πρὸς μέγεθος ἀλλὰ πρὸς ὁμόνοιαν αὐτοῖς
ἐχρήσατο. περὶ μὲν δὴ μεγαλοπρεπείας τοσαῦτα.

(114) Ὥσπερ δὲ παράκειται φαῦλά τινα ἀστείοις
τισίν, οἷον θάρρει μὲν τὸ θράσος, ἡ δ' αἰσχύνη τῇ
αἰδοῖ, τὸν αὐτὸν τρόπον καὶ τῆς ἑρμηνείας τοῖς
χαρακτῆρσιν παράκεινται διημαρτημένοι τινές. πρῶ-

---

[1] γαῖ' ἔστι codd. Hom.: γ' ἐστὶ P.
[2] ταῦτα P.

not be an epiphoneme either. For it is not a later addition, nor is it decorative, nor is it in any way like an epiphoneme, but rather an exclamatory address or a rebuke.

(112) Poetic vocabulary in prose adds grandeur, as, in the words of the proverb, even a blind man can see.[a] Still, some writers imitate the poets quite crudely, or rather, they do not imitate but plagiarise them, as Herodotus has done. (113) Contrast Thucydides. Even if he borrows vocabulary from a poet, he uses it in his own way and makes it his own property. Homer, for instance, says of Crete: "There is a land of Crete, in the midst of the wine-dark sea, beautiful, fertile, wave-surrounded."[b] Now Homer used the word "wave-surrounded" to be impressive. Thucydides, for his part, thinks it right that the Sicilians should act in unity, as they belong to one single "wave-surrounded land."[c] He uses the same words as Homer, "land" instead of "island" and "wave-surrounded," yet he seems to be saying something different. The reason is that he uses the words not to impress but to recommend unity. This concludes my account of the grand style.

(114) But just as in the sphere of ethics certain bad qualities lie close to certain good ones (rashness, for example, next to bravery, and shame to modest respect), so too the types of style have neighbouring faulty styles.

[a] Cf. § 239, Paroem. Gr. ii.156.

[b] Hom. Od. 19.172–73.

[c] Th. 4.64.3 (the speaker is Hermocrates of Syracuse) τὸ δὲ ξύμπαν γείτονας ὄντας καὶ ξυνοίκους μιᾶς χώρας καὶ περιρρύτου καὶ ὄνομα ἓν κεκλημένους Σικελιώτας. The use of περίρρυτος in Hdt. 4.42.2 and 4.45.1 may make the general reference to Herodotus in § 112 more pointed.

DEMETRIUS

τὰ δὲ περὶ τοῦ γειτνιῶντος τῷ μεγαλοπρεπεῖ λέξο
μεν. ὄνομα μὲν οὖν αὐτῷ ψυχρόν, ὁρίζεται δὲ τὸ
ψυχρὸν Θεόφραστος οὕτως, ψυχρόν ἐστι τὸ ὑπερ
βάλλον τὴν οἰκείαν ἀπαγγελίαν, οἷον "ἀπυνδάκωτος
οὐ τραπεζοῦται κύλιξ," ἀντὶ τοῦ ἀπύθμενος ἐπὶ τρα
πέζης κύλιξ οὐ τίθεται. τὸ γὰρ πρᾶγμα σμικρὸν ὂν
οὐ δέχεται ὄγκον τοσοῦτον λέξεως.

(115) Γίνεται μέντοι καὶ τὸ ψυχρὸν ἐν τρισίν,
ὥσπερ καὶ τὸ μεγαλοπρεπές· ἢ γὰρ ἐν διανοίᾳ,
καθάπερ ἐπὶ τοῦ Κύκλωπος λιθοβολοῦντος τὴν ναῦν
τοῦ Ὀδυσσέως ἔφη τις, "φερομένου τοῦ λίθου αἶγες
ἐνέμοντο ἐν αὐτῷ." ἐκ γὰρ τοῦ ὑπερβεβλημένου τῆς
διανοίας καὶ ἀδυνάτου ἡ ψυχρότης. (116) ἐν δὲ λέξει
ὁ Ἀριστοτέλης φησὶ γίνεσθαι τετραχῶς, <. . .>[1] ὡς
Ἀλκιδάμας "ὑγρὸν ἱδρῶτα"· ἢ ἐν συνθέτῳ, ὅταν
διθυραμβώδης συντεθῇ ἡ δίπλωσις τοῦ ὀνόματος,
ὡς τὸ "ἐρημοπλάνος" ἔφη τις, καὶ εἴ[2] τι ἄλλο οὕτως
ὑπέρογκον. γίνεται δὲ καὶ ἐν μεταφορᾷ τὸ ψυχρόν,
"τρέμοντα καὶ ὠχρὰ τὰ πράγματα.[3]" τετραχῶς μὲν
οὖν κατὰ τὴν λέξιν οὕτως ἂν γίγνοιτο. (117) σύνθε
σις δὲ ψυχρὰ ἡ μὴ εὔρυθμος,[4] ἀλλὰ ἄρυθμος οὖσα
καὶ διὰ πάντων μακρὰν[5] ἔχουσα, ὥσπερ ἡ τοιάδε,

[1] lacunam stat. Victorius.
[2] εἰ add. edd.
[3] πράγματα Victorius (cf. Ar. *Rhet.* 1406b9): γράμματα P.
[4] εὔρυθμος Finckh: ἐρρυθμος (sic) P.
[5] μακρὰν Schneider: μακρὸν P.

420

We will discuss first the faulty style which is adjacent to
the grand style. Its name is the frigid style, and frigidity is
defined by Theophrastus[a] as "that which exceeds its
appropriate form of expression," for example "an unbased
cup is not tabled," instead of "a cup without a base is not
put on a table."[b] The trivial subject does not allow such
magniloquence.

(115) Frigidity, like grandeur, has three aspects. It
may be in the thought, as in one writer's description of the
Cyclops throwing a rock at Odysseus' ship, "as the rock
was rushing along, goats were browsing on it."[c] This is
frigid because the thought is exaggerated and impossible.
(116) In diction, Aristotle[d] lists four types, < ... >, for
example Alcidamas' "moist sweat";[e] from compounds,
when the words are compounded in a dithyrambic manner, for example "desert-wandering"[f] in one writer, and
any other similarly pompous expressions; and from
metaphors, for example "the situation was trembling and
pale."[g] These then are the four types of frigidity in diction. (117) Composition is frigid when it lacks good
rhythm, or has no rhythm when it has exclusively long syl-

[a] Theophr. F 686 Fortenbaugh.

[b] TrGF iv Soph. *Triptolemus* F 611.

[c] Author unknown, a grotesque elaboration on Hom. *Od.*
9.481 ἧκε δ' ἀπορρήξας κορυφὴν ὄρεος μεγάλοιο.

[d] Cf. Ar. *Rhet.* 1405b34ff for the four types of frigid diction:
compounds, glosses, epithets, and metaphors. Aristotle helps us
to fill the lacuna in our text, which will have covered glosses and
introduced epithets.   [e] Alcidamas, *fr.* 15 Sauppe, the first
example of frigid epithet in Ar. *Rhet.* 1406a21.

[f] Author unknown, not one of Aristotle's examples.

[g] Gorgias B16 D–K; cf. Ar. *Rhet.* 1406b8–10 χλωρὰ καὶ
ἄναιμα τὰ πράγματα.

"ἥκων ἡμῶν εἰς τὴν χώραν, πάσης ἡμῶν ὀρθῆς
οὔσης." οὐδὲν γὰρ ἔχει λογικὸν οὐδὲ ἀσφαλὲς διὰ
τὴν συνέχειαν τῶν μακρῶν συλλαβῶν. (118) ψυχρὸν
δὲ καὶ τὸ μέτρα τιθέναι συνεχῆ, καθάπερ τινές, καὶ
μὴ κλεπτόμενα ὑπὸ τῆς συνεχείας· ποίημα γὰρ
ἄκαιρον ψυχρόν, ὥσπερ καὶ τὸ ὑπέρμετρον. (119)
καὶ καθόλου ὁποῖόν τί ἐστιν ἡ ἀλαζονεία, τοιοῦτον
καὶ ἡ ψυχρότης· ὅ τε γὰρ ἀλαζὼν τὰ μὴ προσόντα
αὐτῷ αὐχεῖ ὅμως ὡς προσόντα, ὅ τε μικροῖς
πράγμασιν περιβάλλων ὄγκον καὶ αὐτὸς ἐν μικροῖς
ἀλαζονευομένῳ ἔοικεν. καὶ ὁποῖόν τι τὸ ἐν τῇ παροι-
μίᾳ κοσμούμενον ὕπερον, τοιοῦτόν τί ἐστι καὶ τὸ ἐν
τῇ ἑρμηνείᾳ ἐξηρμένον ἐν μικροῖς πράγμασιν.

(120) Καίτοι τινές φασι δεῖν τὰ μικρὰ μεγάλως
λέγειν, καὶ σημεῖον τοῦτο ἡγοῦνται ὑπερβαλλούσης
δυνάμεως. ἐγὼ δὲ Πολυκράτει μὲν τῷ ῥήτορι συγ-
χωρῶ ἐγκωμιάζοντι <. . .>[1] ὡς Ἀγαμέμνονα ἐν
ἀντιθέτοις καὶ μεταφοραῖς καὶ πᾶσι τοῖς ἐγκωμια-
στικοῖς τρόποις· ἔπαιζεν γάρ, οὐκ ἐσπούδαζεν, καὶ
αὐτὸς τῆς γραφῆς ὁ ὄγκος παίγνιόν ἐστι. παίζειν
μὲν δὴ ἐξέστω, ὡς φημί, τὸ δὲ πρέπον ἐν παντὶ
πράγματι φυλακτέον, τοῦτ᾽ ἔστι προσφόρως ἑρμη-
νευτέον, τὰ μὲν μικρὰ μικρῶς, τὰ μεγάλα δὲ μεγά-

[1] lacunam stat. Victorius, e.g. Θερσίτην Maass.

[a] Author unknown (cf. § 42); the second phrase lacks a subject, e.g. "city."

lables, for example "arriving inside our land, since it now is all stirred up" (*hêkôn hêmôn eis tên chôrân, pâsês hêmôn orthês ousês*).[a] Owing to the unbroken succession of long syllables, this sentence is quite unlike good prose and finds no safe footing. (118) It is also frigid to introduce, as some do, continuous metrical phrases, since their continuity makes them obtrude. A line of verse in prose is out of place, and as frigid as too many syllables to the line in verse.[b] (119) In general, there is a sort of analogy between boastfulness and frigidity. The boaster pretends that qualities belong to him even if they do not, while the writer who adds pomp to trifles is himself like the man who boasts about trifles. The use of a heightened style on a trivial subject recalls the proverbial "ornamented pestle."[c]

(120) There are, however, people who hold that we should use grand language on slight themes, and regard it as a sign of exceptional skill. For my own part, I excuse the rhetorician Polycrates[d] who eulogised <...> like an Agamemnon with antithesis, metaphor, and every artifice of eulogy. He was being playful and not in earnest; the very inflation of his writing is part of the play. So play, as I say, is legitimate, but otherwise preserve propriety, whatever the subject; or in other words, use the relevant style,

[b] Or alternatively "as metre which is too regular."

[c] Paroem. Gr. i.459.

[d] Polycrates, *Art. Scr.* B.xxi.11; he specialised in paradoxical encomia of villains and trifles such as pots, pebbles, and mice. In the lacuna add a name such as Busiris, the wicked king who was the subject of his most famous encomium, or the ugly Thersites (cf. § 163). For an extant παίγνιον see Gorgias' *Helen* (cf. *Hel.* 21 Ἑλένης μὲν ἐγκώμιον, ἐμὸν δὲ παίγνιον).

λως, (121) καθάπερ Ξενοφῶν ἐπὶ τοῦ Τηλεβόα ποταμοῦ μικροῦ ὄντος καὶ καλοῦ φησιν, "οὗτος δὲ ποταμὸς ἦν μέγας μὲν οὔ, καλὸς δέ·" τῇ γὰρ βραχύτητι
τῆς συνθέσεως καὶ τῇ ἀπολήξει τῇ εἰς τὸ "δὲ" μόνον
οὐκ ἐπέδειξεν ἡμῖν μικρὸν ποταμόν. ἕτερος δέ τις
ἑρμηνεύων ὅμοιον τῷ Τηλεβόα ποταμὸν[1] ἔφη, ὡς
"ἀπὸ τῶν Λαυρικῶν ὀρέων ὁρμώμενος ἐκδιδοῖ ἐς
θάλασσαν," καθάπερ τὸν Νεῖλον ἑρμηνεύων κατα-
κρημνιζόμενον ἢ τὸν Ἴστρον ἐμβάλλοντα. πάντα
οὖν τὰ τοιαῦτα ψυχρότης καλεῖται. (122) γίνεται
μέντοι τὰ μικρὰ μεγάλα ἕτερον τρόπον, οὐ διὰ τοῦ
ἀπρεποῦς ἀλλ' ἐνίοτε ὑπ' ἀνάγκης· οἷον ὅταν μικρὰ
κατορθώσαντά τινα στρατηγὸν ἐξαίρειν βουλώμεθα
ὡς μεγάλα κατωρθωκότα, <ἢ>[2] οἷον ὅτι ἔφορος ἐν
Λακεδαίμονι τὸν περιέργως καὶ οὐκ ἐπιχωρίως
σφαιρίσαντα ἐμαστίγωσεν· τούτῳ[3] γὰρ αὐτόθεν
μικρῷ ἀκουσθῆναι ὄντι ἐπιτραγῳδοῦμεν, ὡς οἱ τὰ
μικρὰ πονηρὰ ἔθη ἐῶντες ὁδὸν τοῖς μείζοσι πονη-
ροῖς ἀνοιγνύουσιν, καὶ ὅτι ἐπὶ τοῖς μικροῖς παρανο-
μήμασιν χρὴ κολάζειν μᾶλλον, οὐκ ἐπὶ τοῖς μεγάλοις. καὶ τὴν παροιμίαν ἐποίσομεν,[4] "ἀρχὴ δέ τοι
ἥμισυ παντός," ὡς ἐοικυῖαν τούτῳ[5] τῷ σμικρῷ κακῷ,
ἢ καὶ[6] ὅτι οὐδὲν κακὸν μικρόν ἐστιν. (123) οὕτως μὲν
δὴ ἐξέστω καὶ τὸ μικρὸν κατόρθωμα ἐξαίρειν μέγα,

---

[1] ποταμὸν Schneider: *flumen* Lat.: ποταμῷ P.
[2] ἢ add. Roberts.   [3] τούτῳ edd.: τοῦτο P.
[4] ἐποίσομεν Hemsterhuys: ἐποιήσαμεν P.
[5] τούτῳ τῷ P[2]: τοῦτο P[1].   [6] ἢ P[2], om. P[1].

slight for slight themes, grand for grand themes, (121) just as Xenophon does when he describes the small and beautiful river Teleboas, "this was not a large river; it was beautiful, however."[a] Through the conciseness of the construction and the final position of "however" he makes us all but see a small river. Contrast another writer who describes a river similar to the Teleboas, saying that it "rushed from the hills of Laurium and disgorged itself into the sea,"[b] as though he were writing about the cataracts of the Nile or the mouth of the Danube. All such language is called frigid. (122) Minor themes, however, may be magnified in another way, a way which is not inappropriate and sometimes necessary, for instance when we wish to praise a general for some small victory as though he had actually won a major victory; or the ephor in Sparta who scourged a man who played ball with extravagant gestures and not in the local manner. The offence in itself sounds trivial, so we wax eloquent on its gravity, pointing out that men who permit minor bad habits open the way to more serious ones, and that we ought to punish minor offences against the law rather than major ones; and we will introduce the proverb, "work begun is half-done,"[c] arguing that it fits this minor offence, or even that no offence is minor. (123) In this way, then, we may legitimately magnify a small success,

[a] Xen. *Anab.* 4.4.3, cf. § 6.
[b] Author unknown.
[c] Hesiod, *Op.* 40, cf. Paroem. Gr. i.213.

οὐ μὴν ὥστε ἀπρεπές τι ποιεῖν, ἀλλ' ὥσπερ καὶ τὸ μέγα κατασμικρύνεται χρησίμως πολλάκις, οὕτως ἂν καὶ τὸ μικρὸν ἐξαίροιτο.

(124) Μάλιστα δὲ ἡ ὑπερβολὴ ψυχρότατον πάντων. τριττὴ δέ ἐστιν· ἢ γὰρ καθ' ὁμοιότητα ἐκφέρεται, ὡς τὸ "θέειν δ' ἀνέμοισιν ὁμοῖοι," ἢ καθ' ὑπεροχήν, ὡς τὸ "λευκότεροι χιόνος," ἢ κατὰ τὸ ἀδύνατον, ὡς τὸ "οὐρανῷ ἐστήριξε κάρη." (125) πᾶσα μὲν οὖν ὑπερβολὴ ἀδύνατός ἐστιν· οὔτε γὰρ ἂν χιόνος λευκότερον γένοιτο, οὔτ' ἂν ἀνέμῳ θέειν ὅμοιον. αὕτη μέντοι [ἤτοι]¹ ἡ ὑπερβολὴ ἡ εἰρημένη ἐξαιρέτως ὀνομάζεται ἀδύνατος. διὸ δὴ καὶ μάλιστα ψυχρὰ δοκεῖ πᾶσα ὑπερβολή, διότι ἀδυνάτῳ ἔοικεν. (126) διὰ τοῦτο δὲ μάλιστα καὶ οἱ κωμῳδοποιοὶ χρῶνται αὐτῇ, ὅτι ἐκ τοῦ ἀδυνάτου ἐφέλκονται τὸ γελοῖον, ὥσπερ ἐπὶ τῶν Περσῶν τῆς ἀπληστίας ὑπερβαλλόμενός τις ἔφη, ὅτι "πεδία ἐξέχεζον ὅλα," καὶ ὅτι "βοῦς ἐν ταῖς γνάθοις ἔφερον." (127) τοῦ δὲ αὐτοῦ εἴδους ἐστὶ καὶ τὸ "φαλακρότερος εὐδίας" καὶ τὸ "κολοκύντης ὑγιέστερος." τὸ δὲ "χρυσῷ χρυσοτέρα" τὸ Σαπφικὸν ἐν ὑπερβολῇ λέγεται καὶ αὐτὸ καὶ ἀδυνάτως, πλὴν αὐτῷ γε τῷ ἀδυνάτῳ χάριν ἔχει, οὐ ψυχρότητα. ὃ δὴ καὶ μάλιστα θαυμάσειεν ἄν τις Σαπφοῦς τῆς θείας, ὅτι φύσει κινδυνώδει πράγματι καὶ δυσκατορθώτῳ ἐχρήσατο ἐπιχαρίτως. καὶ περὶ μὲν ψυχρότητος καὶ ὑπερβολῆς τοσαῦτα.

¹ ἤτοι del. edd.

but without doing anything unsuitable. Just as major themes can often be usefully depreciated, so can minor themes be magnified.

(124) The most frigid of all devices is hyperbole, which is of three kinds. It is expressed either in the form of a likeness, for example "like the winds in speed"; or of superiority, for example "whiter than snow";[a] or of impossibility, for example "with her head she reached the sky."[b] (125) Admittedly every hyperbole is an impossibility. There could be nothing "whiter than snow," nothing "like the winds in speed." But this last kind is especially called impossible. And so the reason why every hyperbole seems particularly frigid is that it suggests something impossible. (126) This is also the chief reason why the comic poets use it, since out of the impossible they create laughter, for example when someone said hyperbolically of the voracity of the Persians that "they excreted entire plains"[c] and that "they carried oxen in their jaws."[d] (127) Of the same type are the expressions "balder than a cloudless sky" and "healthier than a pumpkin."[e] Sappho's phrase, "more golden than gold"[f] is also in form a hyperbole and impossible, but by its very impossibility it is charming, not frigid. Indeed, it is a most marvellous achievement of the divine Sappho that she handled an intrinsically risky and intractable device to create charm. This concludes my account of frigidity and hyperbole.

---

[a] Hom. *Il.* 10.437 (of horses). [b] Hom. *Il.* 4.443 (of Strife).

[c] Author unknown; cf. Arist. *Acharnians* 82 κάχεζον ὀκτὼ μῆνας ἐπὶ χρυσῶν ὀρῶν. [d] Author unknown, a proverb (Paroem. Gr. ii. 749). In § 161 it describes a Thracian.

[e] Sophron 108 and 34 Kaibel (cf. § 162).

[f] Sappho 156 L–P (cf. § 162 for a longer citation).

Νῦν δὲ περὶ τοῦ γλαφυροῦ χαρακτῆρος λέξομεν, (128) <ὃς> χαριεντισμός ἐστι καὶ[1] λόγος ἱλαρός. τῶν δὲ χαρίτων αἱ μέν εἰσι μείζονες καὶ σεμνότεραι, αἱ τῶν ποιητῶν, αἱ δὲ εὐτελεῖς μᾶλλον καὶ κωμικώτεραι, σκώμμασιν ἐοικυῖαι, οἷον αἱ Ἀριστοτέλους χάριτες καὶ Σώφρονος καὶ Λυσίου· τὸ γὰρ "ἧς ῥᾷον ἄν τις ἀριθμήσειεν τοὺς ὀδόντας ἢ τοὺς δακτύλους," τὸ ἐπὶ τῆς πρεσβύτιδος, καὶ τὸ "ὅσας ἄξιος ἦν λαβεῖν πληγάς, τοσαύτας εἴληφεν δραχμάς," οἱ τοιοῦτοι ἀστεϊσμοὶ οὐδὲν διαφέρουσιν σκωμμάτων, οὐδὲ πόρρω γελωτοποιΐας εἰσί. (129) τὸ δὲ

> τῇ δέ θ᾽ ἅμα Νύμφαι
> παίζουσι· γέγηθε δέ[2] τε φρένα Λητώ·

καὶ

> ῥεῖα δ᾽ ἀριγνώτη πέλεται· καλαὶ δέ τε πᾶσαι·

[καὶ][3] αὗταί εἰσιν αἱ λεγόμεναι σεμναὶ χάριτες καὶ μεγάλαι. (130) χρῆται δὲ αὐταῖς Ὅμηρος καὶ πρὸς δείνωσιν ἐνίοτε καὶ ἔμφασιν, καὶ παίζων φοβερώτερός ἐστι, πρῶτός τε εὑρηκέναι δοκεῖ φοβερὰς χάριτας, ὥσπερ τὸ ἐπὶ τοῦ ἀχαριτωτάτου προσώπου, τὸ ἐπὶ τοῦ Κύκλωπος, τὸ [οὖν][4] "Οὖτιν ἐγὼ πύματον ἔδομαι, τοὺς δὲ λοιποὺς πρώτους," τὸ τοῦ Κύκλωπος

---

[1] <ὃς> χαριεντισμός ἐστι καὶ λόγος ἱλαρός Kassel: καὶ om. P: ὁ γλαφυρὸς λόγος χαριεντισμὸς καὶ ἱλαρὸς λόγος in mg. P.   [2] δὲ om. P.
[3] καὶ del. Schneider.

428

We will next discuss the elegant style, (128) which is speech with charm and a graceful lightness. Some kinds of charm, those of the poets, are more imposing and dignified, others are more ordinary, closer to comedy and resembling gibes, like those of Aristotle,[a] Sophron, and Lysias. Such witticisms as "whose teeth could be counted sooner than her fingers" (of an old woman) and "he has taken as many coins as he has deserved beatings"[b] are exactly like gibes, and come close to buffoonery. (129) Contrast the lines, "At her side the nymphs play, and Leto rejoices in her heart" and "she easily outshone them all, yet all were beautiful."[c] This is the charm that can be called imposing and dignified. (130) Charm is also used by Homer sometimes to make a scene more forceful and intense. His very jesting adds to the terror, and he seems to have been the first to invent the grim joke, as in the passage describing that least charming of figures, the Cyclops: "No-man I will eat last, the rest before him"[d]—the Cyclops' gift of hospitality. No other detail

---

[a] A surprising choice for comic wit (§ 164 is also suspect), and Aristophanes has been proposed.

[b] Lys. *fr.* 1 (cf. § 262) and 93 Thalheim.

[c] Hom. *Od.* 6.105ff (of Artemis).

[d] Hom. *Od.* 9.369–70 (cf. §§ 152, 262),

Οὖτιν ἐγὼ πύματον ἔδομαι μετὰ οἷς ἑτάροισι,
τοὺς δ᾽ ἄλλους πρόσθεν, τὸ δέ τοι ξεινήιον ἔσται.

---

4 οὖν P, om. edd.: fort. delenda sunt verba omnia τὸ ἐπὶ . . . τὸ οὖν Roberts.

ξένιον· οὐ γὰρ οὕτως αὐτὸν ἐνέφηνεν δεινὸν ἐκ τῶν ἄλλων, ὅταν δύο δειπνῇ ἑταίρους, οὐδ' ἀπὸ τοῦ θυρεοῦ ἢ ἐκ τοῦ ῥοπάλου, ὡς ἐκ τούτου τοῦ ἀστεϊσμοῦ. (131) χρῆται δὲ τῷ τοιούτῳ εἴδει καὶ Ξενοφῶν, καὶ αὐτὸς δεινότητας εἰσάγει ἐκ χαρίτων, οἷον ἐπὶ τῆς ἐνόπλου ὀρχηστρίδος, "ἐρωτηθεὶς ὑπὸ τοῦ Παφλαγόνος εἰ καὶ αἱ γυναῖκες αὐτοῖς συνεπολέμουν, ἔφη· αὗται γὰρ καὶ ἔτρεψαν τὸν βασιλέα." διττὴ γὰρ ἐμφαίνεται ἡ δεινότης ἐκ τῆς χάριτος, ἡ μὲν ὅτι οὐ γυναῖκες αὐτοῖς εἵποντο ἀλλ' Ἀμαζόνες, ἡ δὲ κατὰ βασιλέως, εἰ οὕτως ἦν ἀσθενής ὡς ὑπὸ γυναικῶν φυγεῖν. (132) τὰ μὲν οὖν εἴδη τῶν χαρίτων τοσάδε καὶ τοιάδε.

Εἰσὶν δὲ αἱ μὲν ἐν τοῖς πράγμασι χάριτες, οἷον νυμφαῖοι κῆποι, ὑμέναιοι, ἔρωτες, ὅλη ἡ Σαπφοῦς ποίησις. τὰ γὰρ τοιαῦτα, κἂν ὑπὸ Ἱππώνακτος λέγηται,[1] χαρίεντά ἐστι, καὶ αὐτὸ ἱλαρὸν τὸ πρᾶγμα ἐξ ἑαυτοῦ· οὐδεὶς γὰρ ἂν ὑμέναιον ᾄδοι[2] ὀργιζόμενος, οὐδὲ τὸν Ἔρωτα Ἐρινὺν ποιήσειεν[3] τῇ ἑρμηνείᾳ ἢ γίγαντα, οὐδὲ τὸ γελᾶν κλαίειν. (133) ὥστε ἡ μέν τις ἐν πράγμασι[4] χάρις ἐστί, τὰ δὲ καὶ ἡ λέξις ποιεῖ ἐπιχαριτώτερα, οἷον

ὡς δ' ὅτε Πανδαρέου[5] κούρη, χλωρηῒς ἀηδών,
καλὸν ἀείδησιν, ἔαρος νέον ἱσταμένοιο·

[1] λέγεται P: λέγηται edd.
[2] ᾄδοι Schneider: ᾄδει P.

reveals so clearly the grimness of the monster—not his eating two of Odysseus' companions for supper, nor his door made from a rock, nor his club—as this piece of wit. (131) Xenophon is also familiar with this type, and he too uses charm to grim effect, as in the passage describing the dancing girl in armour: "A Greek was asked by the Paphlagonian whether their women accompanied them to war. 'Yes,' he replied, 'in fact *they* were the ones who routed the king.'"[a] This witticism is tellingly forceful in two ways, the implication that it was not mere women but Amazons who accompanied them, and the implied insult to the king that he was so feeble that he was put to flight by women. (132) This, then, is the number and variety of the forms of charm.

The charm may lie in the subject matter, such as gardens of the nymphs, marriage songs, loves, or the poetry of Sappho generally. Such themes, even in the mouth of a Hipponax,[b] have charm, and the subject has its own graceful lightness. No one could sing a marriage song in frenzied anger, nor could style change Love into a Fury or a Giant, or laughter into tears. (133) There is, then, charm in the theme itself, but sometimes diction can give an added charm, as in the lines:

> "Just as Pandareus' daughter, the pale nightingale,
> sings beautifully at the beginning of spring."[c]

[a] Xen. *Anab.* 6.1.12–15.
[b] Cf. § 301.   [c] Hom. *Od.* 19.518–19.

---

[3] ποιήσειεν Hammer: ποιήσει ἐν P.
[4] πράγμασι Victorius: πράγματι P.
[5] Πανδαρέου codd. Hom: Πανδαρέη P.

ἐνταῦθα γὰρ καὶ ἡ ἀηδὼν χάριεν ὀρνίθιον, καὶ τὸ
ἔαρ φύσει χάριεν, πολὺ δὲ ἐπικεκόσμηται τῇ ἑρμηνείᾳ, καὶ ἔστι χαριέστερα τῷ τε "χλωρηῒς" καὶ τῷ[1]
"Πανδαρέου[2] κούρη" εἰπεῖν ἐπὶ ὄρνιθος, ἅπερ τοῦ
ποιητοῦ ἴδιά ἐστι.

(134) Πολλάκις δὲ καὶ τὰ μὲν πράγματα ἀτερπῆ
ἐστι φύσει καὶ στυγνά, ὑπὸ δὲ τοῦ λέγοντος γίνεται
ἱλαρά. τοῦτο δὲ παρὰ Ξενοφῶντι δοκεῖ πρώτῳ εὑρῆ-
σθαι· λαβὼν γὰρ ἀγέλαστον πρόσωπον καὶ στυ-
γνόν, τὸν Ἀγλαϊτάδαν, τὸν Πέρσην, γέλωτα εὗρεν
ἐξ αὐτοῦ χαρίεντα, ὅτι "ῥᾷόν[3] ἐστι πῦρ ἐκτρῖψαι ἀπὸ
σοῦ ἢ γέλωτα." (135) αὕτη δέ ἐστι καὶ ἡ δυνατωτάτη
χάρις, καὶ μάλιστα ἐν τῷ λέγοντι. τὸ μὲν γὰρ
πρᾶγμα καὶ φύσει στυγνὸν ἦν καὶ πολέμιον χάριτι
[ὥσπερ καὶ Ἀγλαϊτάδας],[4] ὁ δ' ὥσπερ ἐνδείκνυται
ὅτι καὶ ἀπὸ τῶν τοιούτων παίζειν ἔστιν, ὡσπερεὶ καὶ
ὑπὸ θερμοῦ ψύχεσθαι, θερμαίνεσθαι δὲ ὑπὸ τῶν
ψυχρῶν.

(136) Ἐπεὶ δὲ τὰ εἴδη τῶν χαρίτων δέδεικται, τίνα
ἐστὶ καὶ ἐν τίσιν, νῦν καὶ τοὺς τόπους παραδείξομεν,[5] ἀφ' ὧν αἱ χάριτες. ἦσαν δὲ ἡμῖν αἱ μὲν ἐν τῇ
λέξει, αἱ δὲ ἐν τοῖς πράγμασιν. παραδείξομεν οὖν
καὶ τοὺς τόπους καθ' ἑκάτερα· πρώτους δὲ τοὺς τῆς
λέξεως.

(137) Εὐθὺς οὖν πρώτη ἐστὶ χάρις ἡ ἐκ συντομίας, ὅταν τὸ αὐτὸ μηκυνόμενον ἄχαρι γένηται, ὑπὸ

---

[1] τῷ τε . . . καὶ τῷ Finckh: τό τε . . . καὶ τὸ P.
[2] Πανδαρέη P.

This passage refers to the nightingale, which is a delightful little bird, and to spring, which is of its nature a delightful season of the year, but the style has made it much more beautiful, and the whole has added charm from "pale" and the personification of the bird as Pandareus' daughter. Both these touches are the poet's own.

(134) Often subjects which are naturally unattractive and sombre acquire a lighter tone from the writer's skill. This secret seems to have been discovered first by Xenophon, who took the gloomy and sombre figure of the Persian Aglaitadas and exploited him for a charming joke, "it would be easier to strike fire from you than laughter."[a] (135) This is, indeed, the most effective kind of charm, and one which most depends on the writer. The subject was in itself sombre and hostile to charm,[b] but the writer virtually gives a demonstration that even with such unpromising material jokes are possible, just as cold can heat and heat can cool.

(136) Now that we have set out the varieties of charm and where it is found, we will next list its sources. As we have already said, it lies partly in the style and partly in the subject. So we will list the sources under both categories, beginning with those from style.

(137) The very first source of charm is brevity, when a thought which would lose its charm if it were expanded is

---

[a] Xen. *Cyrop.* 2.2.15.
[b] The Greek text adds "as Aglaitadas certainly was."

---

[3] $\hat{\rho}\hat{q}ov$ codd. Xen.: $\hat{\rho}\acute{a}\delta\iota ov$ P.
[4] del. Schenkeveld.
[5] $\pi\alpha\rho\alpha\delta\epsilon\acute{\iota}\xi o\mu\epsilon\nu$ Gale: $\pi\alpha\rho\alpha\delta\epsilon\acute{\iota}\xi o\mu\alpha\iota$ P.

DEMETRIUS

δὲ τάχους χάριεν, ὥσπερ παρὰ Ξενοφῶντι, "τῷ ὄντι
τούτῳ[1] οὐδὲν μέτεστι τῆς Ἑλλάδος, ἐπεὶ ἐγὼ αὐτὸν
εἶδον ὡσπερεὶ Λυδὸν ἀμφότερα τὰ ὦτα τετρυπημέ-
νον·[2] καὶ εἶχεν οὕτως." τὸ γὰρ ἐπιλεγόμενον τὸ
"εἶχεν οὕτως" ὑπὸ τῆς συντομίας τὴν χάριν ποιεῖ, εἰ
δὲ ἐμηκύνθη διὰ πλειόνων, ὅτι "ἔλεγεν ταῦτα ἀληθῆ,
σαφῶς γὰρ ἐτετρύπητο," διήγημα ἂν ψιλὸν ἐγένετο
ἀντὶ χάριτος. (138) πολλάκις δὲ καὶ δύο φράζεται δι'
ἑνὸς πρὸς τὸ χάριεν, οἷον ἐπὶ τῆς Ἀμαζόνος καθευ-
δούσης ἔφη τις, ὅτι "τὸ τόξον ἐντεταμένον ἔκειτο,
καὶ ἡ φαρέτρα πλήρης, τὸ γέρρον ἐπὶ τῇ κεφαλῇ·
τοὺς δὲ ζωστῆρας οὐ λύονται." ἐν γὰρ τούτῳ καὶ ὁ
νόμος εἴρηται ὁ περὶ τοῦ ζωστῆρος, καὶ ὅτι οὐκ
ἔλυσε τὸν ζωστῆρα, τὰ δύο πράγματα διὰ μιᾶς
ἑρμηνείας. καὶ ἀπὸ τῆς συντομίας ταύτης γλαφυρόν
τί ἐστι.

(139) Δεύτερος δὲ τόπος ἐστὶν ἀπὸ τῆς τάξεως.
τὸ γὰρ αὐτὸ πρῶτον μὲν τεθὲν ἢ μέσον ἄχαρι γίνε-
ται· ἐπὶ δὲ τοῦ τέλους χάριεν, οἷον ὡς ὁ Ξενοφῶν
φησιν ἐπὶ τοῦ Κύρου, "δίδωσι δὲ αὐτῷ καὶ δῶρα,
ἵππον καὶ στολὴν καὶ στρεπτόν, καὶ τὴν χώραν
μηκέτι ἁρπάζεσθαι." ἐν γὰρ τούτοις τὸ μὲν τελευ-
ταῖόν ἐστι τὸ τὴν χάριν ποιοῦν τὸ "τὴν χώραν
μηκέτι ἁρπάζεσθαι" διὰ τὸ ξένον τοῦ δώρου καὶ τὴν
ἰδιότητα· αἴτιος δὲ ὁ τόπος τῆς χάριτος. εἰ γοῦν
πρῶτον ἐτάχθη, ἀχαριτώτερον ἦν, οἷον ὅτι "δίδωσιν

[1] τούτῳ M: istius Lat.: τοῦτο P.

434

given charm by a quick mention, as in Xenophon: "This man has really nothing Greek about him, for he has (and I saw it myself) both his ears pierced like a Lydian; and so he had."[a] The ending, "and so he had," has charm from its brevity, but if it had been expanded at greater length, "what he said was true, since he had evidently had them pierced," it would have become a bald piece of narrative instead of a flash of charm. (138) Often too the conflation of two ideas in one sentence gives a delightful effect. A writer once said of a sleeping Amazon: "Her bow lay strung, her quiver full, her shield by her head; but they never loosen their belts."[b] In one and the same phrase the general custom about their belts is indicated, and so is the fact that she had not loosened her belt—two things at once. There is a touch of elegance in this brevity.

(139) The second source is word order. The very thought which would have no charm if it is put at the beginning or middle of a sentence, is often full of charm if it comes at the end, for example Xenophon on Cyrus, "He gives him gifts too—a horse, a robe, a torque, and the assurance that his country would no longer be plundered."[a] It is the last item in the sentence ("the assurance that his country would no longer be plundered") that creates the charm, from the novel and unique nature of the gift. And the charm is due to its position. If it had been put first, it would be less attractive, for example, "He

[a] Xen. *Anab.* 3.1.31.   [b] Author unknown. The Amazon custom was to remain virgins.   [c] Xen. *Anab.* 1.2.27.

[2] τετρυπημένον codd. Xen.: *perforatas* Lat.: τετριμμένον P.

αὐτῷ δῶρα, τήν τε χώραν μηκέτι ἁρπάζεσθαι, καὶ
ἵππον καὶ στολὴν καὶ στρεπτόν." νῦν δὲ προειπὼν
τὰ εἰθισμένα δῶρα, τελευταῖον ἐπήνεγκεν τὸ ξένον
καὶ ἄηθες, ἐξ ὧν ἁπάντων συνῆκται ἡ χάρις.

(140) Αἱ δὲ ἀπὸ τῶν σχημάτων χάριτες δῆλαί
εἰσιν καὶ πλεῖσται παρὰ Σαπφοῖ, οἷον ἐκ τῆς ἀναδιπλώσεως, ὅπου[1] νύμφη πρὸς τὴν παρθενίαν φησί,
"παρθενία, παρθενία, ποῖ με λιποῦσα οἴχῃ;" ἡ δὲ
ἀποκρίνεται πρὸς αὐτὴν τῷ αὐτῷ σχήματι, "οὐκέτι
ἥξω πρὸς σέ, οὐκέτι ἥξω" πλείων γὰρ χάρις ἐμφαίνεται, ἢ εἴπερ ἅπαξ ἐλέχθη καὶ ἄνευ τοῦ σχήματος.
καίτοι ἡ ἀναδίπλωσις πρὸς δεινότητας μᾶλλον δοκεῖ
εὑρῆσθαι, ἡ δὲ καὶ τοῖς δεινοτάτοις καταχρῆται ἐπιχαρίτως.[2] (141) χαριεντίζεται δέ ποτε καὶ ἐξ ἀναφορᾶς, ὡς ἐπὶ τοῦ Ἑσπέρου, "Ἕσπερε, πάντα φέρεις,"
φησί, "φέρεις οἶν,[3] φέρεις αἶγα, φέρεις ματέρι
παῖδα." καὶ γὰρ ἐνταῦθα ἡ χάρις ἐστὶν ἐκ τῆς
λέξεως τῆς "φέρεις" ἐπὶ τὸ αὐτὸ ἀναφερομένης.
(142) πολλὰς δ' ἄν τις καὶ ἄλλας ἐκφέροι χάριτας.

Γίγνονται δὲ καὶ ἀπὸ λέξεως χάριτες, ἢ ἐκ μεταφορᾶς, ὡς ἐπὶ τοῦ τέττιγος, "πτερύγων δ' ὑποκακχέει
λιγυρὰν ἀοιδάν, ὅτι ποτ' ἂν φλόγιον †καθέταν ἐπι-

---

[1] ὅπου edd.: ποῦ P.
[2] ἐπιχαρίτως Finckh: ἐπι (sic) χάριτος P.
[3] οἶν Paulus Manutius: οἶνον P.

---

[a] Sappho 114 L–P.
[b] Sappho 104(a) L–P. The text has some uncertainties and

gives him gifts, the assurance that his country would no longer be plundered, a horse, a robe, and a torque." As it is, he listed the customary gifts first, and then added last the novel and unusual gift, and all this combines to give charm.

(140) There is obvious charm from the use of figures, preeminently in Sappho, for example the use of repetition when a bride addresses her own virginity, "virginity, virginity, why have you gone and left me?" and it replies to her with the same figure, "never again shall I come to you, never again shall I come."[a] The idea has clearly more charm than if it had been expressed only once, without the figure. Repetition, it is true, is thought to have been invented more particularly to add force, but Sappho exploits even the most forceful features for charm. (141) Sometimes too she makes attractive use of anaphora, as in the lines on the evening star,

> "Evening star, you bring everything home,
> you bring the sheep, you bring the goat, you bring
> the child to its mother."[b]

Here the charm lies in the repetition in the same position of the phrase, "you bring." (142) Many other examples of this could be cited.

Charm also comes from the use of a single word, for example from metaphor, as in the passage about the cicada,

> "from under his wings
> he pours out a stream of piercing song, as

the second line may contrast the bride who does not return home to her mother.

πτάμενον† καταυλεῖ," (143) ἢ[1] ἐκ συνθέτου [τοῦ][2]
ὀνόματος καὶ διθυραμβικοῦ, "δέσποτα Πλούτων[3]
μελανοπτερύγων—τουτὶ δεινόν, πυρροπτερύγων[4]
αὐτὸ ποίησον." ἃ μάλιστα δὴ κωμῳδικὰ παίγνιά
ἐστι καὶ σατυρικά.[5] (144) καὶ ἐξ ἰδιωτικοῦ δὲ ὀνόματος γίγνεται, ὡς ὁ Ἀριστοτέλης, "ὅσῳ γάρ," φησί,
"μονώτης εἰμί, φιλομυθότερος γέγονα"· καὶ ἐκ
πεποιημένου, ὡς ὁ αὐτὸς ἐν τῷ αὐτῷ, "ὅσῳ γὰρ
αὐτίτης καὶ μονώτης εἰμί, φιλομυθότερος γέγονα."
τὸ μὲν γὰρ "μονώτης" ἰδιωτικωτέρου εἴδους[6] ἤδη
ἐστί, τὸ δὲ "αὐτίτης" πεποιημένον ἐκ τοῦ αὐτός.
(145) πολλὰ δὲ ὀνόματα καὶ παρὰ τὴν θέσιν τὴν ἐπί
τινος χαρίεντά ἐστιν, οἷον "ὁ γὰρ ὄρνις οὗτος κόλαξ
ἐστὶ καὶ κόβαλος."[7] ἐνταῦθα ἡ χάρις ἀπὸ τοῦ σκῶ-
ψαι τὸν ὄρνιν καθάπερ ἄνθρωπον, καὶ ὅτι τὰ μὴ
συνήθη ἔθετο ὀνόματα τῷ ὄρνιθι. αἱ μὲν οὖν τοιαῦται χάριτες παρ' αὐτὰς τὰς λέξεις.

---

[1] locus corruptus, at recte καταυλεῖ· ἢ Finckh: καταυδείη P.
[2] τοῦ del. Finckh.
[3] Πλούτων M[2] Bergk: πλοῦτον P.
[4] πυρροπτερύγων Wilamowitz (qui et personas distinxit):
πρὸ πτερύγων P.
[5] σατυρικά Gale: σατύρια P.
[6] εἴδους Orth: ἔθους P.
[7] κόβαλος Wilamowitz: κόλακος P.

---

[a] Alcaeus 347 (b) L–P. The text is corrupt, the metaphor
probably the attractive conjecture, καταυλεῖ, "flutes." The

in the blazing †heat of summer he flies and†
flutes";[a]

(143) or from dithyrambic compounds, "'Pluto, lord
of the sable-winged'—'that is terrible, make it red-
winged.'"[b] Such freaks of language are best suited for
comedy and satyr drama. (144) Idiosyncratic language is
another source, as in Aristotle: "the more I am a solitary,
the more I have become a lover of stories."[c] So too are
neologisms, as in the same author and passage: "the more
I am a solitary and selfish, the more I have become a lover
of stories." The word "solitary" is already of a rather
idiosyncratic type, and "selfish" is coined from "self."
(145) Many words owe their charm to their application to
a particular object, for example: "this bird is a flatterer
and a rogue."[d] Here there is charm because the author
mocked the bird as though it were a person, and applied
words not usually applied to a bird. These then are the
types of charm from single words.

author is likely to be Alcaeus, since like 347 (a) L–P it imitates
Hesiod, *Op.* 582ff.

[b] Author unknown, presumably comedy (Supp. Com. *Adesp.*
1) rather than lyric (PMG 963). The text is corrupt, but parodies
tragic compounds in "-winged," and is probably a dialogue.

[c] Ar. *fr.* 668 Rose (cf. §§ 97, 164). The surrounding context
involves unusual words and uses, and μονώτης is rare outside
Aristotle, so ἰδιωτικός should here mean "idiosyncratic." If the
text of § 164 were sound (see note), the meaning must be "ordinary," as in §§ 15, 207–8, and it is an accident that we lack proof
that μονώτης was indeed part of ordinary speech (so D. J. Allen,
Mnemosyne 27 (1971) 119–22).

[d] Author unknown, cf. Ar. *Hist. Anim.* 597b23 (of a kind of
owl) κόβαλος καὶ μιμητής.

(146) Ἐκ δὲ παραβολῆς, ὡς[1] ἐπὶ τοῦ ἐξέχοντος ἀνδρὸς ἡ Σαπφώ φησι, "πέρροχος ὡς ὅτ' ἀοιδὸς ὁ Λέσβιος ἀλλοδαποῖσιν." ἐνταῦθα γὰρ χάριν ἐποίησεν ἡ παραβολὴ μᾶλλον ἢ μέγεθος, καίτοι ἐξῆν εἰπεῖν πέρροχος ὥσπερ ἡ σελήνη τῶν ἄλλων ἄστρων, ἢ ὁ ἥλιος ὁ λαμπρότερος, ἢ ὅσα ἄλλα ἐστὶ ποιητικώτερα. (147) Σώφρων δὲ καὶ αὐτὸς ἐπὶ τοῦ ὁμοίου εἴδους φησί, "θᾶσαι, ὅσα φύλλα καὶ κάρφεα τοὶ παῖδες τοὺς ἄνδρας βαλλίζοντι, οἷόν περ φαντί, φίλα, τοὺς Τρῶας τὸν Αἴαντα τῷ παλῷ." καὶ γὰρ ἐνταῦθα ἐπίχαρις ἡ παραβολή ἐστι, καὶ τοὺς Τρῶας διαπαίζουσα ὥσπερ παῖδας.

(148) Ἔστι δέ τις ἰδίως χάρις Σαπφικὴ ἐκ μεταβολῆς, ὅταν τι εἰποῦσα μεταβάλληται καὶ ὥσπερ μετανοήσῃ, οἷον "ὕψου[2] δή," φησί, "τὸ μέλαθρον ἀέρατε τέκτονες· γαμβρὸς εἰσέρχεται ἶσος Ἄρηϊ, ἀνδρὸς μεγάλου πολλῷ μείζων," ὥσπερ ἐπιλαμβανομένη ἑαυτῆς, ὅτι ἀδυνάτῳ ἐχρήσατο ὑπερβολῇ, καὶ ὅτι οὐδεὶς τῷ Ἄρηϊ ἴσος ἐστίν. (149) τοῦ δὲ αὐτοῦ εἴδους καὶ τὸ παρὰ Τηλεμάχῳ, ὅτι "δύο κύνες δεδέατο πρὸ τῆς αὐλῆς, καὶ δύναμαι καὶ τὰ ὀνόματα εἰπεῖν τῶν κυνῶν. ἀλλὰ τί ἄν μοι βούλοιτο τὰ ὀνόματα ταῦτα;" καὶ γὰρ οὗτος μεταβαλλόμενος μεταξὺ ἠστεΐσατο καὶ ἀποσιγήσας τὰ ὀνόματα. (150) καὶ ἀπὸ στίχου δὲ ἀλλοτρίου γίνεται χάρις, ὡς ὁ Ἀρι-

---

[1] ὡς Radermacher: καὶ P.
[2] ὕψου edd.: νύψω P: ἴψω Radermacher.

(146) Charm also comes from the use of comparison, as in Sappho's description of an exceptionally tall man as "preeminent, like the poet of Lesbos among strangers."[a] Here the comparison creates charm rather than grandeur, as would have been possible if she had said, "preeminent like the moon among the stars," or the sun, which is even brighter, or any other more poetic comparison. (147) Sophron uses the same type when he says: "See how many leaves and twigs the boys are throwing at the men —as thick as the mud, my dear, which they say the Trojans threw at Ajax,"[b] Here again the comparison is charming, as it makes fun of the Trojans as though they were boys.

(148) There is a kind of charm from a change of direction which is peculiarly characteristic of Sappho. She will say something and then change direction, as though changing her mind, for example: "Raise high the roof of the hall, builders, for the bridegroom is coming, the equal of Ares, much taller than a tall man."[c] She seems to check herself, feeling that she has used an impossible hyperbole, since no one is the equal of Ares. (149) The same type appears in Telemachus: "Two hounds were leashed in front of the courtyard. I can tell you the actual names of the hounds. But why should I want to tell you their names?"[d] By this sudden change of direction in the middle, suppressing their names, he too is elegantly witty. (150) Charm also comes from parody of another writer's

[a] Sappho 106 L–P.

[b] Sophron 32 Kaibel; cf. Hom. *Il*. 11.358ff, where Ajax' slow retreat is like a donkey being beaten by boys.

[c] Sappho 111 L–P.   [d] Telemachus, otherwise unknown (or, but less natural Greek, an unknown author describes Telemachus, son of Odysseus).

στοφάνης σκώπτων που τὸν Δία, ὅτι οὐ κεραυνοῖ
τοὺς πονηρούς, φησίν,

αλλὰ τὸν ἑαυτοῦ νεὼ βάλλει, καὶ Σούνιον
ἄκρον Ἀθηνῶν.

ὥσπερ γοῦν οὐκέτι ὁ Ζεὺς κωμῳδεῖσθαι δοκεῖ, ἀλλ᾽
Ὅμηρος καὶ ὁ στίχος ὁ Ὁμηρικός, καὶ ἀπὸ τούτου
πλείων ἐστὶν ἡ χάρις.

(151) Ἔχουσι δέ τι στωμύλον καὶ ἀλληγορίαι
τινές, ὥσπερ τό, "Δελφοί, παιδίον ὑμῶν ἁ κύων
φέρει." καὶ τὰ Σώφρονος δὲ τὰ ἐπὶ τῶν γερόντων,
"ἐνθάδε ὦν¹ κἠγὼ παρ᾽ ὕμμε τοὺς ὁμότριχας ἐξορμί-
ζομαι, πλόον δοκάζων πόντιον· ἀρτέαι² γὰρ ἤδη τοῖς
ταλικοῖσδε ταὶ ἄγκυραι·" ὅσα τε ἐπὶ τῶν γυναικῶν
ἀλληγορεῖ, οἷον ἐπ᾽ ἰχθύων, "σωλῆνες, γλυκύκρεον
κογχύλιον, χηρᾶν γυναικῶν λίχνευμα."³ καὶ μιμικώ-
τερα⁴ τὰ τοιαῦτά ἐστι καὶ αἰσχρά.

(152) Ἔστι δέ τις καὶ ἡ παρὰ [τὴν]⁵ προσδοκίαν
χάρις, ὡς ἡ τοῦ Κύκλωπος, ὅτι "ὕστατον ἔδομαι
Οὖτιν." οὐ γὰρ προσεδόκα τοιοῦτο ξένιον οὔτε
Ὀδυσσεὺς οὔτε ὁ ἀναγινώσκων. καὶ ὁ Ἀριστοφάνης
ἐπὶ τοῦ Σωκράτους, "κηρὸν διατήξας," φησίν, "εἶτα
διαβήτην λαβών, ἐκ τῆς παλαίστρας ἱμάτιον ὑφεί-

---

¹ ἐνθάδε ὦν Schneider: ἐνθαδεον P.
² πόντιον· ἀρτέαι Kaibel: πόντιον ναὶ vel ποντίναι P.
³ λίχνευμα apud Athenaeum 86e: ἰχνεύμασι P.
⁴ μιμικώτερα Victorius: μιμικώτερα P.
⁵ τὴν P: del. Schneider.

line, like Aristophanes' mockery of Zeus somewhere because "he does not strike the wicked with his thunderbolts but his own very temple, and 'Sunium, headland of Athens.'"[a] It seems as though it is no longer Zeus who is being laughed at, but Homer and Homer's line, and this fact increases the charm.

(151) Some allegories have a colloquial turn of wit, as in: "Delphians, that bitch of yours is with child";[b] and in Sophron's passage on the old men: "Here I too wait with you, whose hair is white like mine, outside the harbour, ready for the voyage out to sea: for men of our age always have our anchors weighed"; and his allegory of women, when he speaks of fish: "tube fish, sweet-fleshed oysters, dainty meat for widows."[c] Jokes of this kind are ugly and suit only the mime.

(152) There is also a sort of charm from the unexpected, as in the Cyclops' words, "No-man I will eat last."[d] Neither Homer nor the reader was expecting this kind of hospitality gift. Similarly Aristophanes says of Socrates, "He melted some wax first, then grabbed a pair of compasses, and from the wrestling school—he stole a

[a] Arist. *Clouds* 401; cf. Hom. *Od.* 3.278 ἀλλ' ὅτε Σούνιον ἱρὸν ἀφικόμεθ', ἄκρον Ἀθηνέων

[b] Author unknown (= PLG. *Adesp.* pp. 742–43). Text and meaning are both uncertain.

[c] Sophron 52 and 24 Kaibel. In the latter σωλήν, a pipe or tube, is a slang term for the penis as well as a type of fish.

[d] Hom. *Od.* 9.369 (cf. §§ 130, 262).

λετο." (153) ἤδη μέντοι ἐκ δύο τόπων ἐνταῦθα ἐγένετο ἡ χάρις. οὐ γὰρ παρὰ προσδοκίαν μόνον ἐπη-
νέχθη, ἀλλ' οὐδ' ἠκολούθει τοῖς προτέροις· ἡ δὲ τοιαύτη ἀνακολουθία καλεῖται γρῖφος, ὥσπερ ὁ παρὰ
Σώφρονι ῥητορεύων Βουλίας· οὐδὲν γὰρ ἀκόλουθον
αὐτῷ[1] λέγει· καὶ παρὰ Μενάνδρῳ δὲ ὁ πρόλογος τῆς
Μεσσηνίας.

(154) Πολλάκις δὲ καὶ κῶλα ὅμοια ἐποίησεν
χάριν, ὡς ὁ Ἀριστοτέλης, "ἐκ μὲν Ἀθηνῶν," φησίν,
"ἐγὼ εἰς Στάγειρα ἦλθον διὰ τὸν βασιλέα τὸν
μέγαν· ἐκ δὲ Σταγείρων εἰς Ἀθήνας διὰ τὸν χειμῶνα
τὸν μέγαν." καταλήξας γὰρ ἐν ἀμφοτέροις τοῖς
κώλοις εἰς τὸ αὐτὸ ὄνομα ἐποίησεν τὴν χάριν. ἐὰν
δ' οὖν ἀποκόψῃς τοῦ ἑτέρου κώλου τὸ "μέγαν," συν-
αφαιρεῖται καὶ ἡ χάρις.

(155) Καὶ κατηγορίαι δὲ ἀποκεκρυμμέναι ἐνίοτε
ὁμοιοῦνται χάρισιν, ὥσπερ παρὰ Ξενοφῶντι ὁ Ἡρακλείδης ὁ παρὰ τῷ Σεύθει προσιὼν τῶν συνδείπνων
ἑκάστῳ καὶ πείθων δωρεῖσθαι Σεύθει ὅ τι[2] ἔχοι·
ταῦτα γὰρ καὶ χάριν τινὰ ἐμφαίνει, καὶ κατηγορίαι
εἰσὶν ἀποκεκρυμμέναι.

(156) Αἱ μὲν οὖν κατὰ τὴν ἑρμηνείαν χάριτες
τοσαῦται καὶ οἱ τόποι, ἐν δὲ τοῖς πράγμασι λαμβά-
νονται χάριτες ἐκ παροιμίας. φύσει γὰρ χάριεν
πρᾶγμά ἐστι παροιμία, ὡς ὁ Σώφρων μέν, "Ἠπιόλης,"[3] ἔφη, "ὁ τὸν πατέρα πνίγων." καὶ ἀλλαχόθι

---

[1] αὐτῷ M: αὐτὸ P.
[2] ὅ τι M: ὅ τις P.

coat."[a] (153) Here the wit came from two sources: the last words were not only added unexpectedly, they had no connection with what precedes. Such incoherence is called a puzzle; and an example is Boulias making a speech in Sophron's mime[b] (he is utterly incoherent), or the prologue of Menander's *Woman of Messenia*.[c]

(154) Again, assonance often produces a charming effect, as in Aristotle: "I went from Athens to Stagira because of the great king, and from Stagira to Athens because of the great storm."[d] Through the use of the same lexical ending in both clauses, he adds charm. If you remove the word "great" from the second clause, the charm also disappears.

(155) An innuendo also has an effect sometimes which resembles wit. In Xenophon, for example, Heraclides, one of Seuthes' men, goes up to each guest and urges him to give all he can to Seuthes[e] This shows some wit, and it is an example of innuendo.

(156) These then are the varieties and sources of charm in style. Charm in content comes from the use of proverbs, since they are by their nature delightful. Sophron, for instance, speaks of "Epioles, who throttled his own father",[3] and somewhere else, "off one claw he

[a] Arist. *Clouds* 149 and 179.
[b] Sophron 109 Kaibel.
[c] Menander *fr.* 268 Koerte.
[d] Ar. *fr.* 669 Rose (cf. § 29).
[e] Xen. *Anab.* 7.3.15ff.

---

[3] Ἠπιόλης Kaibel: ἐπίης P.

πού φησιν, "ἐκ τοῦ ὄνυχος γὰρ τὸν λέοντα ἔγραψεν·
τορύναν ἔξεσεν· κύμινον ἔπρισεν."[1] καὶ γὰρ δυσὶ
παροιμίαις καὶ τρισὶν ἐπαλλήλοις χρῆται, ὡς ἐπιπληθύωνται[2] αὐτῷ αἱ χάριτες· σχεδόν τε πάσας ἐκ
τῶν δραμάτων αὐτοῦ τὰς παροιμίας ἐκλέξαι ἐστίν.
(157) καὶ μῦθος δὲ λαμβανόμενος καιρίως εὔχαρίς
ἐστιν, ἤτοι ὁ κείμενος, ὡς ὁ Ἀριστοτέλης ἐπὶ τοῦ
ἀετοῦ φησιν, ὅτι λιμῷ θνήσκει ἐπικάμπτων τὸ ῥάμ-
φος· πάσχει δὲ αὐτό, ὅτι ἄνθρωπος ὤν ποτε ἠδίκη-
σεν ξένον. ὁ μὲν οὖν τῷ κειμένῳ μύθῳ κέχρηται καὶ
κοινῷ. (158) πολλοὺς δὲ καὶ προσπλάσσομεν προσ-
φόρους καὶ οἰκείους τοῖς πράγμασι, ὥσπερ τις περὶ
αἰλούρου λέγων, ὅτι συμφθίνει τῇ σελήνῃ [καὶ][3] ὁ
αἴλουρος καὶ συμπαχύνεται, προσέπλασεν[4] ὅτι
"ἔνθεν καὶ ὁ μῦθός ἐστιν, ὡς ἡ σελήνη ἔτεκεν τὸν
αἴλουρον"· οὐ γὰρ μόνον κατ' αὐτὴν τὴν πλάσιν
ἔσται ἡ χάρις, ἀλλὰ καὶ ὁ μῦθος ἐμφαίνει χάριέν τι,
αἴλουρον ποιῶν σελήνης παῖδα.

(159) Πολλάκις δὲ καὶ ἐκ φόβου ἀλλασσομένου
γίνεται χάρις, ὅταν διακενῆς τις φοβηθῇ,[5] οἷον τὸν
ἱμάντα ὡς ὄφιν ἢ τὸν κρίβανον ὡς χάσμα τῆς γῆς,

---

[1] ἔπρισεν Hemsterhuys: ἔσπειρεν P.
[2] ἐπιπληθύωνται M: ἐπιπληθύονται P.
[3] del. Spengel.
[4] προσέπλασεν M: πρὸς ἔπλασσεν P.
[5] φοβηθῇ Schneider: φοβῇ P.

---

[a] Sophron 68 and 110 Kaibel. The former is obscure, but
probably Epioles (or Epiales or Ephialtes), the demon of night-

drew the lion," "he polished even the ladle," and "he split cummin seeds."[a] He uses two or three proverbs in quick succession, to accumulate the charm, and almost all the proverbs in existence could be collected from his mimes. (157) A neatly introduced fable is also attractive, either a traditional fable, like Aristotle's fable of the eagle: "It dies of hunger, when its beak grows more and more curved. It suffers this fate because once upon a time when it was human it wronged a guest."[b] Here Aristotle has used a traditional, familiar fable. (158) But we can often also invent fables which fit closely and match the context, for example one writer on the topic of cats said that they thrive and pine in phase with the moon, and then added his own invention, "and this is the origin of the fable that the moon gave birth to the cat."[c] Not only will the new fiction in itself be attractive, but the actual fable is charming in making the cat the child of the moon.

(159) Release from fear[d] is also often a source of charm, for example a man needlessly afraid, mistaking a strip of leather for a snake or a bread oven for a gaping hole in the ground— mistakes which are rather comic in

mare and cold fevers, chokes the sleeper, its "father" (cf. Arist. *Wasps* 1038–39). The first of the three proverbs, building a whole picture off a detail, is common, as is the third, an example of miserliness (Paroem. Gr. i.252 and ii.178), but the second is attested only here.

[b] Ar. *Hist. Anim.* 619a16.

[c] Author unknown. There was an Egyptian story that a cat's eyes wax and wane with the moon (Plu. *Mor.* 376f).

[d] The text here may be corrupt, but the type of joke is clear from the examples. Compare the parasite frightened by a wooden scorpion thrown into his cloak in Plu. *Mor.* 633b.

ἅπερ καὶ αὐτὰ κωμῳδικώτερά ἐστιν. (160) καὶ εἰκα-
σίαι δ' εἰσὶν εὐχάριτες, ἂν τὸν ἀλεκτρυόνα Μήδῳ
εἰκάσῃς, ὅτι τὴν κυρβασίαν ὀρθὴν φέρει· βασιλεῖ
δέ, ὅτι πορφύρεός ἐστιν, ἢ ὅτι βοήσαντος ἀλεκτρυό-
νος ἀναπηδῶμεν, ὥσπερ καὶ βασιλέως βοήσαντος,
καὶ φοβούμεθα.[1] (161) ἐκ δὲ ὑπερβολῶν χάριτες
μάλιστα αἱ ἐν ταῖς κωμῳδίαις, πᾶσα δὲ ὑπερβολὴ
ἀδύνατος, ὡς Ἀριστοφάνης ἐπὶ τῆς ἀπληστίας τῶν
Περσῶν φησιν ὅτι "ὤπτουν βοῦς κριβανίτας ἀντὶ
ἄρτων." ἐπὶ δὲ τῶν Θρᾳκῶν ἕτερος ὅτι "Μηδόκης ὁ
βασιλεὺς βοῦν ἔφερεν ὅλον ἐν γνάθῳ." (162) τοῦ δὲ
αὐτοῦ εἴδους καὶ τὰ τοιαῦτά ἐστιν, "ὑγιέστερος
κολοκύντης" καὶ "φαλακρότερος εὐδίας," καὶ τὰ
Σαπφικὰ "πολὺ πακτίδος ἀδυμελεστέρα, χρυσοῦ
χρυσοτέρα." πᾶσαι γὰρ αἱ τοιαῦται χάριτες ἐκ τῶν
ὑπερβολῶν εὕρηνται. [καί τι διαφέρουσι.][2]

(163) Διαφέρουσι δὲ τὸ γελοῖον καὶ εὔχαρι πρῶτα
μὲν τῇ ὕλῃ· χαρίτων μὲν γὰρ ὕλη νυμφαῖοι κῆποι,
ἔρωτες, ἅπερ οὐ γελᾶται· γέλωτος δὲ Ἶρος καὶ Θερσίτης. τοσοῦτον οὖν διοίσουσιν, ὅσον ὁ Θερσίτης
τοῦ Ἔρωτος. (164) διαφέρουσι δὲ καὶ τῇ λέξει αὐτῇ.
τὸ μὲν γὰρ εὔχαρι μετὰ κόσμου ἐκφέρεται καὶ δι'

---

[1] καὶ φοβούμεθα del. Denniston, fort. recte (om. Lat.).
[2] del. Spengel.

---

[a] Cf. Arist. *Birds* 486–87, and 490. There it is the Persian
king who (rightly) wears the upright tiara, and purple is not mentioned.

themselves. (160) Comparisons too may be attractive—
for instance, if you compare a cock to a Persian because it
holds its crest up, or to the Persian king because of its
purple plumage, or because at cockcrow we jump up as
though a king had shouted,[a] and we are afraid.[b] (161)
Charm in comedy comes especially from the use of hyperbole. Every hyperbole is impossible, for example Aristophanes on the voracity of the Persians, "they baked oxen
in their ovens instead of bread,"[c] and another writer on
the Thracians, "their king Medoces would carry a whole
ox in his jaws."[d] (162) Of the same type are expressions
such as "healthier than a pumpkin," "balder than a cloudless sky,"[e] and Sappho's "far more melodious than the
harp, more golden than gold."[f] The charm in all of these
comes from hyperbole.

(163) Laughter and charm are, however, different.
They differ first in their material. Gardens of the nymphs
and loves are material for charm (they are not humorous),
Irus and Thersites[g] are material for laughter, and the two
concepts will be as different as Thersites and Love. (164)
They also differ in their actual style. Charm is expressed

---

[b] This last phrase may well be a later addition (so J. D. Denniston, *Classical Quarterly* 23 (1929) 8)

[c] Arist. *Acharnians* 85–87

παρετίθει δ' ἡμῖν ὅλους
ἐκ κριβάνου βοῦς. (Δι.) καὶ τὶς εἶδε
βοῦς κριβανίτας;

[d] Author unknown (cf. § 126, there of the Persians).

[e] Sophron 34 and 108 Kaibel (cf. § 127).

[f] Sappho 156 L–P (cf. § 127) and *fr. Add.* (a) p. 338 L–P.

[g] Irus, the beggar in Hom. *Od.* 18.1ff, and Thersites, the ugly
common soldier in *Il.* 2.216ff.

449

ὀνομάτων καλῶν, ἃ μάλιστα ποιεῖ τὰς χάριτας, οἷον
τὸ "ποικίλλεται μὲν γαῖα πολυστέφανος" καὶ τὸ
"χλωρηῒς ἀηδών"· τὸ δὲ γελοῖον δι'[1] ὀνομάτων ἐστὶν
εὐτελῶν καὶ κοινοτέρων· [ὥσπερ ἔχει· "ὅσον[2] γὰρ
αὐτίτης καὶ μονώτης εἰμί, φιλομυθότερος γέγονα."][3]
(165) ἔπειτα ἀφανίζεται ὑπὸ τοῦ κόσμου τῆς ἑρμηνείας, καὶ ἀντὶ γελοίου θαῦμα γίνεται. αἱ μέντοι
χάριτές εἰσι μετὰ †σωφροσύνης†,[4] τὸ δὲ ἐκφράζειν
τὰ γέλοια ὅμοιόν ἐστι καὶ καλλωπίζειν πίθηκον.
(166) διὸ καὶ ἡ Σαπφὼ περὶ μὲν κάλλους ᾄδουσα
καλλιεπής ἐστι καὶ ἡδεῖα, καὶ περὶ ἐρώτων δὲ καὶ
ἔαρος[5] καὶ περὶ ἀλκυόνος, καὶ ἅπαν καλὸν ὄνομα
ἐνύφανται αὐτῆς τῇ ποιήσει, τὰ δὲ καὶ αὐτὴ εἰργάσατο. (167) ἄλλως δὲ σκώπτει τὸν ἄγροικον νυμφίον
καὶ τὸν θυρωρὸν τὸν ἐν τοῖς γάμοις, εὐτελέστατα καὶ
ἐν πεζοῖς ὀνόμασι μᾶλλον ἢ ἐν ποιητικοῖς, ὥστε
αὐτῆς μᾶλλόν ἐστι τὰ ποιήματα ταῦτα διαλέγεσθαι
ἢ ᾄδειν, οὐδ' ἂν ἁρμόσαι πρὸς τὸν χορὸν ἢ πρὸς τὴν
λύραν, εἰ μή τις εἴη χορὸς διαλεκτικός. (168) μάλιστα δὲ διαφέρουσι καὶ ἐκ τῆς προαιρέσεως· οὐ γὰρ
ὅμοια προαιρεῖται ὁ εὐχάριστος καὶ ὁ γελωτοποιῶν,

---

[1] δι' conieci (iam καὶ δι' Richards): καὶ P.

[2] fort. ὅσῳ Roberts.

[3] del. Hahne.

[4] σωφροσύνης P: κόσμου Schenkeveld: an εὐφροσύνης?
(cf. § 168).

[5] ἔαρος Gale: ἀέρος P.

with decorative, beautiful words, a chief source of charm, for example "the earth is a tapestry of garlands of flowers,"[a] and "the pale nightingale."[b] By contrast, laughter uses ordinary and rather prosaic words [for example "the more I am a solitary and selfish, the more I have become a lover of stories,"[c]] (165) and secondly laughter is actually destroyed by a decorative style and becomes bizarre. Charm may be embellished †in moderation†,[d] but the formal elaboration of a humorous topic is like beautifying an ape.[e] (166) This is why Sappho sings of beauty in words which are themselves beautiful and attractive, or on love or spring or the halcyon. Every beautiful word is woven into the texture of her poetry, and some she invented herself. (167) But it is in a very different tone that she mocks the clumsy bridegroom and the doorkeeper at the wedding.[f] Her language is then very ordinary, in the diction of prose rather than poetry; so these poems of hers are better spoken than sung, and would not suit the accompaniment of a chorus or lyre—unless you could imagine a chorus which speaks prose. (168) But the main difference is in their purpose: the writers of charm and comedy do not share the same purpose, the one aims to give pleasure, the other to make

[a] PMG *Adesp.* 964(a).

[b] Hom. *Od.* 19.518 (cf. §133).

[c] Ar. *fr.* 668 Rose (see also on §§ 97, 144), but neologism at least is a curious example of ordinary speech, and interpolation is more likely (so Hahne). [d] Text corrupt, concealing "with elaboration" or "with resulting pleasure."

[e] Compare the proverbial "ape in purple," which even dressed up is ugly (Paroem. Gr. i.303).

[f] Cf. Sappho 110(a) L–P.

DEMETRIUS

ἀλλ' ὁ μὲν εὐφραίνειν, ὁ δὲ γελασθῆναι. καὶ ἀπὸ τῶν
ἐπακολουθούντων δέ· τοῖς μὲν γὰρ γέλως, τοῖς δὲ
ἔπαινος. (169) καὶ ἐκ τόπου. ἔνθα μὲν γὰρ γέλωτος
τε χρεία¹ καὶ χαρίτων, ἐν σατύρῳ καὶ ἐν κωμῳδίαις,
τραγῳδία δὲ χάριτας μὲν παραλαμβάνει ἐν πολλοῖς,
ὁ δὲ γέλως ἐχθρὸς τραγῳδίας· οὐδὲ γὰρ ἐπινοήσειεν
ἄν τις τραγῳδίαν παίζουσαν, ἐπεὶ σάτυρον γράψει
ἀντὶ τραγῳδίας.

(170) Χρήσονται δέ ποτε καὶ οἱ φρόνιμοι γελοίοις
πρός τε τοὺς καιρούς, οἷον ἐν ἑορταῖς καὶ ἐν συμπο-
σίοις, καὶ ἐν ἐπιπλήξεσιν δὲ πρὸς τοὺς τρυφερωτέ-
ρους, ὡς ὁ Τηλαύγους² θύλακος, καὶ ἡ Κράτητος
ποιητική, καὶ φακῆς ἐγκώμιον ἂν ἀναγνῷ τις ἐν τοῖς
ἀσώτοις· τοιοῦτος δὲ ὡς τὸ πλέον καὶ ὁ Κυνικὸς τρό-
πος· τὰ γὰρ τοιαῦτα γελοῖα χρείας λαμβάνει τάξιν
καὶ γνώμης. (171) ἔστι δὲ καὶ τοῦ ἤθους τις ἔμφασις
ἐκ τῶν γελοίων, [καὶ]³ ἢ παιγνίας ἢ ἀκολασίας, ὡς
ὁ⁴ τὸν οἶνον τὸν προχυθέντα ἐπισκώψας Πηλέα⁵
ἀντὶ Οἰνέως. ἡ γὰρ ἀντίθεσις ἡ περὶ τὰ ὀνόματα
καὶ ἡ φροντὶς ἐμφαίνει τινὰ ψυχρότητα ἤθους καὶ
ἀναγωγίαν. (172) περὶ δὲ σκωμμάτων <τὸ>⁶ μέν

¹ τε χρεία Weil: τέχναι P.
² Τηλαύγους Casaubon: τηλαυγὴς P.
³ Delevi.
⁴ ὁ Gärtner (iam ὁ add. Goeller): καὶ P.
⁵ ἐπισκώψας von Arnim: Πηλέα Sophianus: ἐπίσχων τὰ
σπήλαια P.
⁶ τὸ add. von Arnim.

452

us laugh. They differ also in their results, laughter in the one case, praise in the other. (169) They also fit different contexts. In some there is need of both laughter and charm—in comedy and satyr drama—whereas tragedy often welcomes charm, but laughter is its enemy. No one could really conceive of a tragedy of humour, or he would be writing a satyr drama rather than a tragedy.

(170) Even sensible people will indulge in laughter on such suitable occasions as feasts and drinking parties, and in reprimanding those who are too inclined to a life of luxury. Examples are Telauges' bag[a] and Crates' poetry[b]—and you might well read a eulogy of lentil soup to the profligate. The Cynic manner is very much like this, for such humour is a substitute for maxims and gnomic wisdom. (171) Laughter also gives some indication of character, revealing playful wit or vulgarity. Somebody once mocked the spilling of wine on the floor as "Oeneus turned into Peleus."[c] The punning play on the names and the laboured thought indicate a character lacking taste and upbringing. (172) In gibes too, one type is a witty

[a] The text is uncertain, but probably refers to the *Telauges* of Aeschines Socraticus (= *fr.* 42 Dittmar; cf. § 291). The beggar's bag represents the ostentatiously ascetic life.

[b] Crates VH 66 Giannantoni. For the mocking poetry of this Cynic philosopher cf. § 259. Since he wrote one, the praise of the humble lentil soup is also best taken as his.

[c] Crates VB 488 Giannantoni. The text is uncertain, but the names of two heroes are used to suggest a pun on wine (*oinos*) turned into mud/wine-lees (*pêlos*).

DEMETRIUS

οἷον εἰκασία τίς ἐστιν [ἡ γὰρ ἀντίθεσις]¹ εὐτράπε-
λος. χρήσονταί τε ταῖς τοιαύταις εἰκασίαις, ὡς "Αἰ-
γυπτία κληματίς" <ἀποκαλοῦντες τὸν>² μακρὸν καὶ
μέλανα, καὶ τὸ "θαλάσσιον πρόβατον" τὸν μῶρον
τὸν ἐν τῇ θαλάσσῃ. τοῖς μὲν τοιούτοις χρήσονται·
εἰ δὲ μή, φευξόμεθα τὰ σκώμματα ὥσπερ λοιδορίας.

(173) Ποιεῖ δὲ εὔχαριν τὴν ἑρμηνείαν καὶ τὰ
λεγόμενα καλὰ ὀνόματα. ὡρίσατο δ' αὐτὰ Θεόφραστος οὕτως, κάλλος ὀνόματός ἐστι τὸ πρὸς τὴν
ἀκοὴν ἢ πρὸς τὴν ὄψιν ἡδύ, ἢ τὸ τῇ διανοίᾳ ἔντιμον.
(174) πρὸς μὲν τὴν ὄψιν ἡδέα τὰ τοιαῦτα, "ῥοδό-
χροον," "ἀνθοφόρου χλόας."³ ὅσα γὰρ ὁρᾶται
ἡδέως, ταῦτα καὶ λεγόμενα καλά ἐστι. πρὸς δὲ τὴν
ἀκοὴν "Καλλίστρατος, †Ἀννοῶν†."⁴ ἥ τε γὰρ τῶν
λάμβδα σύγκρουσις ἠχῶδές τι ἔχει, καὶ ἡ τῶν νῦ
γραμμάτων. (175) καὶ ὅλως τὸ νῦ δι' εὐφωνίαν⁵
ἐφέλκονται οἱ Ἀττικοὶ "Δημοσθένην" λέγοντες καὶ
"Σωκράτην." τῇ διανοίᾳ δὲ ἔντιμα τὰ τοιαῦτά ἐστιν,
οἷον τὸ "ἀρχαῖοι" ἀντὶ τοῦ "παλαιοὶ" ἐντιμότερον· οἱ
γὰρ ἀρχαῖοι ἄνδρες ἐντιμότεροι.

(176) Παρὰ δὲ τοῖς μουσικοῖς λέγεταί τι ὄνομα
λεῖον, καὶ ἕτερον τὸ τραχύ, καὶ ἄλλο εὐπαγές, καὶ
ἄλλ' ὀγκηρόν. λεῖον μὲν οὖν ἐστιν ὄνομα τὸ διὰ
φωνηέντων ἢ πάντων ἢ διὰ πλειόνων, οἷον Αἴας,

¹ del. Gale.
² τὸν addidi, ἀποκαλοῦντες post μῶρον iam Radermacher.
³ χλόας Gomperz: χρόας P.

454

comparison, and writers can use comparisons like calling a tall, dark man "Egyptian clematis" and an idiot at sea "sea sheep."[a] This is the kind they can use; otherwise we will avoid gibes as we would crude insults.

(173) Charm in style also comes from what are called beautiful words. According to the definition of Theophrastus,[b] beauty in a word is that which gives pleasure to the ear or the eye, or has an inherent nobility of thought. (174) Pleasant to the eye are expressions such as "rosecoloured" and "flowery meadow,"[c] since images pleasant to see are also beautiful when they are spoken of; and pleasant to the ear are words like "*Kallistratos*" and "†*Annoôn*†",[d] since the double "l" and the double "n" have a certain resonance. (175) In general, it is on account of the euphony that the Attic writers add an extra "n" to the accusative forms of Demosthenes and Socrates (*Dêmosthenên, Sôkratên*).[e] Inherently noble in thought are words like "the men of old" which is nobler than "the ancients," since "the men of old" implies greater nobility.

(176) Musicians speak of words as smooth, rough, well-proportioned, and weighty. A smooth word is one which consists exclusively or mainly of vowels, e.g. Ajax

[a] Both are attributed to the Stoic Chrysippus (SVF i.1 and ii. Chrysippus 11).

[b] Theophr. F 687 Fortenbaugh, an adaptation of the definition in Ar. *Rhet.* 1405b17–8.

[c] Authors unknown.

[d] Probably corrupt. It occurs only here.

[e] I.e. the accusative ending in -*ê* becomes -*ên*.

---

[4] Ἀννοῶν P, vix recte.

[5] εὐφωνίαν Gale: εὐφημίαν P.

τραχὺ δὲ οἷον βέβρωκεν· καὶ αὐτὸ δὲ τοῦτο τὸ
τραχὺ ὄνομα κατὰ μίμησιν ἐξενήνεκται ἑαυτοῦ·
εὐπαγὲς δὲ ἐπαμφοτερίζον καὶ μεμιγμένον ἴσως τοῖς
γράμμασιν. (177) τὸ δὲ ὀγκηρὸν ἐν τρισί, πλάτει,
μήκει, πλάσματι, οἷον βροντὰ ἀντὶ τοῦ βροντή· καὶ
γὰρ τραχύτητα ἐκ τῆς προτέρας συλλαβῆς ἔχει, καὶ
ἐκ τῆς δευτέρας μῆκος μὲν διὰ τὴν μακράν, πλατύ-
τητα δὲ διὰ τὸν Δωρισμόν· πλατέα λαλοῦσι γὰρ
πάντα οἱ Δωριεῖς. διόπερ οὐδὲ ἐκωμῴδουν δωρίζον-
τες, ἀλλὰ πικρῶς ἠττίκιζον· ἡ γὰρ Ἀττικὴ γλῶσσα
συνεστραμμένον τι ἔχει καὶ δημοτικὸν καὶ ταῖς τοιαύταις εὐτραπελίαις πρέπον. (178) ταῦτα μὲν δὴ
παρατετεχνολογήσθω[1] ἄλλως. τῶν δὲ εἰρημένων
ὀνομάτων τὰ λεῖα μόνα ληπτέον ὡς γλαφυρόν τι
ἔχοντα.

(179) Γίνεται δὲ καὶ ἐκ συνθέσεως τὸ γλαφυρόν·
ἔστι μὲν οὖν οὐ ῥᾴδιον περὶ τοῦ τρόπου τοῦ τοιοῦδε
εἰπεῖν· οὐδὲ γὰρ τῶν πρὶν εἴρηταί τινι περὶ γλαφυ-
ρᾶς συνθέσεως. κατὰ τὸ δυνατὸν δὲ ὅμως πειρατέον
λέγειν. (180) τάχα γὰρ δὴ ἔσται τις ἡδονὴ καὶ
χάρις, ἐὰν ἁρμόζωμεν ἐκ μέτρων τὴν σύνθεσιν ἢ
ὅλων ἢ ἡμίσεων· οὐ μὴν ὥστε φαίνεσθαι αὐτὰ
μέτρα ἐν τῷ συνειρμῷ τῶν λόγων, ἀλλ', εἰ διαχωρί-
ζοι τις καθ' ἓν ἕκαστον καὶ διακρίνοι, τότε δὴ ὑφ'
ἡμῶν αὐτὰ[2] φωρᾶσθαι μέτρα ὄντα. (181) κἂν μετρο-
ειδῆ δὲ ᾖ, τὴν αὐτὴν ποιήσει χάριν· λανθανόντως δέ

[1] παρατετεχνολογήσθω Goeller: παρατεχνολογείσθω P.
[2] αὐτὰ Kroll: αὐτῶν P.

(*Aiâs*). An example of a rough word is "devoured" (*bebrôke*)—and this particular rough word has a form designed to imitate its own meaning. A well-proportioned word is one which draws on both and is a balanced mix of rough and smooth. (177) A weighty word has three aspects, breadth, length, and emphatic pronunciation,[a] for example *brontâ* instead of *brontê* ("thunder"). This word has roughness from its first syllable, length from its second because of the long vowel, and breadth because of the Doric form, since the Dorians broaden all their vowels.[b] This is why comedies were not in Doric but in the sharp Attic dialect. For the Attic dialect has terseness, and is used by ordinary people, and so suits the wit of comedy. (178) But let us leave this theorising as rather an irrelevance. Of all the words I have listed, you should use only the smooth, since they have a certain elegance.

(179) Elegance also comes from composition. It is not easy to describe the process, and no previous writer has analysed it, but I must try to do so, to the best of my ability. (180) There will, perhaps, be a pleasing charm if we integrate metrical units into our composition, whole lines or half-lines; yet the actual metres must not obtrude in the general flow of the sentence, but only if it is divided and analysed in minute detail, then and only then should we detect that they are metres, and (181) even an approximation to metre will produce the same effect. The

---

[a] Πλάσμα is vocal inflexion, a fuller sound used by the trained speaker (cf. Quint. 1.11.6 καταπεπλασμένον).

[b] Cf. Theocritus 15.88 ἐκκναισεῦντι πλατειάσδοισαι ἅπαντα.

τοι παραδύεται ἡ ἐκ τῆς τοιαύτης ἡδονῆς χάρις, καὶ πλεῖστον μὲν τὸ τοιοῦτον εἶδός ἐστι παρὰ τοῖς Περιπατητικοῖς καὶ παρὰ Πλάτωνι καὶ παρὰ Ξενοφῶντι καὶ Ἡροδότῳ, τάχα δὲ καὶ παρὰ Δημοσθένει πολλαχοῦ· Θουκυδίδης μέντοι πέφευγε τὸ εἶδος. (182) παραδείγματα δὲ αὐτοῦ λάβοι τις ἂν τοιάδε, οἷον ὡς ὁ Δικαίαρχος· "ἐν Ἐλέᾳ," φησί, "τῆς Ἰταλίας πρεσβύτην ἤδη τὴν ἡλικίαν ὄντα."[1] τῶν γὰρ κώλων ἀμφοτέρων αἱ ἀπολήξεις μετροειδές τι ἔχουσιν, ὑπὸ δὲ τοῦ εἱρμοῦ καὶ τῆς συναφείας κλέπτεται μὲν τὸ μετρικόν, ἡδονὴ δ᾽ οὐκ ὀλίγα ἔπεστι.

(183) Πλάτων μέντοι ἐν πολλοῖς αὐτῷ τῷ ῥυθμῷ γλαφυρός ἐστιν ἐκτεταμένῳ[2] πως, καὶ οὔτε ἕδραν ἔχοντι οὔτε μῆκος· τὸ μὲν γὰρ ἰσχνὸν καὶ δεινόν, τὸ δὲ μῆκος μεγαλοπρεπές. ἀλλ᾽ οἷον ὀλίσθῳ τινὶ ἔοικε τὰ κῶλα, καὶ οὔτ᾽ ἐμμέτροις[3] παντάπασιν οὔτ᾽ ἀμέτροις, οἷον ἐν τῷ περὶ μουσικῆς λόγῳ ἐπὰν φῇ[4] "νῦν δὴ ἐλέγομεν".[5] (184) καὶ πάλιν, "μινυρίζων τε καὶ γεγανωμένος ὑπὸ τῆς ᾠδῆς διατελεῖ τὸν βίον ὅλον"· καὶ πάλιν, "τὸ μὲν πρῶτον, εἴ τι θυμοειδὲς εἶχεν, ὥσπερ σίδηρον ἐμάλαξεν"· οὕτως μὲν γὰρ γλαφυρὸν καὶ ᾠδικὸν σαφῶς· εἰ δ᾽ ἀναστρέψας εἴποις, "ἐμάλαξεν ὥσπερ σίδηρον," ἢ "διατελεῖ ὅλον τὸν βίον," ἐκχεῖς[6] τοῦ λόγου τὴν χάριν ἐν αὐτῷ

---

[1] ὄντα edd.: ὄντι P.
[2] ἐκτεταμένῳ Victorius: ἐκτεταμένος P.
[3] οὔτ᾽ ἐμμέτροις C. F. Hermann: οὔτε μέτροις P.
[4] ἐπὰν φῇ Spengel: ἐπάμφω P.

charm of this pleasing device steals over us before we are aware, and the type is a favourite with the Peripatetics, Plato, Xenophon, and Herodotus; it is also, I think, frequent in Demosthenes, but Thucydides avoids it. (182) Dicaearchus can offer this example: "At Elea in Italy," he says, "when already he was old in years" (*en Eleâ tês Italiâs, presbûtên êdê tên hēlikiân onta*).[a] The close of each clause has a quasi-metrical cadence, but the metre is disguised by the smooth, continuous flow. The effect is highly attractive.

(183) Now Plato's elegance in many passages comes directly from the rhythm, which is given some length but is free from endings which have a perceptible pause and a series of long syllables. The former suits the plain and forceful styles, the latter the grand. Instead Plato's clauses seem to glide smoothly along and to be neither altogether metrical nor unmetrical, as in the passage about music, in the words "we were saying just now,"[b] (184) and again "warbling and radiant under the influence of song he passes his whole life,"[c] and again "first, if he had any symptom of passion, he would like iron temper it."[d] This word order is clearly elegant and musical, but if you inverted it to say, "he would temper it like iron," you

---

[a] Dicaearchus 39 Wehrli. In §§ 182–85 the intended rhythmical effects are most clearly seen from the transpositions in §§ 184–85, which introduce hiatus and the clash of consonants between words and lose the runs of short vowels near the ends of clauses, thus adding ἕδρα and μῆκος.

[b] Pl. *Rep.* 411a (cf. § 51).

[c] Pl. *Rep.* 411a.   [d] Pl. *Rep.* 411b.

---

[5] ἐλέγομεν Victorius e Plat.: λέγομεν P.

[6] ἐκχεῖς Dahl: ἐξέχεις P.

<τῷ>¹ ῥυθμῷ οὖσαν· οὐ γὰρ δὴ ἐν τῇ διανοίᾳ, οὐδ᾽ ἐν ταῖς λέξεσιν. (185) καὶ περὶ τῶν μουσικῶν δὲ ὀργάνων πάλιν χαριέντως ἥρμοσεν, ἐν οἷς δή φησιν, "λύρα δή σοι λείπεται κατὰ πόλιν·" εἰ γὰρ ἀναστρέψας εἴποις "κατὰ πόλιν λείπεται," μεθαρμοσαμένῳ ποιήσεις ὅμοιον. τοῦτο δὲ ἐπιφέρει, "καὶ αὖ κατ᾽ ἀγροὺς τοῖς ποιμέσιν σύριγξ ἄν τις εἴη"· τῇ γὰρ ἐκτάσει καὶ τῷ μήκει πάνυ χαριέντως μεμίμηται τρόπον τινὰ ἦχον σύριγγος. ἔσται δὲ δῆλον, εἴ τις μετασυνθεὶς λέγοι καὶ τοῦτο. (186) περὶ μὲν δὴ τοῦ κατὰ σύνθεσιν γλαφυροῦ ἐπιφαινομένου τοσαῦτα, ὡς ἐν δυσκόλοις. εἴρηται δὲ καὶ περὶ τοῦ χαρακτῆρος τοῦ γλαφυροῦ, ἐν ὅσοις καὶ ὅπως γίνεται.

Καθάπερ δὲ τῷ μεγαλοπρεπεῖ παρέκειτο ὁ ψυχρὸς χαρακτήρ, οὕτως τῷ γλαφυρῷ παράκειταί τις διημαρτημένος. ὀνομάζω² δὲ αὐτὸν τῷ κοινῷ ὀνόματι κακόζηλον. γίνοιτο³ δ᾽ ἂν καὶ οὗτος ἐν τρισίν, ὥσπερ καὶ οἱ λοιποὶ πάντες. (187) ἐν διανοίᾳ μέν, ὡς ὁ εἰπὼν "κένταυρος ἑαυτὸν ἱππεύων," καὶ ἐπὶ τοῦ βουλευμένου Ἀλεξάνδρου δρόμον ἀγωνίσασθαι Ὀλυμπιάσιν ἔφη τις οὕτως· "Ἀλέξανδρε, δράμε σοῦ τῆς μητρὸς τὸ ὄνομα." (188) ἐν δὲ ὀνόμασιν γίγνοιτ᾽ ἂν οὕτως, οἷον "ἐγέλα που ῥόδον ἡδύχροον"· ἥ τε γὰρ μεταφορὰ ἡ "ἐγέλα" πάνυ μετάκειται ἀπρεπῶς, καὶ τὸ σύνθετον τὸ "ἡδύχροον" οὐδ᾽ ἐν

---

¹ τῷ add. Gale.
² ὀνομάζω Gale: ὀνομάζει P.

rob the language of its charm, which comes directly from the rhythm; for it is definitely not in the thought or the vocabulary. (185) He has integrated yet another attractive rhythm in his account of musical instruments, "it is the lyre which you are left with in the town."[a] Invert the order to say, "in the town you are left with the lyre," and you will change the melody. He adds, "and yes, in the fields the shepherds would have some pipe." By the length of the clause and the long syllables he has very elegantly imitated the sound of a pipe, as will be clear to anyone who changes the word order of this sentence also. (186) This concludes my account of elegance which is found in composition, a difficult subject; and it also concludes my account of the elegant style, and where and how it is produced.

Just as the frigid style was adjacent to the grand style, so there is a faulty style next to the elegant style, and I call it by that broad term, the affected style. Like all the other styles, it too has three aspects. (187) It may be in the thought, for example one writer spoke of "a centaur riding himself,"[b] and on the theme of Alexander deliberating whether to compete in the Olympic games, another said, "Alexander, run in your mother's name."[c] (188) It may be in the words, for example the sweet-coloured rose laughed."[d] The metaphor "laughed" is thoroughly inappropriate, and not even in verse could the compound

[a] Pl. *Rep.* 399d.

[b] Author unknown.

[c] Author unknown. The name of Alexander's mother was Olympias.   [d] Author unknown.

---

[3] γίνοιτο edd.: γίνεται P.

ποιήματι θείη ἄν τις ἀκριβῶς σωφρονῶν· ἢ ὥς τις[1]
εἶπεν ὅτι· "λεπταῖς[2] ὑπεσύριζε πίτυς αὔραις." περὶ
μὲν δὴ τὴν λέξιν οὕτως. (189) σύνθεσις δὲ <κακόζη-
λος ἢ>[3] ἀναπαιστικὴ καὶ μάλιστα ἐοικυῖα τοῖς
κεκλασμένοις καὶ ἀσέμνοις μέτροις, οἷα μάλιστα τὰ
Σωτάδεια[4] διὰ τὸ μαλακώτερον, "σκήλας καύματι
κάλυψον," καὶ "σείων μελίην Πηλιάδα δεξιὸν κατ'
ὦμον" ἀντὶ τοῦ "σείων Πηλιάδα μελίην κατὰ δεξιὸν
ὦμον"· ὁποῖα γὰρ μεταμεμορφωμένῳ ἔοικεν ὁ στίχος, ὥσπερ οἱ μυθευόμενοι ἐξ ἀρρένων μεταβάλλειν
εἰς θηλείας. τοσάδε μὲν καὶ περὶ κακοζηλίας.

(190) Ἐπὶ δὲ τοῦ ἰσχνοῦ χαρακτῆρος ἔχοιμεν[5] ἂν
καὶ πράγματα ἴσως τινὰ μικρὰ καὶ τῷ χαρακτῆρι
πρόσφορα, οἷον τὸ παρὰ Λυσίᾳ, "οἰκίδιόν ἔστι μοι
διπλοῦν, ἴσα ἔχον τὰ ἄνω τοῖς κάτω." τὴν δὲ λέξιν
εἶναι πᾶσαν χρὴ κυρίαν καὶ συνήθη· μικρότερον
γὰρ τὸ συνηθέστερον πᾶν,[6] τὸ δὲ ἀσύνηθες καὶ
μετενηνεγμένον μεγαλοπρεπές. (191) καὶ μηδὲ
διπλᾶ ὀνόματα τιθέναι· τοῦ γὰρ ἐναντίου χαρακτῆρος καὶ ταῦτα, μηδὲ μὴν πεποιημένα, μηδ' ὅσα ἄλλα
μεγαλοπρέπειαν ποιεῖ, μάλιστα δὲ σαφῆ χρὴ τὴν
λέξιν εἶναι. τὸ δὲ σαφὲς ἐν πλείοσιν.

---

[1] ὥς τις edd.: ὅστις P.
[2] λεπταῖς Radermacher: δέ γε ταῖς P.
[3] κακόζηλος ἢ add. Goeller.
[4] Σωτάδεια Victorius: σώματα P.
[5] ἔχοιμεν Victorius: ἐκεῖ μὲν P.
[6] πάντων in πᾶν corr. P.

"sweet-coloured" be used by anyone with reliable good sense. This is true also of the words, "the pine was whistling to the accompaniment of the gentle breezes."[a] This is enough on diction. (189) The composition is <affected when it is> anapaestic and like the emasculated, undignified metres, particularly the Sotadean[b] because of its rather effeminate rhythm, as in "having dried in the heat, cover up" (*skêlas kaumati kalypson*) and "brandishing the ash spear Pelian to the right over his shoulder" (*seiôn meliên Pêliadâ dexion kat' ômon*)[c] instead of "brandishing the Pelian ash spear over his right shoulder" (*seiôn Pêliadâ meliên kata dexion ômon*).[d] The line seems to have changed its whole shape, like figures in the world of fable who change from male into female. This now concludes my account of affectation.

(190) In the case of the plain style, we should perhaps keep to subjects which are themselves simple and appropriate to that style, like this passage in Lysias, "I have a small house on two floors, the one above exactly corresponding to the one below."[e] The diction throughout should be normal and familiar, since the more familiar is always simpler, while the unfamiliar and metaphorical have grandeur. (191) Do not admit compounds either (since they too belong to the opposite style), nor yet neologisms, nor any other words which create grandeur. Above all, the diction should be clear. Now clarity involves a number of factors.

[a] Author unknown.
[b] For the dissolute reputation of Sotadeans cf. e.g. DH. *CV* 4, Quint. 1.8.6.
[c] Sotades 17 (meaning obscure) and 4(a) Powell.
[d] Hom. *Il.* 22.133.   [e] Lys. 1.9.

DEMETRIUS

(192) Πρῶτα μὲν ἐν τοῖς κυρίοις, ἔπειτα ἐν τοῖς
συνδεδεμένοις. τὸ δὲ ἀσύνδετον καὶ διαλελυμένον
ὅλον ἀσαφὲς πᾶν· ἄδηλος γὰρ ἡ ἑκάστου κώλου
ἀρχὴ διὰ τὴν λύσιν, ὥσπερ τὰ Ἡρακλείτου· καὶ γὰρ
ταῦτα σκοτεινὰ ποιεῖ τὸ πλεῖστον ἡ λύσις. (193)
ἐναγώνιος μὲν οὖν ἴσως μᾶλλον ἡ διαλελυμένη
λέξις, ἡ δ' αὐτὴ καὶ ὑποκριτικὴ καλεῖται· κινεῖ γὰρ
ὑπόκρισιν ἡ λύσις. γραφικὴ δὲ λέξις ἡ εὐανάγνω-
στος. αὕτη δ' ἐστὶν ἡ συνηρτημένη καὶ οἷον
ἠσφαλισμένη τοῖς συνδέσμοις. διὰ τοῦτο δὲ καὶ
Μένανδρον ὑποκρίνονται <ὄντα>[1] λελυμένον ἐν τοῖς
πλείστοις, Φιλήμονα δὲ ἀναγινώσκουσιν. (194) ὅτι
δὲ ὑποκριτικὸν ἡ λύσις, παράδειγμα ἐκκείσθω[2] τόδε,
"ἐδεξάμην,[3] ἔτικτον, ἐκτρέφω, φίλε." οὕτως γὰρ
λελυμένον ἀναγκάσει καὶ τὸν μὴ θέλοντα ὑποκρίνε-
σθαι διὰ τὴν λύσιν· εἰ δὲ συνδήσας εἴποις, "ἐδεξάμην καὶ ἔτικτον καὶ ἐκτρέφω," πολλὴν ἀπάθειαν τοῖς
συνδέσμοις συνεμβαλεῖς.[4] πᾶν[5] δὲ τὸ ἀπαθὲς ἀνυ-
πόκριτον. (195) ἔστι δὲ καὶ ἄλλα θεωρήματα ὑποκριτικά, οἷον καὶ ὁ παρὰ τῷ Εὐριπίδει Ἴων ὁ τόξα
ἁρπάζων καὶ τῷ κύκνῳ ἀπειλῶν [τῷ ὄρνιθι,][6] ἀποπα-
τοῦντι κατὰ τῶν ἀγαλμάτων· καὶ γὰρ κινήσεις πολλὰς παρέχει τῷ ὑποκριτῇ ὁ ἐπὶ τὰ τόξα δρόμος καὶ

[1] ὄντα add. Kassel.
[2] ἐκκείσθω Finckh: ἐγκείσθω P.
[3] ὑπεδεξάμην Kock.
[4] συνεμβαλεῖς Roberts: συμβαλεῖς P.
[5] πᾶν Victorius: omne Lat.: πάνυ P² in mg., om. P¹.

(192) First, it involves the use of normal words, secondly the use of connectives. Sentences which are unconnected and disjointed throughout are always unclear. For the beginning of each clause is obscured by the lack of connectives, as in the prose of Heraclitus,[a] for it is mostly this lack which makes it darkly obscure. (193) The disjointed style is perhaps better for immediacy, and that same style is also called the actor's style[b] since the asyndeton stimulates dramatic delivery, while the written style is easy to read, and this is the style which is linked closely together and, as it were, safely secured by connectives. This is why Menander, who mostly omits connectives, is acted, while Philemon is read.[c] (194) To show that asyndeton suits an actor's delivery, let this be an example: "I conceived, I gave birth, I nurse, my dear."[d] In this disjointed form the words will force anyone to be dramatic, however reluctantly—and the cause is the asyndeton. If you link it together to say, "I conceived and I gave birth and I nurse," you will by using the connectives substantially lower the emotional level, and anything unemotional is always undramatic. (195) Acting technique offers other aspects to investigate, for example the case of Ion in Euripides, who seizes his bow and threatens the swan which is fouling the sculptures with its droppings.[e] The actor is given wide scope for stage movements by Ion's rush for his bow, by turning his face up to the sky

[a] Cf. Ar. *Rhet.* 1407b13.   [b] Cf. Ar. *Rhet.* 1413b8ff.
[c] PCG Philemon T 22.   [d] Menander *fr.* 685 Koerte.
[e] Eur. *Ion* 161ff.

---

[6] del. von Arnim.

ἡ πρὸς τὸν ἀέρα ἀνάβλεψις τοῦ προσώπου διαλεγο-
μένου τῷ κύκνῳ, καὶ ἡ λοιπὴ πᾶσα διαμόρφωσις
πρὸς τὸν ὑποκριτὴν πεποιημένη. ἀλλ' οὐ περὶ ὑπο-
κρίσεως ἡμῖν τὰ νῦν ὁ λόγος.

(196) Φευγέτω δὲ ἡ σαφὴς γραφὴ καὶ τὰς ἀμφι-
βολίας, σχήματι δὲ χρήσθω τῇ ἐπαναλήψει καλου-
μένῃ. ἐπανάληψις δέ ἐστι συνδέσμου ἐπιφορὰ τοῦ
αὐτοῦ ἐν τοῖς διὰ μακροῦ ἐπιφερομένοις λόγοις, οἷον
"ὅσα μὲν ἔπραξε Φίλιππος, καὶ ὡς τὴν Θρᾴκην
κατεστρέψατο, καὶ Χερρόνησον εἷλεν, καὶ Βυζάντιον
ἐπολιόρκησεν, καὶ Ἀμφίπολιν οὐκ ἀπέδωκεν, ταῦτα
μὲν παραλείψω."[1] σχεδὸν γὰρ ὁ μὲν σύνδεσμος ἐπε-
νεχθεὶς ἀνέμνησεν ἡμᾶς τῆς προθέσεως, καὶ ἀπε-
κατέστησεν ἐπὶ τὴν ἀρχήν. (197) σαφηνείας δὲ ἕνεκεν καὶ διλογητέον πολλάκις· ἥδιον γάρ πως τὸ
συντομώτερον ἢ[2] σαφέστερον· ὡς γὰρ οἱ παρατρέ-
χοντες παρορῶνται ἐνίοτε, οὕτως καὶ ἡ λέξις παρα-
κούεται διὰ τὸ τάχος.

(198) Φεύγειν δὲ καὶ τὰς πλαγιότητας· καὶ γὰρ
τοῦτο ἀσαφές, ὥσπερ ἡ Φιλίστου λέξις. συντομώτερον δὲ παράδειγμα πλαγίας λέξεως καὶ διὰ τοῦτο
ἀσαφοῦς τὸ παρὰ Ξενοφῶντι, οἷον "καὶ ὅτι τριήρεις
ἤκουεν περιπλεούσας ἀπ' Ἰωνίας εἰς Κιλικίαν[3] Τά-
μον ἔχοντα τὰς Λακεδαιμονίων καὶ αὐτοῦ Κύρου."
τοῦτο γὰρ <ἂν>[4] ἐξ εὐθείας μὲν ὧδέ πως λέγοιτο·

---

[1] παραλείψω M: omittam Lat.: περιλείψω P.
[2] ἢ edd.: ὡς P.

466

as he speaks to the swan, and by the way in which all the other details are shaped to exploit acting skills. But acting is not our present subject.

(196) Clear writing should also avoid ambiguities and use the figure termed epanalepsis. Epanalepsis is the resumptive repetition of the same particle in the course of a long sentence, for example "On the one hand, all Philip's activities—how he conquered Thrace, seized the Chersonese, besieged Byzantium, and refused to return Amphipolis—all these, on the one hand, I shall pass over."[a] The repetition of the particle "on the one hand" (*men*) virtually reminded us of the opening and put us right back to the beginning again. (197) Clarity often demands repetition. Brevity may in a way add more pleasure than clarity. For just as men who run past us are sometimes not properly seen, so too the speed of a passage sometimes causes it not to be properly heard.

(198) Avoid also the use of dependent constructions, since this too leads to obscurity, as Philistus' style shows.[b] A shorter example of how the use of dependent constructions causes obscurity is this passage of Xenophon: "and that he had heard that triremes were sailing round from Ionia to Cilicia commanded by Tamus, ships belonging to the Spartans and to Cyrus himself."[c] This sentence could be redrafted without dependent constructions in the fol-

---

[a] Author unknown; cf. Dem. 11.1, also § 263.

[b] FGrHist 556 Philistus T 19. He was noted for his obscure style, e.g. Cic. *Brutus* 66.

[c] Xen. *Anab.* 1.2.21.

---

[3] Κιλικίαν Xen.: σικελίαν P.

[4] ἂν add. Spengel.

"τριήρεις προσεδοκῶντο εἰς Κιλικίαν[1] πολλαὶ μὲν
Λάκαιναι, πολλαὶ δὲ Περσίδες, Κύρῳ ναυπηγηθεῖ-
σαι ἐπ' αὐτῷ τούτῳ. ἔπλεον δ' ἀπ' Ἰωνίας· ναύαρχος
δ' αὐταῖς ἐπεστάτει Τάμος Αἰγύπτιος." μακρότερον
μὲν οὕτως[2] ἐγένετο ἴσως, σαφέστερον δέ. (199) καὶ
ὅλως τῇ φυσικῇ[3] τάξει τῶν ὀνομάτων χρηστέον, ὡς
τὸ "Ἐπίδαμνός ἐστι πόλις ἐν δεξιᾷ ἐσπλέοντι εἰς[4]
τὸν Ἰόνιον κόλπον"· πρῶτον μὲν γὰρ ὠνόμασται τὸ
περὶ οὗ, δεύτερον δὲ ὃ τοῦτό ἐστιν, ὅτι πόλις, καὶ τὰ
ἄλλα ἐφεξῆς. (200) γίγνοιτο μὲν οὖν ἂν καὶ τὸ ἔμπαλιν, ὡς τὸ "Ἐφύρη." οὐ γὰρ πάντῃ ταύτην δοκιμά-
ζομεν τὴν τάξιν, οὐδὲ τὴν ἑτέραν ἀποδοκιμάζομεν,
καθὰ[5] ἐκτιθέμεθα μόνον τὸ φυσικὸν εἶδος τῆς
τάξεως. (201) ἐν δὲ τοῖς διηγήμασιν ἤτοι ἀπὸ τῆς
ὀρθῆς ἀρκτέον, "Ἐπίδαμνός ἐστι πόλις," ἢ ἀπὸ τῆς
αἰτιατικῆς, ὡς τὸ "λέγεται Ἐπίδαμνον τὴν πόλιν."
αἱ δὲ ἄλλαι πτώσεις ἀσάφειάν τινα παρέξουσι καὶ
βάσανον τῷ τε λέγοντι αὐτῷ καὶ τῷ ἀκούοντι.

(202) Πειρᾶσθαι δὲ μὴ εἰς μῆκος ἐκτείνειν τὰς
περιαγωγάς· "ὁ γὰρ Ἀχελῷος ῥέων ἐκ Πίνδου ὄρους
ἄνωθεν μὲν παρὰ Στράτον πόλιν[6] ἐπὶ θάλασσαν
διέξεισιν· ἀλλ' αὐτόθεν ἀπολήγειν καὶ ἀναπαύειν

---

[1] Κιλικίαν Xen.: σικελίαν P.
[2] οὕτως M: *ita* Lat.: οὗτος P.
[3] φυσικῇ Victorius: φύσει καὶ P.
[4] εἰς P, om. M, Thuc.
[5] καθὰ P suspectum; expectes ἀλλά.
[6] Στράτον πόλιν M: *Stratopolim* Lat.: στρατὸν πόλιν P.

lowing sort of way: "Triremes were expected in Cilicia, many of them Spartan, many of them Persian and built by Cyrus for this very purpose. They were sailing from Ionia, and the commander in charge of them was the Egyptian Tamus." This version would perhaps have been longer, but it would also have been clearer. (199) In general, follow the natural word order, for example "Epidamnus is a city on your right as you sail into the Ionian gulf."[a] The subject is mentioned first, then what it is (it is a city), then the rest follows. (200) The order can also be reversed, for example "There is a city, Ephyra."[b] We do not rigidly approve the one nor condemn the other order; we are simply setting out the natural way to arrange words. (201) In narrative passages begin either with the nominative case (e.g. "Epidamnus is a city")[c] or with the accusative[d] (e.g. "It is said that the city Epidamnus . . ."). Use of the other cases will cause some obscurity and torture for the actual speaker and also the listener.

(202) Try not to make your periodic sentences too long. Take this sentence: "For the river Achelous, flowing from Mount Pindus, passing inland by the city of Stratus, runs into the sea."[e] Make a natural break here and give

[a] Th. 1.24.1 (cf. § 201). On theories of natural word order cf. DH. CV 5.

[b] Hom. Il. 6.152.   [c] Th. 1.24.1 (cf. § 199).

[d] The Greek construction for indirect speech after e.g. "it is said that" may have the accusative as the subject (and the infinitive as the verb).

[e] Th. 2.102.2 (cf. §§ 45–47, 206). The inns of § 47 have become signposts (cf. milestones, a Roman adaptation, in Quint. 4.5.22).

τὸν ἀκούοντα οὕτως· "ὁ γὰρ Ἀχελῷος ῥεῖ μὲν ἐκ
Πίνδου ὄρους, ἔξεισιν δὲ εἰς θάλασσαν·" πολὺ γὰρ
οὕτως σαφέστερον, ὥσπερ ἂν αἱ πολλὰ σημεῖα
ἔχουσαι ὁδοὶ καὶ πολλὰς ἀναπαύλας· ἡγεμόσι γὰρ
τὰ σημεῖα ἔοικεν, ἡ δὲ ἀσημείωτος καὶ μονοειδής,
κἂν μικρὰ ᾖ, ἄδηλος δοκεῖ. (203) περὶ μὲν δὴ σαφηνείας τοσαῦτα, ὡς ὀλίγα ἐκ πολλῶν, καὶ μάλιστα ἐν
τοῖς ἰσχνοῖς αὐτῇ λόγοις χρηστέον.

(204) Φεύγειν δὲ ἐν τῇ συνθέσει τοῦ χαρακτῆρος
τούτου πρῶτον μὲν τὰ μήκη τῶν κώλων· μεγαλοπρεπὲς γὰρ πᾶν μῆκος, ὥσπερ καὶ ἐπὶ τῶν [ἡρωϊκῶν][1]
μέτρων τὸ ἐξάμετρον ἡρωϊκὸν [ὂν][2] καλεῖται ὑπὸ
μεγέθους καὶ πρέπον ἥρωσιν,[3] ἡ κωμῳδία δὲ συνέ-
σταλται εἰς τὸ τρίμετρον ἡ νέα. (205) τὰ πολλὰ οὖν
κώλοις τριμέτροις χρησόμεθα καὶ ἐνίοτε κόμμασιν,
ὥσπερ ὁ μὲν Πλάτων φησί, "κατέβην χθὲς εἰς Πειραιᾶ μετὰ Γλαύκωνος"· πυκναὶ γὰρ αἱ ἀνάπαυλαι
καὶ ἀποθέσεις. Αἰσχίνης δὲ "ἐκαθήμεθα μέν,"
φησίν, "ἐπὶ τῶν θάκων ἐν Λυκείῳ, οὗ οἱ ἀθλοθέται
τὸν ἀγῶνα διατιθέασιν." (206) ἐχέτω δὲ καὶ ἕδραν
ἀσφαλῆ τῶν κώλων τὰ τέλη καὶ βάσιν, ὡς τὰ εἰρη-
μένα· αἱ γὰρ κατὰ τὰ τελευταῖα ἐκτάσεις μεγαλο-
πρεπεῖς, ὡς τὰ Θουκυδίδου, "Ἀχελῷος ποταμὸς
ῥέων ἐκ Πίνδου ὄρους" καὶ τὰ ἑξῆς. (207) φευκτέον

[1] ἡρωικῶν del. Spengel.
[2] ὂν del. Radermacher et Roberts.
[3] ἥρωσιν edd.: ἡρώων P.

470

the listener a rest: "For the river Achelous flows from Mount Pindus, and runs into the sea." This version is far clearer. Sentences are like roads. Some roads have many signposts and many resting places; and the signposts are like guides. But a monotonous road without signposts seems infinite, even if it is short. (203) These are a few remarks out of the many possible on the subject of clarity, and clarity is to be used most of all in the plain style.

(204) Next, composition in this style: first, avoid long clauses, since length always has grandeur, just as in the case of metres the hexameter is called heroic because of its length and it suits heroes,[a] while New Comedy is kept confined within the iambic trimeter. (205) So we shall for the most part use clauses of trimeter length[b] and some-times phrases, as in Plato, "I went down yesterday to Piraeus with Glaucon . . ."[c] (here the pauses and endings come close together), and in Aeschines, "we were sitting on the benches in the Lyceum, where the stewards of the games organise the contests."[d] (206) And let the closing words of the clauses reach a secure and perceptible end,[e] as in the sentences I have just quoted. Long delayed end-ings belong rather to the grand style, as in the sentence of Thucydides, "The river Achelous, flowing from Mount

[a] Cf. § 5.

[b] I.e. a length of roughly 15–16 syllables. The phrase is shorter (see note on § 5).

[c] Pl. *Rep.* 327a (cf. § 21). The whole sentence is intended.

[d] Aesch. Soc. 2 Dittmar, probably the beginning of the *Alcibiades*. Compare also the beginning of his *Miltiades* (in *P.Oxy.* 2889), "It happened to be the great Panathenaic festival, and we were sitting . . ."

[e] Cf. § 183.

οὖν καὶ τὰς τῶν μακρῶν στοιχείων συμπλήξεις ἐν
τῷ χαρακτῆρι τούτῳ καὶ τῶν διφθόγγων· ὀγκηρὸν
γὰρ πᾶσα ἔκτασις. καὶ εἴ που βραχέα συγκρου-
στέον βραχέσιν, ὡς "πάντα μὲν τὰ νέα καλά ἐστιν,"
ἢ βραχέα μακροῖς, ὡς "ἠέλιος,"[1] ἢ ἁμῶς[2] γέ πως
διὰ βραχέων· καὶ ὅλως ἐμφαίνεται[3] εὐκαταφρόνητος
ὁ τοιοῦτος τρόπος τῆς λέξεως καὶ ἰδιωτικός, κἀπ'
αὐτὰ[4] ταῦτα πεποιημένος. (208) φευγέτω δὴ καὶ τὰ
σημειώδη σχήματα· πᾶν γὰρ τὸ παράσημον ἀσύνηθες καὶ οὐκ ἰδιωτικόν. τὴν δὲ ἐνάργειαν καὶ τὸ πιθανὸν μάλιστα ὁ χαρακτὴρ οὗτος ἐπιδέξεται. περὶ
ἐναργείας οὖν καὶ περὶ πιθανότητος λεκτέον.

(209) Πρῶτον δὲ περὶ ἐναργείας· γίνεται δ' ἡ
ἐνάργεια πρῶτα μὲν ἐξ ἀκριβολογίας καὶ τοῦ παρα-
λείπειν μηδὲν μηδ' ἐκτέμνειν, οἷον "ὡς δ' ὅτ' ἀνὴρ
ὀχετηγὸς" καὶ πᾶσα αὕτη ἡ παραβολή· τὸ γὰρ
ἐναργὲς ἔχει ἐκ τοῦ πάντα εἰρῆσθαι τὰ συμβαίνοντα
καὶ μὴ παραλελεῖφθαι μηδέν. (210) καὶ ἡ ἱπποδρο-
μία δὲ ἡ ἐπὶ Πατρόκλῳ, ἐν οἷς λέγει, "πνοιῇ δ'
Εὐμήλοιο μετάφρενον," καὶ "αἰεὶ γὰρ δίφρου ἐπι-
βησομένοισιν ἔϊκτην." πάντα ταῦτα ἐναργῆ ἐστιν ἐκ

---

[1] ἠέλιος Victorius: ἥλιος P.
[2] ἁμῶς Finckh: ἄλλως P.
[3] ἐμφαίνεται Victorius: ἐμφαίνεσθαι P.
[4] καὶ αὐτὰ P: κἀπ' αὐτὰ Roberts.

---

[a] Th. 2.102.2 (cf. §§ 45 and 202).

Pindus . . ."[a] and so on. (207) In this style we should also avoid hiatus between long vowels and diphthongs, since any lengthening is imposing. If there is any, we should have it between short vowels (e.g. *kala estin* at the end of the sentence "all that is young is beautiful"[b]) or between a short and a long (e.g. *êelios*, "the sun"), or at any rate shorts in some shape or form. In general, this type of style is unimpressive and ordinary, and that is the very effect it intends. (208) Conspicuous figures should also be avoided, since anything conspicuous is unfamiliar and out of the ordinary. Vividness, however, and persuasiveness will be particularly welcome in this style, so we must speak next about vividness and persuasiveness.

(209) First, vividness: it comes first from the use of precise detail and from omitting and excluding nothing, for example the whole simile beginning "as when a man draws off water in an irrigation channel."[c] This comparison owes its vividness to the fact that all accompanying details are included and nothing is omitted. (210) Another example is the horse race in honour of Patroclus, in the lines where Homer describes "the hot breath on Eumelus' back" and "for they always looked as if they were about to mount the chariot."[d] The entire passage is

[b] Author unknown (cf. § 70).

[c] Hom. *Il.* 21.257ff. "as when a man draws off water in an irrigation channel from a spring with deep black water, and he guides the flow of water along his plants and orchards, and with a spade in his hands, he throws out any obstructions from the ditch, and as the water streams forth, all the pebbles are jostled along, and flowing quickly down it gurgles in its sloping bed, and outruns the man who controls it."

[d] Hom. *Il.* 23.379–81.

τοῦ μηδὲν παραλελεῖφθαι τῶν τε συμβαινόντων καὶ συμβάντων. (211) ὥστε πολλάκις καὶ ἡ διλογία ἐνάργειαν ποιεῖ μᾶλλον ἢ τὸ ἅπαξ λέγειν, ὥσπερ τὸ "σὺ δ' αὐτὸν καὶ ζῶντα ἔλεγες κακῶς, καὶ νῦν ἀποθανόντα γράφεις κακῶς." δὶς γὰρ κείμενον τὸ "κακῶς" ἐναργεστέραν σημαίνει τὴν βλασφημίαν.

(212) Ὅπερ δὲ τῷ Κτησίᾳ ἐγκαλοῦσιν ὡς ἀδολεσχοτέρῳ διὰ τὰς διλογίας, πολλαχῇ μὲν ἴσως ἐγκαλοῦσιν ὀρθῶς, πολλαχῇ δὲ οὐκ αἰσθάνονται τῆς ἐναργείας τοῦ ἀνδρός· τίθεται γὰρ ταὐτὸ <δὶς>[1] διὰ τὸ πολλάκις ποιεῖν ἔμφασιν πλείονα. (213) οἷα τὰ τοιάδε, "Στρυαγγαῖός[2] τις, ἀνὴρ Μῆδος, γυναῖκα Σακίδα καταβαλὼν ἀπὸ τοῦ ἵππου· μάχονται γὰρ δὴ αἱ γυναῖκες ἐν Σάκαις ὥσπερ αἱ Ἀμαζόνες· θεασάμενος δὴ τὴν Σακίδα εὐπρεπῆ καὶ ὡραίαν μεθῆκεν ἀποσῴζεσθαι. μετὰ δὲ τοῦτο σπονδῶν γενομένων, ἐρασθεὶς τῆς γυναικὸς ἀπετύγχανεν· ἐδέδοκτο μὲν αὐτῷ ἀποκαρτερεῖν· γράφει δὲ πρότερον ἐπιστολὴν τῇ γυναικὶ μεμφόμενος τοιάνδε· Ἐγὼ μὲν σὲ ἔσωσα, καὶ σὺ μὲν[3] δι' ἐμὲ ἐσώθης· ἐγὼ δὲ διὰ σὲ ἀπωλόμην." (214) ἐνταῦθα ἐπιτιμήσειεν ἂν ἴσως τις βραχυλόγος οἰόμενος εἶναι, ὅτι δὶς ἐτέθη πρὸς οὐδὲν τὸ "ἔσωσα" καὶ "δι' ἐμὲ ἐσώθης." ταὐτὸν γὰρ σημαίνει ἀμφότερα. ἀλλ' εἰ ἀφέλοις θάτερον, συναφαιρήσεις καὶ τὴν ἐνάργειαν καὶ τὸ ἐκ τῆς ἐναργείας πάθος.

---

[1] δὶς add. Gärtner, cf. δὶς πολλάκις in mg. P.
[2] Στρυαγγαῖος Finckh: στρυάγλιος P.
[3] μὲν P: om. P.Oxy. 2330.

vivid since no detail of what usually happens and did happen is omitted. (211) Consequently repetition is often more vivid than a single mention, e.g. "you are the man who when he was alive spoke to his discredit, and now when he is dead write to his discredit."[a] The repetition of "to his discredit" gives the insult a more vivid impact.

(212) This is relevant to the charge of garrulousness regularly brought against Ctesias[b] on account of his repetitions. In many passages it is perhaps a valid charge, but in many others it is a failure to appreciate the author's vividness. The same word is often put twice to increase the impact, as in this passage: (213) "Stryangaeus, a Persian, unhorsed a Sacian woman (for among the Sacians the women fight like Amazons), his gaze was caught by the Sacian's youth and beauty, and he let her escape. Later, when peace was made, he fell in love with the woman but had no success. He decided to starve to death, but first he wrote her this letter of complaint: 'I saved you, because of me you were saved, yet because of you I am dead.'"[c] (214) Here perhaps anyone convinced of his own brevity might object that there is a pointless repetition in "I saved you" and "because of me you were saved," since both mean the same. But if you take away either, you will also take away the vividness and the

[a] Author unknown (cf. § 26).
[b] FGrHist 684 Ctesias T 14(a).
[c] F 8(a); cf. F 8(b) = P.Oxy. 2330.

καὶ τὸ ἐπιφερόμενον δέ, τὸ "ἀπωλόμην" ἀντὶ τοῦ
"ἀπόλλυμαι," ἐναργέστερον αὐτῇ τῇ συντελείᾳ ἐστί·
τὸ γὰρ δὴ γεγονὸς δεινότερον τοῦ μέλλοντος ἢ γινομένου ἔτι. (215) καὶ ὅλως δὲ ὁ ποιητὴς οὗτος (ποιητὴν γὰρ αὐτὸν καλοίη τις <ἂν>[1] εἰκότως) ἐναργείας
δημιουργός ἐστιν ἐν τῇ γραφῇ συμπάσῃ. (216) οἷον
καὶ ἐν τοῖς τοιοῖσδε· δεῖ τὰ γενόμενα[2] οὐκ εὐθὺς
λέγειν ὅτι ἐγένετο, ἀλλὰ κατὰ μικρόν, κρεμνῶντα
τὸν ἀκροατὴν καὶ ἀναγκάζοντα συναγωνιᾶν. τοῦτο
ὁ Κτησίας ἐν τῇ ἀγγελίᾳ τῇ περὶ Κύρου τεθνεῶτος
ποιεῖ. ἐλθὼν γὰρ ὁ ἄγγελος οὐκ εὐθὺς λέγει ὅτι
ἀπέθανεν Κῦρος παρὰ τὴν Παρυσάτιν· τοῦτο γὰρ ἡ
λεγομένη ἀπὸ Σκυθῶν ῥῆσίς ἐστιν· ἀλλὰ πρῶτον
μὲν ἤγγειλεν ὅτι νικᾷ, ἡ δὲ ἥσθη καὶ ἠγωνίασεν·
μετὰ δὲ τοῦτο ἐρωτᾷ, βασιλεὺς δὲ πῶς πράττει; ὁ δὲ
πέφευγέ φησι· καὶ ἡ ὑπολαβοῦσα· Τισσαφέρνης
γὰρ αὐτῷ τούτων αἴτιος· καὶ πάλιν ἐπανερωτᾷ·
Κῦρος δὲ ποῦ νῦν; ὁ δὲ ἄγγελος ἀμείβεται· ἔνθα
χρὴ τοὺς ἀγαθοὺς ἄνδρας αὐλίζεσθαι. καὶ[3] κατὰ
μικρὸν καὶ κατὰ βραχὺ προϊὼν μόλις, τὸ δὴ λεγόμενον, ἀπέρρηξεν αὐτό, μάλα ἠθικῶς καὶ ἐναργῶς τόν
τε ἄγγελον ἐμφήνας ἀκουσίως ἀγγελοῦντα τὴν συμ-
φοράν, καὶ τὴν μητέρα εἰς ἀγωνίαν ἐμβαλὼν καὶ τὸν
ἀκούοντα.

[1] ἂν M: om. P.
[2] γενόμενα Greg.: γινόμενα P.
[3] καὶ Lockwood: καὶ οὕτω Greg.: om. P.

476

emotional impact of the vividness. Furthermore, the following words, "I am dead" instead of "I am dying," add yet more vividness by the use of an actual past tense, since what has already happened is more forceful than what will happen or is still happening. (215) Altogether, this poet (for Ctesias may reasonably be called a poet) is an artist in vividness throughout his writings, (216) as in the next example. In the case of a disaster we should not immediately say that a disaster has happened but reveal it only gradually, keeping the reader in suspense and forcing him to share the anguish. This is what Ctesias does when the messenger reports Cyrus' death.[a] The messenger arrives but does not immediately say before Parysatis that Cyrus is dead (for that would be the proverbially blunt speech of the Scythians).[b] First he reports the victory of Cyrus. Parysatis feels both joy and anguish. Then she asks, "How is the king?" He replies, "He has escaped." She responds, "Yes, this he owes to Tissaphernes." Again she asks a question: "Where is Cyrus now?" The messenger replies, "where the brave should camp." Moving gradually and step by reluctant step Ctesias at last, in the traditional phrase, "broke the news," and in a style full of characterisation and vividness he presented the messenger's reluctance to report the disaster and stirred the mother's anguish, which he made the reader share.

[a] F 24. The king is Artaxerxes, the elder son of Parysatis (cf. § 3).

[b] Cf. § 297, Paroem. Gr. ii.438.

(217) Γίνεται δὲ καὶ ἐκ τοῦ τὰ παρεπόμενα τοῖς πράγμασι λέγειν ἐνάργεια, οἷον ὡς ἐπὶ τοῦ ἀγροίκου βαδίζοντος ἔφη τις, ὅτι "πρόσωθεν ἠκούετο[1] αὐτοῦ τῶν ποδῶν ὁ κτύπος προσιόντος," ὡς οὐδὲ βαδίζοντος ἀλλ᾽ οἷόν γε λακτίζοντος τὴν γῆν. (218) ὅπερ δὲ ὁ Πλάτων φησὶν ἐπὶ τοῦ Ἱπποκράτους, "ἐρυθριάσας [ἤδη τῇ νυκτὶ[2]], ἤδη γὰρ ὑπέφηνέν τι ἡμέρας, ὥστε[3] καταφανῆ αὐτὸν γενέσθαι," ὅτι μὲν ἐναργέστατόν ἐστι, παντὶ δῆλον· ἡ δ᾽ ἐνάργεια γέγονεν ἐκ τῆς φροντίδος τῆς περὶ τὸν λόγον καὶ τοῦ ἀπομνημονεῦσαι, ὅτι νύκτωρ πρὸς αὐτὸν εἰσῆλθεν ὁ Ἱπποκράτης.

(219) Κακοφωνία δὲ πολλάκις, ὡς τὸ "κόπτ᾽, ἐκ δ᾽ ἐγκέφαλος," καὶ "πολλὰ δ᾽ ἄναντα, κάταντα"· μεμίμηται γὰρ τῇ κακοφωνίᾳ τὴν ἀνωμαλίαν· πᾶσα δὲ μίμησις ἐναργές τι ἔχει. (220) καὶ τὰ πεποιημένα δὲ ὀνόματα ἐνάργειαν ποιεῖ διὰ τὸ κατὰ μίμησιν ἐξενηνέχθαι, ὥσπερ τὸ "λάπτοντες." εἰ δὲ "πίνοντες" εἶπεν, οὔτ᾽ ἐμιμεῖτο πίνοντας τοὺς κύνας, οὔτε ἐνάργεια ἄν τις ἐγίνετο. καὶ τὸ "γλώσσῃσι" δὲ τῷ λάπτοντες προσκείμενον ἔτι ἐναργέστερον ποιεῖ τὸν λόγον. καὶ περὶ ἐναργείας μὲν ὡς ἐν τύπῳ εἰπεῖν τοσαῦτα.

(221) Τὸ πιθανὸν δὲ ἐν δυοῖν, ἔν τε τῷ σαφεῖ καὶ συνήθει· τὸ γὰρ ἀσαφὲς καὶ ἀσύνηθες ἀπίθανον·

---

[1] ἠκούετο Cobet: ἤκουστο P.
[2] ἤδη τῇ νυκτὶ del. Schneider.
[3] ὥστε Plat. codd.: εἰς τὸ P.

(217) Vividness also comes from the use of circumstantial detail, as in someone's description of a countryman walking along, "the clatter of his feet was heard from far away as he approached,"[a] just as if he were not just walking along but virtually stamping the ground. (218) Plato too has an example when he is describing Hippocrates: "He was blushing, for there was already a first glimmer of daylight to reveal him."[b] This is extremely vivid, as anybody can see, and the vividness is the result of his careful use of words and keeping in mind that it was night when Hippocrates visited Socrates.

(219) Harsh sounds are often vivid, as in "He struck them down, and out spurted their brains" (*kopt', ek d' enkephalos*)[c] and "over and over, up and down" (*polla d' ananta katanta*).[d] Homer intended the cacophony to imitate the jerkiness, and all imitation has an element of vividness. (220) Onomatopoeic formations also produce vividness, since they are coined to suggest an imitation, as in "lapping" (*laptontes*).[e] If Homer had said "drinking," he would not have imitated the sound of dogs drinking, and there would have been no vividness; and the addition "with their tongues" (*glōssēisi*) after "lapping" makes the passage still more vivid. This concludes my brief outline on the subject of vividness.

(221) Next, persuasiveness: it depends on two things, clarity and familiarity, since what is unclear and unfamil-

---

[a] Author unknown; cf. Hom. *Od.* 16.6 περί τε κτύπος ἦλθε ποδοῖιν.

[b] Pl. *Protag.* 312a.

[c] Hom. *Od.* 9.289–90 (of the Cyclops) κόπτ', ἐκ δ' ἐγκέφαλος χαμάδις ῥέε, δεῦε δὲ γαῖαν.

[d] Hom. *Il.* 23.116.   [e]Hom. *Il.* 16.161 (cf. § 94).

DEMETRIUS

λέξιν τε οὖν οὐ τὴν περιττὴν οὐδὲ ὑπέρογκον διω-
κτέον ἐν τῇ πιθανότητι, καὶ ὡσαύτως σύνθεσιν
βεβαιοῦσαν¹ καὶ μηδὲν ἔχουσαν ῥυθμοειδές. (222)
ἐν τούτοις τε οὖν τὸ πιθανόν, καὶ ἐν ᾧ Θεόφραστός
φησιν, ὅτι οὐ πάντα ἐπ' ἀκριβείας δεῖ μακρηγορεῖν,
ἀλλ' ἔνια καταλιπεῖν καὶ τῷ ἀκροατῇ συνιέναι καὶ
λογίζεσθαι ἐξ αὑτοῦ· συνεὶς γὰρ τὸ ἐλλειφθὲν ὑπὸ
σοῦ οὐκ ἀκροατὴς μόνον ἀλλὰ καὶ μάρτυς σου γίνεται, καὶ ἅμα εὐμενέστερος. συνετὸς γὰρ ἑαυτῷ
δοκεῖ διὰ σὲ τὸν ἀφορμὴν παρεσχηκότα αὐτῷ τοῦ
συνιέναι, τὸ δὲ πάντα ὡς ἀνοήτῳ λέγειν καταγινώ-
σκοντι ἔοικεν τοῦ ἀκροατοῦ.

(223) Ἐπεὶ δὲ καὶ ὁ ἐπιστολικὸς χαρακτὴρ δεῖται
ἰσχνότητος, καὶ περὶ αὐτοῦ λέξομεν. Ἀρτέμων μὲν
οὖν ὁ τὰς Ἀριστοτέλους ἀναγράψας ἐπιστολάς
φησιν, ὅτι δεῖ ἐν τῷ αὐτῷ τρόπῳ διάλογόν τε γράφειν καὶ ἐπιστολάς· εἶναι γὰρ τὴν ἐπιστολὴν οἷον τὸ
ἕτερον μέρος τοῦ διαλόγου. (224) καὶ λέγει μέν τι
ἴσως, οὐ μὴν ἅπαν· δεῖ γὰρ ὑποκατεσκευάσθαι πως
μᾶλλον τοῦ διαλόγου τὴν ἐπιστολήν· ὁ μὲν γὰρ
μιμεῖται αὐτοσχεδιάζοντα, ἡ δὲ γράφεται καὶ δῶρον
πέμπεται τρόπον τινά. (225) τίς γοῦν οὕτως ἂν δια-
λεχθείη² πρὸς φίλον ὥσπερ ὁ Ἀριστοτέλης πρὸς
Ἀντίπατρον ὑπὲρ τοῦ φυγάδος γράφων τοῦ γέρον-
τός φησιν· "εἰ δὲ πρὸς ἁπάσας οἴχεται γᾶς³ φυγὰς

¹ βεβαιοῦσαν P vix recte: βεβαίαν Dahl: βεβαίαν οὖσαν
Roberts.

480

iar is unconvincing. So to be persuasive we should aim
for diction which is not elaborate or inflated, and for composition similarly which moves steadily along without formal rhythm. (222) These then are the essentials of persuasiveness, along with the advice of Theophrastus,[a] that
you should not elaborate on everything in punctilious
detail but should omit some points for the listener to infer
and work out for himself. For when he infers what you
have omitted, he is not just listening to you but he
becomes your witness and reacts more favourably to you.
For he is made aware of his own intelligence through you,
who have given him the opportunity to be intelligent. To
tell your listener every detail as though he were a fool
seems to judge him one.

(223) We will next discuss the style for letters, since
that too should be plain. Artemon,[b] the editor of Aristotle's *Letters*, says that a letter should be written in the
same manner as a dialogue; the letter, he says, is like one
of the two sides to a dialogue. (224) There is perhaps
some truth in what he says, but not the whole truth. The
letter should be a little more formal than the dialogue,
since the latter imitates improvised conversation, while
the former is written and sent as a kind of gift. (225) Who
would ever talk to a friend as Aristotle writes to Antipater
on behalf of an old man in exile? "If he is a wanderer over

[a] Theophr. F 696 Fortenbaugh.

[b] Perhaps the second-century B.C. grammarian. For the letter as part of a conversation, cf. Cic. *Ad Att.* 13.18, Ovid *Ars.
Amat.* 1.468 *praesens ut videare loqui.*

---

[2] διαλεχθείη Schneider: διαλεχθῇ P.

[3] γᾶς Valckenaer: τὰς P.

οὗτος, ὥστε μὴ κατάγειν, δῆλον ὡς τοῖσγε εἰς
Ἅιδου κατελθεῖν βουλομένοις οὐδεὶς φθόνος·" ὁ
γὰρ οὕτως διαλεγόμενος ἐπιδεικνυμένῳ ἔοικεν μᾶλλον, οὐ λαλοῦντι. (226) καὶ λύσεις συχναὶ[1] ὁποῖαι
<...>[2] οὐ πρέπουσιν ἐπιστολαῖς· ἀσαφὲς γὰρ ἐν
γραφῇ ἡ λύσις, καὶ τὸ μιμητικὸν οὐ γραφῆς οὕτως
οἰκεῖον ὡς ἀγῶνος, οἷον ὡς ἐν τῷ Εὐθυδήμῳ· "τίς ἦν,
ὦ Σώκρατες, ᾧ χθὲς ἐν Λυκείῳ διελέγου; ἦ πολὺς
ὑμᾶς ὄχλος περιειστήκει·" καὶ μικρὸν προελθὼν ἐπι-
φέρει, "ἀλλά μοι ξένος τις φαίνεται εἶναι, ᾧ διελέ-
γου· τίς ἦν;" ἡ γὰρ τοιαύτη πᾶσα ἑρμηνεία καὶ
μίμησις ὑποκριτῇ πρέπει[3] μᾶλλον, οὐ γραφομέναις
ἐπιστολαῖς.

(227) Πλεῖστον δὲ ἐχέτω τὸ ἠθικὸν ἡ ἐπιστολή,
ὥσπερ καὶ ὁ διάλογος· σχεδὸν γὰρ εἰκόνα ἕκαστος
τῆς ἑαυτοῦ ψυχῆς γράφει τὴν ἐπιστολήν. καὶ ἔστι
μὲν καὶ ἐξ ἄλλου λόγου παντὸς[4] ἰδεῖν τὸ ἦθος τοῦ
γράφοντος, ἐξ οὐδενὸς δὲ οὕτως, ὡς ἐπιστολῆς.

(228) Τὸ δὲ μέγεθος συνεστάλθω τῆς ἐπιστολῆς,
ὥσπερ καὶ ἡ λέξις. αἱ δὲ ἄγαν μακραί, καὶ προσέτι
κατὰ τὴν ἑρμηνείαν ὀγκωδέστεραι, οὐ μὰ τὴν ἀλήθειαν ἐπιστολαὶ γένοιντο ἄν, ἀλλὰ συγγράμματα,
τὸ χαίρειν ἔχοντα προσγεγραμμένον, καθάπερ τοῦ
Πλάτωνος πολλαὶ[5] καὶ ἡ Θουκυδίδου. (229) καὶ τῇ

---

[1] συχναὶ Victorius: ἰσχναὶ P.
[2] lacunam stat. Goeller: αἱ τοῦ διαλόγου prop. Roberts.
[3] πρέπει Victorius: πρέποι P.
[4] παντὸς Victorius: πάντως P.

all the world, an exile with no hope of being recalled home, it is clear that we cannot blame men like him if they wish to return home, to Hades."[a] A man who talked like that would seem to be making a speech, not chatting. (226) Yet a series of abrupt sentence breaks such as <...>[b] does not suit the letter. Abruptness in writing causes obscurity, and the imitation of conversation is less appropriate to writing than to real debate. Take the *Euthydemus*: "Who was it, Socrates, you were talking to yesterday in the Lyceum? There was certainly a large crowd standing round your group." And a little further on he adds: "I think he was a stranger, the man you were talking to. Who was he?"[c] All this sort of style in imitation of reality suits oral delivery better, it does not suit letters since they are written.

(227) Like the dialogue, the letter should be strong in characterisation. Everyone writes a letter in the virtual image of his own soul. In every other form of speech it is possible to see the writer's character, but in none so clearly as in the letter.

(228) The length of a letter, no less than its range of style, should be restricted. Those that are too long, not to mention too inflated in style, are not in any true sense letters at all but treatises with the heading, "Dear Sir." This is true of many of Plato's letters, and that one of Thucydides.[d] (229) The sentences should also be fairly

[a] Ar. *fr.* 665 Rose = F 8 Plezia.   [b] Add e.g. "suit the dialogue."   [c] Pl. *Euthyd.* 271a.

[d] An unknown later fiction, unless it is the letter of Nicias in Th. 7.11–15. Neither it nor the Plato letters begin with χαίρειν.

---

[5] τοῦ Πλάτωνος πολλαὶ Finckh: τὰ Πλάτωνος πολλὰ P.

συντάξει[1] μέντοι λελύσθω μᾶλλον· γελοῖον γὰρ περιοδεύειν, ὥσπερ οὐκ ἐπιστολήν ἀλλὰ δίκην γράφοντα· καὶ οὐδὲ γελοῖον μόνον ἀλλ᾽ οὐδὲ φιλικὸν (τὸ γὰρ δὴ κατὰ τὴν παροιμίαν "τὰ σῦκα σῦκα" λεγόμενον) ἐπιστολαῖς ταῦτα ἐπιτηδεύειν. (230) εἰδέναι δὲ χρή, ὅτι οὐχ ἑρμηνεία μόνον ἀλλὰ καὶ πράγματά τινα ἐπιστολικά ἐστιν. Ἀριστοτέλης γοῦν ὃς[2] μάλιστα ἐπιτετευχέναι δοκεῖ τοῦ [αὐτοῦ[3]] ἐπιστολικοῦ, "τοῦτο δὲ οὐ γράφω σοί," φησίν· "οὐ γὰρ ἦν ἐπιστολικόν." (231) εἰ γάρ τις ἐν ἐπιστολῇ σοφίσματα γράφοι καὶ φυσιολογίας, γράφει μέν, οὐ μὴν ἐπιστολὴν γράφει. φιλοφρόνησις γάρ τις βούλεται εἶναι ἡ ἐπιστολὴ σύντομος, καὶ περὶ ἁπλοῦ πράγματος ἔκθεσις καὶ ἐν ὀνόμασιν ἁπλοῖς. (232) κάλλος μέντοι αὐτῆς αἵ τε φιλικαὶ φιλοφρονήσεις καὶ πυκναὶ παροιμίαι ἐνοῦσαι· καὶ τοῦτο γὰρ μόνον ἐνέστω αὐτῇ σοφόν, διότι δημοτικόν τί ἐστιν ἡ παροιμία καὶ κοινόν, ὁ δὲ γνωμολογῶν καὶ προτρεπόμενος οὐ δι᾽ ἐπιστολῆς ἔτι λαλοῦντι ἔοικεν, ἀλλὰ <ἀπὸ>[4] μηχανῆς. (233) Ἀριστοτέλης μέντοι καὶ ἀποδείξεσί που χρῆται ἐπιστολικῶς, οἷον διδάξαι βουλόμενος, ὅτι ὁμοίως χρὴ εὐεργετεῖν τὰς μεγάλας πόλεις καὶ τὰς μικράς, φησίν, "οἱ γὰρ θεοὶ ἐν ἀμφοτέραις ἴσοι, ὥστ᾽ ἐπεὶ αἱ χάριτες θεαί, ἴσαι ἀποκείσονταί σοι παρ᾽ ἀμφοτέραις." καὶ γὰρ τὸ ἀποδεικνύμενον αὐτῷ ἐπιστολικὸν καὶ ἡ ἀπόδειξις αὐτή.

---

[1] καὶ τῇ συντάξει P[2]: τάξει P[1].
[2] ὃς M: ὡς P.   [3] αὐτοῦ del. Spengel.

loosely structured. It is absurd to build up periods, as if you were writing not a letter but a speech for the law courts. Nor is it just absurd to be so formal in letters, it is even contrary to friendship, which demands the proverbial calling of "a spade a spade."[a] (230) We should also be aware that there are epistolary topics as well as style. Certainly Aristotle is thought to have been exceptionally successful in the genre of letters, and he comments, "I am not writing to you on this, since it is not suitable for a letter."[b] (231) If anyone should write in a letter about problems of logic or natural philosophy, he may indeed write, but he does not write a letter. A letter's aim is to express friendship briefly, and set out a simple subject in simple terms. (232) It has its own beauty, but only in expressions of warm friendship and the inclusion of numerous proverbs. This should be its only permitted philosophy, permitted since the proverb is ordinary, popular wisdom. But the man who utters sententious maxims and exhortations seems to be no longer chatting in a letter but preaching from the pulpit [c] (233) Aristotle, however, sometimes even develops proofs, though in such a way that they suit the letter. For instance, wanting to prove that large and small cities have an equal claim on benefactors, he says: "The gods are equal in both; so, since the Graces are gods, you will find grace stored up equally in both."[d] The point being proved suits a letter, and so does

[a] Paroem. Gr. ii.654, literally figs.
[b] Ar. *fr.* 670 Rose = T 4(b), F 16 Plezia.
[c] I.e. as a *deus ex machina*, speaking from on high.
[d] Ar. *fr.* 656 Rose = T 4(c), F 17 Plezia.

---

[4] ἀπὸ add. Cobet (Ruhnkenium secutus).

(234) ἐπεὶ δὲ καὶ πόλεσίν ποτε καὶ βασιλεῦσιν γράφομεν, ἔστωσαν τοιαῦται [αἱ]¹ ἐπιστολαὶ μικρὸν ἐξηρμέναι πως. στοχαστέον γὰρ καὶ τοῦ προσώπου ᾧ γράφεται· ἐξηρμένη μέντοι καὶ² οὐχ ὥστε σύγγραμμα εἶναι ἀντ' ἐπιστολῆς, ὥσπερ αἱ Ἀριστοτέλους πρὸς Ἀλέξανδρον, καὶ πρὸς τοὺς Δίωνος οἰκείους ἡ Πλάτωνος. (235) καθόλου δὲ μεμίχθω ἡ ἐπιστολὴ κατὰ τὴν ἑρμηνείαν ἐκ δυοῖν χαρακτήροιν τούτοιν, τοῦ τε χαρίεντος καὶ τοῦ ἰσχνοῦ. καὶ περὶ ἐπιστολῆς μὲν τοσαῦτα, καὶ ἅμα περὶ τοῦ χαρακτῆρος τοῦ ἰσχνοῦ.

(236) Παράκειται δὲ καὶ τῷ ἰσχνῷ διημαρτημένος χαρακτήρ, ὁ ξηρὸς καλούμενος. γίνεται δὲ καὶ οὗτος ἐν τρισίν· ἐν διανοίᾳ μέν, ὥσπερ τις ἐπὶ Ξέρξου ἔφη, ὅτι "κατέβαινεν ὁ Ξέρξης μετὰ πάντων τῶν ἑαυτοῦ." μάλα γὰρ ἐσμίκρυνεν τὸ πρᾶγμα, ἀντὶ τοῦ "μετὰ τῆς Ἀσίας ἁπάσης" εἰπεῖν [ἢ]³ "μετὰ πάντων <τῶν>⁴ ἑαυτοῦ" φήσας. (237) περὶ δὲ τὴν λέξιν γίνεται τὸ ξηρόν, ὅταν πρᾶγμα μέγα σμικροῖς ὀνόμασιν ἀπαγγέλλῃ,⁵ οἷον ὡς ὁ Γαδαρεὺς⁶ ἐπὶ τῆς ἐν Σαλαμῖνι ναυμαχίας φησί <...>·⁷ καὶ τοῦ Φαλάριδος τοῦ τυράννου ἔφη τις, "ἄττα γὰρ ὁ Φάλαρις ἠνώχλει τοῖς Ἀκραγαντίνοις." ναυμαχίαν γὰρ τοσαύτην καὶ τυράννου⁸ ὠμότητα οὐχὶ τῷ "ἄττα"

---

¹ αἱ del. Spengel.   ² καὶ del. Goeller.
³ ἢ P: del. edd.   ⁴ τῶν add. edd.
⁵ ἀπαγγέλλῃ edd.: ἀπαγγέλῃ P: ἀπαγγελῇ Radermacher, fort. recte.

the proof itself. (234) Sometimes we write to cities and kings: such letters must be a little more elaborate, since we should consider the person to whom the letter is written, but it should not be so elaborate that the letter turns into a treatise, like those of Aristotle to Alexander or that of Plato to Dion's friends.[a] (235) In summary, in terms of style the letter should combine two of the styles, the elegant and the plain, and this concludes my account of the letter, and also of the plain style.

(236) Next to the plain style is its faulty counterpart, what is called the arid style, and it too has three aspects. The first is the thought, as in one writer's account of Xerxes, "he was coming down to the coast with all his men."[b] He has greatly trivialised the event by saying "with all his men" instead of "with the whole of Asia." (237) In diction aridity is found when a writer narrates a great event in trivial language, for example the man of Gadara[c] on the sea battle of Salamis <. . .>,[d] or another writer on the tyrant Phalaris, "Phalaris was a bit of a nuisance to the people of Acragas."[e] So momentous a sea battle and so cruel a tyrant should not have been

[a] Pl. *Epist.* 7.

[b] Author unknown.

[c] The "man of Gadara," the probable text, may but need not be Theodorus of Gadara, a rhetorician of Augustan Rome.

[d] A quotation seems lost.

[e] Author unknown.

---

[6] Γαδαρεὺς edd.: Γαδηρεὺς P.

[7] lacunam stat. ed. Glasg.

[8] τυράννου P²: *tyranni* Lat.: τυράννων P¹.

ὀνόματι οὐδὲ τῷ "ἠνώχλει" ἐχρῆν λέγειν, ἀλλ᾽ ἐν
μεγάλοις καὶ πρέπουσιν τῷ ὑποκειμένῳ πράγματι.
(238) ἐν δὲ συνθέσει γίνεται τὸ ξηρόν, ἤτοι ὅταν
πυκνὰ ᾖ τὰ κόμματα, ὥσπερ ἐν τοῖς Ἀφορισμοῖς
ἔχει· "ὁ βίος βραχύς, ἡ δὲ τέχνη μακρά, ὁ δὲ καιρὸς
ὀξύς, ἡ δὲ πεῖρα σφαλερά·" ἢ ὅταν ἐν μεγάλῳ
πράγματι ἀποκεκομμένον ᾖ τὸ κῶλον καὶ μὴ ἔκ-
πλεων, ὥσπερ τις Ἀριστείδου κατηγορῶν ὅτι οὐκ
ἀφίκετο εἰς τὴν ἐν Σαλαμῖνι ναυμαχίαν, "ἀλλὰ
αὐτόκλητος," ἔφη, [ὅτι]¹ "ἡ μὲν Δημήτηρ ἦλθεν καὶ
συνεναυμάχει, Ἀριστείδης δὲ οὔ." ἡ γὰρ ἀποκοπὴ
καὶ ἀπρεπὴς καὶ ἄκαιρος. ταῖς μὲν τοιαύταις ἀποκο-
παῖς ἐν ἑτέροις χρηστέον. (239) πολλάκις μέντοι τὸ
μὲν διανόημα αὐτὸ ψυχρόν τί ἐστι, καὶ ὡς νῦν ὀνο-
μάζομεν κακόζηλον, ἡ σύνθεσις δ᾽ ἀποκεκομμένη
καὶ κλέπτουσα τοῦ διανοήματος τὴν ἀηδίαν,² ὥσπερ
ἐπὶ τοῦ νεκρᾷ τῇ γυναικὶ μιχθέντος ἔφη τις, ὅτι "οὐ
μίγνυται αὐτῇ αὖ".³ τὸ μὲν γὰρ διανόημα καὶ τυφλῷ
δῆλόν φασιν, ἡ σύνθεσις δὲ συσταλεῖσα κλέπτει
μέν πως τὴν ἀηδίαν⁴ τοῦ πράγματος, ποιεῖ δὲ τὴν
νῦν ὄνομα ἔχουσαν ξηροκακοζηλίαν συγκειμένην ἐκ
δυοῖν κακῶν, ἐκ μὲν τῆς κακοζηλίας διὰ τὸ πρᾶγμα,
ἐκ δὲ τοῦ ξηροῦ διὰ τὴν σύνθεσιν.

¹ ὅτι del. Hahne.
² ἀηδίαν Weil: ἄδειαν P.
³ αὐτῇ αὖ M, fort. recte: αὐτῆς ἄν P: αὖ τῇ ἀνθρώπῳ
Roberts.

described by words like "a bit of" and "nuisance," but in impressive terms appropriate to the subject. (238) In composition aridity is found when there is an unbroken series of phrases, as in the *Aphorisms*, "Life is short, art long, opportunity fleeting, experience deceptive,"[a] or when the subject is important and the clause is abruptly broken off and not completed, as in one writer's accusation of Aristides for not coming to the battle of Salamis, "But Demeter came uninvited and fought on our side in the sea battle, but Aristides not."[b] Here the abrupt ending is inappropriate and ill-timed. Such abruptness should be used in other contexts. (239) Often it is the thought itself which is frigid, or in our current terminology affected, while the composition is abrupt and tries to disguise the unpleasant nature of the thought. Someone says of a man who lay with his wife's corpse: "he does not lie with *her* again" (*ou mignutai autei au*).[c] The meaning, in the words of the proverb, is clear even to the blind;[d] but the wording is so compact that it disguises to some extent the unpleasantness of the subject, and produces what we now term arid affectation, a combination of two faults, affectation in the subject and aridity in the composition.

[a] Hippocr. *Aphorism.* 1.1 (cf. § 4).

[b] Author unknown. Aristides fought at Salamis, and this fiction sounds like a piece of school declamation.

[c] Author unknown, text uncertain but including ugly hiatus and abrupt monosyllables.

[d] Cf. § 112.

---

4 ἀηδίαν Weil: ἄδειαν P.

DEMETRIUS

(240) Καὶ τὰ περὶ τῆς δεινότητος δὲ δῆλα ἂν εἴη λοιπὸν ἐκ τῶν προειρημένων, ὅτι καὶ αὐτὴ γένοιτ᾽ ἂν ἐν τρισίν, ἐν οἷσπερ οἱ πρὸ αὐτῆς χαρακτῆρες· καὶ γὰρ πράγματά τινα ἐξ ἑαυτῶν ἐστι δεινά, ὥστε τοὺς λέγοντας αὐτὰ δεινοὺς δοκεῖν, κἂν μὴ δεινῶς λέγωσιν, καθάπερ ὁ Θεόπομπος τὰς ἐν τῷ Πειραιεῖ αὐλητρίας καὶ τὰ πορνεῖα καὶ τοὺς αὐλοῦντας καὶ ᾄδοντας καὶ ὀρχουμένους, ταῦτα πάντα δεινὰ [ὀνόματα]¹ ὄντα καίτοι ἀσθενῶς εἰπὼν δεινὸς δοκεῖ.

(241) Κατὰ δὲ τὴν σύνθεσιν ὁ χαρακτὴρ οὗτος γίνοιτ᾽ ἂν πρῶτον μὲν εἰ κόμματα ἔχοι ἀντὶ κώλων· τὸ γὰρ μῆκος ἐκλύει τὴν σφοδρότητα, τὸ δὲ ἐν ὀλίγῳ πολὺ ἐμφαινόμενον δεινότερον· παράδειγμα τὸ Λακεδαιμονίων πρὸς Φίλιππον, "Διονύσιος ἐν Κορίνθῳ·" εἰ δὲ ἐξέτειναν αὐτό, "Διονύσιος ἐκπεσὼν τῆς ἀρχῆς πτωχεύει ἐν Κορίνθῳ διδάσκων γράμματα," διήγημα σχεδὸν ἂν ἦν μᾶλλον ἀντὶ λοιδορίας. (242) κἂν τοῖς ἄλλοις δὲ φύσει ἐβραχυλόγουν οἱ Λάκωνες· δεινότερον γὰρ τὸ βραχὺ καὶ ἐπιτακτικόν, τὸ μακρηγορεῖν δὲ τῷ ἱκετεύειν πρέπει καὶ αἰτεῖν. (243) διὸ καὶ τὰ σύμβολα ἔχει δεινότητας, ὅτι ἐμφερῆ ταῖς βραχυλογίαις· καὶ γὰρ ἐκ τοῦ βραχέως ῥηθέντος ὑπονοῆσαι τὰ πλεῖστα δεῖ, καθάπερ ἐκ τῶν συμβόλων· οὕτως καὶ τὸ "χαμόθεν οἱ τέττιγες ὑμῖν ᾄσονται" δεινότερον ἀλληγορικῶς ῥηθὲν ἢ εἴπερ ἁπλῶς ἐρρήθη, "τὰ δένδρα ὑμῶν ἐκκοπήσεται."

¹ ὀνόματα del. Schenkl.

(240) Next, forcefulness. It should be clear from what has already been said that forcefulness, like all the previous styles, has three aspects. Some subjects are forceful in themselves, so that those who speak about them are thought to be forceful, even if they do not speak forcefully. Theopompus, for instance, speaks about the flute girls in the Piraeus, the brothels, and the men playing flutes, singing and dancing;[a] all these are forceful in themselves, and although his style is feeble, he is thought to be forceful.

(241) In composition this style would result, if, first, phrases replace clauses. Length dissipates intensity, while a lot of meaning packed into a few words is more forceful. An example is the message of the Spartans to Philip, "Dionysius in Corinth."[b] If they had expanded it, "Dionysius was deposed from rule and is now a poverty-stricken schoolteacher in Corinth," the result would have been a virtual narrative rather than an insult. (242) In all circumstances the Spartans had a natural inclination towards brevity in speech. Brevity, after all, is more forceful and peremptory, while length in speech suits supplications and requests.[c] (243) This is why expressions which symbolise something else are forceful, since they resemble brevity in speech. We are left to infer a great deal from a short statement, as in the case of symbols. For example, the saying "the cicadas will sing to you from the ground" is more forceful in this allegorical form than if it had been straightforwardly expressed, "your trees will be cut down."[d]

[a] FGrHist 115 Theopompus T 43, cf. § 75.
[b] See note on § 8.   [c] Cf. § 7.
[d] Cf. §§ 99–100.

DEMETRIUS

(244) Τάς γε μὴν περιόδους ἐσφίγχθαι μάλα δεῖ
κατὰ[1] τὸ τέλος· ἡ γὰρ περιαγωγὴ δεινόν, ἡ δὲ λύσις
ἁπλούστερον καὶ χρηστοηθείας σημεῖον, καθάπερ ἡ
ἀρχαία πᾶσα ἑρμηνεία· ἁπλοϊκοὶ γὰρ οἱ ἀρχαῖοι.[2]
(245) ὥστε ἐν δεινότητι φεύγειν δεῖ τὸ ἀρχαιοειδὲς
καὶ τοῦ ἤθους καὶ τοῦ ῥυθμοῦ, καὶ καταφεύγειν
μάλιστα ἐπὶ τὴν νῦν κατέχουσαν δεινότητα. τῶν
οὖν κώλων αἱ τοιαῦται ἀποθέσεις, "ὡμολόγησα τούτοις, ὡς ἂν οἷός τε ὦ, συνερεῖν," ἔχονται μάλιστα οὗ
εἴρηκα ῥυθμοῦ. (246) ποιεῖ δέ τινα καὶ ἡ βία κατὰ
τὴν σύνθεσιν δεινότητα· δεινὸν γὰρ πολλαχοῦ καὶ
τὸ δύσφθογγον, ὥσπερ αἱ ἀνώμαλοι ὁδοί. παράδειγμα τὸ Δημοσθενικὸν τὸ "ὑμᾶς τὸ δοῦναι ὑμῖν
ἐξεῖναι."

(247) Τὰ δὲ ἀντίθετα καὶ παρόμοια ἐν ταῖς περιόδοις φευκτέον· ὄγκον γὰρ ποιοῦσιν, οὐ δεινότητα,
πολλαχοῦ δὲ καὶ ψυχρότητα ἀντὶ δεινότητος, οἷον
ὡς ὁ Θεόπομπος κατὰ τῶν ἑταίρων τῶν Φιλίππου
λέγων ἔλυσεν τῇ ἀντιθέσει τὴν δεινότητα, "ἀνδροφόνοι δὲ τὴν φύσιν ὄντες," λέγων, "ἀνδροπόρνοι τὸν
τρόπον ἦσαν"· τῇ γὰρ περισσοτεχνίᾳ, μᾶλλον δὲ
κακοτεχνίᾳ προσέχων ὁ ἀκροατὴς ἔξω γίνεται
θυμοῦ παντός. (248) πολλὰ μέντοι ὑπ' αὐτῶν τῶν
πραγμάτων ὥσπερ ἀναγκασθησόμεθα συνθεῖναι
στρογγύλως καὶ δεινῶς, οἷον τὸ Δημοσθενικὸν τὸ

<hr>

[1] κατὰ Victorius: καὶ P.
[2] οἱ ἀρχαῖοι M: ἀρχαῖοι P.

(244) Periods should be tightly concentrated at the end. Periodic rounding is forceful, while a loose structure is more straightforward and a sign of simple innocence, like the whole early style; for the early writers were straightforward. (245) It follows that in the forceful style we must avoid old-fashioned qualities of character and rhythm, and resort to the new fashion of forcefulness. Clauses which have endings of the following kind, "I have agreed to speak to the best of my ability in their support,"[a] keep closest to the rhythm I have mentioned (246) Violent collocation also creates a kind of force. For in many passages harsh sounds are forceful, like rough roads,[b] as in Demosthenes' sentence "(he has deprived) you of the power for you to grant" (*hûmâs to dounai hûmîn exeinai*).[c]

(247) We should avoid antithesis and assonance in periods, since they add weight, not force, and the result is often frigid instead of forceful. Theopompus, for example, attacks the friends of Philip but destroys the force by his antithesis, "men-killers by nature, they were men-harlots in behaviour."[d] By having his attention drawn to the excessive artifice, or rather the inept artifice, the hearer loses all sense of anger. (248) We will often find ourselves compelled by the very nature of the subject matter to construct sentences which are compact and forceful, as in this example from Demosthenes: "Just as

---

[a] Dem. *Lept.* 1 (cf. §§ 10–11, 20).

[b] Cf. § 48.

[c] Dem. *Lept.* 2, the end of a long period. Note hyperbaton, assonance, hiatus, and only one short syllable.

[d] FGrHist 115 Theopompus T 44 and F 225(c) (cf. §§ 27, 250).

τοιοῦτον, "ὥσπερ γὰρ εἴ τις ἐκείνων ἑάλω, σὺ τάδ᾽[1]
οὐκ ἂν ἔγραψας· οὕτως ἂν σὺ νῦν ἁλῷς, ἄλλος οὐ
γράψει·" αὐτὸ γὰρ τὸ πρᾶγμα καὶ ἡ τάξις αὐτοῦ
συμπεφυκυῖαν[2] σαφῶς ἔσχεν τὴν σύνθεσιν, καὶ οὐδὲ
βιασάμενος ἄν τις ῥᾳδίως ἑτέρως συνέθηκεν αὐτό.
ἐν γὰρ πολλοῖς πράγμασι συντίθεμεν, ὥσπερ οἱ τὰς
καταβάσεις τρέχοντες, ὑπ᾽ αὐτῶν ἑλκόμενοι τῶν
πραγμάτων. (249) ποιητικὸν δὲ δεινότητός ἐστι καὶ
τὸ ἐπὶ τέλει τιθέναι τὸ δεινότατον· περιλαμβανόμε-
νον γὰρ ἐν μέσῳ ἀμβλύνεται, καθάπερ τὸ Ἀντισθέ-
νους, "σχεδὸν γὰρ ὀδυνήσει ἄνθρωπος ἐκ φρυγάνων
ἀναστάς·" εἰ γὰρ μετασυνθείη τις οὕτως αὐτό, "σχεδὸν γὰρ ἐκ φρυγάνων ἀναστὰς ἄνθρωπος ὀδυνήσει,"[3] καίτοι ταὐτὸν εἰπὼν οὐ ταὐτὸν ἔτι νομισθήσε-
ται λέγειν. (250) ἡ δὲ ἀντίθεσις, ἣν ἐπὶ τοῦ Θεοπόμπου ἔφην, οὐδὲ ἐν τοῖς Δημοσθενικοῖς ἥρμοσεν,
ἔνθα φησίν, "ἐτέλεις, ἐγὼ δὲ ἐτελούμην· ἐδίδασκες,[4]
ἐγὼ δὲ ἐφοίτων· ἐτριταγωνίστεις, ἐγὼ δὲ ἐθεώμην·
ἐξέπιπτες, ἐγὼ δὲ ἐσύριττον." κακοτεχνοῦντι γὰρ
ἔοικεν διὰ τὴν ἀνταπόδοσιν, μᾶλλον δὲ παίζοντι,
οὐκ ἀγανακτοῦντι.

(251) Πρέπει δὲ τῇ δεινότητι καὶ τῶν περιόδων ἡ
πυκνότης, καίτοι ἐν τοῖς λοιποῖς χαρακτῆρσιν οὐκ
ἐπιτηδεία οὖσα· συνεχῶς[5] γὰρ τιθεμένη μέτρῳ εἰκα-
σθήσεται λεγομένῳ ἐφεξῆς, καὶ τοῦτο δεινῷ μέτρῳ,

---

[1] σὺ τάδ᾽ Dem. codd.: σὺ δ᾽ P.
[2] συμπεφυκυῖαν Victorius: συμπεφυκυῖα P.
[3] ὀδυνήσει Goeller: ὀδυνήσειεν P.

you would not have made this proposal if any of them had been convicted, so if you are convicted now, no one will make it in future."[a] This particular arrangement clearly grew naturally out of the subject itself and the order it demanded, and not even by violent dislocation could anyone have easily constructed it differently. In many topics in constructing sentences we are swept along by the subject itself, just as though we were running down a steep slope. (249) It also creates force to put the most striking part at the end, since if it is put in the middle, its point is blunted, as in this sentence of Antisthenes, "for almost a shock of pain will be caused by a man standing up out of brushwood."[b] If you were to change the order, "for a man standing up out of brushwood will cause almost a shock of pain," you will be saying the same thing but will no longer be believed to be saying the same. (250) But to revert to antithesis, which I condemned in Theopompus:[c] it is not suitable either in that passage of Demosthenes where he says, "you were initiating, I was initiated; you were a school teacher, I went to school; you took minor roles in the theatre, I was in the audience; you were driven off the stage, I would be hissing."[d] The elaborate parallelism seems too artificial, and more like word play than honest anger.

(251) A massive series of periods fits the forceful style, though it does not suit the other styles. Put continuously, they will suggest successive lines of metre, and forceful

[a] Dem. *Aristocr.* 99 (cf. § 31).   [b] Antisthenes VA 45 Giannantoni. For the advice cf. §§ 50–53.   [c] Cf. §§ 27, 247.

[d] Dem. *De Cor.* 265.

---

[4] γράμματα add. M, Dem.: om. P.

[5] συνεχῶς edd.: συνεχεῖ P.

DEMETRIUS

ὥσπερ οἱ χωλίαμβοι. (252) ἅμα μέντοι πυκναὶ ἔστωσαν καὶ σύντομοι, λέγω δὲ δίκωλοί τινες, ἐπεί τοι
πολύκωλοί γε¹ οὖσαι κάλλος μᾶλλον παρέξουσιν, οὐ
δεινότητα.

(253) Οὕτω δ᾽ ἡ συντομία τῷ χαρακτῆρι χρήσιμον, ὥστε καὶ ἀποσιωπῆσαι πολλαχοῦ δεινότερον,
καθάπερ ὁ Δημοσθένης· "ἀλλ᾽ ἐγὼ μέν, οὐ βούλομαι
δὲ δυσχερὲς οὐδὲν εἰπεῖν, οὗτος δὲ ἐκ περιουσίας
κατηγορεῖ." σχεδὸν ὁ² σιωπήσας ἐνταῦθα δεινότερος
παντὸς τοῦ εἰπόντος ἄν. (254) καὶ νὴ τοὺς θεοὺς
σχεδὸν [ἂν³] καὶ ἡ ἀσάφεια πολλαχοῦ δεινότης
ἐστί· δεινότερον γὰρ τὸ ὑπονοούμενον, τὸ δ᾽
ἐξαπλωθὲν καταφρονεῖται.

(255) Ἔστι δ᾽ ὅπη κακοφωνία δεινότητα ποιεῖ,
καὶ μάλιστα ἐὰν τὸ ὑποκείμενον πρᾶγμα δέηται
αὐτῆς,⁴ ὥσπερ τὸ Ὁμηρικόν, τὸ "Τρῶες δ᾽ ἐρρίγη-
σαν, ὅπως ἴδον αἰόλον ὄφιν"· ἦν μὲν γὰρ καὶ εὐφω-
νοτέρως εἰπόντα σῶσαι τὸ μέτρον, "Τρῶες δ᾽ ἐρρί-
γησαν, ὅπως ὄφιν αἰόλον εἶδον"· ἀλλ᾽ οὔτ᾽ ἂν ὁ
λέγων δεινὸς οὕτως ἔδοξεν οὔτε ὁ⁵ ὄφις αὐτός. (256)
τούτῳ οὖν ἑπόμενοι τῷ παραδείγματι καὶ τὰ ἄλλα
προσστοχασόμεθα⁶ τὰ ὅμοια, οἷον ἀντὶ μὲν τοῦ
"πάντα ἂν <ἔγραψεν>" "πάντα⁷ ἔγραψεν ἄν," ἀντὶ

¹ γε Goeller: τε P.   ² ὁ Weil: ὡς P.
³ ἂν del. edd.
⁴ δέηται αὐτῆς M: δέῃ τοιαύτης P.
⁵ ὁ M: om. P.
⁶ προσστοχασόμεθα Goeller: προστοχασόμεθα P.

496

metres at that, like the choliambic.[a] (252) These massed periods should, however, be short (I suggest two clauses), since periods with many clauses will produce beauty rather than force.

(253) Brevity in fact is so useful in this style that a sudden lapse into silence often adds to the forcefulness, as in Demosthenes, "I certainly could—but I do not wish to say anything offensive, and the prosecutor has the advantage in accusing me."[b] His silence here is almost more effective than anything anyone could have said. (254) And (strange as it may seem) even obscurity is often a sort of forcefulness, since what is implied is more forceful, while what is openly stated is despised.

(255) Occasionally cacophony produces vigour, especially if the nature of the subject calls for it, as in Homer's line, "the Trojans shuddered, when they saw the writhing serpent" (... idon aiolon ophin).[c] It would have been possible for him to construct the line more euphoniously, without violating the metre, "the Trojans shuddered, when they saw the serpent writhing" (... ophin aiolon eidon), but then neither the speaker nor the serpent itself would have been thought forceful. (256) On this model we can attempt other similar experiments, for example by replacing "he would have written everything" (panta an egrapsen) with "everything would he have written" (panta egrapsen an), or "he was not present" (ou

[a] See on § 301.   [b] Dem. De Cor. 3.
[c] Hom. Il. 12.208. The line scans if the first syllable of ὄφιν is "irregularly" lengthened (as if opphin).

7 "πάντα ἂν edd.: πάντων P: "ἔγραψεν" πάντα add. Radermacher.

δὲ τοῦ "οὐ παρεγένετο" "παρεγένετο οὐχί"· (257)
ἀπολήγοντες δέ ποτε καὶ εἰς συνδέσμους τὸν "δέ" ἢ
τὸν "τέ"· καίτοι παραγγέλλεται φυγεῖν τὴν ἀπόληξιν τὴν τοιαύτην· ἀλλὰ πολλαχοῦ χρήσιμος τοιαύτη
ἂν γένοιτο, οἷον "οὐκ εὐφήμησε μέν, ἄξιον ὄντα,
ἠτίμασε δέ," καὶ[1] τὸ "Σχοῖνόν τε Σκῶλόν τε," ἀλλ'
ἐν μὲν τοῖς Ὁμηρικοῖς μέγεθος ἐποίησεν ἡ εἰς τοὺς
συνδέσμους τελευτή. (258) ποιήσειε δ' ἄν ποτε καὶ
δεινότητα, εἴ τις ὧδε εἴποι "ἀνέτρεψεν[2] δὲ ὑπὸ τῆς
ἀφροσύνης τε ὑπὸ τῆς ἀσεβείας τε τὰ ἱερά τε τὰ
ὅσιά τε"· ὅλως γὰρ ἡ λειότης καὶ τὸ εὐήκοον γλαφυ-
ρότητος ἴδια, οὐ δεινότητός ἐστιν, οὗτοι δ' οἱ χαρακτῆρες ἐναντιώτατοι δοκοῦσιν.

(259) Καίτοι ἐστὶ πολλαχοῦ ἐκ παιδιᾶς παραμε-
μιγμένης δεινότης ἐμφαινομένη τις, οἷον ἐν ταῖς
κωμῳδίαις, καὶ πᾶς ὁ Κυνικὸς τρόπος, ὡς τὰ Κράτητος "πήρη[3] τις γαῖ'[4] ἔστι μέσῳ ἐνὶ οἴνοπι πόντῳ"·
(260) καὶ τὸ Διογένους τὸ ἐν Ὀλυμπίᾳ, ὅτε τοῦ ὁπλί-
του δραμόντος ἐπιτρέχων αὐτὸς ἐκήρυττεν ἑαυτὸν
νικᾶν τὰ Ὀλύμπια πάντας ἀνθρώπους καλοκἀγαθίᾳ.

---

[1] καὶ Radermacher: ὡς P.
[2] ἀνέτρεψεν Weil: ἄν. ἔγραψεν P.
[3] πήρη Victorius: τὸ ποτήρη P.
[4] γαῖ' Victorius: γὰρ P.

---

[a] The negative moves to final, emphatic position. The point
of the first example is presumably that ἄν prefers a weak position.

paregeneto) with "present he was not" (*paregeneto ouchi*);[a] (257) or by ending sometimes with a connective, "on the other hand" (*de*) or "too" (*te*), even though the normal instruction is to avoid such endings. But this sort of closure can often be useful, for example "he did not praise him on the one hand (*men*), though he deserved it; he insulted him, on the other hand" (*de*);[b] or "and Schoenus and Scolus too ..." (*Schoenon te Skôlon te* ...)[c] though in Homer's lines it is grandeur which is the result of ending with a connective. (258) But sometimes it can also produce force, as in this sort of sentence (with repeated *te*), "He overturned, in his folly and his impiety too, things sacred and holy too."[d] In general, smoothness and euphony are characteristic of the elegant style, not the forceful, and these two styles seem to be direct opposites.

(259) Yet mixing in an element of playfulness often produces a kind of vigour, for example in comedy; and the whole Cynic manner is like this, as in the words of Crates, "There is a land of Beggarbag in the midst of the wine-dark sea";[e] (260) and the story about Diogenes at Olympia, when after the race between men in armour he ran forward and personally proclaimed himself victor in

[b] Author unknown.

[c] Hom. *Il.* 2.497 (cf. § 54).

[d] Author unknown.

[e] Cf. § 170. Crates VH 70 Giannantoni, a parody of Homer's description of Crete (quoted in § 113). Demetrius (or a copyist) is too close to Homer: compare the correct version in Diog. Laert. 6.85, Πήρη τις πόλις ἔστι μέσῳ ἐνὶ οἴνοπι τύφῳ, "There is a city of Beggarbag in the midst of wine-dark delusion."

καὶ γὰρ γελᾶται τὸ εἰρημένον ἅμα καὶ θαυμάζεται,
καὶ ἠρέμα καὶ ὑποδάκνει πως λεγόμενον. (261) καὶ
τὸ πρὸς τὸν καλὸν ῥηθὲν αὐτῷ· προσπαλαίων γὰρ
καλῷ παιδὶ Διογένης διεκινήθη πως τὸ αἰδοῖον, τοῦ
δὲ παιδὸς φοβηθέντος καὶ ἀποπηδήσαντος, "θάρρει", ἔφη,[1] "ὦ παιδίον· οὐκ εἰμὶ ταύτῃ ὅμοιος."
γελοῖον γὰρ τὸ πρόχειρον τοῦ λόγου, δεινὴ δ' ἡ κευ-
θομένη ἔμφασις. καὶ ὅλως, συνελόντι φράσαι, πᾶν
τὸ εἶδος τοῦ Κυνικοῦ λόγου σαίνοντι ἅμα ἔοικέ τῳ
καὶ δάκνοντι. (262) χρήσονται δ' αὐτῷ καὶ οἱ ῥήτο-
ρές ποτε, καὶ ἐχρήσαντο, Λυσίας μὲν πρὸς τὸν
ἐρῶντα τῆς γραὸς λέγων, ὅτι "ἧς ῥᾷον ἦν ἀριθμῆ-
σαι τοὺς ὀδόντας ἢ τοὺς δακτύλους"· καὶ γὰρ δεινό-
τατα ἅμα καὶ γελοιότατα ἐνέφηνεν τὴν γραῦν·
Ὅμηρος δὲ τὸ "Οὖτιν ἐγὼ πύματον ἔδομαι," ὡς
προγέγραπται.

(263) Ὡς δ' ἂν καὶ ἐκ σχημάτων γίγνοιτο δεινότης, λέξομεν· ἐκ μὲν οὖν τῶν τῆς διανοίας σχημάτων, ἐκ μὲν τῆς παραλείψεως ὀνομαζομένης οὕτως·
"Ὄλυνθον μὲν δὴ καὶ Μεθώνην καὶ Ἀπολλωνίαν
καὶ δύο καὶ τριάκοντα πόλεις τὰς ἐπὶ Θρᾴκης ἐῶ"· ἐν
γὰρ τούτοις καὶ εἴρηκεν πάντα, ὅσα ἐβούλετο, καὶ
παραλιπεῖν αὐτά φησιν, ὡς δεινότερα εἰπεῖν ἔχων
ἕτερα. (264) καὶ ἡ προειρημένη δ' ἀποσιώπησις τοῦ
αὐτοῦ εἴδους[2] ἐχομένη δεινότερον ποιήσει τὸν λόγον.

[1] ἔφη Greg.: om. P: εἶπεν post παιδίον M.
[2] εἴδους Orth: ἔθους P.

500

the Olympic games over all mankind, in nobility of character.[a] This announcement raises simultaneous laughter and applause, and unobtrusively it also somehow gently bites as it is being said. (261) So do his words to the handsome youth: wrestling with a handsome youth Diogenes somehow experienced an erection, and the boy became afraid and jumped away. "Never fear, my boy," he said, "I am not like you in *that* way."[b] There is wit in the speed of the reply, and force in the meaning hidden below. Generally speaking, to summarise, the whole character of Cynic sayings suggests a dog that fawns as it bites. (262) Orators will also sometimes use it, as they have in the past, for example Lysias when he said to the old woman's lover, "her teeth could be counted sooner than her fingers."[c] He revealed the old woman most forcefully in a most ridiculous light. Homer also used it, as in an example I have already quoted, "No-man I will eat last."[d]

(263) We shall next discuss how force can result from figures. First, figures of thought, beginning with the figure given the name of paraleipsis, for example "I pass over Olynthus, Methone, Apollonia, and thirty-two cities in Thrace."[e] In these words Demosthenes has actually stated everything he wanted, yet he claims to pass over them, to imply that he has other more forceful points to make. (264) The figure of aposiopesis which I have already mentioned[f] is of the same kind, and it too adds

---

[a] Diogenes VB 449 Giannantoni.   [b] Diogenes VB 410 Giannantoni.   [c] Lys. *fr.* 1 Thalheim (cf. § 128).

[d] Hom. *Od.* 9.369 (cf. §§ 130, 152).   [e] Dem. *Phil.* 3.26.

[f] Cf. § 253 (rather than § 103).

(265) παραλαμβάνοιτο δ' ἂν σχῆμα διανοίας πρὸς δεινότητα <ἡ>[1] προσωποποιΐα καλουμένη, οἷον "δόξατε ὑμῖν τοὺς προγόνους ὀνειδίζειν καὶ λέγειν τάδε τινὰ ἢ τὴν Ἑλλάδα ἢ τὴν πατρίδα, λαβοῦσαν γυναικὸς σχῆμα"· (266) ὥσπερ ἐν τῷ ἐπιταφίῳ Πλάτων τὸ "ὦ παῖδες, ὅτι μέν ἐστε πατέρων ἀγαθῶν . . . ," καὶ οὐκ ἐκ τοῦ ἰδίου προσώπου λέγει ἀλλὰ ἐκ τοῦ τῶν πατέρων· πολὺ γὰρ ἐνεργέστερα καὶ δεινότερα φαίνεται ὑπὸ τῶν προσώπων, μᾶλλον δὲ δράματα ἀτεχνῶς γίνεται.

(267) Τὰ μὲν δὴ[2] τῆς διανοίας [καὶ][3] σχήματα λαμβάνοιτ' ἄν, ὡς εἴρηται· καὶ γὰρ τοσαῦτα τὰ εἰρημένα παραδείγματος ἕνεκα, τὰ δὲ τῆς λέξεως σχήματα ποικιλώτερον ἐκλέγοντα ἔστι δεινότερον ποιεῖν τὸν λόγον· ἔκ τε τῆς ἀναδιπλώσεως, ὡς "Θῆβαι δέ, Θῆβαι, πόλις ἀστυγείτων, ἐκ μέσης τῆς Ἑλλάδος ἀνήρπασται" (διλογηθὲν γὰρ τὸ ὄνομα δεινότητα ποιεῖ)· (268) καὶ ἐκ τῆς ἀναφορᾶς καλουμένης, ὡς τὸ "ἐπὶ σαυτὸν καλεῖς, ἐπὶ τοὺς νόμους καλεῖς,[4] ἐπὶ τὴν δημοκρατίαν καλεῖς"· τὸ δὲ σχῆμα τὸ εἰρημένον τοῦτο τριπλοῦν· καὶ γὰρ ἐπαναφορά ἐστιν, ὡς[5] εἴρηται, διὰ τὸ τὴν αὐτὴν λέξιν ἐπαναφέρεσθαι ἐπὶ τὴν αὐτὴν ἀρχήν, καὶ ἀσύνδετον· δίχα γὰρ συνδέσμων λέλεκται, καὶ ὁμοιοτέλευτον διὰ τὴν

---

[1] ἡ add. Hammer.
[2] δὴ Spengel: εἴδη P.   [3] καὶ del. Spengel.
[4] ἐπὶ τοὺς νόμους καλεῖς add. Aesch., M in mg., om. P.
[5] ἐστιν, ὡς Victorius: ἴσως P.

force to what we say. (265) Another figure of thought which may be used to produce force is the figure called prosopopoeia, for example "Imagine that your ancestors are rebuking you and speak such words, or imagine Greece, or your country in the form of a woman."[a] (266) This is what Plato uses in his Funeral Speech, "Children, that you are the sons of brave men ..."[b] He does not speak in his own person but in that of their fathers. The personification makes the passage much more lively and forceful, or rather it really turns into a drama.

(267) The figures of thought may be used as I have described; and the instances above will serve as a sample. As for figures of speech, the more varied your choice, the more forceful their impact on what you say. Take repetition, as in "Thebes, Thebes, our neighbouring city, has been torn from the middle of Greece."[c] The repetition of the name gives force. (268) Or take the figure called anaphora, as in "against yourself you summon him, against the laws you summon him, against the democracy you summon him."[d] Here the figure in question is three-fold. It is anaphora, as I have already said, because the same word is repeated at the beginning of each clause; it is asyndeton because it is expressed without connectives; and it is homoeoteleuton because of the recurrent end-

[a] Author unknown, perhaps an invented pastiche since ancestors and country give the two standard categories of animate and inanimate, e.g. Cic. *Orator* 85.

[b] Pl. *Menex.* 246d.

[c] Aesch. *Ctes.* 133.

[d] Aesch. *Ctes.* 202.

ἀπόληξιν τοῦ "καλεῖς" <τεθεῖσαν>[1] πολλάκις. καὶ
δεινότης ἤθροισται ἐκ τῶν τριῶν, εἰ δ' εἴποι τις
οὕτως, "ἐπὶ σαυτὸν[2] καὶ τοὺς νόμους καὶ τὴν δημοκρατίαν καλεῖς," ἅμα τοῖς σχήμασιν ἐξαιρήσει καὶ
τὴν δεινότητα. (269) μάλιστα δὲ πάντων ἰστέον τὴν
διάλυσιν δεινότητος ἐργάτιν, οἷον "πορεύεται διὰ
τῆς ἀγορᾶς τὰς γνάθους φυσῶν, τὰς ὀφρῦς ἐπηρ-
κώς, ἴσα βαίνων Πυθοκλεῖ"· εἰ γὰρ συναφθῇ ταῦτα
συνδέσμοις, πρᾳότερα ἔσται. (270) λαμβάνοιτ' ἂν
καὶ ἡ κλῖμαξ καλουμένη, ὥσπερ Δημοσθένει τὸ "οὐκ
εἶπον μὲν ταῦτα, οὐκ ἔγραψα δέ· οὐδ' ἔγραψα μέν,
οὐκ ἐπρέσβευσα δέ· οὐδ' ἐπρέσβευσα μέν, οὐκ
ἔπεισα δὲ Θηβαίους"· σχεδὸν γὰρ ἐπαναβαίνοντι ὁ
λόγος ἔοικεν ἐπὶ μειζόνων μείζονα· εἰ δὲ οὕτως εἴποι
τις ταῦτα, "εἰπὼν ἐγὼ καὶ γράψας ἐπρέσβευσά τε
καὶ ἔπεισα Θηβαίους," διήγημα ἐρεῖ μόνον, δεινὸν
δὲ οὐδέν. (271) καθόλου δὲ τῆς λέξεως τὰ σχήματα
καὶ ὑπόκρισιν καὶ ἀγῶνα παρέχει τῷ λέγοντι,
μάλιστα τὸ διαλελυμένον [τοῦτ' ἔστι δεινότητα].[3]
καὶ περὶ μὲν τῶν σχημάτων ἀμφοτέρων τοσαῦτα.

(272) Λέξις δὲ λαμβανέσθω πᾶσα, ὅση καὶ ἐν τῷ
μεγαλοπρεπεῖ χαρακτῆρι, πλὴν οὐκ ἐπὶ τὸ αὐτὸ
τέλος· καὶ γὰρ μεταφέροντα ἔστι δεινὰ ποιεῖν, ὡς τὸ

---

[1] καλεῖς τεθεῖσαν Denniston: καλεῖσθαι P: καλεῖς iam edd.
[2] ἐπὶ σαυτὸν Victorius: ἐπαυτὸν P.
[3] del. Radermacher.

ing, "you summon him." Force is the cumulative result of
the three figures, and if you were to write, "against yourself and the laws and the democracy you summon him,"
you will remove the force along with the figures. (269)
But you should realise that above all other figures it is
asyndeton which produces force, as in "he walks through
the marketplace, puffing out his cheeks, raising his eye-
brows, keeping in step with Pythocles."[a] If the words
were smoothed out with connectives, they will be tamer.
(270) The figure called climax should also be used, as in
this sentence from Demosthenes, "I did not express this
opinion, and then fail to move the resolution; I did not
move the resolution and then fail to serve as envoy; I did
not serve as envoy and then fail to convince the
Thebans."[b] This sentence seems almost to be climbing
higher and higher at each step, and if you were to rewrite
it like this, "after I gave my opinion and moved the resolution, I served as envoy and convinced the Thebans," you
will give a mere narrative of events, with nothing forceful
about it. (271) In summary, figures of speech, particularly
asyndeton, provide the speaker with scope for dramatic
delivery and immediacy [that is to say force].[c] This concludes my account of both kinds of figures.

(272) The diction to use should be entirely the same
as that in the grand style, but with a different end in
view. Metaphor, for example, creates force, for example

[a] Dem. *De Fals. Leg.* 314.

[b] Dem. *De Cor.* 179, the traditional example, e.g. Quint.
9.3.55. Literally ladder, κλîμαξ has a narrower meaning than its
derivative, "climax," since each step must be repeated.

[c] The perverse word order in the Greek seems to demand
deletion.

"τῷ Πύθωνι θρασυνομένῳ καὶ πολλῷ ῥέοντι καθ᾽
ὑμῶν"· (273) καὶ εἰκασίας¹ λέγοντα, ὡς τὸ Δημοσθένους, "τοῦτο τὸ ψήφισμα τὸν τότ᾽ ἐπιόντα τῇ πόλει
κίνδυνον παρελθεῖν ἐποίησεν, ὥσπερ νέφος." (274)
αἱ παραβολαὶ δὲ τῇ δεινότητι οὐκ ἐπιτήδειαι διὰ τὸ
μῆκος, οἷον τὸ "ὥσπερ δὲ κύων γενναῖος, ἄπειρος,
ἀπρονοήτως ἐπὶ κάπρον φέρεται"· κάλλος γὰρ καὶ
ἀκρίβειά τις ἐν τούτοις ἐμφαίνεται, ἡ δὲ δεινότης
σφοδρόν τι βούλεται καὶ σύντομον, καὶ ἐγγύθεν
πλήττουσιν ἔοικεν. (275) γίνεται δὲ καὶ ἐκ συνθέτου
ὀνόματος δεινότης, ὥσπερ καὶ ἡ συνήθεια συντίθησιν δεινῶς πολλά, "τὴν χαμαιτύπην" καὶ "τὸν παρα-
πλῆγα" καὶ εἴ τι ἄλλο τοιοῦτον· καὶ παρὰ τοῖς
ῥήτορσι δὲ πολλὰ ἄν τις εὕροι τοιαῦτα. (276) πειρᾶσθαι δὲ τὰ ὀνόματα πρεπόντως λέγειν τοῖς πράγμασιν, οἷον ἐπὶ μὲν τοῦ βίᾳ καὶ πανουργίᾳ δράσαν-
τος "διεβιάσατο,"² ἐπὶ δὲ τοῦ βίᾳ καὶ φανερῶς καὶ
μετὰ ἀπονοίας "ἐξέκοψεν, ἐξεῖλεν," ἐπὶ δὲ τοῦ δολίως
καὶ λαθραίως³ "ἐτρύπησεν"⁴ ἢ "διέφαγεν," ἢ εἴ τι
τοιοῦτον πρόσφορον τοῖς πράγμασιν ὄνομα.

(277) Τὸ δὲ ἐξαίρεσθαί πως λαμβανόμενον οὐ
μέγεθος ποιεῖ μόνον ἀλλὰ καὶ δεινότητα, ὡς τὸ "οὐ
λέγειν εἴσω τὴν χεῖρα ἔχοντα δεῖ, Αἰσχίνη, ἀλλὰ

---

¹ εἰκασίας M: εἰ εἰκάσειας P.
² διεβιάσατο M: διεβιβάσατο P.
³ λαθραίως Victorius: λάθρα ὡς P.
⁴ an ἐξετρύπησεν?

"Python grew bold and was a rushing torrent in full spate against you,"[a] (273) and so does simile, as in Demosthenes' passage, "this decree made the danger which then threatened the city pass by like a cloud."[b] (274) But detailed comparisons do not suit the forceful style because of their length, for example "as a gallant hound, ignorant of the danger, recklessly charges a boar."[c] There is an element of beauty and precise detail about this sentence, whereas forcefulness needs to be short and sharp, like a close exchange of blows. (275) Compound words also give force, as usage proves in many forceful compounds such as "street-lay," "brain-crazy,"[d] and the like. Many similar examples may be found in the orators. (276) Try also to use words which match their subject, for example say of a man who acted violently and ruthlessly that "he forced his way through," or of a man who acted violently in an open and reckless manner that "he slashed his way out, he hacked his way out," or of a man who acted treacherously and evasively that "he wormed his way, he gnawed his way through," or whatever words similarly match the subject.

(277) Some uses of heightening the tone produce force as well as grandeur, for example "It is not as an orator that you ought not to hold your hand out, Aeschines,

[a] Dem. *De Cor.* 136 (cf. § 80).

[b] Dem. *De Cor.* 188.

[c] Xen. *Cyrop.* 1.4.21 (cf. § 89).

[d] Literally ground-struck (prostitute) and sideways-hit (mad). Compounds also dominate § 276, providing all but one of the examples (to be emended therefore?). Cf. § 93 for the concise power of compound verbs.

πρεσβεύειν εἴσω τὴν χεῖρα ἔχοντα." (278) καὶ τὸ
"ἀλλ' ὁ τὴν Εὔβοιαν ἐκεῖνος σφετεριζόμενος"· οὐ
γὰρ ὑπὲρ τοῦ μέγαν ποιῆσαι τὸν λόγον ἡ ἐπανάστα-
σις, ἀλλ' ὑπὲρ τοῦ δεινόν. γίνεται δὲ τοῦτο ἐπὰν
μεταξὺ ἐξαρθέντες[1] κατηγορῶμέν τινος· ὥσπερ γὰρ
Αἰσχίνου κατηγορία, τὸ δὲ Φιλίππου ἐστίν. (279)
δεινὸν δὲ καὶ τὸ ἐρωτῶντα τοὺς ἀκούοντας ἔνια
λέγειν, καὶ μὴ ἀποφαινόμενον, "ἀλλ' ὁ τὴν Εὔβοιαν
ἐκεῖνος σφετεριζόμενος καὶ κατασκευάζων ἐπιτεί-
χισμα ἐπὶ τὴν Ἀττικήν, πότερον ταῦτα ποιῶν ἠδίκει,[2] καὶ ἔλυεν τὴν εἰρήνην, ἢ οὔ;" καθάπερ γὰρ εἰς
ἀπορίαν ἄγει τὸν ἀκούοντα ἐξελεγχομένῳ ἐοικότα
καὶ μηδὲν ἀποκρίνασθαι ἔχοντι· εἰ δὲ ὧδε μεταβαλὼν ἔφη τις, "ἠδίκει καὶ ἔλυε τὴν εἰρήνην," σαφῶς
διδάσκοντι ἐῴκει καὶ <οὐκ>[3] ἐλέγχοντι. (280) ἡ δὲ
καλουμένη ἐπιμονὴ ἐστὶ μὲν ἑρμηνεία πλείων τοῦ
πράγματος, μέγιστα δὲ συμβάλοιτ' ἂν εἰς δεινό-
τητα· παράδειγμα δὲ αὐτῆς τὸ Δημοσθένους,
"νόσημα γάρ, ὦ ἄνδρες Ἀθηναῖοι, δεινὸν ἐμπέπτωκεν[4] εἰς τὴν Ἑλλάδα . . ." <. . .>[5] οὐκ ἂν οὕτως ἦν
δεινόν.

(281) Τάχα δὲ κἂν[6] ὁ εὐφημισμὸς καλούμενος
μετέχοι τῆς δεινότητος, καὶ ὁ τὰ δύσφημα εὔφημα

---

[1] ἐξαρθέντες Spengel: ἐξαιρεθέντες P.
[2] καὶ παρεσπόνδει add. M, Dem.
[3] οὐκ add. Victorius.
[4] ἐμπέπτωκεν M: μὲν πέπτωκεν P.
[5] lacunam stat. Victorius.   [6] κἂν Goeller: καὶ P.

but as an envoy not to hold your hand out."[a] (278) And similarly: "No, he was annexing Euboea ..."[b] The rise in tone is not aimed to make the style dignified, but to make it forceful. This happens when the heightening is introduced as we attack someone, just as the former passage is an attack on Aeschines, the latter on Philip. (279) It is also forceful to express some points by asking the audience questions rather than by making a statement, for example "No, he was annexing Euboea and establishing a base against Attica— and in doing this was he wronging us and breaking the peace, or was he not?"[c] Demosthenes forces his listener into a sort of corner, so that he seems to be cross-examined and unable to reply. If you were to redraft and substitute this version, "he was wronging us and breaking the peace," it would seem an open statement rather than a cross-examination. (280) The figure called epimone, which is an elaboration going beyond the bare statement of fact,[d] can contribute very successfully to a forceful effect. Here is an example from Demosthenes, "men of Athens, a terrible disease has fallen on Greece" <...> the sentence would not then have had force.

(281) Perhaps some force may be found even in what is called euphemism, language which makes inauspicious

[a] Dem. *De Fals. Leg.* 255. Aeschines may use the hand gestures of the orator, but should not take bribes.

[b] Dem. *De Cor.* 71.   [c] The same passage now illustrates a different point, the use of rhetorical questions.

[d] I.e. the same idea is variously expressed, as in the example from Dem. *De Fals. Leg.* 259, which continues with a list of variants on δεινόν. This will have been clarified in the lacuna. Add e.g. "If it were cut short at this point."

ποιῶν καὶ τὰ ἀσεβήματα εὐσεβήματα, οἷον ὡς ὁ τὰς
Νίκας τὰς χρυσᾶς χωνεύειν κελεύων καὶ καταχρῆ-
σθαι τοῖς χρήμασιν εἰς τὸν πόλεμον οὐχ οὕτως
εἶπεν προχείρως, ὅτι "κατακόψωμεν τὰς Νίκας εἰς
τὸν πόλεμον"· δύσφημον γὰρ ἂν οὕτως καὶ λοιδο-
ροῦντι ἐοικὸς ἦν τὰς θεάς, ἀλλ᾽ εὐφημότερον, ὅτι
"συγχρησόμεθα ταῖς Νίκαις εἰς τὸν πόλεμον"· οὐ
γὰρ κατακόπτοντι τὰς Νίκας ἔοικεν οὕτως ῥηθέν,
ἀλλὰ συμμάχους μεταποιοῦντι.

(282) Δεινὰ δὲ καὶ τὰ Δημάδεια, καίτοι ἴδιον καὶ
ἄτοπον τρόπον ἔχειν δοκοῦντα, ἔστι δὲ αὐτῶν ἡ
δεινότης ἔκ τε τῶν ἐμφάσεων γινομένη, καὶ ἐξ ἀλλη-
γορικοῦ τινος παραλαμβανομένου, καὶ τρίτον ἐξ
ὑπερβολῆς. (283) οἷόν ἐστι τὸ "οὐ τέθνηκεν Ἀλέ-
ξανδρος, ὦ ἄνδρες Ἀθηναῖοι· ὦζεν γὰρ ἂν ἡ οἰκου-
μένη τοῦ νεκροῦ." τὸ μὲν γὰρ "ὦζεν" ἀντὶ τοῦ
"ἠσθάνετο" ἀλληγορικὸν καὶ ὑπερβολικὸν ἅμα, τὸ
δὲ τὴν οἰκουμένην αἰσθάνεσθαι ἐμφαντικὸν τῆς
δυνάμεως τῆς Ἀλεξάνδρου, καὶ ἅμα δέ τι ἐκπληκτι-
κὸν ἔχει ὁ λόγος ἠθροισμένον ἐκ τῶν τριῶν· πᾶσα
δὲ ἔκπληξις δεινόν, ἐπειδὴ φοβερόν. (284) τοῦ δὲ
αὐτοῦ εἴδους καὶ τὸ [ὅτι]¹ "τοῦτο τὸ ψήφισμα οὐκ
ἐγὼ ἔγραψα, ἀλλ᾽ ὁ πόλεμος τῷ Ἀλεξάνδρου δόρατι
γράφων," καὶ τὸ "ἔοικε γὰρ ἡ Μακεδονικὴ δύναμις,
ἀπολωλεκυῖα τὸν Ἀλέξανδρον, τῷ Κύκλωπι τετυ-
φλωμένῳ." (285) καὶ ἀλλαχοῦ που, "πόλιν,² οὐ τὴν
ἐπὶ προγόνων τὴν ναυμάχον, ἀλλὰ γραῦν, σανδάλια

¹ del. de Falco.   ² πόλιν Lhardy: πάλιν P.

510

things appear auspicious and impious things appear pious. A speaker, for example, once recommended that the golden statues of Victory should be melted down and the proceeds used to finance the war: he did not say openly, "let us cut up the Victory statues for the war." That would have been inauspicious and like an insult to the goddesses. He put it more auspiciously, "we will have the support of the Victories for the war,"[a] a version which suggests not the cutting up of the Victories but their conversion into allies.

(282) There are also the forceful sayings of Demades, though they are thought to be of a peculiar, and even eccentric nature, and their force results from innuendo, from the use of an allegorical element, and thirdly from hyperbole. (283) This is an example: "Alexander is not dead, men of Athens; or the whole world would have smelled his corpse."[b] The use of "smelled" instead of "noticed" is both allegory and hyperbole; and the idea of the whole world noticing implicitly suggests Alexander's power. Further, the words carry a shock, the cumulative result of the three sources; and what shocks is always forceful, since it inspires fear. (284) Of the same kind are the words, "I was not the one to write this decree, the war wrote it with Alexander's spear,"[c] and "The power of Macedon after the loss of Alexander is like the Cyclops after his blinding,"[d] (285) and in another passage, "a city which is no longer the city of our ancestors fighting sea

[a] Author unknown, example also in Quint. 9.2.92.

[b] Demades *fr.* 53 de Falco.

[c] *Fr.* 12 de Falco.

[d] *Fr.* 15 de Falco.

ὑποδεδεμένην καὶ πτισάνην ῥοφῶσαν·" τὸ μὲν γὰρ
γραῦν ἀλληγοροῦν ἀντὶ τοῦ ἀσθενῆ καὶ ἐξίτηλον
ἤδη, καὶ ἅμα ἐμφαῖνον τὴν ἀδρανίαν αὐτῆς ὑπερβο-
λικῶς· τὸ δὲ πτισάνην ῥοφῶσαν ἐπὶ τοῦ[1] ἐν κρεανο-
μίαις τότε καὶ πανδαισίαις διάγουσαν ἀπολλύειν[2] τὰ
στρατιωτικὰ χρήματα. (286) περὶ μὲν οὖν τῆς Δημα-
δείου δεινότητος ἀρκεῖ τοσαῦτα, καίτοι ἐχούσης τι
ἐπισφαλὲς καὶ οὐκ εὐμίμητον μάλα· ἔνεστι γάρ τι
καὶ ποιητικὸν τῷ εἴδει, εἴ γε ποιητικὸν ἡ ἀλληγορία
καὶ ὑπερβολὴ καὶ ἔμφασις, ποιητικὸν δὲ μικτὸν
κωμῳδίας.

(287) Τὸ δὲ καλούμενον ἐσχηματισμένον ἐν λόγῳ
οἱ νῦν ῥήτορες γελοίως ποιοῦσιν καὶ μετὰ ἐμφάσεως
ἀγεννοῦς ἅμα καὶ οἷον ἀναμνηστικῆς, ἀληθινὸν δὲ
σχῆμά ἐστι λόγου μετὰ δυοῖν τούτοιν λεγόμενον,
εὐπρεπείας καὶ ἀσφαλείας. (288) εὐπρεπείας μέν,
οἷον ὡς Πλάτων Ἀρίστιππον καὶ Κλεόμβροτον λοιδορῆσαι θελήσας, ἐν Αἰγίνῃ ὀψοφαγοῦντας δεδεμέ-
νου Σωκράτους Ἀθήνησιν ἐπὶ πολλὰς ἡμέρας, καὶ
μὴ διαπλεύσαντας[3] <πρὸς>[4] τὸν ἑταῖρον καὶ διδά-
σκαλον, καίτοι οὐχ ὅλους ἀπέχοντας διακοσίους
σταδίους τῶν Ἀθηνῶν. ταῦτα πάντα διαρρήδην μὲν
οὐκ εἶπεν· λοιδορία γὰρ ἦν ὁ λόγος· εὐπρεπῶς δέ
πως τόνδε τὸν τρόπον· ἐρωτηθεὶς γὰρ ὁ Φαίδων τοὺς
παρόντας Σωκράτῃ, καὶ καταλέξας ἕκαστον, ἐπανε-
ρωτηθεὶς εἰ καὶ Ἀρίστιππος καὶ Κλεόμβροτος

---

[1] ἐπὶ τοῦ Sauppe: ἐπεὶ P.
[2] ἀπολλύειν M[2]: ἀπολύειν PM[1].

battles, but an old hag, wearing slippers and gulping her broth."[a] Here "hag" is used allegorically to describe a weak city in terminal decline, whose impotence it also suggests implicitly and with hyperbole; and "gulping her broth" is also allegorical, describing a city then preoccupied with feasts and banquets and squandering the funds for the war. (286) This is enough on the forcefulness of Demades, a type which has an element of risk and is not very easy to imitate. There is in its nature an element of poetry, if allegory, hyperbole, and innuendo are poetic, but it is poetry with a blend of comedy.

(287) Next, what is called allusive verbal innuendo. It is used by current orators in a ridiculous way, with a vulgar and what one might call obtrusive explicitness, but genuine allusive innuendo is expressed with these two safeguards, tact and circumspection. (288) Tact is shown, for example, when Plato wants to blame Aristippus and Cleombrotus because they were feasting in Aegina when Socrates was imprisoned for many days in Athens, and they did not sail over to visit their friend and teacher, although they were less than two hundred stades from Athens.[b] Plato did not say all this explicitly (for that would have been an open insult) but with some tact, as follows. Phaedo is asked who were with Socrates, and he lists them one by one. Next he is asked if Aristippus and

[a] *Fr.* 18 de Falco.
[b] I.e. roughly twenty-five miles.

---

[3] διαπλεύσαντας P[2]: διαλύσαντας P[1] Greg.
[4] πρὸς add. Gärtner.

παρῆσαν, "οὔ," φησίν, "ἐν Αἰγίνῃ γὰρ ἦσαν"·
πάντα γὰρ τὰ προειρημένα ἐμφαίνεται τῷ "ἐν
Αἰγίνῃ ἦσαν"· καὶ πολὺ δεινότερος ὁ λόγος δοκεῖ
τοῦ πράγματος αὐτοῦ ἐμφαίνοντος τὸ δεινόν, οὐχὶ
τοῦ λέγοντος. τοὺς μὲν οὖν ἀμφὶ τὸν Ἀρίστιππον
καὶ λοιδορῆσαι ἴσως ἀκινδύνου ὄντος ἐν σχήματι ὁ
Πλάτων ἐλοιδόρησεν. (289) πολλάκις δὲ ἢ πρὸς
τύραννον ἢ ἄλλως βίαιόν τινα διαλεγόμενοι καὶ
ὀνειδίσαι ὁρμῶντες χρῄζομεν ἐξ ἀνάγκης σχήματος
λόγου,[1] ὡς Δημήτριος ὁ Φαληρεὺς πρὸς Κρατερὸν
τὸν Μακεδόνα ἐπὶ χρυσῆς κλίνης καθεζόμενον
μετέωρον καὶ ἐν πορφυρᾷ χλανίδι, καὶ ὑπερηφάνως
ἀποδεχόμενον τὰς πρεσβείας τῶν Ἑλλήνων, σχημα-
τίσας εἶπεν ὀνειδιστικῶς, ὅτι "ὑπεδεξάμεθά ποτε
πρεσβεύοντας ἡμεῖς τούσδε[2] καὶ Κρατερὸν τοῦτον"·
ἐν γὰρ τῷ δεικτικῷ τῷ "τοῦτον" ἐμφαίνεται ἡ ὑπερη-
φανία τοῦ Κρατεροῦ πᾶσα ὠνειδισμένη ἐν σχήματι.
(290) τοῦ αὐτοῦ εἴδους ἐστὶ καὶ τὸ Πλάτωνος πρὸς
Διονύσιον ψευσάμενον καὶ ἀρνησάμενον, ὅτι "ἐγώ
σοι Πλάτων οὐδὲν ὡμολόγησα, σὺ μέντοι, νὴ τοὺς
θεούς." καὶ γὰρ ἐλήλεγκται ἐψευσμένος, καὶ ἔχει τι
ὁ λόγος σχῆμα μεγαλεῖον ἅμα καὶ ἀσφαλές. (291)
πολλαχῇ μέντοι καὶ ἐπαμφοτερίζουσιν· †τοῖς ἐοικέναι εἴ τις ἐθέλοι καὶ ψόγους εἰ καὶ ὁ ψόγους εἶναι
[θέλοι τις]†[3] παράδειγμα τὸ τοῦ Αἰσχίνου ἐπὶ τοῦ

---

[1] λόγου Finckh: ὅλου P.   [2] τούσδε edd.: τόνδε P.
[3] locus corruptus, fort. οὐ pro ὁ Grube: θέλοι τις del.
Roberts.

Cleombrotus were also there. "No," he replies, "they were in Aegina."[a] Everything that precedes leads up to the words, "they were in Aegina," and the passage seems far more forceful because the force is produced by the fact itself and not by an authorial comment. So, although he could presumably have openly insulted Aristippus and his friends without any personal risk, Plato has done so allusively. (289) But in addressing a tyrant or any other violent individual, if we wish to be censorious, we often need to be oblique out of necessity, as in the case of Demetrius of Phaleron: when the Macedonian Craterus sat high above him on a couch of gold and in a purple robe and received the Greek envoys with insolent pride, he addressed him, using innuendo to censure him, "We ourselves once welcomed these men as envoys, including this man, Craterus."[b] By the use of the demonstrative, "this man," all the pride of Craterus is implicitly indicated and allusively censured. (290) Under the same heading comes Plato's reply to Dionysius, who had broken a promise and then denied ever making it: "I, Plato, have not made you any promises, but *you* —well, heaven knows!"[c] Dionysius is convicted of telling lies, while the words themselves carry a dignified and circumspect innuendo. (291) People often use words with an equivocal meaning. †If you wanted to be like them and use invective which does not seem invective†,[d] there is an example in Aeschines' passage about Telauges.[e] Almost the whole

[a] Pl. *Phaed.* 59c, similarly interpreted as an attack on Aristippus in Diog. Laert. 3.36.

[b] Dem. Phal. 183 Wehrli.   [c] Cf. Pl. *Epist.* 7, 349b.

[d] Text very uncertain, but the general sense is clear.

[e] Aesch. Soc. *fr.* 48 Dittmar. Cf. § 170.

Τηλαυγοῦς· πᾶσα γὰρ σχεδὸν ἡ περὶ τὸν Τηλαυγῆ διήγησις ἀπορίαν παράσχοι ἄν[1] εἴτε θαυμασμὸς εἴτε χλευασμός ἐστι. τὸ δὲ τοιοῦτον εἶδος ἀμφίβολον, καίτοι εἰρωνεία οὐκ ὄν, ἔχει τινὰ ὅμως καὶ εἰρωνείας ἔμφασιν.

(292) Δύναιτο δ᾽ ἄν τις καὶ ἑτέρως σχηματίζειν, οἷον οὕτως· ἐπειδὴ ἀηδῶς ἀκούουσιν οἱ δυνάσται καὶ δυνάστιδες τὰ αὐτῶν ἁμαρτήματα, παραινοῦντες αὐτοῖς μὴ ἁμαρτάνειν οὐκ ἐξ εὐθείας ἐροῦμεν, ἀλλ᾽ ἤτοι ἑτέρους ψέξομέν τινας τὰ ὅμοια πεποιηκότας, οἷον πρὸς Διονύσιον τὸν τύραννον κατὰ Φαλάριδος τοῦ τυράννου ἐροῦμεν καὶ τῆς Φαλάριδος ἀποτομίας· ἢ ἐπαινεσόμεθά τινας Διονυσίῳ τὰ ἐναντία πεποιηκότας, οἷον Γέλωνα ἢ Ἱέρωνα, ὅτι πατράσιν ἐῴκεσαν τῆς Σικελίας καὶ διδασκάλοις· καὶ γὰρ νουθετεῖται ἀκούων ἅμα καὶ οὐ λοιδορεῖται καὶ ζηλοτυπεῖ τῷ Γέλωνι ἐπαινουμένῳ καὶ ἐπαίνου ὀρέγεται καὶ οὗτος. (293) πολλὰ δὲ τοιαῦτα παρὰ τοῖς τυράννοις, οἷον Φίλιππος μὲν διὰ τὸ ἑτερόφθαλμος εἶναι ὠργίζετο, εἴ τις ὀνομάσειεν ἐπ᾽ αὐτοῦ Κύκλωπα ἢ ὀφθαλμὸν ὅλως· Ἑρμείας δ᾽ ὁ τοῦ Ἀταρνέως ἄρξας, καίτοι τἆλλα πρᾶος, ὡς λέγεται, οὐκ ἂν ἠνέσχετο ῥᾳδίως τινὸς μαχαίριον ὀνομάζοντος ἢ τομὴν ἢ ἐκτομὴν διὰ τὸ εὐνοῦχος εἶναι. ταῦτα δ᾽ εἴρηκα ἐμφῆναι βουλόμενος μάλιστα τὸ ἦθος τὸ δυναστευτικόν, ὡς μάλιστα χρῇζον λόγου ἀσφαλοῦς, ὃς καλεῖται ἐσχηματισμένος. (294) καίτοι πολλάκις καὶ οἱ δῆμοι οἱ μεγάλοι καὶ ἰσχυροὶ δέονται τοιούτου εἴδους τῶν

narrative about Telauges will leave you puzzled whether it is meant as admiration or mockery. This ambiguous way of speaking, although not irony, yet has a suggestion of irony.

(292) Innuendo may be used in yet another way, as in this case: since powerful men and women dislike hearing their own faults mentioned, we will not speak openly, if we are advising them against a fault, but we will either blame others who have acted in a similar way, for example, in addressing the tyrant Dionysius, we will attack the tyrant Phalaris and the cruelty of Phalaris, or we will praise people who have acted in the opposite way to Dionysius, and say that Gelo or Hiero, for example, are like fathers and teachers of Sicily. Dionysius is receiving advice as he listens, but he does not feel insulted; he is envious of Gelo, the subject of this praise, and wants to be praised himself. (293) Such caution is often needed in dealing with rulers. Because he had only one eye, Philip would grow angry if anyone mentioned the Cyclops in his presence or used the word "eye" at all. Hermeias, the ruler of Atarneus, was in other respects good-tempered, it is said, but he resented any mention of a knife, surgery, or amputation, because he was a eunuch. I have mentioned these points to bring out very clearly the true nature of those in power, and to show that it especially calls for that circumspection in speech which is called innuendo. (294) It is also the case, however, that great and powerful

---

[1] παράσχοι ἂν P^2: παρέχοι P^1.

λόγων, ὥσπερ οἱ τύραννοι, καθάπερ ὁ Ἀθηναίων δῆμος, ἄρχων τῆς Ἑλλάδος καὶ κόλακας τρέφων Κλέωνας καὶ Κλεοφῶντας. τὸ μὲν οὖν κολακεύειν αἰσχρόν, τὸ δὲ ἐπιτιμᾶν ἐπισφαλές, ἄριστον δὲ τὸ μεταξύ, τοῦτ᾽ ἔστι τὸ ἐσχηματισμένον. (295) καί ποτε αὐτὸν τὸν ἁμαρτάνοντα ἐπαινέσομεν, οὐκ ἐφ᾽ οἷς ἥμαρτεν, ἀλλ᾽ ἐφ᾽ οἷς οὐχ ἡμάρτηκεν, οἷον τὸν ὀργιζόμενον, ὅτι χθὲς ἐπῃνεῖτο πρᾷος φανεὶς ἐπὶ τοῖς τοῦ δεῖνος ἁμαρτήμασιν, καὶ ὅτι ζηλωτὸς τοῖς πολίταις σύνεστιν· ἡδέως γὰρ δὴ ἕκαστος μιμεῖται ἑαυτὸν καὶ συνάψαι βούλεται ἐπαίνῳ ἔπαινον, μᾶλλον δ᾽ ἕνα ὁμαλῆ ἔπαινον ποιῆσαι.

(296) Καθόλου δὲ ὥσπερ τὸν αὐτὸν κηρὸν ὁ μέν τις κύνα ἔπλασεν, ὁ δὲ βοῦν, ὁ δὲ ἵππον, οὕτω καὶ πρᾶγμα ταὐτὸν ὁ μέν τις ἀποφαινόμενος καὶ κατηγορῶν φησιν, ὅτι "οἱ[1] ἄνθρωποι χρήματα μὲν ἀπολείπουσι τοῖς παισίν, ἐπιστήμην δὲ οὐ συναπολείπουσιν, τὴν χρησομένην τοῖς ἀπολειφθεῖσιν"·[2] τοῦτο δὲ τὸ εἶδος τοῦ λόγου Ἀριστίππειον λέγεται· ἕτερος δὲ ταὐτὸν ὑποθετικῶς προοίσεται, καθάπερ Ξενοφῶντος τὰ πολλά, οἷον ὅτι "δεῖ γὰρ οὐ χρήματα μόνον ἀπολιπεῖν τοῖς ἑαυτῶν παισίν, ἀλλὰ καὶ ἐπιστήμην τὴν χρησομένην αὐτοῖς." (297) τὸ δὲ ἰδίως καλούμενον εἶδος Σωκρατικόν, ὃ μάλιστα δοκοῦσιν ζηλῶσαι Αἰσχίνης καὶ Πλάτων, μετα-

---

[1] ὅτι οἱ edd.: ὅτι δε P.
[2] τοῖς ἀπολειφθεῖσιν Victorius: τοῖς συναπολειφθεῖσιν P.

---

[a] Not a fragment of Aristippus (IV A 148 Giannontoni). We

democracies often need this type of speech just as much
as tyrants, for example the democracy of Athens when it
was ruler of Greece and the home of flatterers like Cleon
and Cleophon. Flattery is shameful, open criticism is
dangerous, and the best course lies in the middle, namely
innuendo. (295) Sometimes we will compliment the very
man who has a weakness not on the weakness but on his
avoidance of it. We will compliment a bad-tempered
man, for example, that he was praised yesterday for the
mildness he showed when so and so was at fault, and that
he is a model to his fellow citizens. Every one likes to be
his own example and is eager to add praise to praise, or
rather to win one uniform record of praise.

(296) In general, language is like a lump of wax, from
which one man will mould a dog, another an ox, another a
horse. The same subject will be treated by one person in
the form of direct statement and accusation, for example
"men leave property to their children, but they do not
leave with it the knowledge of how to use the
legacy"[a]—this is the type used by Aristippus. Another
will, as Xenophon frequently does, put the same idea in
the form of a precept, for example "men ought to leave
not only property to their children, but also the knowledge of how to use it." (297) What is specifically called the
Socratic manner—the type which Aechines and Plato in

have three variations in the styles of Aristippus, Xenophon, and
Socrates of a passage described as open rebuke as if by a *deus ex
machina* in Pl. *Clitoph.* 407b, "mankind, where are you rushing
to? are you not aware of your inappropriate behaviour, devoting
all your energy to making money but with no thought for how
your children, to whom you will leave it, will understand how to
use it justly?" See A. Carlini, *Rivista di Filologia e di Istruzione
Classica* 96 (1968) 38–46.

ρυθμίσειεν ἂν¹ τοῦτο τὸ πρᾶγμα τὸ προειρημένον εἰς
ἐρώτησιν ὧδέ πως οἷον "ὦ παῖ, πόσα σοι χρήματα
ἀπέλιπεν ὁ πατήρ; ἢ πολλά τινα καὶ οὐκ εὐαρί-
θμητα;—πολλά, ὦ Σώκρατες.—ἆρα οὖν καὶ ἐπιστήμην ἀπέλιπέν σοι τὴν χρησομένην αὐτοῖς;" ἅμα
γὰρ καὶ εἰς ἀπορίαν ἔβαλεν τὸν παῖδα λεληθότως,
καὶ ἠνέμνησεν ὅτι ἀνεπιστήμων ἐστί, καὶ παιδεύ-
εσθαι προετρέψατο· ταῦτα πάντα ἠθικῶς καὶ ἐμμε-
λῶς, καὶ οὐχὶ δὴ τὸ λεγόμενον τοῦτο ἀπὸ Σκυθῶν.
(298) εὐημέρησαν δ' οἱ τοιοῦτοι λόγοι τότε ἐξευρε-
θέντες τὸ πρῶτον, μᾶλλον δὲ ἐξέπληξαν τῷ τε μιμη-
τικῷ² καὶ τῷ ἐναργεῖ καὶ τῷ μετὰ μεγαλοφροσύνης
νουθετικῷ. περὶ μὲν δὴ πλάσματος λόγου καὶ σχη-
ματισμῶν ἀρκείτω ταῦτα.

(299) Ἡ δὲ λειότης ἡ περὶ τὴν σύνθεσιν, οἵᾳ
κέχρηνται μάλιστα οἱ ἀπ' Ἰσοκράτους, φυλαξάμενοι
τὴν σύγκρουσιν τῶν φωνηέντων γραμμάτων, οὐ
μάλα ἐπιτηδεία ἐστὶ δεινῷ λόγῳ· πολλὰ γὰρ [τὰ³]
ἐκ τῆς συμπλήξεως ἂν αὐτῆς γένοιτο δεινότερα, οἷον
"τοῦ γὰρ Φωκικοῦ συστάντος πολέμου, οὐ δι' ἐμέ,
οὐ γὰρ ἔγωγε ἐπολιτευόμην πω τότε." εἰ δὲ μεταβα-
λών τις καὶ συνάψας ὧδ' εἴποι· "τοῦ πολέμου γὰρ οὐ
δι' ἐμὲ τοῦ Φωκικοῦ συστάντος· οὐ γὰρ ἐπολιτευόμην ἔγωγέ πω τότε," οὐκ ὀλίγον διεξαιρήσει τῆς
δεινότητος, ἐπεὶ πολλαχοῦ καὶ τὸ ἠχῶδες τῆς
συγκρούσεως ἴσως ἔσται δεινότερον. (300) καὶ γὰρ
τὸ ἀφρόντιστον αὐτὸ καὶ τὸ ὥσπερ αὐτοφυὲς δεινό-

¹ μεταρυθμίσειεν ἂν Schneider: μεταρυθμήσειαν P.

particular are considered to emulate—would redraft the
same idea in the form of questions, in this sort of way:
"'My boy, how much property did your father leave you?
Was it a lot and not easily assessed?' 'It was a lot,
Socrates' 'Well now, did he also leave you the knowledge
of how to use it?'" Socrates unobtrusively drives the boy
into a corner; he reminds him that he does not have
knowledge and encourages him to find instruction. All
this is done with characterisation and in perfect taste, far
from the proverbial Scythian bluntness.[a] (298) This type
of speech was very successful at the time it was first
invented, or rather it stunned everyone by the verisimili-
tude, the vividness, and the nobility of the ethical advice.
Let this then be enough on how to mould speech, and on
innuendo.

(299) Smoothness of composition (of the kind particularly used by the followers of Isocrates, who avoid any
clash of vowels) is not well suited to forceful speech. In
many cases the very hiatus would increase the force, for
example "when the Phocian war broke out, through no
fault in me, as I at that time was not yet active in public
life."[b] If you were to redraft the words more smoothly,
"when through no fault in me the Phocian war broke out,
as I was at that time not yet active in public life," you will
remove much of the force, since in many passages
perhaps the very resonance of the hiatus will be more
forceful. (300) The fact is that words which are unpre-

[a] Cf. § 216.

[b] Dem. *De Cor.* 18. Note especially the jerky hiatus between
the clauses, *polemou, ou di' eme, ou*. On hiatus cf. §§ 68–74.

---

[2] μιμητικῷ Gale: τιμητικῶ P.   [3] τὰ del. Spengel.

τητα παραστήσει τινά, μάλιστα ἐπὰν ὀργιζομένους ἐμφαίνωμεν αὐτοὺς ἢ ἠδικημένους. ἡ δὲ περὶ τὴν λειότητα καὶ ἁρμονίαν φροντὶς οὐκ ὀργιζομένου, ἀλλὰ παίζοντός ἐστι καὶ ἐπιδεικυμένου μᾶλλον. (301) καὶ ὥσπερ τὸ διαλελυμένον σχῆμα δεινότητα ποιεῖ, ὡς προλέλεκται, οὕτω ποιήσει ἡ διαλελυμένη ὅλως σύνθεσις. σημεῖον δὲ καὶ τὸ Ἱππώνακτος· λοιδορῆσαι γὰρ βουλόμενος τοὺς ἐχθροὺς ἔθραυσεν τὸ μέτρον, καὶ ἐποίησεν χωλὸν ἀντὶ εὐθέος καὶ ἄρυθμον, τουτέστι δεινότητι πρέπον καὶ λοιδορίᾳ· τὸ γὰρ ἔρρυθμον καὶ εὐήκοον ἐγκωμίοις ἂν πρέποι μᾶλλον ἢ ψόγοις. τοσαῦτα καὶ περὶ συγκρούσεως.

(302) Παράκειται δέ τις καὶ τῷ δεινῷ χαρακτῆρι, ὡς τὸ εἰκός, διημαρτημένος καὶ αὐτός, καλεῖται δὲ ἄχαρις. γίνεται δὲ ἐν τοῖς πράγμασιν, ἐπάν τις αἰσχρὰ καὶ δύσρητα ἀναφανδὸν λέγῃ, καθάπερ ὁ τῆς Τιμάνδρας[1] κατηγορῶν ὡς πεπορνευκυίας τὴν λεκανίδα καὶ τοὺς ὀβολοὺς καὶ τὴν ψίαθον καὶ πολλήν τινα τοιαύτην δυσφημίαν κατήρασεν τοῦ δικαστηρίου. (303) ἡ σύνθεσις δὲ φαίνεται ἄχαρις, ἐὰν διεσπασμένη ἐμφερὴς ᾖ, καθάπερ ὁ εἰπών, "†οὑτωσὶ δ' ἔχον τὸ καὶ τό, κτεῖναι.†"[2] καὶ ἐπὰν τὰ κῶλα μηδεμίαν ἔχῃ πρὸς ἄλληλα σύνδεσιν, ἀλλ' ὅμοια διερρηγμένοις. καὶ αἱ περίοδοι δὲ αἱ συνεχεῖς καὶ μακραὶ καὶ ἀποπνίγουσαι τοὺς λέγοντας οὐ

---

[1] ὁ τῆς Τιμάνδρας edd: ὅτι ἂν τῆς Τημάνδρας P.
[2] locus corruptus, οὕτως ἴδ' P: οὑτωσί cum praecedentibus Radermacher, fort. recte.

meditated, and somehow spontaneous, will in themselves create some vigour, especially when we show our anger or sense of injustice, whereas careful attention to smoothness and harmony signals not anger so much as a lack of seriousness or a display of rhetoric. (301) As has already been said,[a] the figure of abruptness creates force. The same may be said of abrupt composition on a wider scale. Hipponax[b] is a case in point. Wanting to insult his enemies, he shattered his metre, he made it limp instead of walk straight, he made the rhythm irregular, and therefore suitable for forceful insult. Regular, harmonious rhythm would be more suitable for eulogy than invective. This concludes my account of hiatus.

(302) Next to the forceful style there is, as might be expected, a corresponding faulty style. It is called the repulsive style. It occurs in the subject matter when a speaker mentions in public things that are disgusting and obscene, like the man who accused Timandra[c] of being a prostitute and spewed out over the court her basin, her fees, her mat, and many similar ugly details. (303) Composition sounds repulsive if it seems disjointed, like the man who said, "†this and that being the case, to kill†";[d] and when the clauses are in no way linked to one another, but are like broken fragments. Long continuous periods, too, which run the speaker out of breath cause not only a

[a] Cf. § 269.

[b] Hipponax turned the iambic trimeter into "limping" iambics by making the final iamb a spondee. Cf. § 251.

[c] Author unknown; perhaps Hyperides in his attack on this famous prostitute (= *fr.* 165).

[d] Author unknown, text very uncertain.

μόνον κατακορές ἀλλὰ καὶ ἀτερπές. (304) τῇ δὲ ὀνομασίᾳ[1] πολλάκις χαρίεντα πράγματα ὄντα ἀτερπέ-
στερα φαίνεται, καθάπερ ὁ Κλείταρχος περὶ τῆς
τενθρηδόνος λέγων, ζῴου μελίσσῃ ἐοικότος· "κατα-
νέμεται μέν," φησί, "τὴν ὀρεινήν, εἰσίπταται δὲ εἰς
τὰς κοίλας δρῦς·" ὥσπερ περὶ βοὸς ἀγρίου ἢ τοῦ
Ἐρυμανθίου κάπρου λέγων, ἀλλ' οὐχὶ περὶ μελίσ-
σης τινός, ὥστε καὶ ἄχαριν τὸν λόγον ἅμα καὶ
ψυχρὸν γενέσθαι. παράκειται δέ πως ἀλλήλοις
ταῦτα ἀμφότερα.[2]

[1] τῇ δὲ ὀνομασίᾳ Victorius: ἡ δὲ ὀνομασία P.
[2] Δημητρίου περὶ ἑρμηνείας subscriptio in P.

surfeit but actual aversion. (304) The choice of words often makes even subjects which are themselves charming lose their attractiveness. Clitarchus, for instance, gives this description of the wasp, an insect like a bee: "It lays waste the hillsides, and rushes into the hollow oaks."[a] It is as if he described some wild bull, or the Erymanthian boar, rather than a kind of bee. The result is that the passage is both repulsive and frigid, and in a way these two faults lie next to each other.

[a] FGrHist 137 Clitarchus F 14 (cf T 10).

INDEX

Poetics

Glaucon, 61b1

Haemon, 54a2
Hector, 60a15, 60b26
Hegemon, 48a12
Helle, 54a8
Heracles, 51a22
Herodotus, 51b2
Hippias of Thasus, 61a22
Homer, 47b18, 48a11, 22, 26,
    48b28, 34, 51a23, 54b15,
    59a31, 59b12, 60a5, 19. *Iliad*,
    48b38, 51a29, 54b2, 56a13,
    56b1, 57a29, 57b11, 58a7,
    58b31, 59a31, 59b3, 14, 60a15,
    60b26, 61a2–33 *passim*, 62b3,
    8. *Margites*, 48b30, 38.
    Odyssey, 49a1, 51a24, 53a32,
    54b26, 30, 55a2, 55b17, 57b10,
    58b25, 29, 59b3, 15, 60a26, 35,
    61b5, 62b9

Iphigeneia, *see* Euripides
Ixion, 56a1

Little Iliad, 59b2, 5
Lynceus, *see* Theodectes

Magnes, 48a34
Margites, *see* Homer
Medea, *see* Euripides
Megarians, 48a31
Melanippe, *see* Euripides
Meleager, 53a20
Menelaus, 54a29, 61b21
Merope, 54a5
Mitys, 52a8
Mnasitheus, 62a7
Mynniscus, 61b34
Mysians, *see* Aeschylus, Sophocles

Neoptolemus, 59b6

Nicochares, *Deiliad*, 48a13
Niobe, *see* Aeschylus

Odysseus, *see* Homer, *Odyssey*
Odysseus the False Messenger,
    55a13
Odysseus Wounded, *see* Sophocles
Oedipus, 53a11, 20. *See also*
    Sophocles, *Oedipus Tyrannus*
Orestes, 53a20, 37, 53b24. *See also*
    Euripides, *Iphigeneia in Tauris,
    Orestes*

Pauson, 48a6
Peleus, *see* Euripides, Sophocles
Philoctetes, 59b5. *See also*
    Aeschylus, Euripides
Philoxenus, 48a15
Phineidae, *see* Aeschylus,
    Sophocles
Phorcides, *see* Aeschylus
Phthiotides, *see* Sophocles
Pindarus, 61b35
Polygnotus, 48a5, 50a27
Polyidus, 55a6, 55b10
Prometheus, *see* Aeschylus
Protagoras, 56b15

Sack of Troy, 59b6
Scylla, *see* Timotheus
Sicily, 48a32, 49b7
Sinon, *see* Sophocles
Sisyphus, 56a22
Sophocles, 48a26, 49a19, 56a27,
    60b33. *Antigone*, 54a1. *Electra*,
    60a31. (?)*Eurypylus*, 59b6.
    (?)*Mysians*, 60a32.
    (?)*Odysseus Wounded*, 53b34.
    Oedipus Tyrannus, 52a24,
    53b7, 31, 54b8, 55a18, 60a30,
    62b2. (?)*Peleus*, 56a2.
    (?)*Phineidae*, 55a10.

INDEX

INDEX

On The Sublime

INDEX

On Style

Note: Reference is to the section numbers.

INDEX